INDIA'S POVERTY AND ITS SOLUTION

India's Poverty and Its Solution

CHARAN SINGH

Minister for Agriculture, Government of U.P.

71021

HD2072
S61
2d ed.

ASIA PUBLISHING HOUSE

BOMBAY : CALCUTTA : NEW DELHI : MADRAS : LUCKNOW
LONDON : NEW YORK

PRINTED IN INDIA
BY C. L. BHARGAVA AT G. W. LAWRIE AND CO., LUCKNOW AND
PUBLISHED BY P. S. JAYASINGHE, ASIA PUBLISHING HOUSE, BOMBAY.

Preface

POVERTY OF India is extreme : it is, indeed, now regarded as proverbial. Even elementary necessities of life—food, raiment and shelter—are not available to tens of millions of our people to the required degree. The gap in the levels of living of an average Indian and a citizen of Europe (excluding the USSR) has a ratio of almost 1 to 12. The world average is, at least, three times the Indian. And as time passes, the gap is becoming wider and wider still. Till only a decade ago the energies of the leaders of the country were directed against the foreign rule : the poverty of the masses was usually referred to only as an argument against the continuance of that rule. By implication the masses, and also, through process of auto-suggestion, the leaders themselves came to believe that, as soon as the foreign yoke was thrown off, rivers of milk and honey will begin to flow in the country as in the mystical times of yore. Contact with realities, however, has brought disillusionment and there is much brain-searching. Achievement of political freedom appears, in retrospect, to be an easier task than economic freedom—freedom from want, hunger, ignorance and disease. There is a frantic search for formulae of rapid economic development.

Some of the leaders of the country have hit upon the pooling of individual fields and labour as a sure remedy for creating farm surpluses which are an essential precursor of economic development. It is claimed that co-operative farming will accelerate capital formation by increasing the rate of internal savings and, thus, pave the way for industrialisation of India. Examples, particularly of Russia and China, are suggestively quoted on the basis of surprisingly superficial observation and merest hearsay. The Planning Commission has given consideration to the matter and made certain recommendations favouring the idea, albeit cautiously. The purpose of this book is to urge dispassionate and renewed thinking on this question as also our economic problems, in general, and their integrated solution or solutions. It is proposed to deal with co-operative farming, first.

Zamindari and the like systems have all but disappeared from this country. The peasant is rapidly coming into his own. While the results of this stupendous reform are still in the process of crystallising, word has gone forth from authoritative quarters that the country should switch over from peasant farming to an economy of large co-operative farms established by farmers, pooling their lands and placing them under a common management.

The replacement of farm tenancy by peasant proprietorship effects no change in the soil, nor in the production technique ; yet it raises production. That has been the experience all the world over. Statistics can be quoted in support, but it is unnecessary to do so in view of the wide and unquestioning acceptance of the proposition. The reason is that it generates forces which stimulate the free development of the peasant's personality. The thought that land has become his and his children's in perpetuity, lightens and cheers his labours and expands his horizon. The feeling that he is his own master, subject to no outside control, and has free, exclusive and untrammelled use of his land drives him to greater and greater effort. He receives a psychological fillip which vitalises his attachment and devotion to the land. In other words, although the abolition of landlordism does not affect the farm, it powerfully affects the farmer. Likewise, any system of large-scale farming in which his holdings are pooled must affect the farmer, but in the reverse direction. No longer will he be his own master ; he will become one of the many ; his interest will be subordinated to the group interest ; he will have to submit to the control and direction of the group management. Even if the right to secede at will is preserved in theory, in practice it will nearly always be found that the seceder cannot be given back his land, for such restoration will be detrimental to group interest ; he will have to be content with its money equivalent. The forces released by zamindari abolition will suffer a reaction, and one should in consequence expect a fall in production. This is in fact what happens. Inside these pages will be found factual evidence, derived from various sources and pertaining to several countries whence reliable figures are available, that per-acre production falls as the size of farm increases. In the case of a co-operative farm it will be a case of too many cooks. In a word, if zamindari abolition is psychologically right, co-operative farming is psychologically wrong.

The co-operative principle has undoubtedly a very fruitful mission in the field of agriculture, but when stretched to the point of merger of holdings, it violates the essence of true co-operation. Independent businessmen 'co-operate' to remove individual disabilities, but when independence itself is compromised and the farmer is reduced to a farm hand, it is not a case of true co-operation. It is preparing the ground for authoritarian control. A self-elected few will exploit the simplicity, ignorance, credulity and lethargy of the overwhelming majority and dominate the co-operative farms. They will lean on officialdom for support and support it in return. In place of the intermediaries who have been liquidated, a new class of intermediaries will be created with the same hard core, but more powerfully entrenched and masquerading as the spearhead of a new co-operative movement. Local bosses, which the officials of the co-operative will degenerate into, will slowly but surely undermine the very foundation of our nascent democracy and reduce the peasantry, 'their country's pride,' to the status of mere labourers. Sovereignty resides in the people and for that reason the Constitution guarantees fundamental rights to the individual. To the extent that the individual is hampered in the proper appreciation and free exercise of the fundamental rights, to the extent that his personality is cramped, to the extent that his independence of thought and action is subjected to extraneous control, to the extent that his destiny ceases to be his sole concern, the seat of sovereignty will tend to shift from all to the few, and the country will have taken the road to regimentation and totalitarianism.

Large-scale farming, whether co-operative, collective or of any other pattern, inevitably attracts mechanisation. In fact, the popular but erroneous belief that mechanisation increases production is used as an argument for the introduction of co-operative farming. Whatever may be true of countries with different soils, different climatic and rainfall conditions, and differently placed in the map of the world, in this country with a tropical climate and a thin layer of fertility mechanised tilling will reduce, not enhance the yield. Mechanised cultivation on large farms may pay their few owners in money ; it cannot pay the nation in greater tonnage, while in the circumstances of India every ounce matters.

Our economists and planners, perhaps, do not take into account Indian conditions but are influenced by the theories of Karl Marx who concluded without due examination of facts that the laws regarding industrial development at which he had arrived, applied to agriculture also. In India the amount of arable land is limited and the population dense. The production per acre has, therefore, to be increased. In the USA, Canada, Australia and other such countries, the best results are obtained by large-scale mechanised farming, which increases the production per man, because plenty of land is available and labour is scarce.

The other effects of the displacement of human and animal power by petrol and diesel on the economy of the country may be easily foreseen. Unemployment will be accentuated. In the circumstances of our country, industries and services cannot absorb the number of persons that will immediately be released from agriculture by any large-scale pooling of lands. Co-operative farming as an instrument of national policy has thus a very important human aspect.

Import of machinery and motive power will strain the none too sufficient exchange resources of the country.

It is not generally realised that, with the replacement of the bullock by the tractor, farm-yard manure will become scarce and increasing use will have to be made of chemical fertilizers. Evidence collected in this book will prove that the use of inorganic fertilizers tends to reduce soil fertility, even though the immediate results may be striking. Organic manure, on the other hand, maintains fertility and makes the soil an inexhaustible source of food supply. It is not without good reason that the agricultural experts of this country do not now advise unadulterated use of synthetic sulphates and phosphates. The country should not too hastily embark upon a venture for which posterity may condemn the present leaders.

In short, large-scale farming will reduce production, injure the democratic principles which the country cherishes, invite bureaucratic control and lead to rapid mechanisation with all its consequences. Peasant farming, on the other hand, will enable the country to steer a path which may not be spectacular but which will ensure that it does not abruptly go off the rails.*

Our path to economic development is an uphill one and strewn with thorns. Prosperity cannot be reached through a *mantra*, or one bright idea, but has to be earned the hard and long way. Only

---

* Prime Minister Nehru said in a press conference in New Delhi on February 7, 1959 :
"I want to do something in India, to change India within the few years left to me, to change the peasant in India, to change agriculture, economy and the rest. I may go wrong—as I do often—but it is my intense desire to reach a certain goal." (Vide *Jawaharlal Nehru on Co-operation*, issued by Government of India, 1959, p. 17.)
Any comment is unnecessary. The risk involved is as apparent as the sincerity of our Prime Minister.

if we realised it ! We are faced with formidable impediments of lack of capital, miserably low ratio of capital formation to population growth, large-scale unemployment, still larger scale of under-employment, relatively inadequate land and other natural resources, insufficient agricultural production and an impatient population whose aspirations have been awakened and which is becoming increasingly conscious of poverty and economic differences. These problems will require all the energy, skill, administrative acumen and the statesmanship we are capable of.

There is no example which India can follow in solving her problems because in no other country conditions were identical to ours. We can never attain the standards of the USA because our physical resources per capita are comparatively little, or those of the UK because we cannot build up an industrial structure as the UK did on the exploitation of foreign resources and foreign peoples. Nor can we hope to copy the methods of the USSR or China because, as apart from the far more favourable natural resources—man ratio in the former country and the balance-sheet of results in their totality in both, we have given ourselves a democratic constitution.

The belief that our vast population is in itself a great asset and an incentive for large-scale industrialisation, is unfounded. In view of the paucity of physical resources relative to population, our low purchasing power and the hard fact that capital or financial resources can ultimately be constructed out of physical resources alone, India's huge population is an impediment to economic development or industrialisation—a definite liability, not an asset.

It is well established that non-agricultural employments enjoy superiority over agricultural employments as a source of income. That is why every advanced country has been trying ever since the beginning of the last century to develop its own manufactures and find employment for its nationals in businesses and vocations other than production of raw materials. In the case of our country, however, this trend has been in the reverse direction. Whereas the share of agriculture in the labour force in other countries declined, in this country, for want of sufficient non-agricultural vocations to absorb the year to year growing labour force, it moved up—a phenomenon which should cause alarm to every lover of India. The existing situation, therefore, calls for immediate and earnest measures for diversification of our economy—for the development of non-agricultural resources. In this respect there are two schools

of thought—one is an advocate of capital-intensive large-scale enterprises as exist in advanced Western countries while the other
prefers a pattern of decentralised small-scale industries geared to
agriculture.

For establishing large-scale enterprises, capital in the country
is admittedly scarce. It is possible neither to obtain the necessary
amount of capital from external sources without strings or at the
rates of interest we can afford to pay, nor to raise it from internal
savings, for capital formation continues to be slow and meagre. Employment potential of capital-intensive enterprises is also small.
Disposal of goods produced by capital-intensive industries will present formidable problems, for our own people have a poor consumption capacity and foreign countries have a tendency to restrict imports. Further, *inter-alia*, because of restrictions on consumption
and heavy tax burdens it involves, a policy of rapid large-scale
industrialisation seems to be fraught with economic and political
risks. Except for important qualifications, therefore, we need
not make haste to set up a capital-intensive structure and, in
consequence, have to rely on forced savings which might completely
break the people.

Shortage of capital and redundance of labour being the governing factors in determining the pace of economic development, we
have to begin with, and rely mostly on labour-intensive enterprises
requiring little or small capital. Small units spread all over the
countryside and carried on in cottages and small workshops, covering all branches of human needs, will produce almost all the consumer goods needed by the nation. By virtue of their extensive
employment potential they will help in ensuring equitable distribution of wealth and fostering a democratic way of life. Such a structure is likely to increase the rate of financial savings and, in consequence, will result in capital formation because the time-lag
between the input of labour and the flow of output would be almost
negligible.

Progressive increase in the rate of capital formation and in the
purchasing capacity of the masses will release a chain of economic
reactions : markets will expand and, with the passage of time, a
more favourable technological climate will develop. These, in turn,
will provide the needed impetus for the growth of light, medium
and thereafter large-scale industries. It is this sequence which
would seem to suit our conditions best—and not the other way

round. Capital-intensive industries should form the apex, not the base. That was the path Mahatma Gandhi showed us.

We cannot shun advances in technology. Technology, in fact, is now not confined to big industrial units alone ; small and light units can also be developed with latest methods.

If per capita income or output has to be raised, the rate of capital investments will have to be increased—and increased at a rate higher than the rate of population growth. This means that the rate of financial savings will have to be far greater than today. If capital formation cannot keep pace with, rather ahead of population, there will be a retrogression of economic standards—retrogression of even the miserable standards that we enjoy today. Prudence dictates, therefore, that in addition to taking other steps, we divert by voluntary persuasion, of course, the energies of the idle and the semi-idle labour in the villages to capital-construction schemes on *shramdan* (voluntary labour) basis, if possible, or on nominal wages, if necessary. Either of the alternatives, *viz.*, continued unemployment which the present situation means, or inflation which payment of full wages implies, will result in deferment of economic development and consequent prolongation of misery. To the extent, therefore, that unemployed and under-employed man-power can be so mobilized, will democracy be ensured and strengthened in India. Democracy in our circumstances entails obligations and demands sacrifices in a larger measure both from the leaders and the people, than we realize.

A surplus food supply is the *sine qua non* to industrialisation. We have till now been looking at it all from a wrong angle. Industrialisation, of course, to the extent it is possible in the conditions of a dense agrarian economy like India's cannot precede but will only follow—at the most it can only accompany—increased agricultural production. Our per acre yield, however, is miserably low, much lower than in most of the countries of the world. Despite 70 per cent of the entire population being engaged on land, food production remains short of requirements, necessitating import of millions of tons of foodgrains year after year even after the advent of Independence. Obviously, no country, much less a poor country like India, can afford to go on feeding her people indefinitely in this manner. It is even doubtful if foodgrains in such large quantities would be available in the world market after some years.

More capital investment, improved farming practices and harder work on the part of the peasantry can undoubtedly make our fields yield several times more than at present, resulting in farm sur- pluses. Land being limited, the only practical solution of the pro- blem lies in the intensive utilisation of our land resources. And it is small-scale farming on individual basis, aided by a net-work of service co-operatives, that will utilise our land resources at their maximum, that will increase production per acre—increase it to the extent of being so greatly surplus to the needs of the farmers, that, because of diminishing incentives in farming, people are auto- matically released for absorption in industries and services. Large- scale joint farming, on the other hand, will merely release workers without producing enough of food, to keep them alive and working.

As pointed out in Chapter XX, to put it in a nut-shell : inas- much as industrialisation will progress to the extent men are re- leased from agriculture, and men will be released to the extent agri- cultural production goes up, and agricultural production will go up to the extent agricultural practices improve and more capital in- vested, industrialisation or economic development of the country turns on improvement in agricultural practices we are able to effect and amount of capital we are able to invest in land. We must bear in mind, however, that in spite of our best efforts, inasmuch as our land resources relative to population are meagre and as, in a given area, more men produce a greater total of food than fewer men, we will, like Japan, and unlike the USA and other countries which have comparatively larger land resources, have always to keep a very large percentage of our people occupied in agriculture.

Promotion of innovations or technological improvements is as necessary as accumulation of capital. Only three centuries ago India stood, at least, on the same economic level as Western Europe. To- day, things have considerably changed. The reason lies in the greater propensity of the Westerners to innovate. To that end im- pediments like illiteracy, ill-health, caste-system and a fatalistic atti- tude towards problems of life that most of our countrymen suffer from, will have to be removed. Then alone will the efficiency both of labour and available capital improve.

Stress will have to be laid mainly on bringing about technolo- gical improvements, for example, in indigenous ploughs, in the use of organic manures, in constructing small irrigation works, and in the organisation of handicrafts and small industries, rather than doing things in a big way or reproducing expensive European and

American models—big farms, big factories, big irrigation or hydro-electric projects. Apart from other considerations, big economic projects take time to fructify. Capital is locked up for years together ; meanwhile, with passage of time and increase in population, problems multiply and become more and more intractable.

But there is a limit to all this. The country cannot go on allowing the population to increase indefinitely and, by improvement in the farming practices, producing more and more food and, by reliance on a mixture, howsoever judicious, of labour-intensive decentralised enterprises with capital-intensive forms, staving off poverty and misery for ever. There is a limit to substitution of land by labour, capital or improvements and, in consequence, not only a limit to agricultural production but also to development of services and industries, which means that there is a limit to population the country can support. A deceleration of the rate of population growth, thus, becomes imperative. Various methods of doing this have, therefore, also been briefly discussed in the concluding chapter.

This in brief is the theme of the book. Arguments advanced in these pages may be derided and even attacked as unpatriotic in the present intellectual and political climate of India. But the logical validity of an argument does not depend either on its popularity in intellectual circles, or on its political acceptability. If the book succeeds in making farmers, industrialists, public workers, etc. to think for themselves in the light of material provided herein and come to their own conclusions rather than be led away by mere imitative slogans borrowed from other countries or by the fact that some of the biggest leaders of the country have adopted a particular line of thinking and are very insistent on it, it will have served its purpose.

Perhaps it is necessary to indicate here that views expressed in this book are entirely my own ; they have nothing to do with the All India National Congress or the Government of Uttar Pradesh, of which I happen to be a member.

It is in a spirit of great humility that I approach my country-men with this book. I lay no claim to any originality. In fact, I do not consider myself intellectually equipped to write at all on such controversial subjects, particularly, industrial development. But in course of my duties as a public worker, I felt the need of an integrated picture of our economic problems and their solutions.

Others also have felt a similar need. Shri T. T. Krishnamachari, Finance Minister of the Union Government, in a speech in the Lok Sabha in April 1956, is reported to have said : "It is, however, true that we have not yet evolved an economic philosophy of our own, and such as exists is necessarily ambivalent. We have, perhaps, no clear idea of the entire picture of the economic future that we desire this country to have. We are apt to think in compartments without any attempt at synthesizing the conflicts that thinking in compartments necessarily engenders."* An attempt at supplying this desideratum has been made in these pages. Otherwise, almost everything that has been said here has already been expressed somewhere else and, perhaps, in a better manner. I have, in a way, only pieced together others' ideas to make a connected whole. I have drawn greatly, even in the words and expressions, from David Mitrany's *Marx Against the Peasant* (George Weidenfield and Nicolson Ltd., London, 1952), Horace Belshaw's *Population Growth and Levels of Consumption* (George Allen and Unwin Ltd., London, 1956), Elmer Pendell's *Population on the Loose* (New York, 1951) and Kingsley Davis's *Population of India and Pakistan* (Princeton University Press, New York, 1951). To the authors of these works I owe a deep debt of gratitude.

A special word of thanks is due to the late Shri J. Nigam, ICS (then Land Reforms Commissioner, UP), for his valuable suggestions and revision of a portion of the first part of the book. My next obligation is due to Shri Zahurul Hasan, IAS, Revenue Secretary, UP, who went through the entire draft and made some helpful suggestions. I would also like to thank the Economics and Statistics Department of UP for supplying various figures and statistics which form part of many a table in the book. Finally, I would thank Shri Harish Chandra Sanghi, News Officer in the Information Directorate, for the pains he took in going through the draft more than once and also for the suggestions that he made.

Lucknow   CHARAN SINGH
June 16, 1959

* Introduction to *A Philosophy of Indian Economic Development* by Richard B. Gregg, published by the Navjivan Publishing House, Ahmedabad, 1958.

Preface to Second Edition

IN THIS, the second edition of the book, no change in the arguments or conclusions reached in the first edition is being made. Only some new evidence in favour of the old conclusions has been brought forward. In most of the chapters, there have been only a few verbal alterations, slight additions or a mere re-arrangement of the material. Three or four chapters alone may be said to have been re-written.

The title of the book is being changed from *Joint Farming X-Rayed: The Problem and Its Solution* to *India's Poverty and Its Solution*.

I am extremely indebted to members of my personal staff, who worked extra hours to type out the manuscript. I also owe greatly to Shri R. B. Singh, Research Officer of the Economics and Statistics, Directorate of the State, without whose assistance the various tables in the book could not have been brought up-to-date. My thanks are also due to Shri Ram Krishan, Deputy Development Commissioner (Agriculture), who took great pains in preparing the index of the book.

CHARAN SINGH

Lucknow
May 1963

Contents

List of Tables

PART I

PART I

CHAPTER ONE

Introductory

LIVING CREATES wants, which can be satisfied only by use and consumption of goods, collectively called wealth. By and large, wealth is ultimately derived from land. Raw materials must be produced before they can be processed and distributed, and food which, day by day, is necessary to life is mostly obtained from land. Exploitation of land, or agriculture in the narrower sense, is thus obviously the primary and basic industry. Manufacture and commerce, however important they may be in the economy of a country, must of necessity occupy a secondary place.

While land suffers from the limitation that it cannot be increased by any efforts that man may make, it has the supreme advantage of becoming better and better by proper use. All other forms of capital—houses, factories, locomotives, battleships, etc.—deteriorate or disintegrate and are ultimately destroyed, howsoever carefully they may be used; but land seldom. It is this inexhaustibility of land that gives those directly engaged in working it, a feeling of security, which no other means of occupation can offer. Land never disillusions a man completely ; the hope of plenty in the future always remains, and is not infrequently realised.

Obviously enough, the prosperity of a country depends, in the ultimate analysis, on how efficiently it utilises and, at the same time, conserves this free gift of nature. Even the form of society or civilisation that a country hopes to develop will be influenced by the manner in which it exploits the land, and by its land-tenure. "Measures of land reform", observes the Planning Commission,[1] "have a place of special significance, both because they provide the social, economic and institutional framework for agricultural development and because of the influence they exert on the life of the majority of the population. Indeed, their impact extends much beyond rural economy." This is specially true of countries where large percentages of population earn their living by working directly on the soil.

[1] *Second Five-Year Plan of India*, p. 177.

3

India inherited from the British a feudal or landlord-tenant system called *zamindari*, under which ownership of land was concentrated in the hands of a few, while the vast majority, who worked day and night on the land, were mere tenants. The growth and development of democratic institutions are closely related to the national income of a country and its distribution. In an underdeveloped country like India, income directly derived from land has been the chief source of wealth, and ownership of land has since long been accepted as the prevailing standard of status. Wealth and power in the countryside have been concentrated in the hands of those who controlled rents. Land reform, therefore, was the one economic organisational change which was needed before an overall programme of social reconstruction could be contemplated, a more productive economy could be built up and, in fact, before we could dream of making democracy a success.

With few exceptions, landlords performed no economic function; the lands which were tilled by the tenants would not produce less if the landlords disappeared. They rendered no service in return for the rent they received, and were, in the truest sense of the term, parasites, or 'drones doing no good in the public hive.'

That man alone who is not subservient to another in the economic sphere, is truly happy. Under the *zamindari* system, however, the tenant was not free ; somebody else was the owner of the patch of land on which he toiled along with members of his family. In most parts of the country there was no property he could cherish; and in many cases he was liable to eviction at the sweet will of the *zamindar*. Nor could he claim social equality with the latter, for status in the village was determined by rights in land.

Agricultural data from all over the world show that farm tenancy reduces output. The abolition of landlordism was not, therefore, just a matter of social justice to peasants. If agricultural production was to be increased, and the peasant's energetic participation in the country's economy was to be secured, he was to be given that much hold on the land which met his deepest desire. He was to be made the owner of the land he tilled.

The landlord-tenant system created classes and, therefore, led to class war. While the tenant pined for safeguards against capricious eviction, real security of tenure was odious to the *zamindar*. The state tried to strike a balance. Yet the conflict inherent in the system was never resolved. It led to economic and political unrest.

The big *zamindars* mostly stood for political reaction ; they were the props of British rule and dreaded a democratic set-up.

For these and other reasons, leaders of the country decided years ago that, if the decks were to be cleared for social and economic reform and for political stability, the feudal landlord-tenant system had to go.

CHAPTER TWO

Types of Agrarian Organization

THE LANDLORD-TENANT system has departed from almost all the States and consolidation of holdings is going apace in some. But neither the change in ownership and legal relations, nor consolidation of holdings with all its benefits, can have much effect on either the size of the farm or the type of farming. So the question of the future agrarian organisation as an economic, technical and also as a social problem, has yet to be stated and answered. Is land consolidation the last step or is it merely an intermediate stage—a prelude to something else ? There is confusion in the public mind on this crucial issue.

There are three alternatives before us, *viz.*

(*i*) Land can continue to be operated in small units, not by tenants in bondage as hitherto, but by an independent peasantry with or without the assistance of some hired labour ;

(*ii*) We can have large private farms worked with hired labour ; or

(*iii*) We can have large joint farms constituted by peasant farmers pooling their holdings voluntarily or under compulsion, and worked with joint or collective labour.

Small-scale peasant farming and large-scale private farming need no explaining. Nor is joint farming today an altogether novel device. It has been used for a number of years in several countries, notably in Soviet Russia, Mexico and Israel. The Soviet type, although somewhat different in form in the beginning, had been ushered in China in 1955-56, but soon abandoned in favour of what may be regarded as a still more extreme or developed form—the commune. It will be useful to make a rapid review of the working of the system or systems in these countries.

CHAPTER THREE

Features of Modern Joint Farming [1]

IN SOVIET RUSSIA, as a consequence of the Bolshevist Revolution of 1917 carried out under the slogan of 'Peace and Bread', all land was distributed among the peasants. The result was a splitting-up of all the land into some 25,000,000 small farms, each of them capable of producing barely more than was needed by the peasant's own family. Little, if anything, was left to supply the cities. To run his farm, the small peasant needed credits, and obtained them from the wealthier farmer, the *kulak*. Both the deficiency of marketable output and the dominance of the middle class *kulak* presented to the new Soviet State grave problems which had to be solved in terms of its Marxist ideology.

Following the industrial pattern, the Communists argued that farming had to be mechanized. If the peasants could be induced to pool their land and use agricultural machinery in common, not only would the dominance of the *kulaks* be broken but marketable surplus would also be better mobilised. In addition, large-scale joint farming by mechanical means would reduce the number of hands needed in agriculture, and thus free them for use in industry, the expansion of which was, in turn, the *sine qua non* of the mechanisation of agriculture.

A *Kolhoz* or *Kolkhoz* [2]—collective farm—is formed when several peasants living in the same neighbourhood decide, or are induced to make the decision, to socialise their 'basic means of production', *i.e.* labour, soil, draught animals, farm structures and implements, while keeping their individual homes, a small garden, a few livestock, poultry and the like for themselves. Membership is open to all toilers, who have reached the age of sixteen, and who are willing to comply with the established rules and regulations. Application for membership to an already established *kolkhoz* is taken up, first, by its Management Committee and is, legally, subject to the

---

[1] Account of joint farming in Russia, Mexico and Israel has been mostly taken word for word from Henrik F. Infield's article published in the *Year Book of Agricultural Co-operation*, 1951.
[2] Pl. *Kolkhozy*.

approval of the General Assembly. If accepted, the member pays an admission fee which varies in accordance with his previous status. Excluded from membership are *kulaks* and the people deprived of their civic rights. Exceptions are made in the case of families who count among their members a soldier, sailor, or village teacher who is ready to recommend the applicant. Interesting enough, and a sidelight on the effect of collectivisation when ordered from above, is the provision barring peasants "who, before joining the collective farm, slaughter or sell their cattle, get rid of their stock, or wantonly sell their seed corn".

The collective *Ejido* of Mexico can be considered as a sub-type of the *kolkhoz*. *Ejidos* are the new land settlements which were first formed under the agrarian reforms of 1915. They are the off-spring of discontent among labourers in a country of large-scale capitalist farming. There must be at least twenty eligible males to form a group which petitions the Government for land. They must own not more than 2,500 *pesos*, or be of low income status. If the group can lay claim to land that once belonged to them, the land is 'restored' to them ; if their only claim is landlessness, land expropriated from wealthy land-owners—*hacendados*—is 'donated' to them. Both processes are quite protracted and cumbersome, and open to many profiteering practices on the part of the administrative personnel. The allotted land is given to the group in common possession. The members are free to decide whether they want to divide it up and work it individually, or whether they prefer to run it collectively. No admission fee is charged, but each member of group applying for land must contribute his share to the expenses incurred in the process of land assignment.

While the *kolkhoz* and the *ejido* owe their establishment to administrative measures, the *Kvutza* grew out of the spontaneous decisions of those who first shaped its essential socio-economic structure. A particularly acute situation arose in connection with the requirements of Zionist resettlement in Palestine. The development of Jewish agriculture faced two main obstacles : (*i*) the extremely poor quality of available soil ; and (*ii*) the almost complete lack of agricultural experience on the part of the prospective settlers Progress along the lines of traditional individual settlement proved to be so slow as to make prospects for success in the near future very doubtful. The only alternative which offered itself under these circumstances was that of group-settlement. There was, in fact, hardly a choice in the matter. The question appeared to be rather one of either group-settlement, or no settlement at all. The type of settlement which emerged has since become widely known under the name, *Kvutza* or *Kibbutz*.[3]

It was a small group of people devoted to the task of building a Jewish home in the land of their dreams who, after freeing themselves from the uncongenial supervision of a professional agronomist, step by step, experimentally testing their way ahead, developed out of their own free decision what is today called *kvutza* or *kibbutz*. Once this small group of pioneers had set the pattern, and others in relatively large numbers had begun to emulate it, the formation of a *kvutza* became formalised. Today there are two possible ways in which one can join such a settlement, or a group, which prepares for settlement. To be eligible in both cases, one must be a Zionist over eighteen years of age, in good health, and of good character. In the first case, one serves as a candidate for a period of six months to a year, during which time he enjoys virtually all rights of membership with the exception of a vote. At the end of this period, the case of the candidate is brought before the General Assembly, which decides about his or her admission. No admission or any other fee is paid ; but the new member is expected to put all his possessions into the pool. In the second case, the applicant takes part in a training which often begins prior to emigration to Palestine, in one of the Pioneer Training Farms. This training is so devised as to develop the aspirant's capacity for working and living together with others aiming at the same goal. Groups thus prepared form a 'nucleus' (grain), which stays together after immigration to Israel. They continue for a shorter or longer period their preparation, while handling all affairs communally, until the time when they are assigned land for settlement. The period from the start of preparation to final settlement used to last formally sometimes as long as five years. The establishment of the State of Israel made larger areas available for agricultural settlement, and the waiting period has been shortened considerably.

The *kolkhoz*, the *ejido*, and the *kvutza* are alike in their theoretical adherence to the principles of co-operation. The internal administration of all three is based on the Rochdale Principles. It is only that, true to their nature as communities, all three had to

---

[3] Pl. *Kvutzot* and *Kibbutzim*.

modify some of these principles to make them fit their specific requirements. One of these principles is that of open membership.
Community implies more than limited economic activity ; it means
living as well as working together. Moreover, a community is also
naturally restricted by the extent of the geographic area in which
it is located. Because of these and other reasons, membership in
a community cannot be open in the same sense as it is, for instance,
in a consumers' store. For this reason the admission of members
has to be subject to requirements stricter than those imposed in co-
operatives of more limited aims.

Another principle which had to be modified when applied to
the concrete community situation is that of distribution of dividends
according to the amount of purchase. Since the most important aspect of participation in these joint enterprises is that of shared
labour, distribution of net profits according to the amount of purchase would make little sense. The practice followed in all three
instances is, rather to take the amount of labour contributed as the
main basis for the equitable distribution of profit.

As to the remaining principles, the practice in all three instances
is identical with that in any other genuinely co-operative association. No member has more than one vote ; only nominal interest, if
any, is to be paid on investment ; all members have equal rights,
there being no distinction on account of sex ; there are regular meet-
ings at which the members participate in decisions ; and, finally,
members observe rules of proper auditing.

In all three, it is the General Assembly of all members which
is designed as the highest authority in all the internal affairs of
the group. The practice of delegating the conduct and supervision
of the community's business to elected committees is common. Admission, punishment and expulsion of members vests, by law, in the
hands of the General Assembly.

Although theoretically autonomous, the *kolkhoz* and the *ejido*
are much more dependent on government-controlled agencies than
the *kvutza*. The *kolkhoz* is part of a planned economy. It depends,
therefore, on decisions made by the state authorities, particularly,
the *Gosplan* (The National Planning Commission). What is more
important : it is under the direct control of the so-called Machine
and Tractor Station which started as a machine-lending centre and
has since become the 'heart and centre of the local agricultural
administration'. Today, the MTS provides the *kolkhoz* not only with

all large-scale machinery and the staff, but also trains the members in the required skills, and advises them on rotation of crops, the proper use of fertilisers, soil conservation, and other related problems. Above all, the MTS enforces the delivery of that part of the farm produce which the state claims as its share.

A similar, though less stringent supervision is exercised by the state in the case of the collective *ejido*. Here there are two main supervising agencies : (*i*) The National Agrarian Commission which, through State Commissions, directs the establishment of the settlements ; and (*ii*) The National Bank of Ejido Credit which, in addition to furnishing the funds necessary for the running of the settlements, exerts supervisory functions similar to those of the MTS. The Ejido Bank has been described as a combination of banker, agricultural expert, family doctor, school teacher, lawyer, athletic director, and personal adviser of the *ejido*.

It is true that the *kvutza*, too, has received both land and credits from the Jewish National Fund and the Foundation Fund respectively. From the moment of its formation, however, it has always been essentially on its own. In all its relations with the administrative agencies the role of the *kvutza* has been that of a 'contract-partner' rather than that of a 'controlled dependent'.

More marked than any other is the difference in the extent to which co-operation determines the internal activities of the three farm types. Only large-scale agricultural production is carried on jointly in the *kolkhoz* and the *ejido*. In both, work is done by the members themselves ; outside labour may be hired only in times of emergency. In the *kolkhoz* the members form 'work-brigades' composed of five to fifty members, depending on the specific assignment which is made by the Executive Board. Each brigade is directed by a foreman. In the *ejido*, work is organized less strictly, but each member must obey the orders of the elected work-chief. An indicative provision of the Model Rules, which regulate work relations, is the one that forbids the members to accept any outside work as long as the *ejido* itself is in need of their labour.

Co-operation thus limited requires a rather complicated and cumbersome method of accounting. There are two sources of income for the members of the *kolkhoz* and the *ejido*. One is derived from the individual sector production which still exists but is gradually dwindling away : an acre or less of land, a cow, some pigs, and so on, in the *kolkhoz* ; and some small animals, like poultry and pigs, in the *ejido*. The main source of income, however, is large-scale jointly-run agriculture. In both the *kolkhoz* and the *ejido*, the members' share in the harvest is based on the number of labour-days contributed during the year. In the *kolkhoz*, this share is calculated after deduction for taxes, reserves, construction and repairs, on the basis of a measure called 'Work-day' (*trudoden*). This measure is both quantitative and qualitative ; an unskilled labourer will require more hours than a skilled one to fill his *trudoden*. In the *ejido* there are three kinds of compensation for work : (*i*) wages, which differ according to skill ; (*ii*) piece-rates, paid during the cotton-picking season ; and (*iii*) equal shares in the common profit. Work on community projects, school buildings, meeting-halls, roads, is done without any compensation.

The more restrictive aspect of the work relations in *kolkhoz* and *ejido* is reflected in the measures needed to enforce discipline. Punishment is provided in the *kolkhoz* for violations like failure to carry out assignments or to fulfil social obligations ; for absence from work without adequate excuse ; and for negligence in handling equipment and livestock. The punishment may range from reprimand or warning to temporary suspension and fine, or even to expulsion. In the *ejido* the utmost penalty is imposed for : (*i*) continued lack of willingness to work under the direction of the elected authorities ; (*ii*) creating disorders ; (*iii*) agitation against the collective system ; and (*iv*) robbery and other criminal offences.

Compared with all this, the system of the *kvutza* is simplicity itself. The *kvutza* has no use for work-cards, advance wages, shares in profit ; nor does it need any measures of punishment. In the *kvutza*, production, consumption as well as all social activities are co-operative, and everybody is trusted to work according to his best abilities, and to claim from the commonly available goods a share according to his own needs. If a member works on the outside, his earnings go into the group's common purse. No penalty has to be stipulated for absence from work or, for that matter, for any other offence. This does not mean that violations do not occur. They are dealt with in a spirit of "family" persuasion and admonition. Expulsions are extremely rare.

The organization of *kvutza* or *kibbutz* is probably the most complete form of communism in the non-political sense of the word, that the world has known outside monastic communities. Land is not owned, but leased, usually from the Jewish National Fund. Members, who may be men or women, bring in little or no capital of their own ; initial resources are provided by loans from various Zionist funds, and the 'own capital' of the *kibbutz* is accumulated gradually out of annual surpluses. In its dealings with the outside world, the *kibbutz* is on a money economy, and its accounts are kept in that form. Internally, no money passes. Members eat in the common dining-room and receive from the common store clothing, which is washed and mended at a common laundry. From the common store they draw also personal needs and comforts such as soap and cigarettes. As the settlement becomes established, cottages or small blocks of flats are built, in which each worker or married couple is allotted a room. The furniture of these rooms, books, pictures, wireless sets or musical instruments are their only personal possessions. They may be allocated from the property of the *kibbutz*, given by friends or purchased from the allowance, usually about £20, which each member receives for an annual holiday. There are no wages and no individual allocation of surplus at the end of the year. If there is surplus it is used to improve communal services or amenities. A member who leaves, has no right to any share in the common property of the *kibbutz*. The *kibbutzim* are predominantly agricultural, but many maintain sizable industrial enterprises.

Except in a few *kibbutzim*, children do not live with their parents, but are placed from early infancy in nurseries, where they pass to kindergartens and schools, always living with the children of their own age-group until they are old enough to become working members of the settlement. All settlements provide elementary schools. Education up to fourteen is compulsory in Israel. Some also have secondary schools, or a secondary school is run by a group of neighbouring *kibbutzim*. The decision to release a young worker for university education, and to pay for his or her expenses, is taken by the *kibbutz* as a whole, and is influenced by the *kibbutz'* need for a specialist in any particular field of study. The *kibbutz* takes full responsibility for the medical needs of its members and also for the care of the aged.[4]

The *kibbutz*, although probably the most discussed, is by no means the only form of co-operative agriculture in Israel. It was apparent at an early stage that there were prospective settlers who

[4] The degree to which an ageing population will alter the economy of the *kibbutzim* has hardly yet been considered.

were prepared to accept the ownership of land by a national fund, the avoidance of hired labour and a high degree of mutual aid, but not "the extension of collective discipline in the *kibbutz* to cover all aspects of social and economic life. They sought greater scope of personal initiative and individual variety. They felt, too, that the fundamental importance of the family as the organic unit of society, has been neglected by the *kibbutzim*."[5]

In settlements of this type known as *Moshav* or *Moshav Ovdim*, the land which is leased collectively on a forty-nine-year lease, is divided into small holdings, which may be from four to forty acres, according to the type of agriculture carried on. Not infrequently the earliest settlers received two plots, in anticipation that the second plot would be prepared for handing over to a member of the next generation. Some settlers continued to be part-time workers on private farms while they built up their holdings. The General Assembly of all the members elects a Council, which has to approve all transfers of farms and acceptances of new members. Though a general cropping plan is adopted by the settlement, members are free to carry on the work of their own holdings as they think fit. Mixed farming is general, including dairy cattle, poultry, vegetables, green fodder, sometimes grown in a communal field, fruit and grain, usually with the emphasis on the production of members' own food. The *moshav ovdim* are purely agricultural. Settlers have their own houses, and family life follows the usual pattern. In addition to farmers, the settlement includes workers providing village services—drivers, mechanics, cobblers, shopmen, besides teachers and doctors, amounting to some 20 per cent of the community.

Co-operative organisation is, however, comprehensive and compulsory. In some *moshavim*, a single co-operative looks after all the common interests of the village, social, administrative and economic. In others, there are two organisations, one, virtually a local authority, concerned with land leasing, roads, schools, health services and buildings; the other, a co-operative in the ordinary sense, engaged in the marketing of produce, the supply of domestic and agricultural requirements, and agricultural services such as stock-breeding, mechanical cultivation and water supply. In some cases the consumers' co-operative is a separate society. Credit is usually

---

[5] *Co-operative Farming in Israel*, Itzhak Korn.

made available, sometimes as specific loans, sometimes by the simple process of allowing debts to accumulate till crops are sold.

A variant of the *moshav* is the *Moshav Shitufi*, which may be described as half-way between the *moshav* and the *kibbutz*, in that farming (with the exception of small flower and fruit gardens) is carried on collectively while the members continue to live their family lives in private. Each family has its own house and is responsible for its own domestic services such as cooking, laundry and care of the children (as in the *moshav ovdim*). Unlike the members of *kibbutzim*, they are paid, but in proportion to the needs of their families, not (as in Russia) to work done, and at least in some *moshavim shilufim* payment is made, to a considerable extent, not in national currency but in chits which can be cashed only in the co-operative store of the community.

As regards joint farming in China : originally, the Central Committee of the Communist Party of China laid down four types of organisation for agricultural production : (*i*) the temporary (seasonal) mutual-aid team—a simple form of collective labour. Under this arrangement any group of families, with or without land, might come together and form a labour exchange. The farmers were left in possession of their own fields. "Surplus draught animals and implements are loaned to the team by those members who do not need them for current use. Points are allotted to each member for the work done by draught animals, tools or human labour. The credit would be different for manual labour, use of implements or draught animals and also for quantity and quality or work ; "[6] (*ii*) the permanent mutual-aid team—a certain division of labour and assignment of specific work on the basis of collective labour and a small amount of communally-owned property ; (*iii*) the 'elementary' agricultural producers' co-operative—in which members pooled their land as shares and there was unified management and a greater amount of communally-owned property ; and (*iv*) the 'advanced' agricultural producers' co-operative based entirely on collective ownership of the means of production.

The mutual-aid teams were relatively informal organisations. "In the elementary co-operative, 'the principal means of production

[6] Page 34 of the Report of Indian Delegation to China on Agrarian Co-operatives, 1956, hereafter described as the Patil Delegation after the name of its leader, Shri R. K. Patil.

such as land, draught animals and farm tools owned privately by
members are put under a single, centralised management and gradually turned into their common property', and 'the co-operative pays
each member an appropriate sum as dividend out of its annual income, commensurate with amount and quality of land the member
pools in the co-operative'. The 'advanced' type of co-operative is
'a socialist collective economic organisation' to which 'peasants joining the co-operative must turn over their privately owned land and
other important means of production, like draught animals, large
farm tools, etc., to the collective ownership of the co-operative'."[7]

"In China, a distinction is made between the feudal elements in
agriculture and the capitalist elements. The non-cultivating land-
owner is considered to be a feudal element and his lands have been
confiscated without any compensation. The land-owner who cultivates himself is considered to be a capitalist element. While the
Chinese authorities are pursuing a vigorous policy of substituting
peasant proprietorship, which in their view is essentially capitalist agriculture, by co-operative farms, which is socialist agriculture,
they have not confiscated the lands of any land-owner who cultivates them himself unless he has been accused of crime against the
state and the regime."[8]

Those who are not eligible for admission into a co-operative
include, "according to model regulations, former landlords, rich peasants and counter-revolutionaries whose status has not been changed
and who have not yet qualified for membership under the warrant
of the local people's council, and persons deprived of political rights.
Poor peasants and middle peasants are specially encouraged to join
co-operatives and active steps are taken also to draw in demobilised
soldiers, dependants of revolutionary martyrs, soldiers and government workers and also new settlers."[9]

It was clear, however, that the Chinese agrarian policy was set
towards an ultimate collectivisation of agriculture on the Russian
model ; the first three types were merely intermediate stages.[10]
"Their ultimate objective is to pass on from peasant farming,

---

[7] Page 110 of the Report of the Indian Delegation to China on Agricultural Planning and Techniques, July-August, 1956, hereafter described as the Krishnappa Delegation after the name of its leader, Shri
M. V. Krishnappa.   [8] *Ibid.*, p. 61.   [9] *Ibid.*, p. 112.
[10] As has now transpired, even the collective farm was an intermediate
stage to the commune.

first, to co-operative farming and, then, to collective farming at the earliest opportune moment."[11] They did not tarry at the intermediate stages even for five years. No sooner did the agricultural producers' co-operatives come into existence than they were converted into the 'advanced' or collective type. In July, 1955, Chairman Mao Tse-tung had made an important pronouncement when, following a tour of agricultural districts in Central China, he laid down the plans and the party line on agrarian policy and gave the "go-ahead" signal. In only a hundred days, in the autumn of 1955, according to an article under the name of Chau Hansing circulated by the Chinese Embassy in New Delhi, 5,90,000 new agricultural producers' co-operatives were organised in China. This brought their total number to almost $1\frac{1}{4}$ million. It represented the highest tide, thus far, of a constantly accelerating movement that started in 1951. Then the country had only 300 co-operative farms. At the end of 1953, the figure had risen to 14,000. By the summer of 1955, just before the autumn upsurge, there were 6,50,000, with nearly 17 million peasant households as members.

It is said that by January, 1956, 60 per cent and by March, 90 per cent of the peasant families had joined some sort of a co-operative, of whom 56 per cent were members of the so-called 'advanced' co-operatives or collective farms. By the end of May, according to the Report of the Krishnappa Delegation, co-operatives which numbered a million included 91.2 per cent of the 110 million peasant households, of which 61.9 per cent became members of the 'advanced' type. Collectives or societies of the 'advanced' type in 1955 had numbered only 529. It was felt, initially, that it would take a period of three Five-Year Plans for bringing all households into co-operatives. But "such has been the speed with which co-operation has gone forward that, in most parts of China, the main task of establishing agricultural co-operatives of the advanced type is expected to be completed by the close of the winter of 1956."[12] At the time when the Patil Delegation left China, viz. at the end of September, 1956, a figure of 96 per cent was mentioned.

According to the Economist :[13]

[11] Ibid., p. 61.
[12] Ibid., p. 110.
[13] Quoted in the Pioneer, Lucknow, dated October 27, 1956.

Social changes have been most revolutionary in the countryside, and one is left wondering how Mao Tse-tung has succeeded in advancing without bloodshed where Stalin's path was strewn with corpses. Were tax relief and other incentives for the co-operatives and heavy taxation for private farmers enough to push 500 million Chinese peasants into the system ? Out of the 110 million families now within the system, less than one-third are still in looser units, where a rent is still paid to them ; the remainder are grouped in collective farms which approach the Soviet model.

True, a good deal remains to be done to bridge the gap. There are a million collective farms in China against some 90,000 *kolhozy* in the Soviet Union and the difference cannot be explained merely by the size of the rural population and the character of Chinese farming. Quite a lot of consolidation and amalgamation still lies ahead. The Chinese, however, are in no hurry in this respect ; a decade will elapse before they even get the tools necessary for mechanisation. In the next five years the planned 35 per cent increase in agricultural production will have to come from a more rational use of existing resources, local irrigation schemes and fuller utilisation of natural fertilisers. Only afterwards are vast plans of irrigation and land reclamation to pave the way for the tractor.

China does not possess the resources to produce agricultural machinery in bulk ; capital investment is going mainly into heavy industry, and there is little to spare for the import of agricultural machinery or the setting up of large numbers of state farms and machine-tractor stations. In 1953, only 104 (or 2 per cent) of the 4,926 agricultural producers' co-operatives in North-East China were practising mechanised farming. Of all state farms which numbered 3,000 in 1956, only 140 were mechanised. Again, as in Russia, the administration was faced with the problem of decrease in draught animals. In some districts half the buffaloes and oxen were said to have disappeared. Owing to the poor price paid by the co-operatives, peasants sold their beasts, particularly those too young to be worked, to the butchers. The state was almost overwhelmed with the number of hides offered to it for sale.

As usual the country cadres were blamed for mismanagement and ignorant 'Commandism.' But the *People's Daily* put its finger on one basic spot—"the peasant thinks only of getting as much as possible out of the co-operative and whether its interest increases or decreases is not his business."

Another evil, exposed by a long joint directive of the State Council and Central Executive Committee issued on April 3, 1956.

was the reckless waste of money by managers of co-operatives. "They merge villages together by building unnecessary houses, squander money on recreational facilities, sports grounds, roads and nurseries with toys for children, and make no attempt to economise to meet productive expenses."

But with the advent of the people's communes (*jen-min kung-she*) all that has been said above, became past history in a matter of months. The establishment of the communes is the latest in a series of tremendous, frenzied attempts to transform the whole of Chinese society. The commune began on an experimental basis in Honan province in April 1958. Following Mao's tour of that province four months later, the Central Committee of the Chinese Communist Party passed a resolution on August 29 (published September 4), stating that communes would be the basis of the future communist society in China. As a result, while the world's attention in the third quarter of 1958 was focussed on the Quemoy crisis, 'Red' China went through a new and gigantic domestic upheaval. According to official reports, all but a few of the Chinese peasants, *viz*. 99.1 per cent (126.9 million farm households), had been organised into 26,500 communes by early November, 1958. The first communes, of course, came into existence in the characteristically Chinese manner due to the local initiative of peasants !

A commune was formed by the merger of a number of collective farms, or the 'advanced' agricultural producers' co-operatives, as the Chinese call them. An agricultural producers' co-operative was generally co-extensive with a village while the commune is co-extensive with a *hsiang* (a big village or group of villages forming the lowest administrative level under the Constitution of 1954) and the avowed aim of the Chinese communist leaders was to extend the boundary of the communes still further.

The commune represented a social unit combining industry, agriculture, trade, education, culture, politics, local government and military affairs whereas the agricultural producers' co-operative was a social unit concerned with only one field of economic activity —agriculture. Communes revolutionised ownership, labour, consumption and family life as well. Private ownership was abolished not only in land and housing but even in domestic equipments such as cooking pots and so on. The principle of distribution also underwent a complete change. In the communes the peasant became a worker with a fixed income, paid partly in food eaten at the common mess hall and in other amenities, and partly in cash. Labour was militarised to the extreme : each commune had its own militia, and the members were supplied with rifles and bayonets. Leisure was curtailed with the increasing tempo of regimentation.

Communes were so designed and operated as to wipe out the last vestiges of individualism and of traditional family bonds as understood all over the world. Establishment of communal canteens or public service restaurants, the creches, kindergartens and 'happy homes' for the old revolutionised the family life altogether. The peasants ate in communal mess halls, and individual cooking was forbidden. They slept in dormitories where these had been constructed, and put their children in commune schools and creches. The aim was to double the labour force by freeing women from household chores for work in fields and factories. And in fields and factories, husbands and wives, parents and grown-up children were not necessarily in the same team. "Nursing mothers and those of ailing children," says Dr. S. Chandrashekhar, Director of the Indian Institute for Population Studies, Madras, who had visited China recently, "can visit creches or kindergartens, though this is not necessary as children are under the care of trained nurses and teachers. Parents can give up their bourgeois emotional attachments and stop worrying about their children."[14]

While the commune represented a type of social insurance whereby everybody in the village was assured of a living, a roof above his head and two or three meals a day irrespective of his earning capacity, it also meant the total loss of individual freedom and initiative. The Household Registration Law, promulgated in early 1958, imposed harsh restrictions upon the rights of movement and association. Under that law everyone was required to notify the police before leaving a place and on reaching a new place. Everyone was required to notify the local authorities the arrival of a friend, relation or guest. In the communes all had to take part in military parades in the mornings and evenings and also to attend indoctrination courses and military classes. So that under this latest communist dispensation China had become one vast army camp. As a writer has observed, "even the Soviet Union is a free country compared with Red China."

[14] Article in the *Statesman*, New Delhi, 13 January 1959.

Dr. S. Chandrashekhar remarks: "This is the commune where human beings are reduced to the level of inmates in a zoo. But there is a difference. The animals in a zoo do not have to work hard and, what is more, they do not have to listen to the quasi-compulsory radio, which pours out the latest editorial from the *People's Daily*." "The lack of peace and quiet in the countryside," he adds, "where no one can retire and reflect, and the lack of privacy and solitude are to me more terrifying than all the hells put together."

As a result, there were many complaints and the work done in many a commune was poor. Reports of purges in the northern part of 'Red' China in November 1958, were the first indication to the outside world that the communes had run into serious difficulties. These reports, it may be mentioned, emanated not from propaganda sources but were contained in official Chinese communist publications. Although the party put off for an indefinite period the establishment of large-scale communes in big cities, it had no intention at the time to go back on the 'great leap forward' already taken. According to a resolution passed at its historic meeting held at Weechang from November 28 to December 10, 1958, the party came out with a call that the communes, estimated to total more than 26,000, be 'tidied up, checked up and consolidated' by April, 1959. The job was entrusted to army personnel who constituted a large proportion of the special 10,000-man inspecting teams in each province, which were expected to 'thoroughly reorganise, consolidate and improve' the communes.

The birth of the commune in 1958 was accompanied by propaganda about multiplying farm yields, free food and clothes for peasants, the elimination of the 'last remnants of individual ownership of the means of production' in agriculture, and the early dawn of true communism. A 'great leap forward' was promised and publicised, but in actual fact it did not materialise. Hardly, therefore, had a year passed since their inception that China's communist leaders were forced to undertake a painful revision of their economic plans based on the communes. Members of the Central Committee met in a plenary session at Lushan and conferred for a full fortnight, from August 2 to August 15, 1959, 'under the guidance of Comrade Mao Tse-tung'. The official communique showed that there was continued opposition within their ranks to the experiment in communal living. As usual, a 'rightist deviation' was detected and some of the humbler party-men were blamed for their lack of ambition and unjustified pessimism.

The moderates, however, seemed to have come out on top with a compromise policy slowing down the pace of development while continuing the pledge of allegiance to the principles of the 'great leap forward' programme. This was reflected in an announcement on August 26, reducing the year's grain and cotton targets by about half and sharply scaling down figures originally claimed for these harvests in the preceding year.

Not only that, the claims—both ideological and economic—that were being made for the communes were toned down. The realization dawned upon the communists that if agricultural production was to increase, the peasants needed some incentives and 'small freedoms.' The communes, therefore, are no longer expected to make a significant contribution to China's industrial output, and several features of the co-operative farms from which the communes sprang, were restored :

Instead of working solely for the commune, peasants are now encouraged to grow food, keep pigs and hens in their spare time on individual plots and keep any income they make out of this . . . . Small local markets have been set up in communes where a peasant can sell his own produce to the state. A system of supplying peasants with food and clothing as part of their wages was introduced when the communes started. But now the peasants receive more of their income in cash and less in kind. An incentive plan under which those who work harder earn more, has also been brought in.

At first, mess halls for all the peasants came with the communes. Recent official statements have stressed that the peasants need not eat there if they do not wish to, and they must be allowed to take their meals home or cook at home if they prefer.

Military drills were started with the communes, but now they are never mentioned.[15]

After more than a decade of relentless effort and inhuman sacrifice, the Chinese were admitting that they were hardly closer to solving the nation's essential economic problem—food and agriculture—than when they began. In fact, rushing fast as they could, they have barely managed to stay in the same place. Point 4 of a 10-point plan for 1962 outlined by the Prime Minister, Mr. Chou-

[15] Reuter (*Vide* the *Pioneer*, Lucknow, 31 August 1959.)

en-Lai, in his speech in the secret session of the National People's Congress (Parliament), according to an official communique issued at the end of the session on April 16, 1962, aimed at *reducing the urban population and sending back into farm production the workers and functionaries who had come from the rural areas to the towns.* No further proof of the failure of the communes is required, or could be forthcoming. Land area being practically constant, progressive agriculture, as will appear later, can only mean that innovations in the art of farming are being increasingly introduced, more capital is being invested and farmers work harder, better and longer, so that labour is released from agriculture for absorption in other pursuits. A "back-to-the-land" call shows a reverse trend.

The idea of the commune had been tried out on a much smaller scale in Russia, and the experiment ended in failure. When Stalin later on set out to collectivise farming, he forbade every mention of the commune and, ever since, the commune has remained under something like an ideological ban in the Soviet Union. The Chinese, obviously not content with the collective farm, had startlingly rehabilitated the commune. They decided to move henceforth on the road of collectivism quicker and faster than the Russians, and this despite the fact that in technology their farming was very far behind the Russian. On the other hand, Khrushchev has made a series of important concessions to the peasants, relaxing the Stalinist rigours of collectivisation. He has sold the Machine-Tractor stations, hitherto state-owned, to the collective farms ; he has freed the peasants from compulsory food deliveries and he has attempted to place the economic relationship between state and peasantry on something like a market basis. Thus, the whole trend of Chinese policy in regard to agriculture has been at variance with Soviet policy. In an interview with Senator Hubert H. Humphrey of the USA (published in the *Pioneer*, Lucknow, 21 January 1959), Khrushchev branded the commune system as 'old-fashioned and reactionary'. He said, "we tried that right after the revolution. It just does not work. That system is not nearly so good as the state farms and the collective farms." The reason given was that the principle, *viz.*, 'from each according to his abilities, to each according to his needs,' on which the communes were based was not workable and that 'you can't get production without incentive'.

It may be added that Khrushchev preferred state farms because there a worker gets a remuneration according to the labour put in, and collective farms because he has lately been trying to reform them and provide incentives to its members.

Humphrey writes that he was startled at the leader of world communism rejecting the very core of Marxist theory. The Senator asked if his statement on incentives was not 'rather capitalistic'. "Call it what you will," Khrushchev replied, "it works."[16]

---

[16] Hereafter in these pages we will extensively discuss the primary or the elementary agricultural producers' co-operative alone, because it is only this type of agrarian organisation from China that the Planning Commission and the Government of India want to imitate.

CHAPTER FOUR

Co-operative and Collective Farming

THE SO-CALLED co-operative farm—a farm on the lines of the Chinese agricultural producers' co-operative—about which we hear so much and which so many eminent people in our country seem to regard as the panacea for most of the ills from which our rural body-politic suffers, is advocated as a type of farming which, while not affecting any of our fundamental social institutions or interfering with the framework of private property, will have all the advantages which the USSR is said to have reaped from the *kolkhoz*. The co-operative farm is regarded as representing a golden mean between the capitalist organisation with its stress on individual rights and the complete collectivist system under which all individual rights of property are suppressed and merged in collective or state ownership.

Co-operative farms should be organised, says the Committee on Problems of Reorganisation appointed by the Planning Commission's Panel on Land Reforms, as a first step, on the surplus land obtained on the imposition of a ceiling, Government waste land considered suitable for cultivation, land reclaimed through public effort and land periodically let out by Government wherever such lands are available in sizeable areas. As a rule, these lands should be settled with co-operatives, and individual rights should not be created in them. They will constitute the nucleus for co-operative farming. The displaced tenants, the landless agricultural workers who may be selected for settlement on these lands, and the cultivators below the floor limit who agree to put their lands into the pool, will be admitted as members of the co-operative farm. The farms below the floor limit, which stay out of a co-operative farm at the commencement, should be located contiguously to the pooled area as part of operations of consolidation of holdings to enable them to join a co-operative farm at a later date.

The aim is to enlarge the co-operative sector until the entire farm land in the village is included in co-operative farming societies, in fact, until the entire area of the village, both cultivated and uncultivated, becomes the co-operative responsibility of the community and is managed 'as if it were a single farm'.[1]

As regards the method of pooling of land, the following different forms were considered by the Committee :

(*i*) The ownership of land may be retained by individuals but the land may be managed as one unit, the owners being compensated through some form of ownership dividend ;

(*ii*) The land may be leased to the co-operative society for a period, the owners being paid agreed rents or rents prescribed by law ; or

(*iii*) Ownership may be transferred to the co-operative society, but shares representing the value of land may be given to individuals.

As the surplus and other governmental lands will be settled with co-operative groups and not with individuals, no difficulty regarding pooling of land would arise in their case. With regard to land pooled by individuals, no particular method is recommended and no rigid conditions prescribed.

The following different methods of co-operative management were discussed :

(*i*) The entire area may be distributed into family units, each unit being allotted to a member family or a small group of families (depending upon the extent of land available with the co-operative) for purposes of cultivation, the member family or the group paying rent to the society. Each family or a group of families will, thus, have a separate plot to cultivate. They will, however, co-operate in the non-farm operations such as provision of credit facilities, supplies, marketing, etc., and in such farm operations as may be feasible ;

(*ii*) The whole farm may be managed as one unit for carrying out principal operations such as ploughing, sowing and harvesting. For subsidiary operations like irrigation, weeding, hoeing, etc., the farm may be divided into small units, each being allotted to individual families from year to year, the families getting a share of the produce as remuneration for work on subsidiary operations ; and

(*iii*) The whole farm may be managed as one unit for all agricultural operations which will, thus, be centrally controlled by the society, the members being paid wages either on daily wage or on piece-work basis.

[1] *Second Five-Year Plan*, p. 197.

The adoption of any particular mode of management, says the Committee, will depend on the technique of farming that may be applied and the degree of co-operation which has developed among the members. Each co-operative farm will adopt the mode of management which suits it best according to its own circumstances. It is suggested, therefore, that at this stage all the various methods may be tried, till suitable techniques of co-operative management are fully established by experience.

The description of the working of large-scale joint farming in various countries and the ideas of the Planning Commission on the subject throw into relief three minor differences between an agrarian producers' co-operative or a co-operative farm and a collective farm of the *kolkhoz* type. These are :

(*i*) A co-operative farm is an entirely voluntary organisation, no one having a right to be admitted to membership as a matter of course. Whereas in a collective farm all workers of both sexes in the village or locality have a right to membership and it is doubtful whether any person holding land has a right to stay away ;

(*ii*) Under co-operative farming, ownership of land continues to vest in the members who contribute it, whereas under collective farming it passes to the society as a whole. It is not material to the definition of co-operative farming whether or not the individual owners have the right to withdraw their holdings physically from the co-operative farm though, according to most writers, they should have such a right. Where such right is denied to a retiring member, it is essential that he should receive due compensation for the property finally surrendered by him. In a collective farm, however, its members can decidedly have no such right and, as the ownership of land had already passed to the farm or to the society, no question of compensation either arises ;

(*iii*) A co-operative farm pays wages to workers, whether members or not, at prevailing rates and distributes net profit according to the value of the land and also of the live-stock and the dead stock, if contributed. Or, it may adopt another procedure, *viz.* the net proceeds of the farm arrived at after deducting all the expenses of cultivation including payments to members for the use of their land in proportion to its value, wages paid to outsiders, cost of management and contributions to the reserve fund and other funds, if any are established, may be shared by members in proportion to the labour put in by each. The members of a collective farm, on the other hand, are entitled to a share in the net income only according to the number of labour days put in by them. That is, in a collective farm the participants have only one kind of income from the farm— that due to work ; in a co-operative farm those who have contributed the land or stock are entitled to a dividend or an income on account of their contribution, apart from anything they may earn as workers on the farm.

Apart from these differences in the organisational set-up, there is no difference in the actual working of the two types. Rather, there is much greater significance in their similarities. Both are joint enterprises. Land, labour and capital resources are pooled both in a co-operative and a collective farm, and whatever production technique can be applied to one may be equally applied to the other. The effect on peasants-cum-labourers constituting the farm is similar in both cases and, from the point of view of agricultural production, there is nothing to choose between them. In a co-operative farm the identity of both the farm and the farmer disappears as completely as it does in a collective farm. Whatever criticism applies to one applies equally to the other.

To call an agricultural producers' co-operative or the so-called co-operative farm as distinguished from a collective farm, a co-operative enterprise, will be a misnomer. A co-operative is an'association of free autonomous economic units, whereas a co-operative farm consists of members who have lost their economic autonomy. A co-operative is intended to support the enterprise and the business activities of its members. This aim can only be realised if there are autonomous enterprises of the members who associate in order to support their individual enterprises. It cannot be the purpose of a co-operative association to dissolve the individual enterprises and replace them by a joint or collective enterprise.

One cannot have much quarrel with the Planning Commission's Committee on Problems of Reorganisation. It leaves the suitable method of co-operative management to be evolved by experience. The Prime Minister restated the same approach in his address to the Uttar Pradesh Political Conference in Jaunpur on 29 October 1956. He said :

...the Government did not intend to proceed in the matter arbitrarily. It was for the *kisans* themselves to take into account the pros and cons of co-operation and, if they considered it to be useful for them and the country, they should adopt it. But to him there appeared to be no alternative. At this stage all that he wanted was that they should discuss the matter among themselves thoroughly and try co-operatives as an experimental measure.

The first method advocated by the Planning Commission's Committee under which each family has a separate holding to cultivate is but a variant of what is known as a Better Farming Society. Co-operation is not stretched to the point of merger of holdings, but is limited to non-farm activities where it can find its most fruitful field in the domain of agriculture. This method will be acceptable to all ; but the Planning Commission insists that "co-operative farming necessarily implies pooling of lands and joint management". The only concession it makes is that "at this stage of development" it is not prepared to recommend any particular "manner in which lands may be pooled and operated" (*Second Five-Year Plan*, p. 201). It is this insistence which compels a dispassionate examination of the available evidence for and against large-scale joint-farming. Such examination is all the more necessary in view of the fact that the most powerful political party in the country, *viz.* the Indian National Congress has also, in its plenary session held at Nagpur in January 1959, agreed with the Planning Commission and accepted joint farming as the ultimate pattern for India.

The relevant part of the Nagpur Resolution says :

The future agrarian pattern should be that of co-operative joint farming in which the land will be pooled for joint cultivation, the farmers continuing to retain their property rights and getting a share from the net produce in proportion to their land. Further, those who actually work on the land, whether they own the land or not, will get a share in proportion to the work put in by them on the joint farm.

As a first step, prior to the institution of joint farming, service co-operatives should be organised throughout the country. This stage should be completed within a period of three years. Even within this period, wherever possible and generally agreed to by the farmers, joint cultivation may be started.

Surplus land (obtained by imposition of a ceiling on large farms) should vest in the *panchayats* and should be managed through the co-operatives.

The scheme enunciated by the resolution is not so simple as it looks. While it betrays a confusion of thought there are several aspects which are sinister in their implications :

(*a*) The use of the words 'should be' in the first sentence indicates the mandatory nature of the resolution. The words also involve a notion of obligation on the part of the farmers. As if it is not their right to decide how they will or will not carry on cultivation of their lands. It seems to be forgotten that agriculture is not only a science that had to be learned, but also a way of life that could not be rushed or planned by somebody else for the farmer.

(*b*) The aim is defined as 'co-operative joint farming'. One would like to know whether there is a pattern such as 'co-operative single or several farming' also, from which it was considered necessary to distinguish the type recommended here. Co-operative farming cannot but be joint.

(*c*) In order to allay the fears of the farmers the resolution has laid down that they will continue to retain their property rights, but in view of the annotation that Prime Minister Nehru made in his speech in the *Lok Sabha* on March 28, 1959, the assurance contained in the resolution is not worth a moment's consideration. He said : "Of course, the House will remember that we have said that the ownership of the land will continue. Some people say that this is either a ruse or even if we mean it, we will not be able to stick by it. I do not know ; how can I say about the future ? This concept of ownership is a peculiar concept which has changed throughout the ages. The House knows Acharya Vinoba Bhave thinks there should be no ownership of land at all. There it is ; I respect it and I should be very happy, indeed, if that was so. But I do not think it can be so today..... The whole concept of ownership is changing and yet we are sticking to ownership by sitting on a square yard of land and being proud that this square yard is mine and nobody can take it.... In the cities there used to be roads privately owned, bridges privately owned, all kinds of things. Now, a road has become a public, municipal property, a bridge has become municipal or public property, public utilities and so on. Railways and so many things have become public property. The idea of private ownership changes and the public and the individual benefit by it. So, this changing society changes its ideals about these basic forms of ownership. That will happen. One should not be afraid of it. In fact, one should welcome that, provided it leads to the objectives we are aiming at."

(*d*) It would appear that landless persons also have a right to join the co-operative farm whether landowners want them or not.

It is not clear how their work will be evaluated. If wages are paid in cash on a fixed daily or monthly basis, they will be as good as labourers on private farms with no improvement in their status. If, on the other hand (they are given a say in the management, or greater rights than they enjoyed before, or) wages payable to the labourers are evaluated on the same basis as the landowners, the latter would never agree to join such a venture, or allow labourers to join it. The communists in Russia and China had forced the so-called co-operatives on the people only after land had been distributed to everybody in the village.

(e) The words 'may be started' in the second paragraph of the resolution would, again, seem to indicate as if it is not the farmers or landowners who will start the farms, but somebody else who will do it for them. If it is their volition alone that mattered, there was no need, in a way, to show a signal to anybody to go ahead today or three years later.

(f) It is not necessary, according to the resolution, that all farmers in a village should agree before a joint farm could be established. Only a 'general' agreement is required, and a general agreement could mean, if one so chose, even a bare majority decision. Now, it is not democracy to take away one's means of subsistence by the majority decision of one's neighbours and, thus, force upon him a complete change in his way of life as thrusting a man in a co-operative farm would amount to. Of course, if the nation as a whole so decides, it can do so, but in that case it will have to give itself a different Constitution.

(g) To call a joint farm established on surplus lands obtained by imposition of a ceiling, under the terms of the resolution, a co-operative farm, will be a misnomer. The land constituting the farm will not belong to the members, but to the state or the village *panchayat*. Nor will members, therefore, on resignation or expulsion, be entitled to take away a parcel or any share for individual cultivation. Nor will they earn any income other than that due to, and proportionate with the labour put in by them on the farm. So that, it is, pure and simple, a *kolkhoz*—a collective farm of the Russian type.

It is not without reason, therefore, that the communists welcomed the Nagpur resolution ; rather, they congratulated the Indian National Congress thereon. They suggested only one amendment, *viz.* the surplus lands that will be available on imposition of a ceiling should, for the present, be distributed among the landless.

CHAPTER FIVE

Our Problems and the Basic Limitation

IT WOULD BE axiomatic to state that our economy, industrial or agrarian, should be governed by the conditions of our country and so regulated that it might help to solve the main problems that face us, or help to realise the ideals that we have in view. We cannot just copy or lift an agrarian economy obtaining in any particular country irrespective of the society that the latter hopes to build for itself, or irrespective of its conditions, geographical, climatic, and other which may or may not be applicable in our case. Now, the main problems that call for solution in our country, as in many others, can be formulated as follows :

(*i*)   Increase of total wealth or production ;
(*ii*)   Elimination of unemployment and under-employment ;
(*iii*)   Equitable distribution of wealth ; and
(*iv*)   Making democracy a success.

All our laws, schemes, and projects have to be evaluated in the light of these problems. Those which serve to contribute to their solution are beneficial to the country. Those which do not, have to be rejected.

It will be found that, of the three alternatives mentioned in Chapter Two, it is the first, *viz.* an economy of small farms operated by animal, or, if necessary, manual power, and individually worked, with such farms co-operatively linked with each other in all economic activities other than actual farming or production, which will best answer our needs and solve our problems taken together.

The form of agricultural organisation in a country will depend on the proportion in which the two factors of production, *viz.* labour and capital, either separately or more usually conjointly, are available in relation to the third, *viz.* land. The quantity of land that is available for production in our country today is, for all practical purposes, fixed ; there is little possibility, as we shall see, of extension of agriculture by reclamation and colonisation. In other words, land is relatively scarce and constitutes the limiting factor. On

33

the other hand, because of our large and increasing population, the supply of labour is unlimited. That part of capital which provides traction power, *viz.* draught cattle, is, by no means, lacking, if not actually surplus to our needs. Our agrarian organisation has, therefore, of necessity to be such as would lend itself to the maximum exploitation of land, as will give us maximum yield per acre, even though it may not be consistent with the maximum exploitation of labour and capital. It is only in countries like the USA, Canada, Australia or New Zealand where land is not a limiting factor and labour is relatively scarce, that it may be in the national interest to obtain the maximum output per worker rather than maximum yield per acre. Such countries can afford to have an economy which may be wasteful of land. But we in India, where land is relatively so scarce and, therefore, more valuable than the other two factors, cannot but have an economy which is economical in its use of land resources, though it may be wasteful of labour and capital resources, that is, an economy where we have to apply to land more or increasing units of labour or capital, or of both in order that the fullest use may be made of the former, or, which is the same thing, bigger yields realised per acre. To quote W. J. Spillman : "The greatest profit from the business as a whole involves the greatest profit per unit of the limiting factor. Thus, if land be the limiting factor, the aim should be to make the largest profit per acre. If labour limits the business, the aim should be the largest possible profit per unit of labour. Similarly, if the limiting factor be materials, the aim should be the greatest profit per unit of materials."[1]

Marxism, like capitalism, has everywhere asked : How could one obtain from the existing surface a maximum return with a minimum of labour ? The question for us is different. It is : How could we, on the existing surface, secure a living to a maximum number of people through the use of their labour in the villages ? Land being the limiting factor in our conditions, our aim must be, obviously, not the highest possible production per man or agricultural worker, but highest possible production per acre. That is what will give us the largest total for India as a whole and thus eradicate poverty or want of wealth in the absolute.

[1] *The Law of Diminishing Returns*, p. 43.

CHAPTER SIX

Production of Wealth

SIZE OF FARM

A GOOD FEW think that a compact area of 100 acres will yield a somewhat higher produce than 10 plots of 10 acres each. That is, concentration of land will give greater yield per acre than if it is divided or dispersed into small units. People living in the cities who have before them the example of big economic units working success-fully in the field of manufacturing industry, argue by analogy that big mechanised undertakings would produce more in the field of agriculture also. They consider that increased production of food cannot be achieved unless the peasants abandon small-scale farming and join or merge themselves into societies where large-scale farm-ing is possible and tractors, combine-harvesters and similar mecha-nical devices can profitably be used. They would like to put agri-culture, too, on a factory[1] basis.

The economists in our country and the intelligentsia, in general, have taken their views mostly from Marx, the core of whose econo-mic analysis, as of his theory, was a fundamental belief in the superiority, and hence in the necessity, of large-scale production. To him large-scale production was the first condition for general well-being. That condition was clearly being realised in the field of industry ; Marx took it for granted that the same process was bound to take place also in agriculture.

According to Marx the peasant was doomed because he was a peasant, and the evil to which the peasant was succumbing was just his dwarf holding. Neither the peasant nor his system was com-patible with progress, and the development of the society was over-coming them both. The Communist Manifesto went straight to the goal—the scientific cultivation of the soil upon a common plan by means of armies of labourers.

The small peasant produces mainly for himself ; the capitalist farmer mainly for the market. But capitalist farming was obno-

---

[1] In fact, some of the collective farms in the USSR, devoted largely to one crop, were known as 'wheat factory', 'sugar-beet factory', etc.

35

xious to the very principle of communism and, as the industrial workers depended on purchased food-stuffs and these, the Communists said, could not be obtained from the peasants, the old peasant economy was incompatible with the new industrialised state. The peasant was, therefore, to be transformed into a labourer and the nationalised soil tilled by co-operatives of production under the control of society as a whole.

. As has been pointed out by David Mitrany,[2] no part of Marx's economic theory was more uncritically accepted than this. It was forgotten that when Marx was formulating his theory he was living in England where there were no peasants and no agrarian questions to challenge his outlook. His description of the agricultural situation was based on the life of the English labourer and of the pitiable Irish peasantry about the middle of the last century. It was, further, a period when everything seemed to point to concentration of land in the hands of a few large owners. An important aspect of this phenomenon, *viz.* that the increase in large estates had often been achieved by political and social pressure (through enclosures and partly as the price for emancipation of the peasants), and did not represent simply the victory of the better system in free competition, escaped his notice completely. The original views of Marx on agrarian development have, however, continued to grip the communist mind ever since, in spite of the statement of Engels that Marx had himself begun to doubt their validity in cases where, as in Eastern Europe, farming was not capitalistic.

The explanation why, as a consequence of an increased scale of output, a manufacturer can expect to obtain increasing returns per unit of labour or other economic resources employed, while a farmer cannot, lies in the fundamental difference between the two kinds of industry, which has been admirably brought out by Van Der Post. "The manufacturing process", says he, "is a mechanical process producing articles to pattern in succession from the same machine. The agricultural process, on the other hand, is a biological process, and its products are the result not of a man-driven mechanism, but of their own inherent qualities of growth. In the case of the industrial commodity, therefore, standing room for a machine and its operator will suffice in order that it be multiplied indefinitely. In the case of the agricultural commodity, on the other hand, standing

---

[2] *Marx against the Peasant*, London, 1952, Part I, Chapter I.

room is required for each article that has to be produced."[3]

From this fundamental difference between the nature of the two industries stem several other differences that characterise their working and also affect the size of the industrial and agricultural undertakings.

Agriculture depends on the area of land—on the area in which plants can spread their roots and expose their leaves to the sun, and from which they can draw water and chemical substances necessary for their growth. A plant will take the same space to grow, whether it is sown in a small farm or large, so that a large farm has no advantage over a small farm in per-acre production. Provided, therefore, there is no difference in farming methods and capital employed per man is equal, returns per man will diminish as an increasing number of men are put to farm a limited area of land, because the men have, on an average, less area to work with. At the same time, as more men cultivate the land, returns per acre will increase, because each acre has more labour applied to it. Thus, two men working ten acres of land can produce more than one man working those ten acres, and three men working the same area can produce more than two men. But the increase in product per acre, with the increase in the number of workers, is a diminishing increase : the increase in product is in lower proportion than the proportion by which the number of workers increases. Two men working the ten acres cannot produce double of what the one previously working them was doing ; nor can three men produce as much per man as each of the two men. In other words, each equal additional quantity of work bestowed on cultivation of a given area of land yields an actually diminishing return, and this is what is called the 'Law of Diminishing Returns' in agriculture. It can also be described and, perhaps, more correctly, as the 'Law of Diminishing Increments'.

"Except for diminishing returns", says Dr. Elmer Pendell[4], "quantity of land in the world, or in one country, or on one farm, would have no relation to quantity of production. Except for diminishing returns, a twenty-acre farm would produce as much as a thousand-acre farm. If additional volumes of crops could be had in proportion to capital and labour put on the land, a given outlay of capital and labour would produce as much on a small acreage as on a large acreage."

---

[3] *Economics of Agriculture*, p. 162.
[4] *Population on the Loose*, New York, 1951, p. 40.

On the other hand, manufacturing is not dependent on area. If need be, it can also expand upwards. Land, therefore, does not enter substantially into the calculations of manufacturing or its production. Manufacturing deals with labour, raw materials, machines and other capital, which are not constant or limiting factors like land. Labour is increasing daily and raw materials can be produced and capital created by efforts of man. Thus, manufacturing in most branches can be, and is carried out in such a way that product per man or other economic resources employed, rises as the scale of industry is increased. This means that manufacturing works under the law of increasing returns. Manufacturing units, therefore, tend to grow big, which cannot be true of agricultural units.

Dependence of agriculture on area means that larger the size of the farm, the more scattered its operations. This not only makes large farming more expensive than large manufacturing, but makes it more difficult to supervise. Men concentrated under one roof, as is the case with manufacturing, are easier to supervise, than men spread over a large area.

Besides area or space, there is the time factor which tends to push up the size of an industrial undertaking as compared with agricultural. In manufacturing, as the size of the machine or industrial plant increases with improvement in technology, there is greater and greater operational and functional division of labour and, therefore, less and less time is taken in turning out a given quantity of product than before. Economy of time means economy of effort and expenditure. No such economy or economies, however, are possible in the sphere of agriculture where time, like space, is an irreducible minimum which remains unaffected by the size of the enterprise. An agricultural plant will take the same time to mature, whether it is sown in a small farm or large.

While manufacturing lends itself to specialization by tasks and by products and its production can be standardized, agriculture and its production, thanks to its biological character and, therefore, its dependence so primarily on local and particular contexts and imponderable factors like weather, cannot. Manufacturing, therefore, needs less supervision than agriculture and is susceptible to delegation and differentiation of managerial functions much better. These factors favour a larger scale of operations in manufacturing than in agriculture.

Further, crops (and cattle) need not only more intimate, affectionate and devoted care—they need a twenty-four hours' care. A
workshop has its hours of working and closure, but agriculture
simply has no closing hours. Necessarily, this distinguishing feature
makes a lot of difference in the scale of undertakings in the two
spheres.

The invention of the steam-engine in the eighteenth century
led to an unparalleled economic revolution involving a complete upheaval in methods and rates of industrial production (and in civilization in general). Where hitherto man had scarcely known or used
any but hand tools, he had henceforth at his disposal a machine
driven by an external source of power, which could be harnessed
to an indefinite number of other machines.

The great inventions heralding the birth of the capitalist economy, demanded large numbers of workers, heavy capital investment and world-wide markets. The handicraft workshop in which
the master-craftsman worked alongside a few journeymen or ap-
prentices gave way to the factory and the big firm in which concentration of property and the scale of production steadily increased
and the machines were constantly improved.

While, however, introduction of the steam-engine brought a
hundredfold, even a two hundredfold increase in man's capacity
to produce manufactured goods in a given time and space, it did
nothing of the kind in agriculture, which is a biological process.
Mechanised equipment does not overcome the most important
conditions limiting agricultural yields, *viz.* natural fertility of the
soil and climatic conditions. In mechanical processing, replacement
of hand power by steam power established a new relationship between the size of an undertaking and its production. But it could
not influence the life process of plants, and the relationship between
the size of an agricultural farm and its production necessarily
remained unaffected. It was an 'Industrial Revolution' as it is
rightly called, not an 'Agricultural Revolution'.

However, while in sheer theory, the size of the farm, in and of
itself, did not affect production per acre, in actual practice and
for reasons following, given the same resource facilities, soil content and climate, a small farm produces, acre for acre, more than
a large one—howsoever organised, whether co-operatively, collectively or on a capitalistic basis. And it will continue to produce
more, until a device is discovered which can accelerate nature's

process of gestation and growth—a device which can be used only on a large farm and not on small.

Firstly, a plant is a living organism. As such it requires individual care and attention somewhat in the same manner as an animal or human being does. In industry a worker can be 'functionally' efficient even if he is utterly uninterested in the work because work is highly routinised, impersonalised and mechanised. But farming is not a matter of routine. The yield of the land depends directly on the care with which the farmer conserves the soil and protects the crop. And there are limits to the physical and supervisory capacity of the owner or the manager of the farm—to the regard and solicitude which he can bestow. As no man or woman can satisfactorily look after two dozen cows or two dozen children, so no farmer can tend crops efficiently beyond a certain area or limit.

Nor can such care and attention be forthcoming on a co-operative or collective farm either, where no land or field belongs, or is entrusted to anybody exclusively. Distributed responsibility or responsibility of the many which a co-operative or a collective enterprise involves, unless its members are close blood relations, or are inspired by high idealism, which in the economic sphere of human life is rare, will ultimately boil down to the responsibility of no one, and cannot take the place of individual interest which alone can provide the close, constant and intimate attention that lands and crops require.

A man who comes to have two adult sons living and working jointly with him, will produce more per acre, or which is the same thing, a greater total from the same area of land than when he was alone. Similarly, when he has, say, five sons, who are inspired by the same common good or interest of the family, they will produce a still greater total. If, however, whether during the life-time of the father or after his death, mutual distrust among the brothers emerges and they come to place, even in their thoughts, their ownselves, wives or children, above the family as a whole, the production will definitely decline. When the brothers eventually separate and, thus, the incentive for hard work is restored, the production per acre will again go up and, possibly, will be higher than even when mutual trust and confidence existed between them. Such is the experience of all those who come from amongst the peasantry, or know the urges and the psychology of an average house-holder.

Conversely, when, say, five men who were heretofore separately working their holdings, howsoever small, merge or are made to merge them in a joint farm, they will not produce more per acre by virtue of mere merger. At best, that is, if the members of the farm have, with increase in the area of the farm, also broadened their sympathies and are inspired by a common interest, the produce from the joint farm will only total up to what it was previously on the separate farms. On the other hand, if the farmers have only merged their lands, and not their interests, thoughts and sympathies also—which state of affairs will be the rule if joint farms spring up as a result of a drive of Government or a political party—the production will markedly go down. And the larger the number of such farmers, the less possibility there will be of their working as a willing team—as an enthusiastic unit.

Secondly, a peasant farmer and his family are usually under-employed on their patch of land. They do not have to pay for the time and the labour that they devote to it, so that even for a small extra yield they will apply all the labour they are capable of. In peasant farming land is the limiting factor, and the greatest profits, therefore, lie in the maximum yield per acre. On the contrary, the owner of a big farm has necessarily to engage labour on payment, and unless the extra yield is commensurate with the extra labour that may be applied, the extra labour will not be worth-while. In his case labour is the limiting factor, not land ; for, land is there to which extra labour may be employed but it is too costly for the additional output. The maximum profits in the case of a big farmer will not, therefore, correspond to the maximum yield from land as in the case of a small farmer, but to maximum exploitation of labour.

In this context it may not be irrelevant to point to a non-economic consideration which tends to operate against a large farmer and in favour of a small one. Paid labourers can in no case bring to apply the same attention, the same devotion which members of a peasant family will, whether in tending the crops or the aminals of in performing any other of the varied tasks of cultivation. Agriculture for a peasant is not only a means of living, but a way of life also. His wife, children and old parents labour not merely for gain. Whereas the labourers work for wages, not for love.

If the large farm is a co-operative or collective undertaking, the workers or members will lack the incentive, which a peasant farmer owning his patch of land and being master of his produce has, for working hard. There is bound to be a world of difference between the self-employed farmer who works for himself and his family and uses his own judgment in his work, on one hand, and the farmer in a co-operative farm who has to work under the watchful eye of the supervisors, on the other. The knowledge that the total sum to be divided amongst more than a hundred or two hundred members of the co-operative farm depends upon how hard they all work, has proved too weak and diffused an incentive to be effective. "The farmer will not," write Sydney and Beatrice Webb, "be easily weaned from his habit of seeking always to do less work than his fellow-members, on the argument that only in this way can he hope to 'get even' with them, as they will, of course, be seeking to do less work than he does."[5] That is, the pace in a co-operative or collective enterprise is determined by that of the slowest worker.

A co-operative farm would produce even less than a large private farm of the same size. Because labourers on the latter will be working for definite aims—a fixed quantity of wages which may go up with good work, and member-workers on the former, managed as it will be on the basis of majority vote and consent, would be riven by distrust and strife.

"Generally experts, who advocate co-operative farming", says Dr. Otto Schiller, a German Professor of Agricultural Economics, "have in mind that in contrast to what happened in Soviet Russia, the ownership of land should be preserved at least as a title. But it is questionable whether a legal title to a piece of land which still exists in the records but has in fact disappeared as a visible unit in the fields, can provide the same incentive as real possession of the land, even if the profits of co-operative farming are shared according to the assessed value of the land contributed by each member."[6]

Right of ownership in property, in the ultimate analysis, means only right to control the property—to use it in any manner the owner likes or not to use it at all. Once this right to control disappears or is taken away, ownership is reduced to a myth. Those who argue that farmers need not apprehend liquidation of their indi-

[5] *Soviet Communism : A New Civilisation*, Longmans Green & Co. Ltd., London, 1937, p. 218.

[6] *Co-operative Farming and Individual Farming on Co-operative Lines*, pp. 11-12.

vidual ownership, because it would continue in the form of shares
in the society on which dividends would be paid, ignore the basic
fact that land to a farmer is much more than money or shares in a
company. Merger of a person's land in a joint farm will mean a
world of change in his life; not so the purchase of shares by him in a
company. Today the farmer works on his farm in perfect freedom,
confident that he is the master of all he surveys—though what he
surveys may not be much ; on merger he will become one among
many, subject to discipline of the farm management, and exclusive
master of nothing at all.

Thirdly, a peasant farmer, by dint of the surplus labour resources
of his family available to him, is able to carry more cattle per acre
than the large farmer. His family labour is a fixed factor which
has to be maintained at all events : so he tries to utilize it by keeping
live-stock, which adds to his output. No such labour force, or labour
force commensurate to the size of the farm is available to a large
farmer. Almost all the income is, therefore, confined to what the
farmer is able to get from the crops.

Similarly, the capacity of a large farm to rear and maintain
cattle is not enhanced by its being run on co-operative or collective
lines. Cattle and poultry respond to gentle and affectionate treatment almost just as human beings do. They are, therefore, best
cared for only when they are objects of pride to their proprietors.
If it were not so, far greater concessions in the matter of keeping
private livestock would not have been given to collective farmers
in those areas of the USSR which are devoted largely to breeding
of cattle as opposed to areas devoted largely to production of
grain.

Lastly, inasmuch as a family farm can carry a larger number
of cattle and poultry per acre than a big farm, the peasant farmer
will have comparatively more farmyard manure at his disposal.
Cattle waste is organic in character and, at least, in the long run
more effective as manure than the inorganic chemical fertilisers
which are obtainable in the markets. A large farm, whether private
or co-operative, will, of necessity, resort to these fertilizers, since a
tractor and a harvester combine produce no muck or organic manure.
And while the truth that farmyard manure helps to maintain soil
fertility best is admitted by all agrarian experts, some of them,
at least, are definitely of opinion that artificial fertilizer, particularly when it is applied exclusively, depletes the soil.

It may be pointed out here, in parenthesis, that since the great depression of the thirties, doubts about the efficiency of large units have grown even in the field of industry. A most thorough investigation was made to this effect by the so-called Temporary National Economic Committee in the USA, just before the War, in 1941. Its elaborate studies showed that in none of the mass industries were the biggest units the most efficient in productivity. In a practical way the depression of the thirties had also served to show that even in manufacturing smaller units could more readily adapt themselves to changing conditions and markets.

COMPARATIVE DATA OF YIELDS

The conclusion we had reached in the previous sub-chapter, that production on small farms should be greater per acre of land than on large farms, or, in other words, production per acre will increase as the number of men cultivating a given piece of land increases, is well illustrated by Table I taken from Dr. Elmer Pendell's *Population on the Loose*, New York, 1951, page 37. In all cases below the horizontal line that cuts through the table, there are diminishing returns, which are shown in the column headed 'Average production per man'.

Clearly there is less production per man if more than four men work the 100 acres. The more the workers, the less is their per capita production. Dr. Elmer Pendell says that he chose soil which was not very good and where the farmers had only a little help from tools. Nor would tools make a difference to per capita production, at least, when as many as 18 men have to support themselves on a hundred acres. For, less the ground a man has, less the advantage he has in the use of farming equipment.

According to Dr. Elmer Pendell :

As we proceed down a scale of diminishing returns we eventually arrive at an absolute maximum total and an absolute maximum per acre average. The total production will go up no further with further increases of manpower, and will actually go down instead—further and further down....

We get valuable light on the whole problem by taking a look at China.

John Lossing Buck, in *Land Utilisation in China*, a book published in 1937 by the University of Chicago Press, reported the results of an extensive study of Chinese farms. He classified the farms by size into five groups. A simplified version of the data given by him on page 283 of the book is presented vide Table II.

TABLE I

ILLUSTRATION OF THE LAW OF DIMINISHING RETURNS

No. of men working the land	Acres of land worked by the total no. of men	Total Production of the hundred acres in equivalents of bushels of grain	Production in bushels of grain attributable to the man in the series who is now considered for the first time	Average production per man, in bushels	Average production per acre, in bushels
1	100	200	200	200.00	2.00
2	100	500	300	250.00	5.00
3	100	900	400	300.00	9.00
4	100	1,250	350	312.50	12.50
5	100	1,540	290	308.00	15.40
6	100	1,780	240	296.67	17.80
7	100	1,980	200	282.85	19.80
8	100	2,150	170	268.75	21.50
9	100	2,300	150	255.55	23.00
10	100	2,440	140	244.00	24.40
11	100	2,575	135	234.09	25.75
12	100	2,705	130	225.42	27.05
13	100	2,830	125	217.69	28.30
14	100	2,950	120	210.71	29.50
15	100	3,067	117	204.47	30.67
16	100	3,181	114	198.81	31.81
17	100	3,292	111	193.65	32.92
18	100	3,400	108	188.88	34.00

TABLE II

PRODUCTION ON CHINESE FARMS

Farm group	Men-equivalents per 100 crop-acres	Crop-acres per man-equivalent	Production per man-equivalent in equivalents of bushels of grain	Production per acre in equivalents of bushels of grain
A	25.00	4.0	76.1	19.0
B	31.25	3.2	62.0	19.4
C	38.46	2.6	53.5	20.6
D	47.62	2.1	43.1	20.5
E	66.67	1.5	30.6	20.4

There we have a striking statistical showing of diminishing returns. It is something like our other table except that this one shows a condition at a subsistence level and an arrival at an actually declining yield per acre (*Ibid.*, pp. 57-58).

The two tables taken together present a complete picture. Under conditions of manual and animal labour, or conditions where large agricultural machinery is not used, as more and more men work a given land area, that is, as a farm becomes smaller and smaller, production both per acre and also per man (or worker) increases till land per man is reduced to a point between 33.3 and 25 acres. This point coincides with 27.5 acres. Table I would show that if 4 men instead of 3 work 100 acres, that is, if the area per man decreases from 33.3 to 25 acres, production per acre increases by (12.5 — 9 =) 3.5 bushels. So that, presuming a uniform increase over the entire drop in area, production per acre increases by $3.5/8.3 = 0.42$ bushel with every decrease by one acre. Calculation would show that both a holding of 28 acres and 27 acres will produce in the total less than 27.5 acres. But the larger holding will produce less, and the smaller more per acre than the middling. At 27.5 acres the law of diminishing returns begins to operate and production per additional unit of labour or quantity of work begins to decrease. In other words, with gradual decrease in the area of his holding below 27.5 acres, production per man will go on declining. On the contrary, production per acre will continue to increase, though by smaller and smaller increments, till land per man is reduced to a point between 2.6 and 2.1 acres—say, 2.5 acres.

It would seem from Table II above that when a man has less than 2.5 acres of land, production per acre also begins to decrease. Possibly, it is only a chance variation or decrease that production on Chinese farms belonging to groups D and E, shows in the above table. This decrease is so negligible that no inferences can be drawn on its basis. Or, for ought one knows, there may be a psychological reason affecting the farmer's mind which is responsible for the decrease. At least, there is no physical reason. We, therefore, do not agree with Dr. Pendell that a point can be reached where, with further increase of man-power on a given area of land, the total production will go down, further and further down. All that can safely be said is that there is a limit after or beyond which Mother Earth refuses to yield to human coaxing any further—when there are no additional returns due to additional application of labour. This limit, according to Chinese statistics, is reached when the area per man is reduced to 2.5 acres or so.

There is overwhelming factual evidence from various other countries also which establishes that the return per acre goes up as the size of an agricultural holding goes down. Below are given figures for the English, Danish and Swiss agriculture :[7]

TABLE III

VARIATION IN GROSS RETURN PER ACRE ACCORDING TO SIZE OF HOLDING

	ENGLISH		*DANISH*		*SWISS*	
	Size of Holding in acres	*Gross return per acre £. s. d.*	*Size of Holding in acres*	*Gross return per acre £. s. d.*	*Size of holding in acres*	*Gross return per acre £. s. d.*
1.			Under 25	20 1 0		
2.	1 to 50	11 19 9	25 to 50	15 4 0	7½ to 12½	22 11 7
3.	50 to 100	9 19 2	50 to 75	15 3 0	12½ to 25	19 0 3
4.	100 to 150	7 19 1	75 to 100	13 18 0	25 to 37½	17 17 2
5.	150 to 250	7 5 8	100 to 250	12 8 0	37½ to 75	16 2 3
6.	Above 250	7 4 4	Above 250	12 4 0	Above 75	13 17 7

App and Waller remark in *Farm Economics* (pp. 58-59) :[8]

It is quite evident that the larger the business, the larger will be the receipts. To what extent this would hold true as the size increases, will depend upon the type of farming, the locality, and somewhat upon the ability of the operator. In the surveys made in six States of the USA the results average as follows :

TABLE IV

VARIATION IN RECEIPTS PER ACRE ACCORDING TO SIZE OF HOLDING IN U.S.A.

FARM SIZE	*RECEIPTS PER ACRE*
Small	$ 42.90
Medium	$ 41.30
Large	$ 38.80

[7] *Economics of Agriculture* by Van Der Post, 1937, pp. 170-75.
[8] Published by J. B. Lippincott Company, 1938.

Recently studies on the economics of farm management were undertaken by the Directorate of Economics and Statistics, Ministry of Agriculture, Government of India, in six typical regions of the country, *viz.* Bombay, Madras, Punjab, Uttar Pradesh and West Bengal in 1954-55 and Madhya Pradesh in 1955-56. In each of the six regions two contiguous districts were selected for study in such a way that they represented the most important typical soil in the state concerned. These six regions taken together represent the major cropping pattern of the country. Sixteen villages were selected in each district. The data collected by the cost accounting and survey methods from five of these regions (data for Madhya Pradesh being not available to us) do not bear out the contention that large holdings are more productive than small holdings. The data rather indicate a contrary trend, *viz.* output per acre on small holdings is generally higher than on large holdings :

TABLE V

OUTPUT PER ACRE IN RUPEES
(MADRAS)

Size group (acres)	Cost accounting method	Survey method
0 — 2.5	181.1	254.6
2.5 — 5.0	160.9	141.8
5.0 — 7.5	125.0	91.1
7.5 — 10.0	145.8	109.5
10.0 — 15.0	68.5	66.3
15.0 — 20.0	75.3	64.0
20.0 — 25.0	31.0	96.6
above 25.0	101.0	68.5

SOURCE : *The Indian Journal of Agricultural Economics*, Vol. XIII, No. 1, p. 22, 1954-55.

TABLE VI

OUTPUT PER ACRE IN RUPEES
(PUNJAB)

Holding size group (acres)	Cost accounting method	Survey method
0 — 5	174	184
5 — 10	178	176
10 — 20	155	160
20 — 50	137	137
above 50	122	123

SOURCE : *The Indian Journal of Agricultural Economics*, Vol. XIII, No. 1, p. 24, 1954-55.

TABLE VII

OUTPUT PER ACRE IN RUPEES
(WEST BENGAL)

Holding size group (acres)	Hoogly		24 Parganas	
	Cost accounting method	Survey method	Cost accounting method	Survey method
0.01 — 1.25	307	294	260	169
1.26 — 2.50	285	221	199	160
2.51 — 3.75	238	184	221	162
3.76 — 5.00	223	200	178	144
5.01 — 7.50	248	242	188	161
7.51 — 10.00	250	152	207	172
10.00 — 15.00	278	187	62	108
above 15.00	153	103	—	121

SOURCE : *The Indian Journal of Agricultural Economics*, Vol. XIII, No. 1, p. 25, 1954-55.

TABLE VIII

OUTPUT PER ACRE IN RUPEES
(UTTAR PRADESH)

Size group in acres	Cost accounting method		Survey method	
	1954-55	1955-56	1954-55	1955-56
Below 5	313.5	276.6	311.6	291.4
5 — 10	300.6	239.5	280.9	252.7
10 — 15	253.8	204.1	255.3	240.8
15 — 20	238.9	200.3	252.5	215.6
above 20	252.1	204.9	236.7	190.4

SOURCE : *The Indian Journal of Agricultural Economics*, Vol. XIII, No. 1, p. 28, 1954-55.

TABLE IX

OUTPUT PER ACRE IN RUPEES
(BOMBAY)

Size groups of farm (acres)	Ahmednagar District	Nasik District
0 — 5	119.84	112.71
5 — 10	72.31	95.95
10 — 15	53.92	64.85
15 — 20	41.36	68.61
20 — 25	25.60	51.26
25 — 30	33.88	73.28
30 — 50	34.84	60.69
above 50	29.68	64.32

SOURCE : *The Indian Journal of Agricultural Economics*, Vol. XIII, No. 1, p. 54-55, 1954-55.

It is not only crops or pure agricultural farming that shows greater output per acre on smaller farms than on larger : mixed farming (as also cattle-rearing or dairy farming singly) shows the same results. This is illustrated by statistics drawn from five different countries given in Table X.

TABLE X

GROSS OUTPUT PER ACRE

	DENMARK			NORWAY			SWEDEN			SWITZERLAND			CARMARTHENSHIRE (An English County)		
	Under 25 acres	25—50 acres	50—75 acres	Under 25 acres	25—50 acres	50—75 acres	Under 25 acres	25—50 acres	50—75 acres	Under 25 acres	25—50 acres	50—75 acres	Under 25 acres	25—50 acres	50—75 acres
	£ s. d.	£ s. d.	£ s. d.	£ s. d.	£ s. d.	£ s. d.	£ s. d.	£ s. d.	£ s. d.	£ s. d.	£ s. d.	£ s. d.	£ s. d.	£ s. d.	£ s. d.
Crops	1 11 7	1 4 4	1 13 5	3 7 1	3 2 11	2 14 7	1 2 5	1 4 4	1 18 8	2 3 4	1 19 1	2 1 11	0 0 1	0 1 9	0 0 1
Livestock and livestock products	20 14 5	15 18 8	14 7 1	12 17 6	9 16 5	8 9 10	10 5 3	6 15 1	6 19 10	12 7 2	12 11 0	11 6 5	7 14 8	7 10 8	7 3 7
Other sources	1 7 0	0 15 3	0 12 7	1 18 10	1 1 6	0 19 7	0 17 8	0 10 1	0 17 2	6 3 3	5 10 7	4 2 5	2 19 10	1 0 5	0 15 10
Total	23 13 0	17 18 3	16 13 1	18 3 5	14 0 10	12 4 0	12 5 4	8 9 6	9 15 8	20 13 9	20 0 8	17 10 9	10 14 7	8 12 10	7 19 6

SOURCE: *The Economics of Small Holdings*, Edgar Thomas, (1927), pp. 10-11.

It is not only gross production per acre that increases with the decreasing size of the farm ; there is evidence to show that this is true also of net production. David Mitrany, the author of *The Land and the Peasant in Rumania*, says on page 254 of his book :

The progress in the science of agriculture has shown that the laws of industrial production do not also hold good, for the production of food-stuffs. In agriculture, production follows a natural process which does not allow an indefinite division of labour ; and this form of intensifying production has been proved to bring in returns which, for a number of reasons, diminish in the proportion in which the size of the agricultural undertaking increases, as illustrated by the so-called circles of Thunen. More recent inquiries have shown that this is true not only of the total output which was often conceded but also of net production. It might be useful to quote here one inquiry, because of its clear results and of the great competence of its author. The Director of the Swiss Peasant Secretariat, Prof. Ernest Laur, who is also a member of the League of Nations Committee on Agricultural Questions, worked over returns on capital for various categories of Swiss farms over a period of twenty years (1901-21), and has obtained the following averages, in Swiss francs :

TABLE XI

VALUE OF TOTAL AND SOLD PRODUCE PER HECTARE IN SWISS FARMS (in Swiss Francs)

Size of Farm in hectares	Value of Total production per hectare	Value of sold produce per hectare
3 — 5	1,180	795
5 — 10	1,005	740
10 — 15	900	700
15 — 30	825	660
above 30	710	595

A report of the British Ministry of Agriculture referred to in the monthly journal, *The Agricultural Situation in India*, April, 1952, issued by the Economic and Statistical Adviser to the Government of India, also points to the conclusion that net output per acre is highest on the small farms and declines as the size of farm increases :

TABLE XII

NET OUTPUT PER 100 ADJUSTED ACRES*

Farm size group (acres)	1947-48	1948-49
0 — 50	2,565	3,188
51 — 100	1,830	2,319
101 — 150	1,575	2,025
151 — 300	1,576	2,033
301 — 500	1,577	1,980
500 and above	1,551	1,923

*Adjusted acreage of a farm means the actual area in sole occupation reduced by expressing the acreage of any rough grazing in terms of equivalent acres of crop and grass, which vary from district to district according to local conditions.

Similar results have been obtained from a survey[9] conducted by a method close to the purposive selection method, on behalf of the Indian Peasants' Institute in Nidubrolu during 1957. The area selected was of 10 square miles in Divi Taluq, Krishna District in Andhra Pradesh, which contains rich black cotton soil and is inhabited by efficient and hard-working peasants—*vide* Table XIII.

Both Tables XII and XIII confirm David Mitrany's conclusion. They indicate a gradual increase in the net profits per acre, as well as in gross production, from the least intensive to the most intensive groups.

According to an address delivered by Professor Sering in the Emperor's presence before the German Agricultural Council in 1913, quoted in a memorandum submitted to the British Agricultural Tribunal of Investigation in 1924—"The evidence is conclusive that the new peasant holdings in the eastern provinces not only doubled the number of inhabitants in the colonized area—and that within ten years ; they increased the cattle in the area from two to threefold ; the pigs from three to fourfold ; while the grain crops were, in some cases, half as large again, in others doubled. This was,

[9] *The Peasant and Co-operative Farming*, by Prof. N. G. Ranga and P. R. Paruchuri, published by the Indian Peasants' Institute, Nidubrolu and printed at the New Indian Press, New Delhi, 1957, p. 83.

TABLE XIII

THE SIZE OF HOLDINGS, COSTS AND PRODUCTION

Size of holdings (in acres)	Value of the gross produce per acre*	Average No. of unpaid family workers	No. of annual farm servants engaged on the holding	Total man-days of labour per acre in a year	Total paid costs per acre†	Percentage of paid costs to the value of gross produce	Total costs per acre if family labour is remunerated on par with the annual paid farm servants	Percentage of total cost (including remuneration to family workers) to the value of gross produce	Producer's surplus per acre (including the remuneration to family workers) that is, column 2 minus column 6
1	2	3	4	5	6	7	8	9	10
	Rs.				Rs.		Rs.		Rs.
3–5	391.50	2.00	0.50	241	146.00	37.29	335.00	85.57	245.50
8–10	382.50	2.00	1.25	149	150.75	39.41	237.00	61.96	231.25
13–15	380.25	1.50	1.50	102	143.75	37.80	184.25	48.45	236.50
28–30	355.50	1.00	3.00	75	150.12	42.23	162.62	48.47	205.38
42–45	326.25	1.00	6.00	87	176.75	54.18	185.55	56.87	149.50
55–60	317.25	—	8.00	89	200.75	63.28	200.75	63.28	116.50
70–75	279.00	—	10.00	95	212.75	76.25	212.75	76.25	66.25
90–100	243.00	—	9.00	73	172.00	70.78	172.00	70.78	71.00

SOURCE : Ranga and Paruchuri, *Ibid.*, condensed from the tables on pp. 86-88.

* The value of the gross produce in column 2 is not arrived at on the basis of the price at which farmers actually sold their produce but only by multiplying the physical gross produce with the average of the market price in the specific month of 4 years, under the assumption that multipurpose co-operatives exist.

† Total of the wages of hired labour, out-of-pocket expenditure incurred on draught animals, cost of seeds, out-of-pocket expenditure incurred on manures (the real value of the manure available on the farm itself being not calculated or included) depreciation and maintenance cost of farm-sheds and agricultural implements, land revenue, managerial costs, if any have been paid, and miscellaneous costs.

of course, only by dint of harder work than mere hired labourers would care to perform, and by making use of their children and women and old people to do the extra harvest work for which the great land-owners had to rely on Polish season workers."

These peasant holdings had come into being consequent on the division of large estates.

In Poland the change from extensive corn growing to small-scale mixed farming showed great capacity for expansion in that direction. The number of animals (apart from improvement in quality) increased as follows between 1921 and 1938-39 :

TABLE XIV

INCREASE IN NUMBER OF ANIMALS OWING TO CHANGE IN
FARMING PATTERN IN POLAND

	(1921)	(1938-39)
	(in millions)	
Cattle	7.89	10.6
Pigs	4.8	7.7
Sheep	2.5	3.2

In Czechoslovakia the division of the large estates resulted in an improvement in the number and quality of livestock, an increase in milk production and even a rise in corn yields, because more livestock meant more manure.[10]

The British Agricultural Tribunal of Investigation has the following comment to make about the family farm, that is, the farm worked by the occupier and members of his family with or without some hired labour :

We believe that the productivity of European agriculture, particularly, of that of Denmark, Germany and Belgium, where the output has been the greatest, has been largely due to the attention given to the organisation of the family farming system ; and in Denmark which still offers the most instructive field for comparison, the maintenance and extension of the system have been regarded as the most secure foundation for obtaining the maximum out of the land, while, at the same time, developing a democratic and rural social community (*Report* : 1924, p. 87).

[10] David Mitrany, *Marx against the Peasant*, London, 1952, p. 127

TABLE XV

AVERAGE YIELD* PER HECTARE (IN 100 Kgms.) DURING 1958-59—1960-61

Sl. No.	Countries	WHEAT		BARLEY		MAIZE		RICE (Paddy)		POTATOES		TOBACCO	
		Actual	Relative (USA =1)	Actual	Relative (USA =1)	Actual	Relative (USA =1)	Actual	Relative (USA =1)	Actual	Relative (USA =1)	Actual	Relative (USA =1)
1	2	3	4	5	6	7	8	9	10	11	12	13	14
1.	U.S.A.	16.9	(1.0)	16.4	(1.0)	32.7	(1.0)	37.3	(1.0)	206.7	(1.0)	18.2	(1.0)
2.	United Kingdom	34.2	(2.0)	31.2	(1.9)	—	—	—	—	200.0	(1.0)	—	—
3.	Denmark	38.7	(2.3)	34.2	(2.1)	—	—	—	—	200.0	(1.0)	—	—
4.	France	24.0	(1.4)	24.7	(1.5)	29.5	(0.9)	40.3	(1.1)	148.3	(0.7)	18.7	(1.0)
5.	Germany (F.R.)	32.6	(1.9)	30.1	(1.8)	30.2	(0.9)	—	—	222.0	(1.1)	24.0	(1.3)
6.	Belgium	37.3	(2.2)	35.4	(2.2)	43.7	(1.3)	—	—	218.0	(1.1)	24.9	(1.4)
7.	Netherlands	41.3	(2.4)	39.3	(2.4)	34.2	(1.0)	—	—	260.7	(1.3)	—	—
8.	Norway	22.5	(1.3)	24.2	(1.5)	—	—	—	—	213.0	(1.0)	—	—
9.	Sweden	24.0	(1.4)	23.2	(1.4)	—	—	—	—	127.7	(0.6)	24.4	(1.3)
10.	Switzerland	32.9	(1.9)	29.8	(1.8)	38.2	(1.2)	—	—	245.3	(1.2)	20.6	(1.1)
11.	Japan	23.5	(1.4)	25.4	(1.5)	23.5	(0.7)	47.4	(1.3)	167.7	(0.8)	20.5	(1.1)

SOURCE : *Food and Agriculture Organisation Year Book, 1961, Volume XV.*
* Main crops only.

Table XV shows the average production of some of the agricultural commodities of USA, UK, several western European countries and Japan.

The arable part of an average USA holding according to the 1950 World Census of Agriculture came to 64 acres out of 215, *i.e.* 29.5 per cent of the total area. The average arable holding in western European countries was far smaller, less than one-half, even less than one-sixth of the average arable holding in the USA. It was 10 acres out of 27 in Federal Republic of Germany. The entire average holding in England, Denmark, France, Switzerland and Netherlands had only an area of 82, 39, 29, 15 and 14 acres respectively as compared with 215 acres in the USA. The average holding in Japan was far too small—one-thirtieth of the American arable holding, *i.e.* two acres (including pasture land) as compared with 64 arable acres. However, the USA is seen to produce less than almost all the countries given in the above table, even less than Japan. It may be admitted that there are differences in topography, soil fertility, climatic conditions and the resource facilities that may be available to the farmers in the various countries and, therefore, the figures of production are not strictly comparable. Yet, the wide disparity in agricultural production in these countries, all of which are situated in the temperate zone and fall within the category of 'developed countries', cannot in its entirety be explained by these differences alone. The figures can, at least, be taken to point towards the conclusion that mere largeness of the size of an agricultural undertaking does not lead to increase in production per acre.

Whatever evidence is available of Russian collective farming also proves that concentration of land does not increase production per unit. Although "reliable statistics are not available", says Milovan Djilas, some time Vice-President of Yugoslavia, "yet all evidence confirms that yields per acre in the USSR have not been increased over the yields in Czarist Russia, and that the number of livestock still does not approach the pre-revolutionary figure."[11]

Yields of wheat in the Czarist and Soviet Russia, figures of which crop alone are available to us, when compared with yields of relevant periods in European countries, where the family farming system prevails, do not bring out the communist contention that large-scale joint farming increases production in any mysterious manner:

[11] *The New Class*, Thames and Hudson, 1957, p. 57.

TABLE XVI

YIELD OF WHEAT PER ACRE IN SELECTED COUNTRIES
(1885 — 1950)

Countries	Annual average yield per acre in metric quintals		
	1885-89	1934-38	1949-50
1. Denmark	10.3	12.8	14.4
2. United Kingdom	8.2	9.4	11.1
3. Netherlands	7.6	12.2	15.2
4. Belgium	7.6	11.0	14.3
5. Western Germany	5.7	8.9	10.6
6. Hungary	4.9	5.7	5.4
7. France	4.9	6.3	7.5
8. Rumania	4.4	3.9	..
9. Bulgaria	3.8	5.1	..
10. Italy	3.5	5.8	6.3
11. Yugoslavia	2.7	4.6	4.9
12. Russia (USSR)	2.2	3.2	2.9

SOURCE : *World Population and Production Trends and Outlook*, W. S. Woytinsky and E. S. Woytinsky, Table 249 ; published by the Twentieth Century Fund, New York, 1953.

Every pre-War European country, even such underdeveloped countries as Bulgaria and Rumania, had a higher yield than Soviet Russia ; Denmark, the Netherlands and Belgium outdistanced Soviet Russia by more than 3 to 1. By present showing, collective farms will not be able to achieve even in 1985-89, the yields which Denmark, the UK, the Netherlands, Belgium and Germany had done a century earlier, *viz.* in 1885-89.

Collective farms in the USSR which numbered 2,60,000 in 1952 were reduced by amalgamation to 91,000 in 1955 and the average size rose to 5,230 hectares (12,918 acres), of which 38 per cent was cultivated. With further amalgamation, the number of collective farms was reduced to 54,800 in 1960. Besides, there were 5,140 state farms with an average size of 30,800 hectares (76,076 acres), of which only 17.6 per cent was cultivated. A programme of extending cultivation to virgin areas was inaugurated in 1954, with the result that the number of state farms went up to 6,500, and the total sown area of the Union rose to 195.7 million hectares or 484 million acres in 1960. The main aim of amalgamation and enlargement of collective farms was to increase their productive capacity. But we do not think there are any who can seriously contend that the aim has been realised—that agricultural production in the USSR has increased with the increase in the size of the agricultural undertaking.

There have been constant shifts in internal organisation of the *kolkhoz*. Till 1958 all the MTSs, whose number rose from 158 in 1930 to some 7,000 prior to the outbreak of the last war, to 8,400 in 1954 and to more than 9,000 in 1957, had been run by the state. But after a two-day session held on February 25 and 26, 1958, the Central Committee of the Communist Party of Soviet Union decided to transfer the tractors and farm machinery from MTS to direct ownership of collective farms. According to official Party admission, the system had been a brake on production. "As a matter of fact," the official communique went on to announce, "there were many cases in which stations even hampered the progress of outstanding collective farms and throttled the initiative among farm personnel." Peasants were also freed from payment of compulsory food deliveries.

As recently as on December 22, 1961, in a speech made at Kiev, Premier Khrushchev announced that a new organisation of collective farms would be worked out as soon as the proposed new constitution was adopted. He insisted that it was necessary to give collective farms greater freedom of initiative concerning their working methods, provided they fulfilled their responsibilities to supply sufficient produce to the state.

Apart from frequent changes in the working of the *kolkhozy*, there is another circumstance which evidences, if not failure of joint farming, then, at least, the fact that large farms do not mean large production and the expectations of the founders have not borne fruit. The Soviet Prime Minister bitterly criticised a number of ministers and ministries responsible for administration of state and collective farms at the closing of the Siberian Farmers' Conference in July, 1956, for their negligence. Again at a meeting of the Soviet Communist Party's Central Committee held on January 11, 1961, to discuss agriculture, Prime Minister Nikita Khrushchev declaimed fiercely against collective farm leaders who faked crop figures to hide bad management of the harvest in Kazakhstan during 1959. "This is a crime and such people should be brought to trial, whoever they are", he said. In one case a Minister went so far as to force the collective farmers to buy butter from the market and deliver it to the state as part of their own production quota. The Premier of the Ukraine, Mr. Nihifor Kalchenko and Kazakhstan Agriculture Minister, Mr. Nikhail Rooinets, were sacked.

At the Kiev meeting also, above referred to, Mr. Khrushchev devoted his main attention to the productive programme of the Ukraine, the bread basket of Russia, and strongly criticised Mr. P. A. Vlasyup, president of the Ukranian Academy for Agriculture, for misleading farmers and then blaming the party for it.

The ire of Mr. Krushchev is understandable. If an independent farmer under the system of individualistic farming bungles, crops only in a few acres suffer, but if the management of a large joint farm bungles, crops in hundreds and thousands of acres suffer.

Not to digress further, however. From Table XVII on page 61, we can easily deduce that large area of culturable land per man engaged in agriculture (or large size of the agricultural undertaking) does not mean large production per acre. Table XV enabled us to make a comparison of agricultural yields of some countries with those of the USA. Table XVII will enable us to make a similar comparison of present-day yields with the USSR. It will be found that, leaving out of account India and Philippines altogether (for they are acknowledgedly underdeveloped countries), the USSR, pride of the protagonists of large-scale mechanised farming, is bracketed with Turkey and Yugoslavia and occupies the lowest place, both as regards production per acre and production per man.

If we take mean figures both for agricultural production per acre and per person engaged in agriculture and treat the production of USSR as 100, we arrive at the results vide Table XVIII which will, perhaps, be more intelligible to a layman.

Again, it may be conceded that there is a difference in soil fertility and climatic conditions of the various countries mentioned

TABLE XVII

CLASSIFICATION OF 26 COUNTRIES WITH RESPECT TO THE RELATIONSHIP BETWEEN THE INTENSIVENESS OF CULTIVATION AND AGRICULTURAL OUTPUT PER PERSON ENGAGED IN CULTIVATION

Value of agricultural production per person engaged* (Rs. per year)	No. of persons engaged in agriculture per sq. kilometer of cultivable land					
	0— 5	5—10	10—15	15—20	20—25	25—30
Below 1,000	..	Philippines	..		..	India
1,000-1,500	..	..	Turkey Yugoslavia U.S.S.R.	..	..	..
1,500-2,000	..	..	Poland	Rumania	..	Italy
2,000-2,500	Brazil	Greece	Cyprus Bulgaria	Portugal	..	..
2,500-3,000	..	France Austria	Spain	..	Hungary	..
3,000-3,500	Sweden	Ireland	Syria	..	..	..
3,500-4,000	..	..	Germany Czechoslovakia	Belgium	..	..
4,000-4,500	..	..	..		..	..
4,500-5,000	..	Britain	..	Netherlands	..	..
Over 5,000	..	..	Denmark	..	..	..

SOURCE : An article entitled, 'Population Growth And Living Standards' by Colin Clark, published in the *International Labour Review*, August 1953.

* Value of agricultural production has been given in terms of Indian rupee prices of the year 1948-49.

n the following table. But this difference in conditions can, at most, be taken to explain the difference in production only where the cultivable land per person engaged in agriculture is equal or nearly equal, that is, higher production per acre in the eight countries mentioned in the left-half of the table, as compared with that in the USSR, may be due to their superior soil and climate. It will, however, be straining one's credulity too far to believe or to ask one to believe that higher production per person of the six countries mentioned in the right-half of the table where the area of cultivable

TABLE XVIII

COMPARISON OF AGRICULTURAL INCOME IN USSR WITH SOME COUNTRIES

Countries which have about the same area of cultivable land per person engaged in agriculture as in USSR		Countries which have a smaller area of cultivable land per person engaged in agriculture than in USSR		
Country	Index of production per acre (and, therefore, per person)	Country	Index of production	
			Per acre	Per person
USSR	100	USSR	100	100
Poland	140	Rumania	196	140
Cyprus & Bulgaria	180	Italy	252	140
Spain	220	Portugal	308	180
Syria	260	Hungary	396	220
Germany & Czechoslovakia	300	Belgium	420	300
Denmark	420	Netherlands	532	380

land per person engaged in agriculture is smaller than that in the USSR, is also due to this difference in soil and climate, or that the soil and climate of Germany, Czechoslovakia, Portugal, Hungary, Belgium, Denmark and Netherlands are three to five times superior to those of the USSR, particularly, when the claims of the Soviet Union regarding progress in agricultural research and availability of resource facilities on its state and collective farms are so wide and insistent. It will, therefore, be fair, by all standards, to conclude that the size of its agricultural undertaking, which is hundred times or more than that in any other country shown in the table, has not only not helped the USSR increase its agricultural output but, on the contrary, depressed it. There is no reason to suppose that, had the enormous amount of capital invested in the means to produce agricultural machinery, in land improvements, in supplying chemical fertilizers, etc., been sunk in small, private farms, the results would not have been much better.

The following figures would prove where the U.S.S.R., with a jointly-operated collective farm of fifty times the size of the average private farm in the USA., stands with regard to production of six main crops as compared with the latter : [12]

	U.S.A.	U.S.S.R.
Wheat	16.9	11.0
Barley	16.4	12.4
Maize	32.7	16.9
Rice (Paddy)	37.3	20.3
Potatoes	206.7	91.3
Tobacco	18.2	12.7

Taking the world as a whole, the Food and Agriculture Organisation of the United Nations has recently put out a very valuable survey called *Co-operatives and Land Use* published under its official auspices. On the general problem as to whether co-operative farming is more productive than peasant farming, the report says: "There is much evidence that the rural standard of living in countries extensively collectivised is below that of countries in similar latitudes where farming is individual."[13]

We may apprehend the same results in China, in India[14], or, for that matter, in any other country which adopts the agricultural pattern of the USSR. The main reason is not far to seek. To restate it : incentives for hard work which operate in individual farming and tend to increase its production are absent in large-scale joint farming.

[12] Source : *F.A.O. Production Yearbook*, 1961, Vol. XV. Figures relate to the period 1958-61 and are average yield per hectare (in 100 kgms).
[13] Report, p. 105.
[14] The following report in the *Hindustan Times*, New Delhi, would give an idea of the performance of co-operative farms in our country :

The U. P.'s 334 co-operative farms made a profit of Rs. 2,39,710 last year, disclosed Mr. Mohanlal Gautam, Minister for Agriculture and Co-operation in reply to a question by Mr. M. S. Bharati, in the State Council today.

The Minister said that these co-operative farms had an area of 61,016 acres, and a working capital of Rs. 44,93,443.

In reply to a supplementary question the Minister said that the present membership of these farming societies was near seven thousand.

One cannot end up this array of data in favour of small holdings better than by referring to the achievements of Shri Shrikant
Apte, a worker of the Bhoodan movement in our country. He has
achieved on a quarter acre of land—his farm is at Rander, three
miles from Surat—results which stagger one's imagination. He has
experimented with what he calls *Rishi Kheti*, which is a miracle of
self-sufficiency from beginning to end.

He cultivates his plot in such a way as to get all his necessaries
of life from it—food and cloth—and makes an annual saving of
Rs. 400. He works on his land at an average of four hours a day
with hand tools (no bullocks), fetches water on his head to irrigate
it from the river a mile and a half away. The only manure he uses,
is provided by his own excreta and the droppings of his two goats,
whose fodder is procured by a circular pruning of the hedge round
the farm. It takes six weeks to go round the hedge to get forage
for the goats and by the time the circle is completed the hedge is
ready for the next cycle of pruning.

Shrikant Apte has worked his farm with complete success in
this manner for the last five years. And as if not to be outpaced
by the produce of the modern farm managers, using new-fangled
techniques and synthetic fertilisers, he has contrived to raise prize-
size vegetables at his farm. Ever seen a carrot 4 inches less than
3 feet long ? If not, go to Apte's farm at Rander. Not only gargan-
tuan carrots but you will also see mammoth *moolies* (weighing 5 lbs.
each) and onions as big as ostrich eggs, weighing 1 lb. each.

Cotton is Apte's cash crop. He grows only 20 plants which yield
him between $1\frac{1}{2}$ and $1\frac{3}{4}$ maunds of cotton. His personal requirements are met by about 10 seers ; the rest he sells, just as he sells
the surplus produce of vegetables. That is how he makes his extra
Rs. 400 a year with which he runs a *Balmandir* and a library in the
village.

Shrikant Apte works on his farm only for nine months in a
year. Acharya Vinoba has asked him to propagate his technique,
which, Apte claims, is 'possible for everybody.' It has been described by Acharya Vinoba as 'an introduction to the practical book
of Bhoodan'.[15]

This may be an extreme case, but it shows what man is capable
of, unaided by machinery and artificial fertilisers.

The report of the Krishnappa Delegation to China contains on
pages 92 to 104 several tables showing acreages and production in
China during the period 1949-1955. Two of these on pages 100-101

---

[15] *Hindustan Times*, New Delhi, dated 29 January 1957.

show the per-acre yield of major agricultural crops, and one may argue that the gradual increase from year to year mentioned therein is indicative of the correspondence between larger farming units brought about by the introduction of co-operative farming and higher output. The co-operative movement took shape in 1951 and it recorded its high water-mark in 1955. Between 1952 and 1954 the increases, if any, are insignificant, and it is unthinkable that the large operational unit of 1955 should have produced such immediate effects as are reflected in the significant increase between 1954 and 1955. Whatever increases have taken place must, therefore, be ascribed to the financial and technical assistance so largely extended by the Chinese Government to its farmers. Quite apart from these considerations, judged even from the standards of a statistically backward country like India, the Chinese figures are utterly unreliable. In respect both of area and yield, they are based merely on visual estimation and are, therefore, entirely subjective, in contra-distinction to the figures in the tables quoted earlier, which have been compiled on the basis of objective methods. In China, there is no counterpart to our *patwari* ; there are no scientific measurements ; there are no cadastral maps ; there are no crop-cutting experiments.[16]

Our estimate of Chinese statistics is abundantly reinforced by the following observations made by the Krishnappa Delegation in its report :

By and large, it appears to us that Chinese data after 1952 are not strictly comparable with earlier data. As such, a part of the improvement that is revealed by figures of area and yield of agricultural crops in China after 1952 over those of earlier years may be considered to be statistical (p. 86).

In China, although some village maps were prepared during the land reforms, these were very rough sketch maps only and were not used for statistical purposes (p. 86).

Since in China, the objective method of crop-cutting sample surveys is not followed for estimating the yield of agricultural crops, especially of food crops, and since during the last few years there

[16] The sample surveys carried out by Prof. John Lossing Buck in 1921-25 on 2,866 farms in 17 localities of 7 provinces embodied in *Chinese Farm Economy* (University of Nanking, 1930), and in 1929-33 on 16,786 farms in 168 localities and 38,256 farm families in 22 provinces, embodied in *Land Utilisation in China* (University of Chicago, 1937), are, perhaps, the only examples in China of scientific statistics.

has been a vigorous campaign at all levels for increasing the yield
and a spirit of competition is being fostered between different villages and different farmers, it may not be unreasonable to presume
that the tendency towards psychological bias which we have observed in India should also manifest itself in China to some extent.
When the peasants and members of the co-operative farms, local
agricultural officials as also local party members are told that yield
of crops must be increased from year to year and that their work
will be judged by their record in this regard and when there is a
natural enthusiasm in the whole countryside for increasing yields
and also outdoing others, it will be only human if instead of under-
stating the yield they tend to overstate it (pp. 86-87).

But the important point to find out is how far the yield per
acre is improving year by year as a result of various measures undertaken in India and in China. Here, unfortunately, the statistics are
not strictly comparable because while in India the figures of yield
of foodgrains are at present largely based on crop-cutting sample
surveys subject to no psychological bias, in China they are determined by subjective valuation which must be quite appreciably influenced by the psychological climate prevailing there (pp. 87-88).

The agricultural communes introduced in 1958 were much publi-
cized in China and abroad as the main instrument of the 'Great
Leap Forward' which was said to have doubled China's production.
But how far Chinese statistics are worthy of credence will be clear
from an official announcement made on August 26, 1959.
The announcement sharply scaled down figures originally claimed
for harvests of grain and cotton in 1958. The actual amount of
grain was discovered to be not 375 million tons, but only 250 million;
of cotton, not 33,50,000 tons but 21,00,000 tons. "Owing to lack of
experience in assessing and calculating the output of such an unprecedented harvest," the announcement said, "the agricultural
statistical organs in most cases made an over-assessment"!

Later on, Peking attributed this shortfall in agricultural production in 1959 and also that in the succeeding year, 1960, to natural
calamities. It was repeatedly stated that in 1960 half the acreage
was ravaged by floods and drought, while in 1959 nearly 40 per
cent was affected. The truth, however, is that, while China did
have adverse weather conditions during these two years, the major
cause for decreased agricultural productions was lack of incentive
among the peasants.

In the light of definite factual evidence given above, we have to
consider or reconsider in all seriousness whether the plans and

attempts at agricultural reorganisation in our country with a view to increasing the size of the farming units, are not misconceived.

It is sometimes difficult to follow the logic of the advocates of agricultural producers' co-operatives when some of them are at the same time found pleading for a ceiling being put on the existing large, private holdings. They argue that the size of the farm has no bearing on production per acre and their breaking up and distribution in small units will not lead to decrease in total production. The latter view is certainly correct. But an upholder of this view cannot consistently advocate establishment of producers' co-operatives, which will be large units, with a view to increasing production. The two views are mutually contradictory.

MAINTENANCE OF SOIL FERTILITY

In order that the soil of the country may continue to produce food sufficient to feed our increasing population, we need a farming system which will not only maintain but improve the fertility of the soil. It is submitted that a system of small farms alone can do this. As has been shown in a previous sub-chapter, a family or subsistence farm will have more organic manure at its disposal than a large farm, which will, in all probablity, be mechanised and will consequently resort to inorganic fertilisers. And inorganic fertilisers are not an unmixed blessing. We will here refer to two long-term experiments on the effects of the two kinds of fertilisers.

An experiment to determine (i) the relative utility of the three major nutrients, nitrogen, phosphorus and potash, in the manuring of sugarcane, and (ii) the effects on soil fertility due to continuous application of artificial fertilisers, without being supplemented by organic or green manuring, was started in Uttar Pradesh at Shahjahanpur Sugarcane Research Station in 1935-36. The trial is being conducted in two adjacent fields in alternate years, so that a crop of sugarcane would be available every year, the rotation followed being cane-fallow-cane.

The treatments applied to the cane crop included all the 27 combinations of (i) 3 levels of nitrogen, namely 0, 100 and 200 lbs. N per acre ; (ii) 3 levels of phosphate namely 0, 75 and 150 lbs. P_2O_5 per acre, and (iii) 3 levels of potash, namely, 0, 75 and 150 lbs. K_2O per acre. Nitrogen was applied in the form of ammonium sulphate, P_2O_5 as super phosphate and K_2O as sulphate of potash. The trial has now completed a period of 27 years with 14 crops of sugarcane in one field and 13 in the other. After the first two or three crops the average yields in both the fields began to show more or less continuous fall showing thereby a marked deterioration in soil fertility. The rotation was accordingly changed in 1952-53 by introducing *Sanai* green manuring before cane. 5 crops of sugarcane have now been taken from each field after the introduction of green manuring. The results of this experiment are given in Table XIX.

It will be seen that in both the fields, till the introduction of green manuring, there was a marked deterioration in the average cane yields with the progress of years. The overall average cane yield fell from about 690 mds. per acre to about 325 mds. during a period of 17 years. With the introduction of green manuring the improvement in soil fertility became quite marked as shown by the increase in the cane yields in both the experimental fields. These have now been ranging between about 780—600 mds. per acre in different years depending, in all probability, on weather conditions, favourable or otherwise, during the growth period of sugarcane, in a particular year. With the application of green manure (organic matter) the artificial fertilizers under the given level of irrigations, have again brought the yield of sugarcane to a higher level.

The salient conclusions, according to Dr. R. K. Tandon the Director of the Research Station are :

(*i*) There is a definite fall in the average yields of both nitrogen-manured and unmanured plots. Phosphate and potash applications have not shown any response. The mean values for the overall average fall in yield are :

	Mds. per acre per crop.
Control (No nitrogen)	30.24
100 lbs. N per acre	55.54
200 lbs. N per acre	52.75

(*ii*) Continuous application of sulphate of ammonia without any organic or green manuring has resulted, on the average, in an additional deterioration (as compared with no manure) to the extent of about 25 maunds of cane per acre ;

(*iii*) For sustained high yields over long periods artificials only

TABLE XIX

MEAN YIELD OF MAIN EFFECTS N.P.K. IN MDS. PER ACRE

Year	NITROGEN			PHOSPHATE			POTASH		
	0 lbs. N. per acre	100 lbs. N. per acre	200 lbs. N. per acre	0 lbs. P_2O_5 per acre	75 lbs. P_2O_5 per acre	150 lbs. P_2O_5 per acre	0 lbs. K_2O per acre	75 lbs. K_2O per acre	150 lbs. K_2O per acre

FIELD I

Year									
1935-36	559	887	852	769	753	776	773	763	763
1937-38	357	794	802	641	652	629	647	642	664
1939-40	564	910	898	784	797	791	784	792	797
1941-42	253	627	728	552	512	543	542	531	535
1943-44	396	662	678	568	580	588	584	569	589
1945-46	394	537	595	504	512	510	513	494	520
1947-48	376	462	515	447	445	461	453	447	452
1949-50	219	437	467	354	375	394	387	372	363
1951-52	109	266	341	239	243	235	244	238	234
1953-54*	434	708	718	611	626	624	612	609	630
1955-56*	523	798	817	709	714	714	710	715	712
1957-58	586	718	721	650	691	685	646	678	702
1959-60	613	680	654	639	654	654	642	648	657
1961-62	513	700	732	644	645	656	624	663	671

FIELD II

Year									
1936-37	388	651	795	602	620	613	603	613	619
1938-39	561	832	884	755	761	761	751	758	767
1940-41	389	520	539	490	478	480	486	470	491
1942-43	466	937	1035	822	814	823	814	816	828
1944-45	429	727	785	629	648	663	646	646	648
1946-47	301	551	512	412	418	435	410	426	427
1948-49	289	515	545	441	453	456	445	450	454
1950-51	276	432	531	393	417	429	399	408	432
1952-53*	429	650	703	492	589	601	585	607	590
1954-55*	432	790	850	682	686	703	686	688	698
1956-57	686	813	845	761	781	803	756	783	804
1958-59	644	808	880	744	791	796	750	789	792
1960-61	536	600	642	591	575	613	584	593	602

*After green manuring.

cannot be depended upon ; a proper balance between the organic manures and inorganic (artificial) fertilisers is indicated as a permanent policy for obtaining good yields over long periods.

There is evidence to support the conclusion that in countries like China, Japan and Taiwan, where lot of composts, plant and animal wastes were utilized along with commercial fertilizers, better crop yields of wheat per unit of nitrogen applied were still obtained, while the Law of Diminishing Returns was in actual operation in countries like the Netherlands, Belgium and Norway where unmixed commercial fertilizers alone were applied in heavy doses.

The famous Rothamsted experiment in regard to the effect of organic and inorganic fertilisers on the production of wheat has thus been described by T. B. Wood :[17]

Perhaps, the most famous field at Rothamsted is the Broadbalk Field on which wheat has been grown every year since 1852. This field is divided into nineteen plots, each plot being half or quarter of an acre. The plots are manured differently, but each plot gets the same manure year after year. One plot has been continuously unmanured since 1852. From 1852 to 1861 its average yield was 16 bushels per acre. From 1852 to 1901 it yielded on the average just over 12 bushels per acre. In fifty years, therefore, the productivity of this plot for wheat has only decreased by less than 4 bushels. Wheat is, therefore, a good forager, no doubt in virtue of its deep and extensive root system. The average yield of the unmanured plot over the whole 50 years is 13 bushels per acre.

The average yield of the plot manured every year with mineral manures, i.e. phosphates, potash, and lime is only 15 bushels per acre from which we may conclude that wheat is not specially benefited by these manures. The plot manured annually with sulphate of ammonia has given an average yield of 21 bushels per acre, which shows that wheat is specially helped by nitrogenous manures.

It is not, however, entirely independent of phosphates and potash, for on the plot which received annually sulphate of ammonia, together with phosphates and potash, the average yield has been 31 bushels per acre, an increase of 10 bushels over the yield of the plot receiving nitrogen only.

The best yield is given by farmyard manure—36 bushels per acre on the average of 50 years or 5 bushels more than the plot receiving a complete mixture of artificial manures. This increase is, perhaps, due to the improvement in the physical condition of the

[17] The Chemistry of Crop Production by T. B. Wood, University Tutorial Press Ltd., London, 1920.

soil by the humus[18] resulting from the farmyard manure (p. 172).

Every manure, which disturbs life in the soil and drives away the earthworms and bacteria or other humus-making organisms, makes the soil more lifeless and more incapable of supporting plant life. The dangers of one-sided fertilising are, therefore, obvious especially when one uses strong doses of chemical fertilisers containing soluble salts like potassium or ammonium sulphates, of highly corrosive substances, such as nitro-phosphates (usually under some fancy trade name), or poisonous sprays, such as arsenic and lead preparations. These injure and destroy the micro-organic world. Soils intensively treated with chemical fertilisers alone or orchards sprayed for a long time with chemicals have no longer any biological activity.

Further all crop-increases purely from chemicals are short-term benefits. Chemicals do not add to the fertility of the soil but act as stimulants or drugs resulting in immediate bumper crops and in the end bring about a corresponding exhaustion of the land. Plants raised by these means are also much more liable to pest and disease attacks, the natural laws of growth having been violated and disturbed. Plant disease will cure itself when plants are raised on humus manures.

The great English agriculturist, the late Sir Albert Howard,[19] a former Director of Agricultural Research at Pusa, says of artificial fertilisers :

The feature of the manuring of the West is the use of artificial manures. The factories engaged during the Great War in the fixation of atmospheric nitrogen for the manufacture of explosives had to find other markets, the use of nitrogenous fertilisers in agriculture increased, until today the majority of farmers and market gardeners base their manurial programme on the cheapest forms of nitrogen (N), phosphorus (P), and potassium (K) on the market.

[18] *Humus* literally means soil or earth, but in practice it is used to indicate that decaying and undecayed residue of vegetable and animal waste lying on the surface, combined with the dead bodies of bacteria and fungi when they have done their work—the whole being a highly complex and somewhat varying substance—which is, so to say, the mine or store or bank wherefrom the organisms of the soil and then the plants or the trees draw what they need for their sustenance.

[19] *An Agricultural Testament*, Albert Howard, New York, 1943.

What may be conveniently described as the N. P. K. mentality dominates farming alike in the experimental stations and the countryside. Vested interests, entrenched in time of national emergency, have gained a stranglehold. Artificial manures involve less labour and less trouble than farmyard manure. The tractor is superior to the horse in power and in speed of work ; it needs no food and no expensive care during its long hours of rest. These two agencies have made it easier to run a farm. A satisfactory profit and loss account has been obtained. For the moment farming has been made to pay. But there is another side to this picture. These chemicals and these machines can do nothing to keep the soil in good heart. By their use the processes of growth can never be balanced by the processes of decay. All that they can accomplish is the transfer of the soil's capital to current account. That this is so will be much clearer when the attempts now being made to farm without any animals at all march to their inevitable failure. Diseases are on the increase. With the spread of artificial fertilisers and the exhaustion of the original supplies of humus, carried by every fertile soil, there has been a corresponding increase in the diseases of crops and of the animals which feed on them.

Howard calls attention to the contrast between western farming methods and the processes that nature uses to keep the soil in living, healthy condition :

What are the main principles underlying nature's agriculture ? These can most easily be seen in operation in our woods and forests. Mixed farming is the rule ; plants are always found with animals ; many species of plants and animals all live together. In the forest every form of animal life, from mammals to the simplest invertebrates, occurs. The vegetable kingdom exhibits a similar range ; there is never any attempt at monoculture ; mixed crops and mixed farming are the rule. . . .

Howard goes on to say :

The main characteristic of nature's farming can, therefore, be summed up in a few words. Mother Earth never attempts to farm without livestock ; she always raises mixed crops ; great pains are taken to preserve the soil and to prevent erosion ; the mixed vegetable and animal wastes are converted into humus ; there is no waste ; the processes of growth and the processes of decay balance one another ; ample provision is made to maintain large reserves of fertility ; the greatest care is taken to store the rainfall ; both plants and animals are left to protect themselves against disease.

Even those who are in favour of chemical or mineral fertilisers advocate that they should be used in combination with one or other suitable means of humus maintenance, and farmyard manure is admittedly the best, so that a large farmer to the extent he uses machinery and lags behind the small farmer in the maintenance of cattle, will generally lag behind in the maintenance of soil fertility and, therefore, ultimately in the yield per acre. Green manure could, as the Shahjahanpur experiment has shown, be a substitute for farmyard manure though not a complete one.[20] The cultivation of leguminous and other nitrogen-fixing crops would, therefore, have to be promoted where the supply of farmyard manure is reduced by mechanisation. But this would prevent land from being utilised for cash or more productive crops.

There is a cycle in nature which a small farmer can help best complete : if this cycle is broken nature takes its revenge in returning smaller yields.

The task of agriculture is to transform solar energy into chemical energy stored up in human food. This transformation can be brought about only through the agency of living organisms. Green plants, and particularly, cultivated crops, constitute the best and most efficient among such agencies—the first basis of agriculture.

But only one-quarter of the material of which the crop is composed, occurs in a form suitable as human food. Three-fourth of the produce of plants occurs in the form of residues such as straw, chaff, roots, etc., which cannot serve as human food and other purposes of human consumption. Nature has, however, so ordained that these residues can serve as animal food instead. Not only that : the animals can convert this straw and chaff into other forms of organic matter fit for human consumption. But, as in the case of crops, animals too, on their part, can make available only a quarter of the energy they consume, as products in the form of milk and meat which human beings can use. The rest goes into waste material. The excreta contain all the mineral plant nutrients taken in

[20] Farmyard manure or human and animal wastes are superior to green manures (except leguminous ones which, because of sybiotic bacteria present in nodules on their roots, draw nitrogen from the air and fix it on the plants) inasmuch as they make a net addition to the richness of the soil, while the latter can return to it only a part of the nutrients extracted from what was already present in the soil.

by the animal in its food, and need to be decomposed and the nutrients re-converted into forms available to plants. This decomposed
farmyard waste is usually known by the name 'compost'. The
mineral nutrients originally derived from the plants have to be dug
in or ploughed back in the form of compost into the soil which will
make the nutrients again available to the plants. It is thus that
nature's nutritional cycle becomes complete. It is thus, *viz.* by
ensuring the return to the soil of organic wastes for regeneration by
bacteria, worms, etc., that the fertility of the soil will be
maintained.

If, therefore, we are to raise the productivity of the soil, we
must make live-stock an indispensable element of agricultural economy. Live-stock—another living machine—is the second indispensable basis of agricultural industry. A large farmer can obviously keep a large herd but the very much greater overhead
charges of its upkeep, and insufficiency, if not actual lack, of personal attention required by every individual animal will make the
herd uneconomic. He cannot, therefore, ensure the return of all
the organic wastes which may be primarily derived from his farm
to the latter and cannot, therefore, aid nature in completing the
nutritional cycle.

Speaking at the Lucknow University on the researches carried
out in India and specially with which he had been associated from
1930 onwards, Dr. N. R. Dhar, Director of Sheila Dhar Institute of
Soil Chemistry, Allahabad, said on 17 December 1956 that "cow-
dung used by our ancestors from time immemorial was the best
manure suitable to our soil. Next to it were organic plants such as
weeds and legumes, etc., which liberated a large quantity of energy,
due either to bacterial decomposition or photo-chemical oxidation.
These not only increased the production of crops but also enriched
the nitrogen content of the soil."

"Haber's method", he went on to say, "which was used at Sindri
and other places in this country for the synthesis of ammonia and
its subsequent conversion to ammonium sulphate, had some inherent
difficulties. The soil of India and other eastern countries was more
alkaline and so it could not absorb ammonia properly. Though this
method gave good production of crops, it reduced the nitrogen
content of the soil—an injurious thing for the soil."[21]

[21] *The Pioneer*, Lucknow, dated December 19, 1956.

The role of the peasant or small-scale farming in maintaining soil fertility has been very forcefully put by David Mitrany in his book, *Marx against the Peasant* (London, 1952) :

Besides, perhaps the most important aspect of the matter had almost been lost sight of in the debate about production quantities, namely, the vital need of maintaining the productivity of the soil. That is a need which concerns every country, but not till the shock caused by some disaster, like that in the 'dust bowl' of the western United States, had it received the attention which it merits. Good farming means not only what is got out of the soil but also what is put back into it, to keep it 'in good heart and condition'. Everywhere and at all times experience seems to have shown the same close relation between large-scale farming, especially under tenancy, and the impoverishment of the soil. Even in the United States the policy is now to break up the old cotton lands of the South into small units for mixed subsistence farming, as the best way of redeeming the soil (as well as the health and self-respect of the eight million white and negro share-croppers) exhausted by the endless raising of the profitable commercial crops. The planter and large tenant often treated the land as an investment, to be used as long as it paid and sold as scrap : 'land is with him a perishable or movable property'. Marx, characteristically, had simply laid it down that small-scale cultivation impoverished and exhausted the soil. Yet how could a peasant, who expects to raise generations on the same bit of ground, treat his land otherwise than as a living thing ? The virtue of ancient and recent peasant farming, wrote a reviewer in the scientific journal, *Nature,* is that it returns to the soil the elements of life.

There is a strong element of ideal truth in the old Socialist argument that being God-given, and needed by all, the land should be no man's private property. Yet the land as such would be of little worth unless its bearing powers are perpetuated. It is the function of the land, not its raw substance, that society must possess for well-being and survival and in that sense the claim to individual ownership may be logically rooted in the nature of agricultural production itself. With the factory worker, even the artisan, the quality of his product depends on the quality of the material and on his own skill. Whatever tools or machinery he uses are a passive factor, taken over as they stand from the previous user and passed on to the next, but little affected by their temporary use, or easily replaced. All the variable factors of production, materials and skill, are wholly absorbed in each object produced, while machines and tools are transient. With the farmer or peasant, the matter is very different. His chief tool is the soil itself, or rather it is partly tool, partly raw material, a unique combination in the whole scheme of production. It is unique in that it is both a variable factor, affected by each period of use, and at the same time a constant factor, which cannot be replaced. What the farmer can get out of it depends greatly on the state in which the soil was passed on to him by the previous user, and his own way of treating it will affect the results obtained by the next user. Neglect of the soil by one may make it of little use for many. Quite apart from immediate benefits, therefore, the very nature and spirit of cultivation seem to require that the man who tills the land should have constant use of the same piece of the same instrument (pp. 128-129).

Only when the farmer has the same regard for his soil that he has for his bullocks, the welfare of which he guards daily, can we expect of it a performance commensurate with its capacities, year in and year out, without detriment to it. To the peasant, and, let us be clear in our minds, human nature being what it is, not to a member of a co-operative or collective farm, such care and regard are a matter of his own survival.

The few inches of top soil are the most prolific and universal source of wealth that mankind possesses. Large-scale technology which goes with big farms is, however, busy destroying this wealth. It takes nature, in the most favourable circumstances, from 500 to 1,000 years to make one inch of top soil. But today man, due to his indiscreet use of land, is turning vast areas of fertile land into deserts in much less than a generation, by helping causes of erosion. Modern large-scale farming using chemical fertilisers on a scale without precedent in the history of agriculture, has been most successfully developed commercially in America, but it is there that soil erosion has also proved most widespread and disastrous. The one-crop grain and cotton regions in the USA undoubtedly show a much larger decline in fertility than livestock districts. One hundred million acres of land have already been exhausted in the USA in less than two centuries of cultivation. On the other hand, there is Chinese agriculture based on the use of natural manure, which has endured for 40 centuries without any demonstrable exhaustion of soil fertility. The lesson is clear : only by faithfully returning to the soil, in due course, everything that has come from it, can fertility be made permanent and the earth be made to yield a genuine increase. The only way to preserve soil structure is to add humus—and the most feasible way to obtain humus is through the composted farmyard manure.

The small cultivator has, to repeat, a positive contribution to make in this regard. He depends entirely on his animals and himself for all agricultural operations, works up his land well, has a valuable source of organic manure in his farm and animal wastes, keeps his land covered with one crop or other, and, above all, takes care of his land like a precious treasure, for that means life for him and his family and dependants. In mechanised cultivation, which means replacement of animal and human power by machines, a valuable source of organic matter is lost and, with that, starts the whole series of troubles for the land, animals and human beings. Chemical fertilisers then find increasing use and, if applied exclusively, give rise, in turn, to a number of plant maladies. In spite of insecticides and pesticides, the fact remains that diseases multiply unabated and the vicious circle spreads. [22]

CO-OPERATIVE FARMING UNNECESSARY

Protagonists of large-scale farming—and a co-operative farm is a large-scale farm—contend that it has several advantages over small-scale farming, which will lead to increased production. Firstly, technologies can be used, or scientific cultivation is possible, on big farms alone. According to our Prime Minister, "the argument for co-operative farming is based on the very small holdings that

[22] The argument as to the best scale for agricultural production can be seen yet in another light. Good nutrition is concerned as much with the kind and quality of the food-stuff as its quantity. Recent researches suggest that the healthiest peoples in the world are those who derive their food from their own soil and consume it in a fresh condition, maintaining fertility of the soil at a high level by practising the 'Law of Return', i.e. by returning to the soil all the organic wastes—all that has been removed from it by the crop—in the same way in which nature manages her operations. Experiments (vide *Soil Fertility, Renewal and Preservation* by Dr. Ehrenfried Pfeiffer, Faber and Faber Ltd., London, 1947, Chapter XIII) made by Dr. Pfeiffer and others on rats, chickens and turkeys have shown that the seeds, and still more the leaves, of plants sown in soil fertilized with organic compost have the peculiarity, when used as food for these animals, of increasing their capacity for resisting diseases to a greater degree than the corresponding seeds and leaves sown in soil fertilized with chemicals. An analysis made by Dr. McCarrison showed that no difference chemically existed between the compost-grown food-grain and that grown with artificials. This most revealing experiment, therefore, may be taken to prove that there are vital properties in compost-grown foods which cannot be analysed chemically but

farmers have. In countries where holdings may be twenty or thirty acres or more, this may not be necessary. But where the holding is one or two acres; it is not possible to use many modern methods (I am not referring to tractors for the present) and our technique of farming will not improve. It is only when we employ better techniques that we can improve our yield." Secondly, water, credit and marketing and technological facilities, which go to swell the produce and income of a farmer, are easily available to large farms rather than to small farms. Thirdly, large farms alone possess the financial resources required for effecting land improvements or reclamation of land that may be lying waste. Fourthly, planned crop rotation and a rational use of land, which will increase the double-cropped

which are reflected in the health and general well-being of those who eat them.

Professor F. Rost of Manneheim concluded from his experiments that the increased tendency to thrombosis, as we have observed it in recent years, stands in direct relationship of cause and effect with the increased potassium content in food which, thanks to the plentiful use of artificial fertilizers (and to the practice which has grown in recent years of not pouring off the cooking water of vegetables particularly, spinach, but of utilizing it) is higher than in earlier decades.

Incidence of cancer also is said to increase in societies which undertake mechanised agriculture using artificial manures. Said a doctor who had fled to Tanganyika in East Africa from Nazi persecution of Jews in Germany, but returned to Europe in 1952 and was last heard of in Russia :

"In India, with its teeming millions, in China, in Japan, in Russia, in Asia, and here in Africa, we have vast populations, running into hundreds of millions. The incidence of cancer in these countries is so small that it is completely negligible. Here in Africa the position is even more striking. Cancer among the European population all over Africa is definitely on the increase ; and in many cases alarmingly so. By contrast, the native population, which now increases at a more rapid rate than ever before in the history of Africa, is to all intents and purposes, entirely free of cancer. Such statistics as I have available, go to show that among the natives cancer is almost completely unknown. As you go higher in the scale, there is proportionate increase in the incidence of the disease. How, then, must we explain this startling, but demonstrable fact ?

"It is the food, my friend ; it is the food. The scientist and the botanist are creating cancer all over the world today wherever they interfere with the natural structure of plants and seeds. The Barbanks have given us ten grains of corn where only one grew before. In so doing they have altered the natural structure of the corn-seed. They will feed area and the area under high-yield crops, is possible only on big farms. Fifthly, millions of acres of land will be available for crop production owing to elimination of field boundaries because of merger of individual fields and holdings into a co-operative farm. Sixthly, more than one wasteful operation necessitated by small size of peasant farms will be eliminated, costs reduced and capital resources which are so scarce but are wasted on these tiny farms conserved. Seventhly, large-scale or co-operative farming provides the only remedy of fragmentation and of the increasing number of small uneconomic holdings in the country which are characterised by 'lack of capital resources, low level of technique and productivity, and under-employment'. Finally, as a result of increased food production, co-operative farms will have a surplus which can be marketed to feed the towns, thus obviating food imports. This surplus, which is not available on peasant farms today, or, if available in some degree, is not capable of mobilisation, will provide the necessary capital for rapid economic development of the country.

Now to take the arguments one by one : The average holding in India is not one or two acres as the Prime Minister assumes. Today the population of the country can be put at 450 million persons and the total net area sown stands at 325 million acres. Fifty-six per cent of our people hold land or are cultivators, and an average family has a strength of five. So that we have $\frac{450 \times 56}{100 \times 5} = 50.4$ million cultivating families, which gives an average family holding of 6.0 acres for the country.

thousands more on the same acreage, but they will also kill hundreds more with cancer. When the natural structure of the plants and cereals we eat is altered, it has a detrimental effect on the glands in the human system, and that in turn produces cancer. I give cancer by glandular treatment and I take it away by glandular treatment. At this stage of my experiment each individual case is treated on its merits. I watch reactions and I increase or decrease the strength of the doses as required. Some day I hope to have a standard cure for all cancers. That day may never be, but it is certain that I can, and have, cured many cases to which I have given my personal attention. In the back room there are several mice, healthy and well ; if you will come with me and select as many as you wish, I will guarantee to produce cancer in each of them within forty-eight hours" (*Vide* John F. Burger's *African Adventures*, Robert Hale Ltd., London, 1957, pp. 97-98).

As regards technologies in agriculture, according to James Maddox, they are of three kinds :

One group of agricultural technologies springs from the biological sciences. Illustrations are the high-producing, scientifically-bred varieties of plants and animals, including, of course, various types of hybrids. Also, there is a group of vaccines for the prevention and cure of livestock and poultry diseases which are basically biological in nature.

A second group is what may be called the chemical type of agricultural technologies, because it springs largely from the work of the chemist. Examples of it are the ordinary commercial fertilisers so commonly used in many countries, a large and important list of insecticides and fungicides, and also weed-killers. Still another example is some of the modern supplements to livestock rations.

A third group of agricultural technologies springs from the work of the physicists and the engineers. Examples are tractors, the many complicated farm machines and equipment that go with power farming, and also a long list of other things such as farm buildings, silos, and storage facilities, and even farm-to-market roads, and marketing facilities. All these are basically engineering structures or designs.[23]

Now, as regards the first and the second group, they do not need essentially a large farm to use them. They are being used in the fullest measure on one-and two-acre farms of Japan. The responsibility for development of scientifically-bred varieties of plants and animals, preparation of vaccines, and discovery of fertilisers, insecticides and fungicides, shall, of course, have to be shouldered, as all the world over, by the state. Research takes generations and colossal sums of money, and cannot be the responsibility of individuals.

As regards the third group, i.e. tractors and other large machinery, etc., it is true that they cannot be used on small farms. But at the same time it is also true that these technologies do not increase production per acre that we in India are concerned with.

It may be stated here that use of machinery in agriculture is also called a higher or improved technique as distinguished from

[23] A paper entitled "Transferring Agricultural Technology from Developed to Under-developed Areas" read at the International Conference on Land Tenures and Related Problems in World Agriculture, held at Madison, Wisconsin, U.S.A., 1951, *Report*, p. 343.

bullock-farming which is characterised as a low technique. These erroneous designations have done much to create a bias in favour of the former and against the latter. The Prime Minister may not want tractors 'for the present'[24], but to many people modern farming implies mechanisation and, when co-operative farming is advocated, it is often due to the wrong assumption that great progress automatically follows mechanisation. There are, however, numerous examples where very intensive and modern forms of agriculture have been developed and high production achieved without mechanisation or, at least, a high degree of mechanisation.

That mechanisation is also advocated because it will serve as a chain which will bind the peasant to the co-operative farm once he enters it, will be clear from the remarks of the Indian Delegation on Agricultural Co-operation, known as the Patil Delegation, which went out to China in 1956 :

When cultivation is done through machines, the sharing of the common instruments of production could be a cementing factor. In the measure that a co-operative can become mechanised, the tendency to revert back may be less. (Report, p. 147).

Perhaps, comment on such an approach is unnecessary. It is known that mechanisation has greatly helped communist control of Russian agriculture.

We have already seen that in agriculture, unlike in industry, it is not machinery that produces the commodity but the soil. In fact, there is no work in the sphere of agriculture that human or animal labour cannot perform unaided by machine. In the words of Desmond L.W. Anker :

The building of the pyramids in Egypt or, more recently, of airfields and roads during the war years in China and Burma almost entirely with hand labour indicates what can be done by men

---

[24] In 1960 an Indian firm started production of tractors, the capacity of the unit being 6,800 tractors a year. The Third Plan envisages the production of about 70,000 tractors annually by 1965-66 and licences have already been issued to five firms with a total annual capacity of 74,500 tractors by the end of the plan period. The number of tractors in the country stood at 2,100 in 1956 and 34,000 in 1961.

One is unable to understand what these tractors are meant for. Large private farms are being broken up, and there is not much land to reclaim.

working without machines; with the great amount of under-utilised labour to be found in these areas, would it not be preferable to use labour on agricultural development works, and use capital, the scarcest of the factors of production, for purposes more likely to yield greater economic return ?

There would appear to be much to be said, under the conditions prevailing in heavily-populated underdeveloped countries, in favour of techniques for increasing agricultural productivity with a minimum amount of capital. It is claimed that with the use of such methods as improved seeds and application of fertilisers, yields could be increased by 50 per cent without any substantial change in present systems of farming, and without all the adjustments that mechanisation would make necessary. The experience of Japan is illuminating in this respect.[25]

Had machinery by itself contributed to agricultural production, the yield per unit of land in the United States of America, where the chief means employed in working the farm is the use of large machinery, would have been greater than that in Western Europe where much less machinery is used, and in Japan where land is worked for the most part by human labour. But we find that the reverse is the case. That the production per unit of labour in the United States is several times greater than in Japan is beside the point. That mechanisation of farming operations does improve considerably the yield per unit of labour is admitted ; but it does not increase the yield per unit of land and it is this that matters in India and is in dispute. The USA is able to export agricultural produce not owing to high production per acre, but to her vast total acreage.

That the introduction of mechanised agriculture or cultivation by means of tractors does not lead to any increase in per-acre yield is, perhaps, now admitted by our experts also. The results obtained from some cultural experiments conducted by the Indian Agriculture Research Institute are given vide Table XX.

According to a study, the third of its type since 1948-49, conducted by the Board of Economic Inquiry, Punjab, the tractor-cultivated farm showed an overall average gross income of Rs. 250.86 per acre in irrigated, and Rs. 118.75 per acre in unirrigated areas. On the other hand, the average gross income at a bullock-cultivated farm was Rs. 296.58 per acre

[25] An article entitled "Some Effects of Farm Mechanisation," in *International Labour Review*, March 1955, p. 250.

TABLE XX

VARIATION IN COST OF PLOUGHING ACCORDING TO MEANS OF
TRACTION POWER

Type of Ploughing	Mean yield in mds. per acre (sugarcane)
Co *Desi* ploughing by bullock power..	409.9
C1 Tractor ploughing upto 6 inches followed by twice discing and twice grubbing	361.5
C2 Tractor ploughing upto 10 inches followed by twice discing and twice grubbing	356.2

in irrigated and Rs. 140.12 per acre in unirrigated areas.[26]

In tropical regions or regions of heavy rainfall like India, tractor-ploughing will otherwise prove a curse. "Steel mould-board plows," says Richard B. Gregg, "which turn over the soil, expose too much of the soil to the hot tropical sun, thus killing too many of the soil bacteria and other microscopic lives on which the life and health of the vegetation depend. It is no mere coincidence that soil erosion in America has advanced with the increase of technology in farming.[27] Methods that are continuously effective in temperate climates with moderate precipitation distributed evenly throughout the year are dangerous if applied to tropical lands with monsoon rainfall. Even European methods applied indiscriminately to American conditions did much injury to the soil."[28]

Mechanised cultivation is found suitable only in the conditions of the Russian steppes or prairies and in such other regions where the climate is cold or temperate and there is little or no rainfall, or where, as in Western Europe,[29] the land receives the rainfall distributed in the form of showers all over the year, but not in the conditions of our country which has a tropical or sub-tropical climate and large parts of which receive torrential rainfall during a short period.

The nitrogen and organic carbon contents of our soil are already

[26] Vide *The Times of India*, New Delhi, dated March 31, 1961.

[27] Many farmers in America are now veering round to the view held and propagated by Edward. H. Faulkner, author of *Ploughman's Folly*, for the last two decades or so, that deep ploughing is injurious to soil and crop production.

[28] *Which Way Lies Hope* ? Navjivan Press, Ahmedabad, 1952, p. 54.

[29] It is understood that now under the action of farm tractors soil erosion is appearing in France and Western Germany also.

low and the layer of the humus thin. Mechanisation of agriculture, particularly, of tilling, will lead to erosion and further depletion of our soil. The fine humus structure of the soil cannot be produced or preserved by machines ; they will rather destroy the real creators of natural humus. The soil being an assemblage of living organisms and living creatures—creators of humus—cannot be successfully managed by machines and mechanical processes. Tractors and machinery in our country, therefore, may with advantage be employed only in the eradication of deep-rooted weeds like *kans*, *krankhuri* and *motha*, in opening up and colonisation of new areas, *i.e.* in bringing cultivable, but hitherto uncultivated, waste land under cultivation, or, in clearing land originally under jungle.

The argument that ploughing with mechanical power is more economical than ploughing with animal power is supported neither by logic nor by experience. According to document no. 5 (pp. 19-20), published by the European Conference on Rural Life, 1939:

> While, in the case of tractors, variable costs are high and fixed costs low, in that of draught animals the variable costs are trifling and fixed costs are considerable. In other words, the tractors, though expensive when in actual operation, cost little when idle, while the cost of keeping draught animals, though scarcely higher when they are at work than when they are resting, is continuous since they have to be fed and cared for, whether working or not. Hence the use of tractors is most profitable when a great deal of work has to be done in a short time. Animals, on the other hand, are more economical when the work is divided fairly evenly over the entire year.

Inasmuch as laid-up tractors do not eat, they are worthwhile only when the work is intermittent. They are not profitable for the usual run of agricultural work. In our country where steady and constant work on land throughout the year is generally available, the use of bullocks for traction purposes is not uneconomical as compared with that of machinery. In fact, the bullock in our conditions is far beyond the reach of tractor competition.

The working costs of animal traction are comparatively low also because tractors do not repair their injuries as animals do. Breakdowns of machinery are inevitable and there will be need for repairs. In America, every village and town has a repair garage with spare parts. It is not so in India. If we maintain a Machine and Tractor Station at every co-operative farm or even at more than one, the expenses will more than absorb the economy, if there is any, that pooling of land and labour resources may possibly bring about. Spare parts and repairs are available to farmers today only from the big cities, which means delay of several days and consequent crop losses. Nor, as has already been pointed out, do the tractors produce any kind of manure like animal dung, which is an important means of soil maintenance and improvement.

Yugoslavia found by actual experience before the last Great War that purchase of large machines (specially of tractors) and their maintenance was too expensive even on a co-operative village basis, particularly where, as in our country, working animals were adequate for the purpose and human labour was so plentiful. We believe the experience of owners of the few mechanised farms that exist in India, is also none too different. In our country, mechanisation is likely to prove more expensive than in the USA or the USSR because, at least, for some time to come, petrol and the machines will have to be imported from abroad. In the USA, the cost of kerosene and lubricants represents 42 per cent of the entire cost of tractor work. In India, which is distant from the sources of supply, these costs will be about 25 per cent higher, *viz.* 52 per cent owing to transport and tariffs.

The Chinese experience is similar. A conversation between Prime Minister Chou En-lai and the Krishnappa Delegation, which visited China in July-August, 1956, has been reported thus : "Mr. Chou En-lai went on to say that the heavy pressure of population in China meant that the development of agriculture, at least, for the present could not be based either on mechanisation or on large-scale reclamation. In China, the cost of production in mechanised farms might well prove to be higher than the cost of production in non-mechanised farms where farmers worked with ordinary farm implements. The reason was that labour was still much cheaper in China. These big state-owned mechanised farms when set up even with gift tractors were not, therefore, unmixed blessings. They were causing the state quite a lot of expenditure" (pp. 23-24 of the Report).

Professor John Lossing Buck in *Chinese Farm Economy* (The University of Nanking, 1930, p. 315) examined the possibility of replacing present Chinese methods of cultivation by tractor farming. He found animal power definitely more economical than the use of tractors. (*See* Table XXI.)

TABLE XXI

COST OF PLOUGHING IN CHINA BY TRACTOR AND BUFFALO

				Chinese Dollars
Initial cost of tractor			$	2,300
Initial cost of two gang tractor plough			$	300
Yearly depreciation, interest, repair and risk of the :				
(1) Tractor		$ 832 }	$	909
(2) Plough		$ 77 }		
Cost of tractor-ploughing one hectare				
(a) Yearly non-recurring expenses		$ 4.75 }	$	10.43
(b) Operating costs :		}		
(i) Kerosene	3.78 }			
(ii) Lubricating oil	1.40 }	$ 5.68 }		
(iii) Labour	0.50 }			
Whereas cost of ploughing one hectare with a water buffalo came approximately only to			$	4.00

According to an inquiry conducted by the Board of Economic Inquiry, Punjab, already referred to, mechanised farming implied a heavy capital investment. The total investment in tractor-cultivated holdings worked out to Rs. 224 per acre as against an investment of Rs. 112 per acre in a bullock-cultivated holding.

It is reported that in the reclamation works after the Yangtse flood in China in 1947, bullocks and wheel-barrows were found to be cheaper than bulldozers (and the bullocks were later used as draught animals on the re-established farms).

Leonard E. Hubbard, an impartial writer on Russian agriculture, writing of the comparative costs of animal and mechanical power, observes :

The apotheosis of the machine leads to its use out of season as well as in season. It was the experience of the German farm concession (the celebrated Drusag which until 1932 farmed some 27,000 acres on the Kuban) that ploughing with animal power was often more economical than ploughing with mechanical power. Animals (they use oxen a lot in the North Caucasus) were very cheap to keep and wages were low ; a unit consisting of eight yoke, a four-furrow plough and two men, or a man and a boy, to guide the leading yoke, ploughed a hectare as efficiently and at a smaller total cost than a tractor. The latter, of course, came into its own when speed was a factor; for instance, when autumn rain made the soil just right for sowing winter grain. The Russian, however, is inclined to think that, because the tractor turns over the soil at a prodigious rate and with lots of cheerful noise and bustle, it is doing it more economically and efficiently than any other method. In 1935 the official standard consumption of tractor fuel in spring-ploughing one hectare was 21.6 kilos (vide an article *The Production Cost of Grain in State Farms in Planned Economy* No. 2, 1937), and in 1934 the price of one litre of benzine was about equal to the price of 10 kilos of grain. 21 kilos of benzine would be about 23 litres (one litre of water weighs 1 kilogramme, and the specific gravity of benzine is approximately 0.90), equal in cost to 230 kilos of grain. The quantity of corn and hay consumed by horses during the process of ploughing one hectare could not be more than the equivalent of 30 kilos of oats. According to the same authority, the total consumption of fuel in producing and, presumably, harvesting and threshing one hectare of spring wheat in 1933 was 57.3 kilos, equal in cost to 63 litres, or 630 kilos of grain or very nearly the whole crop ....If these figures are correct, it is no wonder that the state farms were being run at a loss.[30]

Further, we must remember that it is in the USA, Canada, Australia and the USSR alone that mechanisation is synonymous with the big tractor and harvester-thresher, or that mechanised farming means large-scale farming. In the first three countries an average farmer has a large arable area on which large agricultural machinery can be used. Now, a small holder meets difficulties in utilising large farm machinery because of the size of his holding, the fragmentation of his fields, and because he lacks the necessary capital. The Soviets solved this problem by adjusting the size of the holding to the requirements of the machine, that is, by establishing collective farms. That is one way. The other way is to adjust agricultural machinery and its utilisation to the given size of the holding, which in India, as in many other countries, is small. In Europe, mechanisation is increasingly taking the form of electrification of the countryside and the use of labour-saving machinery, leaving the structure of the small holding unaffected. There, the manufacturers of agricultural machinery had begun to turn out, before the last war, machines suitable for use on small holdings, while possessing the advantages of large machines. "Engineers are now designing small implements, machines and tractors, suitable for peasant holdings. Some can be worked by small internal combustion engines and some by electricity ; the use of both was spreading over Europe before the War and we hope will continue to do so

[30] *Economics of Soviet Agriculture*, 1939, Macmillan and Co. Ltd., London, pp. 260-61.

after the War ; either can work a small machine almost as economically as a large one," said Sir E. John Russell, Director of the
Rothamsted Experimental Station, in a paper read in a Conference
held in April, 1943. David Mitrany, the author of *The Land and
the Peasant in Rumania*, had also written even before the last War,
"that 3 *ha* was the smallest area on which machines and implements
could be rationally used" Three hectares come approximately to
7.5 acres or 12 standard bighas only. German experience indicates
that a field between 1 and 2 acres is not too small for a tractor of,
say, 15 to 20 h.p. In Japan, they have devised small tractors which
have 3 to 5 horse-power and can plough one acre a day. (These
tractors which numbered 11,131 in 1950 throughout the country increased to 34,974 in 1953). That is, a large farm is no longer a condition precedent to the use of machinery or application of scientific knowledge.

When the holdings are too small and uneconomic for the use of
bullocks, the inevitable conclusion is not to pool them so that large
machinery may be used. Small holdings can be worked by manual
labour as they are mostly in Japan and as they were worked, at
least, hitherto in China also, and yet, as we have already seen, scientific techniques other than large machinery can be employed on
them. Average size of holdings in Japan, it may need emphasizing,
is, perhaps, the smallest in the world (see page 57 *supra*). Next
came pre-communist China. In parts of France also, where arable
holding of two to five acres abound, if the field is too small for
ploughing, the spade is used for tillage and the average peasant has,
by his industry, converted even the most rocky lands into orchards,
vineyards and corn-fields. Surely, we can also do the same : for,
lest we forget, our aim is, not profit per man, but to get the best
out of the land, to make it yield the maximum production per
acre and, at the same time, to keep the largest number of people
employed. In fact, certain peasant communities in our country
in certain localities are already doing it. For example, in the sub-
urbs of the towns of Uttar Pradesh, vegetable-growers, mostly
belonging to the *Kachhi* caste (the best quality of land, *kachhiana*,
being known after them) usually carry on cultivation on their
tiny holdings of two acres or so, without the aid of animal power,
and produce far more (and derive far greater income) per acre than
farmers in the interior do.

Reference has already been made to the example of a Bhoodan

worker in our country, Sri Shrikant Apte, who possesses no farming machinery.

In any case co-operatives can be established for the purchase of such agricultural machinery as the farmers may need, for example, for operations where the time factor is important, such as planting and harvesting, but either which they have not the means to buy or which would not pay if used on a single small farm. Only, joint use of such machinery will necessitate co-operative cropping schemes, which can be achieved without pooling of the land into a single large unit. But as against whatever advantage large agricultural machinery may possess, we must remember that members of the co-operative would all be wanting it at the same time, which will make the co-operative unworkable.

As regards the second advantage of large-scale farming, it is true that a man of small means, particularly, if he is an uneconomic holder, cannot often afford the facilities, technological and other, that will augment his produce or income. There are, however, two other courses open.

Either, the state should provide the facilities as it is doing to-day in a small measure in the form of canals and tube-wells and provision of *taqavi*, fertilisers and insecticides; or, the peasant farmers combine their resources, find these facilities for themselves, that is, shortcomings of small-scale production be mended by co-operative arrangements. In the latter case, the crucial question is—to what extent should they pool their resources ? What is the right socio-organisation principle which will serve to raise the rural standard of living, and yet not rob the peasants of their liberty ? Shall they pool their land and labour resources and work jointly on a large undertaking into which their holdings would have been merged, or, shall they keep their holdings intact, operate them independently and co-operate in non-farm operations alone, that is, pool their financial resources alone with a view to securing the facilities which actually go to increase the production or income of a farm, but cannot be secured by a small man on the strength of his small means ? In our opinion, as we have already indicated, it is the latter type which will best suit our purpose. It is the co-operative principle, combined with the incentive of individual land use and private ownership of land, that offers the right solution.

Since an increase in the size of the farm does not lead to greater production per acre, it is unnecessary and it will be a mistake to ask the peasant farmers to surrender their holdings, in order to constitute a large farm, or to hustle them into doing so. Co-operation need not extend to the act of farming, to those functions of farm management which can properly be executed within the boundaries of a single small farm. Such functions should remain the object of the independent individual himself. All that peasant farmers need do by co-operative action is to save themselves from the disabilities entailed by the small size of their business and their lack of training in the ways of a commercial civilisation. The real mission of co-operation in agriculture should be to secure to the peasant all the benefits and technical advantages of a large-scale undertaking, while they still retain freedom or advantages of private property. Through it the peasants should be able to secure the same results as a large-scale undertaking without the attendant hardships which this form of production has so often brought to the worker in manufacturing industry. Co-operation is the closer union of otherwise independent units—merely coming together of scattered entities—for purposes of eliminating certain disadvantages attendant upon independent, isolated action. Were the members of the organisation to sacrifice their economic and individual independence, it would amount to a merger, not co-operation. Nor, to repeat, from the nature of the agricultural business, is a merger leading to largeness of size, a condition precedent to increased production.

In agriculture, two kinds of reform are possible. One is institutional and the other technological. Transformation of peasant proprietorship into joint farming is an institutional change that will meet with the peasant's resistance. At best, it will take a long time before its efficiency can be assessed. On the other hand, the peasant will welcome technical improvements or technological facilities — irrigation water, manure, improved seeds, pesticides, and better farming practices in general, which can be easily used or introduced on small farms as well as on big. In the field of farming our model should be not the USSR or present-day China, but Japan which produces more per acre than either of these two countries. And the secret of Japan lies in technological improvements, not in institutional changes.

The report of a survey, *Co-operatives and Land Use* made by the Food and Agriculture Organization of the United Nations, already referred to, has this to say on the point :

During the last half century, the rise in yields due to scientific and technological advance has been general, and has been more rapid in many countries in which individual farming is practised than in those which have gone in for massive collectivisation (Report, p.103)

Advantages of large-scale undertakings, also called 'economies of scale', expected from co-operative or collective farming, are often referred to without necessary distinction being made between operational, commercial and financial economies. As we have already seen, in our conditions of a labour-surplus agriculture, there can be no operational economies, or economies resulting from mechanisation of farm operations; at best, such economies are insignificant. It is, however, only in commercial and financial economies—the economies of organised bulk buying and selling, and cheap credit—that large farms excel. But to achieve these 'economies of scale', no merger of holdings and obliteration of identities of the peasants is necessary ; they can be achieved through service co-operatives, as they have been in several countries, while incentives remain unimpaired.

It is said that, because of the larger resources of a co-operative farm, Government will be able to advance larger credit to it than to small farms. True, but the needs of the large farm will also be large, and those of a small farm small. And inasmuch as money taken on credit will have to be paid back, the lender, even if it be a Government, will have to ensure that the borrower possesses sufficient security. The best security is land, and the total area of the land severally owned by farmers will not increase simply because of the pooling. If today, say, only a loan of Rs. 500 can be advanced to a farmer possessing 5 acres, not more than Rs. 5,000 can be advanced tomorrow to a co-operative farm in which ten farmers possessing 5 acres each would have pooled their lands. If we substitute expected produce per land as security (which, by the way, is a chimerical idea), it will not make any difference.

"Northern Europe", says Dr. C. R. Fay, Chairman of the Horace Plunkett Foundation, "has proved to the hilt that the highest degree of technical excellence is entirely compatible with family farming, but only on two conditions : first, that the land unit is the special subject of state guardianship and, secondly, that individual family effort on the land is supplemented by group effort in purchase, processing and sale."[31] In other words, large-scale farm-

[31] Vide *Year Book of Agricultural Co-operation*, 1943, p. 64.

ing is not essential, and, peasant farming as such offers no hindrance, to technical progress.

We may state here that by state guardianship is meant prohibition by law of agricultural land either from being amassed in large areas by one person, or from being divided by inheritance or sale into too small units.

The Patil Delegation, however, does not think service co-operatives can prove an effective agency for bringing advantages of a large-scale organisation to the doors of the peasants. Improvements have not been carried out nor agriculture intensified in our country even on holdings exceeding 10 acres, which should provide fairly good units of cultivation. The reason, it is said, lies in the limitations inherent in family farming. Schemes of land improvement may be undertaken by a cultivator either with his own labour resources or with hired labour. No considerations of money costs (outlay) and benefit (return) are involved in undertaking the former. As regards the latter, a cultivator will take up only those which are remunerative for him. But in agriculture there are many improvements which are not sufficiently remunerative. This sets a limit to the extent to which a cultivator could go in undertaking improvements through hired labour even if he were to be provided with all the supplies and finances required for the purpose. Such improvements can, therefore, be effected either by the state or by an institution organised for common action based on considerations of community interest, rather than individual interest. A co-operative farm is eminently such an institution, so runs the third argument in its favour, which will bind together those who have got the land but not the necessary labour to work it and those who have got the labour but not the necessary land to keep it engaged. Such farms alone will, through undertaking land improvements and intensification of agriculture, ensure the fullest use of our available man-power, which is our greatest asset but is going waste today owing to unemployment and under-employment.

Service co-operatives, it is contended, cannot finance improvements on petty holdings—and most holdings in our country are petty—even if the improvements are remunerative. For, there is a gap between the actual income of the petty farmers and the requirements of bare necessities of life. The additional income which may accrue from improvements initiated and financed by service cooperatives would hardly cover the gap. Recovery of loans from the petty farmers, therefore, presents serious difficulties.

The answer is simple. The report of the Patil Delegation gives no facts and figures to prove its assertion that even cultivators of holdings exceeding 10 acres do not undertake land improvements which may not be profitable in the economic sense. This may be true of owners of large farms to whom agriculture is a profession, but to an average cultivator in our country it is a way of life. Born as he is and living as he does in the midst of hazards, uncertainties and vicissitudes of nature, he does not reckon in the commercial way, nor does he draw up a balance-sheet of loss and profit. He makes no calculations where his land, the *Dharati Mata*, is concerned. He will sink any amount of money and labour on her improvement : this is proved by the high price which a cultivator is willing to pay for land—a price which if it is considerations of outlay and return alone that mattered, no industrialist or non-agriculturist will ever be willing to pay. Highly developed and well-kept peasant farms in central and north-western Europe, Japan and parts of India can be quoted by way of proof. The report embodying *Studies in Economics of Farm Management in Uttar Pradesh* undertaken in Meerut and Muzaffarnagar districts at the instance of Government of India in the year 1954-55, observed thus about the cultivators' love of land improvement, in the introductory chapter. "The whole of the countryside gives a look of very well-maintained and properly levelled fields . . . . As a result of careful cultivation soil has considerably improved. It owes its dark appearance more to its proper tillage and manuring than to its natural characteristics (p. 1) . . . . The noteworthy feature of farming in these districts is that there are few tracts elsewhere with so much 'made' soil by human efforts. The farmers have taken great pains to redeem the otherwise sandy or stiff clay by manuring, irrigation, drainage and levelling" (p. 2).

As regards the efficacy of service co-operatives, we need only refer to the example of Switzerland, Netherlands, Western Germany, Italy, Norway, Belgium and France where an average arable holding, varies from 7 to 16 acres, but which have made a success of service co-operatives. If, however, it is intended to convey that service co-operatives are of no avail where the cultivators possess only tiny, subsistence holdings, it should suffice to state that, according to the 1950 World Agricultural Census, the average farm holding in Japan (with only 12.5 million acres of cultivated land and 6.2 million farm households) is roughly 2 acres. Farmers who cultivate less than 1.25 acres represent 41 per cent., those who cultivate less than 2.50 acres represent 73 per cent and those who cultivate less than 3.75 acres represent 88.5 per cent of all farmers. It will not be irrelevant to point out here that the strength of a farm household in Japan is 6.0, while in India it is 5.1 and in the USA, only 4.5. Yet, the service co-operatives are a great success in Japan. In this connection we cannot do better than quote from the Patil Delegation's own report :

Although there are no co-operative farming societies, Japan has a highly-developed co-operative structure in the field of credit, marketing and supply. More than 95 per cent of the total farm households are members of co-operative societies, which supply 39 per cent of the total agricultural finance and hold 65 per cent of the total savings of the farm households. 96 per cent of surplus rice and 85 per cent of the surplus wheat and barley are marketed through co-operatives (p. 103).

So far as possibilities of reclamation through co-operative farms are concerned, as will appear later, there is little land waiting to be reclaimed. Also, financial resources required for land improvements or reclamation will be available to large co-operative farms only if their production per acre is greater than on small farms, and this is not borne out by the evidence collected in these pages. Further, experience shows that individual farmers under incentive of a high price of agricultural commodities are better able to reclaim cultivable waste. In the State of Uttar Pradesh, since the Second World War, while the Government could reclaim hardly, 1,60,000 acres, individual farmers have brought under cultivation anew several times this area—more than 25 lakh acres in any case.

As regards the fourth advantage, *viz.* that of planned crop rotation and more rational use of land being possible on co-operative farms, there seems to be some confusion. What exactly is the objective of crop rotation ? Obviously, preventing the soil from getting exhausted and maintenance of its productivity. If so, this objective is better served, as we have already seen, by a system of small farms, wherein big machinery is not used and more farm-yard manure is produced, thus helping maintenance of soil fertility. The charge that small holders are not able to practise crop rotation can possibly be laid only against such of them as are greatly uneconomic or sub-basic holders, but even this does not help the critics much. For, such farmers will not raise commercial crops which exhaust the soil and will, for their own subsistence, resort largely or wholly to food-crops which are not all or so exhausting and along with which nitrogen-fixing legumes can be easily grown. Crop rotation is not essential to good farming in all circumstances; mixed cropping so widely practised by small farmers can serve the purpose equally well. Nor do the small farmers lag behind in double-cropping and raising of high-yielding varieties. Indeed, a recent study in the Punjab shows that the intensity of cropping decreases with the increase in the size of farms. Double cropping is more widely practised on the small-sized farms. This naturally makes for an increase in the gross output per acre in the case of small farms compared to large ones. There are only two stipulations: in order that cattle dung which is so essential to maintenance of soil fertility is not burnt, cheap fuel has to be provided through community planting of non-arable, village lands, and, where necessary, a law has to be enacted preventing, particularly, very small farmers from sowing sugarcane or other exhausting crops, say, in more than one-third of their land in a year.

The argument about availability of large areas of land to a co-operative farm through disappearance of field boundaries is one that only needs to be stated in order to be rejected. Everybody who is conversant with the village conditions or agriculture, will testify that very little land is taken up in boundaries. Nor can boundaries be eliminated altogether; even the land of a co-operative farm will require to be irrigated, which cannot be done without boundaries. Also, land will be washed away during the monsoon but for the boundaries. The following extract from an article is given as typical of the advice that usually flows from our cities to the rustic farmer :

Large areas of land are used in building up bunds to demarcate boundaries as well as to hold water. By destroying a huge portion of these bunds and hedges *the average size of holding can be multi-*

plied several times and more area can be brought under cultivation resulting in higher production.[32]

The sixth argument relates to reduction of costs on a large farm. It is not clear, however, which wasteful operations on a small farm the critics have in mind. Perhaps, they refer to loss of time involved in trips that men and bullocks have to make to the various scattered plots into which a cultivator's holding may be divided, and to loss of water that may be entailed in irrigating such plots whether from a well or a canal. If so, these defects will be removed when these plots are consolidated into compact blocks. It does not take a large jointly-operated farm to eliminate such waste of time or water. In actual experience, peasant methods are usually found to have lower costs than the 'modern' scientific methods and that is the main reason why peasant production has been able to withstand the competition of large estates all over the world. Anyway, reduction of operation costs is not our primary aim, at any rate, at the expense of a higher yield. Small farms require comparatively more human and animal power than bigger ones, and this is not of much consequence because owners of such farms do not have to pay for it. So that even if the money costs are reduced in a big farm, it will still be preferable to have smaller ones in view of their greater yield and the available surpluses of labour and cattle. There are no scarce capital resources which are wasted on small farms in our country. Text-book writers of western countries have mostly 'machinery' in mind while using this terminology. In the context of our conditions, the bullock is almost the only capital resource of a small farmer and is not so scarce.

On the contrary, costs on a large co-operative farm will be far greater than what they are on small farms taken together. Owing to the need of detailed supervision and a complicated system of accounting, overhead costs are bound to be very high, which will more than off-set any economy that may be effected by mechanisation of the farm and rationalisation of labour. "As the size of the unit increases, the difficulties and costs of management also increase faster in agriculture than in industry. The workers are spread

[32] Vide Dr. V. D. Nagar. "Agricultural Prosperity through Co-operative Farming" published in the *AICC Economic Review*, September 15, 1959, page 19.

over a much wider area and the supervision required is much closer than in industry. Thus it becomes necessary to have supervisors for every small group of workers. But, again, because of the nature of the operations the supervisors cannot be fully occupied merely in supervision. In other words, a complete separation of managerial and manual functions is very uneconomical in agriculture".[33] This accounts for the excessive costs of supervision and management in the Russian collective farms about which there has been continuous criticism in Russian economic literature. As much as 41 per cent of the total work-days are reported to have been spent on payment for administration and service personnel in Russian Collectives.[34] It is due to the diseconomies of large-scale management in agriculture that the size of the optimum unit is relatively low in agriculture in most countries—except where the abundance of land and shortage of labour makes the existence of large mechanised farms unavoidable. These diseconomies begin to offset the other economies of scale fairly soon. That is why net returns per acre on smaller family farms are often higher than on large-scale farms.[35]

The above applied only to working costs. The initial costs that will be required in setting up a co-operative farm will not be negligible. New investment of capital in the form of manager's office, cattle sheds, godowns etc., will have to be made while the existing ones owned individually by farmers will have little or no use.

Now to the seventh argument : it is claimed that co-operative farming (as distinguished from collective farming which, some of our public men grudgingly concede, has not proved a success in the USSR and may not be practicable in our conditions of a democratic set-up) provides a solution to the evils of uneconomic holdings and fragmentation. A little thought will, however, reveal that, at least, so far as fragmentation is concerned, we need not resort to co-operative or collective farming in order to obviate it. Fragments of land belonging to one farmer, but lying scattered and at a distance from one another, can be easily consolidated into one block or two, compulsorily through law or voluntarily through co-operation amongst farmers. Consolidation of holdings has been

[33] *Economics of Agriculture*, Cohen, p. 56.
[34] *Co-operative Farming*, Talpade, p. 3.
[35] Vide *Co-operative Farming*, a monograph published by the Indian Co-operative Union, New Delhi, 1957, p. 14.

carried out in several countries, resulting in great benefit and satisfaction to the peasantry.

That there are a large number of uneconomic holdings in the
country is admitted. But it will be pertinent to point out here
that they do not form such a large percentage as is generally assumed. The number of actual cultivators is smaller than might be
calculated on the basis of entries in revenue records. The whole
confusion in this respect, which has marred the conclusions of so
many, otherwise ably-written books and reports, arises from the
fact that persons, families and holdings have all been mistaken,
one for another. For example, the cultivating population of Uttar
Pradesh in 1945 stood roughly at 80 lakh families, but the number
of persons entered as cultivators in revenue records (barring tenants
of *Sir* and sub-tenants which must have counted nearly two million
and a half) stood at 122.8 lakhs and the number of their holdings
at about 200 lakhs. The explanation lies in the fact that smaller
peasants usually possessed more than one holding, sometimes three
and even four, and sometimes names of more than one member belonging to a joint family were entered in the records. In 1945 the
number of holdings, possessing an area of four acres or less each in
Uttar Pradesh stood, according to the Zamindari Abolition Committee Report, at 75.5 per cent, but the actual number of families
which held four acres or less each would be found not to have
exceeded 50 per cent in any case. Dr. Otto Schiller, a German
Professor of Agricultural Economics, who served three half-year
assignments from 1953 to 1956 in West Punjab (Pakistan) on
behalf of the Food and Agriculture Organisation of the United
Nations, and made a survey of two villages on the spot, has also
reached the same conclusion about the conditions in Pakistan.[36]

Points about 'lack of capital resources and low level of technique and productivity,' which characterise small subsistence holdings, have already been dealt with. As regards under-employment
on these holdings, it is true that these holdings do not provide full
employment to the peasants all the year round and are, therefore,
uneconomic, leading to poverty, and should disappear as soon as
possible. But mere pooling of land is no remedy : it does not create
more employment. If one hundred persons possessing, say, two acres
each and operating them separately, have to remain idle today for

[36] Vide *Co-operative Farming and Individual Farming on Co-operative
Lines*, All India Co-operative Union, 1957. pp. 19-20.

a good part of the year because of lack of sufficient land, one fails
to understand how—by what magic—these persons will be able to
find full employment throughout the year, merely because their
land has been pooled into a farm of two hundred acres which they
now work jointly or under a unified direction. The number of
acres in the total has not increased by the pooling, nor has the
number of workers gone down. The proportion of rural population
to the land available remains as before.

Dr. S. Chandrashekhar, Director of the Indian Institute for
Population Studies, Madras, who saw four communes in action,
writes :

Not only do the Chinese work all the time, but in massive numbers. One sees 20 people pulling a loaded cart—some pulling with
ropes like animals and some pushing from behind. One would expect in a 'People's Democracy' that people would not be substituted
for animals. But I have seen men and even women pulling a plough !
The reason for this unhappy phenomenon is that people are at
the beck and call of the regime and they need not be paid high
wages. So the economy can afford to waste human labour which, in
terms of dignity and monetary value, means nothing. What could
be accomplished by two people is done by 20. A hundred people
toil on one acre of land and literally thousands work to put up a
building on a shift basis.[37]

If anything, unemployment in a co-operative farm is likely to
increase, for, more likely than not, the farm management will, in
the interest of smoother management, take to mechanisation.

The final, heavy-weight reasoning in favour of co-operative
farming proceeds thus : we are in desperate need of funds or capital
for making up the leeway. But programmes which have been undertaken for industrialisation and development of communications
already place a heavy strain on the available resources. Nor can
we emulate countries like Japan and England where economic development took place during a period of colonial expansion and a
comparatively monopolistic access to raw materials. At that time,
social consciousness had also not advanced so that internal exploitation could go on unchecked. Thus, through internal and external
exploitation, large stocks of capital were created in these countries
which form the basis of their industrial and economic prosperity.

[37] Vide *The Statesman*, dated January 10, 1959.

We have no colonies which we can or would exploit and, therefore, we have to depend upon our own resources. Capital has to be found out of our own efforts and our own savings. At the same time we have declared ourselves a 'Welfare State' and cannot, therefore, think of exploiting our people—exploiting in the sense a colonial or a capitalist government does. We have, therefore, to so reorganise our economy that it makes fullest use of our man-power which is our greatest asset, that it produces more and saves more. In the present agrarian economy based as it is on family-farming in small units, possibilities for savings and capital formation are severely limited. Co-operative farming offers the only solution for mobilising the national resources in which man-power plays the most dominant part.

The argument is naive. It assumes that as soon as land, dispersed today in small holdings, is pooled and jointly worked and agricultural labourers and, maybe, other landless people also are made members of the joint farm and management, the land will, almost automatically, begin to produce more per acre—produce a surplus to the needs even of the increased number of those who work it, just as large private farms do.

Such would also seem to be the view of Shri U. N. Dhebar, ex-President of the Indian National Congress. He says :

The basic problem in agriculture is not that of supplying good seeds, water, manures, or providing the credit and marketing the commodities. Rather, it is the shape of the agricultural economy itself. On the basis of caste, land has been denied to the Harijans and landless classes, which are increasing and lead a precarious existence. Those who hold uneconomic holdings today will be added to the ranks of the landless tomorrow. The Law of Diminishing Returns is working in the case of small uneconomic holdings.[38]

We do not agree with any of the assertions of Shri Dhebar, except that land in many parts of the country has been denied to Harijans, *inter alia*, on the basis of caste. It is his view about the operation of the Law of Diminishing Returns, however, that needs be examined here. He implies that the law will cease to operate the moment small uneconomic holdings are pooled together to form a large holding. The Law of Diminishing Returns is a much-worked and much abused

[38] *AICC Economic Review*, July 1, 1959.

proposition. It simply says that, provided there is no difference in farming methods and capital employed per man is equal, returns per man will diminish as an increasing number of men are put to farm a limited area of land. One fails to understand how the law which operates in a case when the labour force of a single family working, say, 5 acres of land is increased from, say, three men to four (and thus the area per worker is diminished), ceases to operate when the labour force of ten families jointly working 50 acres of land is increased from thirty men to forty. Forty men will each or severally produce less than thirty from the same total area just as four men each will produce less than three. Operation of the Law of Diminishing Returns cannot be held back simply by pooling of land and labour, but only by improvement in farming methods or increase in capital employed per worker, or both. These two developments can be brought about without pooling of land and labour. Increased capital can be had from Government or through credit co-operatives, and improvement in farming methods is the result of farmers' own experience and enterprise, or of research carried out by Government. They are not the consequence, or do not flow out of a joint farm.

While the increase in product per worker, with the increase in the number of workers on a given area (subject to a floor), is a diminishing increase, more men result in more product per acre and, therefore, more total product, but only when incentives remain unimpaired—when land is divided into as many allotments assigned and worked separately. So, if some persons hold land more than they can efficiently exploit, and substantial areas are available, let us certainly arrange for their acquisition and distribution among uneconomic holders, but not pool the existing holdings. As will be apparent from the following pages, our problem of poverty will not be solved by putting more men on land—whether working jointly or separately—but to move them away to non-agricultural occupations, and this consummation will be brought about only if and when production per acre has increased.

The marketable surplus expected to prove the chief source of investible industrial capital for development of the country will not be available from large joint farms. No pains are taken—no facts and figures are given—to prove how greater production per acre will come about or whether it has actually come about in countries where large-scale joint farming has been introduced.

The argument only displays a pathetic, but unexplained faith in large-scale units in conformity with Marxist thinking.

Dr. Otto Schiller points out :

It is not high productivity per acre which enables the large farms to play a predominant role for the supply to urban markets but the fact that less population and mostly also less livestock are attached to the same acreage as compared with the area of small holdings. The introduction of co-operative farming would improve the supply to urban markets, only if it leads to higher productivity per acre or to a shift of population. Both effects, however, are not automatic consequences of co-operative farming but depend upon other factors which can exercise their influence also under the conditions of individualistic farming.[39]

It is high productivity per acre which is the crux of the matter. Once this is achieved, as it can be on small, independent farms, the peasants will have more to consume and also more to sell. Even today they market the last grain they can. Unless, therefore, it is intended to extract from the peasantry a greater surplus than is left after bare subsistence has been kept back and unless our planners wish to emulate the mode of capital formation adopted in Russia, Eastern Europe and China, where the state (through its direct control of collectives, large, compulsory low-price deliveries, heavy taxes, etc.) forced down the actual consumption levels of the peasantry in the name of capital formation—incidentally, if this is not exploitation which the advocates of co-operativisation professedly want to avoid, nothing else is—there is no case for co-operative farming.

It is true that farms in India are too small—smaller than the best economic unit for profits. They are so small because, land-man ratio in the country being low and other occupations also in which the farmers could engage being limited, the farm land inherited from their fathers has to be re-divided amongst each succeeding generation of sons. It is an irrefutable proof of over-population. But the relevant point here is that, could large-scale agriculture be carried on more successfully, or produce more and give happiness to those engaged in it, should we not expect that logic of technological advance, i.e. economic and other forces by themselves would have, just as they did in manufacturing industry, led to the gradual

[39] *Ibid.*, p. 13.

disappearance of the small independent farm and its replacement, without any pressure from the state, by big units worked jointly by hundreds and thousands of persons ? On the contrary, we find that the larger unit, almost wherever it existed, has been broken into small ones—a unique instance of deviation from the laws operating in manufacturing industry—and the average agricultural "business" all the world over, except where a deliberate imposition has been made from above, remains as small as ever, with the peasant farmer as its owner and worker, manager and financier, all rolled into one. The peasant has refused to be fitted into any slogan: his is a role which has defied all economic theories. Indeed, it is not possible for modern economics, nursed in the field of capitalist agriculture with the background of 'wage and labour' and the criterion of as much rent or profits as possible, to give a true insight into the socio-economic nature of wageless family economy that the peasant agriculture symbolises.

At the time when Marx laid it down that in agriculture, as in industry, property was becoming increasingly concentrated and the large producer was bound to displace the small producer, scientific inquiry into agrarian problems had not yet begun and his plausible parallelism between agriculture and industry seemed incontrovertible. "But soon after the appearance of the third volume of *Capital* in 1894", says David Mitrany, "the planks of the Marxist platform began to give way. The German population census of 1895 (the first since 1882) disclosed the peasant's astounding refusal to die. Between 1882 and 1895 the number of holdings of 2 to 20 hectares had increased by 1.26 per cent and the total surface they covered by 659,259 hectares (about 1,650,000 acres). The same phenomenon was reported from countries as different as the United States and Holland. And the German census of 1907 killed the concentration theory altogether. It showed that notwithstanding the many favours which capitalist agriculture had received from the state during the preceding years, large estates and farms were constantly losing ground".[40]

On the contrary, peasant holdings prospered and multiplied because of the greater care and interest the peasant put into his work, and also because of the fact that his demands were sometimes lower than even those of a rural labourer. His readiness to

[40] *Marx against the Peasant*, George Weidenfeld and Nicolson Ltd., London, p. 25.

work harder and to consume less could be explained by the peasant's attachment to his land, as it explained his readiness to pay almost any price for it. "For the capitalist, property or tenancy is a means of employing his capital ; for the proletarian, artisan and the small peasant, property is rather a means of employing his labour", said Otto Bauer, the Father of Austrian Socialism, some 40 years ago. The excess over the normal price which the small holder is willing to pay and the hard work which he willingly puts in may be called the premium which he pays for his independence. It is this love of the peasant for his plot of land and for his independence that we can mobilise and put to great advantage if we give him the encouragement and co-operation he needs. On the contrary, we are trying to destroy this love or this instinct of his, which could come to our rescue when we want more food and more exportable raw materials from our land. The Patil Delegation, unmindful of what effect it will have on its arguments in favour of co-operativisation, observed as follows :

Every family in the co-operative had been allotted a small plot of land close to their house for vegetable cultivation. If there was no suitable land near the house, a piece of land in the fields close to the village site was given. This appeared to be the general system in all the co-operatives. These plots were very carefully and intensively cultivated and it was a treat to see many of them growing a rich crop of vegetables (Report : pp. 9-10).

We do not know whether the question as to why the Chinese peasants devoted more attention to these plots (and, therefore, presumably produced more on them per acre) disturbed the members of the delegation or not when they signed the report in favour of co-operative farming.

It is sometimes said that in India "land has been further concentrated in fewer and fewer hands and there has been more and more proletarisation of small peasants". This is not a correct appraisal, at least, so far as Uttar Pradesh[41] is concerned, of which figures are available to us (See Table XXII).

Figures of 1931 and 1941 have not been given because in these two censuses the occupation of workers alone has been recorded, and not of the entire population.

[41] *Census Report of Uttar Pradesh*, Part I-A, 1951, Table 79, pp. 96-97.

TABLE XXII

VARIATION IN PERCENTAGE OF AGRICULTURAL CLASSES IN U.P.
(1901–1951)

Principal means of livelihood	1901	1911	1921	1951
Cultivators	48.53	59.80	64.18	67.41
Agricultural Labourers	9.03	9.48	8.68	5.71
Rent receivers	7.11	1.80	1.76	1.06
Total	64.67	71.08	74.62	74.18

According to the *Census Report of India* for 1951 (Vol. 1, Part 1—A Report, pages 155-56), during the twenty years following 1931, the percentage of cultivating labourers to all workers on land had fallen in Uttar Pradesh (18 to 9), Orissa (30 to 19), West Bengal (40 to 28), Madras (38 to 35), Bombay (43 to 18), Madhya Pradesh (43 to 32) and Rajasthan (11 to 4). The percentage remained practically unchanged in Bihar (26-27), Mysore (13-14), Hyderabad (31) and Punjab (11-12). There was only one major state where this percentage had increased—Travancore-Cochin (34 to 47).

The fall in the percentage of cultivating labourers is the natural result of increase in the number of cultivators. According to the Report the proportion of agricultural rentiers, which was already small in 1931, became still smaller in 1951.

Whatever other conclusions may be drawn, these figures are an unmistakable tribute to the inherent internal strength of the system of peasant farming, its adaptability to changing circumstances, its capacity to bear the stresses of modernisation, and above all its power to endure.

CHAPTER SEVEN

Employment

APART FROM the agricultural area, that is, arable and pasture lands that a country may possess, it is the availability of non-agricultural resources and, consequently, the density of agricultural population that will determine whether the country will have large-scale farming or intensive peasant farming. Of the three factors of production, *viz.*, land, labour and capital, the one which is the most scarce and, therefore, dearest will be exploited more than the other two. Where land is plentiful, that is, a cheaper factor, and men few in number, the latter will not make the fullest use of the former. They will not try to obtain the highest yield per unit of land, but will bring a greater area of land under cultivation. In other words, large farms will come into existence and agriculture will become extensive. The more, however, the value of land increases relatively to labour (and capital), that is, the more the population or, to be exact, the more the agricultural population increases and the more scarce the land becomes, the greater yields will the cultivator seek to obtain from it by the use of increasing units of labour (or capital, or of both). In other words, small farms will come into existence and agriculture will become intensive. Extensive methods enable the farmer to obtain the biggest net return per unit of labour (and capital) ; intensive methods, however, give him a smaller net return per unit of labour (and capital) but a bigger gross and, according to some studies, even net return per unit of land.

Table XXIII on pages 108-9 shows the availability of land per capita of the entire population and per economically active person in agriculture in the various countries.

It is clear that Australia, New Zealand, the USA, Canada and the Union of South Africa, with more land relatively to population engaged in agriculture, can afford the luxury of large-scale, extensive farming whereas China or Japan, India or Pakistan, Italy or Germany, Norway or Netherlands, Egypt or Indonesia, with greater population engaged in agriculture relatively to land that is available, must of necessity have small-scale, intensive farming (provided, of course, economic laws are allowed to operate and no external pressure is brought to bear on the peasantry).

India is faced with the problem of unemployment. National interest, therefore, demands an agrarian economy which, while serving to extract the maximum out of land that constitutes the limiting factor in our circumstances, will provide the optimum of employment for the rural folk. Such an economy can only be an economy of small farms as distinguished from that of large farms, whether private or co-operative. In fact, small-scale economy, both in the field of agriculture and industry, is the major solution of our unemployment problem.

Large holdings, private or co-operative, attract the use of large machines, thus displacing labour, whereas small holdings limit the use of machines thus employing more labour. The number employed per 100 acres in countries where small holdings predominate is greater than that employed in countries where large holdings form a large percentage. In the Irish Free State, for example, on equal areas of land in the twenties there were five times as many persons working on farms of 15 to 30 acres and three times as many on farms of 30 to 50 acres as on farms of over 200 acres. Similar results were obtained from English, German and Danish statistics. According to Lord Addison, an ex-Minister of Agriculture, records prepared for the Government in 1930-31 for thirty-five different county council estates comprising nearly 17,000 acres, showed that population on these council lands, after they had been divided into small holdings, had increased from 1,048 to 2,298.

Machinery can be profitably used only to the extent to which it saves labour that might otherwise be productively employed, or to the extent it performs work that hand labour cannot do, or cannot do as well, or cannot complete quickly enough to enable farm operations to be done at the most suitable time for maximum production. But a good proportion of labour in our rural areas is already going unemployed or under-employed today ; there is no work in the sphere of agriculture that human or animal labour cannot perform and, our country being a land of small farms, our farmers can easily procure labour in their village itself or in the neighbourhood, that may be required to complete any farm operation in the quickest possible time.

Not only that mechanisation of agriculture is unnecessary, impracticable in our conditions, or too expensive : it will further increase unemployment. As use of machinery makes it possible

TABLE XXIII

STATEMENT SHOWING AVAILABILITY OF LAND PER CAPITA IN CENTS (CENT=0·01 ACRE) AND PERCENTAGE OF ECONOMICALLY ACTIVE POPULATION ENGAGED IN AGRICULTURAL OCCUPATIONS

Sl. No.	Country	Year	Total Area	Land Area	Arable Land and Land Under Permanent Crops	Permanent Meadows and Pastures	Forests and Wood Lands	Total of Cols. 6, 7, 8	Percentage of Economically Active Population Engaged in Agricultural Occupations (Both sexes)	
									Year	Percentage
1	2	3	4	5	6	7	8	9	10	11
1.	Netherlands	1960	70	N.A.	22	28	6	56	1947	19
2.	Korea (Rep.)	1959	100	100	21	**	39	60	1955	80
3.	Belgium	1960	82	N.A.	26	21	16	63	1947	12
4.	Japan	1960	98	N.A.	16	3	66	85	1959	40
5.	Pakistan	1960	253	N.A.	79	N.A.	10	89	1954-56	65
6.	Germany (F.R.)	1960	115	113	40	27	33	100	1959	15
7.	U.K.	1960	115	114	34	59	8	101	1951	5
8.	Ceylon	1960	164	162	38	N.A.	89	127	1953	53
9.	India	1958	193	N.A.	95	8	31	134	1961*	72
10.	Italy	1960	151	148	79	26	29	134	1960	30
11.	Switzerland	1960	190	184	20	80	45	145	1950	16
12.	Israel	1960	242	237	48	93	9	150	1960	17
13.	China (Main land)	1954	410	N.A.	46	75	32	153	N.A.	N.A.
14.	Portugal	1957	246	245	115	N.A.	69	184	1950	48
15.	Denmark	1960	232	N.A.	150	19	24	193	1955	23
16.	Philippines	1959	275	273	62	11	121	194	1959	59
17.	Austria	1959	294	290	62	81	110	253	1951	32
18.	France	1959	303	N.A.	118	72	64	254	1957	26
19.	Thailand	1960	484	N.A.	75	N.A.	247	322	1954	88

20. Greece	1960	389	381	110	155	74	339	1951	48
21. Ireland	1959	610	598	119	290	14	423	1951	40
22. Malaya (Fed.)	1958	499	498	83	**	360	443	1957	58
23. Norway	1957	2232	2127	58	13	484	555	1950	26
24. Turkey	1960	689	689	225	254	94	573	1955	77
25. Guatemala	1950	960	936	130	51	426	607	1950	68
26. Burma	1959	819	N.A.	104	N.A.	547	651	1931	68
27. Finland	1960	1872	1696	148	10	598	756	1950	46
28. Chile	1956	2639	2608	196	16	582	794	1952	30
29. Sweden	1960	1486	1359	119	23	744	886	1950	20
30. U.S.A.	1959	1080	1062	255	352	357	964	1950	12
31. Mexico	1950	1918	N.A.	194	732	378	1304	1950	58
32. South Africa	1960	1917	N.A.	161	1424	22	1607	1958	33
33. Venezuela	1956	3786	3661	121	739	789	1649	1951	41
34. Columbia	1956	2174	N.A.	93	254	1326	1673	1950	54
35. U.S.S.R.	1956	2778	2770	274	458	1092	1824	1951	39†
36. Peru	1959	2932	N.A.	41	282	1643	1966	1959	62
37. New Zealand	1959	2848	2819	52	1339	992	2383	1940	16
38. Brazil	1957	3431	3413	77	434	2087	2598	1956	58
39. Argentina	1957	3454	3416	373	1406	1236	3015	1950	25
40. Paraguay	1954	6569	N.A.	84	114	3377	3575	1947	54
41. Canada	1956	15331	14132	624	336	6798	7758	1960	12
42. Australia	1958	19345	N.A.	679	10859	1000	12538	1954	13

SOURCE: The above table has been built on the figures of area taken from FAO *Production Yearbook*, 1961, on the figures of corresponding total population used for finding area per capita in different countries taken from UN *Monthly Bulletin of Statistics*, August, 1962, issue excepting Argentina and Mexico for which figures have been taken from UN *Monthly Bulletin of Statistics*, January 1962 issue ; and on figures of percentage of economically active population in agriculture taken from *FAO Production Yearbook*, 1961.

* Figures for India in cols. 10 and 11 have been taken from *Census of India*, Paper No. 1, 1962 (P. 25, Statement no. 18).

† According to UN *World Economic Survey*, 1961, Table 3.6, the percentage of labour force engaged in agriculture in USSR in 1959 stood at 42.2.

** None, in negligible quantity.   N.A. = Not available.

for a smaller number of workers to cultivate a larger area, a large farm served by tractors, combine-harvesters and threshers, employs less labour than small farms covering the same area. When machinery is employed, labour is necessarily saved. In one and a half hours a tractor can plough one hectare of land and a combine-harvester can harvest an equal area in one-third of the time. A labourer who formerly ploughed hardly one acre with a pair of bullocks will be able to plough at least 12 acres a day with a tractor. The average area of land per farm increased in the USA from 136 acres in 1890 to 215 in 1950, while the number of workers per farm in the same period decreased from 2.0 to 1.6, which means that in the USA increasing use of agricultural machinery in these 60 years, on a given area of a farm, led to a fall of 50 per cent in the number of workers. An American expert[1] gives the following estimate of man-hours that were found necessary, at various points of time, as mechanisation advanced, for growing and harvesting an acre of wheat land yielding 20 bushels :

Man-hours

In 1830—55.7 (Seeding and harvesting done by hand)
In 1896— 8.6 (Horse-drawn drill and binder)
In 1930— 3.3 (Tractor-drawn drill and harvester-combine)

In Sweden the use of farm machinery reduced labour requirements by 50 per cent in twenty years only, *viz*. from 1930 to 1950.

In the USSR in 1927, 25.6 million independent peasant farms contained 100.5 million hectares of arable land and, according to the census of 1926, 114 million persons lived by agriculture, thus giving an agricultural population of over 103 per 100 hectares of cultivated land. In 1937, after collectivisation of agriculture, there were a little more than 18.5 million families cultivating 110.5 million hectares which, at 4.8 members per family, works out at 88.8 million persons or 80 per hundred hectares of farm land. There was thus a fall of 23 persons per 100 hectares of land in a decade owing to mechanisation of agriculture.

Even so, wrote Sir E. John Russell, Director of Rothamsted Agricultural Research Station, after his visit to Russia in 1937:

---

[1] *Economist*, London, May 6, 1944, p. 592.

The number of workers per 100 hectares is usually large according to western ideas, especially if one assumes that much of the work is done by tractors and combines. On the farms I visited it was about two to four times as many as would have been needed in England, but the yields were less and the work not so well done, indicating a considerable difference in efficiency of the workers of the respective countries.

If agricultural labour were rationalised and machinery economically and efficiently operated, it would probably be found that about two-thirds of the present available labour on collective farms would be sufficient for the present type of farming. "If we calculate on the basis of West European norms of labour requirements in farming operations", says Dr. Otto Schiller, "the normal labour input of approximately 100,000 large-scale farms composing Soviet agriculture today with about 1500[2] hectares of crop land each, considering their actual present intensity of farming and their actual degree of mechanisation, we arrive at an excess farm population of at least 30 million."[3]

The Government of the USSR, however, as and when it considers necessary, can employ this surplus labour to bring new land in Siberia and Central Asia under cultivation. But in an ancient country like India, where manpower is running to waste and there are no vast areas of virgin soil waiting to be broken up, big mechanised farms would be nothing short of a calamity ; industrialisation alone would not absorb tens of millions of workers that would be released from land.

Mr. Hubbard in *The Economics of Soviet Agriculture*, 1939, says :

Since 1928, industry in the USSR has absorbed probably between 12 and 15 millions of rural population, but since 1932 the rate of increase in wage-earners in all branches of activity has slowed down. Since industrial labour is steadily improving in efficiency and productivity, it is unlikely that demand will again expand at the same rate as during the first Five-Year Plan, when the total number of wage-earners doubled.[4]

[2] 2,000 hectares would be the more correct figure.
[3] An article entitled, "The Resources and Performance of Soviet Agriculture" by Dr. Otto Schiller, published in *The Journal of Farm Economics*, America, May, 1956, p. 306.
[4] *Ibid.*, p. 214.

Even in the USSR, therefore, throughout the buoyant period of economic expansion when tremendous cities and vast industrial enterprises were springing up all over the face of that country, only one million and a quarter persons—not more than one million and half in any case—were being absorbed into gainful employment each year, whereas in India the rate of increase in population alone calculated at the decennial rate of the last census period, comes to nearly nine million a year, not to say anything of the existing tens of millions who cannot be said to be gainfully or fully employed today.

Typical of the view that reduction in employment in agriculture caused by mechanisation will be compensated by a rise in employment in other directions, is the comment of Dr. W. Burns, made in his Note on *Technological Possibilities of Agricultural Development in India* submitted to the Government of India on September 30, 1943 :

Use of machines may mean fewer men per operation, but not per acre. There are numerous examples in which modern progressive farming has actually restored the numbers of men employed upon the land. Mechanisation, in addition, creates several new classes, those who make, those who manage and those who repair the machines. It employs, in addition, men-groups who are the suppliers and distributors of the spares, the fuel and the lubricants. Mechanisation, particularly if it involves the transference of machines from one place to another, involves the improvement of roads and here, again, a large prospect of employment is opened up (p. 127).

It is true that mechanisation of agriculture will lead to creation of certain secondary and tertiary industries in which some of the displaced agricultural labour will be able to find employment. But in a country where most of the rural areas are over-populated, where there is already a pressing problem of surplus agricultural labour even on the basis of the existing technique of agriculture, where the joint-family system contains so much hidden unemployment and under-employment, and where, therefore, expanding industry's demand for labour, for many, many years to come, is likely to be covered by the existing idle hands, there is no economic justification in creating a supplementary labour supply through mechanisation of agriculture. In the USA, Sweden and other countries, surplus farm labour released by mechanisation of agriculture did not create any problems of unemployment because it was absorbed by industries which developed in the meantime. In Soviet Russia, one of the reasons for introduction of collectivised mechanised farming, thirty years ago, was the belief that it is a pre-requisite for the execution of a huge programme of industrialisation, with its increasing demand for human labour. This reason does not operate in India where agriculture is already labour-surplus today— where the marginal productivity of millions of people employed in agriculture is zero, or very close to zero.

In India it is thought that, with the bullocks and ploughs in common use, 100 acres in grain can provide employment for perhaps 15 persons 'gainfully employed' in agriculture ; whereas the average number 'gainfully employed' in India per 100 acres is 30. Allowing for the fact that some of India's agriculture is more intensive than grain, Indian economists estimate conservatively that a quarter of the rural population is surplus, in the sense that its removal from that land would make no difference to agricultural output. This was equivalent to having some 20 million people permanently un-employed about a decade ago.[5]

The Planning Commission itself has stated that "in agriculture, except under certain conditions, in the present stage of develop-ment the possible economic advantages of mechanisation may be more than offset by the social costs of unemployment that such mechanisation would involve" (*Second Five-Year Plan*, p. 113). The surplus of labour in the countryside is already large enough to meet the demand for industrial labour for a long time. And as we will see in Chapter XVI, unemployment both in the urban and rural areas has increased despite implementation of two Five-Year plans.

Mahatma Gandhi had said :

Mechanisation is good when the hands are too few for the work in-tended to be accomplished. It is an evil when there are more hands than required for the work, as is the case in India. I may not use a plough for digging a few square yards of a plot of land. The problem with us is not how to find leisure for the teeming millions inhabit-ing our villages. The problem is how to utilise their idle hours, which are equal to the working days of six months in the year.[6]

[5] *Aspects of Industrialisation*, Cairo, 1953, p. 8, quoted by Coale and Hoover in *Population Growth and Economic Development in Low-Income Countries*, Oxford University Press, 1959, p. 116.

[6] "Man vs. Machine", in *Harijan*, 16th November 1934, p. 316, as quoted in *The Mind of Mahatma Gandhi* compiled by R. K. Prabhu and U. R. Rao, Oxford University Press, 1945, p. 122.

On another occasion Mahatmaji said :

An improved plough is a good thing. But if by some chance one
man could plough up, by some mechanical invention of his, the
whole of the land of India and control all the agricultural produce,
and if the millions had no other occupation, they would starve, and
being idle, they would become dunces as many have already become.[7]

In our country, with its dense population, the practical politician
will have to correct the economic stand-point with the social, and
in many respects the economic problem for him will become a problem of population. He will want employment more than he hates
poverty. Hands, therefore, must have precedence over the machine
in India (even if we equate mechanisation with plenty).

The objection that unrestricted use of machinery will create unemployment is usually met with the argument that the collective
or co-operative farmers, who would include the whole rural population, could work only for, say, three hours a day and take holiday
for the rest, which will mean more leisure for intellectual pursuits ;
that in place of so much poverty and starvation of today we shall
have a perpetually rising standard of life. But the latter contention
does not hold. A large, mechanised joint farm cannot produce
more per acre than small peasant farms do. But even if it does,
it is doubtful whether a holiday of nine hours of day-light could
be regarded as a national gain. That an idle mind is a devil's
workshop, cannot be denied. "Leisure is good and necessary up to
a point only," says Mahatma Gandhi, "God created man to eat his
bread in the sweat of his brow, and I dread the prospect of our being
able to produce all that we want, including our food-stuffs, out of
a conjurer's hat".[8] Too much leisure demoralises society and it
will be an evil day for India when its peasantry succumbs to tempta-
tions of ease and pleasure.[9]

[7] *Young India*, 5-11-1925.   [8] *Harijan*, 16th May, 1936, p. 111.
[9] A series of articles from correspondents in various countries on the
problem that increased leisure poses, opened in the *Pioneer*, Lucknow,
dated July 17, 1960, with the following statement :
"Effective use of increasing leisure in this age of automation is worrying sociologists in many parts of the world. As more and more machines
increase productivity and reduce the need for long hours of manual
work, workers find themselves with more free time than ever before.

The advocates of mechanisation forget that the chief benefit the rational use of machine promises, is certainly not the elimination of work ; what it promises is something quite different—the elimination of servile work and drudgery. A peasant, however, is his own master and his work on his own farm is not, like a labourer's work in a factory, servile or a type of work that the machine was intended to eliminate. We are not opposed to use of all machines by the peasant farmers. Tools and machines which do not dispense with the use of animal power, or take away the need for a peasant farmer's labour and skill, which do not diminish his independence or lead to the disappearance of his very farm, but lighten his burden thereby easing drudgery, and increase the farmer's efficiency and productivity, are to be welcomed. It is to the all-purpose tractor that we are opposed. The tractor strikes at the very basis of independent farming. For, it nullifies the one competitive advantage which the peasant-farmer enjoys over the large farm or farmer, *viz.*, the cheap labour supply of his family.

Lastly, although the advocates of co-operative farming in India are not yet clear in their mind as to the traction power they would like to use, when confronted with the objection that mechanisation is likely to lead to unemployment, they sometimes reply that the co-operative farms of their conception will be run with animal power, instead. Now, this is a novel proposal : in the only countries in which co-operative or collective farms have been working for some time they are mechanised. It is already difficult to organise human labour in the various operations on a mechanised farm or *kolkhoz* : it will be still more difficult to do so if we add the work of looking after, say, 50 pairs of bullocks to the tasks of a farm. The personal attention and devotion which the tending of animals demands, can-

"In countries where standards of living are highest, there is a tendency today to reduce the length of the working week and increase the length of annual holidays. Suggestions and predictions for the future make the present average 35, 40 or 45 hour working week with retirement at the age of 60 or 65, look like slavery.

"In some countries, increased leisure has been blamed for an unusual increase in crime, especially among adolescents, in recent years. In others, boredom is said to be responsible for a big rise in the number of people requiring psychiatric treatment of one sort or another. Most countries are tackling this problem of boredom first and foremost in the adolescent, considering that it is to youth that it constitutes the greatest threat."

not be forthcoming in a community of, say, 100 persons who have only a joint interest and responsibility. Animals can be best looked after only when they are the exclusive responsibility of individuals. It will not be out of place to refer those who would not learn by their own experience or from conditions in their own country, to a press report about China when the co-operative farms were only just in the process of establishment. China has not the resources to produce agricultural machinery in bulk, nor is it in a position to spare resources for its import. The co-operative farms, as and when they came into operation, were, therefore, being run with animal power. The report says :

Another aspect of the same trouble is that when beasts are taken over by a co-operative, many perish from neglect through being left outdoors all night or from sheer lack of food, since it seems to be nobody's business to look after them.[10]

The Krishnappa Delegation to China observes in this connection :

On the whole, Chinese agriculture is weak in animal husbandry. In the production and development plans of co-operatives more emphasis might be given to this aspect of the rural economy. This might require not only a larger allocation of resources but also, perhaps, certain changes of an organisational character. In the breeding and care of cattle, collective maintenance has a part to play but along with it there might be room also for individual families being enabled to breed and look after cattle as much for their own benefit as for the advantage of the community. Since fodder resources are at the disposal of the co-operative, such schemes of animal husbandry development would require special arrangements for making green and dry fodder available to individual families (p. 121 of the *Report*).

Capital formation and, consequently, industrialisation being a very slow process, any reduction of pressure on land is hardly likely, at least, in the foreseeable future. It is said, therefore, we have to think in terms of re-organising our agrarian economy in a manner that would enable us to provide increased employment opportunities within agriculture itself. The advocates of co-operative farming contend that it will not lead to unemployment but will open up

[10] *Hindustan Times*, New Delhi, dated May 15, 1956.

new avenues of employment for those who are unemployed or under-employed today.

It is argued that our villagers today suffer from under-employment while, side by side, there exists a large employment potential. On the one hand, according to the Committee on Problems of Re-organisation appointed by the Planning Commission's Panel on Land Reforms, those who have rights in land do not generally possess an adequate area of land for their own full employment or the employment of surplus labour in the village. On the other, there are wells to be constructed, tanks to be dug and repaired, irrigation channels to be extended, drainage works to be executed, houses and roads to be built, local manure to be conserved and, if soil erosion is to be checked, land has to be terraced, bunded and afforested, etc. Also, there are large areas which have gone out of cultivation due to soil erosion and have to be reclaimed. All these works are of labour-intensive nature. Things have to be so arranged that the huge under-employed (and unemployed) population in the rural areas is utilised in executing these works, *i.e.*, in creating capital or physical assets—assets that will increase the production potential. But as long as peasants are tied down to their small plots of land they are not free to leave it for considerable periods to work on the creation of capital assets. Even if they have to work only for one or two hours a day to look after their cattle or land, they cannot leave the land. The existing pattern of land-use and management, that is, indivi-dual farming, thus impedes full utilisation of man-power. In a way, under-employment is an economic compulsion under conditions of individual farming. This compulsion or under-employment can be removed only by organisation of the existing small and uneconomic holdings into co-operative farms which, through rationalisation of work and pooling of resources, will release labour for capital forma-tion and intensification of agriculture. Such fuller and more conti-nuous employment, it is said, has helped to reduce and to a consi-derable extent, even to eliminate the worst forms of rural poverty in China. This, according to the Krishnappa Delegation to China, is a lesson of great value to India. The delegation, however, is beset with doubt in the very next sentence when it says—"Nevertheless, it may be difficult for a rural economy so greatly dependent on agricultural operations as that of China to continue to expand indefi-nitely work opportunities in farms for which the main resource needed is organised human labour" (*Report*, p. 121).

Earlier in its report the Delegation on this very question observed as follows :

In reply to a question on the effects that the formation of co-operative farms on a large-scale was likely to have on the employment problem, Mr. Chou En-lai said that the problem should be looked at from the point of view of two sectors and two periods. The two sectors were the villages and the cities and the two periods were the present and the future. So far as villages were concerned, in the short period, lots of work had to be done. Apart from cultivation, water conservancy projects had to be undertaken, reservoirs and tanks had to be dug and roads had to be built. All these required a lot of labour and the formation of co-operative farms made some of these activities possible and absorbed a considerable amount of labour of the co-operative farmers. But this state of affairs obviously could not be expected to continue for a long time. Soon a stage was bound to come when all the water conservancy projects in the village would be finished, all the roads would be built, and then there would arise the problem of some surplus labour in the village. Steps have, therefore, to be taken during the interim period for the utilisation of this surplus labour for the production of agricultural by-products. There was a good market for agricultural by-products and if the surplus labour in the rural areas could be absorbed by developing these by-product industries and in other subsidiary occupations in the villages, the problem could be solved to a considerable extent. Of course, during the same period if there was a certain amount of industrialisation in the country, that would draw away a number of surplus labourers from the villages. He felt, however, that, by and large, most of the rural workers would have to be employed in the village itself. It was mainly the educated and trained workers who could migrate to the cities and find some employment there (p. 27).

We leave it to the reader to judge for himself whether the question of additional employment through co-operative farming has been satisfactorily answered by this delegation. The Dissenting Minute of the Delegation, however, has to say the following in this regard :

The argument that if agriculture is collectivised, there will be work for all is not borne out even by our Chinese experience, because there we found that, in a vast majority of the co-operatives, there was great under-employment. The members were not employed even for 200 days in a year. Most of the co-operatives have also to rely on subsidiary occupations. Subsidiary occupation has a loose meaning in China and, in fact, we found examples where working as labourers on a road being constructed by Government was also taken as subsidiary occupation. Payment received by the members on the road-work was very low, so the difference was made up by the co-operative—which meant—at the expense of the members. Even the Minister, Mr. Liao, admitted displacement of labour by formation of co-operatives and said 'extra labour available due to pooling of land is transferred to subsidiary occupations which are suitable for a particular area' (*Report.* p. 212).

The former Food and Agriculture Minister of the Government of India, Shri Ajit Prasad Jain, while inaugurating a two-day conference of representatives of state co-operative institutes in New Delhi on 18 April 1956, was pleased to observe that the scheme of agricultural producers' co-operative societies would not result in a surplus of labour. He said that "the position today was that in addition to a large number of unemployed persons in the agricultural sector there was a good number who were under-employed. The creation of co-operative farms with medium and small-size holdings would provide full employment to many. By the introduction of small-scale industries it would be possible to find employment for others". The Planning Commission's Panel on Land Reforms also holds much the same view when it says that "the other advantage would be that a considerable amount of industrial work for self-use could be organised very much better in these co-operatives".

But, if it is small-scale industries which will have to be established to provide full employment on a co-operative farm, one is intrigued to know why they cannot be established independently of a co-operative farm. Fifty-two per cent of farmers in Japan in 1950 possessing, on the average, a holding of two acres carried on home and small industries in their spare time, without having first organised themselves in agricultural producers' co-operatives.

Perhaps, it will not be out of place to refer here to the belief, often voiced, that peasant-farming cannot be carried on except with the help of hired labourers, who enjoy no security today and eke out their existence somehow in a state of semi or gradual starvation, and that co-operative farming alone offers a solution. Both the beliefs are, however, unfounded. There is no agricultural labour worth the name in the Hariana districts of the Punjab, and whoever does not possess land in western parts of Germany where, too, the holding is almost as small as in the Punjab, is engaged as an industrial worker in the factories. The existence of landless agricultural labour, therefore, is not essential to peasant farming. In both these parts of the world the peasant's wife works in the field shoulder to shoulder with her husband and, instead of being a burden to him, as in certain other parts of India, she is an economic treasure to her life-mate. "The Jat woman in the Punjab does not plough, dig or drive a cart, but there is no other form of agricultural labour which she does not practise and ordinarily adorn", says Dr. Radha Kamal Mukerji.[11] Further, during periods of harvesting and on other occasions when time is a great factor, peasants can and, where necessary, do collaborate among themselves for providing the necessary labour.

As regards availability of employment in a co-operative farm for those who are landless today, well, it is simply not possible. If there is not enough land to go round, or, if it does not suffice even for those who are engaged upon it as cultivators today, we will have to find employment for the landless in occupations other than agriculture. A co-operative farm, if it is mechanised, will, rather, throw out of employment quite a good percentage even of those who are employed today.

[11] *Rural Economics of India*, 1926, p. 71.

CHAPTER EIGHT

Equitable Distribution of Wealth

IN VIEW of the small agricultural area as compared with the number of those who subsist on agriculture today, and will, of necessity, continue to do so tomorrow, there can be no place for large, privately-owned farms if it is our intention to build up an economy where wealth will be equitably distributed. So, taking away of land from large individual farms in excess of whatever ceiling may be decided upon, and its distribution amongst the landless and the holders of uneconomic farms, is an obvious course dictated by the principle of social justice enshrined in our Constitution. The Committee on Tenancy Reform constituted by the Panel on Land Reform appointed by the National Planning Commission has put the case admirably. It says—"There is no doubt that such solution will be welcomed by the large masses of the landless population ; possession of land gives them security, increases their bargaining power and enhances their status as land-holders in the village. Where the landless people belong to the Harijan[1] caste, this is an essential preliminary for the removal of untouchability itself. Existing disparities in ownership of land in agricultural incomes will, to a certain extent, be reduced. This will facilitate co-operation and rural progress and the state will have laid down the fundamental basis for the creation of a socialistic pattern of society" (*Report*, p. 9).

There is one substantial argument advanced against the proposal to place a ceiling upon the existing land holdings, *viz.* that in order to be fair we should place a ceiling on non-agricultural incomes as well. Otherwise, we will be discriminating against the large owners of rural property and be guilty of a bias in favour of the urban rich. This argument, however, does not take account of the fact that, while man cannot create land, he can create other forms of capital. The large farmer has not added to the nation's

[1] It may be stated here that not all Harijans are agricultural labourers or landless. For example, in Uttar Pradesh, according to the census of 1951, 60.9 per cent of the Harijans were cultivators of land or farmers, and 17.2 per cent were agricultural labourers (the corresponding figures for the entire population being 67.4 and 5.7).

wealth in capturing more land than ought to have fallen to his share, whereas the industrialist or the non-agricultural property-owner has, in putting up a factory or a house, created something which did not exist before. Secondly, it is land that in our conditions is a limiting factor while, of the two factors of production with which the non-agriculturist deals, labour is surplus to our needs and capital, though wanting in the measure we need it, is after all not so limited as land.

The Committee on Tenancy Reform has the following observations to make in this connection :

Monopoly in land and the ownership of large areas by a small minority of the agricultural classes is an obstacle to economic development. This does not apply with equal force to industrial development where large-scale organisation may lead both to greater economy and efficiency. Besides, redistribution of land is a simple operation as compared to changes in the much more complex organisation of industry and commerce. Historically also, redistribution of land, in a number of countries, preceded economic changes in the industrial sector (*Report* : p. 42).

It is not necessary to agree with the Committee in its entirety : except in Communist countries, redistribution of land by the state has not been regarded anywhere as a *sine qua non* to economic progress. Nor is imposition of ceilings on industrial ownership an impossible task. The American Occupation authorities successfully did it in Japan in the later part of the forties. The efficiency of large-scale industrial undertakings in all spheres is also, at best, a disputed point.

Ownership of industry is more concentrated—management control incredibly more so—than any other form of property or wealth. National policy in this regard has not only been halting, but faulty—with the result that disparities in incomes since independence have widened instead of being narrowed down. "The path of planned development", points out Dr. N. V. Gadgil in an article in a special number of *Economic Weekly* (Bombay, 1961), "that we have adopted, with its emphasis on forced growth of basic and capital goods industries, is largely modelled on the experience of the Communist countries. But we have not taken steps which the Communist countries did to .destroy economic power residing in private interest groups and to ensure egalitarian distribution of incomes, to control prices and production and distribution of consumer goods. Nor have we assumed responsibility for finding work and food for all. The alternative path in Capitalist countries where initial investment is made in less capital-intensive industries and the industrial classes are left to find their own capital resources, keeps the inequality in distribution of incomes from becoming too great. The attempt in India to follow the Communist route of planning combined with protection to heavy industries but little protection to farmers or consumer industries, has the result that we have the worst of both the worlds."

If breaking up of large organised businesses is not feasible or is not intended, the reasons being what they may, there are two sets of measures which can be easily applied and yet the structure of the operational unit will remain undisturbed. First : a ceiling just as in the case of land may be imposed on ownership of industry, if not directly, then through partnership or shareholdings. Dispersal of ownership will be a measure chiefly helping more egalitarian distribution of wealth and income. Second : without controlling policies of individual companies, Government should be able to ensure that their operations are conducted as befitting concerns affected by public interest. This could be done through imposition of uniform accounting systems, appointment of independent auditors or other measures of surveillance which will prevent acts of evasion, avoidance, collusion, etc. Such control will prevent accrual or accumulation of illegal profits which sometimes exceed lawful gains.

However, to return to land : the governing principle of redistribution of land should, perhaps, be that none is allowed to possess an area of land which under our technique of farming is beyond the capacity of an average man or worker to manage and none possesses less than an area below which, howsoever more labour may be applied to it, land will not produce more per acre. That is, the upper limit of the farm shall be governed by the capacity of one unit of manpower and the lower limit by the capacity of one unit of land. A reference to Table I will show that, as more and more men work a given land area, that is, as area per man decreases, production per acre increases with such great strides that production per man also increases, till land per man is reduced to 27.5 acres. Four men with hundred acres between them are found to produce more per man than three men with the same area. Below 27.5 acres, production per man begins to fall off as the area decreases although production per acre

continues to increase till land per man is reduced to a point between
2.6 and 2.1 acres—say, 2.5 acres (vide Table I). So that if the area a
man possesses amounts to more than 27.5 acres, neither land is fully
utilised, nor labour, because of its dispersal over too large an area,
gets its full return, and if it amounts to less than 2.5 acres per worker
labour is not fully employed and goes waste. At these stages, that is,
when the above level of 27.5 acres and the lower level of 2.5 acres per
man have been passed, both individual and national interests
coincide and suffer equally. In between these levels, the more land
a man or an agricultural worker has, the better for him, for his
total production will rise with every acre added to the holding ; the
less land he has, the better for the country, for the country's total
production will rise with every acre taken away from the holding.

Therefore, it is in the interest of the nation *and also in the interest of the farmers concerned*, if excess land is taken away from all
those families which possess more than 27.5 acres per worker, and
distributed to those which possess less than 2.5 acres per worker.
Also, laws relating to transfer and partition of land should be so
amended and enacted that no holding of less than 2.5 acres per
worker comes into existence in the future. The figures of 27.5 and
2.5 acres have been arrived at with reference to conditions in a country other than India. If in our country we adopt the figures of 25
and 3.125 acres instead, or 40 and 5 standard *bighas* respectively,
we will not be deviating, or deviating far from facts of agricultural
economics.

The Committee on Tenancy Reform set up by the Planning
Commission's Panel on Land Reforms is also of the view that
"peasant farming can be stabilised only if provisions are made to
ensure that units of management do not decrease below a minimum
size."[2]

In order to determine the area of land a family may be allowed
to retain, we will have to look to its labour resources. Indian agriculture has a labour force of 41 per cent so that an average farming
family of five persons has a labour force of $\frac{5 \times 41}{100}$ or 2.05 men-
equivalents. Therefore, for an average family land-holding, we
arrive at a ceiling of $(27.5 \times 2.05) = 56.40$ acres. If we take the area
of 25 acres as the ceiling for one worker, the corresponding figure for
an average family will stand at about 50 acres.

[2] *Report of the Committee on Tenancy Reform*, p. 48.

There may be other criteria to determine the floor and the ceiling, depending upon the preference of an economist or a government concerned, or what ideas an authority holds on 'social justice'. The Size of Holdings Committee set up by the Panel on Land Reforms has suggested that the ceiling be placed at three times a family holding—the latter being defined as land held by an average family of five persons which brings a gross income of Rs. 1,600 per annum or a net income of Rs. 1,200 per annum (including remuneration for family labour) and is less than one plough-unit, that is, an area of land which could be cultivated with one pair of bullocks, or if the soil is inferior, with two pairs of bullocks. A family was deemed to consist of husband, wife, unmarried daughters, dependent sons and grand-children.

This definition of a family holding, however, is not very satisfactory. It speaks of three determinants, *viz.*, income, size of family and its cultivating capacity. Income from land cannot be a reliable guide, for it will depend upon the type of farming, the locality, and the ability of the farmer. Also, it is likely to differ almost every year with the quantity of production and with prices, both of which, in their turn, depend on so many factors that are beyond the control of an individual. Nor is the size of the family a safe criterion. One man may have three minor daughters, and another three adult sons who are still living with him. A young man and an old man may have families of an equal size today, but in course of time, the size of the young man's family is likely to increase. A family holding may, therefore, better be defined solely with reference to the area that an average family may fully exploit. Besides land, there are two other factors of production, *viz.*, labour and capital without which it cannot be worked. It would, thus, be rational to correlate the area of a family holding with the labour resources of an average peasant family and its minimum capital requirements, so that full use of all the three economic factors throughout the year is assured. Now, an average family has two workers, and the minimum capital it requires is a pair of bullocks. So that a family holding should have an area that may provide continuous employment for two workers and two bullocks. Since it is economic factors that determine its size, the holding may also be called an economic holding. Strictly speaking, the area of such holding also in various regions of the country will differ with the kind of soil, the nature of crops grown, the availability or otherwise of irrigation facilities, and the performance of the bullocks, but almost all these factors are remediable. For, in most cases the soil can be improved, the cropping pattern changed, irrigation facilities provided where they did not exist and, where the bullocks are of poor quality, two plough-units may be allowed instead of one.

As for mechanised farms, according to Dr. L. Dudley Stamp,[3] Professor of Social Geography in London School of Economics and world authority on soil use, 100 acres are the optimum for efficient management, so that in the case of mechanised farms a ceiling can, with reason, be placed at 100 acres.

It must be conceded that in this respect, namely, the attainment of the objective of equitable distribution, a system of collective farming, if not that of co-operative farming, scores over an economy of small farms, where disparities in economic status, although greatly reduced, will still remain. It is a different matter, though, as there are various grades in men's capacities, difference in their economic conditions also should and will always remain. According to a decree of the Council of Ministers, dated April 19, 1948, there are nine classes of workers on a Soviet collective farm, ranging from the president, senior tractor-drivers, etc., who are credited with two to five labour-days for each day actually on duty, to watchmen, cleaners, etc., who score only half a labour day for every day on duty.

[3] "Land for Tomorrow", 1956, quoted in *The Peasant And Co-operative Farming* by Prof. N. G. Ranga and P. R. Parachuri, published by the Indian Peasants' Institute, Nidubrolu, 1958, pp. 56-57.

CHAPTER NINE

Making Democracy a Success

WE HAVE deliberately chosen a democratic way of life. Inasmuch as we have emerged into a full-fledged democratic state after centuries of colonial and despotic rule, which has demoralised our people, we have to take special care and special pains to see that the democratic spirit is fostered in our society at every step. All schemes that we frame in the social, economic or administrative sphere have to be tested on the touchstone of democracy, *viz.* whether or not they will serve to strengthen the democratic tendencies, inculcate democratic modes of behaviour and generate an atmosphere of personal freedom and initiative. Those which do not serve these purposes have to be scrupulously eschewed as a matter of national policy. The care and guardianship of this tender plant of democracy becomes all the more incumbent on us in view of the circumstances in which our country finds itself in the East—almost a lone standard-bearer of parliamentary democracy amidst a crowd of nations which either do not understand democracy, or have notions on it far different from ours, or are just struggling to find their feet consequent on the retreat of western colonialism from the region.

It is the individual who forms the base of democracy. It is he who as a voter chooses who will run the village panchayat, the State Government, or the Union Government for him. He should, therefore, be able to form a judgment or take a decision on his own responsibility, untrammelled by any restrictions or apprehensions. Now, it is axiomatic that a man who is not free in his economic life or who is dependent or leans on somebody else for his bread or has to take orders from others all the twenty-four hours of the day, cannot develop an initiative. He will have his personality cramped and, what is the crux of the matter, will not be free to act, much less vote, as he likes. So, an economic system in which the individual is not free, whether he works on land or in industry, will ultimately work out to the detriment of democracy. Political and economic freedom are interdependent—'you cannot have one for long without the other'. In that society alone will democracy, in the true sense, be a success where the individual, the bread-winner, is the master of his tools or means of production. There he does not have to take orders from, or render account to, anybody or any group or association of individuals, in fact, any authority outside of himself. But he is the sole captain of his fate, free to regulate his conduct as best, or, even as worst as he likes. That is what Mahatma Gandhi taught us ; that is the message of the *charkha* on which he laid so much stress.

We have now to decide which of the three alternatives set out in Chapter II will fulfil our purpose. In our opinion, it is the economy of small farms, again, which happens to be the answer. Not only does it produce more wealth and provide more employment, but it also removes glaring disparities from land and will also prove the most secure base of democracy. The liberty of the worker— a condition precedent to successful functioning of democracy—varies inversely with the size of the undertaking in or upon which he is employed. An economy of large private farms or capitalist farming envisages a rural scene where the number of persons who will give the orders, *viz.*, the farm-owners or managers, will be very few and the number of those who will carry out these orders, *viz.*, labourers, will be very large. For example, if we divide or distribute the arable land of Uttar Pradesh into farms of, say, 50 acres each, we will be left only with about eight to nine lakh persons or families of land-owners, and the rest, say, more than ninety lakh of families of divested peasantry, will be added to farm labourers, who already count more than a million and a quarter of families. In such an economy of large undertakings a few will get the whip-hand, who will develop, because of the nature of their business, an imperious attitude hostile to equality and freedom and who will gradually come to dominate the political life and the administration. While the vast majority, accustomed always to receive and obey orders, free though according to law, will not count either in social life or counsels of the States and the Union.

Under the Weimer Republic, concentration of large estates in pre-war eastern Germany, where a group consisting of three per cent of the population owned 20 per cent of land and was roughly characterised as *junkers*, resulted in a feudal society of poorly educated, poorly paid, and ill-housed farm labour population and in an educated and powerful land-owning 'elite'. This group formed the kernel of social and political 'reactionary-ism' in Germany. The majority of the *junkers* supported and encouraged all movements aimed at the overthrow of the Republic. They were consistent and active opponents of democratic government.

A proposition of an economy based on large, private farms has, therefore, only to be stated in order to be rejected, and we need not tarry long over it.

Now, as regards the co-operative farm which will be a big economic unit with hundreds, sometimes thousands of workers jointly working under one direction or management—Will such an organisation ensure freedom to the individual or full expression of his personality ? Will an economy based on large mechanised undertakings produce self-regulated individuals who are the first postulate of democracy ? No, it cannot. Such an economy can efficiently be run only on the basis of planned management and over-all regulation by the state. Whether we take the case of the Russian *kolkhoz* or the Chinese producers' co-operative, the degree of control, apart from the manner in which it is exercised, which the state has necessarily to apply to keep these organisations functioning, shows unmistakably the futility of imitating them in a democratic set-up.

In the USSR, the state through the State Planning Commission assisted by the Rayon and Provincial Commissions, lays down a production plan for each farm containing directions about the acreage to be put under different crops. It also decides how and when labour shall be applied, the agronomic measures the *kolkhoz* must apply, the amount of gross revenue that should be saved, that is, reinvested in means of production, and so on. The only freedom that a *kolkhoz* enjoys in this regard, is to decide matters of purely domestic nature, such as proportion of the surplus produce to be sold, the proportion to be distributed among its members and the percentage of the net revenue to be set aside for communal purposes, such as club-rooms and creches.

The measure of the external control to which the *kolkhozy* are subject in their day-to-day working can be realised from the fact that, apart from the internal accounting a *kolkhoz* has to render, it has to submit, at least, eleven returns at intervals ranging from days to six months to the Commissariat of Agriculture, showing the progress of field work, the state of crops, sowing and harvesting operations, etc.

In addition to the production plan and all it implies, the state lays down a rigid price policy for the greater part of the marketable produce of the farm. Every *kolkhoz* is compelled to deliver to the state its quotas or fixed quantities of grain and other crops and meat per unit of cultivated land to the amount laid down for each region, for which it receives payment at the state purchasing price, nominally based on the cost of production. The prices paid are, however, extremely low in comparison with prices of manufactured goods bought by the peasant or the open market prices for the same commodities. These compulsory deliveries[1] are generally and appropriately referred to as a tax in kind as the state obtains a large part of its budget revenue by the sale, at greatly inflated prices to the consuming population, of the produce it has bought cheaply from the farms.

The same remarks apply *mutatis mutandis* to the Chinese producers' co-operative. It will be sufficient to quote from the Report of the Krishnappa Delegation to China :

The co-operative must work to plan. It should draw up plans both for the production and sale of products in the light of its own conditions and gear these plans to the production and purchase plans of the State (Article 4 of the Model Regulations for Elementary Agricultural Co-operative quoted on p. 113).
To ensure fulfilment of the annual production plan, the co-operative shall draw up schemes for the progress of work in the various farming seasons and stages of work, set definite production tasks and definite dates for their completion (Article 29 of the Model Regulations quoted on pp. 114-115).

It is out of the money extracted from the peasantry or the land-worker by an unrelenting dictatorship that heavy industries were built up in the USSR and are proposed to be built up in China. As the Report observes : "It should be pointed out here that the main emphasis in Chinese planning is not on agriculture but on industries, especially heavy industries" (p. 40 of the Report).

As an organisation both the *kolkhoz* and the Chinese producers' co-operative are political subordinates to the Communist Party— they have no independent thought or say of their own. Their primary organisational role is political propagation, *rather than agricultural production*. The joint farm by whatever name it may be designated in the two countries, was adopted because political instruction can be more effectively conducted among an associated

[1] See p. 23, however.

group than separate units. As a matter of fact, today, it is wrong to talk of co-operative farming in China as something distinct from collective farming in the USSR. The 'advanced' co-operatives, into which all 'elementary' agricultural producer co-operatives were later on converted, according to the Chinese themselves, were nothing but collectives.

The aims and considerations which impelled the Communist Governments to establish collective farms—the role which these farms were intended to fulfil—cannot be stated better than in the words of Leonard E. Hubbard :

Apart from the inconsistency of permitting agriculture to be based on private capital and enterprise while industry was completely socialised, and the possible danger to the Communist State if a large and influential class of prosperous peasant farmers were allowed to grow up, the Bolsheviks decided on the collectivisation of peasant farms because this was the only practical way of forming large-scale and economic farm units under effective government control. A collective farm could be made to grow whatever crop was considered best in the eyes of the Government, irrespective of whether it was the most profitable to the growers themselves ; a large proportion of the harvest could be taken away from a collective farm than could easily be recovered from a number of independent farmers cultivating, in the aggregate, the same area ; a collective farm could be compelled to introduce intensive methods of cultivation, including the use of modern machinery even if it raised product costs, while the independent peasant, even if a comparatively large farmer, was often too conservative and obstinate readily to adopt new and scientific methods, and in any case required to be convinced that it would be to his pecuniary advantage. Finally, as against State farms, the collective farm was less calculated to involve the State in a loss. A State farm has to pay fixed wages and salaries and its overhead and working expenses were relatively inelastic : a collective farm, on the contrary, reimbursed its members out of its net proceeds in kind and money. If its proceeds were small the *kolkhozniki*[2] had to reduce their own consumption, and the State had to come to their assistance only if they were actually starving. For all these reasons and because cultural and political instruction can be more effectively conducted among an associated group than separate units, the collective farm was adopted as the standard farm of agricultural enterprise (*The Economics of Soviet Agriculture*, 1939, Macmillan and Co., Ltd., London, pp. 98-99).

[2] Members of a *Kolkhoz* or collective farm.

Article 8 of the Model Regulations quoted in the Report of the Krishnappa Delegation at page 120 proceeds thus :

The co-operative should take all measures which will bring about a steady rise in the level of political understanding of members; it should give them regular education in socialism and patriotism, and see to it that every member abides by the laws of the country. It should be ready to respond to the call of the Communist Party and the People's Government, and lead its members in the advance to socialism.

The Report goes on to say :

Yet, at this stage, it is difficult to escape the conclusion that local co-operatives depend heavily on direction and stimulus provided from county and district branches of the Communist Party and from cadres sent down to work in the villages by the People's Councils at higher levels (p. 120).

It should be clear, then, that the Chinese producers' co-operative has little liberty as an organisation. That advocates of co-operative farming in India are also actuated by some such temptation will be clear from remarks in the Patil Delegation's Report : "Without the producers' co-operatives, the needs of each one of the 50 million families engaged in agriculture have to be ascertained and provided for. With the producers' co-operatives, the State will have to deal alternately with less than half a million co-operatives which will become the organ of the State in implementing its welfare programmes" (p. 134).

It would seem that people of the way of thinking typified in the Patil Report have despaired of the slow processes of democracy, or are afraid of the vast number of individuals in the country who will have to be approached, persuaded or dealt with, and, therefore, would herd them into co-operatives or joint enterprises so that they may be better managed. They would very much like to copy communistic methods or programmes but, owing to circumstances beyond their control, have to resort to democratic terminology in order to achieve their purpose.

The liberty which its members enjoy as individuals is even less. We shall quote again from the Report of the Krishnappa Delegation :

Each production brigade consists of a number of working teams.

.... The management committee appoints the leaders of production brigades and of working teams.... A supervisory committee is also elected by the general meeting or by delegates elected by a general meeting, its functions being to see that the chairman and members of the management committee abide by the regulations of the co-operative and the resolutions of the general meeting, that the accounts of the co-operative are in order, and that there is no corruption, theft, sabotage, waste, or damage to the co-operative's property. The chairman of a co-operative is a person with much power and responsibility as he 'represents the co-operative in its dealings with other parties'........ there are considerable reserve powers, especially with the leaders of production brigades and with members of the management committee, through which failures in team work, lack of application and indiscipline can be dealt with .... To put the piece-work system into practice each co-operative has to decide upon suitable norms for various jobs and to fix rates of payment.... The number of work-days a member earns for fulfilling the norm for each job is decided on the basis of the skill and intensity of labour involved and the importance of the job to the production of the co-operative as a whole (pp. 115, 116 and 117).

Election of committees and office-bearers has to be made from names given by the Communist Party.

Translated into capitalistic terminology, the farmers become wage-earners with the same widely varying wage-scales as the factory workers and with the same subordination. With this difference that a man not fulfilling the norms would not merely get less remuneration for less work, but would actually be punished. The Delegation sums up by saying :

It is not improbable that in many co-operatives there exist doubts and criticisms to which there may or may not be satisfactory answers. It is not easy for a visiting delegation to grasp such elements in a new situation in which large numbers of men and women are thrown together rather suddenly in a complex set of social, economic and organisational relationships such as a large agricultural co-operative represents (p. 118).

In his voluminous study of Soviet agriculture Naum Jasny comes to the conclusion that the contrast between theory and practice is most flagrant. Instead of voluntary participation there is coercion ; instead of democratic decisions by the General Assembly there is dictatorship of officials who themselves are only small cogs in a big administrative machine. There is a tendency to shirk duties, to defraud the group for the sake of personal gain, and instead of a spirit of partnership the actual state of affairs makes the 'analogy to serfdom' increasingly justified. Jasny concludes : "the misnamed *kolkhoz* is the nutshell of a co-operative without the nut". The same is true of the Chinese venture in the field of co-operative farming.

The truth is that economic motives are only secondary. All the motive power comes from the social theory that the peasant is a capitalist and must, therefore, be uprooted from his land, eliminated as an independent unit and reduced to a proletarian, for otherwise he will remain a potential source of internal opposition to the Communist regime.

David Mitrany says :

Pure Marxists were moved much more by political needs than by scientific arguments, and even less by any understanding or sympathy for the countryside. The Communist Manifesto had lumped the peasant together with handicraftsmen and small traders, etc., in the 'petty bourgeoisie' as an unstable and reactionary class and never thought of allotting him a place of his own in the revolutionary procession. If one considers not only *Capital* but his whole scientific and political activity, nowhere will one find signs that Marx had seriously studied the actual state of the peasants in any one land. His way had been to formulate a general theory and simply sweep them into it, never considering them as a subject fitted for a special plan or reform. It was a sentence without a trial. All his life, not only as an economist, but also as a townsman and a revolutionary, Marx was filled with undisguised contempt for the peasant (*Marx against the Peasant*, 1952, pp. 40-41).

None of the top leaders of the Russian Revolution who forced the co-operatives upon the peasantry, had a peasant origin or any connection with the village. They belonged to the urban intelligentsia or the proletariat and were, therefore, unable to appreciate peasant needs, and entertained no sympathy for peasant longings. The same is true of most of the ardent supporters of joint farming in India.

The aim of Communism is to gradually convert the independent peasants, through the system of collective farms, into a landed proletariat. Everywhere it has climbed to power on the backs not of capitalist bourgeoisie which did not exist, or were insignificant but on the backs of the working peasant masses. It first encouraged the peasants to help themselves to land, only so that it might have its hands free to grasp political power, and then used that power to deprive peasants of land.

To implement this scheme, the Soviet Government sent out 25,000 industrial workers into the country in 1929 to become the first *kolkhozy* presidents. An equal number of members predominantly belonging to the urban proletariat was again despatched into the country in 1933 who were distributed among more than 5,000 political centres to exercise political supervision over the attached *kolkhozy*. According to an announcement in the *Pravda*, the Soviet leaders decided as late as in April, 1955, that a 'shock brigade' of 30,000 city-trained specialists or 'experienced workers' was to be sent into the countryside within the next four months to 'ensure the guidance of agriculture'. These men were to be 'recommended' as chairmen of those collective farms where weak leadership was responsible for inefficiency and shortage in output. It is almost superfluous to say that these specialists were chosen for their loyalty to the Party and their Communist single-mindedness, and not for their knowledge of agricultural conditions. It is these 80,000 persons who were the forerunners of a class of professional presidents and other functionaries who to-day rule the *kolkhozy*. It is these 80,000 persons and other technical personnel drawn from the town who assumed the leadership of the village : very few presidents of the *kolkhozy*, indeed, were local men or men of rural origin.

To quote again from the report of the Krishnappa Delegation in regard to China : "No less important than these technical and economic considerations was the view held by the leaders of the Communist Party that a socialist society could not be built up unless co-operative farming took the place of peasant proprietorship and, step by step, all vestiges of individual ownership in land were discarded. As they put it, 'the nation could not stand with one foot on socialistic industry and the other on a peasant economy.' Or, in the words of Chairman Mao Tse-tung, 'if positions in the countryside are not held by socialism, capitalism will assuredly occupy them'. It was for these various reasons that the Central Committee of the Communist Party declared a year ago that :

The aim of the co-operative movement is to lead about 110 million peasant households from individual to collective farming and then go on to bring about technical reform in agriculture ; it is to eliminate the last vestiges of capitalist exploitation in the rural areas and establish socialism. The building up of socialism is the cause of hundreds of millions of people (p. 107).

The Communist Party and its cadres at all levels have played a fundamental role in the organisation of producers' co-operatives as they did earlier in land reforms. They provide the core of the organised effort in every local community and in the future also the success or failure of co-operatives will turn largely on their performance, behaviour and leadership (p. 190).

But behind this organisation of the Chinese farmers into co-operatives and the mobilisation of the resources of the entire nation, there is a force which should not be lost sight of. It is the Communist Party of China which has 10.7 million well-organised, disciplined and hard-working members. It is the members of the Party working in the remotest villages who have brought about a fundamental change in the rural structure of China within a short period of seven years. It is also these party members who provide the necessary drive for increasing production and ensuring that the targets are fulfilled. There are writers on China who have spoken of the ruthlessness which might have marked the early phases of the new regime as a factor in the subsequent transformation from individual to co-operative cultivation. This may or may not be so, but we cannot comment on the suggestion from our own direct observations (pp. 191-92).

It is abundantly clear from these observations that the motive power for the Chinese co-operatives came not from the Chinese farmer but from the active members of the Communist Party. Comparing the conditions with India the delegation observes:

In Indian villages in areas where development programmes are undertaken and the right kind of leadership is forthcoming, there is, perhaps, more voluntary effort, local initiative and general awareness than we were able to observe in China (p. 192).

There may be a view that in China the rural leaders lack flexibility and depend more on directions from the party as well as from the Government than on their own initiative or on the support of the local people. If this occurred, they would not compare favourably with rural leaders in countries with a long history of economic development on democratic lines, and in the long run this may prove to be a serious handicap and may limit the degree of technical as well as social progress which is achieved by the rural population (p. 191).

No fundamental reform can be divorced from ideological considerations. The ideology which has been responsible for the pheno-

menal growth of what is called co-operative farming in China, has
been deliberately rejected by us. Can we transplant a seedling which
has been sown, tended and nourished in a communist climate into
our climate of fundamental freedoms ? As observed by the Krishnappa Delegation on page 43 of its report : "The system of Communism in China, however it may have been adapted to the needs and
conditions of Chinese society, does not, of course, provide for freedoms such as those of information, expression and association in the
manner familiar to us in India. In this sense, it shares inevitably
several typical political features with communist countries in the
west." In the concluding sentence of its report the Delegation
rightly cautions us thus : "We must emphasise, however, that any
measures that we may adopt for economic development or technical
progress should be fully in accord with our democratic institutions"
(p. 199).

How the thinking of advocates of co-operative farming in this
country is confused is well illustrated by a correspondent of a New
Delhi newspaper dated June 1957 :

In India democratic socialist thought has yet to define its attitude
to the small peasant clearly. Remnants of the archetypal Marxist-
Leninist theory of the small peasant's doom, largely irrelevant in
the context of India's man-land ratio, mixed with a genuinely democratic concern for the small peasant, produce a schizophrenic policy
bristling with contradictions. Yields can be greater on small farms
than on large farms and yet we regard an enlargement of the scale
of farming operations as a pre-condition of increased output. We
know that the small peasant is not an exploiter and yet we would
treat him as a 'capitalist'. We wish to help the small peasant but
we continue to believe in his doom. We know that in our peasant
democracy the small peasant must predominate and yet it is for his
proletarianisation that we work. Our administrative and co-operative structure has yet to prove equal to the supreme task of redis-
tributing land and carrying enough resources to the small farmers,
but we are already dreaming that it will soon co-operativise a
substantial proportion of agricultural lands. We know how attached
our peasants are to their holdings and yet we desperately wish to
believe that they will pool them 'voluntarily'.

It is high time we—all of us socialists now—come down to earth
and squarely face the problems of the small peasant and give him
what he needs, before delivering our *ex-parte* judgment that he
cannot deliver the goods, unless we run him as a wage-labourer in
a huge collective. The small peasant is not a person to be disposed
of by starry-eyed logic ; he is a harassed human being to be under-

stood and helped to help himself and to feed us. If we, who feed on him, mistreat him, collectivise him and write him off, inspite of the unprecedented peasant franchise that characterises our democracy, the results can only be fatal. Indian socialism must be for the small peasant, not against him.

A society based exclusively or overwhelmingly on big economic units, whether in the field of agriculture or of manufacturing industry, must inevitably lead to concentration of power in the hands of a few. The larger the size of an undertaking, the less the active participation of the members or workers in its affairs and fewer the opportunities for office-bearers to come into direct contact with them. This will affect the understanding of the members about the problems of the organisation and there will be a danger of decisions being taken by the few which may not be in its true interest. Ordinarily, majority of the people have little time and little inclination to think and learn all the facts necessary to make wise decisions on public affairs of a large institution. They prefer to follow someone else who is willing to think or in a position to think. So, in large matters people must delegate decisions to a relatively few representatives. This will be particularly true in the case of joint farming in India where few villagers can read and write.

"A society based on big economic units leads", said Acharya Kripalani, "to bureaucratic and dictatorial exercise of power. The rulers in that case not only regulate the political but also the economic life of the people. If political power has a tendency to corrupt the holders of power, this tendency is doubly increased by the combination of political and economic power in the same hands· Capitalism killed democracy because the capitalist class wielded, directly or indirectly, political power. Communism puts in the hands of the political dictator and bureaucrat the entire control of economic power. Herein lies as great a danger to democracy as under capitalism.

"Therefore, if democracy is to survive, it must discover a means of avoiding concentration of economic power in the hands of the ruler or rulers, however selected or elected. Even a political democracy can be a dictatorship if there are no spheres of free activity left to the individual."[3]

[3] Presidential Address delivered by Acharya J. B. Kripalani at the 54th Session of the Indian National Congress in November 1946, in Meerut.

The plant of freedom cannot thrive on the soil of collectivised farm which is a large joint undertaking, nor was it intended to thrive by its founders. When we find in India, therefore, persons who profess belief in democracy yet advocate establishment of huge, jointly-operated units of production as the remedy of our rural problems, one can only sympathise with them and wish they knew the country-side and the object of their arm-chair solicitude before offering solutions. No lover of the peasantry and the country would be enthused by the prospect when our countryside will be turned into huge barracks or gigantic agricultural factories. Such an economy would enslave the people and take away their freedom which is material to all definitions of happiness. Assuming a collectivist economy leads to a powerful and prosperous state, it is doubtful whether there is any advantage in having such a state if it is to be achieved at the expense of human freedom and happiness.

In a speech in New Delhi in the early half of 1955 the Prime Minister said that "India is trying to achieve economic prosperity without abandoning democratic institutions and would not sacrifice democratic institutions at the altar of economic progress". He went on to add that, "in the long run, economic prosperity based on a denial of human freedom and dignity could not carry a country far", and that progress had been achieved in Russia "at the cost of the freedom of the individual".

Whatever emphasis may be placed upon the differences[4] between a co-operative farm and a collective farm, so far as internal working is concerned there is, and there can be, no difference. Land, labour and capital are pooled in both and, the size being large, they cannot be managed without a plan and without orders issuing from some central unified authority. In both, the peasants will have to be assigned to brigades and the latter divided into teams, individual work evaluated, a complex accounting system adopted, a code of punishments provided, and so on. Nor is there a difference

[4] Even if there is a difference, transition from a co-operative to a collective farm is but a short step. The Nagpur Resolution already lays down that even those who do not possess land, can become members of the farm and will be entitled to "a share in proportion to the work put in by them on the joint farm". As time passes and people are reminded that land is a national asset and, therefore, belongs to all, the conception of private property will weaken, and the share payable to members in proportion to the land contributed by them would gradually dwindle and finally disappear altogether.

in the motives underlying the two. To the extent—and this extent in a joint undertaking will necessarily be large—the peasant, the member of the farm, is not free to obey his own desires, his liberty is curtailed ; he is not independent. And to that extent democracy in the country will suffer.[5]

It is true that some control of the individual is inherent in all organisations, and that organisations—social, economic and political —are essential to all civilised existence. It is, therefore, on the degree of control that the question turns. *That society is best where control over the individual is the least.* Such is a society of small autonomous organisations usually consisting of a family, both in the sphere of agriculture and also, as far as we can help it, in the sphere of industry. Large organisations are inevitable in some branches of manufacturing, but not at all necessary in the sphere of agriculture.

A system of agriculture based on small enterprise, where the worker himself is the owner of the land under his plough, will foster democracy. For, it creates a population of independent outlook and action in the social and political fields. It is true that the peasants have to earn their living the hard way : only a few are able to accumulate a surplus. They may be conservative, but will not be reactionary ; they may be in favour of a private economy, but are not exploiters, either. The peasant is an incorrigible individualist ; for, his avocation, season in and season out, can be carried on with a pair of bullocks in the solitude of Nature without the necessity of having to give orders to, or, take orders from anybody. That is why the peasant class everywhere is the only class which is really democratic without mental reservations. The system of family-size farms also ensures stability because the operator or the peasant has a stake in his farm and would lose by instability.

Peasant farming also makes for a happy community and a satisfied individual. Security to the peasant owner is a matter of course.

To own the land and to be free to farm it in the traditional peasant

---

[5] Delivering the inaugural address at the annual session of the Federation of Indian Chamber of Commerce and Industry in New Delhi on March 7, 1959, Prime Minister Nehru said :
"As for somebody telling me that *co-operative* farming will lead to collectivisation, and, therefore, to communism, well, if it does I am not frightened" (vide a booklet *Jawaharlal Nehru on Cooperation* issued by Government of India, 1959).

way is to him nothing less than the equivalent of that 'social security' which has become the aspiration of industrial masses even in
the advanced countries of the West. The life-line which in the west
the State has to throw to the worker whenever he is in difficult
circumstances, through the complex of insurances against unemployment, against sickness and want, for old age and so on, the peasant
has always found in his traditional economy. As Miriam Beard says
in her *History of the Business Man*, discussing his part through many
centuries, 'men suffered on the land but survived ; while in the
cities they flourished—and faded'. The peasant's way to security
may not provide him with such great material benefits as those now
given in the West by the State, but it is a security which he can
achieve with his own hands and which leaves him free to stand on
his own feet.[6]

Inasmuch as the character of political institutions was determined by the fundamental laws respecting property, Jefferson, one
of the architects of American democracy, firmly believed that a wide
dispersion of private property—a wide diffusion of rights in land
which makes for individual freedom and creative individualism, and
an opportunity to acquire such rights—was essential to the establishment of democracy and the safest assurance that it would endure.
Freedom is founded upon ownership of property. It cannot exist
where, as under a system of state and collective farms in Russia and
communes in China, it is the rulers who own everything. Against
such a state the individual who owns nothing, has neither the
means of defence nor anything to defend. Nor has he any freedom
of action or any means of self-expression like houses to modify and
crops to tend, or trees to plant and cows—even offsprings—to rear.

F. C. Howe states:

Farm ownership and the small farm are the economic bases of
Danish life. To these economic conditions other things are traceable. The kind of land tenure that prevails is the mould of the civilisation of a State. This is true of nearly all countries. It is hardly
a coincidence that wherever we find hereditary landlordism, as in
Great Britain and Prussia, there we have political reaction. There
is, so far as I know, no exception to this rule. It was this that explained old Russia. It was land monopoly that lay at the back of
the Irish question and the long-continued poverty of the Irish people. On the other hand, wherever we find the people owning their
own homes and cultivating their own land, there we find an entirely

6 David Mitrany, *op. cit.*, p. 130.

different spirit and a different political system. With ownership we find democracy, responsible government, and with them the hope, ambition and freedom that prevails in France, Holland, Switzerland and the Scandinavian countries. For these are the countries where the people, rather than the old feudal aristocracy, own the land.[7]

[7] *Denmark : A Co-operative Commonwealth*, 1922, p. 71.

CHAPTER TEN

Impracticability of Large-scale Farming

THE NUMBER of persons holding cultivable land in India is vast : it was more than 226 million in 1961. The corresponding figure for the biggest state in India, *viz.* Uttar Pradesh, stood at about 47 million. In the context of these figures a pertinent question is whether large-scale farming as a method for general adoption in this country is really practicable.

Quite apart from the merits of the proposal, it is simply not possible for any democratic government to divest these people of their lands with a view to set up an economy of large farms. The psychology of the peasant will have to be considered. Habits centuries old are not changed in a day, and habits rooted in the soil are with difficulty changed at all. A large collective undertaking may be well adopted to the needs and mentality of the agricultural or industrial labour, but not one tenant in a hundred or one owner in a thousand wishes to be turned into a collectivist as long as he can make a living, however modest, on his farm. He is too tenacious of his independence and, if an owner, too attached to his land and too jealous of his social prestige. In membership of a co-operative or collective farm he sees a loss of all the three—his land, independence and prestige. Hardly any farmer, therefore, is a candidate for membership of such a farm.

The Food and Agriculture Organisation of the United Nations, in a survey report entitled *Co-operatives and Land Use*, 1957, very truly says :

In general, those to whom the co-operative farm appeals are either intellectuals without previous farming experience ; the technically-minded, to whom machines and all that goes with them are more important than the bare ownership of land ; the more dependent type of share-croppers and labourers with no experience of managing farms of their own ; or tribal peoples who have no tradition of individual ownership. Experience shows that labourers and tenants, though they may at first accept land pooling, tend to develop the traditional peasant attitude as their experience increases, and to demand the division of land into individual holdings. It is possible that the attitude of tribal peoples will undergo a

similar change and that they may come to resent what they feel
to be an attempt to force them back into the undifferentiated herd.
Any kind of uprooting or migration makes the introduction of
collective farming less difficult, since the sense of ownership is
weaker and a shock makes easier the entry of new ideas (pp.
105-106)

Attachment to the land is a universal trait in the peasantry of
all countries. The French peasant, for instance, calls his land his
'mistress'. Here is an extract from a French author, Michelet, which
correctly depicts a peasant's passion towards his land :

If we would know the inmost thoughts, the passion, of the French
peasant, it is very easy. Let us walk out on Sunday into the country
and follow him....I perceive that he is going to visit his mistress.
What mistress ? His land.
I do not say he is going straight to it. No, he is free today, and
may either go or not. Does he not go every day in the week ?
Accordingly, he turns aside, he goes another way, he has business
elsewhere, and yet he goes.
It is true, he was passing close by ; it was an opportunity. He
looks but apparently he will not go in ; what for ? And yet he
enters.
At least, it is probable that he will not work ; he is in his Sunday dress ; he has a clean kerchief and blouse. Still, there is no
harm in plucking up this weed, and throwing out that stone. There
is a stump, too, which is in the way ; but he has not his tools with
him,he will do it tomorrow.
Then he folds his arms and gazes, serious and careful. He gives
a long, very long, look, and seems lost in thought. At last, if he
thinks himself observed, if he sees a passer-by, he moves slowly
away. Thirty paces off he stops, turns round, and casts on his land
a last look, sombre and profound, but to those who can see it, the
look is full of passion, of heart, of devotion.[1]

Human nature is the same everywhere. Here, our peasant calls
his land *Dharati Mata*—Mother Earth—inasmuch as it provides
sustenance for all living things.
Everywhere the peasant is a firm believer in property striving
for independence. Hence a collectivist economy will meet with his
emotional resistance from the start. Ultimately it is not a question
of economic efficiency or of form of organisation, but whether individualism or collectivism should prevail. Peasantry represents not

[1] *Vide* N. Gangulee, *The Indian Peasant and his Environment*, Oxford
University Press, 1935, p. 59.

only a certain form of economy but also a certain way of life. Within the peasantry those characters, traits and moral forces are most pronounced which resist the tendency towards collectivism and of being levelled down into a uniform mass. On the other hand, the co-operative idea of self-help by voluntary association which does not efface economic independence, appeals to peasants. It is significant that communists try to overcome the individualistic thinking of peasants by using co-operative slogans.

Any government with democratic pretensions, run by any political party whatsoever, attempting to establish an economy of large farms in India will either founder in the attempt never to recover, or, will turn dictatorial in the process. Constituting a majority of the total electoral strength as they do, the peasants cannot, even if all other sections of population combine against them, be coerced into accepting a course against their will. That is why in every instance the Marxist agrarian programme has had to be applied by force and to rely on force for its survival. The socialists who wanted to remain democrats had, in every instance, to abandon the programme.

The advocates of collectivisation commit the mistake of appraising India in terms of the psychology and the living conditions of old Russia and do not make an allowance for 'differences in political experience, social background and emotional response'. Possession of land had been in some sense joint and communal throughout Russian history. The *mir* or the *commune*, in which the village communities were organised, was a distinctive and peculiar attribute of traditional Russian civilisation. The characteristics of communal land-holding were :

(*i*) Distribution in strips,
(*ii*) Compulsory adherence by all members of the commune to a common rotation of crops,
(*iii*) Temporary occupation by the individual of his allotment, and
(*iv*) Periodical alterations in the size of the allotments.

The coming of the *kolkhoz* is, therefore, a purely Russian event that must be seen, understood and-evaluated as such. "The *kolkhoz* is the collectivised farm emerging out of a primitive peasant economy", says G. D. H. Cole, "which had neither wholly lost nor forgotten the collective characteristics of serfdom and feudalism. It could not be developed out of a system of middle-sized tenant farms such as existed in Great Britain, or out of a developed and civilised peasant proprietorship like that of France, or again out of the homestead farming characteristic of the United States and Canada".[2] Nor can it emerge, in our opinion, in India where individual ownership has a very long history and is deeply rooted in the consciousness of the peasantry.

The idea of peasant ownership came to the fore in Russia only in the latter half of the last century. It was after a long agitation beginning with the Emancipation Act of 1861 that on November 22, 1906, an ukase was promulgated depriving the *mir* of its authority and giving the peasants a right of separation from the commune, which laid the foundations of a class of true peasant proprietors. In 1928, therefore, when the Government of the USSR embarked on compulsory collectivisation, peasants whose ownership of land had some history behind it, were a small fraction of the entire peasantry, *i.e.* 10.7 per cent, the vast majority having come into ownership (a fact never openly recognised by the Communist Government) only in 1917 when the big landlords, the church and the crown were liquidated. Nevertheless, even in Russia collectivisation was bitterly resented by the peasants as a class who had hoped to enjoy the land some day in individual ownership as a result of the Revolution.

Some of the believers in collectivisation may, perhaps, like to argue that the desired end can be brought about by persuasion and that, provided the necessary propaganda, education and demonstration are forthcoming, the peasants can be converted to a voluntary acceptance of collective farming. So far, however, the experience of the USSR, Yugoslavia and other eastern European countries tells a different tale.

While, on the one hand, propaganda as a result of a resolution of the Fifteenth Party Congress held in December 1927, which decided upon collectivisation, was unleashed by the Soviet Government in 1926 for popularising the *kolkhozy*, and a few collective farms were set up to serve as demonstration, the Government introduced, on the other, a so-called contract system under which an independent peasant was bound to deliver to Government grain-collecting organisations the whole of his surplus harvest at the price fixed by the Government. It was the Government collecting agency

[2] *Practical Economics*, 1937, pp. 49-50.

itself which decided what quantity of grain was surplus to the needs of a particular peasant. In case a peasant or *kulak* failed to deliver his quota, his grain was confiscated under Article 107 of the Criminal Code and 25 per cent of it made over to the poor peasants of the village. All these measures and other restrictions, however, failed to attract the peasant into the *kolkhoz*. He remained unconvinced of its superiority, with the result that during two years from the spring of 1927 to the spring of 1929, percentage of peasant housesteads collectivised rose from 0.8 to 3.9 only. In January 1930, therefore, the Central Committee of the Communist Party took a most decisive turn in policy. It resolved to eliminate the *kulaks* as a class by wearing down their resistance in open battle and depriving them of the productive sources of their existence and development (the free use of land, *viz.* the means of production, the renting of land, the right to hire labour, etc.). Instructions were issued that by coming spring 30 million hectares of land should be brought under collectivisation. This was about 25 per cent of the total area under crops in 1929. Peasants labelled rich were *ipso facto* condemned to liquidation, and taxes far heavier in proportion to those borne by the other groups, middle and poor, were imposed on them ; if they paid the first time, they were reassessed at twice or three times the original sum. Sooner or later the peasant failed to pay his taxes ; thereupon, his property was handed over to the nearest *kolkhoz*. Those who showed the least signs of resistance or gave cause for doubt or offence to the local party bosses, were liquidated or silenced by measures which are now part of history.

An attempt at coaxing the peasantry into collectivisation was made next in Yugoslavia, but it must be confessed that it met with the same disappointing results so far as the reactions of the peasantry were concerned. A movement to wean the peasants into collective farms was set afoot with open and covert official pressure, soon after the country had been liberated from the yoke of the Nazis in 1945. With the relaxing of official pressure, however, the movement evidently lost its momentum. As against 3,500 collective farming societies started in 1949, in 1950 only 353 societies came into existence. In the summer of 1951 the total number stood at 7,000 comprising 22 per cent of Yugoslavia's arable land and 4,20,000 households. Signs of discontent began to grow in the older societies. Management was inefficient and the credits were expended chiefly on buildings. There were many applications to withdraw, over 2,500 in

Macedonia and more than 3,000 in Croatia. The Communist Government, led by Marshal Tito, therefore, decided not to force the peasants into collectivisation at the point of the bayonet, and it is this deviation from the orthodox communist policy that formed one of the major causes which led to the breach of diplomatic relations between the USSR and Yugoslavia. The Yugoslav parliament, on 27 April 1957, formally passed a resolution abandoning altogether the system of collectivisation. It pointed out that collectivisation had shown negative results—loss of interest on the part of peasants and decrease in production all round. The country is now committed to what is called 'socialistic co-operation'—co-operation between farmers farming their own private land on one hand and co-operative societies dealing with marketing and machinery on the other. On 4 June 1957, Marshal Tito declared in Belgrade that the Soviet-style 'forcibly formed co-operatives' in farming had not worked in Yugoslavia and this was why she had switched to a compromise between collectivisation and private enterprise. According to a recent report, hardly 500 collective farms were extant today.

Nor have the peasantry of East Germany, Czechoslovakia and Hungary taken kindly to joint or collective farming, efforts of the local Communist Governments and the USSR, which holds these countries in its grip, notwithstanding. It is imposition of collective farms which is largely responsible for political unrest in the rural parts of these countries. Such farms, wherever they had been established, are now in the process of being broken up over large parts of eastern and central Europe.

... In Hungary the socialised sector in 1955 included one-third of the arable land area, with 1.3 million hectares in co-operatives and 700,000 hectares in state farms ; but between October 1956 and January 1957 there was a 50 per cent decline in the area and number of co-operative farms. In Poland the rate of formation of co-operatives was slower than in other Eastern European countries. By early 1956, the socialised sector comprised 23 per cent of the agricultural land area, with two million hectares, or 10 per cent in co-operative farms, and 13 per cent in state farms. Since the political events of October 1956, three-quarters of the co-operatives have dissolved. New policies, designed to increase output on peasant farms, and even to encourage land purchase, are now being introduced.[3]

[3] An article entitled "Changes in European Peasant Farming," by Doreen Warriner published in *International Labour Review*, November 1957, p. 463.

According to press reports, Gomulka, the new Communist leader of Poland, in his first policy statement made at the Eighth Plenum of the PZPR Central Committee, on 20 October 1956, said that "in agriculture it is only the private sector which has prospered and that it was a mistake to collectivise the *kulak*." He told the Committee that "individual peasant production per hectare was 16.7 per cent higher than in co-operative farms and 37.2 per cent higher than in state farms." He summarised his speech in the following words :

This is, in brief, an outline of the economic picture of co-operative farming. It is a sad picture. In spite of great outlays they had smaller returns and greater costs of production.

In an article, dated May 1957, on the alarming situation in the 6,000 state farms, General Ochab, the newly appointed Polish Minister of Agriculture, revealed "that in 1956 the deficit on the state farms amounted to £ 427,000,000. This was double the losses suffered last year. There was moreover no hope of any immediate improvement." The Minister ordered the dismissal of many hundreds of administrators and officials whose education and training had proved below the required standards. At the same time, the Government was presenting a new bill providing for the reorganisation of agriculture on the lines of 'peasant autonomy' suggested by Mr. Gomulka a few months before. This was designed to give greater freedom to peasants of state farms, collectives and other types of farms to plan the running of them 'from below', and thus make them share more fully in the responsibilities of everyday management and profits. Individual farms, in particular, were to be given much greater encouragement, and the process of giving freehold title deeds to peasants on the land they cultivate was to be expedited.

This picture of the agrarian situation in Poland is true of what obtains in all the East European countries under the orbit of the Soviet Union. The tide is now beginning to turn again in favour of the individual farmers.

The collective farm or *ejido* is proving a failure in Mexico also. Its production per acre is far less than on individual farms and only very recently members have been given the right to break away from the farm and take to individual farming.

It is claimed that the agricultural producers' co-operatives had been a success in China. If so, one could naturally like to know, why was it necessary to convert and consolidate them into the 'advanced' or collective type of Russia ? The truth is that in pursuance of their communist philosophy the Chinese Government regarded the co-operative farms merely as an intermediate stage to their ultimate goal of collectivisation, or shall we now say, communisation. Almost the same words, the same reasoning and the same technique which the Bolsheviks used in the USSR have been employed by their pupils in China. Chinese peasants, however, being what peasants are all the world over, these co-operatives, notwithstanding all the propaganda, could not have come into existence so suddenly as if by a magic wand and were, without question, a result of coercion. One can plan and, perhaps, also achieve physical targets at break-neck speed, but not targets which require or depend on progress in human consciousness to fulfil, as the organisation of co-operative farming does. With absolute political and military power resting in the hands of the Government, from which there was no escape and no appeal, the Chinese peasants, just as their brothers in Russia, had no choice, but voluntarily—'voluntarily' in the sense of the Communist dictionary—to opt or vote for the collective farm.

According to Peking, the people "volunteered" even for the communes. In an interview with Julius Burgin, secretary-general of the Polish-Chinese Friendship Association, Mao asserted : "The old organisational forms proved too narrow.... As a result of pains-taking search for new forms, the idea for people's communes was born to meet the needs of hundreds of millions. Even the name of this new organisation was given by the peasants themselves : 'The people's communes'. . . . The peasants wanted the communes very much. They need them very much. They help to build Socialism, which the peasants desire and need because they want to live better. The people know what they need. We, I myself, wanted to be careful and thought it would be better if the communes were created gradually in order to accumulate experience, but the masses changed our ideas. They did not want to procrastinate."[4]

[4] Vide Introduction (p. 5) to Richard L. Walker's *Letters from the Communes*, published as a supplement to the *New Leader*, New York, June 15, 1959. (A critic must be forgiven if he sees a family resemblance between this statement of Mao Tse-tung and the *claims* of a section of our political leadership that co-operative farming is the 'demand' of the peasantry and that it is only 'vested interests' which are opposed to it !)

To come back to the co-operative farm : it was the utter poverty of the Chinese peasants which was exploited by the Chinese Government to fulfil its ideology. Says the Krishnappa Delegation to China on page 108 of its report :

... land reform in China meant an extraordinarily wide distribution of ownership in land. Altogether about 118 million acres of land were distributed among 300 million peasants, men and women, an average of one-third of an acre per head. Besides land, houses belonging to landlords containing about 38 million rooms, about 30 million draught animals, 39 million agricultural implements and about 5 million tons of foodstuffs were confiscated from landlords and redistributed. Many former landlords were allotted land on the same basis as tenants and labourers.

Again, on page 109 :

Agricultural co-operation followed naturally from land reform. Arrangements for state purchase of foodgrains and other farm products and the organisation of credit co-operatives closely linked with the People's Bank were important supporting developments. Together, they helped eliminate the rural trader, the urban merchant and the landlord, so that the ground was fully prepared for agricultural co-operatives.

Still, again, on page 62, the Krishnappa Delegation has this to say :

We were told that there was no attempt to compel the Chinese peasants to join a co-operative farm. All that the Chinese authorities did was to carry on intensive propaganda and to regulate the Chinese peasants indirectly through sales and purchases and other controls and also through the monopoly of credit and to offer them other inducements for joining a co-operative farm. ... Price policy, technical assistance, provision of consumers' goods as well as producers' goods like fertilisers and, in some cases, contracts for purchase of the produce at a pre-determined price are the various means through which the Chinese Government is trying to make the Chinese farmers follow the planned pattern.

It was against this background—a background created by giving everyone one-third of an acre, destroying the freedom of sale and exchange, and displaying unrelenting ruthlessness—that the Chinese peasant was welded into what is called the voluntary Chinese Producers' Co-operative. The theoretical freedom of the peasants to keep out of co-operatives was meaningless since it was impossible for them to function independently. The dissenting minute to the Patil Delegation's report says :

Our colleagues do not see the evident contradiction between the professed principle of voluntariness and the simultaneous setting of high targets of the number of co-operatives to be established from year to year. How a 'voluntary' movement can progress according to the targets fixed by the State is something beyond our comprehension. We may here refer to a remarkable passage in Gomulka's famous report of 20 October 1956, in which he says, 'that a quantitative development of producers' co-operation cannot be planned, because on the basis of voluntary entry to a co-operative, this would amount to planning the growth in human consciousness, and that cannot be planned.' In the same report Gomulka says that the principle of voluntariness means not only threats or psychological compulsion but economic compulsion as well are excluded. Tax assessments and the establishment of the size of quota deliveries could also be an instrument of compulsion.
(p. 200 of the Report)

Nor could these co-operatives be called a success in the economic sense. Sufficient time had not yet elapsed, nor were any reliable statistics available, to show that pooling of land into co-operatives has in any way contributed to increase in agricultural production. The Krishnappa Delegation to China clearly acknowledges that pre-war yields had not yet been attained.[5]

It was pure propaganda inspired by political considerations that was let loose on the world to the effect that as soon as China was taken over by Communism, food production went up by leaps and bounds and the offer, again inspired by political considerations, that China made to India of 50,000 tons of rice or so was cited as proof of the same. But what are the facts ?

Mr. G. F. Alexandrov, leader of the Russian Delegation to the 41st session of the Indian Science Congress, told pressmen in Hyderabad on 6 January 1954 :

In 1950, Russia had begun implementing a five-year plan, which would be completed this year. The main feature of the plan was that side by side with the development of heavy industry, light industries and agriculture would also be developed. Russia was producing plenty of food-stuffs and was exporting a considerable

[5] Vide p. 89 of the Report.

quantity to *China*, France, Italy and other European countries (Italics ours).

In spite of the much-boosted rise in agricultural production in China, the prices of essential commodities continued to rule very high. The Krishnappa Delegation observed : "But we noted that the cost of living in China was substantially higher than in India. For instance, at the time of our visit, the retail price of ordinary rice was Rs. 0-9-3 per seer in Shanghai, of wheat Rs. 0-9-9 per seer, vegetable oil for cooking Rs. 2-2-0 per seer, potatoes Rs. 0-3-6 per seer, peas Rs. 0-3-6 per seer, mutton Rs. 2-3-0 per seer, sugar Rs. 2 per seer, cotton shirting Rs. 4 per yard, cotton suiting Rs. 8 to Rs. 10 per yard, woollen suiting Rs. 45 to Rs. 50 per yard and shoes Rs. 30 to Rs. 40 per pair" (p. 41 of the Report).

China, with such dense population, will suffer far more grievously owing to this venture of their Government. The USSR had a vast area of culturable land, compared to her population, on which men and machinery could be employed. Mr. Aneurin Bevan, the left wing leader of the British Socialist Party, who himself had visited China as a guest of the Communist Government, said in a public meeting in Delhi on 2 April 1957, "that the failures of the Soviet Government in the field of agriculture were covered up by the opening up of virgin lands. These new fields provided a cushion to Soviet rulers." He went on to advise India that "she could not afford to make the mistakes that Russia had committed because she did not possess empty spaces which could be called upon to make up for the failures and mistakes of agriculture. She had to bring about an economic revolution in harmony with the needs of the countryside."

In the country of its origin, the Soviet Union, the *kolkhoz* or collective farm to which a co-operative farm is admittedly only an intermediate stage, is not regarded as the final, logical form of agrarian organisation. Before his death, in *Economic Problems of Socialism in the USSR*, Stalin foresaw[6] that the *kolkhozes* should

---

[6] In the fifties there was a relative growth in state farms at the expense of collective farms. The tendency towards gradual elimination of differences between state and collective farms was reflected in the introduction of the guaranteed minimum wage in a sizable proportion of collective farms. Two of the reasons were that the state farm is ideologically more acceptable, and it produces more cheaply (especially because

become *sovkhozes* or state farms, which is to say that the bureaucracy should become their real owner. Criticising Stalin for his excessive use of purges, Khrushchev did not, however, renounce Stalin's views on property in *kolkhozes*. It will be a strange commentary on our wisdom that just when reports from the Soviet Union show that the *kolkhoz* has not given the results expected of it by ts founders and the Communists are in desperate search of remedies and palliative, our leadership is enthusiastically recommending the preliminary form, the co-operative farm, for adoption in India. There can be no manner of doubt that in looking towards the USSR or the People's Republic of China for a tenure pattern we are looking in the wrong direction.

In this connection we have further to remember that educated persons living in the towns have not been able to make a success even of the Co-operative Stores, or Consumers' Societies which were concerned merely with marketing. Speaking at the 13th meeting of the All-India Handloom Board in Bombay on June 20, 1959, Mr. Lal Bahadur Shastri, Union Minister for Commerce and Industry expressed surprise that the private weaver who was not in the co-operative sector was able to compete easily with co-operatives and had almost monopolised the export trade in handloom fabrics. "And mind you" he said, "weavers in the private sector do not get any financial assistance for development purposes, nor any rebate. Only recently some facilities in regard to import of dyes and chemicals had been given to them. I would no doubt like it very much that they should all come under the umbrella of the co-operative system. However, there can be no compulsion."[7]

Nor are credit societies in the countryside yet a success in spite of so much time and effort that have gone into their organisation. Village panchayats, too, which are meant only to administer muni-

higher prices were being paid to the collectives). Latest reports indicate, however, that the Russians are again having a second or third thought in this connection. Proposals to fuse the collective and state farms are "profoundly wrong", according to the *Kommunist*, which points out quite frankly that this would mean that the state would have to bear the losses. This journal of the Central Committee of the Soviet Communist Party goes on to state that "anyone at all acquainted with life in the *Kolkhoz* village" knows that the time for the abolition of the private plot "has not come, and will not come as soon as some people imagine" (vide *London Times*, dated June 21, 1961).

[7] *The Indian Express*, New Delhi, June 22, 1959.

cipal functions or common lands, have run into difficulties and are posing a problem. This is so because they are elected bodies and election on the basis of majority and minority votes, not to create factions, requires largeness of heart which is rare among villagers and even well-educated town-dwellers. How much more difficult it would be to organise agricultural production, which is such a complex task, on a co-operative basis and through an elected management, in a community of illiterate and semi-literate peasantry, can therefore, well be imagined. In fact, co-operative farming in the true sense of being voluntary, has not been a success anywhere in the world (except in Israel)—even where the farmers are cent per cent literate.

The initial success of co-operative farming in Israel is due to the peculiar situation which arose in connection with the requirements of Zionist resettlement. The abortive Russian revolution of 1905 brought to Palestine (then a part of the Turkish Empire) a number of young Russian Jews of some education, no agricultural or industrial experience, no private means, but of strong socialist convictions. Fundamental to these convictions was a belief in the immorality of employing labour. The exact form of the first settlements, and, in particular, the completely communist society which they evolved, thus owed something to the theories which the pioneers had brought with them to Palestine and something to their handicaps and environment—lack of means for individual settlement, lack of experience, and the need for mutual protection against a hostile Arab world. Something also may be attributed to their urban and intellectual background, which gave them interest and aspirations unlike those of the typical peasant. It should be remembered, too, that a great majority were, at that time, unattached young men and it was natural that their life should be modelled on the camp rather than the home. The Jewish refugees that trickled to these settlements, particularly, after the Balfour Declaration, had suffered prolonged persecution all over the world. United by this common distress, a common religious faith and a common desire to find a new homeland, they were determined to sacrifice all individualism for the sake of collective success of their new refuge. Also, the success of these settlements was greatly facilitated by the technical and other resources that the world Jewry placed at the disposal of the settlers.

Even so, the number of these settlements was not large. Only half a dozen successful collective settlements were founded under Turkish rule, though a few more, which failed after a struggle, were later refounded. Under the British mandate their number increased fairly rapidly. A score or more dating from the 'twenties' and the number increasing steadily through the 'thirties' and 'forties', till by the time of establishment of the State of Israel (May 15, 1948) there were in all 136 *kibbutzim*. By mid-1955 the number rose to 279, but by December 1957, it fell to 228.

Difficulties in the working of the *kibbutz* have now begun to arise and multiply. There is no complete answer yet to questions such as : Are socialism and greater family cohesion incompatible ? What about the care and education of children ? What are the inalienable rights of individuals in a co-operative community? What about the dining-hall ? What about hired labour ? Many of the married couples left the *kibbutzim* because they felt that the *kibbutz* did not provide an opportunity for the kind of family life which they desired—the opportunity for the wife to keep her own house, raise her children by herself, and provide for her husband's personal needs. There is an increasing demand for personal comforts; there is increasing lack of participation in the General Assembly. Many members leave simply because they do not like their colleagues. A human being is not a very fit subject for governance by rules, howsoever perfect or flexible. Particularly, none can be devised to meet temperamental problems. From the establishment of the State of Israel and the requirements of unrestricted immigration have also stemmed such problems as loss of the most active members, tendency on the part of the state to interfere in the internal affairs of the settlements and disinclination on the part of the new immigrants to join the ranks of the *kibbutz*. The past ten years have, therefore, seen a striking development in the *moshav* type of village, which has become the dominant form of social organisation in Israel today. It has grown in number from some 91 villages before the establishment of the State of Israel in 1948 to 356 in December 1957 (out of a total of 743 villages in the entire country). The *moshav*, because it answered the desire for individualistic living while providing a practical solution to economic problems in a co-operative frame-work, has proved more attractive to the incomer —the post-1948 type of immigrant.

Deriving from these developments there is a widely-held view that the *kibbutz* is a passing phenomenon incidental to the ea·

colonisation stage of the country and destined to disappear within the foreseeable future. Great masses of people can continue such idealism for only a limited period of time. The State was no longer to be built ; nobody was any more personally involved. Until the emergence of the State, the *kibbutz* movement was the very distillation of Zionist idealism. Personal realisation of the Zionist ideal, Jewish self-defence, the absorption of immigrants, and a high degree of idealism in social relations were placed above all other interests. The individual *kibbutznik* felt he was not only creating a new society by his efforts—a unique accomplishment in itself : he was shouldering the burden or responsibility for the future of the whole *Jewish* people. At least, the new immigrants no longer feel that way. An over-powering reason—a reason which can become personal—which will make a person willing to live his way with people with whom he had no previous intimate relationship, did not exist in their case.

However, notwithstanding the problems that confront the *kibbutz*, it cannot be said yet that it is on the way out. Evolutionary changes are taking place within the *kibbutz* and it is still strong, vital and prospering.

Anyway, the Israel experiment can be regarded only as an extreme case that can hardly serve as a model for general application where similar conditions do not exist. Israel representatives attending the International Agricultural Producers' Conference in India in 1959, clearly stated that there seemed little scope of success for their experiment in India.

We will have to make a distinction between the adoption of co-operative farming in new settlements and its introduction in old villages of the traditional peasant structure. Perhaps, there are no examples where peasants in an existing old village have voluntarily given up individual use of their land, pooled it for joint utilisation and worked it as one undertaking for any considerable length of time.

Says the German expert Dr. Otto Schiller in a report submitted in 1959 to the Planning Commission which had asked him to make a study of co-operative farms in the country :

Pooling of land, however, is a hard decision for those land-owners who are cultivating their land by their own labour and that of their family members. For these farmers the transition to co-operative farming is combined with a complete change in their working and living habits. While so far they managed their small holdings under their own responsibility and themselves had to decide how to organise their day's work, they now receive daily orders as to what to do, and have to work in a group. They also must be prepared to have their work supervised and evaluated by others which may entail that this evaluation does not coincide with their own opinion. Considering the peculiarities of the farmer's way of thinking, it is understandable that, under normal conditions, it is not a very promising attempt to persuade farmers to voluntarily change to co-operative farming. Few examples of this type, therefore, exist in the non-Communistic world.[8]

Peasants will not be persuaded easily to give up their independent way of living and will always prefer retaining their own individualities and prospects of bettering themselves by their own efforts to sinking or merging their identities into a collective enterprise or, for the matter of that, into a co-operative farm. By far the most eloquent proof of the ineradicable individualism of the peasants is furnished by the fact that "in 1941 during the first months of German occupation, in remote villages where, after the retreat of the Soviet Army, the Russian peasants felt free to act according to their own wishes, in all cases they dissolved the *kolkhoz* farms at once and turned to individual farming. The young *kolkhoz* members were no exception."[9]

The Bhoodan leader, Acharya Vinoba Bhave, who was originally inclined in favour of co-operative farming, told a public meeting in Gaya on 13 January 1961, that co-operative farming is entirely unsuitable for India where most of the farmers are illiterate. According to him, only the managers of the farm or a handful of large farmers will be profitted by a co-operative farm. He said that most of the co-operative farms in the country have been established merely with a view to take loans from Government. He went on to say that service co-operatives, which have not been opposed by any political party in the country can, of course, be a success in India.

An Indian Communist leader, Shri E. M. S. Namboodiripad, former Chief Minister of Kerala, also does not consider co-operative farming a practicable proposition. In reply to a question on the subject he said that, "service co-operatives which would supply seeds, manure, implements, etc. would be welcome in the State

[8] *Pioneer*, Lucknow, dated 7.10.1959.
[9] *Farm Economics*, Dr. Otto Schiller, May 1956, p. 308.

but joint farming co-operatives where the whole process of cultivation was done by co-operatives would not be feasible *at present.*"[10]

The use of the words 'at present' is significant. Shri Namboodiripad knows that joint farming is not a practicable proposition
under the present democratic Constitution of India. That is why,
again, the Communist Party of India would distribute the surplus
land that may be available after imposition of a ceiling on large
holdings, among the landless, for individual cultivation rather than
have it jointly cultivated, as would Congressmen in pursuance of
the Nagpur Resolution of the Indian National Congress passed in
January 1959. The Communists are a clever people and realise
that the time for pooling of land and labour will arrive only when,
after securing the good-will of the peasantry, they have attained
absolute political power and clamped down a dictatorship.

Sometimes, it is argued that just as the state has abolished the
landlord tenant system by law, similarly it can eradicate the attachment of the peasantry to the land by enactment of legislation,
that is, by making them work jointly on their lands, on pain of
law. It is forgotten, however, that efficient operation of the farm
will require willing consent of the farmers, and this cannot be
evoked by law. Just as you can take a horse to a pond but cannot
make it drink, so you can pool the land of a thousand farmers but
cannot make them jointly work hard and well by fear of law.
Law can award damages for failure to honour a contract to work,
but should not force a party to work. Law that can extract work
under the threat of the lash will convert a free citizen into a slave
—a voluntary worker into a prisoner. It can certainly be done as
demonstrated by the USSR and China, but then India will cease
to be a democracy (and its agricultural production, of course,
will go down).

In 1955 the Planning Commission carried out a survey of 22
Co-operative Farming Societies in the country. They were not a
representative sample by any means because the State Governments recommended only the more successful societies for study.
It was found that joint cultivation was practised only in 16 out of
the 22 societies. In seven of these societies the land had been
obtained from the Government ; in three of them it had been
obtained in one block or two by lease or purchase from a landlord.

Thus, there were only twelve societies in which members had pooled their existing holdings. But in eight of these twelve, most or all the members did not perform any farm work. In seven societies out of twenty-two, members also held land outside the farm ; in one, their parents did so. It appears, therefore, that most of the so-called co-operative farming societies were either settlement societies or societies run on capitalist lines by groups of absentee landowners having all the work done by hired labour—a kind of joint stock estate farm established by joint families or extended families merely to secure the concessions given by Government in the form of loans or subsidies to co-operative farms. Some of the societies formed with Government land continued to exist only because members had no rights of transfer in the land which was allotted to the societies. If rights were given to the individual members, the societies would most likely be dissolved. The majority of the societies could be written down as failures, although it was only five years or so since they were established.

According to the Working Group on Co-operative Farming appointed by the Government of India in the middle of 1959, with Shri Nijalingappa as Chairman, there were 1,440 co-operative and collective farming societies on June 30, 1958 : of them 1,098 were reported to be working. The membership was 39,075, but only 24,687 were working on the farms. The rest were sympathisers, absentees or non-working members. The Working Group visited 34 societies in eight States and found that while 9 had been started with a genuine desire to increase production and improve the economic conditions, 25 had been started with such objects as ejecting tenants or preventing them from obtaining better rights, obtaining Government land or financial assistance, settling the landless, purchasing a tractor, utilisation of effluent water from a factory, consolidation of scattered holdings, resisting eviction, and settlement of refugees.

How co-operative farming is being abused or exploited for fostering absentee landlordism will be clear from an extract of Dr. Otto Schiller's report just referred to above :

The share of the non-working group in the membership is actually much higher than could be expected. This may obviously be explained by the fact that pooling of the land does not call for a difficult decision on the part of those land-owners who do not apply their own labour in cultivating the land. Instead of having their land operated by relatives, tenants or hired labour thus receiving a rent, they now have it operated by the co-operative society. This may offer the advantage that their annuity thus is better secured and may be even higher.

Not only that : The amusing aspect of the whole situation is that instead of being deprecated as an undesirable development, emergence of absentee landlordism—or opportunity of leasing out one's lands without the risk of losing them, with the only difference that tenants will work collectively rather than individually—is being held up as an argument in favour of the co-operative movement. Addressing the villagers in a Kisan Mela-cum-Cattle Show at Bandi· in Basti district on 28 January 1960, Shri Mohan Lal Gautam, the then Minister for Agriculture and Co-operation, Uttar Pradesh, is reported to have said :

A man possessing five bighas of land could very well manage to hand it over to the joint farming society and himself take to some other work aiming at increasing the overall income of the family. His ownership of the land was not going to be affected in the least, contrary to what happened in the case of private land-owners and their tenants.[11]

Both the Planning Commission and the Working Group presided over by Shri Nijalingappa found, *inter alia*, that some of the so-called co-operative farms sprang into existence merely in order to secure financial concessions extended by Government with a view to encourage joint farming. Yet, public men and public servants continue to make lavish promises of monetary aid to induce farmers to pool their lands. The Working Group proposed setting up of 3,200 pilot projects and 20,000 other new societies during the Third Plan. It recommended per society an amount of Rs. 3,050 as subsidy for the manager's salary and a godown-cum-cattle shed, Rs. 2,000 as share capital to be subscribed by the Government and Rs. 7,750 as loan. Cost during the Third Plan period of education and training over these societies was estimated to be of the order of Rs. 424.40 lakh and over the technical, advisory and organisational staff, of the order of Rs. 237.44 lakh. The total outlay came to Rs. 3,526.44 lakh.

The question arises : if mere pooling of lands has all the virtues claimed for it by its advocates and can solve the problem of increa-

[11] *National Herald*, Lucknow, dated January 30, 1960.

sed agricultural production, then why should special financial concessions be at all necessary ? And if financial aid to farmers is necessary, as we think it is, then why cannot this aid be extended to farmers individually, particularly when a large part of the aid to co-operative farms will be spent on salary of staff and construction of buildings which are unnecessary on individual holdings? If liberal aid is necessary even after merger of individual holdings, then joint farming has evidently no merits which a service co-operative does not possess.

And will all the aid that is being promised be forthcoming ? Have the Union Government and the State Governments the necessary financial means ? A co-operative farm, with a view to put up farm buildings of various kinds, to purchase various kinds of equipment and draught power, to pay overhead charges, etc. will require far greater amounts of capital than the individual farmers would have required.

The only merit of a co-operative farm compared with a collective farm, which lies in the fact that members remain owners of the land they contribute, proves its undoing. Cultivation is a work of such nature as to depend, for its efficiency, upon the personal qualities of the cultivator. Joint cultivation cannot be carried on, unless it is marked by a great degree of mutual confidence and liberality of heart between the participants. These qualities being not common, occasions when members will fall out, will be frequent. Says Mr. Phiroj J. Shroff, a former Principal of Sir Lallubhai Shah Law College and Deputy Secretary in the Ministry of State, Government of India :

Co-operative farms will be breeding grounds of interminable disputes. The frayed tempers of the disputants are not likely to be pacified by the thought that they will have to pay for the services of the adjudicators of avoidable disputes. On the co-operative farms there will be endless disputes about the right approach to farming operations. When the majority will foist its will on the minority, the latter will be resentful and unco-operative. Sabotage cannot be ruled out by embittered members. Disputes about the division of the produce will be fierce and prolonged. All this will undermine the basic object of agriculture which is to produce increased yields of quality crops.[12]

[12] "Co-operative Farming : A Psychological Searchlight" published in the *Kalki*, a leading Tamil weekly of Madras, dated September 13, 1959.

Solution of the disputes and differences will be sought through resignation or expulsion. And whether they resign or are expelled, members will or should be free to withdraw their land from the pool. The area of the farm, therefore, will soon dwindle. If, on the other hand, the would-be members are told at the outset that they will not be entitled to take away their lands in any eventuality, they will not join at all.

Shri Shriman Narayan, Member, Planning Commission, however, claims to have found a solution of the problem. He says:

It is being propagated by the critics of co-operative farming that once an agriculturist joins such a farm, it would never be possible for him to opt out of the farm. This is wholly erroneous. It is true that once a farmer joins a co-operative venture he should give it a fair trial for some years. But, if after a few years, he unfortunately finds it impossible to continue his membership of the co-operative farm, he can leave the farm, provided he gives due notice, say, of one year, repays all his loans and other liabilities, and deposits adequate compensation with the co-operative farm for improvements on his plot of land. After discharging these obligations, he may be returned either his original piece of land or another plot of land equivalent in value. All this would depend upon the terms of the original contract at the time of forming the co-operative farm.[13]

The learned member of the Planning Commission may rest assured that, if he is given the choice, no farmer would be foolish enough to walk into what would obviously sound as a trap. For, he will not be slow to conclude that while an increase in his income is, at best, problematic, his liabilities will definitely soar up— liabilities which, if he wants to disassociate himself from the farm, he will be able to clear off only by selling up his part of the land.

The kind of farming that is advocated by the Planning Commission and others in our country will lack both the advantage of joint farming in the USSR and China, *viz.* compulsion, and the advantage of individual farming practised in the rest of the world, viz. incentive for personal profit. Co-operative farms will fail as soon as they are set up, and we will have either to retreat to individual farming, or advance like the Chinese to the advanced agricultural producers' co-operative, which is a synonym for the Russian collective farm.

[13] "Advantages of Co-operative Farming", published in *AICC Economic Review*, dated September 1, 1959.

In fact, if we have to take the Chinese as our model, we will have to travel much faster than a democratic country like India has bargained for. As we have already seen, the Chinese have gone one step further than even the Russians. Agricultural producers' co-operatives, primary or advanced, have now been superseded by the communes.

Granting that the co-operative farm has certain advantages over the collective farm or the commune, the organisation is likely soon to fall apart: the centrifugal forces making for its disorganisation will be powerful. For, we should remember that it is not a problem of members alone, but of their respective families also. From a worker on his own individual plot of land the peasant will have become a cog in a vast land factory. It will mean an overwhelming change in his life—social and economic. Women and children from different families will come into closer contact and rub shoulders with each other far oftener than previously. Members will be working side by side, day after day, and depending on the co-operative farm for all or nearly all of their income. A co-operative farm is, thus, very different in this respect from other co-operative enterprises, e.g., a co-operative consumers' store or a co-operative brick-kiln where a member's interest is very much limited. A farmer's joining a co-operative farm means voluntarily giving up a great deal of his individual authority which joining a non-farming society does not.

The reaction of the peasant to joining a co-operative or collective farm where all the three factors of production, viz. land, labour and capital, will be pooled, is, therefore, understandable. Human nature being what it is, even brothers born of the same mother usually separate from one another after the head of the family has been removed by death or other cause. In the circumstances it is utopian to expect that an average householder will, all of a sudden, identify his interests with the interests of those hundreds of persons in the village or neighbourhood who were total strangers to his life hitherto. A co-operative farm brings together indiscriminately under its banner persons with no long-established ties of kinship or social level—Hindu and Muslim, Brahmin and Harijan—owner, tenant and labourer. Were a man to reach the heights wherefrom he could see his own good in the good of every other human being, he will cease to be a householder that very day. The ties of family, language, religion and country would no longer have any meaning for him. In such ideal conditions planning will not be

necessary. Economic laws will become infructuous and, indeed,
even government will itself be a costly luxury. The mother is able
to nurse and nourish her child because she is selfish, because in
the child she sees her own image. Did every other child in the
village, or in this wide, wide world occupy the same position in her
eyes as her own, she might as well turn a *sanyasini*. In our enthusiasm for a millennium right now in our own lives, we must
not forget that man is. not entirely a rational being. He is governed more by heart than by mind, and the heart has not yet made
(whether it ever will make, being doubtful) the same advance as the
mind which has narrowed down physical space and made the world
a smaller place than it was in the days of our forefathers. Scientific
progress or progress in control of the outer world has not resulted
in greater control of the inner world of the self, without which a
large joint economic undertaking cannot be run smoothly or
successfully. Man remains as selfish or greedy, proud or jealous,
and ambitious as ever.

Recommending collective cattle farming, Mahatma Gandhi wrote
in the *Harijan*, dated February 15, 1942 :

I firmly believe too that we shall not derive the full benefits of
agriculture until we take to co-operative farming. Does it not stand
to reason that it is far better for a hundred families in a village to
cultivate their lands collectively and divide the income therefrom
than to divide the land anyhow into a hundred portions ? And what
applies to land applies equally to cattle.

As has been shown in previous pages, however, it does not stand
to reason that a large area jointly operated as one unit should
produce more per acre than when it is divided into small portions
and operated severally. Nor does it do so in practice.

When advocates of co-operative farming buttress their case
by reference to Gandhiji's opinion, they should remember that he
was a world teacher, and world teachers in every clime and country
have believed in and preached a widening of one's affections so as to
embrace the whole village, the country and, in fact, the entire
world in their compass. *Vasudhaiv Kutumbakam* (वसुधैव कुटुम्बकम्)
meaning that the world is one family, is an old ideal enshrined in
our religious lore. But political parties or administrators do not
work or plan for a kingdom of God on earth. They work for what
is practicable in the not too distant future.

Mahatmaji himself had warned that co-operative farming "would be possible only if people became friends of one another and as one family. When that happy event took place, communal trouble would be a thing of the past.... He, however, warned that co-operation must not be brought about by force or compulsion, it was not to be imposed from above, it should be based on strict non-violence and grow from below." [14]

Whether the 'happy event' or stage in their mutual relations of which Mahatmaji spoke,had arrived, was for the peasants themselves to judge, and not any external agency.

Further, Mahatma Gandhi suffered from no inhibitions or complexes. Nor did he claim a monopoly of wisdom. The remarks made by him in respect of joint farming were made—if we may say so with respect—in a somewhat casual manner. Had he been able to devote some time to the problem and gather experience in the actual field, he would not have hesitated to own up his error. He never allowed prestige, rather false prestige to stand in his way.

Nor as men made of ordinary clay, do we, in all other matters, conform or are able to conform to what Gandhiji said and preached. For example, he had advocated self-restraint as the only desirable means of population control, but the Planning Commission and the Government of India are enthusiastically propagating all the modern contrivances, which were a taboo to him.

The Patil Delegation admits that there are inherent difficulties in the way of introduction of co-operative farming. It says :

The difficulties inherent in the change from individual farming to agrarian co-operatives are great and must never be minimised. Individual owner is his own master. If he joins a co-operative, he has : (i) to surrender his right of individual management of his farm, and accept the discipline of a group ; (ii) to place his capacities for production at the disposal of the group, and accept their valuation of them ; and (iii) to accept some diminution in the transferability of his individual interest in land. These disadvantages appear formidable to him. His apprehensions could, indeed, be removed to some extent by a demonstration of successfully-run agrarian co-operatives. It could be shown, for instance, how techniques of working can be introduced which provide for maximum individual participation, do away to a large extent with the

---

[14] Prayer speech, February 15, 1947, vide the *Harijan* dated 9-3-1947 and *Mahatma Gandhi—The Last Phase* by Pyare Lal, Navjivan Publishing House, Ahmedabad, pp. 543-44.

evils of bureaucratism and commandism and thereby to ease the acceptance of group discipline. Evolution of norms and targets can provide respectively for the preservation of individual and group incentives. Co-operatives also offer opportunities for sharing much wider responsibilities than in individual farming, thus mitigating the possibility of a wrong judgment of individual capacities. Though joining an agrarian co-operative does mean a diminution in the transferability of individual interest, it is partly provided for by allowing the free exercise of the right of a member to leave the co-operative at his will. Once he is out, his transferability is restored. Moreover, the members could be permitted to transfer their ownership interest, *i.e.* the right to rent (p. 145). . . Thus, by evolving suitable techniques and procedures, the disadvantages which a farmer may feel in joining a co-operative could be minimised, but their basic character would not be altered. As against these disadvantages, there would be prospects of increased production and possibilities of a higher standard of living which would be demonstrated as years go by. In joining a co-operative, the farmer will naturally weigh these advantages against the disadvantages. His decision will naturally be subjective because, the disadvantages are not capable of economic valuation as the advantages. It is possible that to some the material advantages of increased production would outweigh the sacrifice they would be called upon to make in accepting group discipline, group estimation of their abilities and the restrictions on transferability. To many others, the sacrifice involved in accepting the new way of life may be too great to be compensated by material gains. It has been a common experience of group-working, whether within a family or outside it, that considerations of material benefits often fail to keep the people together, unless there are higher considerations of social value. For inducing peasants to join co-operatives on any scale and later to keep them together, it would be necessary, we feel, that considerations of material gain are combined with higher considerations of socialism and patriotism (p. 146).

The issue has not been put squarely. The summing up of the case by the Patil Delegation assumes that co-operative farming will lead to increased production. Facts and figures given in these pages do not, however, support this view. But even if the assumption made by the delegation is correct, for the overwhelming majority of the peasants increased material benefits brought about by co-operative farming will not compensate for loss of the individual freedom that they enjoy today on their independent farms. As if in proof of this realisation the report goes on to provide two safeguards which, in their view, should satisfy even the most extreme advocates of democratic values :

We are insisting that the principle of voluntariness should be scrupulously adhered to and there should be no coercion of any type in inducing farmers to join co-operatives. And, secondly, a person should be free to leave a co-operative whenever he chooses to do so, his decision being effective at the end of a season. In such an event he should be given a plot of land outside the area of the co-operative so that the compactness of the co-operative is preserved and he should be made to accept liability, if any, for any improvements on the plot of land made by the co-operative. And, finally, all efforts by the state to persuade farmers to join co-operatives must aim at producing in them a conviction to join a co-operative and not act, directly or indirectly, as leaving them no alternative but to join. Various examples of this could be given. If, for instance, under the pretext of making preferential supplies to co-operatives, supplies to individual farmers are barred, they would have no alternative but to join. These examples can be multiplied. The test of farmers joining voluntarily or not is whether the last decision to join is with them. State efforts should produce acceptance by the farmers of the co-operatives born of conviction and not compulsion (p. 150 of the Report).

The Planning Commission, however, does not believe in any policy of self-denial or *laissez-faire*! According to it while all cultivators in the village can avail of the general departmental services and the common facilities offered by the multi-purpose, better farming or large-sized credit societies, those alone who pool their lands in co-operative farming societies are to get special subsidies for administrative expenses, credit on specially liberal terms, preference in consolidation proceedings, preference in technical assistance, preference in the supply of seeds, fertilisers and construction materials, and special financial and technical assistance for developing ancillary occupations.

This discriminatory treatment is sought to be justified on the argument that just as under the Indian Income-Tax Act, the taxable limit in the case of a joint-stock company is higher than in the case of individuals, so nobody should have any objection if a co-operative farm is granted more loans or subsidy or given priority in matters of supplies as compared with individual farmers. It is contended that this is one of the well-accepted principles of encouraging socially desirable patterns of organisation. The argument, however, is fallacious. First, it is taken for granted that a large joint undertaking in the sphere of agriculture is a more desirable form of organisation, just as it is in industry and commerce.

Second, income-tax rates of joint-stock companies, when worked out against the share-holders severally, are actually found not to be lower than if the share-holders carried on the business individually.

A pertinent question that arises in connection with co-operative farming is whether we have—in fact, whether any country has—the necessary human material. Individual families who cultivate their small holdings, a few acres in size, keep no accounts : they do not need to. It is all their own concern. They look after the entire agricultural process from sowing to harvesting of the crop. There are no fellow-members whose work has to be evaluated or supervised, or to whom account has to be rendered. They are self-employed persons—owners and workers, managers and financiers—all rolled into one. But in a large-scale undertaking, particularly, in one which is to be organised on the basis of voluntary co-operation, problems are bound to crop up which would demand leadership and character of the highest order. The organisers will be faced with several weighty problems, such as, relation between the co-operative farm and the Government, selection of members, the taking over of land, draught animals and farm tools ; internal management or relation of members *inter se*, the formulation and implementation of production plans, the organisation of the labour force into working teams and production brigades; the utilisation of Government subsidy, if any, in terms of finance, equipment and expert advice ; sale of necessaries and marketing of produce ; the setting up of funds to meet production expenses, to acquire means of production, to provide relief and welfare, and for reserves ; the provision of cultural and welfare services, and the education of members in the spirit of collectivism (which, in China, is undertaken under the 'guidance' of the Communist Party and the People's Government), etc.

A far more difficult and important task, however, than any mentioned above, is the assessment of performance of various agricultural and other operations and their proper remuneration. Differences in skill and consciousness are wide. Unless a proper system of measurement and evaluation of different types of farm work are evolved, jealousies between the efficient and the inefficient worker can easily wreck the society. Production in agriculture does not lend itself to specialisation by task and standardisation by products as it does in manufacturing. Measurement and evaluation of various farm operations, therefore, requires extra-ordinary intelligence and scrupulous impartiality. If the farm operations are valued and paid for without much differentiation, inefficiency and light work get a premium and labour costs are inflated ; if accurate differential evaluation is attempted, over-head costs are inflated. The Chinese, as the Russians, have tried to solve the problem by adoption of a system of norms for impor-tant items of work. 'Norm' is a standard of daily performance in regard to quantity and quality of output expected of an average member working on a specified job. It is to be seen whether the Chinese will succeed where even after 25 years of experience the Russians have not yet succeeded; for, we still hear of grave 'short-comings in the standardisation of work, in the laying down of standards of production and the valuation of labour involved in work-days on the Soviet Collective Farms.

Will the requisite enlightened leadership be forthcoming in our countryside ? In India which suffers from an acute shortage of competent managerial personnel and general illiteracy of farmers, the disadvantage of large-scale farming is obvious. It will be clear that a co-operative farm would be too big an affair, too big for ordinary peasants to control. We will have to draw upon the towns, which will rule the countryside and rule it unimaginatively, with all the evils that are associated with an unsympathetic bureaucracy. Also, by and large, a city-dweller has always looked down upon a villager as intellectually deficient and culturally backward. The villager has, on the other hand, always considered an urbanite as morally degraded. It is doubtful if the two, with the above back-ground, can work harmoniously, at least, in the immediate future.

Lastly, there are two very important considerations or impedi-ments that stand in the way of mechanisation and, consequently, of joint farming in India. Impediments to mechanisation have to be considered because whether we desire it today or not, joint farms will come to be mechanised some day. First, we do not manufacture large agricultural machinery, nor do we produce petroleum in the quantities that will be needed. Where will we find the colossal amounts of money that will be required for invest-ment in the means to produce large agricultural machinery—the tractors, the threshers, the harvester-combines, etc.? People are finding it difficult even to pay the present taxes. What will we do to our huge existing capital—the bullocks ? Perhaps, they will have to be slaughtered. And, finally, what will happen to our land itself—eroded and damaged as it will be by tractors and chemicals ? If so, India will soon become a desert.

Second, India does not possess enough petroleum even for her existing industries and transport and, if tractors are added, the problem of supply of fuel oil will become very difficult, indeed Nor can we cover our sky with a network of electric wires which will supply the motive-power to the tractors, combines and threshers all over the countryside. We will, therefore, have to depend on a foreign country to keep the machines going so that our teeming millions may have food. It will be nothing short of lunacy to plan for such an economy. The Nazi hordes in the last Great War had rushed towards the Caucasus not without reason ; they wanted to capture the oil wells so that by cutting the vital artery of Russian economy they could more easily and quickly starve their enemy into surrender.

Let the enthusiasts of large-scale joint farming, therefore, pause and reconsider. Let there be a full and frank debate : let the people, viz., the peasants who are most concerned themselves decide. The recommendations made by the Congress Planning Sub-Committee, viz., "we shall experiment with the Cooperative joint farming wherever possible" (p. 53), in its report submitted to the All-India Congress Committee held in the last week of September 1959, in Chandigarh, represented an approach to which nobody can take an exception. The plenary session of the Congress held at Bangalore in January, 1960, endorsed this approach when it said, "Cooperative farming should be developed wherever it is desired by the *farmers concerned* and is considered feasible. It should be realized that cooperation in all its forms is a voluntary movement." Similar was the recommendation made (in February 1960) by the Working Group under the Chairmanship of Mr. S. Nijalingappa, appointed by the Ministry of Community Development, Government of India. The mere idea of compelling unwilling farmers to join a co-operative farming society was abhorrent to the Group which was hostile even to certain States' legislative enactments that went against the principle of voluntariness. Such laws, though not enforced so far, should be repealed—recommended the Group. Where voluntary experiments in co-operative farming can be promoted and assisted, and are truly understood by those engaged in them, they are well worth the trouble and initial expenditure. If successful, they will inevitably find imitators. [15]

[15] Perhaps, all controversy about co-operative joint farming, so far as the Indian National Congress was concerned, would seem to have been set at rest by Prime Minister Nehru's statement at his monthly conference held in New Delhi in March 1960. He said that the proposal regarding establishment of a few large state farms on the Suratgarh model "had nothing to do with the normal agricultural pattern of the country comprising peasants' small holdings, peasant proprietorship and service co-operatives."

A few days later, while addressing the Federation of Indian Chambers of Commerce and Industry at Calcutta on March 27, he declared as follows :

"Therefore, the conclusion was inevitable that there was no escape from cooperation, that cooperatives—service cooperatives for the present—was the right way for Indian agriculture, not to be imposed upon them. Our basic approach to agriculture is the approach of peasant proprietor cooperating with other farmers in service cooperatives."

Mr. Nehru said that the next point for consideration was whether there should be joint cultivation or farming. "That I admit may be an arguable point. Therefore, we have said that this is a thing which may— we approve of it as an ideal—depend on so many circumstances, first of all, willingness of the people. Apart from that it may be feasible in some conditions and it may not be in other conditions. There is neither any compulsion nor a rigid approach to the problem."

The *Hindustan Times*, New Delhi, dated March 28, commented on the above report as follows :

"Mr. Nehru's latest observations on joint farming are different from his first thoughts on the subject. An ideal which is not a principle and which may not be held to be rigidly applicable the whole way through is certainly not the same thing as a settled programme for enforcement according to a fixed time-table. Peasant farming, after all, is to stay ; and to service cooperatives, of course, there has never been any objection from the critics of the Nagpur pattern."

PART II

PART II

CHAPTER ELEVEN

Possible Solutions

SOLUTION to the problem both of the uneconomic holdings, or the too small size of the farms and of the landless labour in rural areas, in fact, of the entire economic problem of our poverty lies, first, in bringing about—to the extent it is possible—a more favourable ratio or more productive combinations than obtain at present between the factors of production, viz., land (and other natural resources), labour and capital both on the basis of an individual or an earning unit and of the nation ; secondly, in increasing the efficiency of labour and capital and, thirdly, in maximising the utilisation of the natural resources, their quantity and quality being already determined by Nature.

Land and other natural resources being naturally formed, will remain practically constant. Arable area of the country can, however, be increased to some extent by reclamation, that is, by drainage and bringing culturable waste under cultivation. The average size of the farm may also be increased by emigration to other regions and countries, or by transferring. some farmers to non-agricultural pursuits, both of which remedies will lead to reduction of pressure on arable land. Apart from an incidental increase in the size of the farms, this transference of workers from agricultural to non-agricultural pursuits will result in an increase in output of goods and services which are required to meet the varied wants of a civilised people, and thus raise their living standards. Today, the marginal productivity of labour of a vast multitude in our villages, who are entirely unemployed or ineffectively employed in agriculture, tends to zero.

Labour includes not only manual or physical labour, but every kind of human activity directed to producing goods and services. Labour force is a variable factor and, with increase in population, it is fast increasing.

Capital is largely a product of human labour, set aside for and used in further production, or, in other words, a product of work carried out in the past, which was not consumed. It is also a variable factor. Means which aid production, agricultural or non-agricultural, for example, draught animals, tools and other equipment, sources of irrigation, manures and fertilizers, improved seeds and insecticides, factories or machines can all be classed as capital and practically be increased indefinitely, provided, of course, that man is prepared to make the necessary sacrifice of not consuming all the product of his labour immediately it is produced.

Both labour force and capital being variable, man can help retard or accelerate their growth. This retardation of population growth or acceleration of capital formation or both have to be so effected or effected in order that production per head or national real income grows faster than population. Obviously, some method or methods of population control will have to be devised and the rate of capital investment will have to be increased.

Even if population continues to grow at the present rate, production per head can rise, if the rate of capital investment exceeds the rate of population increase. Capital investment is *inter alia* required to bring about technological improvements or innovations which will increase the efficiency or performance both of land and labour. Labour may also become more efficient by better health measures, better training or changes in attitudes towards work.

Land can produce and continue to produce more if resource facilities are available, if technologies referred to in a previous chapter are applied and correct farming methods are practised. These means will both conserve and improve the soil.

We have seen that small farms produce (and employ) more per acre than large farms. And it is increase in productivity per acre which is the essence of economic progress. In order, therefore, that the arable land may be better and more fully utilised, large farms may be broken up and the area surplus to a minimum divided into small farms and distributed to those who hold no land today although they work on land, or to those who own little land.

Remedies of our poverty, therefore, boil down broadly to reclamation and redistribution of land, emigration to foreign countries, development of non-agricultural resources, intensive utilisation of our land resources and population control.

CHAPTER TWELVE

Reclamation, Redistribution and Emigration

RECLAMATION and colonisation seem scarcely a solution, since land for such extensive colonisation as would be needed is limited. According to the Survey-General of India the total geographical area of the country is 806.3 million acres and, according to revenue or village records, 724.1 million acres. Land utilisation statistics in 1958-59 were available for 725.1 million acres only, which are as follows :

TABLE XXIV

FIGURES OF LAND UTILIZATION IN INDIA IN 1958–59

	Million Acres (Provisional)
Forests	128.1
Not available for cultivation	116.6
Permanent pastures and grazing lands	32.4
Groves and miscellaneous tree crops	14.2
Culturable waste	50.8
Fallows ;	59.4
(a) Current 29.4	
(b) Other 30.0	
Net area sown	323.6
Total	725.1

SOURCE : *Basic Statistics Relating to Indian Economy* issued by Planning Commission for the years 1950-51 to 1960-61, published in December, 1961, p. 13.

Out of the culturable waste, which includes weed-infested areas, some 35 million acres can be reclaimed and brought under the

177

plough. Also, inasmuch as technical research and improvements have now reduced the necessity of letting lands lie fallow—which practice was resorted to in order that the exhausted soil may recuperate—half the area of the land now shown as fallows, can be kept permanently under cultivation.

In spite of the pressure of population, relatively small extension of cultivation to waste lands has taken place during the last 40 years. This is due, partly, to the fact that the exploitation of such waste lands has not been within the resources of the ordinary cultivator, but, perhaps, more due to the fact that such lands are inferior in quality and otherwise unsuitable. Reclamation of any considerable part of these areas, which are relatively inaccessible at present, will be a very difficult and time-consuming process even for the state as it involves large-scale tree or bush-clearance, road-making, anti-malaria operations, water-supply, house-building etc. Considerations of soil conservation will also have to be borne in mind before large-scale tree-clearance is undertaken. Any reclamation which accentuates soil erosion cannot be desirable from the long-term point of view, although it may give some additional production in the immediate future. Anyway, we will thus be able to settle only four million families in the entire country which will not solve any problems. According to latest statistics, our population is growing at the rate of about 2.0 per cent or 9 million persons, which means an addition of 1.8 million families every year.

REDISTRIBUTION OF LAND

As regards the second solution, viz. redistribution of land in excess of a certain area that may be reserved to the family of a large owner, it is not going to yield substantial results in all parts of the Union. In some it may not yield results at all worth the name. For, the area of three family holdings throughout the country, in terms of the definition as suggested by the Size of Holdings Committee and referred to in Chapter VIII, will measure up to more than 30 acres and, in some parts, even more than 45 acres, and holdings in excess of these areas are not many. If we adopt the second definition which is more scientific, that is, leave an area of 27.5 or 25 acres to every male adult, perhaps, the area that will be available, may be even less.

A census of *Land Holdings and Cultivation* was held in most of

TABLE XXV

AREA OF SURPLUS LAND AVAILABLE IN VARIOUS STATES IN INDIA

(In Lakh Acres)

States	Area Required		Surplus Area with Ceiling at 30 acres					Surplus Area with Ceiling at 45 acres					Surplus Area with Ceiling at 60 acres				
	To make up sub-basic holdings to basic size	For settlement of landless at a basic holding	Percentage of holdings affected	Extent	% to area owned	% to col. (2)	% to col. (3)	Percentage of holdings affected	Extent	% to area owned	% to col. (2)	% to col. (3)	Percentage of holdings affected	Extent	% to area owned	% to col. (2)	% to col. (3)
1	2	3	4	5	6	7	8	9	10	11	12	13	14	15	16	17	18
Andhra	53	47	3.3	21.7	12.0	41	47	1.5	13.4	7.4	25	20	0.8	9.2	5.1	17	19
Bombay	199	52	6.3	61.4	13.0	31	118	2.7	34.9	7.5	18	67	1.3	23.0	5.0	11.5	44.2
Madhya Pradesh	230	94	4.3	55.9	15.0	24	59	2.0	37.3	10.0	16	40	1.2	27.6	7.4	12	29
Madras	77	57	2.4	41.9	12.9	55	74	1.1	29.9	9.2	40	53	0.7	23.9	7.3	31	42
Punjab	8	8	2.0	10.4	7.4	127	135	0.8	6.2	4.4	76	80	0.4	3.9	2.7	49	49
Hyderabad	73	66	13.0	95.5	20.2	130	144	6.5	61.0	12.9	84	90	3.7	42.7	9.0	58	64.5
Madhya Bharat	58	17	5.6	16.5	11.3	29	95	2.3	9.0	6.2	16	52	1.2	5.8	3.9	10	34
Mysore	26	9	3.3	9.0	10.1	35	96	1.5	5.5	6.2	22	59	0.8	3.9	4.4	15	43
PEPSU	1	3	3.4	4.2	8.1	323	124	1.3	2.2	4.3	169	63	0.7	1.4	2.8	140	46.5
Rajasthan	64	12	..	13.0	9.0	20	108	..	10.0	7.0	16	83	..	8.0	5.0	12.5	66.6
Saurashtra	3	9	29.7	18.6	21.9	547	211	12.2	8.6	10.1	253	98	5.3	4.4	5.2	146.5	48.8

I. The surplus area in Hyderabad is in terms of 'converted dry acres.

II. In Punjab, PEPSU and Mysore the census was confined to holdings of 10 acres and above. In Rajasthan it was conducted in 22 selected tahsils only. The State Governments have, however, given estimates of area comprised in all owned holdings.

III. A basic holding has been assumed to consist of:
(1) 10 acres for Bombay, Madhya Pradesh, Hyderabad, Madhya Bharat, Rajasthan and Saurashtra, and
(2) 5 acres for Andhra, Madras, Punjab, Mysore and PEPSU.

the States under the advice of the Planning Commission some eight years ago. The census related to agricultural lands comprised in holdings which consist of cultivable area including groves and pastures. All unoccupied area such as forest lands and other uncultivable lands and also land held within urban limits were excluded. The entire agricultural land held by a person as owner throughout a State constituted a single holding. In case of joint holdings the area of each co-sharer was treated as a separate holding. Table XXV shows the surplus land that will be available, according to the census, in case the ceiling is applied at 30, 45 or 60 acres of the area owned, and the estimates of the area that will be required to settle landless agricultural workers and build up the sub-basic holdings to basic size in the various States. The data relate generally to the year 1953-54.

The area under lease in the various States in which the tenant does not hold permanent and heritable rights, included in the three categories of large holdings, according to the above census, is shown in the following table :

TABLE XXVI
TOTAL AREA OF LARGE HOLDINGS IN VARIOUS STATES IN INDIA
(in Lakh Acres)

States	Holdings of more than 30 acres	Holdings of more than 45 acres	Holdings of more than 60 acres
Andhra	7.41	6.00	5.08
Bombay	27.48	21.54	17.40
Madhya Pradesh	22.55	17.90	15.47
Madras	21.63	18.61	16.56
Punjab	16.97	13.26	10.88
Mysore	3.46	2.70	2.20
Madhya Bharat	6.23	4.62	3.65
Hyderabad *	48.85	27.70	17.20
PEPSU	3.88	2.80	2.17
Saurashtra	6.73	4.50	3.26

* Area converted into 'dry acres'.

Area 'owned' in Table XXV includes land held by a person as owner as well as land held by him as tenant under permanent and heritable rights. Leased area, shown in Table XXVI, is included in the area owned by his landlord. Land in the various States that needs to be redistributed, that is, land under personal cultivation or possession of the owners, will, therefore, be arrived at by deducting the acreages given in Table XXVI from the corresponding 'owned' acreages shown as available for redistribution in columns 5, 10 and 15 of Table XXV. In Uttar Pradesh, where no census of land-holdings was held, it is estimated by the Revenue Department that under the Imposition of Ceiling on Land-holdings Act, 1960, hardly two lakh acres of land will be available for redistribution.

According to the Second Five Year Plan (pp. 196-97) :

There would appear to be an advantage in exempting the following categories of farms from the operation of ceilings which may be proposed :
(i) Tea, coffee and rubber plantations ;
(ii) Orchards where they constitute a reasonably compact area ;
(iii) Specialised farms engaged in cattle breeding, dairying, wool-raising, etc ;
(iv) Sugarcane farms operated by sugar factories ; and
(v) Efficiently-managed farms which consist of compact blocks, on which heavy investment or permanent structural improvements have been made and whose break-up is likely to lead to a fall in production.

In the nature of things, remarks the Planning Commission, these are general suggestions which should be adapted to the needs and conditions of each state.

If we deduct the area of plantations and other farms suggested by the Planning Commission as fit for exemption, and of farms that may have been broken up or reduced in size by succession or transfers since the census was taken and also take into account the additional area that will have to be left to families which consist of more than five persons, the area in the various States that will actually be available for redistribution today will be found to be much smaller than the figures collected several years ago and given above, indicate. Meanwhile, through sheer increase in population, the number of agricultural labourers would have gone up by not less than 20 per cent.

In order that glaring disparities in possession of land might be eliminated there was an alternative method available to that of redistribution directly by the state. Instead of, first, allowing the owners to resume the area in possession of non-permanent tenants and then putting a ceiling on the holdings thus enlarged, as the Planning Commission recommended, the better course would have been to confer permanent rights on the tenants, impose a heavy graduated tax on the area actually under personal cultivation or possession of the owners so that inefficient or too large farms would have had to sell up, and fix a ceiling on future acquisitions at a low level, say, 12.5 acres for an adult including the spouse and the minor children. So that land surplus to what a person might efficiently cultivate will have been distributed automatically, that is, without the state coming into the picture at all. The state would not have had to pay any compensation (rather, it would have got a substantial amount as tax), nor would it have to incur any administrative responsibility that cutting down of large farms and the distribution of surplus land necessarily involve. Any feeling of bitterness, justified or unjustified, in the minds of the large farmers that they were being discriminated[1] against as compared with owners of large urban property, would have been avoided and the state saved the burden of financing the would-be settlers. Nor will have any feeling of uncertainty been created in the mind of those middle-class cultivators who may not be affected by the ceiling today (for the ceiling, at whatever area we fix it, will appear as arbitrary and there is no guarantee—these cultivators will argue to themselves—that it will not be brought down to a lower limit tomorrow), or a feeling of discontent among those landless labourers and sub-basic holders who may be or have been left out of the redistribution. Last, but not least, the redistribution would have been effected without having 'unleashed a class conflict', as the State Communist Party, Uttar Pradesh, in its meeting of April 20-21, 1959, held at Lucknow gleefully said, the Nagpur Resolution of the Indian National Congress passed in January, 1959, had done.

There are two dangers inherent in acceptance of the principle

[1] In the non-agricultural sector, only a tax is payable on incomes more than Rs. 3,600 or Rs. 4,200 a year. In the rural or agricultural sector, on the other hand, nobody will at all be allowed to exist or function who derives an income in excess of these figures.

of redistribution of land, however theoretically sound, in a country like India where there is little land per capita and little land that will be, or has been available by imposition of a ceiling. First, the situation created by acceptance of the principle will arouse, or has aroused land hunger not only among agricultural labourers which was understandable, but also among all non-agriculturists in the villages. Second, in the class conflict so unleashed, various political parties will try to outbid each other in the matter of fixing as low a ceiling as possible—a still lower ceiling in the future—and the Communist party, which aims at collective farming, will be the gainer.

Anyway, if we have ultimate interest of the country at heart and not only slogans, we should take care to see that redistribution of land does not increase the number of agriculturists in the country. The feeling generated by the Bhoodan Movement of Acharya Vinoba Bhave that our economic problem will be solved the day everybody gets a patch of land to cultivate, is entirely unfounded. As the following chapters will show, economic development of a country means gradual decrease in the percentage of its population which is engaged in agriculture, and corresponding increase in the percentage which is engaged in non-agricultural occupations. Therefore, the suplus lands obtained by putting a ceiling on large holdings should preferably be or have been distributed among sub-basic holders rather than landless people. The latter have to be drawn to industries, trade, transport and other non-agricultural avocations : if agriculture still continues to be the chief attraction it means we are making little or no economic progress. It was the problem of the excluded heirs that is regarded as one of the causes of industrialisation of Germany. The State Governments and the Union Government are likely to become complacent or have less anxious moments over the people's poverty if all those who are landless or unemployed today are tied up to land. The word 'tie' has been used because there is a strange attraction in land ; it is with difficulty that a man moves from his land in search of another occupation. For, although there are bad years, the land never disillusions the holder completely, and hope for plenty in the future always remains.

Finally, howsoever we may proceed in the matter of redistribution of land, taking the country as a whole, it will not make or have made any appreciable difference to the economic situation and will not solve or have solved any problems for us.

EMIGRATION

In theory, some relief might be obtained by emigration—a more even distribution of population of the world in relation to land resources of the various countries—but, in practice, emigration is not likely to have much effect in lessening the pressure of population in the homeland itself. As Dr. Kingsley Davis has pointed out in his *Population of India and Pakistan* (Princeton University Press, New York, 1951), emigration from India, which was never large in proportion to the total population, has declined in volume since 1930. The factors that have led to this decline—the treatment of the Indians abroad, the growth of local labour, the increasing nationalism of colonial areas—show no real signs of slackening in the future. Latin America now has a policy of Asian exclusion. Burma is now independent and does not welcome Indians in addition to those that are resident there. South and East Africa are continually embroiled with their Indian communities. Australia maintains its White-Australian policy. All over the world, migration is confronted with tremendous and increasing obstacles, and there is little sign that Indians will be welcome anywhere. The division of India into Pakistan and the Union of India has weakened the Indian sub-continent as an international power and, apart from its desirability, lessened the chances of forcing an outlet for the citizens of either Pakistan or the new India. Only a major world catastrophe would seem to alter the situation. Short of such a catastrophe, it seems unlikely that migration will constitute a relief—a solution—for our population problem.

CHAPTER THIRTEEN

Need for Non-agricultural Vocations

A MORE constructive solution lies in the development of non-agricultural resources which might permanently draw off some of those peasants who possess uneconomic holdings and landless labourers who find their wages unremunerative, and which might further serve as a subsidiary source of income to those who still remain in agriculture. Provision of employment opportunities will bring income and, as we will see, non-agricultural employments, at the present stage of world development, bring greater income than agricultural for the same amount of energy expended.

All economic activity, industry or production, may be classified as Primary, Secondary and Tertiary.[1] Agriculture is commonly grouped with mining, forestry, hunting and fishing under the head of primary industries. Manufacturing and construction (of buildings and public works) are grouped together under the head of secondary production or industries. Tertiary industries are defined by difference as consisting of all other economic activities, the most prominent of which are commerce and finance, transport and communications, public utilities (electricity, gas and water) as well as public and private services. The actual classification, however, differs with the preference of the particular economist. Some put mining and public utilities under the second head. In that case the three sectors are better called Agriculture, Industry and Services.

In a just society labour should be rewarded according to the amount of energy expended and the skill required so that an hour's labour devoted to, say, ploughing, should earn about the same reward as an hour's work by an ordinary factory machine-minder. But, in actual fact, the net reward of farm labour, almost all

---

[1] Latterly, some economists have divided these activities into four sectors—the primary sector representing agriculture and ancillary activities, the secondary manufacturing and mining activities, the tertiary commerce, communications and transport, and the quarternary the professions, the government services, the domestic services, etc.

the world over, is far inferior to that of factory labour. The agricultural class has, always and everywhere been comparatively poor, that is, poorer than the industrial, trading and other sections of the community. Sir William Petty had written in 1691 :

"There is much more to be gained by Manufacture than Husbandry ; and by Merchandise than Manufacture—Now here we may take notice that as Trades and Curious Arts increase, so the Trade of Husbandry will decrease, or else the wages of Husbandmen must rise and consequently the Rents of Lands must fall."[2]

Commenting on the high level of income per head in the Netherlands at that time as compared with other European countries, Sir William shows that this was associated with the employment of a large proportion of the Dutch population in manufacture and commerce. In England, he points out, the wages of a husbandman at that time were four shillings a week while a seaman's wages were as much as twelve shillings a week. "So as a Seaman is in effect three Husbandmen, wherefore there is little ploughing and sowing of corn in Holland and New Zealand, or breeding of young cattle,"[2] a considerable proportion of Dutch food supplies being obtained by importation.

Mihail Manoilesco, President of the Union of the Chambers of Commerce and Industry, Rumania, in his book entitled *Theory of Protection and Exchange* (1929) bases his entire argument in favour of protection of agricultural produce on the greater productiveness of labour in non-agricultural pursuits than in agricultural. He quotes statistics showing the total income of twenty-two countries, the proportion of agricultural income to total income, and the proportion of agricultural workers to the total number of workers in each country. Taking the twenty-two countries together it was found that 20 per cent of the total income was produced by 52 per cent of the total number of workers engaged in agriculture, and 80 per cent of the total income by 48 per cent of the total number of workers devoted to non-agricultural occupations. A simple calculation shows that "all other human activities were, on an average, approximately 4.35 times more productive than agricultural activity."

Inasmuch as wealth consists of industrial goods also, countries

[2] *The Conditions of Economic Progress*, by Colin Clark, 1951, p. 395.

which have a larger proportion of their nationals engaged in industries (and, therefore, also in services) are bound to enjoy a higher
per capita income. In fact, only. those persons are called wealthy,
a major portion of whose income is spent on use and consumption
of non-agricultural goods and enjoyment of services rendered by
others. Those who are hardly or, with difficulty, able to provide
for food, raiment and shelter are poor. Food is the first necessity
of man, with raiment and shelter closely following in order ; but
a man has, or as the supply of these three is assured, develops other
desires[3] also. And the means of satisfaction of these desires can
be provided only by the secondary and tertiary sectors of the
economy.

Wealth, prosperity or economic development, therefore, means
greater growth of the non-agricultural sectors as compared with
the primary or agricultural sector. Its basis lies in man's increasing
ability to transform natural resources into useful products and
services. Table XXVII shows that in all the prosperous or
advanced countries it is industry (the term including mining,
construction and utilities besides manufacturing), transportation
and services, i.e., non-agricultural occupations that contribute a
far larger share to national income than agriculture.

The method of converting the national product of various countries as estimated in their national currencies, into a common
currency unit, such as a United States dollar, is, however, not
quite satisfactory. It assumes that the average relation between the
internal purchasing powers of the different currencies is the same as
the rate of exchange used in foreign trade. But it is obvious, points
out the *Economic Snrvey of Asia and the Far East*—1961 (p. 8),
that most of the goods and services included in national product
do not fall within the orbit of foreign trade. Even in the case of

---

[3] Says Dr. E. M. Ojala : "The total welfaie of a people is the sum
of all the satisfactions enjoyed by all the individual persons
comprising the group. Some come from the possession or consumption of material things, such as housing, clothing and
food ; some are yielded by the services of persons, and these include
medical attention, the delivery of letters, and the work of housewives, and
finally some are contributed by non-mateiial factors such as friendships,
science, views and attitudes to life. In the last analysis all satisfactions
arise fiom services, whether the services are directly derived from personal, material or non-material resources" (*Agriculture and Economic
Progress*, Oxford University Press, 1952, p. 7).

TABLE XXVII

PERCENTAGE DISTRIBUTION OF GROSS DOMESTIC PRODUCT*
1950–1960†

Country	National income per capita in 1960 (in dollars)	Agriculture	Industry	Transportation	Services
1	2	3	4	5	6
United States	2286	5.7	39.6	6.5	48.2
Canada	1536	10.6	40.2	8.8	40.4
Sweden**	1377	8.0	50.0	..	42.0†††
New Zealand††	1285	22.8	31.2	9.1	36.9
Australia§	1236	20.8	29.4§§	..	..
United Kingdom	1071	5.1	48.2	8.6	38.1
Denmark	1036	17.7	37.5	9.3	35.5
Belgium	989	8.1	48.7	7.6	35.6
Norway	971	13.3	38.1	17.4	31.2
France‡	964	12.2	47.5	5.7	34.6
Germany (FR)‡	927	9.7	49.4	7.5	33.4
Finland	821	23.2	41.4	7.7	27.7
Netherlands‡‡	807	12.5	40.4	9.3	37.8
Austria	644	13.4	53.7	4.9	28.0
Italy	509	22.9	41.5	6.6	29.0
Japan	341	21.0	33.6***	8.7***	36.7

SOURCE : (For the second col.) : *U.N. Monthly Bulletin of Statistics*, April, 1962.

(For the rest) : *U.N. World Economic Survey*, 1961, table 2–1, p. 61.

   * Except for Japan and the United States, where net domestic product was used, data are at current factor cost except for Australia, Austria and France, where they are at current market price.

   † Average of 1950–51 and 1959–60.

   § Average of 1950-51–1951–52 and 1958–59–1959–60.

   §§ Excluding construction.

   †† Two year average of 1952–53 and 1954–55.

   ** 1956.

   ‡ Average of 1950–51 and 1958–59.

   ††† Including transportation.

   ‡‡ Average of 1950–51 and 1957–58.

   *** Utilities included in transportation.

Note : Countries are arranged in descending order of national income per capita in 1960.

goods traded internationally, there must be a stable or consistent exchange rate if conversion is to be meaningful ; in the context of the gamut of exchange controls, quantitative restrictions, tariff protection and transportation costs, this assumption is obviously unrealistic and misleading. Even if there were a stable 'normal' exchange rate, final values to domestic buyers of internationally traded goods would differ widely because of variations in domestic tax rates and distribution costs. For an example, the Survey points out on p. 81, that while, at current rates of exchange, the *per capita* product of India in real terms in 1960-61 *viz.*, Rs. 322 at 1958-59 prices, would come to approximately 68 dollars, in terms of its real purchasing power it would be equivalent to 150-200 dollars.

Notwithstanding these drawbacks, however, this method is the best that can be thought of.

Table XXVIII shows that in all countries an agricultural worker earns less than a non-agricultural worker. The figures relate to a point of time roughly thirty to forty years later than the one when Mihail Manoilesco wrote his book. During this period, in comparatively under-developed countries a proportion of population had further been transferred from primary to secondary and tertiary sectors. The proportion between agricultural and non-agricultural incomes, *viz.* 1 : 4.35, that obtained thirty years before, therefore, moved up to 1 : 3.

A feature common to nearly all the countries shown in the two tables is that the share of agriculture in the net domestic product falls notably short of its share of the labour force. This shortfall appears to be particularly marked in the less developed countries. As a corollary, the share of industry and service combined in the net domestic product exceeds that in the labour force for nearly all the countries shown. This also holds true for each of the two sectors separately, although to varying extents. The extent to which the percentage share of the net domestic product exceeds that of the labour force is generally much higher in the service than in the industry sector. This implies that in most of the countries under consideration, the net output per worker is highest in the service sector. The disparity is more pronounced in the less developed countries.

We arrive at the firm conclusion that a high average level of real income per head is usually associated with a high proportion

TABLE XXVIII

PERCENTAGE DISTRIBUTION OF LABOUR FORCE AND NET DOMESTIC PRODUCT BY ECONOMIC SECTOR OF SELECTED COUNTRIES

Country	Year	Agriculture		Industry		Services		Comparative Net Output per Worker By Sector (Agriculture=100)		Per capita product at factor cost for years 1952-54 averaged over population at mid-year 1953 (U.S. dollars)	Per capita national income in U.S. dollars 1960
		Labour Force	Net Domestic Product	Labour Force	Net Domestic Product	Labour Force	Net Domestic Product	Industry	Services		
1	2	3	4	5	6	7	8	9	10	11	12
AFRICA											
Union of South Africa	1946	49	14	21	33	30	53	570	650	300	834
AMERICA											
Canada	1951	19	16	36	38	45	46	130	130	1,310	1,536
U.S.A.	1950	13	7	37	40	50	53	190	130	1,870	2,286
Argentina	1947	27	19	30	29	43	52	130	170	460	378
Brazil	1950	61	35	13	18	26	47	240	310	230	108(1959)
Mexico	1950	61	20	17	24	22	56	450	770	220	278

ASIA											
India	1951	74	50	10	17	16	33	260	300	60	69
Japan	1954	45	22	22	31	33	47	280	300	190	341
Pakistan	1951	79	61	8	6	13	33	110	330	70	52
Thailand	1947	86	60	2	11	12	29	620	350	80	93
EUROPE											
Austria	1951	33	15	37	50	30	35	300	260	370	644
Germany (F.R.)	1954	21	11	46	56	33	33	230	190	510	927
Italy	1954	41	25	32	40	27	35	210	230	310	509
Netherlands	1947	20	12	34	36	46	52	180	190	500	807
Turkey	1950	86	54	7	13	7	33	280	780	210	164(1959)
United Kingdom	1951	5	5	49	47	46	48	95	105	780	1,071
U.S.S.R.	1950	50	N.A.	30	N.A.	20	N.A.	N.A.	N.A.	N.A.	747
OCEANIA											
New Zealand	1951	18	27	35	30	47	43	60	65	1 000	1,285

SOURCE for column 11 : *United Nations Statistical Paper, Per Capita National Product of Fifty-Five Countries* : 1952-54 (Series E No. 4), pages 8 and 9.

SOURCE for last column : Calculated on the basis of figures of National Income given in the *United Nations Monthly Bulletin of Statistics*, April 1962 (Vol. XVI, No. 4).

SOURCE for the rest : *International Labour Review*, May 1956, p. 158 for all countries, and p. 503 for the U.S.S.R. According to *UNO World Economic Survey*, 1961, p. 92, table 306, labour force in agriculture in the U.S.S.R. had come down to 42.2 per cent in 1959.

Note : The net national or domestic product represents that part of a nation's total output of goods and services which has become available for final consumption and capital formation. Commodities used up in the production of other commodities are excluded, because from the point of view of the economy as a whole, they are only intermediate products fed back into the system. When such commodities are included, it is called gross domestic product. It is derived from the combined efforts of the factors of production employed (labour, enterprise and capital), and thus corresponds to the sum of their remunerations (factor cost), that is, the sum of compensation of the employees, interest, rent and profits, and, for the nation as a whole is identical with the national income. Factor costs differ from market prices, because of the inclusion in the latter of indirect taxes (such as sales tax, customs duties, etc.) minus subsidies (which tend to reduce prices).

of the working population engaged in secondary and tertiary industries, and with the transfer of population away from primary industry. For various reasons, the chief being the difference between natural resources : man ratio in the various countries (and social and economic attitudes of the peoples concerned), the correlation between the growth of real income per head, on the one hand, and the growth of secondary and tertiary employment on the other is not uniform, and the co-efficient of correlation varies widely between country and country. Yet, of the broad validity of the generalisation itself there seems little doubt. *Land and mineral resources per head of the population being equal, and the quality of these resources and climatic conditions being similar, that country or region is comparatively more prosperous than others where more men are employed in non-agricultural activities than in agricultural.*

Explanation for relative inferiority of average agricultural incomes might be found, first, and chiefly in the law of supply and demand, or the low price elasticity of demand for many basic agricultural products. Except when a population is living at starvation levels, the demand for food or agricultural products as compared with that for non-agricultural products and services is low. While there is a limit to the consumption of the former, there is none to that of the latter. Increased supplies of an agricultural product, therefore, cause a more than proportionate fall in prices—other factors remaining unchanged—so that the gross receipts of farmers from sales of the product are reduced. Fall in prices resulting from over-production is not balanced for a considerable time, or, at least, immediately by reduction in production costs.

Secondly, agriculture, both in the sphere of production and marketing, has to work under comparatively higher competitive conditions than other sectors of the economy. Food being man's first necessity, its production has, since the dawn of civilisation, been his first or main concern and occupation and, despite development of other necessities and interests, with the exception of one or two countries, food production or agriculture still claims more workers than should be necessary. Also, in view of the fact that the varieties of food products can only be limited in number and there is not much difference in quality, there is little scope for exercise of ingenuity or innovations on the part of agricultural producers. While, man's wants other than for food being so diverse, secondary or tertiary production is capable of great differentiation and, therefore, commands a far wider market than primary or agricultural production. Also, further, while in the final analysis agricultural expansion has upper limits imposed by such natural factors as land and climate, manufacturing offers opportunities for potentially unlimited expansion.

Thirdly, annual average hours of work per person are definitely higher in industries and services than in agriculture owing to the seasonal nature of agricultural work and the large number of part-time family workers.

Fourthly, agriculture being a biological process, power and machinery are not such effective aids to man's capacity to produce in the sphere of agriculture as they are in that of manufacturing, which is a mechanical process. In order that an agricultural worker may produce as much as an industrial worker, large areas of land are required which are not available in most of the countries. Even if large areas are available, they cannot be so easily managed as large industrial units.

Fifthly, "The truth is that in manufacturing," says Ehrenfried Pfeiffer, "we are dealing with something primarily inorganic. Its general calculability as well as the calculability of its individual factors are all easily controlled. Agriculture, on the other hand, works with living factors, with the growth, health and diseases of plants and animals. It has to do with the enlivening of the soil. All of its factors are variables. In their individual characteristics they are independent of one another ; yet they unite to form a higher unity, a whole, that is to say, an organism.

"Raw materials are received by the factory and transformed into finished goods. Between these two poles in manufacturing—the pole of the raw materials on one side and of the finished commodity on the other—there stands the machine. The machine is not a variable factor except for deterioration. Agriculture, on the other hand, has for its one pole fertiliser and seed as raw material. It furnishes vegetables, grain, fruits, etc., as the finished product. But between the beginning and the end of agricultural production stands the life process (biological process). Economic thinking could form a correct idea of what takes place in agriculture only if this life process could be taken into its calculation."[4]

But this life-process is not easy to calculate. Just as animals

---

[4] Vide p. 606 preface to his book, *Soil Fertility, Renewal and Preservation*, 1947, Faber and Faber Ltd., 24, Russell Square, London.

and human beings, in respect of manifestations of their life, are not an arithmetical problem, so also soil. Just as the performance of a horse does not depend on feeding alone, and the gallons of milk that may flow out of a cow are not directly proportionate to the pounds of proteins and salts that may be fed to it, so is the productive capacity of a cultivated field also not directly proportionate to the amount of seed and fertiliser applied. A cultivated field is a biological organism like the horse or the cow and, as such, subject to organic laws. From this peculiarity flows the corollary that agriculture is liable to great hazards of weather, blight, plant disease, insect pests, flood and fire. Some of these hazards may be mitigated by science and the worst effects of them may be mitigated by organised efforts ; but it is clear that agriculture will always have to reckon with the unforeseeable and largely uncontrollable natural conditions which are the basis of its productive processes. Manufacturing does not suffer from any such hazards and its productive processes can be controlled by man.

Sixthly, there is a vast difference between industry and agriculture as regards their capacity of adjustment to changed conditions. Labour and capital in agriculture have a low mobility compared with industry. "The manufacturer can discharge labour, introduce new machinery, change his product, reduce costs, or shift to other fields, not easily but with comparative facility. The growth of a corporate organisation of horizontal or vertical consolidations, and trade cooperation, the development of a more generalised type of professional industrial management, and, above all, the availability of abundant liquid capital, together with the fundamental fact that in most cases industrial costs are an expression of the time involved in production and marketing, all have combined to make the adjustment to changed conditions in manufacturing relatively easy, and hasten the elimination[5] of a surplus of workers or enterprises in any field. In agriculture, on the other hand, with its numerous, scattered, largely unrelated establishments, its small proportion of hired labour, its relatively large fixed capital, its slow turnover, its combination of business and industry with a home and

---

[5] According to *Twentieth Century Socialism* by Socialist Union, Penguin Books Ltd., Harwordsworth, Middlesex, 1956, pp, 91-92, inefficient firms in British industry, however, have survived and not been eliminated, because labour, capital and demand have never been sufficiently mobile for choice to switch automatically from the worse to the better firm.

a way of life, its lack of corporate or other flexible forms of organisation, the perishability of its products, and the fundamental control of its productive process by natural processes in which time is an irreducible factor, adjustment is slow and difficult."[6] This difference in the two occupations leads to greater wastage of labour and capital in agriculture, and is reflected in the income derived from them.

Seventhly, the continuance in agricultural production of superfluous resources of labour and superseded resources of land and capital brings down their remuneration and thus leads to lower incomes in agriculture. Superflous labour continues in agriculture because of lack of an alternative occupation ; superseded land is taken under agriculture because of lack of better land ; and superseded or outmoded capital is not written off, primarily because of poverty of the agriculturist and, secondarily, because of lack of propensity to innovate on his part due to illiteracy. The fact that in the UK an agricultural worker earns the same rate of return as his countrymen in the other two sectors shows that a balance between employment opportunities has been reached, i.e. employment opportunities in the various sectors are readily available in this country to all those who seek them. The result is that those who remain in agriculture need not take to marginal or sub-marginal land, and there is parity in the two incomes—agricultural and non-agricultural. In other words, from the point of view of economic development, an ideal situation has been realised in the UK. In Canada also the 'rural exodus' is nearly completed. The benefits deriving from a movement of agricultural workers into more productive occupations elsewhere in the economy are largely exhausted. Incidentally, it is this situation—parity of incomes between various classes—that a just society should aim at in any country. Of the 18 countries mentioned in Table XXVIII New Zealand is the only exception[6a] where agriculture or primary occupations

---

[6] *The Condition of Agriculture in the United States and Measures for its Improvement* (p. 174) : A Report by Businessmen's Commission on Agriculture appointed in 1926.

[6a] There are some other countries, not given in the table, where the share of industry in total output is low, yet their per capita incomes are relatively high. This is due to their fortunate natural resource endowment ; through production and export of primary commodities, they have exploited the strong advantage which they enjoy in international trade as a means of raising their national income. In recent history, the clearest examples are the petroleum exporting countries like Venezuela, Trinidad and Saudi Arabia.

are more profitable than those falling in the secondary or tertiary sectors, the main reason being that in this country the conditions are exceptionally favourable for livestock production for export. We should not be surprised, therefore, if, in course of time, workers from the secondary and tertiary sectors shift to the primary sector in New Zealand.

The question why a farmer still stays in agriculture—why, barring a country or two, diversion of workers from agricultural pursuits with lower incomes to non-agricultural pursuits with higher incomes has not proceeded or proceeded fast enough to achieve income parity between agricultural and other production —has already been partly answered. The answer is, in part, provided by some of those very reasons which are responsible for smaller incomes to agricultural producers than to non-agricultural producers. Alternative opportunities of employment are not available or easily available to the farmers in every country. Where such opportunities in manufacturing and service industries are ample, at least, the wage-worker, or a farmer's son, whose net contribution to the value of the farm's production is of a value about equal to the income of a wage-earner, if he is educated, usually makes no delay in quitting the farm. The farmer, more often than not, lacks resources in fluid capital (savings or realized assets), which keeps him tied to the village or agriculture. Land and buildings that he possesses are immovable, and largely unrealizable assets. Sentimental attachment of the farmer apart, they cannot always be sold at remunerative prices. And a farmer, on moving to a non-agricultural employment in an urban centre, experiences a wrench which an industrial worker moving from one industry or factory to another does not. He faces a complete break with the way of life he was hitherto leading—with the family and social ties rooted in the village and neighbourhood.

A farmer also stays in agriculture because of the self-sufficient nature of his profession. He is practically sure of raising, at least, as much as he needs for maintaining himself and his family, and this fact makes him, to a large extent, independent of the existing economic conditions and enables him to defy the trend of economic forces for a long period. Moreover, in certain countries like India, the people continue in agriculture because they are not, in general, inspired by any urge to improve their economic conditions. Even if they are so minded, the farmers, because of their illiteracy and lack of knowledge of ways of the modern world, do not know where to seek better prospects, granting that any are available. Further, many persons prefer to enter or remain in agriculture, because of the non-material satisfactions that rural life affords or is supposed to afford.

However, the reasons for difference in the two kinds of income and for the farmer to stick to his land being what they may, industry and commerce today are found, by experience, to enjoy a superiority over agriculture as a source of income. That is why the government of every advanced country has tried to develop its own industries and manufactures and to find increasing employment for its nationals in businesses and vocations other than production of raw materials.

Figures for various countries given in Tables XXIX and XXX taken from two different sources, can be quoted in evidence.

These two tables only show the shifts in employment in the three sectors of the economy of the countries mentioned, at various points of time, but not the corresponding national income per capita. Were the figures available, they would show that these countries, maybe, with one or two exceptions, possess a progressive economy—an economy in which the overall production per head of material things has *gradually* increased during the last century. Table XXVIII depicts the situation both regarding employment and income in the three sectors of the economy in the various countries, but only as it existed in a particular year, or at a particular point of time. Table XXXI however, gives percentage figures both of employment and income in agriculture (corresponding figures of other sectors combined being deducible by subtraction from 100) relating to three countries, viz. the United Kingdom, Sweden and the United States, over a long period or at various points of time— countries for which alone such figures were available. This table illustrates that as the percentage of the working population engaged in agriculture in a country gradually declines and, therefore, the percentage of those engaged in industries and services rises, so the proportionate contribution of agriculture to economic welfare steadily declines and the economy progresses, that is, the national income per capita or the standard of living rises (despite population growth).

Importance of agriculture as a source of income in these countries had declined relatively as their standard of living has risen. Coale

TABLE XXIX

VARIATION IN PERCENTAGE DISTRIBUTION OF WORKING POPULATION OF SELECTED COUNTRIES

	Year	Primary	Secondary	Tertiary
United States				
	1870	54.9	20.5	24.6
	1880	51.6	22.0	26.4
	1890	45.3	23.7	31.0
	1900	40.6	24.8	34.6
	1910	34.2	28.5	37.3
	1920	30.2	30.3	39.5
	1930	23.9	28.9	47.2
	1940	21.3	29.2	49.5
Australia				
	1871	43.9	26.5	29.6
	1881	38.6	29.8	31.6
	1891	32.2	30.6	37.2
	1901	32.8	26.9	40.3
	1911	30.3	28.8	40.9
	1921	25.9	31.5	42.6
	1933	27.0	26.0	47.0
	1939	23.1	31.8	45.1
	1947	18.6	35.8	45.6
Great Britain				
	1870	18.5	45.1	36.4
	1880	15.9	44.4	38.7
	1890	15.5	38.5	46.0
	1900	14.2	40.5	45.3
	1910	14.6	39.4	46.0
	1920	14.4	40.3	45.3
	1930	12.0 (5.6)	38.3	49.7
	1938	11.1 (4.6)	41.6	47.3
Belgium				
	1880	24.5	38.7	36.8
	1890	18.2	40.5	41.3
	1900	16.7	43.9	39.4
	1910	17.6	50.1 (6.2)	32.3
	1920	16.0	49.5 (7.1)	34.5
	1930	13.9	50.0 (6.2)	36.1
Canada				
	1901	45.7	25.4	28.9
	1911	42.4	24.2	33.4
	1931	34.5	26.3	39.2
	1941	31.5	29.5	39.0
	1945	28.6	31.3	40.1
	1946	27.4	32.5	40.1

TABLE XXIX—(*contd.*)

	Year	Primary	Secondary	Tertiary
New Zealand				
	1881	40.3	29.5	30.2
	1886	38.3	31.3	30.4
	1891	37.0	28.7	34.3
	1896	37.0	28.6	34.4
	1901	35.2	27.5	37.3
	1911	30.1	28.4	41.5
	1921	28.9	25.5	45.6
	1936	27.0	26.8	46.2
	1945	23.2	30.6	46.2
France				
	1866	43.0	38.0	19.0
	1901	33.1	42.0	24.9
	1921	29.4	36.1	34.5
	1926	26.1	39.5	34.5
	1931	24.5	41.0 (2.4)	34.5
	1936	24.2	37.1 (2.0)	38.7
	1946	20.6	34.8 (1.6)	44.6
Netherlands				
	1899	28.5	35.9	35.6
	1909	25.7	36.1	38.2
	1920	22.9	37.8	39.3
	1930	22.4	37.6	40.0
	1938	19.7	34.2	46.1
	1947	15.9	33.3	50.8
Germany				
	1882	41.9	38.9	19.2
	1895	35.7	48.2	21.5
	1907	23.8	50.6 (4.3)	25.6
	1925	17.8	48.9 (3.1)	33.3
	1933	16.9	47.4 (2.7)	35.7
Denmark				
	1901	42.4	27.6	30.0
	1911	37.3	27.6	35.1
	1921	31.7	28.8	39.5
	1930	30.6	30.1	39.3
	1940	28.9	32.6	38.5
Norway				
	1875	48.8	24.1	27.1
	1890	45.2	26.7	28.1
	1900	37.1	31.6	31.3
	1910	37.5	29.5	33.0
	1920	34.1	31.4 (1.6)	34.5
	1930	34.0	28.1 (1.1)	37.9

TABLE XXIX (*contd.*)

	Year	Primary	Secondary	Tertiary
	1939	38.9	23.0	38.1
	1946	35.4	26.6	38.0
Japan				
	1872	84.8	4.8	10.4
	1887	78.0	9.1	12.9
	1912	62.8	17.1	20.1
	1920	55.5	20.0	24.5
	1930	51.3	18.5	30.2
Italy				
	1871	51.9	32.6	15.5
	1881	46.8	36.4	16.8
	1901	50.0	30.0	20.0
	1911	46.7	31.9	21.4
	1921	47.7	29.0	23.3
	1931	43.0	32.5	24.5
	1936	41.1	31.7	27.2
Switzerland				
	1888	32.9	44.6	22.5
	1900	27.6	47.0	25.4
	1910	22.8	48.2	29.0
	1920	22.1	46.4	31.5
	1930	21.7	44.6	33.7
	1941	20.9	45.8	33.3
Sweden				
	1900	49.7	20.9	29.4
	1910	40.8	30.4 (0.7)	28.8
	1920	34.9	35.0 (0.9)	30.1
	1930	30.5	35.3 (1.3)	34.2
	1940	26.5	37.1 (1.2)	36.4
India				
	1881	60.2	28.1	11.7
	1911	63.3	15.8	20.6
	1921	64.4	14.5	21.1
	1931	64.2	13.6	22.2
Russia				
	1926	81.0	5.6	13.4
	1939	57.8	17.2	25.0

SOURCE—*The Conditions for Economic Progress* by Colin Clark. 1951

Note 1—Except Great Britain figures for 'Mining' are included in the secondary sector and wherever available, are shown in brackets.

Note 2—Figures in this table cannot be compared strictly with corresponding figures given in the next table.   In fact, figures from no two sources are strictly comparable for reason of difference in concepts and methods as well as in institutional arrangements for collection of the statistical material.

TABLE XXX

TRENDS IN DISTRIBUTION OF LABOUR FORCE BY ECONOMIC SECTOR IN TWELVE COUNTRIES

Country	Year	Labour force (in thousands)				Percentage of Labour Force in		
		agri-culture	industry	services	total	agricul-ture*	indus-try†	ser-vices‡
France	1866	8,535	4,384	3,724	16,643	51	26	23
	1881	7,890	4,444	4,210	16,544	48	27	25
	1896	8,501	5,660	4,774	18,935	45	30	25
	1906	8,855	6,338	5,528	20,721	43	30	27
	1921	9,024	6,662	6,034	21,720	41	31	28
	1936	7,204	6,379	6,677	20,260	36	31	33
	1954	5,280	7,154	6,786	19,220	28	37	35
Germany**	1882	7,133	5,990	3,372	16,495	43	37	20
	1907	8,556	9,982	6,099	24,637	35	40	25
	1925	9,762	13,478	8,769	32,009	31	42	27
	1939	8,934	14,418	10,917	34,269	26	42	32
Germany (F.R.)	1929	5,274	7,347	5,256	17,877	30	41	29
	1939	5,399	8,424	6,232	20,065	27	42	31
	1954	5,076	11,424	8,142	24,643	21	46	33
Great Britain	1881	1,638	6,372	4,785	12,795	13	50	37
	1891	1,582	7,176	5,888	14,646	11	49	40
	1901	1,385	7,158	6,851	15,394	9	47	44
	1911	1,550	9,023	7,269	17,842	9	51	40
	1921	1,381	9,142	8,236	18,759	7	49	44
	1931	1,258	9,717	9,919	20,894	6	47	47
	1951	1,116	11,086	10,281	22,482	5	49	46
Italy	1881	8,600	3,850	2,600	15,050	57	26	17
	1901	9,443	3,879	2,640	15,962	59	24	17
	1911	9,086	4,387	2,929	16,402	55	27	18
	1921	10,264	4,508	3,659	18,431	56	24	20
	1931	9,356	4,924	4,001	18,341	51	27	22
	1936	8,843	5,375	4,128	18,346	48	29	23
	1954	8,468	6,454	5,615	20,537	41	32	27

SOURCE :—*International Labour Review*, May, 1956, pp. 508-09.
* "Agriculture" comprises agriculture, forestry, hunting and fishing.
† "Industry" comprises mining and quarrying, manufacturing, construction and utilities (electricity, gas and water).
‡ "Services" comprises commerce, transport, storage and communications, as well as public and private services.
** Frontiers of 1934.

TABLE XXX—(contd.)

Country	Year	Labour force (in thousands)				Percentage of Labour Force in		
		agri-culture	industry	services	total	agricul-ture*	indus-try†	ser-vices‡
United States	1870	6,910	2,830	3,185	12,925	53	22	25
	1880	8,682	4,139	4,571	17,392	50	24	26
	1890	10,121	5,973	7,225	23,318	43	26	31
	1900	11,122	7,894	10,058	29,073	38	27	35
	1910	11,834	11,622	13,916	37,371	32	31	37
	1920	11,719	13,951	16,763	42,434	28	33	39
	1930	10,753	15,498	21,242	47,492	23	33	45
	1940	9,317	17,560	23,197	50,074	19	35	46
	1950	7,331	21,623	29,488	58,442	13	37	50
Australia	1911	480	668	790	1,939	25	34	41
	1921	532	790	974	2,296	23	34	43
	1933	588	935	1,150	2,673	22	35	43
	1947	498	1,140	1,368	3,006	17	38	45
Egypt	1907	2,440	380	605	3,425	71	11	18
	1917	2,626	429	949	4,003	65	11	24
	1927	3,525	556	1,169	5,250	67	11	22
	1937	4,308	610	1,177	6,095	71	10	19
	1947	4,398	835	1,495	6,729	65	13	22
India	1931††100,037		15,352	25,300	141,035	71	11	18
	1951	103,014	13,733	22,592	139,339§	74	10	16
Japan	1920	14,661	5,721	6,350	26,733	55	21	24
	1930	14,687	5,951	8,411	29,049	51	20	29
	1954	18,060	8,880	12,990	39,930	45	22	33
Mexico	1900	3,177	934	401	4,512	70	21	9
	1910	3,596	1,106	436	5,138	70	22	8
	1921	3,488	561	454	4,504	77	13	10
	1930	3,626	743	587	4,957	73	15	12
	1940	3,831	746	1,117	5,694	67	13	20
	1950	4,824	1,319	1,774	7,917	61	17	22
Sweden	1910	1,016	565	535	2,116	48	27	25
	1920	1,058	808	699	2,565	41	32	27
	1930	1,041	927	904	2,872	36	32	32
	1940	864	1,070	1,032	2,966	29	36	35
	1950	632	1,267	1,183	3,082	21	41	38
Union of South Africa	1911	2,186	577	935	3,698	59	16	25
	1921	3,018	547	666	4,231	71	13	16
	1946	2,418	1,026	1,466	4,910	49	21	30

†† Pre-partition India.   § Including earning dependents.

TABLE XXXI

RELATIONSHIP BETWEEN NATIONAL INCOME AND AGRICULTURAL EMPLOYMENT

United Kingdom					Sweden						United States				
period	population	national income at factor cost	index no. of persons occupied in agri.	% of agricultural income to national income	period	population	national income	agrarian population as % of total	% of agricultural income to national income		period	population	national income	% of gainful workers employed in agriculture	% of agricultural income to national income
1867-69	100* (2,97,50,000)	100 (962 £m)	100	20.2	1861-65	100 (3993,000)	100 (773 m. kronor)	74.3	49.1	Average of	1819 and 1829	100 (212,52,000)	100 (1134 $m)	72.3 (1820)	45.9
1870-76	108	113	95	18.5	1866-70	104	109	72.9	51.8		1829 and 1839	134	139	70.8 (1830)	45.2
1877-85	117	117	88	15.4	1871-75	107	149	71.1	49.8		1839 and 1849	183	212	69.0 (1840)	42.4
1886-93	126	136	86	11.3	1876-80	113	160	68.7	48.8		1849 and 1859	243	330	64.8 (1850)	38.4
1894-1903	136	168	80	8.3	1881-85	115	164	66.2	46.0		1859 and 1869	312	562	60.2 (1860)	34.5
1904-10	148	202	78	7.7	1886-90	119	160	63.3	42.6		1869-78	395	700	53.5 (1870)	31.8
1911-13	153	237	78	7.1	1891-95	121	186	60.1	40.9	Decade averages	1879-88	503	744	50.0 (1880)	20.6
1920-22	158	502	80	7.8	1896-1900	126	232	56.5	35.9		1889-98	618	1100	43.4 (1890)	24.3
1924-29	152	417	55	4.3	1901-05	130	266	53.3	32.8		1899-1908	740	1831	38.2 (1900)	22.3
1930-34	156	387	53	4.3	1906-10	131	351	49.9	31.2		1909-18	883	347	31.6 (1910)	21.9
1935-39	159	472	51	4.1	1911-15	141	444	47.3	31.2		1919-28	1020	6541	27.6 (1920)	14.8
					1916-20	145	1023	44.9	30.0		1929-38	1130	5518	21.9 (1930)	11.4
					1921-25	150	909	42.9	21.1						
					1926-30	152	988	41.2	18.2						

SOURCE—*Agriculture and Economic Progress* by Dr. E. M. Ojala, Oxford University Press, London, Geoffry Cumberledge, 1952 (Condensed from tables No. 6, 12, 20, 30, 31, 46, 49, 50, 55).
* These figures relate to period 1860-69.
Note : 'Agriculture' in all the countries includes horticulture, forestry and fishing.

and Hoover refer to this phenomenon in the economy of the developed countries as follows :

As per capita output rises, the output of agriculture rises less than in proportion to total national output : while the output of industry, and the non-agricultural part of the economy generally, rises faster than overall output. This tendency has been considered sufficiently consistent to permit the statement as a quantitative empirical 'rule'. For example, Egbert De Vries has derived from the data in 34 countries the generalisation that for every 10 per cent increase in per capita real income, the fraction of national income arising from agriculture drops by 1.5 percentage points (vide *The Balance Between Agriculture and Industry in Economic Development*, a paper for the 4th Meeting of Technicians of the Central Bank of the American Continent, May 1954).[7]

The percentage share of agriculture in the labour force in all the countries mentioned in tables XXIX and XXX has shown a downward trend, and that in the industry and service sectors an upward trend, over a long period. In the case of India, however, the proportion of workers in the primary sector since 1881 has steadily increased, and that in the secondary and tertiary sectors combined, has steadily declined—a phenomenon contrary to the experience of all the other countries considered here and one that should cause concern to every lover of India. What is most alarming is the fact that *implemantation of two Five-Year Plans in the 1950's has brought about little or no difference in percentage of workers in the primary sector in 1961 as compared with 1951.* According to a statement No. 18 on page XXV of Paper No. 1, 1961 *Census of India*, the relevant figures are as follows :

TABLE XXXII

PERCENTAGE DISTRIBUTION OF WORKERS IN GENERAL AND BY SEX IN INDIA IN 1951 AND 1961

Year		Primary (including mining)	Secondary	Tertiary
1951	P	72.12	10.62	17.26
	Male	69.08	11.59	19.33
	Female	79.57	8.26	12.17
1961	P	72.28	11.70	16.02
	Male	67.98	12.68	19.34
	Female	81.58	9.59	8.83

[7] *Population and Economic Development in Low-income Countries*, Oxford University Press, 1959, p. 121.

Things in India, however, were not so bad before. It was not always a poor, undeveloped country depending solely on agriculture. The Indian Industrial Commission of 1916-18 presided over by Sir Thomas Holland opened its report with the statement :

At a time when Western Europe, the birthplace of the modern industrial system, was inhabited by uncivilised tribes, India was famous for the wealth of her rulers and for the high artistic skill of her craftsmen. And even at a much later period, when merchant adventurers from the West made their first appearance in India, the industrial development of this country was at any rate not inferior to that of the more advanced European nations.[8]

It is to the policy of our erstwhile British masters that the plight of the country can largely be traced. Indian handicrafts and industries were systematically rooted out by the British manufacturers who had the state power in the country at their disposal. When the Britishers arrived in India, it was not "a purely agricultural country ; it was an important manufacturing centre, exporting finely worked merchandise to Europe, Arabia, Egypt and China. Delicate silks, muslins, laces, embroidery, jewellery and rugs were sent abroad. Pere Vatue, in his history, says that India was rising out of her Middle Ages, and her relative prosperity was the product of transitional economy, moving from a closed medieval system into a nascent factory capitalism. Rural artisans were coming to the cities to work in factories, and laying the foundations for an industrial development which could raise the national income and living standards ever higher. There were still occasional famines, a heritage of the medieval period, just as there were in Europe. But famine was on the way out, and it certainly would have disappeared with the development of industrialism just as it did in Western Europe. It was the intervention of the English with their insatiably greedy traders that violently cut short India's economic revolution and forced the country back to a medieval economy and into a permanent starvation."[9]

To give an example of the foreigner's greed : weavers, silk-winders and other artisans and manufacturers of Bengal in the latter part of the 18th century were often required by the East

[8] *Indian Industrial Commission Report*, p. 6.
[9] Vide *Geography of Hunger* by Josue De Castro 1952, Victor Gollancz Ltd., London, pp. 157-58.

India Company to supply a fixed quantity of goods, at a fixed time and at a fixed price which was 15 to 40 per cent lower than the market rates. According to a letter written by an English merchant, William Bolts, which was published in 1772, "Weavers, also, upon their inability to perform such agreements as have been forced upon them by the Company's agents, universally known in Bengal by the name of *Mutchulcahs*, have had their goods seized and sold on the spot to make good the deficiency ; and the winders of raw silk, called *Nagoads*, have been treated also with such injustice, that instances have been known of their cutting off their thumbs to prevent their being forced to wind silk."[10]

Not the industries alone, but agriculture also declined in Bengal under this system ; for, the manufacturers of the country were largely peasants as well.

"For the Ryots," Bolts goes on to say, "who are generally both landholders and manufacturers, by the oppressions of *Gomastahs* in harassing them for goods, are frequently rendered incapable of improving their lands, and even of paying their rents ; for which, on the other hand, they are again chastised by the officers of the revenue, and not infrequently have by those harpies been necessitated to sell their children in order to pay their rents, or otherwise obliged to fly the country."

Bengal was thus rendered a vast scene of oppression. It was this state of affairs which led Mir Kasim to revolt.

Such rapacity notwithstanding, the silk and cotton goods of India up to earlier part of 19th century could be sold for a profit in the British market at a price from 50 to 60 per cent lower than those manufactured in England. Consequently duties as high as 70 to 80 per cent of their value were imposed on the Indian imports. When even high duties did not deter English nobility from buying superior Indian goods their use was declared a penal offence.[11] Says H. H. Wilson, historian of India :

Had this not been the case, had not such prohibitory duties and decrees existed, the mills of Paisley and Manchester would have been stopped in their outset, and could scarcely have been again

---

[10] *Economic History of British India* by Romesh Dutt, London, Vol. I, pp. 26-27.

[11] For reference see *Bharat Men Angrezi Rajya* by Sri Sunder Lal, pp. 900-03, Vol. II, 1938, Onkar Press, Allahabad.

set in motion, even by the power of steam. They were created by the sacrifice of the Indian manufacture. Had India been independent, she would have retaliated, would have imposed prohibitive duties upon British goods and would thus have preserved her own productive industry from annihilation. This act of self-defence was not permitted her ; she was at the mercy of the stranger. British goods were forced upon her without paying any duty, and the foreign manufacturer employed the arm of political injustice to keep down and ultimately strangle a competitor with whom she could not have contended on equal terms.[12]

Even if the British Government did not discriminate against the Indian fabrics they would not have, perhaps, in the long run, been able to compete with mill-made products of Britain, unless specifically protected by the state. On the other hand, if India were free she would have, in all likelihood, profited from the lessons of the Industrial Revolution, equally well with Western nations. It is now all a matter of speculation. The fact remains that, along with the spread and tightening of the British stranglehold on the country, our industry began to decline and was stifled. The result was that the class of artisans was completely ruined, and the nation's economic strength shattered. It was not only the old manufacturing towns and centres that were laid waste, and their population driven to overcrowd the villages ; it was above all the very basis of our old village economy, the union of agriculture and domestic industry, that received its mortal blow. The millions of ruined artisans and craftsmen, spinners, weavers, potters, tanners, smelters, smiths, alike from the towns and from the villages, had no alternative save to crowd into agriculture. Also, many an Indian peasant who practised weaving or other handicrafts in the slack period of agriculture, found his subsidiary occupation gone for ever. In this way India was forcibly transferred, from being a country of combined agriculture and industry, into an agricultural colony of British manufacturing capitalism. This conclusion is illustrated by Table XXXIII.

It will be found that in 1931 only 26.0 per cent of the non-agricultural workers were engaged in their traditional occupations and 68.0 per cent of those who had given it up, or 50.0 per cent of the total, had taken to agriculture and other allied pursuits. "The proportion of artisans in India", says Josue De Castro, "fell

[12] Romesh Dutt, *op. cit.*, pp. 262-63.

TABLE XXXIII

CASTES AND OCCUPATIONS IN INDIA IN 1931

Caste, Tribe or Race	Earners and working dependents	Those who returned their traditional caste occupation as principal means of livelihood	Those who returned exploitation of animal and vegetation as principal means of livelihood
1. Barhai	760,060	336,176	283,300
2. Bhangi	555,529	310,983	118,838
3. Bhat	50,186	3,871	31,324
4. Chamar	5,077,307	386,197	3,558,939
5. Darzi	212,359	123,687	38,727
6. Dhobi	951,058	436,699	345,881
7. Jhinwar	933,368	152,499	443,996
8. Khatik	103,582	22,258	51,609
9. Khatri	185,173	92,992	17,712
10. Kumhar	995,300	369,023	390,887
11. Lohar	763,482	270,453	268,014
12. Momin	1,234,393	409,656	520,340
13. Mali	360,938	15,061	248,823
14. Nai	1,079,229	502,552	351,164
15. Od, etc.	50,620	23,339	9,383
16. Pinjara	1,098	268	231
17. Sansi	10,664	402	3,991
18. Sonar, etc.	274,134	166,256	53,178
19. Tanti and Koshti	427,344	112,571	104,915
20. Teli and Chanchi	1,783,788	383,465	935,926
Total	15,809,612	4,118,408	7,877,178

SOURCE: *Census of India*, 1931, Vol. I, India, Part II—Imperial Tables, pp. 416-17.

during the nineteenth century, from 25 percent of the population to 10 per cent while the population of agriculturists rose from 60 to 75 per cent."[13]

It is in these facts and figures largely that lies hidden the cause of our poverty. It consists not so much in scarcity of natural resources as in the pattern of our economy where too many people are living on land but do not find full employment thereon, and produce little. Apart from the political circumstances that obtained in the country since the beginning of the eighteenth century, this pattern is traceable, in a great part, to our social and economic attitudes and a fatalistic outlook on life in general— to absence of conditions which, despite far less natural resources per head of population than India, made Japan reduce the percentage of agricultural workers from 45 in 1954 to 36 in 1960 and increase the per capita income of 190 dollars in 1953 to 341 dollars in 1960. Whereas India stands practically where it did before.

"At the root of much of the poverty of the people of India, and of the risks to which they are exposed in seasons of scarcity," the First Famine Commission, 1880, rightly diagnosed, "lies the unfortunate circumstance that agriculture forms almost the sole occupation of the mass of the population, and no remedy for present evils can be complete which does not include the introduction of diversity of occupations through which the surplus population may be drawn from agricultural pursuits and led to find the means of subsistence in manufactures or some such employments."

It is thus agreed between all economists and well-wishers of the country that measures for diversification of employment and production have to be taken, that industrial or non-agricultural outlets have to be provided for a good many of our people. The question now is : what form this diversified production or industrial development should take and how far we should go, rather how far it is possible for us to go, on the path to non-agricultural employments. There are two schools of thought on this question : the one contends that we should rely chiefly on large-scale mechanised industry and, the other, that small-scale decentralised industry geared in with agriculture should predominate. The latter would lay great emphasis on handicrafts and cottage or village industries.

The advocates of the first school contend that the first place

[13] Josue De Castro, op. cit., p. 169.

has to be given to the establishment of heavy industries because
only then the foundation for industrial growth and economic revolution could be laid. At the initial stage heavy industries brought
about upsets. The machines displaced persons following old professions and unemployment resulted. But, it is contended, only
through big industry could vast employment opportunities be
ultimately created. This school is best represented by Prime Minister Jawahar Lal Nehru. In January, 1956, he expressed himself
before the National Development Council as follows :

If you want India to industrialise and to go ahead you must go
to the root and the base and build up that root and base on which
you will build up the structure of industrial growth. Therefore, it
is the heavy industries that count ; nothing else counts, except
as a balancing factor, which is, of course, important. We want
planning for heavy-machine-making industries and heavy industries;
we want industries that will make heavy machines and we should set
about them as rapidly as possible because it takes time.[14]

According to the advocates of the second school, heavy industries will occupy the least part of the vast national economic activity which will mainly be carried on in the villages. It was no
less a person than Mahatma Gandhi, the *zeitgeist* of India's awakening, who first expounded this view-point. "If I can convert the
country to my point of view," said he, "the social order of the
future will be based predominantly on the *charkha* and all it implies. It will include every thing that promotes the well-being of
the villagers. I do visualise electricity, ship-building, iron works,
machine-making and the like, existing side by side with village
handicrafts. But the order of dependence will be reversed. Hitherto
the industrialisation has been so planned as to destroy the villages
and the village crafts. In the state of the future it will subserve the
villages and their crafts. I do not share the socialist belief that
centralisation of the necessaries of life will conduce to the common
welfare when the centralised industries are planned and owned
by the state."[15]

On another occasion, he said : "Instead of production by the

[14] Vide p. 174 of WS Woytinsky's *India : The Awakening Giant*,
Harper & Brothers, New York, 1957.
[15] *Why the Constructive Programme* ? an Indian National Congress
Publication, New Delhi, 1948, p .19.

fewest possible hands through the aid of highly complicated machinery at a particular centre, I would have individual production in people's own homes multiplied by a million of times."

CHAPTER FOURTEEN

Case for Industrialism

THERE HAS always been lack of equilibrium, rather, a sort of antagonism between the cities and the countryside. This is particularly so in our land where the gulf of inequality between the capitalist class and the working-class pales into insignificance before that which exists between the peasant farmer in our village and the middle-class town-dweller. India is really two worlds—rural and urban. The relationship between the countryside and the cities is, therefore, a vital problem to us.

There is no example which India can exactly follow in solving the problem of reconciling the development of the countryside with growth of industries. Britain had, consequent on the Industrial Revolution of the 18th century, destroyed its countryside in the effort to industrialize herself. So had the Soviet Union, consequent on the Bolshevik Revolution of 1917. Will India succeed where both Capitalism and Communism have failed?

Advocates of industrialism plead that in this modern age advances in science and technology have made it possible for man to produce the means of satisfaction of his wants with minimum expenditure of energy. It has increased man's power to produce wealth a ten-fold, nay, a hundred-fold what it was previously. At this stage it is unthinkable that we in India remain content with, or continue to have, an economy where her natural physical resources remain unutilised while the nation leads a life of want and misery —that it will be an act of utter folly on our part if we refuse to make use of the power that science and technology have placed at the disposal of man for betterment of his lot. India is one of the poorest countries of the world and it is through intensive industrialisation alone—through marriage of man with the machine— that her poverty can be eradicated.

All former civilisations and cultures were fundamentally based on slave labour. The Greek poets and philosophers had the leisure to discuss abstruse subjects for long hours only because there was slave labour to work on their behalf and create an economic 'surplus' to maintain them while they engaged in these abstruse discussions. Today in the machines we have our slaves. Scientific technique has today reached a stage where we can, if we would, organise plenty and leisure for all—yes, 'freedom from want' for all.[1]

In the developed countries great strides have been made in the techniques of manufacture. There, automation is ushering in a new revolution in industry. The average American worker produces nearly eight times as much as the British worker, and five to six times compared to the Italian worker. We at present stand no comparison with the productive capacity of the workers of these industrially advanced countries. Productivity is the ratio of the goods or services produced, *i.e.* output of wealth, to the input of resources required for the production. The resources include men, power, capital, machines and raw materials. We possess men and materials. The former need to be supplied power, capital and machines so that out of the latter—raw materials—goods may be produced which will wipe out our poverty.

Advocates of industrialism point to the immense wealth and high standards of living in all the industrialised countries of the world, particularly, the example of the USA, as a complete and irresistible proof of their contention. Judging from the percentage of the people engaged in the secondary and tertiary sectors, next to United Kingdom, USA is the most non-agricultural or highest industrialised country and with only seven per cent of the world's land area and six per cent of its population, turns out about one-third of the world's total goods and one-half of all manufactured products.[1a] Contrary to general belief, however, she exports only five per cent of this vast produce and consumes the rest herself, excepting, of course, what she sets aside for capital formation (which will further increase national income in the years ahead). That is why the USA enjoyes the highest material standards of living yet known anywhere. An average factory worker now works only 40 hours a week and earns $2 per hour. And these standards are rising every year ! In 1949 the per capita income in the USA stood

[1] Dr. P. S. Loknathan's article entitled, "A Matter of Bottlenecks" published in *The Eastern Economist*, New Delhi, dated 30th July 1943, p. 378.
[1a] According to Table 2.6 given in UN's *World Economic Survey*, 1961, while the percentage share of the USA in world's manufacturing output rose from 35.7 in 1938 to 51.2 in 1950, it came down to 43.8 in 1960.

at 1,433 dollars ; the average for 1952-54 stood at 1,870 dollars.

According to a news-item there was a rise of 5.5 per cent in the personal income of Americans in the first ten months of the year :

Washington, Nov. 18—Personal income of Americans during the first ten months of 1957 was at an annual rate of 342,500 million dollars—17,500 million dollars above the corresponding period a year ago, the Commerce Department reported today.

The Department said this represented a 5.5 per cent rise in personal income which embraces wages and salaries, net income on business proprietorships, dividends, interest and rents received from real estate and other kinds of individual income.

The October income flow this year was put at 11,500 million dollars—3.5 per cent above October last year—UPI—AFP.[2]

And lest we forget—it is the introduction of machines that has increased the productivity of the USA, and the current emphasis on automation will increase it still further. In 1850, 65 per cent of total power requirements were supplied by men and animals. Today, the figure is 2 per cent, power machines providing the remaining 98 per cent.

Cannot India, it is asked, which also has rich material resources and potentially a much larger internal market, provide the same living standards to her people through large-scale mechanised industries ? Thirty-six per cent of the employees in large-scale industrial establishments of USA in 1947 were working in establishments with more than 1,000 employees each and an average labour strength of 2,423.

In this fast-changing world in which countries are coming closer and closer no nation can live a life of seclusion. We must have commerce and intercourse with other peoples. Not to have large industries of our own, therefore, is to make our economy subservient to the economy of foreign countries. Further, large-scale industry alone can provide the means of national security and independence.

Large-scale industrialisation, it is contended, will also help solve our population problem and that in two ways. First : the majority of industries and services in the modern community including most forms of large-scale manufacture, transport, postal communications, banking, insurance and the like are quite specifically benefited by increasing population. Colin Clark considers that

[2] *Pioneer*, Lucknow, dated November 11, 1957.

these industries "work under the law of increasing returns rather
than the law of diminishing returns. The law of increasing returns
prevails in any industry where, as a consequence of increased scale
of output, we can expect to obtain increasing returns per unit of
labour or other economic resources employed. In fact, most of the
economic operations of a modern community are carried out in
such a way that, if there were an increase in the population and the
size of the market, organisation would become more economical and
productivity per head would increase, not decrease. Without the
large and densely settled populations of North America and Western
Europe, most modern industries would be working under great
difficulties and at very high costs—it is doubtful, indeed, whether
they would have come into existence at all".[3]

It is pointed out that, when Britain stood on the threshold of
industrial revolution at the end of the 18th century, she was regarded as grossly over-populated. But not only did capitalism or
industrialism absorb the existing hands : it positively resulted in a
tremendous upsurge of population. Great Britain's population
greatly increased in the 19th century ; similar phenomenon was
observed in the early stages of industrial development in Germany
and Japan. Comparing the conditions of India and European countries, the British Communist leader, Mr. Rajani Palme Dutt, indirectly refers to the population-sustaining capacity of industrialism
in the following terms :

The decisive difference between India and the European countries is not in the rate of growth of population, which has been more
rapid in the European countries. What makes the difference between the conditions of India and Europe is that the economic development and expansion of production which have taken place in the
European countries, and have facilitated a more rapid growth of
population, have not taken place in India.[4]

This is as regards the early stages of industrial development.
In the long run—and this is the second reason, it is said, how the
process will help solve our population problem—industrialisation
will encourage the development of new urban patterns of living

[3] Colin Clark's article, "Population Growth and Living Standards"
published at pp. 101-02, *International Labour Review*, Vol. LXVIII—
No. 2, August 1953.
[4] *India Today*, People's Publishing House, Bombay 1949, p. 57.

which lead to the control of the high birth-rate. It is almost a truism to say that increasing incomes by changing psychological motivations and economic desires tend to bring about small families. This tendency is strongly reinforced by increasing urbanisation, rising cost of technical education, more facilities of recreation, availability of effective and clean contraceptives, etc., etc. This has been the experience of most of the advanced industrialised nations of the West and Japan. There is no reason, it is said, why India should not conform to this experience of other countries where industrialisation has ultimately led to deceleration of the growth rate, if not to decreased fertility.

Large-scale industrial economy, it is again contended, does not stand in the way of realisation of our third aim either, *viz.* equitable distribution of wealth, even where it is private economy that obtains. The distribution of income is in most countries now more equal than it was before the second world war. This is proved, particularly, by the example of the two most highly industrialised nations, *viz.* the UK and the USA, where a comprehensive system of social insurance covering the whole population has been established from the cradle to the grave. Through far-reaching measures of social security, — old-age assistance, subsidies for housing, labour legislation, agricultural price supports, minimum wage laws, and changes in taxation methods (of which the graduated income-tax is the outstanding example),—not only has the worker and the salaried employee's real income in recent years grown but his proportion of the total national income increased materially. At the same time, the average income of the top people both in the UK and the USA has decreased substantially.

According to a British Socialist Union publication :

Income-tax in the United Kingdom has so far proved to be the best instrument for cutting away income differences. It is nicely flexible ; it can be graduated steeply, so that the higher the income the higher the rate at which it is taxed ; it can be relaxed to allow for special needs. As a result of generations of stiff income-taxing, the gap between the extremes of wealth and poverty has been narrowed in this country. Something like a national maximum of net income (that is, income after taxation) has been established. To retain much more than this, so very much more has to be earned —because most of the extra will be taxed away—that very few can manage it. Out of the revenue gained by taxation, the government has been able to build up what amounts to a national minimum at

the other end of the scale. All sorts of 'social incomes' are distributed—pensions, family allowances, national assistance, sickness
benefits and so on—which between them go a long way to ensure that
everyone has at least the minimum on which to live.[5]

Figures showing how the gap between the extremes of wealth
and poverty has been narrowed in the UK during the period,
1938-1952, are given vide Table XXXIV. According to *Blue Book
On Income*, an annual publication, in 1961, after tax 45 per cent of
the people earned less than 500 sterling, 41 per cent between 500
and 1000 sterling, 13 per cent from 1000 to 2000 sterling and
1 per cent over 2000 sterling. A look at col. 3 of the table would
show that, as compared with 1952, the gap between incomes in
1961 has narrowed still further.[5a]

As regards the USA, no figures of earners in the various income-
groups are available to us, but it is known that in the 1930's an
extensive body of federal legislation was enacted to correct the
abuses of unbridled capitalism. This dealt with strict government
control of the monetary system, strengthening of the labour unions,
and extensive social welfare legislation.

Originally established at low rates, the income tax in the USA
together with a high inheritance tax has become the greatest economic and social force. By a system of graduated rates, which
range from 22 per cent to 91 per cent of net income in the highest
brackets, the income-tax has deterred the excessive amassment of
wealth. The tax structure has become a major force in the development of a large middle-class.[6] In terms of 1955 dollars the consumer
units (families, etc.) which earned over $4000 a year have increased
25 per cent since 1941. In 1929, only 20 per cent of the consumer

[5] *Twentieth Century Socialism* by Socialist Union, Penguin Books,
1956, pp. 77-78.

[5a] A Reuter's report published in the *Pioneer*, Lucknow, dated September 25, 1962.

[6] The following report appeared in the *National Herald*, Lucknow,
dated June 10 :

COONOOR, June 9—Dr. C. P. Ramaswami Aiyar stated here that
America was now "practically a socialist state" where the gap between
the rich and the poor was getting eliminated. This phenomenal change
had been brought about by wise legislation and taxation policy, he
added.

Dr. Aiyar was inaugurating a seminar on economy of the American
people, sponsored by the United States Information Service at Coonoor.

TABLE XXXIV

REDISTRIBUTION OF PERSONAL INCOMES IN THE U.K.

Name of Income	Number of Incomes (in thousands)		Total income before tax (£ million)		Total income after income and super tax (£ million)		Proportion of income retained after deduction of taxes		Proportion of income that would have been retained in 1952 at 1938-39 rates of tax*
1	1938	1952	1938	1952	1938	1952	1938	1952	
	2	3	4	5	6	7	8	9	10
Personal income which can be allocated to different ranges									
Under £250	Not available	9,090	2,589	1,405	2,585	1,394	99.8	99.2	99.1
250—499	1,890	9,600	631	3,530	611	3,395	96.8	96.2	96.1
500—999	939	5,805	361	3,737	322	3,454	89.2	92.4	91.6
1,000—1,999	183	740	247	980	202	767	81.8	78.3	83.7
2,000—9,999	98	254	361	878	256	501	70.9	57.1	72.1
10,000 and over	8	11	163	192	69	42	42.3	21.9	45.8

SOURCE : CSO Blue Book on National Income and Expenditure, 1946-52, HMSO, August 1953. p. 27.
* This column indicates the proportion of income in 1952 that would have been retained if the 1938-39 tax rates were to be applied. The egalitarian effect of direct taxes may be seen by comparison of columns (9) and (10).
Notes : 1. A married couple is for income-tax purposes counted as one individual.
2. In addition to the income shown in this table there are amounts accruing to persons that cannot be allocated to particular ranges of income. These are estimated to have been £673 million in 1938 and £1,906 million in 1952.
3. The estimates of income in this table relate to calendar years ; the tax rates used are those that were current in the fiscal years, 1938-39 and 1952-53.

units earned more than four thousand dollars. Today, 48 per cent do. The average income of the poorest one-third of American families in the fiscal year of 1935-36 was $470 in terms of 1950 prices. In 1950, the average income of the poorest third had risen to about $ 1250. In contrast, wealthy people's share in the national income had been drastically reduced. In 1929, the one per cent of the population in the highest income group got 19 per cent of the national income. In 1946, it got only 8 per cent. In view of the rising real income per head in the country the increase in strength of the middle class is due as much to persons from the lower income-groups moving up as to those in the higher groups being made to move down.

If, on the other hand, an industrialised country has a socialist structure, the problem of gross inequalities between the income of one man and another will have disappeared in the very process of its establishment.

As regards the fourth aim, *viz.* that of a political democracy, the advocates of industrialism point to the example of so many countries where it abides side by side with large-scale industry. A country can become a great industrial state and yet remain a democracy. The USA has become an economic giant that it is "without giving up any of the principles basic to a free society. Freedom of speech and of the press, the right to criticise, the right of assembly and of petition, equality of opportunity are more firmly entrenched than ever".[7]

These observations are equally true of the United Kingdom In both countries, it is pointed out, laws have been framed to pro-hibit trusts, cartels, monopolies or agreements intended to restrict trade or production or to maintain prices, so that concentrated eco-nomic power may not affect or prejudice free working of the political apparatus.

Monopolies have not multiplied, points out Prof. W. W. Rostow of the Massachussetts Institute of Technology, that is, the degree of industrial concentration has not increased significantly in the last fifty years either in the U.S.A. or West European countries. Where concentration has increased, it has been more on the basis of the economies of large-scale research and development than because

[7] Vide the USA Ambassador, Ellsworth Bunker's speech at a luncheon meeting of the Indian Junior Chamber of Commerce in New Delhi on April 21, 1957.

small firms could not survive the market environment and, where it has persisted, it has increasingly been forced to operate on terms set by the political progress.

Finally, the advocates of industrialism argue, the industrially advanced countries of the West no longer look down upon small-scale industry as outmoded remnants of a backward economy. It is a mistake, they say, to assume that the big firm is the enemy of the small business and that it would ultimately eat it up. Far from being a relic of the past, the small-scale sector in Europe exists in its own right and has a definite economic and social part to play. In fact, industry and handicrafts are complementary. Large-scale industry cannot do without the help of small *handicraft workshops*, and in some countries the work is shared among firms according to the kind for which they are best suited. In Western Germany in the manufacture of motor-cars, motor-cycles and bicycles, and even in ship-building, industry often makes use of *handicraft firms* to manufacture or assemble components. Quite apart from the fact that a prosperous handicraft business is a valuable customer for firms manufacturing machinery, tools and production equipment, there is a striking parallel between the economic and industrial development of a region and the development of the handicraft trades.

CHAPTER FIFTEEN

Conditions for Industrialism in India not Favourable

IT IS a formidable case that the advocates of industrialism or further large-scale industrialization of India bring forward. Let us, however, look at the facts a bit closely.

The total real income of a country is a function of the three factors of production—a function both of the size and efficiency of labour and capital relative to the size and quality of the natural resources. The size or quantity of these factors is a concept which needs no definition or elaboration. The quality of natural resources is judged by such things as the character of the soil, the forest resources, the topography as favouring or hindering cheap transportation, the mineral resources, the availability of water power, and the rainfall and temperatures. The quality of labour or human factor includes the efficiency of the rank and file of the industrial and agricultural workers, the ability of entrepreneurs and managers, and the skill of the engineers and technicians. While the quality of natural resources is a gift of God or Nature, and is almost wholly beyond human control, the quality or degree of excellence of a people is very much of its own making : it depends upon historical and cultural factors, environment, quality of health and education, and also the kind of leadership provided by government and the social elite. Deficiency in quality and quantity of natural resources can, to a great degree, be overcome by the quality of the working population. The quality of the third factor, *viz.*, capital, is convertible with its efficiency or productivity, which, in effect, leads or contributes to productivity or performance of labour.

A technique or technology means the way or method in which the three factors of production are used, applied or exploited. Broadly, an innovation means a change or an improvement in this method. So that, though not a factor of production, technological innovations are equally important. The nature and extent of these innovations, however, —in fact, whether these innovations will at all come into existence—turn, again, on the human factor— its health, its training and its attitudes to work.[1]

[1] Chapter XVIII *supra.*

While the quality and quantity of natural resources of any country are fixed or constant, the quality and quantity of labour and capital are variable. Obviously enough, therefore, economic development in the sense of a progressive increase in production per head can only mean that an increase in quality and or quantity of one or both of the variable factors, *viz.* labour and capital, helps to increase output more rapidly than population. Labour varies in direct proportion to population. India's population is growing at the mean rate of nearly nine million yearly and, over the foreseeable future or several decades to come, will continue to grow. Which means that we do not lack in quantity of labour ⌐it is only its quality that poses or will pose a question. On the other hand, capital is scarce. There are only two sources : it can be accumulated through domestic savings, voluntary and involuntary, or secured from foreign countries. As regards the quality of capital, it will turn almost wholly on the technology that we may choose to apply.

Now, some estimable persons consider that production per head will increase as a result of population increase *per se*—that, in the words of Acharya Vinoba Bhave, man need not starve because while God has given him only one mouth to eat, He has equipped him with two hands to work. That is why the huge population of India or China is sometimes referred to by some economists as 'human resources'—as an asset, and not a liability. They see in over-population a favourable condition for the establishment and success of industrialism. For, every expansion in population is a potential expansion in the markets. To a layman, however, each hundred million of people in India would seem to make the conditions harsher, not better for the other hundreds of millions of them.

Says Elmer Pendell :

A curious malapropism—a distortion of language is seen occasionally in recent years in the term 'human resources'. The expression probably originated because of its emotional tone : a seemingly complimentary connotation in classifying human beings as resources, because resources are helpful. But most human beings are, in net effect, the opposite of helpful. A resource is a basis of benefits. When people are in excess numbers, any random portion of them is, for the rest of them, exactly the opposite of a basis of benefits. They constitute not a resource but a liability.[2]

[2] *Population on the Loose*, Elmer Pendell, New York, 1951, pp. 4-5,

The statement of Colin Clark on p. 215 suggests that an increase in population will itself increase productive power per head of population, irrespective of capital or other requirements. Labour itself is capital, Lord John Maynard Keynes has said, inasmuch as until the point of full employment is reached labour put to use is investment which creates its own equivalent amount of 'saving'.

This proposition however, is, not true in all circumstances. In highly developed or industrialised countries, unemployment usually arises not out of a shortage of capital or equipment but of effective demand. "In an advanced industrial economy," say Coale and Hoover, "progress may be inhabited by overall deficiency of demand because the attempted saving (savers refraining from consumption out of income) exceeds the attempted investment (investors creating capital). When this happens, there is unemployment of all types of productive resources. A spurt in population may cure it by stimulating the savers to spend a larger part of their incomes on consumer goods and the investors to invest more on facilities needed to accommodate the new population and its wants. No new natural resources or technological improvements are required."[3]

A growing population may, therefore, provide an incentive to investment making it easier to approach a position of full employment or recover from depression and, thus, constitute a source of capital. But in India and other under-developed countries which have a dense agrarian economy, the nature of unemployment is different. Here unused productive resources or equipment does not exist side by side with jobless labour. There is no danger in these countries of level of savings outpacing the availability of investment opportunities, thus leading to unemployment of productive resources. These countries suffer from a surfeit of labour supply relatively to their resources in land and capital. In order that the unemployed labour may be put to work, there must be unutilised physical resources. Unemployment in these countries, is, thus, largely under-employment which originates in a disproportion between different factors of production rather than in a shortage of effective demand. The problem of full utilisation of labour in our country, therefore, is related not to increasing effective

[3] *Population and Economic Development in Low-income Countries*, Oxford University Press, 1959, p. 241.

demand or utilisation of idle capital and equipment but to the removal of under-employment which, in a predominantly agricultural economy and a social structure based on the joint-family system, takes the form of seasonal and disguised unemployment. Any increase in our population and, for the matter of that, many other Asian countries *per se* will not constitute an asset or a capital resource but a definite liability. It is a liability because there is rarely enough work for the additional hands to go round. Consequently, they will produce little, if at all. An increase in population, therefore, will be a drag on growth : it will tend to reduce output per head—to decrease the *per capita* share in the national dividend. Conversely, if the population of these countries decreases, or is 'spirited away, say, to another planet', *per capita* income would rise and poverty would decrease. For, there will be fewer mouths to feed and hence more for each. In such communities, over-population is a cause of poverty.

The Keynesian thesis that unemployed persons are a source of benefit for the community, holds good only for developed countries where there is no lack of fixed capital and, the wages-fund being already there, putting the unemployed labour force to work does not result in inflation. An increase of population in these countries tends to increase inflationary pressures only when there is already full employment. But in a backward country where the fixed capital itself is scarce or non-existent and has to be built up through a laborious process there would be a considerable time-lag between the input of labour and the flow of output, that is, a considerable time-lag between the creation of a wages-fund and the resultant savings. It is this time-lag which negatives the widely held belief that deficit financing will not raise prices if there is a subsequent increase in output. Such increase in output implies the earning of higher incomes, and thus cannot serve to offset the earlier creation of money which will have already raised money prices and incomes. Therefore, simply putting the unemployed labour force to work or employing all the hands that continually come into existence as a result of increase in population, will involve a large measure of inflation. The problem of putting the unemployed labour force to work is precisely the problem of finding sufficient wages-fund to support labour during the time it is non-existent —during the while new machinery and factories are being built up. "The Keynesian view", says Dr. Gyan Chand, the eminent economist,"that deficit financing may, under certain circumstances, be necessary and desirable to utilise idle resources of a country, does not hold good in India as our only important idle resource is unemployed and under-employed labour in the villages, and it cannot be mobilised for productive purposes merely by the issue of currency notes."[4]

To the extent, however, this idle and semi-idle labour in the villages can be utilised without payment of wages as community projects in our country have proved, there need be no wages-fund or only a very meagre fund and, therefore, no inflation. This labour in our villages can be employed on formation of capital for a wide variety of common purposes : land-levelling, construction of roads, wells, irrigation dams and canals, flood protection and drainage works, contour and other soil and water conservation structures, digging of ponds, establishment of fuel plantations, as well as improvement in amenities through the construction of community buildings, village sanitation, and so on. These types of capital formation require technologically only very small amounts of equipment. They can be constructed with the maximum of labour and minimum of capital resources. In fact, in some cases, the large supply of seasonally idle labour may obviate the use of machinery and other capital in the process of capital creation altogether, especially in respect of public works. In others, some finance capital may be required by way of loans or grants-in-aid. Only the people must want the things for which their labour is necessary (and on which Government has or may have to spend public funds today) or be persuaded to want them. They have to be made aware of the potentialities for betterment in the reservoir of labour power lying unutilised today. The labour power is already there and the road or irrigation dam might be required. Yet it might never have occurred to the villagers that the means are at hand.

Seen in this light, the problem is primarily one of organisation. In our villages where there is greater social integration and the element of common advantage is easier to demonstrate, this should not present much difficulty. If wages have at all to be paid, in view of the fact that a large supply of idle labour is almost always

[4] *Some Aspects of Population Problem of India* by Gyan Chand, published by Patna University, Bihar (India), 1956, p. 133.

available, the wages[5] paid need only be subsistence wages. In using methods of capital construction described above, there will, thus, be little or no inflationary effect. If any money expenditures are involved, they will be more than offset by the increases in food production to which the land and village improvements that will be effected, will immediately lead.

It would not be out of place here to emphasize that victory in the mortal battle of economic development in India will be greatly facilitated if we can mobilise the idle labour force of the country-side—if we can somehow or other persuade the peasants to help themselves. It is less than full, even less than half utilisation of the labour power of tens of millions of our people that partly explains our desperately low productivity and miserable standards of living. All our efforts will be wasted, all success in the sphere of heavy industry and elsewhere will be in vain if we are unable to mobilise the rural labour force for productive purposes or capital creation. The problem does not arise in totalitarian countries, for the consent of the people is not required. The *shramdan* or voluntary work that was started some years ago in India has not been very widespread, or has totalled only a few days a year. The limited enthusiasm it initially aroused is dying down, and the *shramdan* is now becoming a movement of the past. And what little effort is being made scarcely boosts actual production, but is used mainly on roads and buildings. Success in mobilisation of the rural labour force on *shramdan* basis will be possible only if there is full realisation, on the part of our people as well as Government, of the implications of the social and economic situation that the country faces, and all the political parties are agreed on the need of free and voluntary labour---labour by those who are not gainfully employed today and are wasting their time in idleness.

The proposition that all that is needed for production per head to rise, is for population to increase, has till now been demonstrated only in pioneer societies or under-developed countries having abun-

---

[5] The Punjab Government has recently enacted a legislation entitled The Punjab Compulsory Service Act (1961), under which all able-bodied persons residing within an area that is notified, may be required to render compulsory service on executing works connected with the development of drainage or the prevention or clearance of water-logging, without payment of any remuneration for a period not exceeding five days within a total period of three months.

dant unused resources but a sparse population like the USA in the nineteenth century. There are a few countries still, located chiefly in Africa and Latin America, which are in the increasing returns stage, where a larger population would mean better use of public utilities such as transport and communications, electricity, gas and water, and of facilities for some of the factory or manufacturing industries such as those which process the metal ores and make basic chemicals. In such countries an increase in population in excess of capital will be associated with marked economies and a larger output per head, as both are applied to readily available land and other resources or equipment.

At the same time, however, in order to make progress, the population must be actuated by a spirit to improve its economic conditions and, therefore, actuated by a propensity to innovate.

Horace Belshaw makes two pertinent observations on the statement of Colin Clark :

(*i*) If increasing returns to population had applied, an increase in population in India and other under-developed countries might have been expected to lead to increasing income per head and the problem of economic development would have been solved already. In fact, production per head has increased little, if at all, in such countries despite some increase in capital and some technological improvement. This leads to a strong presumption of decreasing factor returns to population growth *per se*, and no economies of scale to population growth of itself.

(*ii*) The reference to the density of population in North America and Europe does not quite hit the target ; some degree of population density in these areas would be necessary for optimum economies of scale ; but beyond this diseconomies may well arise. While a large and dense population may be necessary for optimum economies, a larger and denser population may bring no further advantages, and indeed bring disadvantages. Moreover, it may well be that the economies result not from the demographic situation but from this situation plus something else. Population in some under-developed countries is larger and denser than in some of the developed countries,[6] and in terms of these demographic factors alone might derive economies of scale equivalent to those in the areas referred to ; but the something else is lacking. *The question at issue, however, is whether further increases in population would result in increasing returns in under-developed countries, i. e. whether output per head would be higher with a faster than with a slower rate of population increase*[7] (Italics ours).

[6] Vide Table XXIII on pp. 108-109.   [7] *Ibid*, pp. 72-73.

Horace Belshaw's 'something else' is no other than capital and technological innovations. With a growing population, income or output per head will ordinarily rise only if the rate of growth of capital, or of improvements in technology, or of both is greater than the rate of growth in population.

While there are, and can be many simple technological innovations which will increase the physical productivity of labour, and can be effected without any capital outlays or only with insignificant amounts, there are many important innovations which are incorporated in new equipment, thus requiring some net investment. So that, although there may be others, capital or capital formation is unequivocally a *sine qua non* of economic development.

Capital formation presupposes savings, or increase in savings. Savings are, to state it in a homely way, the difference between what one earns and what one eats. In a country of dense agrarian economy, however, where incomes are low and levels of consumption are close to the subsistence level—where the bulk of the aggregate money income of the population is spent on food and relatively primitive items of clothing and household necessities—an increase in savings is not easy to achieve.

We are caught in a vicious circle. In a manner of speaking, our country is poor because it is poor. Poverty means lack or scarcity of material goods required for satisfaction of human wants. There is lack of goods because the level of productivity is low. And productivity is low largely because of our inability to invest capital in production. We are unable to invest capital because of our low capacity to save. Low capacity to save, in turn, derives from low money incomes. And incomes are low because productivity is low. *So productivity is low largely because productivity is low.*

In the ultimate analysis, capital is a product of labour applied to physical resources. Capital (goods or machinery) cannot be created by man out of nothing, or with bare hands out of having nothing to work upon. Financial resources can be constructed only out of physical resources. The truth has to be faced that India does not possess sufficient physical resources relative to her population (and, therefore, relative to her industrial ambitions) and, while a nation can find the financial means to do anything which it has the physical resources to do, no amount of financial jugglery can take the place of the latter. Nor can any mere redistribution of an existing physical asset or product, nor any mere regulation thereof, take the place of expanded production and rising productivity.

It is the ratio between our huge population (with its potential growth) on the one hand and natural resources and capital on the other, that the advocates of rapid large-scale industrialisation or intensive capital structure in the industrial sector are apt to over-look. The point of time in world development at which we have arrived on the stage, when people and resources of other lands cannot be exploited and foreign markets are not so readily available, is also a relevant factor ; as also our way of life, *viz.*, a democratic constitution which we have given ourselves and which precludes exploitation even of our own people beyond a point. It is these considerations which make advocates of high capital-intensive enterprises or heavy industries wrong and those of low capital-intensive, decentralised industries right.

The economically advanced countries of today, whether those which had an earlier start and achieved industrialisation in the nineteenth century, or those which joined the race later and became industrialised only recently, can be divided broadly into two classes, —those which had a high population density relative to natural sources, and others which had comparatively a low population density relative to resources.

Of natural resources, land is the most important. A reference to Table XXIII will show that countries like Netherlands, Belgium, Japan, UK and West Germany do not possess much land resources relative to their population. In fact, the land-man ratio in these countries is lower than in India. Yet they are economically advanced because they had grabbed colonies and dependencies, thus making up for lack of resources at home. The industries in these countries (as in a few others) were built up on the exploitation of the vast natural and human resources of the territories held in subjection. Industrial development in these countries would not have been possible, had it not been for the existence of less indus-trialised countries and newly opened territories together with the predominance of free trade. Prosperity in these countries resulted from (*i*) the draining off of excess people to the New World and other colonies, (*ii*) the stimulation of sales of manufactured goods in new areas, and (*iii*) the flow of cheap food and raw materials to them.

The development of the age of inventions or success of the

Industrial Revolution in England or Western Europe depended not simply on some special and unaccountable burst of inventive genius in the English or European races, but on the accumulation of a sufficient fund of capital. The introduction of expensive implements or processes involves a large outlay, and it is not worth while for any man, however enterprising, to make the attempt unless he has a considerable command of capital, and has access to large markets. Both the capital and the markets were supplied by the colonies and dependencies of European countries spread all over the world. In the case of England it was India which largely fulfilled this role.

Says Brooks Adams :

The influx of the Indian treasure, by adding considerably to England's cash capital, not only increased its stock of energy, but added much to its flexibility and the rapidity of its movement. Very soon after Plassey, the Bengal plunder began to arrive in London, and the effect appears to have been instantaneous ; for all the authorities agree that the 'industrial revolution', the event which had divided the nineteenth century from all antecedent time, began with the year 1760. Prior to 1760, according to Baines, the machinery used for spinning cotton in Lancashire was almost as simple as in India : while about 1750 the English iron industry was in full decline because of destruction of the forest for fuel. At that time four-fifths of the iron used in the kingdom came from Sweden.

Plassey was fought in 1757, and probably nothing has ever equalled in rapidity of the change which followed. In 1760 the flying shuttle appeared, and coal began to replace wood in smelting. In 1764 Hargreaves invented the spinning jenny, in 1776 Crompton contrived the mule, in 1785 Cartwright patented the powerloom and, chief of all, in 1768 Watt matured the steam engine, the most perfect of all vents of centralising energy. But though these machines served as outlets for the accelerating movement of the time, they did not cause the acceleration. In themselves inventions are passive, many of the most important having lain dormant for centuries, waiting for a sufficient store of force to have accumulated to set them working. That store must always take the shape of money, and money not hoarded, but in motion. Before the influx of the Indian treasure, and the expansion of credit which followed, no force sufficient for this purpose existed ; and had Watt lived fifty years earlier, he and his invention must have perished together. Possibly since the world began, no investment has ever yielded the profit reaped from the Indian plunder, because for nearly fifty years Great Britain stood without a competitor. From 1694, when the Bank of England was founded, to Plassey (1757) the growth had been relatively slow

Between 1760 and 1815 the growth was very rapid and prodigious."[8]

These opportunities are not open to us. The ethics of the matter apart, we have no colonies or dependencies to exploit. Also, all under-developed countries are trying to make up the lee-way so that soon there will be left few or no external markets to buy our industrial goods. Capital or means for India's large-scale industrialisation, therefore, will have to be found from within the country itself, that is, our own savings.

The last twenty countries mentioned in the table on pages 108-109 possess immense land resources of their own—resources far greater relatively than India. Of these, nine, viz., Norway, Finland, Sweden, the USA, South Africa, Venezuela, New Zealand, Canada and Australia have already achieved a high degree of industrialisation. Their resources not only produced raw materials that fed the factories, but food in quantities that left a surplus over rural requirements to feed industrial workers and those engaged in capital formation. This surplus also increased the income of rural populations—which initially constituted a high percentage of the total—so that they could buy industrial goods.

Two of these twenty countries, viz., Chile and the USSR are still in the midst of economic transformation and the peak justified by their natural resources has yet to be reached. The remaining nine[8a] are still poor and under-developed. Judged by our reasoning, they are also destined to achieve great economic progress, sooner or later.

There is no complete inventory of mineral resources that the various countries may possess. Yet, the available data shown in Table XXXV will indicate India's relative position in respect of the more important ones. The minerals which are used in, by far, the greatest physical quantities in manufacturing industry, transport, etc., as a whole, are coal, iron ore and petroleum. Coal is essential in production of steel, and steel in fabrication of most machines.

[8] "The Law of Civilization and Decay", pp. 259-60 quoted by R. P. Dutt in *India Today*, 1949, People's Publishing House, Bombay, pp. 107-08.

[8a] A reference to Table XXVIII in Chapter XIII will show that, instead of progressing, the economies of Turkey, Brazil, and Argentina during the period 1953-60, have definitely retrogressed. This means that besides natural resources, there are some other pre-conditions also which are essential to making and keeping a country prosperous.

TABLE XXXV

STATEMENT SHOWING ESTIMATES OF RESERVES OF IMPORTANT MINERALS

Sl. No.	Name of the country	Year	Population in '000	Coal (including Lignite)		Iron Ore		Petroleum	
				total estimated reserves (m. tons)	per capita reserve (tons)	total estimated reserves (m. tons)	per capita reserve (tons)	total estimated reserves (m. barrel)	per capita reserve (barrels)
I	2	3	4	5	6	7	8	9	10
1	India*	1952	367,000	42,649a 45,423h 79,000b	116.21 123.77 215.26	21,240b 10,137i	57.87 27.62	300d	0.82
2	USA	1953	159,629	2,400,000g	15,034.86	25,488b 3,800i	159.67 23.81	24,702g 30,500d	154.75 191.07
3	Canada	1951	14,009	30,319a 100,000g	2,164.25 7,138.27	2,221b 1,500g	158.54 107.07	1,200h 3,600d	85.66 256.98
4	Mexico	1950	25,791	..	..	189b 100i	7.33 3.88	850h 2,500c 3,000d	32.96 96.93 116.32
5	Argentina	1947	15,894	50a (probable)	3.15	32b	2.01	250g 350c 2,300d	15.73 22.02 144.71
6	Australia	1952	8,649	20,900a 20,000g	2,416.46 2,312.41	198b 400i	22.89 46.25	..	..
7	Union of South Africa	1953	13,153	7,914d 200,000h	601.69 15,205.65	5,089b 1,000j	386.91 76.03	..	..
8	United Kingdom	1953	50,857	129,500a 190,000g	2,546.36 3,735.97	918b 3,100i	18.05 60.96	7d	0.14
9	France	1952	42,545	6,000ag	141.03	9,333b 4,500i	219.37 105.77	150d	3.53
10	Germany (West)	1950	48,994	80,440a 110,000g	1,641.83 2,245.17	840b 1,250i	17.14 25.51	365d 540g	3.06 7.45
11	Italy	1953	Under 47,756	1a 1,000g	0.02 20.94	30b 60i	0.63 1.26	200d (including Sicily)	4.19
12	Sweden	1953	Under 7,171	97a 1,000g	13.53 139.45	1,000b 1,250i	139.45 174.31	..	..
13	Norway	1953	3,359	11,000g	3,274.78	738b	219.71	..	..

15	China	1947	463,198	1,500,000g / 444,000e	7,240.38 / 958.55	3,100i / 1,215b / 4,168e	14.98 / 2.62 / 9.00	23,000 / 750d	111.11 / 1.63
16	Japan	1951	84,300	5,895a / 6,500e	69.93 / 77.11	38b / 24i	0.45 / 0.28	25d	0.30
17	Indonesia	1947	76,360	500e (Proved reserves)	6.55	720b	9.43	1,100h / 3,000d	14.41 / 39.29
18	Belgium	1953	8,778	less than 11,000a	less than 1,253.13	62i / 50b	7.06 / 5.70	..	..
19	Netherlands	1953	10,493	212a	20.20a	1,500**b / 100i	142.95 / 9.53	.. / 110c	.. / 10.48
20	New Zealand	1953	Under 2,047	560a / 1,000g	273.57 / 488.52	less than 50b	24.43		
21	Brazil	1950	51,976		..	4,000i	76.96	..	..
22	Chile	1952	5,933	5,000g	842.74	120i	20.23	..	..

* According to Dr. R. C. Misra, Head of the Department of Geology, Lucknow University, the figures of 45,423 million tons for coal and 10,137 million tons for iron-ore reserves seem to be more likely. According to the Planning Commission, reserves of coal estimated for beams of thickness 4 feet and above are of the order of 50,000 million tons, of which coking coal accounts for 5.6 per cent, or above 2,800 million tons. Inferred reserves are placed at 80,000 million tons. In addition, about 2073 million tons of lignite are estimated to be available. Reserves of iron ore are estimated at 21,870 million tons (vide Third Plan, pp. 191 and 193).

** Figures relate to Netherland Indies.

SOURCE: (a) (i) India's Resources by V. P. Sondhi and D. R. S. Mehta, 1957
(ii) Bulletin of Economic Minerals XVI by E. R. Gee
(b) (i) World Iron Ore Resources and Their Utilization, U.N.O. Publication, 1950
(ii) Figures of possible reserves according to:
(i) Iron Ore of India by Dr. M. S. Krishnan (1958), p. 150;   (ii) Geology of India, May (1957). p. 7,
a pamphlet published by the Ministry of Information and Broadcasting, Publications Division,
Government of India; and   (iii) The Progress of the Mineral Industry of India (1951), published
by the Mining, Geological and Metallurgical Institute of India.
(According to these sources the proved reserves of iron ore are only 6,421 million tons).
(c) Indian Minerals, Vol. XI, No. 2   (Reserves for 1955)   (d) World Petroleum Report (1958)
(e) Development of Mineral Resources in Asia and the Far East (1953)
(f) Economic Mineral Deposits by Allen M. Bateman (1952) and 12th International Geological Congress, Canada,
1913   (g) Mineral Resources of the World by Von Royen, Bowels and Prehson (1952)
(h) Bharat Me Koyle Ke Sansdhan by Chintamani Tripathi, published in the Indian Minerals, Vol. II, No. 2. (June
1957)   (i) Figures of total estimated reserves according to Proceedings of U.N. Scientific Conference on
Conservation and Utilization of Resources (1951) and Records Geological Survey of India, Vol. 85, II (1954). p. 264.

For several countries more than one figure for a mineral reserve has been given in Table XXXV because they relate to estimates, not to proved actuals, and, therefore, vary according to sources.

It is clear that we are not as richly endowed by nature as many of us think. Our economic potentiality is not of an order which may be comparable with the USA or the USSR. It will be a mistake, therefore, on our part to entertain visions of our economy on the pattern of the USA or the USSR, in fact, any developed country whatsoever whose material circumstances differ so greatly from India. China is the only country with which India can be compared. While she possesses less arable land *per capita*, the usable land resources, as a whole, *per capita* in China are greater than in India. While China possesses more coal, India possesses more iron.

The USA had nearly three times the land area and far less than half the population, *viz.* 41.5 per cent of India (it was much less a hundred years ago).[9] Her usable land resources *per capita*, including forests, are more than eight times those of India. As a consequence of this land-man ratio in the two countries, the USA can afford to have large-scale farming, that is, produce enough food for herself and more, without putting or forcing too many persons on land, whereas India cannot do without intensive farming under which relatively more persons are employed on the same area. As partially evidenced by Table XXXV, USA's resources in minerals, petroleum, coal, iron and water-power also were, and are a vast advantage compared to India. The rate of capital growth was, therefore, far higher in the USA than it can possibly be in India. Obviously, then, we cannot hope to develop in the same way as the USA did. The American system which grew up on a continent rich with natural resources and almost empty of human beings, cannot be duplicated in India.

As the advocates of industrialism point out, our huge population does constitute a tremendous potential internal market. Once purchasing power of our people is raised, their own manufactures may not or will hardly be sufficient to meet the pent-up demands of four hundred and fifty million customers or more for a long time to come. But this purchasing power cannot be developed in a day or by rush methods. We will have to produce more food with fewer people on the land—food sufficient to feed the farmers and those

[9] The USA had an area of 93,63,000 sq. km. compared with 32,63,000 of India and, in the middle of 1961, a population of 183.65 million as compared with 443 million of India.

who have gone to the factories. Farm surpluses are required to provide the farmers with purchasing power with which to buy the goods that factory workers will be producing. Then alone will we be able to develop our internal market, not earlier. But this consummation will require a far greater application of capital to land, and improvement in farming methods than we possibly imagine, and than we have hitherto been able to ensure. Anyway, unless increased food production per acre can be achieved, there is no reasonable hope of India achieving any marked improvement in her economic conditions by manufacturing, because there is too little market anywhere in the world for the things she might manufacture, and our farmers will not be having the wherewithal to buy the products manufactured by their countrymen.

According to Prof. W.W. Rostow, it was in 1860 that the USA had achieved and passed the point of economic "take-off", *viz.*, the point from which onwards it could sustain its economic growth through its own surplus of capital and normal channels of international investment. Russia followed some fifty years later. The eminent economist locates the periods of this transformation of American and Russian economy as extending from 1843 to 1860 and from 1890 to 1914 respectively. The Russian take-off like the concurrent Canadian take-off was aided by the world rise in grain prices which occurred in the mid-90's ; for this rise made attractive, in both countries, the laying of vast railway nets. It was the railway, with its multiplying impact on growth, points out Prof. Rostow,[10] that took Russia through its take-off by the outbreak of the first world war. Coal, iron and engineering surged ahead, as did a modern cotton industry to meet the expanded home demand. The Baku petroleum field expanded to its natural limit ; the Ukranian coal-iron complex was brought to life, as the Ruhr and the Pennsylvania and Mid-Western complexes had been half a century earlier. Russia's industrial output as a whole, for two decades before 1914, had been increasing, on the average, about 8 per cent per annum. So that the foundations of self-generating economy had already been laid in Russia when the Bolshevik Revolution engulfed it in 1917. Like America, the USSR also had the advantage of huge economic resources—'huge' relative to population—which gave it a high

[10] "Rostow on Economic Growth" in *The Economist*, London, August 15 and 22, 1959.

potentiality for rapid industrial progress compared with many other nations in the world.

But, actuated by their belief in big economic units which Communism inculcates and their desire to outstrip the West in shortest possible time, they started building the 'biggest' and the 'most up-to-date' factories, some of which were so colossal that they were not finished till 8 or 10 years later. This required a huge amount of capital which was locked up and, for all practical purposes, lost during this period. It was with a view to find capital for these industrial giants that collective farms were established which meant enormous suffering for the masses that could, perhaps, have been avoided. Despite large capital outlays in agriculture, collectivisation damped productivity with the result that quite a large proportion of the labour force had to be kept on land.

The People's Republic of China followed suit, and did not make secret of the purpose behind her agrarian co-operatives. The primary aim of agrarian co-operatives in China, which was only an initial name for collective farms, was officially declared to be the accumulation of capital for industrialisation by increasing the marketable surplus of food-grains.

In an article entitled "Develop Agricultural Cooperation to Accumulate Capital for the Industrialisation of the State", Chang Ching-Tai said in the Communist theoretical journal, *Hsueh-hsi* ('Study'), dated December 2, 1955 :

The development of industry, particularly the development of heavy industry, needs a colossal amount of capital, which must be earned over a considerable period of time. As we all know, the capital needed for our own industrialisation can only come from accumulation within our own country, and accumulation in the agricultural field is an important factor. Due to our technical backwardness, many kinds of modern industrial equipment and various heavy-type or precision instruments cannot yet be produced in the country and they must be imported from abroad, first, from our fraternal countries. To import these things, we must first organise exports. At the moment when our industry is still backward, our major exportable goods are only agricultural produce, native goods and minerals. It will thus be seen that the development of agricultural production is of great significance for the support of the industrialisation of our State.

However, the present situation is that the development of agriculture does not fully satisfy the needs of industrial development. As an example, the rate of the increased output of marketable grain is very low. Many light industries, for the lack of sufficient supply of raw materials, cannot make the fullest use of their machinery equipment. If such conditions continue, the speed of industrialisation must be affected.

Our agricultural development is backward because today the small peasant economy still occupies an important proportionate share in our agricultural economy. The sole means to solve this question is to lead the small peasant economy to the road of co-operation. . . According to the data collected from various areas, the existing agricultural producers' cooperatives in our country, during the first one or two years of their formation, have registered a production increase of between 10 and 20 per cent. Generally speaking, the output of cooperatives is higher than that of mutual aid teams, and, of course, much higher than that of the individual peasants.

The reader will recollect with interest that some of the reasons advanced by the Patil Delegation in favour of co-operativisation of agriculture in India sound like a paraphrase of the arguments given in the above article from the Chinese journal.

The article was written in 1955 ; by the end of 1956, 96 per cent of the Chinese peasantry had been organised into co-operatives, of which two-thirds were of the 'advanced' type or collectives.[11] We have, however, already seen that pooling of land cannot by itself lead to increased production. People in China have been led into Co-operatives or Collectives just as they were in the Soviet Union, and in exactly the same stages : first, confiscation of land and physical liquidation of landlords ; then, its distribution into small bits and loud professions of support to peasant economy ; the discovery that peasant economy, which is after all a capitalist economy, breeds individualism and leads to inefficient production ; encouragement of peasants' societies where at first labour and livestock alone are pooled ; then land also till the *kolkhoz* is reached, with an announcement to the world that the advantages of collective farming were found by the farmers to be so great that they all only too gladly opted, rather rushed into the *kolkhozy*, or 'advanced' co-operatives in a 'surging tide'. The reasons for dragooning the peasants into collective farms in Soviet Russia were similar, *viz.* the collective farms will be in the grip of the state and will be forced to yield farm produce to the state at rates far lower than those

[11] As we said in Chapter III, the collectives were converted into communes within a period of less than three months in the latter half of 1958.

prevailing in the market. This produce will be sold in the cities or the outside world at far higher rates, and the difference will go towards purchasing equipment for heavy, large-scale industries. An economy of millions of independent peasants could not be made to yield these compulsory deliveries, misnamed 'surplus produce', to the state.

Some such picture would seem to be the ideal of our leaders in India also. Declared Prime Minister Nehru in the *Lok Sabha* on March 28, 1959 : "Ceilings, cooperatives and state trading (of food-grains) are all correlated and should be looked at as one picture." Actually our speed is more rapid in a sense—in the sense of our intentions. In the USSR and China, co-operatives came only after the *kulaks* had been completely liquidated. Here we are covering or trying to cover both the stages in one stride. If there is delay, it is the Constitution which is to blame !

The communists claim that they alone possess the key to material prosperity of the densely-populated, under-developed countries. In proof of their claim they point to the example of Russia which. according to them, was totally undeveloped in 1917, but was today well within sight of an American standard of life. 'In the last 40 years, Russia, a defeated and backward country which had to fight a civil war and a World War as well, has become one of the two mightiest powers of the world.' Russia owes all to the new doctrine---it is said.

We are not concerned with military might here,[12] but as regards standards of living it may be sufficient to state that the American standard is three times higher than the Russian. In fact, the living standard of many a European country is higher than that of Russia. As for comparison with India and China and, for that matter, any other over-crowded and backward country, there are two important points in which Russia differed from them, which the communists slur over. First : at the time of the 1917 Revolution,

[12] Although even the claim that communism raises the military strength of a country miraculously, is untenable. Before and during the last World War, Germany, comparatively a small country, was singly the mightiest country in the world. Russia possessed more than double the human and natural resources of Germany and more than two decades since the Bolshevik Revolution had passed when she entered the War in 1941. Yet, despite its vast spaces, it would have been beaten to the knees in no time, had it to contend singly against Germany. And Germany was a non-communist country !

it was industrially not a backward country at all or, at least, not so backward as it is often depicted to be. British and French capital and technology had already set up enclaves of industrial expansion in the Czarist economy. As we have already seen, according to W. W. Rostow, its economy had achieved the 'take-off' stage before the first World War. India and China have still to achieve this stage. Says W. S. Woytinsky:[13]

Czarist Russia was a backward country in comparison with some of her western neighbours, but she had the largest and most efficient cotton mills in Europe, possessed shipyards able to build battleships and submarines, turned out locomotives second only to those of the United States, had the largest steel bridges in the world, built by her engineers, with domestic materials. Illiteracy was rapidly disappearing in a large part of Russia. The country had a net-work of first-class institutes for advanced technical studies. The Czarist government was reactionary, corrupt, weak, and commanded no respect from the people, but after the overthrow of the democratic government that succeeded the Czar, the Communists came into an economic inheritance far greater than that left to India after the end of the colonial rule.

Second, along with relatively vast untapped mineral resources which China and India could not claim, the land : man ratio in the USSR was far higher. The Soviet Union had a much smaller population, millions of acres of unused or virgin arable land, and sizeable food surpluses for export in 1917. Thus the Kremlin could even afford a decline in agricultural output while it pressed forward on the industrial front, as long as a higher proportion of total food produced found its way to the cities. China and India have no such margins. As compared with Russia's 274 cents of arable land *per capita*, China and India have 46 and 95 cents only, and new lands or culturable wastes in both countries are scarce (vide Table XXIII). Instead of being exporters of food, both countries have been facing food shortages, while, on the other hand, China's population grows by 17 million each year and that of India by 10 million or even more.

If experience of Russian agriculture is any guide, the aim of the Chinese Government to find capital for rapid industrial growth from collectivisation of land will hardly be realized. In fact, the Central Committee of the Communist Party of China has already,

[13] *India : The Awakening Giant*, Harper and Bros., New York, 1957, pp. 190-91.

in its eighth plenary session held at Luchan in August, 1959, admitted the failure of the commune, however diluted the admission may be by rhetoric. The Committee's decision, referred to in Chapter III *antea*, it may be hoped, will now serve to disillusion those of our countrymen, who have been inclined to regard the Chinese experiment as a model for rapid economic development.

It would seem the implications flowing from fundamental facts of the Chinese economy have dawned, at least, upon the Russians somewhat more clearly. The *Hindustan Times*, New Delhi, carried the following report from Moscow in its issue dated October 1, 1959:

> Moscow, Sept. 30 :—Mr. Khrushchev said in Peking today that the Russians realized after the Communist revolution in China that 'the building of socialism in such a vast and formerly backward country presented considerable difficulties.'
> Speaking at a reception marking the 10th anniversary of the Communists coming to power in Peking, he added that they also realized what vast upsurge of enthusiasm had been produced.

A communistic system of Government, or a 'vast upsurge of enthusiasm' whipped up by it may, at best, or possibly—and only possibly—make up for lost time, but cannot make up for lack of physical resources. With her vast physical resources and, in particular, so favourable a land : man ratio, the USSR would have, under any system of democratic government, whether on the pattern of the UK or the USA, but which was efficiently administered, achieved equal, if not greater, economic development, than the Communist Government during the same period. "I think that in the long run," observed Prime Minister Nehru in a speech in the early half of 1955, "the democratic and peaceful method is more successful even from the point of view of time and much more so from the point of view of results." Both democracy and communism rely equally on technology, and technology knows no ideological frontiers.[14]

[14] The USSR has claimed innumerable times over the last decade, in fact, almost since its very inception, that very soon it will excel the USA in economic production and, thus, become world's country No. 1. The following statement by the *Pravda* is typical of such propaganda :

> MOSCOW, Oct. 12.—*Pravda* said today that Russia would outstrip the United States in production per man within five years after completion of the current seven-year-plan, which began in February
> The newspaper, quoted by *Tass*, said this would give Russians the

Statistical evidence is also forthcoming that, as a matter of actual fact, the gap in the economic positions of the USA and the USSR in 1955 was exactly what it was in 1913. Communism could do nothing to abridge that gap. In *The American Economic Review* of May, 1957, Mr. Warren Nutter's study of "Soviet Economic Developments : Some Observations on Soviet Industrial Growth" includes a chart showing industrial production per head of population for Russia, 1880-1955, and the United States, 1870-1955. This chart takes 1913 as 100 and covers 37 industries. The median lag in 1955 is 56 years of growth, and the whole Soviet curve is set below the American by an amount that does not vary greatly in terms of time lag. What emerges is that the relative position in 1955 remains surprisingly what it was in 1913. The lags are not uniform ; in some industries they are under 20 years, in others well over 50. But if one takes the growth sequence as the basis for comparison, Mr. Nutter is correct in his four conclusions :

highest standard of living in the world—an achievement which would constitute the "historical victory of communism over capitalism" (*Hindustan Times*, New Delhi, dated Oct. 13, 1959).

A reference to Tables No. XV and XVII combined, and XXIII, XXXV, and XXXVIII in this book will, however, show that the claim of the *Pravda* is likely to remain a mere boast. The USA possesses per head more coal, iron and petroleum reserves, and more arable lands and permanent pastures, and produces more crude steel and electricity than the USSR. According to tables on pp. 112 and 116 of the Annual Number of the *Eastern Economist*, New Delhi, 1960, the average production of hard coal, pig iron and crude steel in the USA and the USSR over three years, 1955-57, amounted, in percentages of world production, to 27.8, 35.4 and 37.3 and 18.0, 17.7 and 17.2 respectively. Also, USA's agricultural production per acre is higher. Only, it possesses less forests and woodlands· And in exploitation of natural resources, democracy, as we have seen, does not lag behind communism. On the basis of known material facts, therefore, the USSR will be able, if at all, to catch up with the USA only with difficulty, and is not likely ever to outstrip it.

Although material standards have little or nothing to do with knowledge of cosmic space or advance in rocketry, yet most people are dazzled by Russian achievements in these two spheres, and are, therefore. in a mood to believe its propagandist claims in the economic sphere also. But if Russia has got a big enough lead over America in missiles and outer space it arises, not from any general superiority in scientific development and production techniques, but from two special reasons : Russia has concentrated a much higher proportion of its engineers and, especially, its first-class break-through scientists on military work, particularly, on missiles and on cosmic research ; (2) investment in the Soviet

Soviet industry seems still to be roughly three and a half decades behind the United States in levels of output and about five and a half decades in levels of *per capita* output.... Second ... the development of Soviet industry is roughly equivalent to what took place in the United States in the four decades bracketing the turn of the century—in *per capita* terms, to an even earlier period ending around the turn of the century. Third, over the Soviet era as a whole, Soviet industries have generally lost historical ground to their American counterparts—the lags have generally increased—in terms of both total and *per capita* output ... Fourth, while

Union is concentrated on heavy industry and industry related to military potential as opposed to the American diffusion of investment over heavy and light industry, consumers' goods and services.

Advocates of Communist Russia can certainly point to the fact that, for the last five years or so, its economy is expanding at an annual rate markedly higher than the USA. But it will be wrong to draw from these figures the conclusion that the *Pravda* does. The present higher Soviet rate of increase in gross national product is the consequence, firstly, of a peculiar concentration of its investment in heavy industry. The huge capital locked up in huge projects for so long, is only now gradually coming to fruition. Secondly, an adolescent's rate of growth is always higher than an adult's. In an industrially mature country like the USA the benefits deriving from a movement of agricultural workers into non-agricultural occupations are largely exhausted. Consequently, the chief major factor through which further increases in over-all productivity in the USA may be obtained is additional capital investment. Not so in the Soviet Union where about more than forty per cent of the labour force is still occupied in agriculture, and from where it can be easily diverted to the more productive secondary and tertiary sectors. In the USA substantial additions to the capital stock when it is already very large, are not easy to bring about : in the USSR the labour force, which will increase non-agricultural production is already there, and has not to be created. As and if, with passage of time, international tensions relax and a sense of security and satisfaction develops in the USSR, the demand for consumers' goods grows and there is less and less scope for absorption of rural workers in urban pursuits, its economy will move closer and closer to the high consumption economies of the West and the rates of growth will also become more alike. This tendency is already being reflected in Soviet allocations : in agriculture, for example, where it is now a major goal to increase supplies of better food, to some degree in housing and in such consumers' goods as television sets, washing machines, refrigerators, motor cycles and even cars. But, ultimately, as in any country, the amount of natural resources the Soviet Union possesses will impose a ceiling on the growth of its economy : assuming that the efficiency of the labour force in the two countries is equal, the living standards of the USSR, communism notwithstanding, cannot surpass those obtaining in the USA.

Soviet industries have tended in recent years to gain ground in terms of total output, they have continued to lose ground in terms of *per capita* output.[15]

In China, physical means are not available in such abundant measure as in the USSR. That is why 'the building of socialism in China presented considerable difficulties.' Perhaps, Mr. Nikita Khrushchev, for obvious reasons, chose to blink over the harsh truth.

Surplus or idle labour power could make a road, a bridge or a building in record time, provided the materials were available It can dig out coal, manufacture steel or reclaim lands, but the coal and iron deposits and unused lands must first be there or have been created by Nature. That some people in China also, even within Communistic ranks, are having some such thoughts will be clear from their condemnation by the Chinese Prime Minister, Chou En-lai, in the usual choice communist language in an article published in Peking on October 6, 1959 :

Imperialists, bourgeois elements and 'rightist opportunists in our own ranks' said it was impossible for China to achieve her aim of achieving greater, faster, better and more economical results in building socialism.
But we firmly reply that it is quite possible because what we depend on are the masses of the people, the creators of history.[16]

Mr. Chou En-lai forgets that although 'the masses of the people' can create history, they cannot create natural physical resources Human beings, in the circumstances of China, are not a 'resource', but a liability. Despite her frantic efforts, China will never attain the economic standards of the USSR much less the USA. She will, therefore, seek *lebensraum*, sooner or later, and cast avaricious eyes towards the plains of Outer Mongolia, Siberia and Turkistan and the territories bordering her on the south. The vast plateau of Tibet has already been drawn into her bowels, not so much as a subject-territory but as a colony.

To turn to India : we differ even from China in two vital respects, *viz.*, first, we are faced with immense problems presented by the

[15] "Rostow on Economic Growth" in *The Economist*, London, August 22, 1959.
[16] The *National Herald* dated October 7, 1959.

backward classes and the prevalence of ancient and strongly entrenched customs inimical to economic progress ; second, we are a democracy and not a dictatorship. We cannot order our people about : we can only persuade them. So that our circumstances differ from every other country that has been mentioned.

To repeat and re-emphasize : we have neither an abundance of physical resources relative to population, nor colonies and dependencies to exploit; further, almost every country in the world has now entered the competition for rapid economic development and we are, in a way, burdened with a fully democratic Constitution and the problem of backward classes coupled with the fatalistic attitude of our people. The mental tools with which we usually start and which are derived from the advanced philosophies of the welfare States of Europe—the philosophy of rich countries or countries favourably circumstanced from the point of view of history or economic resources—will have to be discarded. In our case the complementary development of agriculture and industry will have to take place within the framework of our own economy, and—a still greater handicap—within the framework of democratic freedoms which prevent exploitation of the peasant and the labourer beyond a point, and within the limitations set by our low land or natural resources : man ratio.

Although it is now about a century since India began establishing some factories on the Western pattern, the percentage of employment in the industry or secondary sector, according to Table XXIX, came down from 28.1 in 1881 to 13.6 in 1931, and, according to Table XXX, from 11.0 in 1931 to 10.0 in 1951. According to the latest census, it rose from 10.62 in 1951 to 11.70 in 1961. We may, therefore, regard 1947, the year of her independence, as the starting point of her economic development in earnest. Now, it would appear that with the exception of Japan which had, at the beginning of its industrial expansion (1870), a density of about 1,500 per square mile of arable land, India had a population more crowded than that of any country on the eve of its industrialisation, viz. 649 per square mile of arable land. That a dense agrarian economy tends to impede industrialisation, there can be no doubt. For, the extent of industrialisation is in a large measure determined by the degree to which machinery is substituted for human labour and, in a dense agrarian economy, labour is, at least, immediately cheaper than machinery.

The amount of land per cultivator in India is steadily declining, which tends to increase poverty, to limit investment in the land and thus to hold down productivity. If personal labour[17] is taken into account, farming is a deficit undertaking in many parts of the country. When agricultural productivity is so low, the satisfaction of elementary needs like food and clothing absorbs a high proportion of the country's active population, leaving only a few for production of non-agricultural goods and services. And a high ratio of farm population in a country like India where there is little land, or man-land ratio is high, in turn, means that most of the land is devoted to food crops for sustenance rather to export crops for an investment surplus or to crops that provide raw materials for industries. The situation reaches its ultimate futility when agricultural productivity is so low or food requirements of the swollen population so great that an agricultural country becomes an importer of agricultural produce.

The masses are so greatly deprived of the immediate necessities, points out Dr. Kingsley Davis, that all the pressures are on the side of more and immediate personal consumption and, thus, everything is expended on sheer maintenance of life. As bare necessities are met, further increases are made to the population so that the supply of immediate necessities must be constantly expanded. As somebody has said, it is like Alice running merely to stand still. This leads to a situation where the future has to be sacrificed for the present—a situation which makes it hard to accumulate any surplus at all, much less the surplus necessary to develop an industrial system of high capital-intensity.

In 1949-50 India had a national income of Rs. 88,70 crores. The Planning Commission or the Government of India proposes to double the national income by 1967-68 and the *per capita* income by 1973-74, that is, in 18 and 24 years respectively, since the first Five-Year Plan was launched. Can these goals be realised? What are the premises for such an assumption?—one may legitimately ask.

The Planning Commission had, for the period of the First and Second Plans, *viz.* 1951-61, assumed a mean annual population

[17] According to Farm Management Surveys held by the Planning Commission in Uttar Pradesh, Punjab, West Bengal and Madras during 1954-55 to 1956-57, and in Bombay during 1957-58, the value of the personal labour of the farmer and his family averaged to 21.5 per cent of the total costs in crop production.

growth rate of 1.20 per cent. The estimates of the 1961 Census reveal, however, an actual rate of 1.95 per cent. Assuming, in agreement with the Planning Commission, that a capital : output ratio of 3 : 1 is valid for the entire economy, it will take an investment of Rs. 3 to produce an income of Re. 1. Just to maintain the present standard of living, therefore, we need to make an investment of (1.95 x 3) 5.85 or about 6 per cent of the national income annually. An increase of 1 per cent of output per head will require an additional investment of 3 per cent, *viz.* about 9 per cent in all. Thus, calculated by the logarithmic method, it will require capital formation at the average rate of 9 per cent and a period of 106 years to double our present standard of living ! Whereas the ratio of savings to national income which was estimated by the First Plan document to rise from 5.0 per cent in 1950-51 to 6.75 per cent in 1955-56, and 11.0 per cent in 1960-61, actually turned out to be 6.3 per cent in 1955-56 and 8.5 per cent in 1960-61 ! !

There is a source of capital, however, to which we can look for assistance, *viz.* the international market. Even the USA, Canada, Australia, Sweden and the USSR resorted or had to resort to foreign capital for developing their economy. But there are two limitations on the extent to which we can utilise such assistance. Loans must pay interest. And, as Horace Belshaw has pointed out, it is not all kind of economic or developmental activities that are able to pay their way or necessarily and automatically lead to proportionate improvement in the balance of payments. For example, investment in social overheads like power, communications, transport, water supply, health and education is often a type of investment in which returns are long deferred, and which has a low output : capital ratio. Similarly, although investments in irrigation or land development will improve nutritional levels, they may not immediately reduce imports or increase exports and thus have only remote and indirect effects on improving the balance of payments. The increase in food production may be completely absorbed by the producers themselves, and not lead to any increase in the volume of commercial transactions. The second limit is imposed by the necessity to 'marry' the imported capital with local savings or capital formation. This may pose no problem to the extent to which imported equipment (and skill) can utilise our idle and semi-idle labour. But this extent cannot be large or unlimited, and our capacity to absorb foreign capital will ultimately be governed by the rate of our internal savings, which is low.

There is yet another consideration which should stand in the way of resort to lavish or massive inter-governmental foreign aid, or aid from international institutions. Such aid is bound to have adverse psychological reactions both in the political and economic fields. In the political field, if we are not cautious, it is likely to inhibit our freedom in terms of foreign policy; in the economic field, it takes the edge off the need for maximizing domestic effort in the mobilization of domestic resources as also that for maximizing vigilance in regard to details of expenditure on the Plan projects. Foreign economic aid, in certain circumstances, may actually do more harm than good. To the extent it permits importation of foreign-made machinery and equipment for projects which, though they may satisfy our vanity, are unremunerative, it may set off an inflationary spiral increasing and aggravating the existing social and economic tensions in the country.

There are examples of countries which have imported large quantities of foreign capital for long periods without any substantial transformation in their economies, e.g. the Argentine before 1914 and Venezuela down to recent years. The imports may result only in a brief spurt of expansion which is not subsequently sustained. For, there are so many factors or conditions, other than mere amount of foreign capital, that contribute or make a difference to the economic development of a country, e.g., quantity and quality of its natural resources; the rate of internal savings; the choice of techniques or the composition of capital in individual projects, that is, whether they will be capital-intensive or labour-intensive; the priority that will be allotted to the various sectors and sub-sectors of the economy; the extent to which free or private enterprise will or will not be allowed to function; the availability of a trained and healthy labour force and an aggressive and forward-looking class of entrepreneurs; the social system and the economic organisation which determine the incentives and mobility of the workers; the political philosophy and efficiency or otherwise of the administration on which depends whether the citizens will or will not enjoy a sense of security; and, above all, *the attitudes of the people*, that is, whether they really desire progress, and are prepared to innovate and work hard for it.[18]

Perhaps, it would be a better course to attract private foreign

[18] Chapter XVIII *supra*.

investors, instead, who may themselves prefer to participate in
the establishment of plants and factories of various kinds (provided,
of course, many large factories or capital-intensive industries are
at all needed or desirable, which we do not consider they are). In
addition to providing employment, such factories will make available
the technical knowhow and managerial skills that we do not possess.
At the same time, no question of repayment of capital and its interest will arise, nor any question of political strings being attached.
Private foreign investors, however, usually tend to shy away from
industries working for the domestic market in an under-developed
country like India and to concentrate, instead, on primary production mostly in extractive industries such as oil-fields, mines
and plantations. There is no conspiracy behind this attitude, but
two economic considerations, *viz.* poverty of local consumers in
backward areas and vigorously expanding markets for primary
production in the world's industrial centres.

Further, as it is, investment of private foreign capital has not
succeeded to any marked degree in promoting the economic development of the country in the past; obstacles or apprehension of
obstacles such as the possibility of nationalisation, inconvertibility
of currencies or other impediments to repatriation of capital or
profits, and higher returns possible in developed countries, stand
in its way today.

Thus, foreign capital, even if it becomes available in the most
desirable forms, is not enough. It can have only a limited
role to play: it cannot become a substitute for earnings from
abroad or automatically provide a solution to the problem of
capital accumulation within the country itself. The *World Economic
Survey*, 1961, 14th in a series of comprehensive reviews of world
economic conditions, published by the UN on July 12, 1962, is
categorical that "external aid can never be more than a supplement
to the foreign exchange which under-developed countries earn
from their own exports".

Such being the position with regard to capital formation within
the country and availability or utility of capital from outside,
and the need for economic development being admitted, the speed
and scope of the development call for profound statesmanship
on the part of India's leaders. We are faced with a problem as,
perhaps, no other country is. The problem is: *How to bring about,
within the context of a free society*, a take-off or break-through from

economic stagnation to economic development; from a situation where the people live at subsistence levels and whatever efforts at improving the income or output per head we are able to make, are largely cancelled or liable to be cancelled by the population growth or its increasing rate, to a situation where the rate of output of goods so greatly outstrips the rate of population growth that the economy is able to develop a self-sustaining and self-accelerating movement; that is, a situation where economic growth becomes more or less automatic—where the economy begins to expand by its own internal momentum—and increases in incomes and levels of living become possible without undue strain or pressure on the individuals composing the society. On the manner how we solve the problem will depend, in a large measure, the course of world history, at least the future of Southern Asia, of the Middle East and of Africa. On what happens in India during the next ten years or so, will turn the answer to the question whether it is possible to raise the masses of over-crowded and backward countries out of their lowly ways of life without their passing under the sign of Communism—without 'sacrificing the life of many, and the comforts of most, of a whole generation'.

The goal—a higher standard of living by means of industrial growth—being quite acceptable, it draws popular support for our Five-Year Plans. But as the means—the sacrifices involved in the plans—*viz.* high taxes and inflation, have become known in detail, they are meeting stiff opposition. In a democracy where the government has to win willing co-operation of the electorate, politically it is more difficult to secure these means than in a totalitarian country, where consumption can be cut down to any extent that may be desired by Government and all the savings needed, therefore, raised without difficulty, because the consent of the people is not required. In Russia and China the peasantry as a whole, the majority of the population, evidently opposed collectivisation, which was a means of finding capital for heavy industries. Only a dictatorship could have forced through such a programme.

It is hard, indeed, to convince people who are hungering for food, clothes, houses, education and medicine to make sacrifices for basic industries which do not benefit them so immediately. Why, indeed, should people want economic development sufficiently to do something about it, that is, to pay high taxes, if their living standards remain unchanged? Unless the food and clothing of most of them improve at a pace and in a manner perceptible to and approved by them, political freedom and democracy will have little meaning for them, and they will increasingly incline to accept the promises of Communism, little knowing its costs.

Obviously then, as the rate of savings must necessarily be low, a policy of rapid large-scale industrialisation is fraught with political risks. It is not so easy for a democracy that we are, as it may be for a dictatorship, to enforce the policy of 'Jam Tomorrow' and of keeping the people reasonably contented with make-do goods or none at all on the plea that at the end of another Five-Year Plan, the nation will be all the stronger and all the wealthier.

Prime Minister Nehru has observed in several speeches that in India and other newly independent countries political rights or independence had preceded economic revolution while in Western Europe and the USA the reverse had been true. Long before the masses in the latter countries came into the picture through adult franchise, etc., they had been able to build up their industry and perfect their techniques and begun to produce enough resources to meet the demands made by democracy or the political revolution. Capital accumulation in these countries was facilitated by denying the worker his due share in the increased production that followed from application of new and newer methods and techniques of production. The capitalist employer was thus enabled, out of his higher profits, to make larger investments till the economy was able to 'take-off.' Exploitation of the worker was possible because, in the transitional period, not only had the right of vote been denied to him, but also the right of association, the right to strike, etc., with which he could have taken organised action to wring larger economic benefits from the employer. Democratic freedoms were granted to the worker only after economic development had been achieved (In communist countries the transition from economic development to democratic freedom is still in doubt and may not take place at all). On the other hand, in the former countries which are economically under-developed, people's wants had become or could become pressing before the means to satisfy them became available. While population density and growth hamper economic improvement, people's aspirations have been awakened by the political democracy which they have come to enjoy. They are becoming increasingly conscious of poverty and economic differences. They are becoming impatient.

But the question is whether our leadership also will become impatient—so impatient as to try to force the pace of history. No kind or amount of planning can make up for non-existent resources, or neutralize our huge population. Nor, as the experience of the USSR and other countries would show, will forced industrialisation bring about speedy improvement in the economic conditions of our people. "It is doubtful," says W. S. Woytinsky, "whether the *per capita* income of the masses of Russian people, in terms of food, housing, clothing and other material comforts of life, hours and conditions of work, and personal economic security, has risen appreciably under communist rule. It is certain, however, that the experience of the Iron Curtain countries does not support the contention that economic and social progress can be accelerated by forced industrialisation".[19]

Finally, as we will see later, there can be no *rapid* industrialisation of the country unless agricultural surpluses are *rapidly* available and our social and economic attitudes that will enable us to innovate, to acquire the necessary skills and put in the necessary efforts, undergo a *rapid* change. And Nature—animate or inanimate, human or physical—particularly, under the Indian sky, cannot be rushed.

Perhaps, therefore, except for important qualifications, we need not make haste to set up a capital-intensive structure on the lines of the USSR and, in consequence, to have to rely on forced savings, as she did, to provide us with sinews of investment, and a better balance can be maintained between handicrafts or home industry, small-scale or light industry and heavy industry. If, as a result, industrialisation does not proceed at break-neck speed, it will develop on a sounder basis with less waste and suffering for the people.

[19] *Op. cit.*, p. 190.

CHAPTER SIXTEEN

Industrial Structure Suitable for India

THE KIND of capital structure that will suit India depends upon the answer to the question as to what do we aim at ? If we aim merely at the highest output per person employed, output being positively correlated with capital per head, we must have a capital structure on the lines of western industries where this amount is large. But we have three other aims also, *viz.*, to provide optimum employment, to ensure equitable distribution of the national product and to promote a democratic way of life.

An example or two showing the relationship between capital and output in the cotton industry will serve to show that, on the whole, it is less capital-intensive structure that meets India's needs best. According to Dr. P. S. Loknathan, textile fabrics in India were manufactured in the 'forties, broadly speaking, by four different methods of production involving an ascending degree of capital-intensity (that is, capital investment per head of worker). Firstly, there was the ordinary handloom cottage industry, using crude methods, having low capital-intensity, giving low output per head and employing a large number of workers. Secondly, there was the improved handloom or automatic handloom with higher capital-intensity, *e.g.*, the Salvation Army loom, the Chittaranjan loom and the Hattersley loom. In the Hattersley loom, almost all the motions are automatic and capital-intensity is also rather high. Thirdly, there was the small-scale industry— single-unit powerlooms worked in cottages and small-loom factories. Fourthly, there was the modern textile mill. Relevant details are roughly as given in Table XXXVI.

According to another writer, Shri A. K. Sen, quoted by *UN's World Economic Survey* 1961, p. 54, figures of relative productivity of capital and labour for five different techniques in the Indian cotton weaving industry would stand as shown in Table XXXVII.

The figures presented in these tables, though they will differ from industry to industry, may be taken to illustrate the broad relationships obtaining as among the various techniques or technologies within a particular industry.

252

Table XXXVI

CAPITAL AND OUTPUT IN COTTON WEAVING IN INDIA*

Method of Production	Capital intensity (or capital investment per head of worker)	Output (or net value added) per head	Capital coefficient (or ratio of value of output to capital)	Amount of labour employed per unit of capital
I	2	3	4	5
	Rs.	Rs.		
1. Modern mill or large composite factory consisting of spinning-cum-weaving establishments (large-scale industry)	1,200	650	0.54	1
2. Power-loom or small factory consisting of weaving establishments alone (small-scale industry)	300	200	0.66	3
3. Automatic loom (cottage industry)	90	80	0.90	15
4. Handloom (cottage industry)	35	45	1.29	25

* A table given in an article by P. S. Loknathan entitled *Cottage Industries and the Plan* published in *The Eastern Economist* dated July 23, 1943, p. 340

Table XXXVII

ESTIMATES OF PRODUCTIVITY OF CAPITAL AND LABOUR IN INDIAN COTTON WEAVING INDUSTRY USING ALTERNATIVE TECHNIQUES

Technique	Value added per unit of fixed capital	Value added per worker
	Rs.	Rs.
Fly-shuttle handloom	9.0	450
Semi-automatic handloom	7.5	1,500
Cottage power loom	1.5	2,250
Factory non-automatic power loom	1.5	6,000
Automatic power loom	0.6	48,000

Source : Derived from data published in A. K. Sen, *Choice of Techniques : An Aspect of the Theory of Planned Economic Development* (Oxford, 1960), Appendix C.

The data in the above tables bring into relief the conflict between two (or three) possible tests, *viz.*, output (and employment) per unit of capital and output per head. Different ends seem to compete with each other, but so far as our country is concerned the conflict is not real and, therefore, the choice not difficult. According to both the tables, undertakings of high capital intensity or those employing higher technology produce far more per worker employed than undertakings of low capital intensity or those employing cruder technology. For the same amount of capital invested, however, industrial undertakings of low capital intensity produce more goods and provide far more employment than undertakings of high capital intensity. In order to calculate the total output for different types of technologies in Table XXXVI, one will have to assume a given quantity of capital and multiply it by the capital coefficient as given in column 4 of the table. If this were done, one will find that on an assumed capital of Rs. 1,200, the output under different forms of technology beginning with the modern mill would be Rs. 648, Rs. 792, Rs. 1,080 and Rs. 1,548.

While, therefore, highly capital-intensive enterprises may be advantageous to the persons who are employed therein, for they will get higher wages, it is low capital-intensive enterprises that are advantageous *to the country as a whole*—a country where capital is scarce (for such enterprises require less capital), poverty is extreme (for they yield larger product in the total), and labour is plentiful (for they provide more employment). In our country where capital is much the scarcer factor of production than labour, the optimum adaptation of scarce means to unlimited ends would be achieved only when we use capital-economising and labour-intensive methods of production. In other words, we shall have to use less 'capitalistic' methods of production or cruder technology.

A highly capital-intensive undertaking results in keeping a majority of the labour force unemployed or renders them unemployed and, at the same time, tends to concentrate wealth in the hands of a few—to concentrate wealth that would have otherwise gone as wages or earnings to small men or workers, into the pockets of the mill-owners as profits (or of the few workers that will be employed, as high wages). That is why, it would seem, *inter alia*, disparities in incomes in India are so great and, despite a fairly large number of factories, little or no difference in the living standards or levels of consumption of the masses is discernible. In a way, unemployment and consequent misery of millions of persons is the price that the country pays for profits of a few at the top (and employment of a few at high wages).

The capital coefficient or the ratio of the value of output to the amount of capital used, owing to differences in environment and demand, will differ from industry to industry in the same country and identical industries with similar capital structure in different countries. For *enterprises similar in size and with similar capital structure*, the capital coefficient or productivity of capital will be higher in regions or countries where technical efficiency is comparatively higher, managerial skills more developed, educational and training facilities ampler, and social overhead in the form of power, transport, and monetary and marketing institutions more developed. As a general rule, however, the coefficient or productivity of capital in low capital-intensive industries which use cruder technology, for example, in the cottage and handicraft industries will be higher than in more modern industries which use advanced technology. In a country like India, therefore, where capital is scarce and labour not only abundant but redundant, and therefore, the rate of interest higher relatively to the rate of wages—it will not be economical to use the latest, highly automatic, costly machines which require more capital relatively to labour. Here we should expect the structure of economic organisation to be such that the ratio of output to labour would be lower, and that to capital higher, than in economically advanced countries where capital-intensity or capital invested per head of worker is greater.

Speaking as an advocate of heavy industry in the meeting of the All-India Congress Committee held in Chandigarh on September 28, 1959, Prime Minister Nehru said :

The primary thing about an integrated plan was production and not employment. Employment was important, but it was utterly unimportant in the context of production. It followed production and not preceded production. And production would only go up by better techniques which meant modern methods.[1]

The Prime Minister's argument about the relation or sequence between employment and production is naive, indeed. It assumes

[1] *Hindustan Times*, New Delhi, September 29, 1959.

that, while handicrafts or small enterprises may provide comparatively more employment, they produce little or very little compared
with large enterprises. It is this assumption which is responsible for
an undue emphasis on heavy or capital-intensive industries in our
country. The two tables above, however, are a complete refutation of
any such assumption. Large-scale or capital-intensive enterprises
produce less per unit of capital invested than small enterprises.

Large plants or projects do not make much difference, or such
difference to the prosperity or the bulk of the people as is sometimes
supposed. Industrialisation in the modern sense of mills and
factories began in India in the middle of the nineteenth century,
yet the contribution of the organised industrial sector to the total
product of the Indian Union in 1948-49 stood only at 6.3 per cent.
After thirteen years of disproportionately heavy investments the
figure could be raised to 9.5 per cent only in 1960-61. As
between constituent States of the Union : despite its iron and steel
industry, the people of Bihar have remained poor and, although
the Punjab has no large industry, by devoting greater attention to
agriculture and small-scale industries, its people have come to
enjoy a higher standard of living than people elsewhere in the
country. It is not without reason, therefore, that Mahatma Gandhi
had said : "An increase in the number of mills and cities will
certainly not contribute to the prosperity of India" (vide *Swaraj
Through Charkha* compiled by Kanu Gandhi, AISA, Sevagram,
Wardha, 1945, page 5). And the reason is obvious': the number
of workers employed in large plants or projects is small, rather—
in view of our huge population—insignificant, and the return per
unit of capital investment low, indeed, the lowest of all other types
of economic enterprises.

In the conditions of our country, establishment of capital-intensive industry is not likely to mean an improvement in the physical
productivity of the community as a whole for yet another circumstance, viz., *it will throw out of work those who are already employed
today*. "Strange as it may appear", said Mahatma Gandhi, "every
mill generally is a menace to the villagers. I have not worked out
figures, but I am quite safe in saying that every mill-hand does
the work of, at least, ten labourers doing the same work in their
villages. In other words, he earns more than he did in his village,
at the expense of ten fellow-villagers. Thus, spinning and weaving
mills have deprived the villagers of a substantial means of liveli-

hood. It is no answer in reply to say that they turn out cheaper, better cloth, if they do so at all. For, if they have displaced thousands of workers, the cheapest mill cloth is dearer than the dearest *khadi* woven in the villages. Coal is not dear for the coal-miner who can use it there and then, nor is *khadi* dear for the villager who manufactures his own *khadi*."[2]

In this context, it would not be inapt to refer to Shri Nehru's own observations :

Gandhiji has, I think, done a great service to India by his emphasis on village industry. Before he did this, we were all thinking in a lop-sided way and ignoring not only the human aspect of the question, but the peculiar conditions prevailing in India. India, like China, has enormous man-power, vast unemployment and under-employment . . . Any scheme which involves the wastage of our labour-power or which throws people out of employment is bad. From the purely economic point of view, even from the human aspect, it may be more profitable to use more labour-power and less specialised machinery. It is better to find employment for large numbers of people at a low income level than to keep most of them unemployed.[3]

It is obvious that it is not desirable—perhaps, not even possible— for us to copy blindly labour-saving techniques and organisation specially designed for the industrially advanced countries of Europe. Here, account has to be taken of cheap labour and high cost of capital, the level of local technical skill and experience, and the use of local raw material. Our economy has, of necessity, to be such as would lend itself to the maximum exploitation of capital, that is, such as will give us maximum yield per unit of capital invested, even though it may not be consistent with the maximum exploitation of labour employed—an economy which is economical in its use of capital resources, though it may be wasteful of labour resources. It would, therefore, be necessary to safeguard against any unintelligent imitation of the West which may be self-defeating and hold back the pace of industrialization by waste or misuse of the country's scarcest factor, capital, and the inadequate utilization of the cheapest factor, labour.

Addressing a distinguished gathering at Calcutta University

[2] *Harijan* dated November 16, 1934.
[3] Foreword to *China Builds for Democracy* by Nym Wales, 1942.

on July 21, 1961, the United States Ambassador, John Kenneth Galbraith, who is also an eminent economist, said as follows :

> Borrowing technology was highly desirable, in principle, but much of the technology of the more advanced countries represented an accommodation to labour shortages or reflected other special requirements. The mechanical cotton-picker or the modern heavy farm tractor were innovations of this kind. On U. S. farms they reflected the fact that hired labour was exceedingly scarce. This technology should not be taken over by countries in the earlier stages of development. To do so is to waste scarce resources and handicap development and, much more than incidentally, add to unemployment.
>
> While it was a mark of wise development planning to copy from the countries in the more advanced stages, it was also a mark of wise planning not to do so. The advantages of late arrival in the field of development should certainly be exploited, but they are all too few.[4]

The Ambassador listed high-yielding maize hybrids, the Japanese method of rice cultivation, improved fertilizer use and the L-D process of steel production as advances or technologies of general application. They economise all resources, and are as appropriate and important for the less as for the more developed country. He went on to emphasise that the greatest danger lay in borrowing methods of organisation. Many institutions and services in more advanced countries were luxuries the developing nations could ill afford.

The social and economic conditions of our country constituted one of the reasons why Mahatma Gandhi was so greatly opposed to the establishment of heavy or large-scale mechanised industries in the country and which made him such a strong advocate of handicrafts and small scale enterprises. "I can have no consideration for machinery," he said, "which is meant either to enrich the few at the expense of the many, or *without cause*, to displace the useful labour of many" (vide the *Harijan*, dated 22-6-1935). "Men go on saving labour," he said on another occasion, "till thousands are without work and thrown on the open streets to die of starvation. I want to save time and labour, not for a fraction of mankind, but for all. I want the concentration of wealth not in the hands of many, but distribution in the hands of all. Today machinery

[4] *Hindustan Times* dated July 22, 1961.

merely helps a few to ride over the back of millions."[5]

But, while all that has been said in the preceding paragraphs is true, in the long-term interest of the country, we will have to have certain—a minimum unavoidable number of—heavy or capital intensive projects and industries, even if their capital coefficient and labour intensity, i.e., the ratios of net value added and of labour employed per unit of capital invested, are comparatively lower. Gandhiji, too, was not averse to this course. He aimed not at eradication of all machinery but at its limitation. As we have already seen, he was prepared to "visualize electricity, ship-building, iron-works, machine-making and the like existing side by side with village handicrafts."[6] Obviously, he would also have had no objection to organisation of defence industries on a large or heavy scale. The motives underlying the pattern of defence industries cannot be primarily social or economic: their organisation and capital-intensity will be dictated largely by considerations of security.

Once a friend asked Gandhiji whether he proposed to replace the railways with bullock-carts and, if he did not, how he expected to replace mills with spinning wheels. He wrote :

I told him that I did not propose to replace railways with carts because I could not do so even if I wished. Three hundred million carts could not destroy distance. But I would replace mills with wheels. For railways solved the question of speed. With mills it was a question of production in which the wheel could easily compete if there were enough hands as there were in India.[7]

In this age, electric power and steel are the key to economic development, whether it be in the field of large-scale operations, or that of cottage industry. It is the extent of substitution of mechanical for manual or physical power that indicates the extent of industrialisation or economic development of a country. Machines are made of iron or steel and run with (coal or) electric energy. Therefore, unless there is a great disparity in possession of natural resources and availability of raw materials, there is, in the various countries, a broad relationship between steel and energy production on one hand and national income on the other.

[5] Mahadeo Desai's article in the *Young India*, dated 13-11-1924.
[6] *Why the Constructive Programme*, New Delhi, 1948, p. 19.
[7] *Young India* dated May 28, 1925.

TABLE XXXVIII
RELATION OF CONSUMPTION OF ENERGY AND CRUDE STEEL
TO NATIONAL INCOME FOR 1960

Sl. No.	Country	Consump-tion* of energy per capita (in kilo-gram-mes)	Per capita actual produc-tion of electric energy (in K.W.H.)	Production per capita (in kg.)		Consump-tion of crude steel · per capita (in kilo-gram-mes)	Per capita National Income (in U.S. Dollar)
				Pig Iron and Ferro-alloys	Crude Steel		
1	2	3	4	5	6	7	8
1.	United States	8,013	4,654	345	498	501	2,286
2.	Canada	5,679	6,399	225	295	308	1,536
3.	United Kingdom	4,920	2,609	306	471	425	1,071
4.	Belgium	3,968	1,655	716	785	275	989
5.	Germany (F.R.)	3,651	2,187	486	641	525	927
6.	Sweden	3,496	4,652	218	425	545	1,377
7.	U.S.S.R.	2,847	1,363	218	305	296	747
8.	Denmark	2,821	1,131	16	· 64	259	1,036
9.	Netherlands	2,820	1,438	117	169	278	807
10.	Norway	2,732	8,738	199	136	275	971
11.	Venezuela	2,558	456	..	..	76	891
12.	Union of S. Africa	2,411	1,585 ·	136	144	145	824
13.	France	2,402	1,584	315	379	306	964
14.	Austria	2,180	2,255	316	447	268	644
15.	Ireland	2,014	797	..	..	56	530
16.	Switzerland	1,941	3,557	9	51	293	1,377
17.	Finland	1,637	1,934	31	57	229	821
18.	Israel	1,266	1,094	..	..	170	911
19.	Italy	1,186	1,139	57	167	187	509
20.	Japan	1,164	1,239	132	238	208	341
21.	Argentina	1,069	518	9	14	76	378
22.	Mexico	1,012	307	15	28	50	278
23.	Chile	883	603	36	57	70	503
24.	Greece	569	227 (1958)	..	..	40	325
25.	Columbia	509	265	8	11	27	215 (1959)
26.	Brazil	372	329 (1959)	23	..	41	108 (1959)
27.	Portugal	362	365	5	5	43	· 226
28.	Peru	355	210 (1959)	..	..	16	113 (1959)
29.	Korea (Rep.)	254	71	..	2	..	111
30.	Fed. of Malaya	241	172	..	..	29	211 (1959)

TABLE XXXVIII (*contd.*)

Sl. No.	Country	Consumption of energy per capita (in kilogrammes)	Per capita actual production of electric energy (in K.W.H.)	Production per capita (in kg.)		Consumption of crude steel per capita (in kilogrammes)	Per capita National Income (in U.S. Dollar)
				Pig Iron and Ferro-alloys	Crude Steel		
1	2	3	4	5	6	7	8
31.	Turkey	237	104	89	10	22	164 (1959)
32.	Guatemala	146	67 (1959)	..	..	..	155
33.	India	140	46	10	8	11	69
34.	Philippines	138	85 (1959)	..	..	15	135
35.	Ceylon	105	30	..	..	9	120
36.	Paraguay	87	71 (1959)	..	..	..	101
37.	Pakistan	67	16	..	..	5	52
38.	Thailand	63	..	..	..	8	93
39.	Burma	55	19	..	..	..	50
40.	China (Mainland)	..	64 (1959)	43	29	27	59 (1957)

SOURCE : (1) *U. N. Statistical Year Book*, 1961.

(2) Exchange rates for conversion of National Currency units into U. S. Dollars from *U. N. Monthly Bulletin of Statistics*, April 1962 and *I. M. F. International Financial Statistics*, March 1962.

Note : (1) The figures relate to the year 1960. In case of those countries whose figures for 1960 were not available, their latest available figures have been taken and the year in question shown within brackets.

(2) In case of China (Mainland) per capita figure in col. 4 has been worked out by the total population in 1960 as the corresponding population for 1959 was not available.

(3) The figures shown in cols. 3 to 8 against Union of South Africa relate to South Africa.

(4) Per capita figures in cols. 4, 5 and 6 have been worked out by dividing the total production data of a country by its corresponding population.

* Consumption data are based on the apparent consumption of coal lignite, petroleum production, natural gas and hydro-electricity.

Table XXXVIII would show that for nearly all nations a large use of steel and energy means a high standard of living and *vice versa*.

Sweden's lower consumption of energy than U.K., Belgium and Germany (F.R.) although it enjoys higher *per capita* income, is compensated by higher consumption of steel. Denmark's higher *per capita* income than Belgium, Germany (F.R.) and U.S.S.R. despite lower *per capita* consumption both of energy and steel is explained by highest agricultural production per acre in the world, taking crop and dairy together. Switzerland is a class by itself : a large part of its income is derived from tourist traffic.

Around 1850 Britain's iron production was 1.3 million tons per year. A spectacular effort took this figure to 6 million tons by 1870. The iron and steel output of India in 1950-51, at the threshold of her own economic development, was of about the same order as Britain's 100 years ago. India's output rose to 3.5 million tons by the end of the Second Five-Year Plan, and it is expected to rise to 9.2 million tons by the end of the Third Five-Year Plan. But to rank as an equal in this regard with Britain of today, India will have to produce 100 million tons of steel a year. To reach that objective India has reasonable expectations with regard to raw materials. Her iron ore deposits are singularly rich with a metal content of up to 61 per cent as against the 15 per cent to 30 per cent which iron and steel works in other countries find it worthwhile to process.

Like steel and electric energy, development of nuclear energy will also require heavy industry. India is particularly fortunate in possessing mineral resources of nuclear power in an abundant measure which, in course of time, can be developed to great economic advantage of the country. "India has the largest known thorium reserves in the world, equalling in amount, the total world reserve of uranium. Several deposits of uranium also have been discovered in various parts of the country, which are still being proved by drilling. A deposit containing several thousand tons of uranium has already been established in Bihar" (*Vide* 'Third Plan', p. 196).

Mahatma Gandhi laid down the criterion for heavy industry thus : "The heavy industry for works of public utility which cannot be undertaken by human labour has its inevitable place".[8] He listed printing presses, surgical instruments and Singer's Sewing

[8] *Harijan* dated June 22, 1935.

machines as examples of works of public utility which could not be made with one's hands and, therefore, required heavy industry for their manufacture. In fact, he was prepared to have heavy industry for manufacturing all kinds of tools, implements or instruments and machinery which did not deprive the masses of the opportunity to labour, but which helped the individual ease his effort and added to his efficiency—"which saved individual labour and lightened the burden of millions of cottages"—and which a man could handle at will without being their slave. His exceptions in favour of such machines—machinery, for manufacture whereof, heavy industry was permissible—would end just where they began to cripple or atrophy the limbs of man, or where they ceased to help the individual and encroached upon his individuality.

Perhaps, it would be a correct representation of Gandhiji's position to say that he approved establishment of heavy or capital-intensive industries for—and only for—purposes which could not be carried out on small scale, or for production of things which could not be manufactured by hand labour, that is, on the scale of handicrafts, or cottage industries. "But heavy industries," he emphasized, "will occupy the least part of the vast national activity which will be carried on mainly in villages".[9]

The question, however, arises whether such heavy or capital-intensive projects and enterprises as may be in public interest shall be set up in the public or the private sector.

Labour being cheap and machinery relatively costly in the country, the best results for the private entrepreneur in most cases should be obtainable by applying large amounts of labour to a single machine. He will, therefore, left to himself, cut down his costs by selecting labour-using methods in preference to capital-using ones. However, the organisation of labour into trade unions and the various laws governing relations between labour and industry, tend to push up the wages and, in consequence, to make the machines cheaper comparatively to labour. The prophecy of Karl Marx that the economic condition of depressed classes in industrial societies must progressively deteriorate, has not been fulfilled in Western democracies, simply because workers have organised themselves to exercise political power and do away with the free supply and demand of human labour. Ideas about the polarisation of society into the bourgeoisie and the proletariat and ever-increasing misery of the

[9] *Why the Constructive Programme ?*, New Delhi, 1948, p. 28.

proletariat, ending in class-war, have been superseded through the joint operation of political democracy and labour organisation. This has happened in India also. The entrepreneur, therefore, in actual practice, would prefer a higher capital structure, that is, a structure which uses comparatively less labour. As shown by the experience of the USA and other countries, however, private capital ordinarily shies from investment in those capital-intensive projects which are ultimately calculated to develop an economy. In the pre-take-off period, particularly, private capital is invested in lucrative but unproductive fields, like trade and commerce. There is also scarcity of private initiative and enterprise at this stage. In the circumstances it devolves on the state to step in and help "shift investments from unproductive to productive and from static to dynamic avenues". It will be a mistake, and not conducive to public interest, to allow the capital structure of the economy to be determined entirely by the interests or preferences of the private entrepreneur, or by the forces of the free market, that is, left to be dictated by the fact that only a small volume of capital is available in the country relative to the large supply of labour. The role of the state in the economic field is underlined by the philosophy that its resources should be directed for the welfare of the people. Basic heavy or capital intensive industries in the country, therefore, should be established by the state.

According to Gandhiji also, the minimum and inevitable heavy industry that the country must have, was to be owned by the state and, of course, used entirely for the benefit of the people. "I am socialist enough to say," he said, "that such factories should be nationalized or state-controlled."[10] In fact, as a matter of principle, he "would have state ownership where a large number of people have to work together."[11] He would have no large-scale or heavy industry in the private sector at all, except where, for unavoidable reasons, the state might itself allow an entrepreneur to set up such industry subject to certain conditions. But while he did not totally reject socialism or an economic system based on public ownership of means of production, he did not totally accept it. For shortage of capital and redundance of labour, he argued, our economy will need to be carried on predominantly in the form of handicrafts or on a small scale—dispersed over the countryside. Mahatma

[10] Mahadeo Desai's article in the *Young India*, dated 13-11-1924.
[11] *Harijan*, dated 1-9-1946.

Gandhi held "that to industrialize India in the same sense as Europe was to attempt the impossible,"[12] and that "no amount of socialization could eradicate the evils of capitalism inherent in industrialism".[13] The economy that will suit us will be an economy where (private) capitalism is eliminated almost altogether and (state capitalism or) socialism is retained to the minimum—an economy which is based predominantly on self-employed persons, artisans and workers, with the owner and the worker, the employer and the employee, the entrepreneur and the financier all rolled into one.

Here we may notice an apprehension sometimes voiced by the advocates of small or labour-intensive industry, *viz.* that an exception in favour of certain types of heavy industry will prove the thin end of the wedge. It will be difficult to draw a line where one can stop and ultimately the entire industrial culture of the West will have been established. The noted historian, Arnold Toynbee, says : "The truth is that every historic culture-pattern is an organic whole in which all the parts are inter-dependent, so that, if any part is prized out of its setting, both the isolated part and the mutilated whole behave differently from their behaviour when the pattern is intact. This is why 'one man's meat' can be 'another man's poison' : and another consequence is that 'one thing leads to another'. If a splinter is flaked off from one culture and is introduced into a foreign body social, this isolated splinter will tend to draw in after it, into the foreign body in which it has lodged, the other component elements of the social system in which this splinter is at home and from which it has been forcibly and unnaturally detached. The broken pattern tends to reconstitute itself in a foreign environment into which one of its components has once found its way."[14]

But in arguing as above, three things are forgotten. First, left to himself the private entrepreneur, in the conditions of our country, mostly finds it profitable to use only labour-using techniques. The logic of economic facts is all against capital-using techniques. Second, even if there is a fallacy in the above reasoning or, owing to other causes, he finds it profitable to establish capital-intensive forms, the state will or should simply not allow him to do so. The heavy capital goods industries that come into being, will be estab-

[12] *Young India*, dated August 6, 1925.
[13] *Harijan*, dated September 29, 1940.
[14] Footnote on p. 133 of the *Harijan*, dated June 25, 1955.

lished in the public sector as part of a plan. Third, the splinter from the western body social may, in course of time, instead of drawing the parent body in its wake, find its level in the new environment or the latter may so adjust itself as to make the splinter an unrecognisable part of itself. That Toynbee's thesis does not represent an inviolable rule of human and social behaviour has been proved time and again by the Indian social system whose capacity of absorption and adaptation is great.

Be that as it may, barring the industries that have been mentioned and those, if any, which cannot be established or run on small scale, it is not capital-intensive but labour-intensive industries that are the key to our problems. Wherever we can help it, we should not substitute capital for labour—machines for men. In particular, it is labour-intensive enterprises or handicrafts and small-scale industries alone that will fulfil the second aim of our economy, *viz.* provision of maximum employment.

The Planning Commission also while favouring capital intensive techniques for heavy or producer goods industries, conceded that, so far as consumer goods industries are concerned it is in the national interest that labour-intensive techniques are used. "It is only", the Commission observes, "when we come to the production of consumer goods that the choice between techniques of production may raise difficult issues. The use of capital-intensive techniques irrespective of other considerations involves a double loss in the form of (a) displacement of labour which has in any case to be maintained, and (b) a greater draft on the scarce resources for investment, particularly foreign exchange resources. The issues involved in this field go to the roots of the problem of economic and social development. . . . The long-term objective of having a rising rate of investment, which cannot be sustained without an adequate level of savings out of current output, has to be accepted. It is particularly when the capacity of decentralised production to accumulate surpluses is challenged that the conflict among different desirable objectives becomes a matter of some concern. The surplus generated per person in a comparatively labour-intensive technique may be less than in a more advanced technique, but the total surplus available per unit of output for capital formation, taking into account the social and economic cost of maintaining those who would otherwise remain unemployed may, perhaps, be larger in the case of labour-intensive methods. In an under-developed economy where the distribution of doles to the unemployed is not practicable, the balance of advantage from the standpoint of equity lies decidedly in favour of labour-intensive techniques. From the point of view of development, however, the difficulty in the adoption of such techniques lies in the mobilisation of the available surplus from a large number of smaller units ; but this is an organisational problem and requires to be faced".(Vide Second Five-Year Plan, pp. 113-114).

Unemployment not only involves a huge economic waste, but constitutes a threat to our social and political stability. According to the Planning Commission the number of unemployed persons in the country in 1955 stood at 5.3 million—2.5 in urban areas and 2.8 in rural areas. The new entrants to the labour force during the next five years, *viz.* 1956-61, were estimated at 10 million. In actual fact, this figure has proved to be an under-estimate for the simple reason that the Planning Commission had under-estimated the growth rate of our population.

Even if the unemployment situation existing at the beginning of the Second Plan were to remain unchanged, some 10.0 million more jobs would have had to be created by the end of the Second Five-Year Plan. But the additional work, or employment opportunities outside agriculture that were likely to be created as a result of the Plan would have, according to the original estimates of the Planning Commission itself, been able to absorb only 8.0 million persons. The Commission, therefore, went on to observe that "it would be incorrect to hold out the hope that full employment can be secured by the end of the Second Plan" (p. 112). There was no question of holding out or not holding out any hope ; the revised estimates put the figure of additional jobs at 6.5 million only, thus leaving 3.5 million *new* entrants to the labour force of the country at the end of the Second Plan to fend for themselves.

About the actual employment or unemployment situation at the end of the Second Plan, the Third Five-Year Plan has the following observations to make on page 156 :

In the course of the Second Plan the additional employment opportunities created amounted to about 8 million, of which about 6.5 million were outside agriculture. The back-log of unemployment at the end of the Second Plan is reckoned at 9 million. This estimate is admittedly rough. It takes account of the estimate of unemployment as at the beginning of the Second Plan (5.3 million), the larger increase in labour force during the Second Plan period than had been visualised earlier (1.7 million), and the estimated shortfall in the employment target originally proposed for the Second Plan (about 2 million). In addition, under-employment in the sense of those who have some work but are willing to take up additional work cannot be precisely estimated, but is believed to be of the order of 15-18 million.

According to the Third Five-Year Plan, on such estimates as were at the moment possible, the addition to the labour force during 1961-66 might be of the order of 17 million, about a third of the increase being in the urban areas. Thus, the number of unemployed people for whom jobs must be found during the Third Plan period must be placed at 26 million, but the most optimistic estimate is that not more than 14 million (3.5 million agricultural + 10.5 million non-agricultural) jobs at best can be created during the Third Plan period. This implies that the back-log of the un-employed at the end of the Third Plan period will be larger, *viz.* 12 million, than the back-log at the beginning of the Second Plan period, *viz.* 5.3 million !

The estimates of the unemployed do not take into account the widespread under-employment in the rural areas, both among the cultivating and non-cultivating classes. From the information collected some years ago by the National Sample Survey (although it suffers from certain limitations) it would seem that nearly 20 million persons normally work one hour or less per day, 27 million work two hours or less per day, and nearly 45 million persons are engaged in gainful work for four hours a day or less. In NSS (5th and 6th rounds : December, 1952—March, 1953) it was found that nearly 30 million persons have gainful work for less than five days, 39 million less than 10 days, and 53 million less than 15 days in the month. In another inquiry (NSS : 7th round, October 1953—March, 1954) it was found that about 45 million persons were working part time. Among them 23 million (or about half) gave reasons of an economic nature such as lack of demand for their labour, lack of tools and raw materials, slack and off season, etc. In NSS 9th round, May 1955 to August 1955, in reply to a specific question, nearly 12 million persons stated that they were seeking additional work and would be available for four hours of work or more per day (vide the *Sankhya*, Calcutta, vol. 20, p. 78). The following table prepared in NSS 11th and 12th round, August 1956—August 1957, gives still more up-to-date and comprehensive figures of the extent of under-employment in our country. Of the persons who may be called 'gainfully employed', 15.29 per cent were under-employed in the villages, and 11.1 per cent in the towns :

TABLE XXXIX

PERCENTAGE DISTRIBUTION OF GAINFULLY EMPLOYED
BY WEEKLY HOURS AT WORK AND THE PROPORTIONS
AVAILABLE FOR ADDITIONAL WORK IN EACH
GROUP OF HOURS AT WORK

Weekly hours at work	Rural			Urban		
	per cent of persons	per cent reporting availability for addl. work	$(2) \times (3)$ / 100	per cent of persons	per cent reporting availability for addl. work	$(5) \times (6)$ / 100
1	2	3	4	5	6	7
1. 0	4.77	5.43	0.26	3.83	5.83	0.22
2. 1–7	1.33	37.24	0.50	1.21	35.87	0.43
3. 8–14	4.27.	39.83	1.70	2.53	32.53	0.82
4. 15–28	12.34	37.02	4.57	8.34	36.21	3.02
5. 29–42	18.37	27.83	5.10	18.38	20.85	3.84
6. 43–56	32.09	7.79	2.50	38.62	5.47	2.11
7. 57–70	24.14	2.66	0.64	21.06	2.76	0.58
8. above 70	2.69	0.81	0.02	6.03	1.30	0.08
9. Total	100.00	15.29	15.29	100.00	11.10	11.10
10. Number of sample persons	68,447	..	..	16,736	..	..

SOURCE : *The National Sample Survey*, Eleventh and Twelfth Round, August 1956—August 1957, Number 52 (Table 2.4).

Today, *viz.* nearly 8 years after the survey, these figures must have gone still higher.

These figures show that the extent of under-employment is far greater than that of unemployment. This is also proved by sample inquiries held by the Economics and Statistics Department of

Uttar Pradesh in 6,709 rural households covering all districts of the State during the period 1956-61 according to which, while only 1.26 per cent of the total male labour force were completely un-employed, 16.08 were found to be under-employed.

Land-holdings are becoming smaller and smaller, and even the traditional non-agricultural employments in the villages are shrinking. This is broadly confirmed by the Second Agricultural Labour Enquiry, the National Sample Survey and the Studies undertaken by the Programme Evaluation Orga-nisation. The reasons are obvious : the Planning Commission and our Governments have not placed the necessary emphasis on the most potent remedy, *viz.* the development of handicrafts and small-scale industries in the countryside, and on labour-intensive techniques in all possible spheres. The unemployment situation is a reflection of our industrial policy, as a consequence whereof while the share of factory establishments in the national product has increased from 6.3 per cent in 1948-49 to 9.5 per cent in 1960-61, that of small enterprises, which would have provided several times more employment per unit of capital invested, has during the same period, decreased from 10.1 per cent to 8.0 per cent ! [15]

It will be a paradox, on the basis of increase in aggregate nation-al income or on the assumption of increase in the *average per capita income*, to claim that India is achieving economic progress, if at the same time the number of the unemployed and the under-employed goes on increasing. The objective of development should be not only to raise the level of per capita real income, but also to provide employment to all our countrymen and thus secure them the barest necessities of life.

Mahatma Gandhi laid great emphasis on eradication of un-employment and under-employment of our people, and reverted to the subject again and again :

The disease of the masses is not want of money so much as it is want of work. Labour is money. He who provides dignified labour for the millions in their cottages, provides food and clothing, or which is the same thing, money. The charkha provides such labour. *Till a better substitute is found, it must, therefore, hold the field.*[16]

[15] Vide *Estimates of National Income* 1948-49 *to* 1960-61, February, 1962, issued by Central Statistical Organization, Department of Statistics, Cabinet Secretariat, Government of India, New Delhi.

[16] *Young India*, dated June 18, 1925.

Idleness is the great cause, the root of all evil, and if that root can be destroyed, most of the evils can be remedied without further effort. A nation that is starving has little hope or initiative left in it. It becomes indifferent to filth and disease. It says of all reforms, 'to what good?' That winter of despair can be turned into the 'sunshine of hope' for the millions only through the life-giving wheel, the *charkha*.[17]

Say the critics, the spinning wheel is not exciting enough, it is an occupation only for women, it means a return to the middle ages, it is a vain effort against the majestic march of scientific knowledge for which machinery stands. In my humble opinion India's need is not excitement, but solid work. For the millions solid work itself is excitement and tonic at the same time. The fact is that we have not given the spinning wheel enough trial. I am sorry to have to say that many of us have not given it a serious thought.[18]

India has to live, that is, her millions have to live. There is no other country in the world where so many millions of people have only partial employment and where, in spite of the civilization being predominantly rural, the holdings are barely two acres per head. To manufacture the whole of her cloth requirements through steam or electricity, or any other than the human power behind the wheel, is still further to deepen the unemployment of the population. An industrialized India must, therefore, mean utter extinction of many millions.[19]

The spinning wheel represents to me the hope of the masses. The masses lost their (economic) freedom, such as it was, with the loss of the *charkha*. The *charkha* supplemented the agriculture of the villagers and gave it dignity. It was the friend and the solace of the widow. It kept the villagers from idleness. For the *charkha* included all the anterior and posterior industries—ginning, carding, warping, sizing, dyeing and weaving. These in their turn kept the village carpenter and the blacksmith busy. The *charkha* enabled the seven hundred thousand villages to become self-contained. With the exit of the *charkha* went the other village industries, such as oil press. Nothing took the place of these industries. Therefore, the villages were drained of their varied occupations and their creative talent and what little wealth these brought them .... Hence, if the villagers are to come into their own, the most natural thing that suggests itself is the revival of the *charkha* and all it means.[20]

Mahatma Gandhi held that "the method of doing or manu- facturing a thing by machinery was harmful when the same thing could be done or manufactured easily by millions of hands *not*

[17] *Young India*, dated August 27, 1925.
[18] *Young India*, dated December 26, 1924.
[19] *Harijan*, dated October 27, 1933.
[20] *Harijan*, dated April 13, 1940.

otherwise occupied".[21] "With crores of human beings going idle," he emphasized, "India cannot afford to have large machinery which will displace their labour. It would spell their unemployment and their ruin. Our problem is how to find employment for all the crores of our people, not how to save their labour. Continuous unemployment has already induced in them a kind of laziness or listlessness which is most depressing."[22]

One-fourth of India's population today lives on a daily expenditure of less than 4 annas or 25 *naye paise*, and one-fifth of the total population lives on considerably less (*Sankhya*, Calcutta, Vol. 20, p. 74). Handicrafts and small-scale industry, however, can provide employment and income to all these people, and employment for all is any day preferable to plenty for the few. For example, an average skilled spinner working on the traditional or the *Ambar charkha* for three to four hours a day can earn between 3 to 5 annas. In the case of most other village industries, the level of earnings per day is considerably higher. We would, therefore, do well to keep our people employed even with the *charkha*, the handloom and other hand-driven employments rather than let them eat out their heart in unemployment.

It may be conceded for argument's sake—and for argument's sake only—that handicrafts and small-scale industries are not able to produce all the wealth that we can possibly need or consume. In order to improve production, therefore, we may make all attempts to reach electric power to villagers, and to improve the existing techniques. But if modern technology cannot be reached to the villagers just today, this does not mean that in the meanwhile the villagers should remain or be kept under-employed and unemployed. It will be suicidal and must mean certain death to millions of India's population, if the solar power stored in their hands is allowed to run waste while an attempt to replace it with steam, electricity or such other power is being made.

It has to be realised—and one who cannot realise it, cannot serve India and her teeming masses—that the measure of removal of unemployment and underemployment is the true measure of happiness of our people *as also of the Union and State Government's achievement.*

Richard B. Gregg, an exponent of Gandhian economics has discussed, in an admirable manner, how millions of engines in

[21] *Young India*, dated July 2, 1931.
[22] *Harijan*, dated January 2, 1937.

India, in the form of unemployed and under-employed persons, are lying idle, how easily and cheaply the machines or devices, on one hand, and the raw materials, on the other, are available, and yet it does not occur to us that the engines can be attached to the machines and, thus, our poverty eradicated in a large measure. He says :

We do not usually think of the *charkha* as a machine, but it really is so. It uses the available mechanical energy of a man, woman or child for producing material goods. The handloom does likewise. That mechanical energy is derived from the food eaten by the person. The energy in the food came from the sunshine that fell on the fields where that food grew. Though in a different degree, manner and mode, the process is the same as that occurring in a steam engine or hydraulic power plant —namely, the transformation of solar energy into mechanical motion.

There are today great numbers of unemployed Indians. They are, in effect, engines kept running by fuel (food), but not attached to any machines or devices for producing goods. Gandhiji proposed to hitch them to *charkha* and thus save a vast existing waste of solar energy.

If we want to increase the use of mechanical power in India, this is the quickest and cheapest way. The 'engines' are all present ; a man is as efficient a transformer of fuel energy into mechanical motion as a steam engine is; the spinning and weaving machinery to be used is ready at hand in large quantity and could in a very few years be increased enough to supply all needs. Any additional needs can be quickly and cheaply produced in India by artisans who need no further training in technical skill for this purpose ; the speed and quantity of output possible with *charkha* and handloom are more closely adapted to the needs of the Indian villages and Indian producers than any other type of machinery ; no foreign capital is needed to purchase the machinery ; and, therefore, there will be no expensive interest and capital payments or difficulties arising from absentee control ; the maintenance of such a factory is inexpensive and can be done entirely by available workers without further training ; the amount of training needed for an operative is minimum and of a sort more easily acquired than for any other type of machinery ; the 'fuel' or power cost for the man-*charkha* system will be nothing above the present food bill of the nation ; the material to be used is available in every Indian State but Kerala, the smallest, at a minimum transportation cost ; and the market is everywhere in India.[23]

Therefore, while the Commission's approach in regard to consumer goods industries is to be welcomed, one cannot but definitely dis-

[23] *A Philosophy of Indian Economic Development*, published by the Navjivan Publishing House, Ahmedabad, 1958, pp. 5-6.

agree with it when it goes on to opine that, besides heavy industries in whose case considerations of size and technology cannot possibly be set aside in favour of employment, machinery should also be used or continue to be used in construction of roads, houses, railway tracks and the like, and not human labour. If man in ancient Egypt could build the pyramids and, in medieval India, the Taj Mahal, or, if more recently, during the war years in China and Burma, he could build airfields and roads entirely by manual labour, there is no reason why he cannot construct almost all kinds of public works without the aid of machines.

It is clear from Tables XXXVI and XXXVII that our unemployment problem can be relieved only by small-scale decentralized industries with low capital-intensity, including cottage or handicraft industries using lower techniques of production, and not by capital-intensive undertakings. The former provide several times larger employment than the latter. The conclusions of the tables as regards employment potentialities of the different kinds of industrial units are confirmed by the Report of the Textile Enquiry Committee (September, 1954). The Report says that the organised cotton textile industry in 1953 provided direct employment to approximately 2,50,000 workers ; powerloom units in the country, both large and small, which had been given texmark numbers by the Textile Commissioner, provided direct employment to 55,000 workers, and the handloom industry to 15,00,000 workers (in terms of whole-time workers). "The mill production is of the order of 4,800 million yards while the powerloom industry produces under present conditions approximately 200 million yards a year. The handloom industry is estimated to produce 1,400 million yards a year. For a production $3\frac{1}{2}$ times as large, the mill industry provides direct employment approximately to one-sixth as large a number of people as are engaged in the handloom industry (assuming that 2.5 lakh workers, including assistants, are directly employed in both shifts on nearly 2 lakh looms). The employment potential in the handloom industry is, therefore, nearly twenty times what it is in the mill industry, yard for yard."

What an unrealistic dream it is to think that large-scale industrialisation will ever be able to provide a solution to our social problem as it has in the case of the United Kingdom or the USA, will be clear from the following table which gives figures relating to manpower and large-scale industrial employment in the three countries stated in juxtaposition, and from the fact that while the number of factories had risen from 8,143 in undivided India in 1931 to 30,836 in the Union of India in 1951, *viz.* about fourfold, the number of persons employed rose only from 1.43 million to 2.54 million, *viz.* from 0.93 per cent to 1.81 per cent of the entire working force of the country. In 1958 the number of factories[24] in the country had risen to 41,579, and persons employed to 3.41 million—which means that, out of about 23 million persons

TABLE XL

COMPARISON OF LABOUR FORCE AND INDUSTRIAL EMPLOYMENT
IN INDIA WITH GREAT BRITAIN AND USA

(In thousands)

Country	Population (Year)	Total labour force (Year)	Percentage of employment of labour force in industry	Labour force engaged in large-scale establishments (Year)	Yearly increase in labour force in the quinquennium 1951-56
1	2	3	4	5	6
Great Britain	5,07,72 (1952)	2,24,82 (1951)	49	70,64* (1949)	81
USA	15,69,81 (1952)	5,84,42 (1950)	37	1,32,590† (1947)	1,072
India	36,70,00 (1951)	13,93,39 (1951)	10	2,540‡ (1951)	1,886

SOURCE : Figures in columns 3 and 4 have been taken from Table XXX of this book.

Figures in column 5 have been taken from *International Labour Review*, June, 1956, pp. 640-644.

Figures in column 6 have been worked out on the basis of percentage of labour force given in Table XXX *ante* operating on figures of population given in the *U.N.O. Statistical Year Book*, 1957.

* Establishments with more than 9 employees.

† Establishments with more than 19 employees.

‡ Establishments with more than 9 employees when they are carried on with the aid of power and more than 19 employees when they are carried on without power.

[24] Excluding Jammu & Kashmir and Mysore (SOURCE : *Statistical Abstract of India*, 1958-59).

added to the labour force of the country since 1951, only 0.87 million or 3.8 per cent could be absorbed in large-scale enterprises. The unrealism of the dream will become all the more evident when it is remembered that, owing to almost continual advance in technology, we require fewer and still fewer men to produce the same amount of goods, as time passes.

We should consider ourselves fortunate if large-scale industries can absorb all those who are completely unemployed today and so many of the under-employed that those who are left behind, get full employment in their present occupations. But it is obvious that large-scale industries cannot possibly provide increasing employment for 4.0 million people every year, which is the natural increase in the labour force of the country. The hopes of those who advocate large-scale industrialisation as a means of enabling the size of land-holdings to be increased by drawing people off the land in large numbers, are doomed to disappointment. So that the basic agrarian picture will not only remain as it is, with land-holdings as pitifully small as ever, but it will deteriorate still further. Quite a good percentage of the increase in the working force engaged in agriculture today, will remain on land making the holdings smaller and smaller still.

In view of the fact that large-scale industrialisation is not going to make any appreciable dent in our economy, any hope of reduction in the birth-rate as a consequence of urbanisation is also a forlorn hope and should not deter us from following any policy that we may otherwise consider suitable.

Advocates of capital-intensive types concede that in the very short run a unit of investment in a labour-intensive industry or process will provide a greater amount of employment than a unit in capital intensive type. But they contend, first, that although in the case of agriculture the producer in our country is also the major consumer, it is not so in the case of industry. Consumers' interest must, therefore, receive special consideration : prices of the basic necessities have to be brought down to a level at which the ordinary householder can, after meeting his basic necessities, have some surplus left which may provide him with some comforts also. The application of advanced technology and automatic methods constantly reduced the capital cost per unit of annual. capacity which is reflected in lower cost of the product. Also, advanced technology leads to a lower cost of production in another manner, *viz.* it utilises the raw materials more fully than crude technology. For instance, a cottage worker cannot produce the same quantity of cloth from a given weight of cotton as a modern textile mill can. The wastage is so much greater at various stages of the operation. Similarly, a crude worker cannot expect the same extraction from sugarcane as a mill. Second, that although output in labour-intensive types is greater relatively to the amount of capital used and there is economy of capital, output per man-hour or labour productivity goes down, and even though the total output would increase, it has to be shared by an increasingly larger number of workers in the industry. When this happens, the standard of living of the workers declines. Third, that economic development consists not in the maximum utilisation of available resources, but in a rapid increase in these resources, particularly in capital resources, and, over the long period, capital-intensive types will generate a greater surplus for capital formation and so make a bigger contribution to employment and national income. Capital-intensive enterprises have the effect of concentrating additional income in the hands of those who are more likely to save and invest it in further industrialisation of the country. If production is distributed into so many workers having low income, all or a large part of it is likely to be used up in consumption and little or nothing saved for capital formation, which is so essential for economic development. Fourth, that in trying to substitute labour for capital in any given sphere of production, which is what the adoption of cruder or low capital-intensive techniques implies, we may actually create labour scarcity. Last, that under a low capital-intensive economy we may produce goods which may not be acceptable to the consumer.

There is no doubt that advanced technology leads to better utilisation of the raw materials. But, in fact, it is capital that matters most. Did we possess it in the measure we need, then, perhaps, no discussion, planning or laying down of priorities was necessary. In a country where the progress of capital accumulation is slow and, in view of the low levels of income, is bound to be slow, and the fraction of the individual's income which is expended on the purchase of consumer goods is not large, the somewhat high price of the goods produced by the less efficient means of production is not an excessive price to pay for conservation of capital and provision and maintenance of employment. Planning for economic security—let us never forget—means, particularly, in the conditions of our country, first and foremost, planning to create and to maintain full employment. Also, in labour-intensive industries spread all over the country-side the producers themselves will constitute a large segment of the total number of consumers—far larger than what they will do in an economy with a capital-intensive structure where the number of worker-consumers is comparatively far smaller. So, the point about cheaper goods to the consumers being made available only through a capital-intensive economy loses much of its edge : the producers in labour-intensive industries, in most cases, are consumers also.

As regards the standard of living, capital-intensive industry will increase the standard only of those who are employed. The level of living of the masses can rise only when there is full employment and this is far more ensured by labour-intensive, decentralised industry. It is conceded by critics that the total national product will be greater in an economy of low capital-intensity or cruder technology—and it is this that should matter most, not the standard of living of a limited number of individuals.

As for the third argument, *viz.* in regard to the capacity of owners and entrepreneurs of capital-intensive enterprises to save and invest: it seems to be forgotten, first that a producer cannot sell his product unless there is enough money in the pocket of the consumer. And workers are the consumers. If most of the work force remain unemployed as they will be in a capital-intensive economy, they will have no money to buy the products and the factories will simply either not start or will have soon to close down. Second, the assumption that the whole of the excess over wages will go to capital formation, is not correct. Much of it will have to be set aside for capital replacement and a good portion is likely to escape into conspicuous consumption by the proprietorship and the management. Further, the long-run advantage of capital-intensive industry over labour-intensive industry in regard to capital formation should only be an argument in favour of special efforts to encourage and mobilise the small units of voluntary savings and of diverting income to capital formation through taxation. The argument is partly based on the assumption that the total amount of non-wage income is lower in small industry than in large industry, and that wage-earners do not save at all. Both these assumptions are unproved. On the contrary, "it has been found that where the proprietor is a craftsman-entrepreneur (rather than a merchant) who has moved up the ladder by proficiency in his craft, the tendency to plough back the surplus into business is very prominent. This trend is particularly evident among the refugee craftsmen who have set up small industries in recent years."[25] Lastly, the choice between maximum utilisation of available resources, on the one hand, and increase in these resources, on the other, is hardly open to a country like India where the masses are clamouring for bare necessities and the delay in providing these necessities, which establishment of a capital-intensive structure implies, may make all the difference between democracy and dictatorship.

The argument about labour scarcity becoming a problem, in case low capital-intensive undertakings are used, needs only to be stated in order to be rejected. There is so much unemployment, overt and hidden, that we are all at our wit's end as to how to solve it. Labour scarcity in a country becomes a problem only when, under given techniques, the given labour cannot produce all the goods that the country wants. When that happy situation arises, if ever it does, we can easily shift a part of our economy to labour-economising, capital-intensive techniques. As to the last argument : the past record of this country shows that the fingers of our workers can produce as fine and artistic goods as any that the machines can do. In fact, they can cater for individual tastes of individual customers with far greater ease, and possess an adaptability which cannot be matched by machines.

Further, the time factor in investment returns cannot be neglected. A part of the problem of increasing labour efficiency is to change attitudes and cause people to work harder, longer and better; and one necessary condition for this is to produce consumer goods which the people want. Such goods can also be called incentive goods inasmuch as they encourage people to earn more income. Indeed, in the final analysis, the distinction between consumption and investment breaks down since man himself remains an instrument as well as the beneficiary of economic growth. Nutrition, health and education are as much a part of people's assets as they are objects of immediate satisfaction.

Two facts stare us naked in the face today, viz. aspirations are growing fast, perhaps faster than production, and death rates are

[25] *Small-scale Industries in Delhi*, P. N. Dhar, Asia Publishing House, Bombay, 1958, p. 82.

definitely falling faster than birth rates, leading to growth in population at a fast pace. So that more and more the emphasis we place on capital-intensive projects and investments, which require long periods to mature, and produce mostly capital or producer goods and, therefore, postpone the time when levels of consumption will or can be raised, larger and larger the percentage of people who are getting impatient. And impatient people usually do not realize that means are as important as ends. If returns on their hard-earned money paid to the state in the form of taxes, are unduly delayed, they may become desperate, conclude that the democracy is no good and hand over the reins of government to those who promise quick relief from poverty by any means whatsoever. Looked at from this angle, therefore, labour-intensive forms of investment or industries of low capital-intensity, which ensure early returns, are preferable. They will provide consumer incentive goods earlier (and thus provide an earlier capacity to create more income and saving for more capital).

The *U. N. Economic Survey of Asia and the Far East*—1961 and the *U. N. World Economic Survey*—1961 must make depressing reading for anyone who has been lulled into a feeling of complacency by the comfortable assumptions of the Third Plan. After being told that "India's economy must not only expand rapidly but must, at the same time, become self-reliant and self-generating", it is disconcerting to find that our country, with a *per capita* growth rate of 1.1 per cent and a national growth rate of 3.0 or 3.1 per cent in industrial production and gross domestic product in the 1950s, figures very low in performance. The record of even the so-called less industrialized among under-developed countries is considerably better than India's (*Vide* Tables XLI and XLII).

As we have seen in the introductory pages of this chapter, the growth rate depends upon the choice of technological alternatives for investment, and these correspond to different values of the capital-output ratio.

"India's high incremental capital-output ratio", says the ECAFE Report, "reflects partly unmatured investment and partly the country's strong preference for a highly capital-intensive form of development which, in the short run, has yielded only a slow rate of product growth" (p. 24).

We have chosen to build first an infra-structure for industry—a "basic" structure of heavy industry, for example, steel and che

TABLE XLI

ECAFE COUNTRIES : AVERAGE RATES OF GROSS FIXED CAPITAL
FORMATION, GROWTH OF REAL DOMESTIC PRODUCT, GROWTH
OF *PER CAPITA* PRODUCT AND INCREMENTAL CAPITAL-OUTPUT
RATIOS 1950-1959*

Country	Average rate of gross fixed domestic capital formation (per cent per annum of gross domestic product)	Average rate of product growth (per cent per annum of real domestic product)†	Average rate of per capita growth (per cent per annum of aggregate product)‡	Incremental capital-output ratio
Japan	21.6	9.1	7.9	2.4
Burma	17.1	5.1	3.0	3.4
India	14.9	3.1	1.1	4.8
Thailand	14.4	5.5	1.9	2.6
China (Taiwan)	13.1	7.9	4.2	1.7
Korea (South)	12.3	5.1	2.1	2.2
Ceylon	11.3	3.9	1.4	2.9
Pakistan	7.8	2.6	0.4	3.0
Philippines	7.0	6.0	2.7	1.2
Indonesia	6.2	3.6	1.6	1.7

SOURCE : *U. N. Economic Survey of Asia and the Far East*—1961. (Bangkok,
1962, pp. 11 and 24).

* The period begins with 1951 for Burma, Cambodia, China: (Taiwan) and
Indonesia; 1952 for Thailand; and 1953 for South Korea.

† For all countries, the figures of 'aggregate product' and 'real domestic
product' in the two tables on pp. 11 and 24 respectively of the UN Survey are
identical. For Thailand, South Korea and Indonesia, however, the figures of
'aggregate product' on p. 11 are given as 5.0, 5.0 and 3.0 respectively. Perhaps, this may be the result of outflow of capital from these countries.

‡ For India, Japan, South Korea, Pakistan, the Philippines and Thailand,
the population deflators to derive *per capita* growth rates were taken from
data according to the 1960-61 censuses. For other countries, *viz.* Burma,
Taiwan, Ceylon and Indonesia, population deflators, taken from United
Nations or national sources, relate to material based on earlier information.
From the experience with recent censuses, it is safe to assume that these are
underestimates. The corresponding growth rates of *per capita* income have,
to that extent, been overestimated for these countries. Burma's growth
rates of aggregate and *per capita* product, in particular, seem to have been
overestimated ; growth of its aggregate product cannot be reconciled with
that of agricultural production, and growth of *per capita* product is further
exaggerated by the use of an unusually low deflator for population growth.

TABLE XLII

RELATIONSHIP BETWEEN GROWTH OF MANUFACTURING PRODUCTION AND OF GROSS DOMESTIC PRODUCT

Country	Annual rate of growth (percentage)	
	Manufacturing production	Gross domestic product
Republic of Korea	19	5
China (Taiwan)	15	8
Venezuela	12	8
Brazil	11	6
Philippines	11	6
Jamaica	10	10
Pakistan	9	3
Rhodesia and Nyasaland	8	7
Congo (Leopoldville)	8	6
Greece	7	6
El Salvador	7	5
Honduras	7	3
Israel	6	9
Algeria	6	8
Turkey	6	6
Colombia	6	5
Peru	6	4
Thailand	6	4
Mexico	5	5
Ecuador	5	5
South Africa	5	5
Panama	5	5
Portugal	5	4
Tunisia	4	3
Morocco	4	2
India	3	3
Chile	3	3
Cyprus	2	5
Indonesia	2	4
Ireland	2	1
Argentina	1	2

SOURCE : *U. N. World Economic Survey 1961*, p. 21.

micals—even though these require large capital and long gestation periods and are heavily dependent on imports. Both the Second and the Third Five Year Plans have been based on the premise that heavy industry was fundamental to rapid growth, that its presence largely determined the pace at which the economy could become self-reliant and self-generating, and that it would, in turn, stimulate the growth of medium and small industry producing its components and utilizing its products, and thus ultimately provide a large employment potential.

This policy is best explained in the words of Prof. Mahalanobis's *Draft Plan Frame* :[26]

In the long run, the rate of industrialisation and the growth of national economy would depend on the increasing production of coal, electricity, iron and steel, heavy machinery, heavy chemicals, and the heavy industries generally which would increase the capacity for capital formation. One important aim is to make India independent, as quickly as possible, of foreign imports of producer goods so that the accumulation of capital would not be hampered by difficulties in securing supplies of essential consumer goods from other countries. The heavy industries must, therefore, be expanded with all possible speed.

With a view to conform to the Government's declared objective of building "a socialistic pattern of society", allocation to modern or heavy industry rose from 8 per cent in the First Plan (1951-56) to 23 per cent in the Second Plan (1956-61), and 25 per cent in the Third Plan.

This emphasis on creation of an infra-structure as the essential pre-requisite of growth has inevitably led to too much investment in infra-structure and too little in direct production. Even in agriculture, preference for capital-intensive (and import-intensive) projects like Bhakra Nangal, Hirakud and Damodar Valley, has directed attention away from less spectacular but high-yielding projects like masonry wells, tanks and *bandhies* which would have been more economical in regard to capital (and foreign exchange). As regards returns : "We were disappointed to find," remarks the Third Finance Commission, 1961, "that in a number of cases the returns in multi-purpose river valley and other major

[26] "Draft Recommendations for the Formulation of the Second Five Year Plan", March 17, 1955, included in *Papers Relating to the Formulation of the Second Five Year Plan*, Planning Commission, 1955, p. 43.

irrigation projects are insufficient to meet even the working expenses and, in the majority of cases, insufficient to cover the additional incidence of interest liability".[27] So that there is a serious lag in agricultural progress which has, moreover, held back the growth of the rest of the economy,

In view of the enormous potential of hydro-electric power, large deposits of coal and iron ore, and the size of its potential domestic market, India would, in any case, become a producer of heavy capital goods some day. The question, however, is whether it was more economical to proceed with heavy industry at the early stage or whether it could be or could have been deferred to a later stage. In most countries, the development of both agriculture and light industry came first, and this policy has paid them handsome dividends.

Says W. S. Woytinsky in *India : The Awakening Giant :*

Heavy industry and specially heavy-machine-making industry, has never been the "root and base"[28] of economic growth. The basis of economic growth in the early phase of industrialisation was agriculture, trade and handicrafts. In all the great industrial powers except the USSR and Japan, heavy industry grew on the basis of consumer goods industries, responding to their demand and adjusting itself to their needs. This refers not only to the United States, Great Britain and Germany but also to France, Italy, Canada and so on. The opposite course of development in Russia and Japan was due to exceptional historical conditions. In Russia after Peter the Great and Japan after the Meiji Restoration industrialisation was promoted and largely controlled by the Government and subordinated to its political aims. In both countries heavy industry was pushed ahead as the basis of military power rather than the foundation of further industrialization. The Soviets in Russia and the military party in Japan on the eve of World War II took over and carried forward this policy with increased ruthlessness (p. 175).

Looked at more critically, it is agriculture and agriculture alone which is the root and base of economic progress. Unless farmers produce more than their needs, they will have nothing to sell and,

---

[27] *Report of the Third Finance Commission,* 1961, published by the Manager, Government of India Publications, Delhi, 1962, p. 42.

[28] 'Root and Base' are the words used by Pt. Jawaharlal Nehru to describe the role of heavy industry in the development of our economy (*vide* p. 210 *ante*).

therefore, no wherewithal to buy. Which means that in the absence of increased agricultural production, there will be even no trade and no handicrafts.

Subject to unavoidable exceptions or those that may be dictated by considerations of national defence—and which may be protected by tariffs or otherwise supported by the state—heavy or large-scale mechanised industries, in our circumstances of a dense agrarian economy, should come, in course of time, as the apex of an industrial structure with handicrafts or village industries as its base. The process of growth will be generated from below—as incomes increase and technologies improve—through small-scale industries, then light or medium industries, and finally to heavy industries. Treating heavy industries as the base and handicrafts and small or consumer industries as an evil to be tolerated or the end or culmination of process of economic growth, will amount to forcibly reversing the trends that should automatically develop in a backward country, which desires or has begun to progress. Russia and Japan cannot serve as examples for us. We have no military aims (except those of defence) and neither the internal resources of Russia nor, like Japan, any dependencies to exploit.[29]

Our policy of starting the growth process from the end of heavy industry has posed a dilemma, viz., while achievement of freedom from dependence on imports is the basic aim of India's development, capacity to import is crucial to achievement of this aim. Our import needs today are virtually insatiable, not only for capital goods, but also for raw materials (and even food). But how are the imports to be financed ? The outlook for primary exports is far from encouraging, and it has not been easy for India to dispose of in world markets large supplies of manufactured goods, especially textiles. Foreign aid has been increasingly helpful, but India cannot count upon aid indefinitely on the present scale.

As already said, while there can be no doubt that we must develop certain lines of heavy industry, "better results would probably be

[29] According to the United Nations' *Economic Survey of Asia and the Far East*, 1961, the shift from light to heavy industry in Japan, which had already started before the Second World War, formed a special feature of the country's post-war economic growth and was greatly accelerated after 1956, followed, and was firmly based on an earlier and considerable development of both agriculture and light industry (pp. 68 and 116).

obtained", says W. S. Woytinsky, "if a country engaged in an industrialisation programme began with the development of processing of domestic raw materials for the domestic market and export, encouraging at the same time the import of capital goods for those industries which best utilise domestic labour and capital, whether these are light or heavy industries and whether they produce consumer or capital goods. This sequence does not exclude the building of automobile and aircraft factories by countries which are now considered under-developed, provided such factories are built because of economic considerations and not for prestige or other ideological reasons" (Ibid, page 177).

There are examples of countries which are both highly prosperous and industrialised without having had a capital goods industry of all kinds, of their own, and without, as a consequence, having sacrificed their economic independence. They have developed lines of production which are most advantageous for them and have been exchanging the surpluses in various goods for articles which they cannot produce on a competitive basis. Canada, Australia, New Zealand, Denmark, Norway, Finland and Switzerland import steel and machinery and show no desire to abandon this practice. Japan can also be included in this list. Other highly developed nations import certain types of machinery and export others. But even if establishment of a closed economy of the Soviet type be our aim, the heavy industry that will needs be established, may still increase our dependence on imported food for a number of years as it is bound to retard the development of agriculture.

As already noticed, it is contended by advocates of capital-intensive economy that it does not, of itself, predicate a society where there should be gross inequalities of income between one man and another. In this connection reference is made to the example of America which is *par excellence* a country of big industry. But the contention is not correct in its entirety. Taking up theory first : if it is an economy where free enterprise rules, an industrial undertaking will cease to function as soon as the entrepreneur's profit falls below a certain point. He has invested huge capital ; if the return thereon does not come up to what he considers to be the minimum, the entrepreneur will simply close down his business. This minimum is bound to be much higher than what a worker in the undertaking, howsoever highly he may be paid, will earn as wages.

Second, while it is true that in the USA the living standards of labour are the highest of any in the world and a substantial middle class has been developed through the mechanism of differential taxation, the disparities are wide and the cartels and monopolies still flourish. Commenting on a statement of the American ambassador to India to the effect that almost a classless society had been achieved in his country the *National Herald* of Lucknow said in one of its editorial notes :

Mr. Herbet H. Lehman, a former Governor of New York and Director of UNRAA, in an article recently in the *New Leader* of New York revealed how big business controls the American economy. He reeled off these astonishing figures :

Fifty large insurance companies control 90 per cent of all the assets of all insurance companies. Of the 325,000 manufacturing companies in the country, fifty large ones make 27 per cent of the sales of all. The fifty largest firms in all fields of the national economy together effect sales of 86 billion dollars, which comes to twenty-eight per cent of the gross national production of the country. In one year—1955—alone the famous firm of General Motors made a net profit of one billion dollars, or one-sixth of the total assets of the firm, on a sales turnover amounting to three per cent of the national production. "How big is too big ?" Mr. Lehman asks, looking at these figures, and answers the question by saying that when a firm attains a net sales volume equal to more than one per cent of the national production it becomes 'just too big for the health of the national economy'.

The speed at which mergers of firms are taking place in the United States—big firms swallowing the small ones—lends emphasis to the point, says Mr. Lehman, "that if the United States wishes to retain an economic system based on competition, new rules must be written very soon to protect the ants against the giants, and the consuming public against both". He adds : "The leaders of big business and Government today pay lip service to individualism and individual enterprise. In fact, their support is being given to the new philosophy of action identified with Madison Avenue, with its emphasis on form and approach rather than content and substance.[30]

Granting that capital-intensive forms of industry which may, in the long run, increase national income and capital formation and thus raise consumption levels more than investment in less intensive forms, they will obviously tend to concentrate wealth

[30] The *National Herald*, dated September 28, 1957.

and economic power in the hands of a few, and thus further widen
the gap between incomes, particularly in a country like ours where
labour is so redundant. They are likely to result in such distribution of the national dividend that, though the average productive power and consumption per head may show an increase, large
masses benefit very little, if at all. Despite eleven years of economic
planning and fourteen years of political independence disparities in
incomes in India have worsened. The main reason lies in our over-
emphasis on big projects and heavy industry.[31] (Two other reasons
might lie in the system of Government-controlled permits, licences
and quotas, and in the evasion of tax by the wealthy classes.) Having
regard to the growing demands of the people for improved economic
conditions, however, it is unlikely that this situation would be
passively accepted for long. Human nature being what it is, the
degree of discontent depends, not so much on the absolute level
of *per capita* incomes, as on their relative ranking.

If it is a socialist economy, even then the disparity between
the income of the manager and that of the worker will be very
large. At least, that is what the experience of the Soviet Union
would tell us. Under Lenin, the wage differences in industry were
one in three. Today the wage differences in all the great factories are one in twenty.[32] An ex-Vice-President of Yugoslavia
says :

In his *Stalin Au pouvoir* published in Paris in 1951, Orlov
states that the average pay of a worker in the USSR in 1935 was
1,800 *rubles* annually, while the pay and allowances of the Secretary
of a rayon committee amounted to 45,000 *rubles* annually. The
situation has changed since then for both workers and party functionaries, but the essence remains the same. Other authors have
arrived at the same conclusions. Discrepancies between the pay of
workers and party functionaries are extreme ; this could not be

[31] Long ago this future was predicted by Mahatma Gandhi in his
characteristically mild words. In a book recently published, *Letters to
Raj Kumari*, he said in 1939 that "Jawaharlal's Plans would be a sure
waste, but he was one who would not be satisfied with anything that was
not big".

[32] During his visit to India a couple of years ago, Mr. Anastas Mikoyan,
First Deputy Prime Minister of the USSR, acknowledged that the difference between the lowest and the highest paid in Russia ranged from 1 to
59. According to others, the difference is 1 : 100 or more (*vide* "Bureaucratic Plans Stifle Economic Enterprise" *Capital*, Calcutta,17-12-1959).

hidden from persons visiting the USSR or other communist countries in the past few years.[33]

This approximates to the conditions in Britain where in industrial concerns there is a bottom wage of about £ 250 per year and a top rate for the directors and managers of about £ 5000 per year. There is one important difference : in capitalist Britain there is a more severe form of income tax.

Writes *The Pioneer* :

Leafing through the typed pages of FNS (Foreign News Service) —we came across this depressing item which spotlights the fact that millionaires will erupt in any society, however strictly egalitarian :

Andre M. Timoshenko, Charge d'Affaires of the Soviet Embassy in Bonn, recently delivered a speech at the Munich 'Politechnic'. The purpose of his lecture was to defend the thesis that the Soviet system enables the working class to raise its standard of living.

His listeners learned that a new class of millionaires had come into being in the Soviet Union. In the year 1940 there were only two. In 1954 this figure had increased to 980, and currently it stands at 2,000 (of whom some 780 are multimillionaires).

Soviet millionaires are composed of a privileged group of poets, marshals of the Soviet Union and high officials, and of the heads of large heavy industrial concerns. The millionaire group also includes one jockey.

The millionaires continue to benefit from the existing law which maintains income tax on a very low level.[34]   At the last meeting of the Supreme Soviet, Khrushchev announced a further income tax reduction.[35]

A factory is a big and complicated unit. A man who can manage it must have high intellectual and supervisory attainments and must, necessarily, be paid highly for them. Between the salary of the manager and his assistants, on the one hand, and that of the workers, on the other, there is bound to be a large disparity. Whereas in a small-scale economy the worker himself or his family is the

[33] *The New Class* by Milovan Djilas, Thames and Hudson, London, 1957, p. 46.

[34] Income tax in the USSR plays a very small part in the Soviet Budget, *viz.* it brings only a little more than 7 per cent of the total revenue. It starts at 5 per cent of a man's income, rises to 13 per cent and then stops. There is no steeply rising scale, and there are all sorts of exemptions.

[35] "Signs of the Times," the *Pioneer*, dated June 10, 1960.

master of the means of production : the question of gross inequalities between the income of one and another, therefore, does not arise. Or, if he employs outside labour, the extent of labour being limited by the size of the business and also, if necessary, by law, his profits cannot be unduly large.

As regards our fourth aim, *viz.*, maintenance of democratic values : big owners of urban industrial property are as anti-democratic in their outlook as zamindars or landlords—big owners of rural, agricultural property. Nor will replacement of private ownership by public ownership which, in practice, is not distinguishable from state capitalism, make much difference. Every form of concentrated economic power is inherently dangerous, even when that power is concentrated in the hands of the state. Already in Russia there is a social and political hierarchy and a new class of managers. Big economic units, where hundreds and thousands of men work under a central unified management, militate against the growth of a truly democratic society.[36] A manager of a state-owned factory is as prone or susceptible to the heady wine of power as the manager of any private factory. The psychology of both kinds of managers gradually gets equally corrupt and the atmosphere of both kinds of factories equally hostile to the plant of personal initiative and freedom. The ordinary worker in the USSR is, in fact, less free and a less willing partner in the enterprise in which he earns a living than the employee of capitalist industry. Labour has no right to strike ; all labour is compulsory. There is job-freezing ; there is periodic raising of work quotas without raising pay. Penalties include dismissal for lateness of 20 minutes or for tardy return to work after lunch. Dismissal from jobs means the forfeiture of food rations and eviction from homes.

Further, the evils of bureaucracy—its slowness, waste and corruption—will multiply a hundred-fold under state capitalism. That is why Government organisations nowhere in the world have

[36] "With the Government taking more and more responsibility on itself in its attempt at building a welfare state," said Acharya Vinoba Bhave at Indore while answering questions from a group of Sarvodaya workers from Punjab on August 13, 1960, "the people would gradually lose their industrious nature, life would become dull and there would be no scope for the development of mind, no compassion and no chance for sharing the common good in life" (vide the *National Herald*, Lucknow, dated August 14, 1960).

been found suitable for conducting industrial enterprises in an efficient manner. The fault does not lie with the officials and the staff as such. It is the centralisation of authority, the order of things, administrative red tape and the fear of public censure without the compensating factor of public applause and monetary reward that account for lower efficiency. As regards freedom of the worker, if the factory-owners of the nineteenth century, having political influence but not unlimited political power, were in a position to exploit the workers, a socialist state in the twentieth century or its agents and managers, possessing not only unlimited political power but also unlimited economic power, through ownership (that is, control) of the instruments of production, are infinitely better equipped to exploit the workers. Today, the state has to keep up some sort of impartiality between the labourer and the private mill-owner. Under a socialist system along with elimination of private capitalism and landlords, free labour movements are also eliminated and the labourer becomes a subordinate employee of the state itself—with none to arbitrate between him and the employer.

The basic problem with which all those who are dissatisfied with capitalism have grappled, is how to bring economic power under social control. The simplest way of doing this, so it seemed, was to replace the private ownership of all property which represented power, by some form of common ownership. For some, viz. Socialists and Communists, common ownership meant state ownership. Communists differ from Socialists only in regard to the method of transfer of power. The latter believe that the change from private to public ownership must be effected by democratic methods involving fair compensation and majority consent, while the former advocate one all-embracing revolutionary act, by which the political power of the state and the economic power of capitalists would be seized and held by a 'dictatorship of the proletariat'.[37]

[37] The Communist Party of India, by a resolution of the Central Committee in its session held from 6th February to 11th February, 1958, which was endorsed by the party Congress in the second week of April 1958, in Amritsar, changed its creed to 'full democracy and socialism by peaceful means' and through Parliament, perhaps, as a consequence of the heart-searchings that had shaken Communism all the world over after the death of Stalin, particularly, since the Twentieth Party Congress of the USSR in March, 1956. Mao Tse Tung's speech also in 1957

But transfer of ownership from private hands to the state has not realised all the hopes pinned on it. The advances towards common ownership in Britain under its post-war Labour or Socialist Government have raised doubts about the efficacy of the usual methods of political democracy in controlling publicly-owned industry. Parliament cannot effectively control—and, indeed, it is often argued that it should not control the internal working of the vast industrial organisations which it has created. Less independent the public boards or corporations are, more they suffer from risks of centralisation and lack of enterprise. On the other hand, however, more independent they are, more they have exercised power without responsibility. Selfless men of outstanding ability devoted wholesale to national interest are not numerous in any country. As regards the worker, British experience shows that he does not automatically work harder for a government than for a private employer. Nationalisation (or public regulation, for that matter) has not been accompanied by a strengthening of the worker's identification with the plant or with the job to be done. Nor has it given him a sense of a new status. Even with the support of powerful trade unions in all the nationalised industries, the individual employee continues to feel that he has no real control over most of the circumstances of his working life, and has merely been transferred from one set of bosses to another. The idea of further nationalisation, therefore, becomes increasingly unpopular, and Socialists, not only in Britain but in West Germany and Japan also, have recently been revising theory and practice. Classical capitalism and classical socialism both are now regarded as nineteenth century doctrines which no longer have clear meanings, and have been left behind by the onward rush of science and technology. Today, it is ideals that matter or should matter, not ideology.

Even compared to capitalism, the communist method of capture of power has made matters worse for the people. In the Soviet Union and, later, in other communist countries Marxism has been taken to its logical conclusion. "All economic power has been

which pleaded for allowing 'a thousand schools to contend' was a straw showing the direction in which the Communist mind was thinking— direction of liberalism and relaxation of authoritarian control. Still more recent events, however, indicate that the Soviet and Chinese Communists are having second thoughts and reverting to their old stand. This is likely to affect the policy of the Indian Communists also.

transferred to the state and the result is not a 'society of the free and equal'—as Marx believed—but a totalitarian tyranny. The state also commands all political power, and so is subject to no effective restraints at all. It is an even sorrier fate for the worker to be at the mercy of the state than to be the victim of private capitalists, for the state—unlike the capitalists—is ubiquitous. If capitalism is individualism run riot, then communism is collectivism run riot ; the remedy is no better than the disease".[38] In the West or what are known as capitalist countries, it would be fair to say that, while the property concept was never challenged openly, the authority of the managers has been reduced considerably and exploitation of workers in any extreme or crude form of the arbitrary powers of management, by and large, eliminated.

So that the abolition of private property alone has not led to the end of exploitation. The problem of checking the bureaucracy remains and, because human conduct is involved, shows little or no signs of solution.

It is in an economy of predominantly small units alone, small family farms and small industry or handicrafts, that democracy prospers, that there are no glaring discrepancies between the status of one man and that of another, that one man is largely independent of the other in the ordering of his life, that the personality of the individual blossoms forth. Only a broad distribution of private economic power can guarantee individual freedom, and this distribution of economic power is assured in an economy of decentralised enterprises of low capital intensity. Such an economy will contribute to an increase in the number and dispersal of those exercising initiative and making decisions, and thus strengthen the roots of democracy in the country.

Marcel Laloire says :

Handicraft[39] work has a great advantage over industrial work in that those engaged in it are fully aware of the purpose of their work. Many workers, after a number of years in the same factory, have never seen where the materials they use come from or where they go. . . . The handicraft worker, on the other hand, begins, machines and finishes the same article himself. . . . He chooses his

---

[38] *Twentieth Century Socialism*, p. 124.
[39] The industry which goes by the name of 'Handicrafts' in western countries is carried on in small mechanised workshops, and is different from the art-crafts or home-crafts as we understand them in our country.

own tools and his own way of doing the work. He is master of his own time and job and not only directs the work but at the same time helps to perfom it, giving full scope to his imagination, initiative and abilities.

Moreover, the personal relationship between a handicraft worker and his assistants usually leads to a more pleasant social atmosphere than that found in very big firms, where the workers hardly know and, in some cases, have never been near 'the boss'. The handicraft worker belongs to the same world as his assistants. He went through the same stages as they did before setting up in business himself.[40]

Small industries and handicrafts do not create a large demand for supervisory staff—a valuable asset in countries where supervisors are still scarce and take time to train : they can draw on centuries of accumulated experience and traditions handed down from father to son, or master craftsman to his pupil.

An economy of cottage and small-scale decentralised units will avoid congestion of population and social disintegration which might result from movement or transference of rural workers to urban areas. As they are closely bound up with the local life, small industries and handicrafts will help to maintain the necessary equilibrium between town and country and check the drift away from the rural areas which drains away both the health and wealth of the villages. Workers engaged in these industries in the rural area will already be living in some sort of houses, thus relieving the governments from the burden of having to construct millions of houses in a short period, and permitting funds to be diverted for meeting more urgent needs. It will also eliminate unnecessary use of transport and reduce the costs of distribution, in turn, leading to a lower cost of amenities available to the rural community. Decentralisation would to a large extent also obviate conflict between labour and capital. "When production and consumption both become localized," said Mahatma Gandhi, "the temptation to speed up production, indefinitely and at any price, disappears. All the endless difficulties and problems that our present-day economic system presents, too, would then come to an end."[41] The Second Five-Year Plan which lays so much emphasis on heavy industry also goes on to concede : "In a country like India with vast distances and a large potential market, the demands can and ought

[40] "Handicrafts in Europe" published in the *International Labour Review*, October 9, 1955.
[41] *Harijan*, dated November 2, 1934, page 301.

to be met through production in efficient, decentralised units. There are other reasons also which weigh in favour of wide diffusion of industry."[42]

Similar is the experience and advice of J. B. Taylor, one of the leading organisers of war-time Chinese Industrial Co-operatives. He says : "India and China are alike in this : that the fundamental need is to improve the life of the rural people who for generations must form the majority of the population. To take away a few millions of them into industrial cities is no solution. Urban industrialisation in China, as in various European countries, has worsened rather than improved matters in the villages, by undermining the rural crafts. Small industries must be spread throughout the countryside on an organised federated basis, such as Indusco's. This not only means fostering, organising and improving cottage industries and putting electric power at their disposal where possible, but also making them a part of a system, including workshops and small factories related to them. This system must integrate with agriculture and give optimum employment to the rural communities."[43]

It is such a system that will furnish purchasing power to the masses for enlarged educational and medical services and a richer social and cultural life. To do this is to retain on a higher level something of the rationality of earlier days, when production and consumption were directly related to largely self-sufficient communities. Self-sufficiency may not be an aim today, but it would be an extravagant commercialism which saw no economy in the local provision of needs when this is possible with local raw materials and local labour for which there is no more profitable alternative.

Small-scale decentralised industries of low capital intensity dispersed in the countryside, Horace Belshaw points out, would be an organic growth at comparatively little cost. They will strengthen saving and investment motives, because concrete results of their frugality and investments will be there to be seen. The wealthier villagers, or groups of villages, might not be tempted by 10 per cent to invest in the capital market in far-off cities, even if the facilities existed to do so, but might be more disposed to establish a small private or co-operative enterprise in the village.

[42] p. 32.
[43] *The Bombay Co-operative Quarterly*, March, 1944, Volume XXVII, pp. 259-60.

There is another great economic advantage which handicrafts and small-scale industry enjoy over specialised industry on a factory scale, which Lewis Mumford, the American sociologist, puts as follows :

And there is still a further reason to give an important position to the handicrafts and machine-crafts as subsidiary forms of production, run on a domestic scale. For both safety and flexibility in all forms of industrial production it is important that we learn to travel light. Our specialised automatic machines, precisely because of their high degree of specialisation, lack adaptability to new forms of production : a change in demand, a change in pattern, leads to the scrapping of very expensive machinery. Wherever demand for products is of an uncertain or variable nature, it is an economy in the long run to use non-specialised machines ; this decreases the burden of wasted effort and idle machinery.[44]

Finally, it will not be amiss to recognise here one advantage that small industry enjoys over big industry even in the sphere of defence and was brought to light by the Second World War. Large industry provides a sure target to aerial bombing by the enemy, resulting in dislocation and destruction of the entire economy of the nation, while small industry can be carried on undetected throughout the countryside. It was this discovery which, during the Second World War, enabled China in a large measure to brave the onslaught of Japan.[45]

One cannot, therefore, but arrive at the conclusion that existing industry in Europe or America, either private or socialised, does not present a pattern which can exactly be borrowed by India. She will need to create her own pattern. In taking a decision on the type, scale and location of industries, we shall not be trammelled by preconceived notions or what a particular country has done in the past or is doing today. Our industries, at least, those which are established in the future will have to meet two conditions above all: to produce things needed by the mass of the people and, using indigenous or locally produced materials in the process, to give employment to as large a number of men as possible. For this

[44] *Technics and Civilization*, 1934, p. 416.
[45] In view of the profound, qualitative change that has come over the methods of making war during the last fifteen years, however, it is problematic whether small-scale industry will continue to enjoy this advantage over big industry in the future also.

reason, industries will mostly have to be scattered widely in smaller units across the land. Such industries might be of two kinds. One may provide all-the-year employment for redundant labour and thus draw off people permanently from the land. The other might not relieve over-population in a direct way by reducing numbers on the land, but supplement agricultural labour by providing subsidiary or seasonal employment. We must not forget that it is seasonal and disguised unemployment in the countryside that is our greatest problem. Although the latter kind of industries will mostly be processing agricultural products and will, therefore, be seasonal in character, yet, in view of their low capital intensity, it will be possible to operate them economically because the loss through idle plants is small.

Land-holdings in Japan are, perhaps, the smallest in the world. Her farmers, however, have been able to improve their standard of living considerably by devoting their spare time to home industries and small industries which have been fostered by Government with almost loving care. Japan has fifty thousand factories in villages and their number is increasing constantly.[46]

The Karve Committee on Village and Small-scale Industry (1955) points to some such pattern when it says that while all possible efforts should be made to provide efficient services to industrial units now located in cities, and especially to the smaller units among them, the definite policy of the Government must be not to permit the growth of a city beyond a roughly prescribed limit. The pattern of industrial activity that should gradually emerge is that of a group of villages having its natural, industrial and urban centre. These small urban centres will be similarly related to bigger ones. Thus, a pyramid of industry broadbased on a progressive rural economy will be built up. In such an organisation, small centres can experience a co-operative interest in the bigger ones and these latter would develop a genuinely supporting, instead of an exploitational relationship towards the smaller towns and the countryside.

The fact that the great cities already exist creates the tendency further to centralise industrial, commercial and service developments in them. Under the new pattern this tendency will be halted.

[46] *Cottage Industries and Agriculture in Japan*, Chaman Lal, New Book Co. Ltd., Bombay, 1949, p. 191.

In view of the shortage of capital and redundance of labour in the country, therefore, we would suggest, for the pattern of our industrial development, a sequence of cottage or handicraft—small-scale—light or medium-scale—heavy or large-scale industries. Such a sequence is all the more desirable because one stage helps provide markets for the next. Cottage or handicraft industries will, perhaps, always be needed ; at least, they cannot be a temporary phase for some decades to come. As for small-scale industries, they have a permanent place in the economy of even the most advanced countries.

It may be pointed out here that, although the priorities enunciated by the Chinese Planning Commission in 1957 were upset when the 'Great-Leap-Forward' movement was launched in August, 1958, bitter experience born of hard social and economic facts of the country, which were sought to be ignored because of ideological considerations, has led the communist government of China to revert to the position taken up in 1957. According to the programme endorsed at the 3-week secret session of the National People's Congress, which ended on April 16, 1962, the priorities have been reversed again, and agriculture gets the first place, with light industry second. Heavy industry, the first priority of the 'Leap Forward' stage, is now put third. Point 10 of the programme is intended "to improve planning and ensure an all round balance between the branches of the national economy *in the order of agriculture, light industry and heavy industry*.[47]

[47] *The Times of India*, New Delhi, April 17, 1962.

Small-Scale Industry and Technology

WE MUST be clear about one thing in our mind : Modern life calls
for the advantage of technology. While it is an essential condition
of a good society that man should be free—not a slave either to
another man, an organisation or a machine, it seems natural and
right that the poor villager should desire the advantage of technology which will enable him to produce ten or twenty times as much
within an hour's work. This would earn him a comfortable living
and some surplus time for his other interests—for fulfilling his
normal and desirable purposes. These two conditions, *viz.* freedom
and leisure can be realised by bringing technology and the small
machines together. Special attention will, therefore, have to be
given to organising innovations or promoting technological improvements in cottage and small-scale enterprises dispersed over the
countryside, so that the output per head is increased even while
the capital used is not large.

Slight modernisation of village crafts and rendering each village
wholly or mostly self-sustaining by its own industrial effort, alone
will, perhaps, not do ultimately. Efficient production, at least
in some spheres, calls for operation on a larger scale than is possible
if the market is just one village. We should never forget that the
industrialised world is moving fast and such halting steps may leave
India lagging fifty years behind. It is an age not only of electrically-
driven machines, but an age of atomic energy and automation,
where machines will act without human intervention or will, and, in
a way, think for themselves, and produce far more at far less cost,
that is, in far less time and with far less human energy expended.

In Britain and the USA they have already developed electronic
thinking machines capable of rapidly solving exceedingly complex
mathematical problems and of exercising certain types of judgment.
The automatic machines contain built-in controls which enable
them to adjust to changing conditions of production, correct their
own mistakes, inspect the product and even replace their own worn-
out parts—and thus ensure a continuous flow of production. Automation will eliminate many a tedious and hazardous task and help

create goods which could not be developed by ordinary methods and which will possess a high and uniform quality never attainable when control was left to human judgment. Although automatic methods are most suitable for large companies which make great quantities of a standardised item and their introduction involves inordinately high capital costs, machines are being perfected to bring some of the advantages of automation even to the small, short-run manufacturer. These two discoveries or developments, *viz.*, automation and atomic energy, will revolutionise the objective conditions in which we live today and will lead to much rethinking and revaluation of old habits and standards.

It would not do, therefore, to think of tools and implements at a pre-determined technological level. Improvements have increasingly to be introduced in the tools used for production of goods by hand. Gandhiji himself had said that "*Charkha* was to hold the field only till a better substitute was found." The invention of the *Ambar Charkha* has shown that technology can improve the little machines powered by human hands. As the Planning Commission has said "continued efforts will have to be made to put the traditional techniques of these crafts on a more efficient basis" (*vide* Second Five-Year Plan, p. 144). Japan is an outstanding example which demonstrates that large numbers of small technical improvements, none of them involving a radical departure from traditional methods or requiring substantial investments, can have a spectacular cumulative effect. Improvement in techniques will, however, depend on availability of electric power in the villages, ability of our artisans to master the new techniques and the capacity of the market to absorb the increased volume of output.

It comes to this that we cannot and should not turn our back on advance in technology, while we can certainly turn it on large scale industry : that is, technology has to be divorced from size.

We can have small units spread all over the countryside covering almost all branches of industry or human activity, and yet use in them—if not today then tomorrow—the latest techniques that science has placed at the disposal of man. Such units—it will bear repetition—will give us all the goods that the nation needs, provide employment to the unemployed and under-employed in their homes, ensure equitable distribution of wealth and foster the democratic way of living. Mahatma Gandhi, the torchbearer of village industries and handicrafts, had a clear mind on this question. He once said:

If we could have electricity in every village home, I should not mind villagers plying their implements and tools with electricity.[1]

He would 'welcome every improvement in the cottage-machine', but he attached four riders : first, that 'where there was no electricity and no machinery' hand-driven implements should continue to be used instead of keeping the people idle. Second, that nobody was thereby rendered unemployed, for 'it was criminal to displace hand labour unless one was at the same time ready to give millions of villagers some other occupation in their homes'.[2] Third, that the improved tools and machines were made in the villages. Fourth, that they were not used as a means of exploitation, that is, they were used for 'manufacturing goods mainly for use'[3]

On the one hand, we have a labour force that is not only abundant but redundant, and our capital resources are scarce; on the other, like other under-developed countries, we are faced with a technology which increases output per worker through increase in capital investment (per worker), but saves labour. This technology suits developed countries which enjoy high incomes and, therefore, possess a high capacity to save. It is out of tune in industrially backward countries with low incomes and low margins of domestic savings—in countries with plentiful labour and little capital. Our problem is to work out production methods or techniques which will economise capital or require less capital per man than do the methods that are most efficient in countries with more capital per man. In our conditions, obviously, it will be more conducive to development to apply the available capital extensively to a large fraction of the labour force than intensively to a small fraction. We will have to maximise productivity per man employed, not per unit of investment.

The scientific study of production techniques, however, has till now been confined almost entirely to Western countries where the main goal in view has been the reduction of labour costs rather than capital costs. With the result that in our country, where most of the equipment has been western-designed and industrial engineers largely western-trained, improved techniques even in small-scale

[1] *Harijan*, dated June 22, 1935.
[2] *Young India*, dated November 5, 1925.
[3] *Harijan*, dated August 29, 1936.

industry are based on a context of high wages and cheap capital. If, therefore, India has to make the best use of its resources, its engineers have to make a research into production techniques and equipment that are appropriate to our conditions of low wages and dear capital. Our engineers will not prove unequal to the task, provided they are set the task specifically. Says K. Santhanam :

There is an erroneous notion that India cannot develop economically unless not only machinery but also raw material for industry can be imported to a large extent. This idea has led to a sterilization of all the inventive capacity of Indian engineers and scientists. There is a considerable degree of expert opinion that if we had relied exclusively on Indian talent for the great irrigation and power projects for the first two Plans, there would have been a saving of many crores of rupees.[4]

To re-state in different words : Our problem is to retain the advantages of technological progress and at the same time to minimise its social cost in terms of unemployment. As industrial techniques develop and production becomes more and more automatic, the number of men employed in production of the same amount of goods falls rapidly, leading to unemployment. We have to reconcile the need for utilisation of modern technology with the need for creation of more and more employment opportunities. This situation poses 'a new economic problem and demands new technical methods for its solution.' Mr. D. S. Morse, Director-General of ILO, said in a report[5] to delegates to the International Labour Organisation's Asian Regional Conference in Tokyo (September, 1953) :

More specifically, the problem will be to develop a new type of industry—radically different from the present cottage and handicraft industries and from the present large-scale factory industries—which for the same amount of capital investment, can at the same time produce more than the former and provide more employment than the latter.[6]

[4] *Kalki*, dated August 17, 1958.
[5] *ILO News*, Volume VI, No. 6, September, 1953.
[6] We may make it clear here that if this problem cannot be solved we will prefer, as said in the last chapter, to keep our vast man-power employed with hand-operated machines rather than have a few capital-intensive automatic machines which may produce the required quantity of goods but will render vast numbers unemployed. As time passes and unemployment mounts, Mahatma Gandhi's approach is finding increasing confirmation and seems to be the only solution of our economic ills.

As far as textiles, the biggest industry, is concerned, the problem posed by Mr. D. S. Morse does not arise : We have seen in the last chapter that units on the cottage and handicraft scale, in this sphere, yield more production and provide more employment for the same amount of capital investment.

Hitherto, it is technology which has largely determined the relationship between the size of plant and efficiency. Higher technology has meant a bigger plant with greater efficiency. But, in sheer theory, science and technique are not concerned primarily with size or appearance ; nor can science be confused or equated with technology. Fortunately, as if to meet the challenge set by dense populations to economic growth, technological improvements today are tending in most industries to reduce the optimum size of the enterprise.

Consequent on the Industrial Revolution of the eighteenth century, the scale of industrial operations had tended to become larger and larger. The only limitation was placed by competition which compelled a firm not to carry its scale of output beyond the point where neither increasing nor decreasing returns prevailed but where, instead, the rate of return was constant. Behind this long-term trend there were certain technological forces which were to be found, basically, in the use of new sources of power (steam), new types of materials (steel), new machines and processes (expensive, single-purpose machines and mechanical processes) and new forms of transportation (rail-roads). Each of these developments was, in itself, a powerful force towards large-scale operations, and each of them inter-acted among the others, thereby imparting a cumulative impetus towards the centralisation of production units, towards greater and greater internal economies, towards larger and larger profits to the entrepreneur.

But John M. Blair has brought forward evidence[7] suggesting that this long-term, general and pervasive increase in plant size throughout most industries has now come to an end. Taking the number of employees as an index of size, it would appear that there has been in the past thirty or forty years no spectacular increase in the size of industrial establishments. This increase has been halted by new technological developments which tend to promote

[7] An article "Does Large-Scale Enterprise Result in Lower Costs ?," in *American Economic Review*, Vol. XXXVIII, No. 2, May, 1948, pp. 121-52.

a smaller rather than a larger scale of operations—which make possible a larger increase in output with only a small increase in capital or, correlatively, the same amount of output with a much smaller amount of capital.

The more important of these new techniques fall into the same categories of technological change which underlay the Industrial Revolution—power, materials, machines, and transportation—but they are qualitatively far different and their effect upon size is the reverse of the nineteenth century technology. Just as steam replaced water wheels as the prime source of industrial power, so is steam in turn being replaced by electricity ; as steel replaced wood as the basic material of industry, so is it in turn being replaced by light metals, alloys, plastics, and plywood ; as single-purpose, highly specialised machines replaced hand labour, so are they being replaced by newer, more flexible and adaptable multi-purpose machines and extremely efficient chemical and mechanical processes ; and as rail-roads replaced the canal, the wagon, and the bullock cart, so are rail-roads being replaced by the motor truck and the automobile.

Of these technological improvements or discoveries, electric energy is by far the most far-reaching in its decentralising effect. In the earlier stages of the Industrial Revolution, the location of industry was very largely decided by the availability of coal. The result was that the factories came to be located either near coal mines or near rail-roads and docks where cheap coal could be made available. The harnessing of electric power has revolutionised the situation in this connection. Electric power can be derived from a variety of things, not only from coal, but also from water-falls, flowing rivers, and even the tides of the sea, and can be carried over long distances. The development of high voltage transmission has widened the radius around the primary energy sources within which electricity could be made economically available in large quantities. This means that industry need no longer be located at certain specific points but can be spread out far and wide over the countryside.

There is yet another development known as the process of standardisation which electrical energy fosters, and which has helped decentralise industry. Machinery makes it possible to turn out the same product or part of a product any number of times over without the slightest change in its size, shape or quality. This is as true of a small machine worked by hand by one person as of the huge monsters on which hundreds of workers attend. "The increasing use of electrical power makes it less and less necessary for industrial processes to be concentrated under one mammoth roof. Parts of the process can just as well be decentralised ; it is certainly no more expensive in terms of social costs to move the finished components once a month to a central point for assembly than it is to move men backwards and forwards every day".[8] It is possible, for instance, for the soles of shoes to be made in one workshop, for the heels to be made in another hundreds of miles away and the upper cover to be made in a third, and for these three parts to be then assembled in a fourth place—producing thousands of pairs of exactly identical and standardised shoes. It is this process of standardisation which has enabled Japan to succeed in integrating small industries into the pattern of large-scale industries so well.

Writing of the factory of Messrs. Daihatsu Ltd. in Japan who manufacture three-wheeler trucks, Shri N. K. Biswas, Deputy Director of Industries, West Bengal, who visited it as a member of a delegation on November 26, 1956, says in his tour diary :

Although the lay-out of their own factory is completely modernised they have not dispensed with the system of getting components from subsidiaries. Messrs. Daihatsu have 32 subsidiary factories working as their subcontractors. In many of them they have participated in capital also. As automobile is a highly technical industry I enquired about the quality control of the parts supplied by their subsidiaries. I was told that with regard to the subsidiaries in which they have participated in capital they have full control as they have a voice in their management. As regards the other sub-contractors where they have not participated in capital, they assist them with all possible assistance, namely, technical know-how, the latest technological information from their development and research laboratory, and the supply of special materials, where necessary, as also credit facilities through their own bankers by issuing guarantees. . . . They also maintain a very well-equipped Test and Research Division from which their sub-contractors draw the up-to-date technological advices and information.

This description is also true of the production methods of Messrs. Tossiba at Tsurumi who are the largest electrical plant manufacturers of Japan, and also of some other industries which in

[8] *Twentieth Century Socialism* by Socialist Union, Penguin Books, 1956, p. 49.

other countries are listed as 'heavy' or 'strategic' and are run on a large scale. Japan's policy of decentralisation, diversification and dispersal of both small-scale and heavy industry has paid handsomely. Sub-contracting is widespread in Japan, particularly in producing special kinds of paper, lanterns, fountain-pens, cutlery, and light engineering products.

Switzerland can also be cited as another example, where many separate village families make wheels or other parts of watches which are assembled in the big factories and go to make the famous Swiss watches (Great care will, however, have to be taken by the state to ensure that factory-owners in such cases do not exploit the workers who manufacture the standardised parts in their homes or small work-shops).

As a result of these 'capital-saving' techniques, as they have been called, or 'decentralising' techniques, as they may also be called, modern technology has tended in recent years to shift towards a smaller size the point at which internal economies of scale cease and diminishing returns to scale begin to operate. These techniques or developments have exploded the basic assumption of manufacturing industry, *viz.*, the bigger the production units, the better and more efficient they are. It has now been established, first, that modern science and technology can be harnessed to small machines which will not require huge capital ; second, that small machines can be a commercial proposition and do not necessarily follow the big ones, but can also precede or substitute them.

In a paper on the 'Sizes of Factories and Firms in the Cotton Industry', read before the Manchester Statistical Society on 9th November, 1949, Dr. Robson, Director of Statistics of the United Kingdom Cotton Board, points out that in the UK textile industry, whether among weaving sheds in which more than one firm operates, or in the case of weaving firms, the most frequent size is under 100 looms. He states : "The main reason for this is that in weaving— in contrast to spinning—there is virtually no technical lower limit to size." He points out further that in the post-war period, between 1947 and 1949, out of 50 new weaving firms, 40 began operating with less than 20 looms each. In Japan, as against 74,000 looms spread over 116 concerns owned largely by the 'Big Ten', there are 251,000 looms belonging to the so-called 'independent weavers' spread over 5,876 units. At any rate, in the weaving section of the industry it is evident that the small unit can hold its own against the larger unit.

Atomic power which has become the basis for a new method of generating energy may well prove to have greater decentralising effects than all of the other techniques combined. If the costs of generation in atomic power plants can compare rather favourably with the costs in coal or hydro-electric plants, then the other attributes of atomic energy—its mobility and infinitesimal transportation costs—should lead to its widespread utilisation, particularly, in under-developed areas, thus giving a great fillip to the whole decentralisation movement.

Incidentally, the atomic or nuclear energy will also solve the problem of fuel. Reserves of uranium which is used as fuel by the nuclear power stations today are, however, as limited as those of coal and oil. It is the hydrogen isotopes—denterium and tritium—that are, therefore, the fuels of the future. "The energy obtainable from a tiny amount of denterium contained in a litre of ordinary water," point out V. Shatunov and V. Kozlov, "is equivalent to the heat produced by the burning of 300 litres of petrol. Hence, the reserves of basic thermo-nuclear fuel—denterium and tritium—locked up in the seas and oceans, will last mankind for billions of years. But, to use it, man has to learn to control thermo-nuclear reactions and to develop special structures—reactors—in which power could be generated by thermo-nuclear fusion."[9]

Current indications of the progress towards controlling thermonuclear reactions fortunately point to a future of great hope. The most thrilling prospect is the reported possibility of converting fusion energy directly into electricity, dispensing with the heat exchangers, boilers and turbines of the conventional cycle. The mechanism for this direct generation has not yet been perfected, but experiments on a small scale have shown that it is, at least, theoretically possible.

"When that happens," said Dr. Bhabha at the Geneva Conference of 1955, "the energy problems of the world will truly have been solved for ever, for fuel will be as plentiful as the heavy hydrogen in the ocean."[10]

The impact of nuclear energy upon present-day, rather older technology, is thus going to be more far-reaching, in no case less

[9] *Pioneer*, Lucknow, dated April 24, 1960.
[10] From an article entitled "Inexhaustible Power from Water—Prospects of Controlled Nuclear Fusion" by Amalendu Das Gupta published in the *Statesman*, dated January 15, 1958, pp. 6-7.

than the impact of electric power upon the steam.

There is, however, not a single reactor in the world today producing power at a price comparable with conventional sources. When this development materialises, that is, when nuclear power becomes an economic proposition, the reasoning in these pages, particularly the one based on the amount of reserves and production *per capita* of coal, petroleum and electric energy in the various countries, will largely become invalid.

The Planning Commission is entirely on the right track when it suggests in the draft outline of the Third Five-Year Plan, 1961-66, that the possibilities of demarcating the spheres of production of large and small units and fixing separate targets of production for the two sectors should be examined in industries producing consumer goods or industrial equipment. In fact, there is no need for any examination left : the matter has been debated thread-bare for decades.

Subject to the exceptions that have already been mentioned, those industries alone should be allowed to be carried on, on large or factory scale, which cannot be run in small workshops or as handicrafts on small-scale. Standardised parts or components even of such industries shall, as far as possible, be produced in small units and, thereafter, assembled in a centre. Laws will have to be enacted to this effect and, if necessary, the Constitution amended. For, in a free market, benefits of decentralised, less intensive types are insufficient, as a general rule, to offset financially the superior technology of the modern mill. Taking the cotton industry as an example : left to itself, even the *Ambar Charkha* is not able to compete with the mills and is facing difficulties. The remedies that suggest themselves are : the production in existing mills should be utilised for the expanding needs of the state and for export. The selling rates of such goods, if any, as are at all allowed to be sold in the internal markets should be fixed by the state so that they are more favourable to decentralised cottage textiles. The difference, leaving a small margin to the owner, should be taken away by the state and spent for furtherance of cottage textiles. Another solution can be to nationalise them and control their production. In no case, however, should licences be given for establishing new units. We should be able to produce all the extra cloth that we need from the *charkha* and the handloom or power-loom. No calamity will befall us if we have to face a shortage of cloth for sometime. This step alone will give employment to several times the number of workers employed in these mills today—dispersed in their homes all over the country and masters of their time. It is needless to add that these small industries and workshops, dispersed in the countryside, and employing, say, not more than ten persons or twenty persons (which is the limit for small-scale industries in the USA), whether electrically-operated or otherwise, should not be allowed to increase their scale and grow into 'giants'. Ultimately we should have urban villages which will take the place of rural hamlets and overcrowded cities of today, without any chimneys emitting smoke, and without any slums.

While handicrafts and small-scale industries will have to be protected by the state from competition of large-scale industries, this alone will not be enough. Those engaged in handicrafts and small industries will have to combine themselves in co-operatives in order to make credit facilities available to such of themselves as need it, to find the necessary equipment, to purchase raw materials for its members and to market their finished products. The craftsmen are often at the mercy of the middleman-seller, or employer-seller, who takes advantage of the former's lack of resources and ignorance of market conditions in every possible way. Provision will also have to be made to make technical know-how available to them and for research and refresher courses. In short, economies of scale and organisation can and should be secured for small units through organised co-operative working. Electricity will have to be provided to every cottage worker by the state, as in Europe and Japan. The state will, in fact, have to serve as a guiding angel in all their activities, till our artisans, long neglected, are rehabilitated and put on their feet. With this reorientation in our policy, they will, in no time, recover their old skill which was once the wonder of the world but, owing to inability of domestic handicraft industries to compete against mill-made articles, is declining today—and which will furnish purchasing power to the masses and thus help start a kind of beneficent chain reaction that will result in higher levels of living all around.

Means of assistance to handicrafts, village industries and small-scale industries, some of which are already in use, have been enumerated by Coale and Hoover. [11] They include :

[11] *Population Growth and Economic Development in Low-Income Countries*, Oxford University Press, 1959, pp. 221-22.

(*i*) Publicly-supported research and development work on new methods and equipment ;

(*ii*) Instruction in use of improved methods ;

(*iii*) Loans to producers (with the Reserve Bank of India charged with overall responsibility) ;

(*iv*) Government aid in setting up improved organisation for marketing (either to final consumers, as in the case of handicrafts and handloom cloth, or to factories in the case of small enterprises producing parts, sub-assemblies, or supplies) ;

(*v*) Preferential Government purchasing of small industry products for departmental use ;

(*vi*) Government action to improve or assure the supply of materials for small producers (*e. g.* by requiring spinning mills to produce enough surplus yarn to supply handloom weavers, or "encouraging" large-scale tanneries to produce surplus findings for small shoe-makers) ;

(*vii*) Adjustment of rail and road transport rates to the advantage of small-scale receivers and shippers ;

(*viii*) Adjustment of electric power rates to the advantage of small-scale power users ;

(*ix*) Tax adjustment to ease the burden of successive sales taxes on the many stages of distribution often involved in marketing the output of small producers ;

(*x*) Government advertising and other sales promotion of small-scale products, at home and abroad (particularly in the case of handicrafts and handloom cloth);

(*xi*) Government assistance in establishment of grading facilities and quality control ;

(*xii*) Government-subsidised provision of improved working facilities for small industries : workshop space, with mechanised "central facilities" such as power saws or heat-treating equipment for use by a number of enterprises ; also, provision of more fully serviced "industrial estate" facilities in larger towns ;

(*xiii*) Direct subsidies to producers (wherever possible on a temporary basis) ;

(*xiv*) Restraint of large-scale competition in order to protect small-scale enterprises, involving :

(*a*) excise taxes on large-scale output,

(*b*) reservations : *i.e.* the designation of certain items for small-scale production exclusively, and

(*c*) restrictions on further expansion of large-scale capacity, by agreement or by denial of licences to expand ; and,

(*xv*) Encouragement in the development of rural exchange systems for non-monetised production along lines already pioneered in some areas in West Bengal.

To look back and summarise : With certain exceptions, we

have to lay emphasis on handicrafts and small-scale decentralised industries of low capital intensity which will form the main pattern of our industrial economy. It is from labour intensive enterprises, that is, handicrafts and small-scale industries that we will progress, as and when real incomes rise, to light and medium industries and thence to capital intensive or heavy industries, to the extent that the economy of the country as a whole can bear. The techniques of the handicrafts and small-scale industries will have to be continually improved, subject, of course, to the paramount considerations, first, that no unemployment is created and, second, that there is greater production for the same amount of capital investment. "I would favour," said Mahatma Gandhi, "the use of the most elaborate machinery, if thereby India's pauperism and resulting idleness could be avoided."[12]

It is true, if there are no improvements or innovations, *i. e.* if we do not avail of what science and technology have placed or will place at the disposal of man, we will keep our economy backward and will not reap as much advantage out of our physical resources as we can. But again—we will do well not to forget—in the development of countries which are today highly industrialised, technical innovations were adopted only when they were economically justified. Labour was replaced by capital wherever this was justified by a reduction in costs. Introduction of automatic machinery in our country, however, where tens of millions of people are going idle, would certainly mean not a reduction, but a considerable increase in costs.

The question, then, arises : What are these innovations and what has, in the past, stood in the way of these innovations—innovations such as we can possibly effect and our economy absorb ?

12 *Young India*, November 3, 1921, p. 350.

CHAPTER EIGHTEEN

Attitudes and Innovations

WE HAVE seen that our material resources are not abundant relatively to the size of our population and, contrary to popular belief, our industrial potential appears to be far lower than that of the USA, USSR and several other countries. But whatever the amount of our natural resources may be, economic development of the country, of course, to the limit that this amount permits, depends on our power to exploit these resources or to convert them into instruments of production—production of consumer goods and services—that is, on our power to convert the potential into the actual. For this we require capital and the necessary skill or knowledge coupled with hard work.

As already noticed, however, owing to the existing low consumption levels of our people, adoption of a democratic system of Government and other reasons, the rate of capital formation within the country is bound to be low. Also, we may not, perhaps, for whatsoever reasons, obtain capital from external sources indefinitely or in the quantities that we need. But there need be no cause for despair on this score. For, while capital investments are necessary for economic development, there is no fixed relationship between new capital investment and future rise in national income. As the reader must have concluded from the tables on page 253 *ante*, output per head greatly depends upon the mode of capital utilisation. National income can be raised substantially through judicious utilisation of available capital and innovations in the field of agriculture and handicrafts or small-scale industries without any or with only insignificant new capital outlay.

The idea that economic development is primarily a matter of investment or introduction of new machines and production processes, is not well-founded. There is no uniform pattern of the behaviour of the variables—the national output, the proportion of the output invested, and the capital-output ratio. We cannot assume as a matter of course that, provided the required supply of capital is forthcoming, the process of economic growth will work itself out in India as it has done or is doing in the advanced countries of the West. This assumption has resulted in the neglect of other influences and factors which, in under-developed economies, are as relevant as capital, if not more, such as the advance of technical knowledge ; the emergence of appropriate economic attitudes and qualities, for example, the urge for material progress, the need for hard work, the inclination to change or improve old ways, and an effective desire to accumulate ; changes in economic and other social relationships, in institutions, and forms of organisation : in short, a wide range of innovations. Mr. P. T. Bauer, Smuts Reader in Commonwealth Studies, Cambridge University, points out in an article :[1]

Any functional relationship between investment and the growth of income clearly depends greatly on the composition of the investment, on its method of finance, and also on the institutions and attitudes of society. This should be obvious in India, where so many social customs and attitudes are adverse to material advance. Here, even more than elsewhere, it is inappropriate to think in terms of capital-output ratios, or to concentrate largely on massive investment in heavy industry.

That is, productivity or economic development of a country depends as much on the quality of its human material as on the quality and quantity of its natural resources or capital. Differences in literacy and skills, human institutions, attitudes to work and social relations generally make a big difference to productivity. What an efficient and determined people or labour force by itself, that is, largely unaided by new capital investments, can do to build up or rebuild their economy, is highlighted by the example of post-war Germany and Japan. Says W. S. Woytinsky :

Prosperity in modern countries is based not on the accumulation of capital but on the people—the labour force, in the broad sense of the term. The experience of Germany and Japan after World War II illustrates this point. Their cities, ports, rail-roads, bridges, factories, and power stations, all the riches accumulated by half a century of hard work, were reduced to heaps of rubble and ashes. Half-naked people were living among ruins. All they had left was their hands and their brains—trained for collective, creative work—and determination. With these assets they started rebuilding. A decade later they came back as greater economic powers than before the war.[2]

[1] *Capital*, dated December 17, 1959
[2] *India : The Awakening Giant*, Harper and Brothers, New York, 1957, pp. 185-86.

The following table taken from an article entitled "Trends in National Productivity" published in the *International Labour Review*, Volume LXXIX—No. 3, March 1959, pp. 315-24, which shows cumulative changes in material productivity of Germany and Japan, along with six other countries, from 1950 to 1957 in the form of index numbers, lends statistical support to W. S. Woytinsky :

TABLE XLIII

INCREASE IN GROSS DOMESTIC PRODUCT IN EIGHT COUNTRIES
FROM 1950 TO 1957 (1950=100)

Sl. No.	Country	Real gross domestic product	Labour force employed	Gross domestic product per worker
1.	U K	120	106	114
2.	U S A	128	110	116
3.	Canada	134	115	116
4.	Belgium	123	104	118
5.	Netherlands	139	113	123
6.	Norway	129	103	126
7.	Germany (Federal Republic)	172	122	141
8.	Japan	176	121	146

According to the United Nations' *World Economic Survey*, 1960 (New York, 1961), p. 16, the annual rate of growth of gross domestic product of the three countries who lost the last world war, *viz.* Japan, Germany (Federal Republic) and Italy during the fifties, came to 9.5, 7.6 and 5.9 respectively. With the exception of Jamaica (whose figure stood at 10), the rate of Japan was the highest in the world. That of the USA and the UK was only 3.3 and 2.7.

W. S. Woytinsky cannot be taken to imply that capital has no part to play in the development of an economy. While it is true that the economy of Western Germany and Japan accomplished such rapid advances largely owing to their highly efficient and flexible labour force as also a large number of aggressive and imaginative managers of enterprises, it will be a mistake to assume that the entire fixed capital which these two countries possessed, had been destroyed by the War, and that they started from scratch. In fact, high rates of increase in the gross domestic product per worker registered in these countries during the early post-war years largely constituted a "rehabilitation effect" : in. 1950 Germany and Japan (as also Italy) were performing well below their potentialities. Further, the financial aid which the USA made available under the Marshall Aid Plan had no mean part to play in the economic recovery of these countries.

W. S. Woytinsky can only mean that capital is not the only or even the most important thing that matters. The quality of labour a country possesses—its vigour, intelligence and character—is as much a controlling factor of its economic and, particularly, industrial development as the ratio that its national resources or capital bears to the population. Capital or natural resources out of which alone capital can ultimately be constructed, though essential and basic, are useless unless the people have the necessary will and the necessary skill and organisation to harness them to productive ends. Several of the national communities in the Middle East have rich sources of oil revenues for investment ; yet they are poor. On the other hand, if natural resources relative to population and, consequently, capital are short, attitudes of a people and innovations or technological improvements—which themselves depend on economic attitudes—can serve to make up for the shortage considerably by increasing the efficiency of labour or the available capital or both. That is, deficiency neither in quality nor in quantity of its natural resources need be a fatal obstacle to economic development of a country, as it can largely be overcome by the high quality of its human resources. Besides Japan, the truth of this conclusion is being illustrated by Israel which has no sources of revenue comparable with its Muslim neighbours, yet enjoys a relatively high and rapidly rising living standard. In our country, the town of Ludhiana offers another example, where hundreds of small enterprises, with little capital outlay, are springing into existence simply on the strength of hands and brains of the workers.

The amount of natural resources, however, is an inexorable factor—a factor, scarcity whereof cannot be entirely overcome by any changes or improvements in technology that man may make or by any ingenuity and efforts that he may bring to bear. As time passes, the gap that existed between the USA and Canada, on one hand, and Germany and Japan (and even the UK), on the other, whether before the war or today, will widen. Efficiency of labour in all the four or five countries being equal or almost equal, the difference in the amount of the natural resources these countries possess—with the closed or autarkik systems to which countries the world over are tending—will ultimately decide the level of their national incomes.

But to revert to the subject-matter of the chapter : What are innovations, and how are attitudes of a people relevant in this connection ?

According to Horace Belshaw, innovations cover all aspects of life, material as well as non-material. Economic or technological innovations are changes affecting human behaviour especially related to economic processes or arts directly applied to the production of goods and services. For example, he points out, deciding to save more, or to transplant paddy instead of broadcasting the seed is an innovation. Better machines which raise productive power per head are but results of human behaviour embodied in concrete things and are innovations. Change in religious beliefs is primarily motivated by other than material or economic ends, yet has economic results. Horace Belshaw's definition of an innovation seems roughly to coincide with a layman's definition given by us in Chapter XV.

Joseph A. Schumpeter, however, gives a wider definition. He assigns the key-role in economic development to innovations and classifies them into five types (p. 66)[3] : (i) conquest or discovery of a new source of supply of raw materials ; (ii) carrying out of a new organisation of industry ; (iii) introduction of a new method of production ; (iv) introduction of a new good, or a new quality of a good ; and (v) the opening of a new market. Horace Belshaw would also include in the concept any change affecting the efficiency of labour, capital or organisation other than the one resulting from a change in the ratio of population to capital and natural resources, or economies of scale.[4]

The case of North America would serve to illustrate the role of innovations in the economic development of a country. There was no dearth of physical resources in the territory now known as the USA and Canada before the Euro peans arrived to colonise it. The

[3] *The Theory of Economic Development*, George Allen & Unwin, 1957.
[4] *Population Growth and Levels of Consumption*, Footnote, pp. 4-5.

few inhabitants or 'human resources' that were there, were sunk in depths of poverty because they lacked the will and knowledge to improve their economic conditions. The farming and non-farming arts, if there were any at all of the latter kind, had ceased to improve. There was no continued technological progress. The territory, rather the entire continent had reached a state which might be described as 'technological stagnation'. When this state is reached, particularly, in countries where levels of consumption are close to the subsistence level, any increase in national income has a tendency to be absorbed, first, in an increase in consumption levels and, second, in an increase in population. The result is that there are no savings and no capital formation. Thus there is no economic progress. It is in such conditions that technological innovations play their greatest role as a generating force which will start a sort of a nuclear chain reaction and achieve a break-through.

Innovations or improvements are important in another sense. Many of them require capital for their expression : for example, a technical improvement may require a new machine for its utilisation, which means more capital. To the extent increased capital is congealed in technological innovations, it is saved from being frittered away in objects that do not lead to economic development of a country. In our conditions, therefore, where an increase in the rate of capital formation is difficult to bring about and the rate of population growth is likely to increase, while the need for more capital has to be stressed, special importance must be attached to promoting innovations—innovations that may be embodied in new machines or technical improvements—in order to prevent the effects of any initial increase in capital formation being absorbed by population increase.

Horace Belshaw says :

Three or four centuries ago the civilizations of India and China were more closely comparable with those in the West in economic forms and achievement than they are today. The capacity to create capital was probably no less than in the Occident ; but the urge to seek material advancement and ability to promote changes to that end proved much weaker. Had the advantage of the West been merely an early superiority in capital accumulation rather than in the ability to develop significant innovations such as the use of steam power, the joint stock company, or an efficient civil service, the process of improvement in levels of consumption would have slowed down. The progressive widening of the gap in wealth and levels of consumption are primarily attributable to the greater propensity to innovate in the West. In particular they are due to the emergence of the social phenomenon of planned innovations ; more recently, to organised research as a part of the planning, and, at a rather late stage, to innovation in the form of family limitation. These made it possible to increase investment faster than population increase.[5]

A good few think that, had India, consequent upon decline of the Moghul Empire, not fallen apart and been divided into warring factions and, later on, not fallen a slave to the British and, thus, become subject to economic exploitation by foreigners, it would have achieved economic progress on the lines of Western countries. This is far from proved. For, while political independence and stability of a country may be, rather is the pre-condition of its economic progress,[6] it cannot, by itself, be the cause thereof. Iran and Thailand are two countries of Asia which enjoyed political stability and escaped the colonialist yoke of Europeans. Yet, they are at about the same general level of destitution and want that has been the rule in India and its ex-colonial neighbours. The same is true about the availability or otherwise of natural resources and/or capital. While England, on one hand, and the latter-day USA and Canada on the other, achieved economic progress, Spain and, as we have already seen, North America of only three centuries ago, that is, before the Europeans arrived to colonise it, failed to do so—although Spain was, perhaps, the greediest of all colonial empires and, at one stage of European history, enjoyed unparalleled prosperity because of economic exploitation of its colonies and dependencies, and North America possessed vast natural resources of its own. Besides favourable political conditions and availability of ample natural resources or capital, therefore, there is something else that would seem to be required for a country to develop economically. That 'something else' is the human factor of requisite quality. The reason for our economic backwardness lies ultimately

[5] Horace Belshaw, *ibid*, pp. 152-53.
[6] A reference to Table XXVIII in Chapter XIII *ante* will show that during the period, 1953-60, economies of Argentina, Brazil, Pakistan and Turkey, instead of progressing, have retrogressed. The reason lies partly in their disturbed political conditions during this period. Whether these conditions can ultimately be traced to the quality or disquality of the human factor is another question.

not in the British domination, nor in our stars or miserliness of Nature towards our country, but in the quality or disquality of its inhabitants—in us and us alone.

The speed of economic development of a country will be governed by the basic motive-springs of its people—by the fact whether people want material advancement and want it sufficiently to work hard for it—whether they are prepared to introduce changes or to apply science and technology for bettering their economic conditions. Our economy suffers from poverty and stagnation primarily because innovations have not been welcomed. Inquiry and exploration, with readiness to examine old ways in the light of new conditions, have been inadequate. Barring a few communities[7] like the Sindhis, Gujratis, Marwaris and Punjabis, we, as a people, are not actuated by any spirit of enterprise or imbued with any urge for material prosperity. Our people are easy-going and unambitious: they are not prepared to work hard, of their own free will, with a view to improve their economic and social status. They are afraid of new ideas and ways, of taking chances, of incurring temporary defeat and loss.

Economic progress will not occur unless the people work hard for it, and they will not work hard unless they desire progress, and progress will not be desired in a community where the people do not think progress is necessary or possible.

Planning in under-developed countries is based on the assumption —which in view of the extreme poverty of the people would seem logical—that the desire for higher levels of living is inherent and more or less universal among the masses being planned for. It is a natural assumption that a poor man who does not have enough for his 'absolute' needs, e. g. food, clothing and housing, would want to have more. But the assumption is unfounded. It is not every-body in the world that wants to improve his economic conditions.

"In the United States for more than a century", said the American Ambassador to India, John Kenneth Galbraith, at the Gujarat

[7] It is noteworthy that these communities reside in those regions of the country which had to face most of the foreign invasions and where the most radical social and religious reform movement in the country, viz. the Arya Samaj, took shape and influenced people's minds greatly. The climate of these regions is arid : they receive comparatively little rain-fall and have, therefore, suffered from numerous visitations of famine. Whether these factors have anything to do with the enterprising spirit of these communities is, however, for a sociologist to say.

University, Ahmedabad, on March 23, 1962, "the Navajo, one of
the great aboriginal tribes of North America, remained stolidly aloof
from what most people would agree was a considerable national
ambition for economic improvement in the rest of America. The
Navajo tended their flocks, spun their yarn, wove their cloth, ate
their sparse simple food, and slept in their hogans. By the standards
of everyone else in Arizona and New Mexico they were poor and
it was partly because they did not ask for wealth." Although
attitudes to work and to self-improvement differ from area to area
and from class to class in India, Mr. Galbraith's description of the
Navajo is true of most of our rural communities also, that is, they
do not share in the concept of an ever-increasing standard of living.
The upper level they are prepared to strive for is limited, very
limited, indeed. There are many persons in our villages who, if
they feel that their requirements are just two bags of paddy per
year, would work for two bags but not for more. There are many
others who would choose to stop work at mid-day despite extreme
poverty.[8]

Peasant communities in many parts of the country often react
to improved agricultural opportunity—to irrigation or improved
methods of cultivation—with the argument that, after all, they
have enough ! Unless a man feels a desire to have more material
wealth, he cannot be expected to have much interest in new techniques ; there will be little attempt on his part to innovate. The

----

[8] Kusum Nair in her recent book, *Blossoms in the Dust*, 1961, Gerald
Duckworth & Co. Ltd., 3 Henrietta Street, London W. C. 2, dwells on
contrasting mental approaches which she noted in the course of her talks
with various types of rural and urban people. Among farmers, for instance, the better workman is able to get better results even in poorer
conditions than the less efficient and less industrious workman succeeds
in producing in much better material conditions. The district of Tanjore
in the South, she points out, is richly endowed by way of natural resources
and irrigation facilities. The adjacent district of Coimbatore is less
favourably situated in these respects. Yet, the farmer in Coimbatore
produces a better crop than the farmer in Tanjore.

Throughout India, she says, the best farmers are to be found not necessarily in communities most favourably endowed with material resources
but in those that are traditionally agriculturist by caste, such as, the
Sadgops in West Bengal, the *Jats* in Punjab and the *Patidars* in Gujrat.
Significant difference exists not only in attitude to manual work, but
in such traits as thrift, industry adaptability, and readiness to exploit
opportunities for a better standard of living.

Japanese method of paddy cultivation was introduced in the paddy-growing areas about a decade ago. But rarely has it been adopted in its entirety anywhere. The average yield of rice in the country, Kusum Nair points out, continues to be the lowest in the world. While there are areas where as soon as canal water reaches them there is clamour for more, there are others where not one single peasant has cared to avail himself of the irrigation facilities from the canal that passes through his village. This, even though for the first three years the water was being offered free of any charge. The result is that at the end of Second Plan in 1961 some 3.25 million acres of irrigable lands remained unirrigated. Of the irrigated area, hardly 15 per cent was under double-cropping. The argument of our experts that the irrigation potential usually takes ten to fifteen years to fully utilise, is not true of every region and every class of peasantry. The average area irrigated per cusec day in the command of the four canals in the western districts of Uttar Pradesh, during the period, 1950-60, stands at 1.20 acres, while that in the command of the Sharda canal in central districts, during the same period, at 0.81 acre, despite the fact that the latter has been in commission for the last more than 30 years. Making all possible allowance for difference in climate and crop pattern, if any, the difference between the performance of the canals in the two regions is largely a reflection of the difference between the attitudes of the inhabitants. It must be remembered in this connection that irrigation of crops is, by no means, a twentieth century innovation. Nor is it a borrowed concept. It has been in practice in parts of India as long as history.

According to an official of the Tungabhadra project in Mysore :

We carry manures and improved seeds in a trailer and offer to deliver them right at the doorstep to induce these cultivators to use them. We offer them loans to buy the seeds and manures. We go to their fields and offer to let in the water for them. We request them to try it out first in two acres only if they are not convinced. They could quadruple their yields if they would only take our advice and at least experiment. Still they are not coming forward.[9]

There is even a belief in certain parts of the country that sowing of new crops or adoption of new methods will bring the wrath of evil spirits. Objection in certain parts of Uttar Pradesh even to

9 Kusum Nair's *Blossoms in the Dust*, 1961, London, p. 48.

castration of scrub bulls and inoculation of cattle against disease is common. In Bundelkhand, there is a class known as *Chaitwas* (inasmuch as their work is done in the month of *Chait* or *Chaitra*) who alone are expected and, perhaps, have a right to harvest the *rabi* crop. If they are delayed for any reason, no cultivator will think of harvesting his own crop even if it is wasted. In fact, no innovation is welcome if it implies deviation of some individuals from the rest of the community or if it tends to arouse personal insecurities in any other way. Almost every change or break from tradition seems to conflict with one assumption or other of many of our people—whether about ancestors or marriage or life after death or personal dignity and so on.

Further, "progress occurs only where people believe that man can, by conscious effort, master nature." Most of our people, on the contrary, are content with their lot or *kismet*, and do not believe that they themselves are the captains of their fate. Instead of relying on their own efforts, they look to agencies outside of themselves to come to their aid, be it God or Government. They are still steeped in the age-old inertia, and advent of independence would, perhaps, seem to have made matters worse in this regard, at least, in certain layers of our society. What use is it having got *Swarajya* if people are not able to get bare food, raiment, shelter and medicine—and get them free or without hard work ! Such are the questions that some people ask themselves or political workers of various parties insidiously suggest to them.

This fatalism or want of initiative, rather refusal to improve their economic conditions by their own efforts may be due as much to existing poverty and consequent inability to provide against natural hazards including disease, and to illiteracy, as to religious beliefs and customs.

Poverty stands in the way of adoption of new methods or innovations, because the latter usually involve some additional outlay and also risks. The western farmer or manufacturer is more disposed to try new methods and lines of production because he has the financial means to make the necessary investment and to bear possible losses. The income of a peasant or a handicraft-man in India and other eastern countries, on the other hand, is so small that he cannot purchase, for example, a better plough if one has been discovered or a small power-driven loom, if he wishes to. Also, losses may mean all the difference between existence and starvation or involve him in debt from which recovery is very difficult. This difference in incomes makes all the difference in their approach to economic problems.

Among the conditions associated with poverty may be mentioned high death rates, disease and insufficient nutrition. A high death-rate, especially among juveniles, leads to great economic and social wastage. It is also inescapably associated with a high rate of morbidity. For one man who succumbs to a disease in a year there must be several who suffer from it, so that the prevalence of sickness is several times higher than the incidence of mortality. Disease and ill-health thus result in reducing the amount of working time. Not only that : inadequate nutrition and disease sap energy and induce lethargy and low receptivity to new ideas. Improved health will not only reduce the amount of lost time but also increase the output per head of total population. Healthy people are also more receptive to new ideas and inclined to make changes.

According to Table XLIV, nearly 42 per cent of the newly-born population in our country died before they reached the age of 20, i.e. before they could make any contribution to national income, and only 22 per cent or so reached the age of 60. The corresponding figures for Sweden stood at 3 and 84 per cent and for Netherlands at 4 and 83 per cent.

This table also shows that it was not only at birth that expectation of life in our country was lower than in other countries—it applied to each age-group. Having reached the age of entry into production the Indian worker contributed to production for a shorter period. The ratio of working to total life in India was comparatively less, very much less. During the last decade, however, disease, particularly in an epidemic form has been greatly controlled, and the death-rate has gone down appreciably. Although the Census figures of 1961 are not yet available, the Planning Commission estimates that the expectation of life since the 1951 Census has increased by 15 years—directly leading to proportionate increase in the period of working life of our countrymen.

Next, it is universally accepted that without a system of technical education related to the life and needs of society, economic progress is not possible. But our system of education, instead of equipping young men for the battle of life that lies ahead, usually disables them from all but clerical or desk work. It creates in their mind even an aversion for the profession of their forefathers, while equipping

TABLE XLIV

EXPECTATION OF LIFE, MORTALITY RATES AND SURVIVORS AT CERTAIN SPECIFIED AGES OF MALES FOR 17 IMPORTANT COUNTRIES

			AGE IN YEARS																	
			0			5			20			40			60			80		
Sl. No.	Countries	Year	Expectation of life	Mortality rates	Survivors	Expectation of life	Mortality rates	Survivors	Expectation of life	Mortality rates	Survivors	Expectation of life	Mortality rates	Survivors	Expectation of life	Mortality rates	Survivors	Expectation of life	Mortality rates	Survivors
1	2	3	4	5	6	7	8	9	10	11	12	13	14	15	16	17	18	19	20	21
1.	United States	1959	66.5	29.6	1,000	63.9	2.8	966	49.5	8.8	954	31.2	22.9	915	15.7	130.1	736	6.1	493.7	241
2.	Canada	1955-57	67.61	34.7	1,000	65.45	0.8	959	51.19	1.6	947	32.74	2.9	912	16.54	20.4	766	5.89	106.1	281
3.	Newzealand	1955-57	68.20	27.5	1,000	65.56	0.8	966	51.29	1.8	954	32.82	2.6	919	16.11	19.9	782	5.70	111.9	266
4.	Sweden	1959	71.69	17.6	1,000	68.26	0.7	978	53.84	1.1	969	35.03	1.9	943	17.75	14.1	840	5.86	100.5	351
5.	Australia	1953-55	67.14	25.2	1,000	64.32	0.8	968	50.10	1.9	955	31.65	3.0	919	15.47	22.2	763	5.47	119.6	237
6.	England and Wales	1960	68.3	32.7	1,000	65.2	0.8	972	50.7	1.3	963	31.8	2.9	938	15.3	23.7	790	5.5	136.3	238
7.	France	1960	67.2	40.8	1,000	64.4	0.7	968	49.9	1.5	959	31.4	4.0	922	15.6	23.2	754	N.A.	133.0	N.A
8.	Belgium	1946-49	62.04	64.0	1,000	62.01	1.5	925	48.02	2.6	908	30.61	5.4	849	15.45	22.7	673	5.18	128.6	209
9.	Denmark	1951-55	69.79	31.7	1,000	67.48	0.7	963	53.01	1.2	954	34.30	2.2	926	17.40	15.4	809	5.80	104.2	326
10.	Norway	1951-55	71.11	25.3	1,000	68.40	0.9	969	54.11	1.4	957	35.54	2.2	927	18.52	13.2	820	6.39	90.8	374
11.	Germany (F.R.)	1959-60	66.69	37.9	1,000	64.71	3.2	956	50.38	9.2	945	31.98	16.7	909	15.53	123.5	765	5.11	559.9	243
12.	Netherlands	1953-55	71.0	23.7	1,000	68.2	0.8	971	53.7	0.8	961	34.8	2.1	939	17.8	15.2	827	5.8	101.8	345
13.	Finland	1951-55	63.4	35.7	1,000	61.3	1.1	956	47.0	1.7	942	29.2	4.8	889	14.1	27.3	688	4.8	139.9	171
14.	Austria	1949-51	61.91	75.2	1,000	62.70	1.4	913	48.69	2.3	897	30.74	4.0	851	15.12	23.4	686	5.05	131.0	202
15.	Italy	1954-57	65.75	54.9	1,000	65.27	1.0	935	51.04	1.4	922	32.52	2.9	890	6.23	19.4	749	5.17	123.1	261
16.	Japan	1959	65.21	36.5	1,000	63.45	5.6	952	49.31	10.6	938	31.30	20.5	892	15.16	122.6	738	5.00	586.3	214
17.	India*	1941-50	32.45	190.0	1,428	40.86	17.1	1,000	33.03	10.5	827	20.53	20.2	620	10.13	57.3	314	3.99	186.3	32

SOURCE: *U.N. Demographic Year Book—1961*, Tables 24, 25 and 26 (pp. 622-674).

Note: 1. 'Expectation of life' implies the average number of years of life remaining to persons surviving to exact age specified.

2. 'Mortality rate' represents the number of deaths during specified year of age (or age interval) per 1,000 persons alive at beginning of year of age (or age interval).

3. 'Survivors' represent the number of persons who would survive at the exact age specified, out of 1,000 born alive.

* Data are survivors out of 1,000 alive at age 5. Values for ages under 5 and for 60 years and over are estimated.

them for no other practical or productive work that might earn them a living. Generally, the educated son of a peasant, though he may own sufficient land, prefers to remain idle than work on the land, because that to him is wholly inconsistent with education. Not only that; the academic education that our young men usually receive, has been a positive hindrance, because it has strengthened desires for consumption without providing the means of satisfying them. The 1951 census gave the number of professional, technical, administrative, clerical and related workers in India as only 2 per cent of the economically active population, whereas the corresponding percentages were 15 in Japan (1950), 19 in the United Kingdom (1959) and 29 in the United States (1950).[9a] We will, therefore, have to modify our educational system a great deal, relate it to economic needs of society and, with that end in view, to undertake research and train people. The need and importance of technical training, particularly in our conditions where capital is short, will become still clearer when we realize that, *while increasing capital per head usually tends to lower the yield of capital, increasing technical knowledge tends to raise it.* Investment in research and training, however, being not profitable for a private entrepreneur, it is one of the barest duties of the state to invest in these directions—for increasing the nation's technical knowledge and capacities so that productivity may be raised. Research or testing has to be followed by professional training which has, in turn, to be followed by advisory services or extension activities in the field.

How the improvement of their skills and capacities increases the productive potentialities of human beings will be clear from the example of the USA. During the period from 1929 to 1953, total national real income in the USA was a little more than doubled, although resources in terms of total man-hours in the labour-force increased only by 17 per cent. The only explanation for this increase in income at a relatively faster rate lies in the improvement in the human factor—a result of increased training, education, and additional capabilities based on health and new knowledge. The USA has invested in the education of her people on a mass scale right from elementary schools to graduate schools and technical institutions—on a scale larger than Britain and many other

[9a] *UN Economic Survey of Asia and Far East,* 1961, Bangkok, 1962, p. 22.

countries.[10] In a speech delivered at the University of Rajasthan in 1961, the US Ambassador to India, John K. Galbraith, said:

The fact is that education is of high importance both as an object of immediate consumption and as a form of investment for future production. It is neither consumption nor investment, but both. Like bread it is something we use or consume. But, like a dam or a canal, it is something in which we invest to produce more in the future. A developing country may, however, rightfully regard its outlays for education as an investment. The fact that these have also the characteristics of consumption, and are rewarding to the individual in their own right, must not be allowed to confuse the issue. That something is both a consumer service and a source of productive capital for the society does not detract at all from its importance as an investment. Rather, it enhances that importance.

Besides technical education for the few, primary or elementary education for all the people is equally important. Popular education releases the energies not of the few but of the many. And it opens men's minds, as they can be opened in no other way, to new methods and new techniques. Needless to say, therefore, popular literacy is, thus, a first indispensable step to any form of economic progress. Nowhere in the world is there an illiterate people that is progressive. Nowhere is there a literate people that is not. According to the Report of the 1961 Census, hardly 24 per cent of the people in India can be counted as literate or having received some kind of education. In Japan, six-year compulsory universal education dates back to 1873. This provided a literate population in rural areas, more skilled in farming, and a supply of labour available to industry more sophisticated than European countries at the time.

"A dollar or a rupee invested in the intellectual improvement of human beings", pointed out the US Ambassador, "will often bring a greater increase in national income than a dollar or a rupee devoted to railways, dams, machine tools or other tangible capital goods." But the estimated investment on the three steel plants, during the Second Plan, amounted to Rs. 510 crores—perhaps, actual investment came to Rs. 526 crores—whereas the investment on the entire field of education by the Union and all the States together amounted only to Rs. 208 crores. Expenditure on each of the steel plants

[10] The USA has also been fortunate in its human resources in another way. It has had the indispensable boon of a steady flow of restless, dynamic, vigorous, diversified immigrants from various countries of Europe.

was twice as great as total expenditure on the development of primary education. In the Third Plan, the outlay on education has been increased to 418 crores. (Of these amounts, cultural programmes claimed 4 crores during the Second Plan, and 10 crores during the Third Plan). Money allocations to education are clearly inadequate and need to be stepped up.

Inasmuch as our financial resources are scanty, we cannot afford to scatter them over all kinds of desirable objectives. Significant achievement in urgent and inescapable tasks is far better than a feeble effort in a multitude of directions. Public expenditure for education would, therefore, at present be better concentrated on enforcing universal, compulsory primary education, organising technical education so as to produce the necessary personnel for every technical job from the lowest to the highest, and making provision for scientific research. Progress in other directions should be left to private initiative and effort with minimum public assistance needed to induce such effort.

Last, but most important, come our religious beliefs and customs, which so largely determine a people's attitude to life. All kinds of human activity, social and economic, are born in the mind. So, the economic conditions of a society can largely be ultimately traced to the thought processes or mental attitudes of its members. The cause of prosperity or poverty of a country can, thus, be seen to lie in the minds of its inhabitants. If we are a poor and economically backward society today, the reason can be sought in our defective mental attitudes. As a corollary, if we now want to make our country prosperous, we will have to bring about a change in the present social and economic attitudes of our people. It is only after there is such a change, that is, a change in the ends or values we have been seeking hitherto, that is, after we have come to entertain a desire for economic progress—a desire to occupy a position in the comity of nations that our forefathers once occupied—that we will set about to acquire the means of achieving it, *viz.* to gain the necessary skills or knowledge and the necessary health or physique, and to work hard. Seen in this manner, economic development "is not exclusively—maybe not even primarily—an economic progress; it also involves a deep cultural and social change—a change in values, habits, knowledge, attitudes, ways of life, social ideals and aspirations."[11] This change or social, cultural and religious reform is

[11] Peter Drucker quoted in *Which Way Lies Hope?*, 1957, p. 196.

part of the price we will have to pay for getting out of the morass in which we find ourselves.

For several centuries the Hindu religion, as interpreted by certain schools, has been placing great reliance on asceticism of an individualistic and functionless kind and gives an extreme rationalisation for ignoring the material world. Because animal drives often play us false, many pious Hindus have reached the conclusion that all such drives are inherently evil. They speak of "the world, the flesh and the devil" in the same breath. To them the world is nothing but *Maya*—an illusion. Great stress has, therefore, been laid on other-worldliness and little positive inducement offered to hard work and accumulation of wealth. Simplicity or unostentatious living has been confused with an inferior mode of living. The result is a society steeped in fatalism and consequent poverty.

Next to religion, custom is singly the most powerful force in every society. A people's conduct or behaviour is largely governed by its social tradition or cultural inheritance, which has perpetuated or transmitted from generation to generation the socially accumulated experience, skills, judgment and wisdom of men who have gone before. With the weakening or disappearance of animal drives, the cultural tradition in every country tended to assume greater and greater authority over men's actions and attitudes, and gradually came to be the chief guide or source of control of human conduct. In fact, it became so important that no human society could survive without it. As a result of this dependence, the ways of the fathers were entrenched and strengthened by every possible means, and gradually took the form of manners, customs, laws and morals (According to some, religion also is no more than a part of people's social tradition or cultural inheritance). Being a very ancient people, there is no wonder, therefore, if a web of customs envelops the Hindus from the cradle to the cremation-ground.

Our customs or cultural traditions, however, like those of any other country, are not all good or unmixed good. While stubborn conservatism has served to preserve precious values—qualities of character and conduct—which give strength, stability and refinement to our society, and might otherwise have been lost, it has also perpetuated traditions which are not so helpful. They include superstitions, bad habits and folkways which are often the product of some mistaken generalisation, or rules that once were good, but are no longer applicable. Such traditions have made the process of living for the mass of the people a heavy, dull burden, and blocked progress.

The caste system—a dominant part of our cultural inheritance—is one such custom or institution that is out of date. This system, as at present practised, under which social status is determined by birth has come down as a special feature of Hindu social organisation for some thirty centuries. Today it is one of the built-in features of the Hindu, rather the Indian mind. In the process of expanding and as time rolled by, the pristine teaching became blurred, with the result that the four castes or divisions of society as originally conceived, based on qualities, actions and aptitudes, were superseded by hundreds of castes and thousands of sub-castes in which neophytes within the Hindu fold were accommodated.[12] The method of combining functional skill with new castes was an ingenious way of establishing social harmony by giving the newcomer an assured economic position within Hinduism, and this continued to hold the field as long as the economic basis of the Hindu social order remained stable. The system served as a social insurance for the weak and the unsuccessful. Instead of being thrown in a maelstrom, every member of the society knew his place and had a source of living which was secure from encroachments or grasping proclivities of his neighbour. Division of functions and power among the four classes—Brahmin, Kshatriya, Vaishya and Shudra—was so arranged, and interests of one class were so different from those of others that control over society as a whole could not be gathered, as today in a communist or purely capitalist society, in the hands of any class or group of individuals. The caste system represented an attempt at organisation of society on the doctrine of checks and balances, separation of powers and diffusion of sovereignty.

Today, however, the caste system, leading directly to the fragmentation of Indian society is a great hindrance to common economic endeavour. With membership of a caste being fixed for life and hereditary, choice of the marriage partner being limited to members of one's own caste, and restrictions placed on dining with or eating food cooked by outsiders and even on touching them,

[12] In 1901 when an attempt at a complete tabulation of all castes was made, the number of "main" castes and tribes was found to be 2378 (vide Census of India, 1901, vol. i, Part I, p. 537).

the caste system bases the organisation of life on the principle of division and disintegration and, thus, represents "a most thorough-going attempt known to human history to introduce absolute inequality as the guiding principle in social relationships".[13] Community projects become a fantastic paradox in such a society which denies the entire theory of community altogether, or restricts it to a very narrow circle. The tragedy has been, to quote an eminent thinker, that "emphasizing the unity of the whole world, animate and inanimate, India has yet fostered a social system which has divided her children into watertight compartments, divided them from one another, generation to generation, through endless centuries, and exposed her to foreign conquests which have left her weak and poor."

The conception of a hereditary occupation is exactly the opposite of the idea of free opportunity, open competition and individual mobility, associated with a dynamic industrial economy. The fact that Japan had a much less rigid caste system than India, helps explain, *inter alia*, why Japan could industrialise more rapidly. A man's caste in India is immutable. It confers or imposes a definite social status on him, virtually eliminating prospects of promotion through hard work. A man can change his religion, but not his caste.

Further, the system serves to inject in every Hindu[14] mind since childhood ideas of high and low, superiority and inferiority, and puts a premium on membership of certain castes and a discount on that of others. It runs counter to the conception of dignity of labour. Manual work is considered degrading : it is more respectable to do nothing at all than to supervise, let alone toil. There is an English adage that 'he that by the plough would thrive, himself must either hold or drive', but there are some high castes in certain parts of India whose members will not 'hold' the plough themselves, nor will their women-folk attend even to milch-cattle. Those who do not work at all or put in comparatively less work occupy higher rungs in the social ladder, and those who put in more work are assigned to lower rungs. It is not surprising,

[13] *Population of India and Pakistan*, Kingsley Davis, New York, 1951, p. 170.
[14] In fact, the caste system applies to nearly every person in India, regardless of his religion. Muslims and Christians also, who are almost all converted from Hinduism, suffer from this malady more or less.

therefore, if in spite of all the learning of our forefathers, India is so poor.

Also, it is caste that lay at the root of our political slavery. The very weaknesses of a caste-ridden society make it incapable of political unity over a large territory, and virtually helpless against an invader. India, therefore, hardly ever needed to be conquered in the military sense by the foreigner ; he always found it bound hand and foot, and ready, in a way, to welcome the aggressor without a struggle or much of a struggle. India had no jealousy or hatred of the foreigner because it had no sense whatever of patriotism or national unity. There was no Indian and, therefore, logically speaking, no foreigner. The notion of patriotism presupposes compatriots or men bred up in a community which may be regarded as a large family, so that it is natural for them to think of the land itself as a mother. But if the community is composed of thousands of castes and sub-castes with no common interest or aspirations and never meeting on the same social plane, then patriotism or love of the country cannot simply take root in such a society.

True, one of the leading elements of nationality is a common religion and a sense of kindred and common interest engendered by it. In Hinduism which was prevalent throughout the country, India had a germ out of which, sooner or later, an Indian nationality might have sprung. And foreign invasions which succeeded each other through so many centuries supplied precisely the pressure which was most likely to favour the development of this germ. But those hopes were belied : Hinduism did not pass into patriotism and failed to arouse a united India against the invader, simply because the caste system had enfeebled it as a uniting principle.

The Moghuls conquered India almost without apparent means. Babar did not come with a mighty nation at his back or leaning on the organisation of some powerful state ; yet he succeeded in working a miracle, *viz.* the establishment of the Moghul Empire which lasted two centuries. This miracle was possible only because hundreds of millions of Hindus who inhabited this country had not developed the habit of thinking all together, like a single nation. A mere mass of individuals or a conglomeration of groups not connected with each other by any common feelings or interests, the Hindus were easily subjugated just as they had been by previous conquerors, from Mahmud Ghazni onwards, because they could be

induced either to remain apathetic or to act against each other.
The same story was repeated in the case of conquest by Britain.
When authority in India had fallen on the ground through the
decay of the Moghul Empire it was picked up in the major part of
the country by the Marathas. They had it within their power to
unite India but failed to do so because they placed their narrow
interests before those of the country as a whole. The idea of a
united India was foreign to them. Not only this : they even failed
to build up a united Maratha State, and·soon split up into five
principalities each based on a separate clan or sub-caste. Answering
the question why the Marathas failed to create an enduring State,
Sir Jadunath Sarkar cites the Hindu caste system as the major
cause. Victories of Shivaji and Baji Rao I created a reaction in
favour of Hindu orthodoxy which accentuated class distinctions
and ceremonial purity of the daily rites :[15]

In the security, power and wealth engendered by their independence, the Marathas of the 18th century forgot the past record
of Muslim persecution ; their social grades turned against each other.
The Brahmans living east of the Sahyadri range despised those
living west of it, and the men of the hills despised their brethren of
the plains, because they could now do so with impunity. The head
of the state, viz. the Peshwa, though a Brahman, was despised by
his Brahman servants belonging to other branches of the caste—
because the first Peshwa's great-grandfather's great-grandfather
had once been lower in society than the Deshastha Brahmans'
great grand-fathers' great-grandfather ! While the Chitpawan
Brahmans were waging a social war with the Deshastha Brahmans,
a bitter jealousy raged betwen the Brahman ministers and governors
and the Kayastha secretaries : We have unmistakable traces of it
as early as the reign of Shivaji. 'Caste grows by fission.' It is
antagonistic to national union. In proportion as Shivaji's ideal of a
Hindu Swaraj was based on orthodoxy, it contained within itself the
seed of its own death. As Rabindranath Tagore remarks :

A temporary enthusiasm sweeps over the country and we
imagine that it has been united ; but the rents and holes in our
body-social do their work secretly ; we cannot retain any noble
idea for long.

Shivaji aimed at preserving the rents ; he wished to save from
Mughal attack a Hindu society to which ceremonial distinctions
and isolation of castes are the very breath of life. He wanted to

[15] *Shivaji and His Times* by Sir Jadunath Sarkar (fifth Edition),
pp. 374-75, published by M. C. Sarkar and Sons Ltd., Calcutta, 1952.

make this heterogeneous society triumphant over all India! He wove ropes of sand; he attempted the impossible. It is beyond the power of any man, it is opposed to the divine law of the universe, to establish the *swaraj* of such a caste-ridden, isolated, internally-torn sect over a vast continent like India ("Rise and Fall of the Sikh Power", as translated by Sir Jadunath Sarkar in *The Modern Review*, April 1911).

It was this division of the Hindu or Indian society into innumerable fragments and not some enormous superiority on the part of the English race that made their empire in India possible. England conquered India and held it by means of Indian troops paid with Indian money.

It is the rigid caste system, again, with its notions of high and low that drove millions of Hindus into other religious folds in spite of the fact that the spiritual teachings of the latter were in no way superior to those of Hinduism. It is only human nature if members of the despised castes resented the injustice and tyranny which the caste system has meant in practice and, in the bitterness of public humiliation, sought to be avenged on the persecuting church by going over to other faiths. The irony of the situation lay in the fact that men who were looked down upon by their co-religionists, because of their birth, usually found recognition as equals at the hands of their erstwhile co-religionists as soon as they forsook the religion of their fathers ! !

Yet, again, it is the caste system which, more than anything else, made it difficult, if not impossible for the different religious groups of India to come closer together, socially and politically—to weld into one society—and ultimately led to the partition of the country. When the system kept one Hindu away from another it could not possibly tolerate or encourage Hindus as a community to partake in cultural and social activities in common with non-Hindus. Despite sincere protestations on behalf of the Indian National Congress, Muslims continued to apprehend that, after the British had left, they will not get a fair deal from the Hindu majority which was not prepared to accord equal treatment even to its own co-religionists. Indian nationalism fostered by common hatred of the British, thus, always bore the mark of a conflict within itself.

In spite of the attainment of *Swarajya* and partition of the country, however, the social integration of Hindus is no nearer achievement. No lessons seem to have been learnt from history. The hold of the caste in the psychology of the people is still very strong. Caste influence in political and economic matters is still great. In fact, instead of being on the decline, it would appear to be on the increase. This was demonstrated during the last two General Elections of 1957 and 1962 when voting for legislatures in many parts of the country took place strictly on caste lines. Even those who are robed in high political offices are accused of a caste bias, and not always without reason ; and not all public servants are able to rise above this weakness. In the circumstances, democracy may yet be regarded only in prospect and not a reality in India.

Another feature of our social tradition or organisation distinguishing India from Europe, and militating against industrialisation, is the joint family system. Such a system, like caste, with all the countervailing advantages that it might have possessed or still possesses, limits social mobility and social change, because it binds an individual to others on the basis of birth and forces him to contribute to the support of a larger group independently of their ability. It serves as a haven for members of the family who may be lethargic, if not actually tends to make them so.

To caste and joint family may be added our various taboos and customs which have a blighting effect on economic progress. For example, among many communities the expense of religious feasts, ostentatious marriage ceremonies and even funeral customs consumes the greater part of the family resources. Even those who are in some position to save, spend their savings in non-productive or low-productivity outlays—temples or monuments, voyages to sacred places, personal ornaments and the like. Till the end of the last century there was a ban on sea voyage among Hindus throughout the country. In Malabar a Hindu had to forswear his religion if he wanted to become a sailor.

Directly deriving from our social tradition are our attitudes towards the having of children. Birth of a numerous progeny, in particular, sons, is regarded not as a calamity but with an air of approval. These attitudes only serve to retard the slow rate of economic progress that we are somehow able to make—and to keep the country poor.

Added to these drags of our cultural inheritance, there is the question of regionalism often associated with language that has come to the fore since Independence. It bedevils the progress of the country as one economic unit and diverts much energy and emotion that could otherwise be harnessed to useful purpose. Political power is for the first time a reality and the country's democratic system is an encouragement to every element in national life to obtain, sometimes alone, sometimes in combination with others, a predominant share in the country's political life. Antagonism between the North and the South is the most obvious of these conflicts. Some of these hatreds and antagonisms are inherited—fundamentally, perhaps, they are a legacy of unequal economic and political development—but in the last decade they have, without a doubt, grown in sharpness. Only God help us if our selfishness or loyalty to caste and region comes to dominate or undermine our paramount loyalty to the country as a whole ! ! In that case, we will have gone under again, perhaps, never to recover.

As has already been said in these pages, we have to work far harder, better and longer, indeed, than we have been doing. One can sit down to eat only after there is something to eat—after something has been produced. With her immense population and comparatively scanty resources, India cannot flirt with the idea of plenty for all out of minimum work. But we are trying to do exactly this, *viz.* to become a Welfare State before creating the means of welfare or the basic economy to sustain it. As somebody has said it : "we want the blessings of the Welfare State today, complete with old-age pensions, unemployment insurance, family allowances, health insurance, forty-hour week, and all the trimmings." In a word, comfort is being given priority over production, and rights over duties. Curiously enough, race for material prosperity, instead of urging our people on to greater and still greater mental and physical efforts, has turned into a clamour for "getting more and working less."

Economic and, particularly, industrial development is the major goal of Indian policy. But the labour legislation that has been enacted in the country is acting as a brake rather than an aid or accelerator to achievement of the goal. Industrial labour in India had from the beginning a status higher and enjoyed more rights and amenities than labour in other countries as judged in relation to the national income *per capita* or the stage of economic development achieved in the country. For example, our wage costs in the textile industry are some 50 per cent higher than those in Japan while the *per capita* national income in that country is more than five times that in India.

The British Government was not anxious to speed up Indian industrialisation ; so, the device of bringing up Indian labour laws to the level of the advanced industrial nations came handy as one of the insidious ways of slowing down the country's economic progress. When India obtained freedom, all our leaders also— all the political parties—plumped for the support of labour. We have treated the recommendations of the International Labour Organisation as the sacred word to be unquestioningly accepted, and thus frittered away the one asset or advantage, *viz*. cheap labour, that we so abundantly possessed.[16] It has been forgotten that for under-developed countries, like India, where living standards are pitifully low, it is absurd to act upon all the recommendations of the I. L. O. or to think in terms of providing the same amenities to workers as the highly advanced countries of the West are able to provide. In our conditions it is a mistake to risk a fall in production, or to so manage things that production is sacrificed in order to make work more meaningful or comfortable for the workers. But this is exactly what we are doing. Especially, the minimum wage legislation, and the requirements of compensation payment to dismissed workers, tend to inflate industrial costs, raise prices, restrict employment opportunities and retard efficient industrialisation.

In order to cultivate and expand the internal market and to promote exports the prices of the products of our mines and factories have to be reduced, or kept at a low level. But such reduction, or maintenance of low price is found to be difficult, basically, because of the recalcitrance of labour. A rural labourer who is unemployed or earns hardly a rupee per day secures a job in a factory, state transport services or a harbour, and then strikes work because a far higher daily wage that he now gets is considered insufficient by him. He forgets entirely that there are millions, of whom he was one only till yesterday, who would be glad to earn even one rupee a day. This sudden transformation that takes place in the psychology of the worker is surprising, indeed, but what is still more surprising is the fact that Government by its policy assiduously fosters this development. However, the result is that the gulf which already exists between organised industrial workers (and Government servants), on the one hand, and the vast army of unemployed and semi-employed agriculturists, artisans and others, on the other,

[16] It is the cheap labour of eastern UP rather than any other factor that made Kanpur the principal industrial centre in Northern India.

goes on widening. The wages and emoluments of those who produce the industrial goods are higher than the incomes of those more than eighty per cent of our people who live in the villages and constitute the largest market for these goods. The result ? Prices rise beyond the means of the consumers, exports decline, stocks accumulate in the godowns of factories, and industrialisation is retarded. According to "The Times of India" News Service, in a grim warning to India's industrialists, the Union Minister for Food and Agriculture, Mr. S. K. Patil, said on March 26, 1961, that even after implementing three Five-Year Plans at a total cost of Rs. 18,000 crores, the country, despite its proverbially cheap labour, might find itself producing articles for which there was no market anywhere in the world. The time had come, he told the Federation of Indian Chambers of Commerce in New Delhi, for the Government and the industrialists to sit together and consider whether India could produce articles which would compete in the world market in quality and price!!

Stating its view on wage policy, the Central Pay Commission observed : "A minimum wage pitched above the level of *per capita* income, and intended for very wide application is obviously one beyond the country's capacity ; in ignoring the country's vital need for savings and investment, such a wage gives no thought to the future "[17]

The second notable result of labour legislation, especially minimum wage legislation, is that it retards absorption into employment of rural and urban unemployed as they cannot secure employment by offering their services more cheaply than the prescribed wages. Instead of industrial wages being determined on the basis of the supply and demand of labour, the tendency today is to fix wages on the basis of the capacity of the prosperous industrial undertakings to pay. As a result, any depression leads to the closure of the weaker units, thereby throwing out of employment even some of those who are employed today.

In every industry, whether privately or publicly owned, it is labour that rules the roost. There is hardly a factory or workshop in which the management is not almost in perpetual fright and does not prefer to turn a blind eye to indiscipline and inefficiency rather than invite a clash with labour. Trade unions, because of the way they have been exploited, have become a crippling burden on the economy and inhibit economic progress, rather than an instrument

[17] *Report*, March 1960.

of increasing the productivity of labour and clearing the ground for rapid economic development of the country.

The consequences of our unimaginative labour policy are high-lighted in the following report :[18]

MADRAS, March 17—Mr. E. F. G. Hunter, Chairman of the Employers' Federation of South India, said yesterday that higher wages without increased productivity, absenteeism and heavy excise duties, were slowly pricing Indian goods out of world markets. Addressing the annual meeting of the Federation, Mr. Hunter said Indian labour had in recent years become much more expensive than in the past, particularly when compared to output. Wage boards and tribunals had been 'generous' in reviewing wage structures ignoring the vital factor of productivity, he added. Employers, Mr. Hunter said, have no objection to paying higher wages, provided increased wages go hand in hand with greater productivity.

Mr. Hunter complained that absenteeism had increased 'in a most alarming fashion'. The way employees' insurance scheme was implemented had also increased absenteeism.

He alleged that under the scheme, 'it is possible for fit men to obtain generous quantities of medical leave on proportionate wages'.

As regards labour participation in management, Mr. Hunter said, judged from results in Madras, it could not be regarded as successful. The Government, he said, would be well advised to approach only establishments with a record of industrial harmony to implement the scheme.

Mr. Hunter also wanted outside leadership of trade unions to be removed or reduced in the interests of labour, industry and the country.

The reason is not far to seek : purely financial incentives prove ineffective unless there is attitudinal readiness for a positive response. In the absence of such readiness, higher wages have brought greater absenteeisms, and extra leisure has been preferred to an increase in earnings.

It is significant that labour troubles are conspicuous by their absence in communist countries. Apparently, the first victim of dictatorship is labour. It would be a sad day for Indian labour, as for Indian democracy, if the conviction is to spread that under political democracy there can be neither discipline nor efficiency in our factories and offices. It is desirable, therefore, that Indian labour voluntarily abandons the strike and substitutes it by con-

[18] *Pioneer*, Lucknow, dated March 18, 1962.

ciliation or other more democratic methods. For this a reorientation in the attitude of political parties would be necessary. We have an example of good relations between labour and capital as in the days of Mahatma Gandhi in Ahmedabad and as in Japan. Japan is a fully democratic state ; yet one seldom hears of lock-outs or strikes in that country. If we do not want external regulation by the state on the lines of communist countries and yet want our country to develop economically with all speed, while retaining the democratic freedoms, the only way is that of self-regulation or voluntary discipline—such as that serves the larger interests of the country. The existing labour legislation must be scrapped in a great part, allowing the law of supply and demand to operate, subject, of course, to the requirement that no undue exploitation or ill-treatment of labour takes place. At the same time, in order, however, that profits are productively utilised by the entrepreneur that part which is ploughed back into the economy within a given period may be exempted from taxation, and that which is not, heavily taxed. Indeed, if our economy takes on the character advocated in these pages, need for much of the labour legislation will have disappeared altogether.

Minimum wages, leave and holidays have been guaranteed and maximum hours of work prescribed by legislation for agricultural labourers also. The enactment will, however, remain a dead letter unless agricultural production increases *pari passu*. If the wages are fixed at a level which the farmer would not otherwise pay or which his farm production cannot bear, the farmer will prefer to do without a labourer as he is doing largely in the Punjab or West Germany. Holidays are meaningless, particularly, on small farms as there are, and can be, no opening or closing days or hours in agriculture. Similarly, employers in shops and commercial establishments have been guaranteed minimum leave and holidays and other benefits. Employers have been prohibited from requiring or even *allowing* any employee to work more than eight hours a day. The same is true of Government servants. Judged in the light of our *per capita* income, the wages of Government servants in India compare very favourably with those in other countries, and the number of public holidays here is larger than anywhere else. Those employed in state banks, postal and telegraph departments, transport services and even some defence establishments have been given rights including the right to strike which workers in other countries have come to enjoy only after great economic progress has taken place and a national consciousness and sense of responsibility developed. Yet, an agitation in many a department in the States and throughout the Union for more and more salaries, allowances and other rights, and less and less work, continues unabated.

Even the prisoners are being pampered in the name of Jail Reform. Living conditions in jails are being made more comfortable than normal life outside. Attempts are being made, particularly in the State of Uttar Pradesh, to convert jails into hostels attached to educational institutions. Differences between a prisoner and a free man are being reduced to the minimum on the ground that, after all, *i. e.*, looked at fundamentally or analytically, we are all criminals in the true sense of the term, the only difference being that those who are outside prisons could not be caught within the net of law as it is defined, or have succeeded in escaping the eyes of the custodians of law and order !

In the morning, the convicts in Uttar Pradesh do P. T. exercises and sing patriotic songs. For breakfast they get *dalia* of wheat. Their meals consist of *chapatis* of wheat *atta*, fresh and tempting vegetables produced in jail gardens, and *dal*. Special meals have been allowed twice a month as also on the occasion of important festivals and anniversaries of Republic and Independence Day. Friends and relatives of convicts can deposit for their use articles of food like *gur*, sugar, pickles, honey, *ghee* and dry or fresh fruits ; articles of toilet like soap, oil, tooth-paste or powder and toothbrush ; articles of indoor games like playing-cards and chess ; cheap musical instruments such as flutes, calendars and newspapers or periodicals (in addition to those allowed at Government cost), provided they are not on the prohibited list ; and boot polish, *biris*, cigarettes, chewing tobacco and snuff.

"With a view to avoiding wastage of man-power in unproductive and irksome work" and to utilise it in a better way, electric flour-mills have been installed in many jails and the system of grinding corn by prisoners is being gradually given up. Drawing of water from wells by manual labour has been abolished as a form of jail labour. Games and sports like football, volley-ball and wrestling are being encouraged and prisoners are allowed to play matches even with outsiders. "In order to break the dull monotony of their lives," prisoners are allowed to stage dramas, to engage in music or *kirtans*, to visit places of interest and even to witness cinema shows. The Information Department has been asked to arrange for exhibition of documentary films in jails. Radios have also been installed in many jails.

Rules regarding interviews have been greatly liberalised. Small rooms have been constructed in Central Prisons "to ensure reasonable privacy and decency in interviews." The period of interview has also been extended from 20 to 30 minutes. A system of release on 'Ticket of Leave' has also been introduced under which prisoners of specified categories can be granted leave for 15 to 21 days in a year to enable them to visit their homes and 'to renew their family ties'. 'Seasonal Parole' is granted to those prisoners who possess productive lands but have nobody to look after them, in order to enable them to attend to agricultural operations.

A number of schemes have been introduced in certain jails for payment of wages to prisoners for the work done by them which helps in 'the restoration of their self-respect and appreciation of the dignity of labour'. An opportunity is also provided to them for working in open camps under conditions of freedom approaching normal life. Prisoners in these camps are allowed enhanced scale of remission at 30 *days per month* served at the camps subject to a maximum of half the sentence. They also enjoy the privilege of home leave during which their sentences stand suspended. They receive wages for their labour according to market rates on piece-work basis. After deducting a part towards the cost of their maintenance, the balance of the wages is credited towards their accounts. For example, during the financial year, 1961-62, 120 inmates of the Model Jail, Lucknow, and 1,700 inmates of the Camp Jail, Ghurma, in Mirzapur District, respectively earned Rs. 388.0 and Rs. 376.6 per head out of which they paid Rs.264.6 and 213.0 to Government as maintenance charges. The rest of the money was credited to their private accounts. The State's *per capita* income in 1960-61 was estimated at Rs. 262.0 only.

The Planning Commission introduced a village housing scheme in 1957, which provided for the selection of villages in groups of four to six and the preparation of lay-out plans for the villages. Assistance in the shape of loans up to two-thirds of the cost of construction subject to a maximum of Rs. 2,000 per house was given for carrying out improvements in the existing houses. During the Second Plan, about 3,700 villages were selected and socio-economic and physical surveys of about 2,000 villages were completed. Lay-out plans of 1,600 villages were drawn up and loans amounting to Rs. 3.6 crores were sanctioned for construction of about 15,400 houses. About 3,000 houses, however, were alone completed and the remaining houses were under different stages of construction.

Under the Third Plan, an amount of Rs. 12.7 crores has been allocated for this scheme. For scheduled castes and tribes in particular, besides funds available under the village housing scheme, assistance by way of subsidy is also provided out of the outlay of Rs. 25 crores intended for health, housing and other schemes under the programme for the welfare of the backward classes.

It is not realised that houses have little value, unless means of living have been first improved, or that we will be creating a political problem for ourselves by providing funds only for a small percentage. There are about 75 million houses in the countryside. Granting that only two-thirds of them need to be reconstructed, and none of the remaining one-third needs to be renovated, a colossal amount of Rs. 15,000 crores will be required, which we will simply never be able to find.

The following report published in the *National Herald*, Lucknow, dated September 3, 1962, is evidence either of our love of show and ostentation or an inordinate desire to be counted as a developed country immediately, irrespective of costs or means :

STOCKHOLM, Sept. 2: A group of young Swedes is about to leave by car for India where they intend to transform the village of Dhanaura in northern India into a 'model village', it was revealed here yesterday.

The group, consisting of fifteen persons, have one year in which to perform their task.

The voyage has been organised in collaboration with the Swedish-Indian Cooperation Committee, and with various Swedish youth groups.

In one of the major States of India, provision has been made for old-age pensions. As if by the mere act of this single scheme, the State will be entitled to rank among the developed or socially advanced states of the world overnight ! Actuated by similar motives, besides 'cultural programmes', we incurred, during the Second Plan an outlay of Rs. 15 crores, and have provided during the Third Plan for an outlay of Rs. 28 crores, for 'social welfare' activities—amounts which could have otherwise contributed to much-needed agricultural production.

Our passion for providing comforts and living standards of European countries to all those of our people to whom they can be provided by budgeting or legal enactments, knows no limits. That these comforts and standards cannot be available to the vast masses of our people living in the villages, and what effect this will have on their minds, or how it will ultimately affect the social and economic development of the country does not seem to bother our leaders and policy-makers.

To raise living standards, however—let us remember—production will have to be raised and, to raise production, a higher investment in actual man-hours provided by the peasants and industrial labourers, would be necessary. Let there be no doubt that belts will have to be tightened. Symbols of modernity or acts of economic extravagance and showmanship like costly Government buildings, glittering air-ports and palatial residences of senior officials cannot be confused with economic growth and will have to be eschewed, and all emphasis laid on measures calculated more generally and pervasively to increase the productivity of our economy. We will have to pay a price for economic development whether we live in a democratic society or are governed by a dictatorship. The only difference is that in a democracy the costs are willingly borne : in a dictatorship they are extracted. The difference is a difference between a willing human being and a beast of burden. Sacrifices have to be made in both cases—in the form of hard work and vigorous thrift—so that more may be produced and more may be saved.

In the past we had developed not many wants. Whatever wants there were, were, on the whole, adapted to economic activities of the society, and the people were in equilibrium with their environment. They had developed a tradition of contentment in the face of adversity and poverty. They never rated the pursuit of material wealth high among life's objectives. Therefore, there was no problem of economic discontent and frustration. In the present times, however, we have been captivated by the European sense of values—by the 'demonstrative effect' of wealthy countries—and have developed wants to an extent that they have outstripped the means of their satisfaction simply because, it will bear repetition, simultaneously we are not prepared to change our attitudes towards work or to work hard enough. We forget that, while it is easy to get converted to new ways of living on the side of wants and aspirations, it is not so easy to secure the means of their satisfaction : strenuous efforts will be required to match the desire for a change in living standards by a corresponding increase in the output of goods and services.

If we have to make progress, the social and psychological barriers from which the western countries were particularly free and from which we particularly suffer, will have to disappear. Change of the present motivations of our countrymen—the "deep cultural and social change" of which Peter Drucker speaks—has to come, if not today, then tomorrow. But the question is : how exactly can this change be made to come or brought about ?

It is difficult to say why any society starts developing and to what social agents this process is actually due. Human conduct knows few rules and no science. Its response under given conditions cannot be easily assessed or foretold with any accuracy. It will, therefore, be a mistake to conclude that all under-developed countries would respond to much the same prescription. Perhaps only a negative statement can be made, *viz.* economic development is not merely a consequence of capital formation or economic factors.

More often than not, the economic motives for seeking economic progress converge with some non-economic motives, such as the desire for increased social power and prestige, national pride, political ambition and so on. Lord Keynes has observed in this connection : "If human nature felt no temptation to take a chance, no satisfaction (profit apart) in constructing a factory, a mine or a farm, there might not be much investment merely as a result of cold calculation."[19]

In the USA, after the Civil War, men did the things needed to industrialise a continent not merely to make money, but also because power, adventure, challenge and prestige were all to be found in the market place and the game of expansion and money-making was rewarding in terms of the full range of human values. As a matter of historical fact, points out Prof. Walt Whitman Rostow of the Massachussetts Institute of Technology, USA, xenophobic nationalism has been the most important motive force in the transition from traditional to modern societies—vastly more important than the profit motive. Men have been willing to uproot traditional societies primarily not to make more money, but because the

[19] *General Theory*, p. 150.

traditional society failed, or threatened to fail, to protect them from humiliation by foreigners.

"In Germany it was certainly a nationalism based on past humiliation and future hope—the Junkers and the men of the East, more than the men of trade and the liberals of the West—that did the job. In Russia, a series of military intrusions and defeats were the great engine of change : Napoleon, the Crimea, the Russo-Japanese War, the First World War. In Japan it was the 'demonstration effect' not of high profits or manufactured consumers' goods, but of the Opium War in China in the early 1840's, and Admiral Peary's seven black ships a decade later, that cast the die."[20]

True, our conditions (and, therefore, our economy will) differ from the USA, the USSR, Germany and Japan and other advanced countries in many a respect. The aggression committed by China on our borders and the long-term threat it poses to our security, however, provides us with an opportunity of the kind which came the way of some of these countries and, if the national leadership so wants it, can be utilised to great economic advantage of the country.

Anyway, if we have to progress economically, new enterprising men have to come forward who would be willing to mobilise savings and to take risks in pursuit of profit. Some others must be ready to undergo the strains and risks of leadership in bringing the flow of available inventions productively into the capital stock. Others, again, must be prepared to lend their money on long term, at high risk, to back the innovating entrepreneur—whether in the sphere of handicrafts, labour-intensive industry or capital-intensive one. Above all, patriotic men in the field of science and economics must come forward who will be able to manipulate and apply modern science to the conditions of our country—to think out solutions of our problems which will not merely be a replica of the Western patterns.

But the emergence of a social or cultural elite alone will not do. The determined passion of a whole society—the entire people— is required to achieve the transformation we seek. Unless the will to individual progress and co-operation exists among the hundreds of millions of our people living in the villages and the towns studded over the vast expanse of India, and is released and activated—

[20] "Rostow on Economic Growth" in the *Economist*, London, August 15 and 22, 1959.

unless they stand up to take their destiny in their own hands, ready to rise out of long ages of stagnation and destitution, determined to create a better life for themselves by individual and collective effort—there will be no economic progress. As Sri Jyotiswarup Saksena has put it : "Economic growth is not automatic : it is rooted in the need for self-awareness and the self-consciousness of a whole culture rather than of the few at the top. It implies the regeneration of the will, the liberation of the creative energies in the whole society."[21]

That a change in our outlook or attitudes is all important—more important than removal of illiteracy and supply of trained personnel —is highlighted by one circumstance. While Prime Minister Nehru has been rightly laying stress on the need of more and more scientists, engineers, and other technical personnel for economic development of the country, the *Hindustan Times*, New Delhi, dated July 13, 1959, carried the following report :

NEW DELHI, Sunday.—Of the 578 scientists, engineers and other technical personnel who returned from abroad recently, nearly 256—44 per cent—are without jobs.

Till April this year, 2,800 Indian scientific personnel now abroad had got themselves registered in the National Register.

Investigations also show that only a small percentage of scientific personnel—trained in India or abroad—are employed in industry. The Government is their major employer. Forty-one per cent of scientists are employed by universities and other academic bodies, 52 per cent by the Government and only 7 per cent by private industry. Seventy-one per cent of the engineers and 52 per cent of technologists are employed by the Government as against 18 and 34 per cent respectively by industry.

As against this, nearly three-fourths of a million scientists and engineers are employed by American industry.

The report does not mention the fact that many technically qualified Indians, who receive their training in western countries, do not return to their motherland at all, or go back after wasting a considerable time here in idleness, largely because of want of opportunities of service in India.[22] Sometimes even graduates from

[21] An article "Ten Years of Nehru" in the *Quest*, Calcutta, July-September, 1959.

[22] According to the National Register maintained by the Council of Scientific and Industrial Research, the number of highly qualified Indian scientists serving in foreign countries in 1962 came to 6,800.

technical colleges within the country itself, who cannot be absorbed, are forced to go abroad or take up appointments as clerks and ordinary school teachers. This would seem to suggest that while it is true that physical resources of a country cannot be exploited without the aid of engineers, etc., it does not follow that mere availability of technical personnel will automatically lead to a demand or create conditions for their absorption. The trained personnel will be absorbed only if our economy expands and acquires a momentum. But our economy cannot expand or develop at the rate we would desire or at which the technical personnel in the country is forthcoming, unless our people develop proper social and economic attitudes.

Perpetuation of the growth process set in motion by the *elite* and technicians, requires that the society as a whole responds to the impulses generated by the initial changes and regularly accepts and absorbs innovations. In this connection, we may refer to what an American economist, W. S. Woytinsky, says in *India: The Awakening Giant*: "To build a modern industry it is not enough to train workers for specific technical performance The task is to educate *the people, all the people*, for a new organisation of economic and civic community life" (p. 186). Unless all the people are healthy and educated, unless their social and economic attitudes undergo a change, all the Five-Year Plans, all the foreign loans and all the assistance extended to the people, whether in the field of industry or agriculture, will have gone down the drain. As we all know by now, the widely advertised Community Development Projects are not as great a success as they were expected to be : the reason lies not so much in the deficiencies of the official agency as in the faulty attitudes of our people. To quote W. S. Woytinsky again: "If it were possible to transplant overnight all the factories of Michigan, Ohio and Pennsylvania to India without changing the economic attitudes of her people, two decades later, the country would be about as poor as it is now" (p. 187).

In their enthusiasm for bringing about an early economic change, our political leaders and economic planners have concerned themselves primarily with provision of capital and improvement of technology, but have over-looked the central problem, *viz.* the creation of the necessary social, cultural or psychological premises. As we have seen, basically, economic reform means a specific cultural or attitudinal change.[23] This does not imply, however, that only a psychological treatment of people is required, and no physical or institutional change is necessary. Sometimes, such a change almost automatically moulds the attitudes of the people concerned, *but this is rare*. New institutions are short-lived and innovations introduced by government officials soon forgotten unless they are accompanied by attitudinal change. No schemes of economic development will, therefore take root—there will be no marked, permanent results—unless people's attitudes and behaviour, unless, in fact, their inner motivations or beliefs underlying the attitudes and the behaviour, are first or simultaneously changed.

Leaders from all walks of life and sections of society have to be taken into confidence and a vast educational effort launched. It may take a full one, even two generations to produce results. In any case, we will have to be patient with our people and, if we are unable to inspire an early change, we shall not seek to coerce them. Inertia of the vast masses accumulated through centuries has to be broken through democratic means. We have to prove that it is possible to conquer poverty without the sacrifice of human rights—without resorting to totalitarian methods. With this end in view public workers will have to recapture or develop again a sense of identity with the masses and not tend to become divorced from them in thought or in feeling as we are unfortunately doing. They have to be actuated by a sense of mission as in the days of Gandhiji. Simple, if not austere lives by the leaders will have to be lived again. Basic moral values which are in danger of being dimmed, if not lost altogether, will have to be kept unimpaired. In fact, the price for a break-through from economic stagnation to economic development will have to be paid by all—the masses, the classes and the leadership. By the masses in the form of harder work, consistent discipline and higher savings—both voluntary and involuntary ; by the classes, *viz.* the entrepreneurs, managers, engineers, bankers, doctors, teachers, civil servants, etc. in the form of lesser personal incomes and emoluments for still harder and more

---

[23] In absence of the necessary attitudinal change, even laws will often remain ineffective. The Bengal *Sati* Regulation, 1829 (Bengal Regulation No. XVII of 1829), the Hindu Widow Remarriage Act XV of 1856, the Child Marriage Restraint Act XIX of 1929 and the Untouchability Act XXII of 1955 are four examples.

efficient service; and by the leadership at all levels in an attempt to live up to Mahatma Gandhi's definition of a leader: "A true leader is he," he once said, "who does not want riches, rewards or comforts for himself, but works day and night and remembers God all twenty-four hours of the day."

The Hindus, in particular, have to understand that there is no contradiction between thrift, hard work and wealth on one side, and the pristine teachings of their religion, on the other. Spiritual values in concrete terms are the same as human values in politics and economics: Justice, equality, respect for human dignity, compassion, unselfishness. In order to be God-fearing, religious-minded or a believer in spiritual values, one need not shun material advance. It is only the materialistic outlook which regards the 'good things of life'—the higher economic standards—as the end of existence that Hinduism like all great religions deprecates or discourages. And it is this pursuit of material ends divorced from moral and spiritual considerations that is taking the world towards self-destruction, not material advance as such. No man can live without bread, just as he cannot live by bread alone. Materialists regard bread or material things as the *summum bonum* of life. Spiritualists, on the other hand, lay undue emphasis on spirit and would ignore the material or physical world altogether. Man, however, is not synonymous with spirit, just as he is not a mere bundle of matter. The physical world is very much with us, and while flesh calls out the 'devil' in man, inasmuch as it is flesh or physical body that encases the soul or the spirit, the 'god' in man will also depart or cease to exist without flesh. We have, therefore, to take care of both: they are not direct opposites. Man's problem is not to displace one source of management of life by another—materialism by spiritualism or *vice versa*—but to place them in right relations with one another.

Though the connection between material progress, on one hand, and moral and cultural values, on the other, is still a matter of debate, yet the wisdom of striking a balance is now beginning to be realised in the West. Exhortations are now heard in Europe and America that mankind should begin to think of the spiritual perils of prosperity and to cherish higher values. The following letter from Shri Phiroze J. Shroff of Bombay, published in the *Pioneer*, Lucknow, dated October 7, 1959, shows the questionings that are troubling the minds of thinkers in the West:

Canada has the second highest *per capita* income in the whole world, it being about 25 times that in India. She has more cars, radios, TV sets, refrigerators, elaborate all-electric cooking ranges, luxurious living accommodation, telephones and other amenities per family unit than any other country in the world with the exception of the USA.

Advanced technology, superior managerial skill, hard work and enterprise have enabled the Canadians to achieve a very high standard of living. A judicious import of foreign capital, mainly from their southern neighbours, has enabled the Canadians to exploit their vast resources and greatly accelerate the tempo of economic development.

Yet this near achievement of material paradise with abundance of food, clothing, housing together with all the modern gadgets and accessories of economic progress, has caused a great searching of hearts amongst the thinking section of the Canadian people. Not only the enlightened Canadians but leaders of thought in other Western countries are questioning the wisdom of the all-engrossing material drive of the people which often brings in its train a very high rate of crime, juvenile delinquency, suicide, insanity, immoral traffic, alcoholism, drug addiction and broken homes.

The following excerpts from a speech recently made at Oxford by Mr. Lester Pearson, the Canadian Opposition leader, will prove an eye-opener to some of our top leaders, who have been seized with an obsession for raising the standard of living of our people at all costs and to the neglect of all spiritual values in life :

Having a car in every garage, a fridge in every kitchen and a colour TV in every room is not a sign of superior civilization. We, especially on the North American Continent, should wake up from that dream. Defence of our values is more important than defence of our standard of living, of our scientific or engineering or economic achievements. It is quite as important as the defence of our borders.

The threat to Western civilization from within is shown in the decline of belief in the spiritual values of our free society and the irresponsible demands we make on Government for material security and an easy way of life. The central value of our civilization is its stress on the integrity, dignity and worth of the individual. Lose this and we lose everything. From that all our freedom flows. The necessity for cooperation in this matter transcends national sovereignty and national policy or power.

We shall never achieve a society of free men if material advance becomes the chief end of life, or if we dismiss the quiet man who thinks as our egghead, and cheer the loud man, who rants as a great leader.

In our country, however, where tradition never put any premium on the pursuit of material wealth, the pendulum has swung for centuries to the other extreme—the extreme of other-worldliness. We have tried to run away or made a pretence of running away from this world or material things of life too long and to an extent that the country is steeped in poverty and large sections of our people are unable to meet even their barest physical needs.

We have to banish fatalism. We must come to regard our physical environment not as an immutable factor but as an ordered world which can be made to yield to productive change. It is not ordained by Providence that our children should remain ignorant or live in want and penury. Human will is free—our people have to be reminded—and one can, by one's efforts in present life (पुरुषार्थे), negate or largely negate the effects of fate or actions in previous life (प्रारब्ध). Fatalism or absolute determinism is not a part or teaching of the doctrine of karma. Man is not merely a creature, but also a creator of circumstances. The idea of progress through human effort is not only not foreign to Hinduism but is a part of its teaching. Dr. Sarvapalli Radhakrishnan has put it admirably.

The cards in the game of life are given to us. We do not select them. They are traced to our past karma, but we can call as we please, lead what suit we will, and as we play we gain or lose, and there is freedom.[24]

Similarly, had Swami Dayanand, the zeist-geist of social and much other change in India, reminded the Hindus that the soul is free and action is the generator of destiny. "An energetic and active life," he wrote in the Satyarth Prakash, "is preferable to the acceptance of the decrees of destiny. Destiny is the outcome of deeds. Deeds are the creators of destiny. Virtuous activity is superior to passive resignation... The soul is a free agent, free to act as it pleases. But it depends on the grace of God for the enjoyment of the fruit of its action."

The caste based on birth or heredity has to go lock, stock and barrel. Heredity and Prarabdha (प्रारब्ध) or samskars of previous life do mould a man, but environment and free will leading to Purshartha (पुरुषार्थे) play an equal part, if not greater. Men must come to be valued not for their birth or connection with a particular caste,

[24] The Hindu View of Life, p. 75.

but for their individual ability—for their actual merits. But the question is : how to eradicate the caste ?

Attempts have been made by great teachers since the days of Gautam Buddha, but to little or no avail. The reforming zeal of organisations like the Arya Samaj and individuals like Swami Dayanand and Mahatma Gandhi in recent times burst against the rock of the caste system and has spent its fury or vehemence, leaving the problem practically unsolved. Had there been only two or three castes, with all their members equal between themselves, the task of abolishing the institution would not have been so difficult. But there are hundreds and thousands of castes or divisions, with sharp differences of rank among themselves and often between members of the same caste. For example, there is no sense of kindred or equality among the various depressed castes severally, who have equally suffered from serious social, economic and political handicaps owing to the system. Said Mahatma Gandhi once : "All the various grades of untouchables are untouchable among themselves, each superior grade considering the inferior grade as polluting as the highest class of the caste Hindus regards the worst grade of the untouchables."[25]

The caste system has deep psychological roots : A Marathi poet describes the Hindu society as made up of "men who bow their heads from kicks above and simultaneously give a kick below, never thinking to resist the one or refrain from the other." It is this balance of psychological compensation provided in the hierarchical system of caste that has kept it going in spite of so many onslaughts that it had to face and so many disasters that it brought upon the country.

There are only a few Hindus today who are educated, and yet openly argue that caste has not outlived its usefulness. Many forces are helping in its dissolution, e.g. the spread of education, political democracy, equality of all citizens before the law guaranteed by the Constitution, new technology and economic influences. Forces or influences falling within the last category are the most potent. It cannot be disputed that changes in the economic life of a people bring in their wake social and psychological changes, that there is no leveller like prosperity, that social prejudices easily sustained on agricultural farms begin to loosen fast on the factory bench, that,

[25] Kingsley Davis, *Ibid.*, p. 167.

working on the same assembly line, the Brahmin has to shed some of his Brahminity and the Shudra some of his Shudraness. With the result that, as pointed out by Kingsley Davis, there is a noticeable loosening of restrictions on interdining, widespread violation of food taboos, gradual removal of untouchability and pronounced growth of social mobility up and down the caste hierarchy.

Yet these influences are insufficient to make any appreciable dent on the fortress of caste in the immediate future : they amount to mere tinkering. While social and economic revolutions, to a large measure, are complementary to each other, yet, as we have seen in the previous pages, it is the social revolution—the change in our norms of behaviour—which will play the primary and leading role. Once we have 'taken off' socially—to adapt the term used by Prof. W. W. Rostow—we will be able to take off economically and, thereafter, changes in both spheres can proceed simultaneously. The state can play an effective role in bringing this social revolution nearer—and in this manner :

The central and most essential trait of the caste system *viz.* the practice of endogamy or choosing of the life-partner within the confines of one's own caste, remains almost as vigorous as before. So, if the evil has to be tackled successfully, steps have to be taken which will rob the caste of its relevance or significance in the matter of marriage. That is, the evil has to be tackled at its source. While laying down rules for recruitment to government services, we prescribe all sorts of qualifications in order to ensure that a man fit and suitable for the job alone gets in. But these qualifications have only the candidate's body and head in view. There is no test laid down to measure his heart—to find out how large his sympathies are, whether he will be able to act impartially, whether his heart is big enough to embrace all those with whom he will have to deal in the course of his official duties, etc. In the context of the caste system, this test will be fulfilled in a large measure if we require candidates, at least, for gazetted jobs, in the first instance, to marry outside the narrow circle of their own caste. By enacting such a provision, we will not be compelling anybody to marry against his will, just as we do not compel anybody to become a graduate today, which is the educational qualification required for many a government job. Of course, this qualification of the marriage being an inter-caste will apply only to marriages that take place after a certain date in the future. An unmarried young man will be free to enter the services but if, later on, he marries inside his caste he will have to resign. The remedy suggested here may sound as too drastic or an undue interference in the personal life of a citizen. But the evil is deep-rooted, and the legal code of the country already contains several restrictive or regulatory provisions regarding marriage and divorce.

Under the impact of economic forces the ties of the joint family are already gradually loosening themselves. And, as education proceeds, superstitions and burdensome customs also are disappearing. Relaxation of these inhibiting factors would both promote development from within, and facilitate absorption of the technical advances and achievements of other countries.

There is, however, little evidence of a propensity to save, developing; the 'demonstration effect' of highly developed economies like the UK and the USA lures us into more and more consumption expenditure rather than productive investment. That is, the trends in our country are just the reverse of those required of a developing economy : the propensity to consume is high, and the rate of saving is low. But, unless there are savings, unless the incomes above minimum levels of living are shifted, voluntarily or involuntarily, into the hands of those who will invest the amount in schools and economic enterprises, resource facilities for agriculture, roads and railways, consumption goods will not be available.

Attitudes towards the having of children are changing, but not fast enough. Unless there is a decline in birth rates, India will be landing itself in a disaster. Gone are the days when our ancestors laid down that a man will go to heaven only if he leaves behind a son to offer oblations to his spirit : now there is little land to go round, or sustain an increasing population in comfort. If even the richest country in the world, *viz.* the USA considers it necessary to practise family limitation, not much argument should be required to convince us of its need in our conditions.

As regards inter-State or linguistic jealousies, perhaps, as in the case of the caste system, inter-linguistic marriages as an indispensable qualification for admission to superior services under the Union Government would be found to be one of the major remedies. We should not be misled by the recent outburst of popular will and enthusiasm to resist and throw back the Chinese hordes from India's soil. While some basic trends or springs common to the entire race do exist in our Collective Unconscious, they have begun to weaken or dry up and need to be strengthened or re-charged. We will, therefore, do well to implement the recommendations made by the States Reorganisation Commission in 1955. The Commission had recommended that the Service of Engineers, the Forest Service and the Medical and Health Service should be reconstituted on an All-India basis, and 50 per cent of the new entrants in the All-India Services and one-third of the number of judges in the High Court should be from outside the State concerned. Further, inasmuch as, in the opinion of the Commission, a common national language had everywhere proved the greatest integrating force, Hindi, as already provided by the Constitution, should progressively replace English for official purposes of the Union. While candidates from non-Hindi speaking areas may be required to pass a qualifying examination in Hindi, those from Hindi-speaking areas may be required to pass a similar examination in one of the Indian languages other than Hindi, preferably a South Indian language. This is necessary so that candidates to All-India Services from the various parts of the country may be put on a par, and may not suffer from any sense of handicap or discrimination. We may add that as a further safeguard, percentage of recruitment from each State may, for a limited period, be fixed in proportion to its population.

It is contended by some that a mobile and progressive economy is not consistent with the teachings of the Hindu religion, nor is the Indian character, formed as it is by these teachings and influenced by a bounteous Nature, which demanded little of man in return for sustenance, capable of evolving such an economy. Now, this is pure bunkum. Much of what goes by the name of Hindu religion today does not correctly represent its teachings. During its passage through the corridor of time, over thousands of years, this most ancient religion has gathered much dross, which will have to be, and is, being gradually shed. Further, India can maintain her religious and cultural identity and, at the same time, adjust herself to the changing conditions of modern life. She has not to adopt wholesale the institutions of other civilisations in order to modernise herself. Modernisation cannot be identified with westernisation. The social and material aspects of our life can undergo a change, and yet the springs of our religion and culture need not be affected. The people can remain rooted in thought and tradition, basically Hindu or Indian, just as the tradition of Europe continues to be,

in spite of the changes of the last hundred and fifty years, basically
Christian. The change in our mental attitudes that the need for
material progress dictates, is only intended to call forth a greater
endeavour on our part. While it will certainly mean abandonment
of ideas, habits and customs that stand in the way of economic
progress, it does not mean the abandonment of all old values, art,
literature, etc. Nor is a change in dress and food habits inevitable.
In other words, we need not try to escape from our basic self : true
democracy does not exclude the affirmation of a noble heritage.
An Asian country, *viz.* Japan, has already shown the way by blend-
ing her ancient traditions and skills with the requirements of modern
industrial development and technology..

The great achievements of ancient India—her missions of culture
and enlightenment carried to large parts of the world beyond the
seas, her immense irrigation works and splendid temples, and the
long campaigns of her armies—do not suggest a devitalised people.
A race which could, during a brief space of two centuries and only
as recently as 1627-1839, give birth to two such movements of political revival as those of Marathas and Sikhs that swept away the
mighty Moghul Empire and effectively blocked the gateway of
foreign invasions from the North-west, and produce two such
military organisers as Chhatrapati Shivaji and Maharaja Ranjit
Singh, is still alive and kicking. The distinguished author of
Shivaji and His Times[26] ends up his work with the following two
paragraphs:

Shivaji has proved that the Hindu race can still produce not
only *jamadars* (non-commissioned officers) and *chitnises* (clerks)
but also rulers of men, and even a King of kings (*Chhatrapati*).
The Emperor Jahangir cut the *Akshay Bat* tree of Allahabad down
to its roots and hammered a redhot iron cauldron on to its stump.
He flattered himself that he had killed it. But lo ! within a year
the tree began to grow again and pushed the heavy obstruction to
its growth aside !
Shivaji has shown that the tree of Hinduism is not really dead,
that it can rise from beneath the seemingly crushing load of centuries
of political bondage, exclusion from the administration, and legal
repression ; it can put forth new leaves and branches ; it can again
lift its head up to the skies.

[26] *Shivaji and His Times* by Sir Jadunath Sarkar, M.A., C.I.E., published by M. C. Sarkar and Sons Ltd., Calcutta, 1952 (Fifth Edition),
p. 389.

Evidence of latent reserves in our people is also suggested by the social reform movements during the last hundred years, leading to sweeping away of some of our superstitious beliefs and customs, by the energy, enterprise and resourcefulness displayed by large numbers of traders and industrialists, by the readiness of Indians to emigrate in order to improve their lot, and by their performance in their countries of adoption.

Besides cultural traditions or social customs and organisation, a people's attitudes are reflected in its economic, legal and political institutions which play a great part in creating an atmosphere favourable or unfavourable to economic development. No peasant or artisan will seek to enhance his income if he knows from his experience that anything over subsistence will be appropriated by the landlord, the merchant or the money-lender. Arrangements under which wealth (and political power) are the monopoly of a small minority of the population cannot conduce to economic progress. "Man is not so constituted that he will bend his best energies for the enrichment of someone else"—said American Ambassador John Kenneth Galbraith in a lecture delivered in the University of Madras in 1961. Impediments inherent in the old systems of land tenure, marketing and credit, therefore, will have to be removed. But the removal or abolition of the old systems will have a desired effect or be successful only if countervailing or alternative, effectively competing agencies are established, offering the services previously provided by the landlord, the merchant or the money-lender. So, positive action is required in establishing and encouraging new agencies or institutions, say, in the form of village *panchayats* or rural development councils, co-operative societies and banks for mobilising savings, which will secure to the farmer or the artisan as far as possible the undivided benefit of the industry, skill and economy he may exert, and also provide cheap and adequate working capital to those who may need it.

Finally, inasmuch as injustice and exploitation is identified with misgovernment, we arrive at the need of good and stable government. "There must be a body of enforced law", says Horace Belshaw, "which enables the individual to enjoy the fruits of his labour and, as a corollary, prevents him from appropriating the fruits of the labour of others, a system of taxation which does not unduly deter enterprise, and a system of administration which is not conducive to arbitrary and unpredictable decisions by officials, petty or otherwise."[27] Under disturbed political conditions, or in a misgoverned society, industrial enterprise cannot prosper. Unless there is good and effective government—unless the minimal requirements of public law and order and impartiality are fulfilled —there can be no economic development. While some well-governed and stable countries may also be poor, the growth of wealth requires stability in social institutions. It is idle to imagine that good development plans can be created or carried out without a good government to do it. Provision of capital, technical assistance or trained personnel is of no avail where administration is indifferent or bad or open to influence in favour of a friend, relative or party man of the political or administrative boss.

In a densely populated country, with a high ratio of farm population to agricultural resources which means that most of the land is devoted to food crops for sustenance rather than to industrial crops or export crops for an investment surplus, with a rapid population growth, with labour so abundant that it is cheaper than machinery, with a low rate of savings or capitalisation, with economic effort, of necessity, focussed on consumption goods rather than producer goods industry, with a low state of public enlightenment, with so great poverty and with a democratic Constitution— perhaps, more democratic than anywhere else in the world—as India, political stability is not easy to maintain. As pointed out by Kingsley Davis (p. 218), in such conditions, "the citizenry is a prey to any rumour or illusion that will promise relief from the round of disaster and despair. *Personalismo*, intrigue, corruption, and revolts tend to thrive." The bulk of the citizens are scarcely conscious of their duties and responsibilities and do not hesitate, on occasions, to disobey lawful orders and even destroy public property. They regard the government as an institution different from and foreign to themselves, forgetting that the government is the creature of their vote and, in the ultimate analysis, represents them. Governments have to carry on under constant threats of *satyagraha*, demonstrations in the streets and walk-outs in the legislatures. Government employees in the administrative cadres organise, and are allowed to organise Demands Days and hold spectacular demonstrations and rallies all over the country. At the

[27] *Ibid*, p. 176.

same time, Governments also are sometimes unimaginative and would seem to be impervious even to reasonable popular demands and grievances which could be met and remedied without any injury to long-term interest of the country or the State concerned. On the other hand, at other times, they yield to pressure and unconstitutional agitation against their better judgment, which only creates a vicious circle. Also, not all the governments in the country have been able to create confidence in the people about the integrity of their administration, so that the very foundations of the country's democratic existence are threatened. As yet we have been able to maintain the political stability which was inherited from the British. The question is: whether we shall continue to maintain this stability or go the way that many a country in the Middle and Far East has gone?

CHAPTER NINETEEN

Economic Progress Through Agricultural Production

INDIA WILL eventually achieve a far greater measure of industrialisation than today, but here should be sounded a note of warning. It will be a mistake to over-stress industrialisation on the basis of Western experience. There are certain broad facts which stand out, and should always be kept in view while discussing economic development of the country.

Our huge population relative to land resources, *i.e.* our low land-man ratio is a deterrent to industrialisation. Because more men under given conditions will produce a greater amount of food from the same area than fewer men, and men must have food above all, they will continue to stick to land rather than move to factories. People leave agriculture and take to manufacturing when food is not only available for all, but is cheaper than manufactured goods that is, when for the same amount of skill and energy expended, there is a greater return in manufacturing than in agriculture. So, in a crowded land the scantiness of food—which results from diminishing returns in agriculture—tends to prevent manufacturing. Withdrawal of labour from agriculture (beyond a certain point) will accentuate food shortage, resulting in still higher food prices. In a new area, with a high land-man ratio and, therefore, with abundance of food supplies it is the other way round: diminishing returns in agriculture stimulate manufacturing—because of diminishing incentives for agricultural production owing to its cheapness.

Supposing that the cultivable area of a country produces or is able to produce food only in the quantity which suffices for its population. If an overwhelming percentage, say, 90 per cent are engaged in agriculture, they will have very little to sell. Most of the food will have to be kept back for personal consumption. With little or no food available in the market, nobody will take the risk of giving up agriculture for the sake of taking to manufacturing. And with little or no surplus food to sell and, therefore, with little or no purchasing power at its disposal, the peasantry which will be constituting 90 per cent of the people, will not have the wherewithal to buy the non-agricultural goods even if any at all are manufac-

360

tured in the country. So, a dense agrarian economy finds itself in a vicious circle. Density of population on land can be decreased (and the standard of living raised) only if a good proportion of the people take to manufacturing. But they cannot take to manufacturing because of the fact of this very density. Those who do so will be able to get food supplies with difficulty and there will be few purchasers of the products they manufacture. No programme of industrialisation in a densely-populated country like India can, therefore, be sufficiently far-reaching unless this circle is broken— unless the programme involves, rather is preceded by a revolution in agricultural production—a technological revolution which will ensure far greater production per acre than today. As we shall see in the succeeding chapter, this circle can be broken.

As men must have food above all; it is the greatest need of densely-populated countries like India and China. Factory production does not increase the amount of food and is, therefore, no cure for the misery that stems from food shortages. Not only is there no improvement in the food situation from industrialisation : if we look back at Table II entitled 'Production on Chinese Farms' on page 45, it would appear that reduction of people working the soil above 'B', possibly even above 'C' (and their transference to non-agricultural occupations) would reduce the total food production of the country.

Apparently, under existing conditions, there are two ways out of the difficulty. First, we may draw or transfer to the factories. people corresponding only to groups 'D' and 'E' in the Chinese example, that is, people from those regions where the pressure of population against the existing soil is so great that the stage of a static yield per acre has been reached, in which case there is likely to be no change in total food production from the transference. The family holding in these regions is so small that if some members of the family obtained other employment, the remaining members could cultivate the holding just as well. (Of course, they would have to work harder : the argument includes the proposition that they would be willing to work harder in these circumstances). The marginal productivity of the members leaving the family farm is negligible or zero : their continuance in agriculture would add no food to the total. To this source, viz., the hidden unemployment in the rural sector, can be added the whole range of casual jobs, the petty traders, and the retainers (domestic and commercial) in the urban areas. With this labour, new industries may be created, or old industries expanded, with a view to manufacturing *for export*. This labour needs to be paid very cheaply, *viz.*, at subsistence level only. We cannot, therefore, be worsted or outbid in a world where in most countries labour is dearer, provided *laissez faire* or free competition prevails. But free trade or competition is no longer in vogue anywhere today. Almost all countries are resistant to manufactured goods from outside so far as they can help it and, if they find it necessary, will erect tariff barriers. Also, the demand for higher wages even on the part of this labour, which though superfluous for the land, can under our existing laws easily organise itself and acquire bargaining power, will have to be reckoned with. As regards the internal market, inasmuch as the vast mass of the people who remain on the farms will be living not much above subsistence level, they will not constitute a very active market for the manufactured goods, except in bumper crop years. The limited industrialisation that we will be able to achieve in this case, will thus result neither in eradication of unemployment and underemployment that exists in our villages today nor in increased *per capita* income of the country.

Second, we may draw upon people not only corresponding to groups 'D' and 'E' but also those corresponding to group 'C' and, in exchange of our industrial products, buy the necessary food from foreign countries to meet the needs of our growing population. It is this course which some countries of Europe, notably the United Kingdom, adopted when they developed their economy. It is true, in this case, that is, if a large enough part of the rural population shifts to the cities which permits larger *per capita* income for the remaining farmers, there will be an active internal market to absorb the manufactured goods. But the snag lies in whether the possibility of our obtaining food or continuing to obtain it in future also from outside, will materialise.

Great Britain developed in this way during the last century. But she was fortunate because she was first in the field and developed her industries and foreign trade at a time when the productivity of cultivation in the world as a whole was developing at a faster rate than the population of the world as a whole. A whole New World was being opened up by modern transportation. Virgin land with fertile soil was plentiful and yielded an abundant return in relation to the effort and expense involved in bringing it under cultivation. Also, the industrial trend in Great Britain and in the West generally had set in before the rural population had increased excessively, and since then any surplus had been continuously drawn away to the towns, or to countries beyond the seas by migration. The number of emigrants from Europe to the new continents from 1815 to 1914, has been estimated at more than sixty million, twenty million of whom came from the British Isles alone.

World conditions, however, are fast changing. Now there are no more vacant fertile lands to exploit, and soon there will be no surplus food in outside countries available for export, and little or no demand for industrial goods that India may produce. Richard B. Gregg, an admirer of Mahatma Gandhi's economics and programmes, says :

Industrial nations make machines, tools, conveniences and luxuries and sell them to other nations in exchange for food cereals, meat and fruits. England began this policy ; Europe and America followed. Japan later did likewise. Having done so, the population in all those countries rapidly and greatly increased. They became very prosperous. But the prosperity was only as reliable as the outside food supply, and the amount of food produced in other countries was and still is out of the control of the food importing countries. As long as there was surplus food anywhere in the world— Canada, the USA, the Argentine, Siam, Burma etc.—it could be drawn into the more advanced industrialised countries. The people with surplus food were glad to sell it in order to get the products of the machines in places like Great Britain and Europe.

But now there is a new situation in the world. Population has increased mightily not only in Britain and Europe but in every land. And the amount of land capable of producing food has increased very little. . . . The result is that food-producing areas are exporting less and less. . . .

This puts Great Britain and Western Europe into the same dilemma that India faces : too many mouths for the local land to feed. Right now, if it were not for the United States money and food subsidies, Western Europe, Great Britain and Japan would be suffering severe famines and millions of deaths from them. Japan is now receiving over a million dollars a day in subsidies from the United States. With the best will in the world, the United States cannot continue this long, for her own soil is eroding and her own population steadily increasing. Between 1900 and 1950 her population has doubled, from 76 million to over 150 million.

For these reasons the past successes of industrialism are not a valid argument for further industrialisation of India. She cannot import endless food from abroad as did Britain and Europe in their heyday. By the export of manufactured goods, India will soon thereby be able to buy very little food from the outside, for that outside exportable food supply is steadily and inevitably shrinking. And the export of hides and bones of her cattle, in payment for outside food, only robs her soil of calcium and phosphorous, and lowers the fertility of her soil and hence her own food production. Export of minerals and fibres would help a little, of course. But jute products are the only fibres which would not meet severe competition from outside.[1]

We may add that our monopoly in jute manufactures is no longer secure. Pakistan has already emerged as a formidable competitor, and there is a growing tendency in some of the erstwhile importing countries, especially in the Middle East and Far East, to become self-sufficient in jute goods. South American countries are making experiments in growing jute in which, looking to their climatic conditions, they may well succeed. Also, since the post-war period some of the major overseas consumers are increasingly turning to substitutes and bulk handling methods. Indeed, substitutes abroad have already played havoc with our jute market. It will, therefore, be dangerous to rely on any expansion of our jute industry.

Tea, our largest foreign exchange earner, is also losing ground in some of the major consuming countries. It is meeting formidable competition from China, Japan, East Africa and Indonesia. Their production costs are lower. Iran and the Argentine, although at present not in a challenging position, have nevertheless succeeded in exporting their tea for auction in London, the traditional world market for tea. The Chairman of the Indian Tea Association told its annual meeting recently that India's share of the 500 million lbs. in British market had dropped from 65 per cent to 58 per cent during the last ten years, viz., 1950-59. The potential of China as a producer and exporter of tea is great. The chances of expanding our tea exports, therefore, are not promising—apart from competing beverages pushing tea out of customary tea-drinking countries.

Along with jute and tea, cotton textiles have, hitherto, been our important earners of foreign exchange. But their exports are shrinking. There are three reasons. First, some of the importing countries are developing their own industrial economy and setting up cloth and yarn mills. Second, artificial fibres such as rayon

[1] *Which Way Lies Hope*, Navjivan Press, Ahmedabad, First Edition, 1952, pp. 50-52.

and nylon are posing a challenge to cotton textiles all the world over. Third, prices of our textiles are getting high—thanks to high wage demands.

Minerals apparently are in some demand, but markets abroad are capricious and undependable.

India must, therefore, produce her own food and for this, because of its low land-man ratio, she will have to put or retain a far greater proportion of workers on the soil than most other countries. If instead of doing this, she adopts the policy of forcing the exports of industrial products and relies on the purchasing power thus acquired in order to back steadily increasing demands for food, she would only succeed in injuring herself. Any product sold by as large and populous a country as India in the world market in sufficient quantity to help her economy measurably will represent a substantial portion of the world trade in that commodity. It will, therefore, affect seriously the other major countries exporting the same or similar products, and they may be expected to protect themselves by various measures, including possible price reductions. The price of food required by India will, therefore, go up and that of manufactured products will go down so that increasing quantities of industrial products will have to be sold by us in order to procure the same amount of food. Our economic growth will become dependent upon the rate at which exports can be expanded, but it will not be possible to continually expand exports as food prices will have risen relatively to all others. A rise in food prices will lead to a rise in industrial costs, and also impede release of workers from agriculture for absorption in industries. "It is inconceivable," said Shri C. Rajagopalachari, "that we can, by any process of modernisation, convert the Indian continent into an industrial country, depending for food on imports from abroad, to be paid for by exports of steel, textiles or sugar or even tea."[2]

India will never become industrialised in the sense, or to the level of ‚Western countries. She will become industrialised, as we will see in the succeeding pages, only to the extent she is able to release workers from agriculture, which, looking to our low land-man ratio and the rate of population growth, can never exceed 50 per cent of her total man-power.

Says the 1951 Census Report of India in this connection :

[2] *Vide* the *Swarajya*, Madras, dated August 23, 1958.

This does not mean that development of industry is unnecessary or unimportant. Far from it. But we should be clear about why we need it. We need it, in order to provide ourselves with those goods and services which add to the comforts and conveniences of life and to make life and work less laborious. Industrialisation will not help to solve our food problem, except indirectly to a limited extent in so far as it can provide the materials needed for the development of agricultural productivity.[3]

We are led to two conclusions : first, that industrialisation is not the answer to the food problem : the widespread belief to the contrary is a fallacy based on a misreading of history. Second, industrialisation, in order to sustain itself, must be based overwhelmingly on the internal market : hundreds of millions of potential consumers in the country must be converted into effective purchasers.

In order, however, that a man may purchase some thing, he must have purchasing power, which is derived from income. Before discussing whence this income can, in its turn, be derived, let us see how growth of income, rather real income per head leads to industrialisation (and, therefore, is associated with the rise of secondary and tertiary and fall of primary employments). It may be explained thus :

Inasmuch as, in order to live, a man must eat, the demand for food cannot be staved off. At low levels of income, therefore, the demand for food is relatively intense and that for manufactured goods and personal services low, or, in other words, the proportion of expenditure on food to total income is far higher than the proportion spent on other items. But as real incomes increase the relative importance of food in the consumer's conception of economic welfare and, therefore, in his budget, decreases, and that of manufactures and services increases. Says Dr. Ojala :

When men acquire, through increasing productivity and income, the capacity to experience and to satisfy an ever-widening range of competing wants, the basic food wants are met first but soon begin to lose their power to compete with non-food wants in the human consumption budget.[4]

As real incomes rise, the constant endeavours of consumers to

[3] Volume I, Part I-A, p. 210.
[4] *Agriculture and Economic Progress*, Oxford University Press, London, 1952, p. 6.

maximise their economic welfare result in a diminishing proportion of their total expenditure being devoted to food. Which means that, although the amount spent for food, as for manufactures and services, increases, yet the. proportion of the former to the total income is less, and that of the latter higher than before. For, while there is a limit to the consumption of food-stuffs, no limit can be placed on use or consumption of manufactured goods and utilisation of services. Said Adam Smith long ago :

The desire for food is limited in every man by the narrow capacity of the human stomach ; but the desire for the conveniences and ornaments of buildings, dress, equipage and household furniture seems to have no certain boundary.[5]

Stated differently, with food for existence and comfort being easily available, the income elasticity[6] of demand or expenditure for most of the basic foodstuffs begins to fall and that for manufactures and services begins to rise (Even among food products, with progressive rise in incomes, consumers want less and less grain products, more and more fruits and vegetables, and more and still more animal products). Finally, as incomes increase still further, a point will come when the amount spent for food will not increase at all—rather in the case of the upper, sedentary and rich classes, it may actually decrease—and all the increments in income, except for what it may be proposed to save or set aside for investment, will be spent for manufactures and services. But most of the services being non-transportable from outside, they must invariably be found or provided by the workers within the country, and it is also advantageous to produce the manufactured goods within the country rather than import them. The rate and extent of increase in real incomes, therefore, becomes the governing factor in the shifting of population or workers from primary to secondary and tertiary occupations. Says A. G. B. Fisher :

[5] *Wealth of Nations* Book I, Chapter XI, Part II.

[6] Income elasticity of demand or expenditure for any item means the relation between a certain ratio of change in income and the ratio of the resultant change in expenditure on that item. This relation is unity when any change in income results in a proportionate change in the expenditure for the item. If following, say, an income increase of 10 per cent, expenditure on food also rose by 10 per cent, the income elasticity of expenditure on food is equal to 1.

If the average income level rises, some money will constantly be spent on things different from those now purchased. If these things are to be purchased, they must first be produced. They cannot be produced on any adequate scale without shifts in employment.[7]

Increased real income per head is, thus, the basic reason behind the shift of the working population from primary to secondary and from both to tertiary industries or services.

On the other hand, once industrialisation gets under way, *per capita* incomes, instead of remaining a mere cause, begin to rise as a *consequence* of the industrialisation. There being a great diversity of human wants, various industries, particularly those which are mutually complementary, that is, which provide a market for, and thus support, each other—and most industries fall under this definition—begin to spring up one after another. Economic development thus becomes a cumulative process, that is, one which, in accordance with the arithmetic of compound interest, gathers in force and size owing to its own internal momentum. And *per capita* incomes go on increasing further and further. As real incomes increase, the consumer demand increases and becomes more and more diverse, part of the increase in incomes is set aside for capital investment, and new and still newer opportunities of plough-back into productive investment are opened up—thus ultimately leading, through a process of action and reaction, to a change in the structure of production and a shift from primary to secondary and tertiary employments. It is through this process— the accelerated development of domestic manufacture of consumption goods over a wide region in substitution for imports—not through heavy industry that Australia and the Argentine achieved economic progress.

To return to the point immediately under discussion : In India, the real income or output per head today is low. So there is greater resistance to reducing consumption of food than of manufactured goods and services. A poor man will forego a pair of shoes for himself or even the education of his son, rather than reduce consumption of food below a point. Large sections of our people are not only under-nourished but under-fed, and intensely desire more and better food. So that increase in incomes leads to a proportionate or more than proportionate increase in the amount spent for

[7] *Economic Progress and Social Security*, London, 1945, quoted in Ojala's book on p. 3.

food. In other words, the income elasticity of demand for food among these large sections of the people is as high as unity and, in some cases, even higher than unity. As a corollary, the income elasticity of demand for manufactured goods and services is little or practically nil, wherefore there is little industrialisation in the country.

The reason or the main reason for low incomes in the country today is that the overwhelming majority of our people depend on agriculture, and agricultural production per man is low. According to the census of 1961, 68.2 per cent of the people are engaged directly in agricultural production and only 11 per cent in production other than agricultural. The remaining 20.8 per cent are engaged in commerce, transport and other services. Granting that, of these tertiary services, industrial or non-agricultural production claims three times its share, viz., 6.8 per cent, we are left with 14.0 per cent who may be taken to render some service or other to the cultivator and, therefore, to depend directly on income derived from agriculture. *Thus, it is agricultural production that determines or provides the real income of (68.2 + 14.0 =) 82.2 per cent of the people. Obviously, then, if agricultural production can be increased, real incomes of the people will rise and industrialisation will be speeded up.*

While increase in agricultural production will furnish purchasing power to the masses with which to buy the manufactured goods and the services, it will also, as pointed out in the beginning of the chapter, release workers from agriculture for transference to industrial and tertiary employments. At the present level of efficiency of our agriculture, release of manpower from it is not easy.

Investigation of the productivity per head of the primary industries of different countries shows that on the basis of each country's average output per head in the primary industries, New Zealand would occupy only 6.4 per cent of her labour force for supplying its entire population with a scientifically arrived at optimum diet, Australia would occupy 9.7 per cent of her labour force and that in Japan, Russia, India and China the attainment of the optimum at the present *per capita* output would require more than their entire labour force in each case. That these countries have an industrial population shows that food consumption is below the optimum, while the excess in the more prosperous countries shows consumption above the optimum or export of the surplus. It is the release of man-power from agriculture which goes with the growth of secondary and tertiary employments with higher *per capita* output.[8]

If output per worker increases more rapidly in one industry or sector of the economy than in others, or so greatly that the supply exceeds the demand, part of the labour force in the former will become superfluous and tend to move away to the latter. This is particularly true of agriculture. When pressure of demand keeps the price of an agricultural commodity high in relation to its cost of production, an increased flow of supplies is the usual result which, owing to inelasticity of demand for basic foods, has the effect of lowering the prices. *Paradoxically enough, therefore, an increase in agricultural production will entail a proportionate decrease in the number of farmers. The continuous rise of productivity in agriculture without which labour from agriculture cannot be diverted, thus emerges as a basic condition of progress in the whole economy.* Unless the community is to suffer food shortage, the only possibility of releasing workers from food production is advancing productivity in agriculture. If this release is impeded by static output per worker in farm production, economic progress of the community as a whole is impeded.

People anywhere in the world will engage in industry, commerce, transport and other non-agricultural occupations only if they have an assured supply of food—the prime necessity of man—whether from local sources or from outside. Food will be obtainable locally only if the farmers produce surplus to their needs, or the needs are depressed and the people go underfed. In the latter case, efficiency of labour will suffer and there will be little purchasing power in the pockets of the farmers, with the result that economic development will not proceed far. Food will be obtainable from outside either if, along with raw materials, particular skills are also available locally so that it is more economical to import food in exchange of manufactured goods than in exchange of raw materials, or if an outside source or sources of food are under political control of the manufacturing country so that the economics of food production and supply are irrelevant.

Not only that there can be no industrialisation unless food or farm surpluses are available (within the country or their supply, of course, in exchange of manufactures is assured from outside) :

[8] An article by Dr. P. S. Loknathan entitled "Occupational Planning' published in the *Eastern Economist*, dated July 1943, p. 265.

the speed and scope or pattern of industrialisation will depend on the rate and amount of the surpluses which can be realised. Farm surpluses, if any, in a country where labour is relatively abundant and capital scarce, that is, men are cheaper than machines, call for an economy in which hand-operated industries or handicrafts and cottage industries will predominate. When agricultural productivity goes up resulting in a further increase of farm incomes and, consequently, a higher demand for manufactured goods, a cumulative process is set into motion, that is, more and more industries are set up and the industrialisation that has already been effected itself becomes a cause rather than merely remain a consequence of increase in incomes. Gradually, a point is reached where, owing to growth of various kinds of industries and services, labour becomes relatively scarce and capital abundant, that is, when men cease to be cheaper but become dearer than machines. It is at this stage that an economy takes on a character or develops into one where machine-operated or mechanised industries will predominate. The progression from handicrafts to mechanised industries—from labour-intensive techniques to capital-intensive techniques—is governed by the rate at which capital becomes available relatively to labour that is released from (or not required in) agriculture.

Economic development or transference of population from agricultural to non-agricultural occupations, therefore, in countries like India which are under-developed today and cannot or do not want to exploit lands and labour of other peoples, will ultimately be governed by the extent of agricultural surpluses that they can achieve internally (and the mineral wealth they possess and can exploit)—by the rate at which they can increase production per acre with fewer and still fewer men on the soil.

Failure to realise the role or importance of agriculture in the economic development of the country will do—in fact, has already done—immense harm. Industrialisation cannot precede, but will follow, at best, accompany agricultural prosperity. Surpluses of food production above farmers' consumption must be available before non-agricultural resources can be developed. Where the surpluses do exist, the villages tend to become cities. Where food surpluses are not present, or are not easily available, villages must remain villages, and the cities must remain few. "Wherever the fertility of the soil, or the state of agricultural arts has produced a surplus of food and raw materials beyond the needs of the produ-

cers," says Roland R. Renne, "towns and cities have developed."[9]
A comparison of the western and eastern parts of the State of Uttar
Pradesh in India will confirm this conclusion : there are more towns
and cities in the west which produce food surplus to the needs of
the farmers, than in the east which has no food surplus.[10] People
moving to the non-agricultural jobs in the cities and towns must
have food. When there is scarcity of food, the Law of Diminishing
Returns will compel them to remain on land.

The truth, therefore, has to sink into the consciousness of our
political leaders and administrators that it is ever-rising productivity of our own agriculture, that is, greater and greater production
per acre with fewer and still fewer men on the soil, that is the key
to economic development of India—and no other. If viable industry
is to emerge in India on a substantial scale, agricultural output
must first increase greatly. To think of or seek industrial development without prior or simultaneous agricultural development
would amount to chasing a will-o'-the-wisp. It is a developing
agriculture alone—agriculture whose productivity increases faster
than demand—that is the key to our prosperity, and no other. And
in this manner :

[9] *Land Economics*, Harper, 1947, p. 57.
[10] The difference in food production per acre in the eastern and western
regions of Uttar Pradesh averaged over years 1944-58, is hardly of the
order of 7.0 per cent. Yet while, in the latter, there are substantial
surpluses or food more surplus to the needs of the farming population
than indicated by this figure, there are little or no surpluses in the former.
The reason is that in the eastern region more men are engaged in farming
the same area of land than in the western. More men in the eastern
region working on a soil whose inherent fertility, if anything, is comparatively higher, are producing only about as much per acre as fewer men
in the western, because, in the latter, farming practices are superior,
capital employed per man is greater and farmers individually work harder.
In other words, greater capital investment, improved farming practices
and harder individual work in the west are being balanced by application
of more hands, or by putting more men on the same area in the east.
Only if and when mental attitudes of people in the eastern districts
change, that is, they come to have an urge for material prosperity and,
to that end, put in greater efforts both of mind and body, farming practices are improved, more capital in land is invested and ravages of nature
become less frequent or they are countered, or, at least, minimized by
human effort, will men be released from agriculture for employment in
industries and services, and *per capita* income rise or economic conditions
in the region improve.

(a) Inasmuch as a developing agriculture makes it possible to secure the production of more and more food and raw materials with fewer and still fewer men on the soil, it will release man-power required for running industries, transport, commerce and other services.

(b) A developing agriculture will provide larger and still larger food-surpluses for feeding increasing number of workers that may be engaged in urban or non-agricultural occupations. Nobody will engage in these activities or occupations unless he is assured of the supply of food—the first necessity of man. If food is not available, these workers will move back to land, or not leave it at all initially. For, lest we forget, under given conditions, more men produce more from the same area than fewer men.

(c) A developing agriculture will secure continuous and increasing production of raw materials for feeding the wheels of industry. (In this context 'agriculture' may be taken to include forestry, animal husbandry, fisheries and mining.)

(d) It is only when there is purchasing power in the pockets of the farmers that a demand for non-agricultural or industrial goods arises. Inasmuch as, and to the extent, therefore, a developing agriculture will bring income and furnish purchasing power to the farmers, it will convert them into a ready market for industrial goods and, thus, promote, and become a direct cause of, industrial growth. The future of *khadi* and village industries or handicrafts, too, depends upon the rate at, and the manner in which, income of the farmers in the rural areas is raised. A farmer cannot buy even a pair of shoes unless he has acquired some purchasing power.

The same is true of services or tertiary industries, especially those engaged in providing education, medical aid and public transport. Experience shows that there is an immediate demand for, and strong response in rural areas to, the provision of schools, hospitals, railways, motor services for the carriage both of goods and passengers, etc. which is directly proportionate to the increase in the farmers' purchasing power. With increase in exchange of agricultural for non-agricultural goods (and one service for another), commerce also begins to flourish.

Industrialists, transport workers, tradesmen, educationists, doctors, and others of their kind, will automatically spring into existence once agricultural productivity goes up, and there is a demand for their services.

India's public men, who had to wrestle with the foreign domination of the country, have mostly been holding that it was the wickedness of the British capitalists or their exclusive concern with raw material supplies that was mainly or wholly responsible for keeping us economically backward and preventing us from enjoying the benefits of manufacturing industry and modern amenities. In actual fact, limitation of the domestic market for manufactured articles and non-agricultural services was equally responsible, if not more (It is a different matter, though, that our agricultural production would, perhaps, have gone up and domestic market expanded, had we been a free nation).

Agriculture provides purchasing power not only to those directly engaged in it, but to others also who have gone to industries and services depending for existence or maintenance on agriculture. For example, in the USA, although only 13 per cent of the workers were engaged in agriculture, it provided purchasing power to about 50 per cent of the population. Looked at in this manner, the figure of 7.0 per cent in Table XXVIII, showing the contribution made by agriculture to the net domestic product in the USA did not convey a correct idea of the role of agriculture. Says Louis Bromfield :

In general both the citizens of the United States and of the world think of the United States as a nation whose power and wealth is almost wholly based upon industry. This is logical in view of the fact that the United States produces more of many industrial commodities than the rest of the world put together. It is largely unknown or unrecognised that the total investment in agriculture in terms of land, building, livestock, machinery, etc., in the United States is larger than the total investment in industry. It is also unrecognised that agriculture provides in one way or another the wages, salaries, and, consequently, the purchasing power for industrial commodities of around fifty per cent of our population. This includes by far the greater part of the small towns and villages whose economy is almost entirely based upon agricultural purchasing power and many larger cities, such as Omaha, Kansas City, Miniapolis, Des Moerics, Memphis and others whose insurance companies, real estate values and general markets are largely based upon livestock and agriculture. There is the whole of the vast meat and food processing industries, the huge agriculture machinery industry and large segments of the automobile, steel, rubber industries and other industries which are dependent for prosperity and employment upon agricultural purchasing power.[11]

A progressive or developing agriculture will, thus, not only provide a growing industrial population but also feed it and keep it employed, and, further, go on contributing to its growth, as time

[11] *Vide* an article entitled "Agriculture in the United States" by Louis Bromfield, Writer, Farmer, Economist, in *Profile of America*, edited by Emily Davie, New York, 1954, pp. 179-80.

passes, till a balance between agricultural and industrial, rather non-agricultural incomes is achieved.

Lastly, surplus raw materials and food stuffs that a developing agriculture will make available, can also play a role in earning foreign exchange with which we can finance imports of capital goods for industrial development. In fact, agricultural surpluses have, as a matter of history, generally preceded or accompanied economic development of many a country in the world. Expanded yield of primary industries created from natural resources has served to finance the import of capital equipment during their take-off periods—grain in the USA, the USSR and Canada, timber and pulp in Sweden, dairy products in Denmark and silk in Japan. Even today there is more than one country in which exports of agricultural produce as complementary to imports of raw materials and other requirements of industry, are a regular and important feature of their economy. Exports of agricultural products by China, wrung at great human and administrative cost through the communes, are intended[12] to play the same role as they did in the USA, Canada and other countries.

The reverse of the proposition formulated in the previous pages is also largely true. That is, agriculture will develop and farmers thrive when industry prospers. Just as agricultural development will foster industrial development, so a growing industry, on its part, will contribute to the development of agriculture or prosperity of the agricultural population. Besides iron tools and materials like fertilisers, where needed for development of agricultural productivity, a growing industry (and along with it, as a necessary concomitant, a growing commerce, transport and other services) will provide agriculture with an expanded market due to the increased demand of the urban population and processing and manufacturing industries for agricultural products, without which expansion in agricultural production will not proceed beyond the point where the farmer has satisfied his immediately felt needs. This increased demand for farm products from the industrial centres will increase the *per capita* income of the farmers. Also,

---

[12] It is a different matter, though, that, as we have already seen, collectivisation or communisation in itself does not increase production, and whatever foodgrains are exported will be done largely at the cost of nutritional or other living standards, that is, by depressing them still further.

since development of industries will require workers, owners of under-sized and uneconomic holdings will tend to migrate to the new industrial areas in their own interest—in order to find work with a higher income—with the result that such holdings will cease to multiply and gradually disappear. This will, as already pointed out, lead to an increase in the area of the land-holdings of the remaining farmers which, again, will increase their income and purchasing power. The arrival of migrants from congested agricultural areas to the sites of industry will, in turn, create a demand for rooms, meals, transportation, entertainment, electricity and other services and thereby provide a ready market for an expanding urban economy, which, again, will attract a still greater amount of surplus agricultural population.

Thus the processes of agricultural and industrial development are complementary to each other. Each is both a cause and effect of the other. But agriculture plays the primary role—the role of a precursor. Agriculture can do without industry, but not industry without agriculture. Also, while man can conveniently do without almost every other thing, he cannot do without food at all. At least, he can do without heavy or mechanical industry, but not without agriculture and handicrafts.

Both economic development and retrogression are cumulative processes : once an area has started to expand, it tends to expand cumulatively ; and once it has started to decline, it tends to decline cumulatively. To elaborate even at the risk of repetition : if in a country supply of food is assured to the entire population and, *over a period of time*, prices of food and other agricultural goods continue to fall or remain lower in relation to those of non-agricultural goods, then people will increasingly take to secondary and tertiary employments—originally to such employments among these as do not require a greater degree of skill and amount of physical labour than agricultural production. As a consequence, land-holdings of those who are left behind in agriculture will become larger and larger, yielding greater and greater surpluses to the farmers[13] and, thus, putting more and more purchasing power at their disposal. This purchasing power, in turn, will lead to an in-

---

[13] As we will see in the next chapter, with land in the total remaining constant in area, but workers on land reduced, production per acre will be maintained at the previous level only if farming practices are improved or more capital per worker is invested, or both. If increased production

crease in demand for more and more non-agricultural goods with the result that more and more people will be required to produce, transport and distribute these goods and, as the prices of agricultural goods will be comparatively lower, these additional people will be provided by or released from agriculture. It is thus that the process or spiral of economic development goes on ascending : growth of secondary and tertiary employments becomes a cause rather than remaining merely a consequence of increased incomes in the primary sector. A country will go on developing economically to the extent supply of food allows it—till the stage when parity between agricultural and non-agricultural incomes has been reached as in the UK, that is, when it is no longer profitable for farmers to leave their profession.[14]

As for economic retrogression : today the UK, which offers an example of perfect economic development, has to obtain her food supplies partly from foreign countries.[15] She is able to do so because she has the advantage of possessing specialised skills and specialised industrial equipment as compared with many a country which are not equally developed but can give her food in exchange of industrial goods. But when other countries, too, would have, in course of time, become industrialised so that they no longer need industrial goods from the UK in exchange of food and, investment of more capital and application of advanced technologies notwithstanding, she is unable to increase her agricultural production with the present strength of workers on the soil, then, provided migration to take off the increasing population is not possible, she will have to release people from the secondary and tertiary sectors in order to work on land, for, as we have seen, under given conditions more people produce a greater total from a given area than fewer people.

is the aim, farming practices will have to be improved still further and capital invested in still greater quantities.

[14] Sometimes we hear a demand being made on the political level in our country that Government bring about by law a parity between agricultural and non-agricultural incomes. Such parity, however, is the endproduct of a long process of economic growth and cannot be achieved and maintained artificially by Government. The demand only betrays ignorance of the cultural and economic forces that shape the growth of a society.

[15] According to Dr. B. R. Sen, Director-General of FAO, before 1939, food and feeding-stuffs accounted for more than 45 per cent of all Britain's imports. Today they represent 38 per cent (vide, the Pioneer, Lucknow, June 3, 1959).

She would then have entered upon a period of economic retrogression resulting in a gradual decrease in the area of landholdings and the demand for industrial goods. Factories will close down, transport will decline and commerce will decay, the released workers being thrown back on land. This cumulative process of retrogression, where low incomes in one sector are both the cause and effect of low incomes in other sectors, could be arrested only when agricultural production per acre again begins to increase at a greater rate than the rate of population growth.

When agricultural productivity within a country does not increase faster than demand, or food is not easily and cheaply available from outside, then food prices will rise relatively to all others. Industries will not only cease to develop, but will decline : more and more men will take to agriculture because more men on given area produce a greater total of food. Large parts of India, for example, Bihar and Uttar Pradesh, find themselves caught in this process of economic retrogression since the day the Britishers came to the country two centuries ago. Farming practices have ceased to improve and/or more capital is not being invested in land, or both, with the result that farmers do not produce food surplus to their requirements and the proportion of workers on land, instead of going down, is going up. This Gordian knot has to be cut if India has to be saved, in the economic sense, and it can be cut only if determined attempts at increasing agricultural production per acre are made. There is simply no other way.

If we cannot produce raw materials to feed the industries and food-stuffs to feed the workers, but have to import them, even the existing industries in the country will have to be closed own, sooner or later. Food imports mean higher food prices and, as food constitutes the largest item in a poor man's or worker's budget, these imports mean higher production and transportation costs. Similarly, insufficient production of raw materials in the country results in imports which means still higher prices of the finished products and shrinkage in the volume of exports. Our industrial products will, therefore, not be able to compete in foreign markets as our textile manufacturers are already finding it to their dismay, their markets being rapidly captured by cheaper Chinese and Japanese textiles.[16] Ginning factories standing idle or dismantled in various

[16] According to a report in the *Hindustan Times* of New Delhi, dated April 6, 1960, the Textile Commissioner, who presided over a meeting

towns of southern and western Uttar Pradesh are a grim reminder of the truth that it is agricultural (and mineral) production which is the key to economic or industrial growth. With the inability of our farmers to produce raw materials to feed the industries, and food-stuffs surplus to their own consumption, also shrinks or disappears the internal market which, if and when developed, could keep tens of times the present number of industrial enterprises working and, to repeat, which in the U.S.A. absorbs 95 per cent of her total production (except for the part that may be saved and is re-invested) that is equivalent to about thirty per cent of total production of the world.

It has to be remembered, however, that, as we have already seen in the last chapter, there can be no economic progress unless there is a change in our attitudes to life. Without the necessary social and economic attitudes there will be no movement of workers from primary to secondary and tertiary employments *even if there is an agricultural surplus*. That is, in order to achieve economic progress, both conditions must co-exist, *viz.*, increased agricultural production and the necessary social and economic attitudes. An increase in agricultural production entails a proportionate decrease in the number of farmers. Increased agricultural production will, therefore, lead to less employment and more under-employment in the rural areas, unless it is accompanied by a shift of workers from agricultural to non-agricultural employments. And this shift cannot come about unless there is a change in the attitudes of our people.

When both the requirements subsist together in a society or a region, it takes rapid strides towards economic prosperity as is illustrated by the example of the Punjab. In a speech delivered in a meeting of the Association of Manufacturers in April, 1957, Prime Minister Nehru said that one of his colleagues had recently made a quick survey of the small-scale industries that had been

of the Cotton Textile Advisory Committee in Bombay, on April 4, said that the abnormally high prices of cotton paid by the industry had had their inevitable result on the exports. It was anticipated that exports during 1960 would be fairly high, reaching the 1,000 million yardmark. He observed :

"It is regrettable that our position in the export has worsened and the expectation now is that we may not exceed very much the exports of 1959."

During the year 1962, India was importing Rs. 70 crores worth of cotton !

started in Punjab since Independence and was very much impressed
with what had been done both by the permanent residents there and
those who had come from Pakistan as refugees. Pandit Nehru said :
"I believe he listed 26,000 small enterprises that had grown up in
the last few years in Punjab with a relatively small capital but
with a great deal of energy and enterprise. That is the kind of
thing which heartens one and increases one's self-confidence."[17]

These enterprises in Punjab have come into existence, first,
because the tillers there produce food (and other materials) surplus
to their needs. Second, because inhabitants of Punjab, particularly,
displaced persons from West Pakistan are imbued with an urge
to seek material advancement and, therefore, have a greater propensity to innovate. Displaced persons from Sindh and Punjab,
who had recently come over to Uttar Pradesh, have also established small industries and enterprises in parts of the State where
none existed before. Prepared to change old ways and to face
risks, they have penetrated into remote corners of the Pradesh
with a view to exploiting or setting up new lines of production and
commerce. Even the few large factories that came into existence in
U.P. before partition of the country are a result of the enterprise
and ability of outsiders—Punjabis and Marwaris. This unmistakably proves that it is the economic attitudes of a people that make
all the difference between economic stagnation and development.
The economic and climatic environment of Uttar Pradesh is what
it has been in the past, but the original inhabitants had not the
necessary urge for material advancement and did not make the
needed effort. There is also a marked difference between the attitudes of these people coming from West Pakistan and those coming
from East Pakistan. The latter are affected or inhabited by a
'listlessness of the spirit' and an inertia which are a handicap to

[17] *Hindustan Times*, New Delhi, dated April 14, 1957. Speaking at
the foundation-stone-laying ceremony of a plant for manufacture of
antibiotics, on May 2, 1960, Mr. Pratap Singh Kairon, Chief Minister
of Punjab, said that there were 680 registered factories in the State at
the time of Independence : today their number exceeded 3,200 giving
employment to one lakh workers and technicians. Besides, the State was
dotted with a large number of cottage industries providing jobs to nearly
three lakh people. In all, 680 units had been set up in the small-scale
textile industry with an estimated annual output of Rs. 10 crores.
Striking progress had been made by the manufacturing concerns of
cycles, sewing machines, hosiery and sports goods.

any economic progress. The fatalistic attitude on life of the people of Uttar Pradesh is shared by those of Bihar and Bengal.

As regards prospects of material prosperity from industrialisation, the fact has to be borne in mind that, in the conditions of our country, even when industrialisation has been achieved at the maximum that is possible, we will not be able to attain the living standards of the West. The case of Japan is in point. Her industrialisation was facilitated, in the first place, by the fact that, as already pointed out, she became a colonial power and was able to bolster up her economic life by exploitation of other peoples and their resources. Secondly, but in no case less important, the productivity of Japanese agriculture has always been high—higher than that of India. But even though Japan industrialised despite her *initial* high density, *viz.* that of 1500 per square mile of arable land, the initial population plus the subsequent population growth (which brought the number to 4250 by 1953) caused the standard of living to rise much more slowly than it would have otherwise done. We will ask the reader to look back at Table XXVIII on pp. 190-191 and find the place which Japan occupies. The *per capita* national product of Japan in 1952-54 with 55 per cent people engaged in the industry (22) and service (33) sectors, came to 190 dollars only, while that of the Union of South Africa, Brazil and Mexico, with only 51, 39 and 39 per cent engaged in these two sectors, stood at 300, 230 and 220 dollars respectively. The *per capita* incomes of the USA, Canada and New Zealand stand at a much higher figure. The reason is apparent from the preceding pages: natural resources of these countries *per capita* are comparatively by far greater than those of Japan. In fact, Japan has the highest population density in the world per square mile of arable land and has little or no mineral resources. When to this basic fact of her economic life we add the circumstance that she has recently lost all her colonies and dependencies, it can be safely predicted that the percentage of her agricultural population, despite the skill, the vigour and the enterprising ability of her people is not likely to come down to the figures of the USA, Canada and New Zealand, and her national income *per capita* will not touch the levels of these countries. As food-exporting countries also gradually learn the necessary skills and develop industrially, she will need to keep comparatively a large percentage of her workers on its soil, because, to repeat, more men working on a given land area produce greater food than fewer men. According to the U.N "Economic Survey of Asia and Far East—1961", page 170, Japan's working population in 1960, numbering 44.7 million was distributed in the various industries on economic activities as follows :

Industries	Percentage
1. Agriculture, Forestry and hunting	35.90
2. Mining	1.40
3. Manufacturing	19.45
4. Construction	5.03
5. Commerce	17.40
6. Transportation, Communications and other public utilities	5.26
7. Services (Non-Government)	15.56
	100.00

The reduction of 9 per cent or so in the percentage of her agricultural population in the brief period of 7 years is a great tribute to the people of Japan. But this has been possible because cheaper food is still obtainable from outside.

Though in regard to land and other industrial resources India is in a better position than Japan, she faces almost the same prospect : there should be no illusions on this score. Her pace of industrialisation will be slow and the standard of living will not rise with industrialisation as fast and to the extent as if she had a smaller initial density or more natural resources and faced a less rapid population growth.

Japan has a relatively low *per capita* income and, therefore, low standards of living because she has to import raw materials for her factories from outside, and has to pay low wages to her workers in order to keep down the cost of her industrial product so that it may compete in external markets. Ultimately it is the physical resources of a country which matter and set her economic standards. We may, therefore, continue to be comparatively a poor people even after the proportion of men and women engaged in industry, trade and transport, that is, in secondary and tertiary occupations, has increased at the expense of agriculture and allied occupations.

It is said on the experience of Australia, New Zealand, the USA, Canada and other western countries that when we succeed in achieving industrialisation on the latest pattern—when energy will be derived from atom, not from coal, and when automation and the electronic eye will require fewer hands to operate 'giants' —the largest employment will be found not in the agricultural or industrial sector, but in the service sector. This, however, is a mistake. No draught power, chemical discovery or mechanical invention being able to increase production in the sphere of agriculture a hundred-fold as it is in the sphere of manufacturing, the largest proportion of the Indian population, looking to our meagre land and other material or physical resources, will always remain engaged in agriculture rather than in either of the other two sectors. India, therefore, can never aspire to attain the material standards of these countries. The second alternative mooted in the beginning of the chapter, *viz.*, economic development through export of industrial goods in exchange of food imports, is hardly open to us, or to any under-developed country with a dense agrarian economy

We ought to be careful lest we set our sights too high. The *National Herald*, Lucknow, very aptly remarks :

If, instead of recognising the limits set by nature and history, the people of India or other countries, similarly placed, strain to keep up with naturally richer countries, and if their efforts should fail, they will suffer from a feeling of deficiency, and that might generate emotional tensions which would be dangerous to themselves and to their neighbours.[18]

To conclude, therefore, broadly speaking, the economic conditions of our country are an expression of the relation that its physical resources and the level of their exploitation bear to the size of its population and the rate of population growth. Although the extent of the physical resources is a factor beyond human control, the level of their exploitation can vary and be raised. Similarly, although we can do nothing about the existing size of our population, at least, its rate of growth can be checked. We have, therefore, to address ourselves to the tasks which alone are open to us, *viz.*, to better exploitation of our physical resources and to checking the growth of our human 'resources', which will improve our economic conditions.

[18] *National Herald*, dated July 18, 1960.

CHAPTER TWENTY

Measures for Agricultural Production

IT HAS already been seen that under existing conditions in India where land is limited and labour so plentiful, we cannot but have intensive farming—a system of small farms in which relatively more labour is employed per unit of land and the object is to realise the highest yield per acre. It is a case of Hobson's choice : even if we would, we cannot have extensive farming—a system in which relatively less labour is employed per unit of land and the object is to realise the highest net return per man. We have already discussed why production per acre rises with the decrease in the area of a farm. Reference has also been made to the data for Chinese intensive agriculture, given in John Lossing Buck's *Land Utilization in China*, which show that increase in average production per acre continues up to the point where each worker has about 2.5 acres.

More men working a given land area result in more product per acre and more total product, and fewer men result in less product per acre and less total product. If the reader turns back to the table entitled 'Illustration of the Law of Diminishing Returns' on page 45, it will be observed that, with 18 men working the 100 acres, though they produce relatively little per man, there is relatively high average productivity per acre and a high total production. If 9 of the 18 men are taken off from the 100 acres, the average productivity of the 9 that are left is higher. But the average production per acre and, therefore, the total production are now only about 68 per cent of what they were with 18 men working those 100 acres. When we reduce the number of men per unit of land, we find that, though the *per capita* productivity of the remaining farmers increases, the total production decreases, that is, *per capita* production or availability of food averaged over the total population is reduced, obviously because those who left the villages and moved to the towns for factory jobs would still be a part of the total population and be in need of food. So, if the 68 per cent is an ample supply for all the 18, then, since the men in towns will make useful goods, the diversification of occupations

to include manufacturing would be advantageous, provided the
factory product could all be sold year after year. But if that 68
per cent of former total production were not enough to go around
among both the factory workers and peasants still on the land,
then the change would mean still greater poverty, that is, still
lower level of food consumption.

In so far as standard of living is judged by the use of commodities
other than food, factory production would appear to make for a
higher standard. Since, however, it does not increase the amount
of food available for the people, it is no remedy to the misery that
arises from the shortage of food. Human energy in our country
must, therefore, concentrate on that one objective, FOOD, because
it is the prime necessity, that is, the land must be worked intensively—must be worked far down the scale of diminishing returns
—in order to provide enough food. A policy of reliance on an international market to sell our manufactured products in, and to buy
food from, will not be a wise policy. Such a policy or solution of
our food problem might well be defeated by an adverse turn in the
terms of trade, or trade restrictions against India's exports, or
both. As time passes, countries from which we purchase our food
today, with increase in their population and erosion of their soil,
will not be able to sell it to us any longer, nor will countries in
which we sell our manufactured products today, with their inhabitants increasingly taking to manufacturing and the policy of
their Government aiming at self-sufficiency, buy our manufactured
products any longer.

Says Dr. Elmer Pandell:

There seems to be a widespread illusion about the depth and
stability of industrial prosperity. The industrial revolution has been
a cause of confusion in many minds concerning the relation of men
to earth. The reason is that while there has been surplus food
anywhere, it could be drawn to the areas where the industrial
revolution was most advanced. The people with extra food were
glad to sell their surplus in order to get the purchasing power to
buy the products of the machines. Actually the people working with
the machines have often, if not usually, been better off than those
who produced the food. But that advantage could apply only when
food was in surplus. When food is scarce, those who produce it have
the advantage. In the years of scarcity that lie ahead, the people
who have come to depend on other lands for food have painted
themselves into a corner. Assembly lines, power shovels, fast autos

and airliners—these are toys and trinkets; a man must eat.[1]

Size of population in countries which possess comparatively little land relative to their population today but which got a start by exploiting labour of other peoples and natural resources of other countries and are at present maintaining themselves with food obtained in exchange of industrial goods which they are able to produce with their specialised equipment and specialised skills, will ultimately, that is, when other countries will also have been industrialised, be governed by the amount of food they are able to produce in their own country.

According to the Census Report of 1951, India was normally surplus in food-grains in or about 1880, including both rice and wheat, and the surplus was of the order of 12-lakh tons per annum. Figures for subsequent years which are available, averaged over five-year periods, are as follows :

TABLE XLV

EXPORT AND IMPORT OF FOODGRAINS BY INDIA DURING
1890-1920
(In Lakh Tons)

Five-year period	Exports	Imports	Net exports
1890-91 to 1894-95	14.5	2.1	12.4
1895-96 to 1899-1900	11.0	4.8	6.2
1900-01 to 1904-05	16.6	6.2	10.4
1905-06 to 1909-10	14.8	9.6	5.2
1915-16 to 1919-20	15.9	11.9	4.0

1915-20 was the last five-year period when undivided India was a net exporter of food-grains. Thereafter, there was net import during every five-year period as shown by the Table XLVI.

The subsequent changes during and since World War II may be briefly narrated. During 1940-41 and 1941-42, net imports diminished to 9.6 lakhs and 4.3 lakhs. During 1942-43 imports were

[1] *Population on the Loose*, New York, 1951, p. 34.

TABLE XLVI

EXPORT AND IMPORT OF FOODGRAINS BY INDIA DURING
1920-1940
(In Lakh Tons)

Five-year period	Imports	Exports	Net Imports
1920-21 to 1924-25	11.4	9.8	1.6
1925-26 to 1929-30	15.9	8.3	7.6
1930-31 to 1934-35	18.4	5.7	12.7
1935-36 to 1939-40	20.7	6.9	13.8

cut off and India supplied Ceylon and a few other places ; net exports reappeared for about one year though the quantity was small—only 2.9 lakhs. The Bengal Famine occurred during 1943-44 when India received, under international allocations, a net supply of 3.0 lakhs. The next two years were managed with imports of only 7.3 and 9.3 lakh of tons. The shortage was made good mainly by eating into the carry-over ; the stocks normally carried by farmers, traders and consumers were reduced, thus adding greatly to the difficulties of distribution, and creating the risks of break-down which was the nightmare of 1946. The first full post-war year, 1946-47, saw India importing 25.8 lakh tons and the next year, 1947-48, 26.6 lakhs. At that stage, the Census Report goes on to say, the agitation against state trading commenced. These imports seemed to be both enormous and unnecessary ; hence the demand for stoppage of imports and lifting of controls. This did not, however, work. During 1948-49, the first full year after partition, India imported 30.5 lakhs. Then it was reduced to 28.6 and 27.2 lakhs. This was followed by two successive years of very large imports. The report of the Planning Commission mentions 32.7 lakhs as the average level of imports per annum during 1947-52.

There is, however, another view of the whole matter according to which the cry of food shortage, at least, until a decade ago, was the result of faulty reasoning based on wrong data, and whatever under-nourishment and even under-feeding there was, it was due to low purchasing-power of large segments of our population.

Imports of Burma rice, says Shri P. C. Bansil in an essay entitled "Indian Food Resources and Population" published in the *Eastern Economist*, dated August 21, 1953, were due to their cheapness as compared with the indigenous variety, and not to any shortage. Mahatma Gandhi rightly pointed out that the import of Burma rice was 5 per cent of Indian production while the loss entailed in polishing came to 10 per cent. As for wheat it was being exported and was, in fact, rotting at Lyallpur, because when transported to Calcutta, it was dearer than the Australian wheat, on which an import duty of Rs. 2 per maund had been levied since March, 1931. The Crop-Planning Sub-Committee, 1934, was thus forced to cry halt to any further expansion of rice cultivation.

It was the War and the Bengal Famine that brought the question of the food resources of India to the forefront. It may, however, be added that the Bengal Famine was not so much due to the actual food deficit resulting from poor crops in Bengal and from the loss of imports from Burma, Siam and Indo-China, as to breakdown of transport because of military demands, the inflation of prices because of wartime conditions, and the hoarding of grain because of profiteering and insecurity.

Shri Pheroze Kharegat made an elaborate and exhaustive study in 1946. He vividly highlighted the then food resources as shown in Table XLVII.

Anyway, if we were short of anything, concludes Shri P. C. Bansil, it was in milk, meat, fish, eggs, pulses and vegetables. The Diet Survey Report for the period, 1935-48, confirmed that the cereal consumption in the country was more than what is required on the basis of nutritive levels. But the Government continued to harp on the old tune of increasing our cereals. Instead of exploring our real resources, the Food-Grains Policy Committee, 1943, had already recommended an immediate import of foodgrains.

Shri P. C. Bansil goes on to point out that besides major food-grains, there are subsidiary foods which are almost as good as any cereal, but can be grown in *bhur* or sandy areas that are generally of poor fertility. He quotes Dr. P. J. Thomas as follows :

In all thickly-populated countries, carbohydrate requirements are not all drawn from cereals, but also from tubers, which are easy to raise and heavy yielders. In the colder Western countries it is the potato, in the warmer countries of South-East Asia it is tapioca.

TABLE XLVII

AVAILABILITY AND REQUIREMENT OF FOOD IN PRE-INDEPENDENT INDIA

	Quantity required for a balanced diet	Quantity available	Total quantity required	Total quantity available
	(in ounces per day per adult)		(in million tons for the whole nation)	
Cereals	16	18.5	48.0	55.5
Pulses	3	2.5	9.0	7.5
Sugar	2	1.8	6.0	5.3
Vegetables	6	3.0	18.0	9.0
Fruits	2	2.0	6.0	6.0
Fats & Oils	1.5	0.6	4.5	1.9
Whole Milk	8*	1.5	32.0	6.3
Butter-milk	..	3.0	..	12.5
Meat, Fish, Eggs	2 to 3	0.5	6 to 9	1.5

* Per Capita

It is an admitted fact that the whole production of potato and sweet potato is consumed by human beings and practically similar is the position regarding other subsidiary foods like groundnut, tapioca, yam, papaya, turnips, carrots, banana, coconut, cassava and parsnips. According to the Marketing Report on Groundnut, 1941, nearly 7 per cent of it was consumed for edible purposes. It has almost the same nutritive value as almonds. Shri P. C. Bansil refers to Prof. B. G. S. Acharya as saying :

It (groundnut) ranks with the microbial protein of yeast and closely approximates animal protein as found in milk, eggs and mutton.

He concluded that with nearly $1\frac{1}{2}$ million tons[2] of its production India can make available some 7 lakh tons of the finest food from

[2] In 1960-61 the annual production of groundnut in the country was of the order of 4.35 million tons. (*Vide* "Agricultural Situation", August, 1961, Table No. 24).

this crop. Prof. D. L. Sahasrabudhe is all full of praise even for groundnut cake, which he says is a highly nutritious food material for human consumption.

The other important tuber, tapioca, which has been named as *Kalpa Vriksha*, after coconut, is for the working classes, what 'manna' was to the worn-out Israelites in the wilderness. The Tapioca Enquiry Committee set up by the Government of Travancore-Cochin (now Kerala) states in its report (1952) :

Today the population of Travancore draws more of its food requirements from tapioca than from rice and wheat.   ·

In Malabar, tapioca is extensively grown and is consumed as a substitute for and a supplement to rice. Hyderabad also along with tapioca has introduced *coorka* (Chinese potato). These two crops are now being grown there practically in every district.

We have yet other foods like *singhara* (*paniphal*) whose cultivation is known from ancient times and whose food value compares quite favourably with wheat. The *Ain-i-Akbari* (1590) mentions levy of revenue on this crop. Even today UP, Madhya Pradesh, Bihar and Kashmir have large areas under it. Another hitherto neglected food is mango-seed kernel. Mahatma Gandhi said that it is rich in carbohydrates and fats, and can make available every year some 70 million lbs. of digestible protein and 780 million lbs. of starch.

But in spite of all that has been so forcefully said by Shri P.C. Bansil, on the authority of many eminent persons, the need for increasing agricultural production remains, and is insistent. For, population continues to increase and the rate of increase since 1951 has been more rapid than previously. Not only has our land to produce more food per acre in order to meet this increase in total population, but also our farmers have *individually* to work harder and better and, thus, to produce food more and more surplus to their needs so that the increasing number of urban workers and town-dwellers may be fed. Larger the food surpluses, more the number of workers that agriculture will be able to release for absorption in non-agricultural employments and larger the purchasing power with the farmers with which they will buy non-agricultural goods and services. Which means—to put it reversely—that without increase in per acre food production far above the existing levels, there will be no appreciable development of non-agricultural resources—whether it be industry, commerce, transport or social services.

Table XLVIII gives figures of India's production of food-grains as also indices of food-grains and all agricultural commodities.

These figures reflect a series of bad years followed by a series of good. The Ministry of Agriculture, however, under-estimated the harvests up to 1953, but became more accurate when it was made responsible for the Plan. So that part of the increase shown in 1953-54, and since then, is due to statistical error of previous years.

The First and Second Five-Year Plans set targets of 65 and 76.0 million tons of food-grains respectively, which were both achieved. But there is no uniform increase over the years ; rather there are wide fluctuations in the figures which shows that whatever improvements we may have been able to make in farming practices or provision of technological facilities, they have not been sufficient to off-set the vagaries of weather. Of the 39.9 per cent increase in agricultural production that has been made in the First and Second Plans, making an allowance for sub-marginal nature of most of the new land to which cultivation was extended, nearly one-half can be attributed to increase in the net area sown, which rose from 293.4 million acres in 1950-51 to 314.9 million acres in 1954-55[3] and 323.6 million acres in 1958-59.[3a]

Table XLIX shows the per hectare yields of five principal crops during the years, 1934-38 and 1956-60, in 27 countries including India. With the exception of Brazil and Pakistan our yields are not only lowest all along the line : they are just static if they have not actually decreased. On the other hand, barring Finland and Turkey, all the other countries have achieved substantial increases during the intervening period though they had the disadvantage of starting from much higher initial levels.

Table L taken from the United Nations *Economic Survey of Asia and the Far East*—1961 (Bangkok, 1962, p. 13), shows that the *percentage increase* in agricultural production in India in the period, 1957-60, over the period, 1952-55, is lower than the

[3] *The Agricultural Situation in India*, July, 1956, Table 23.1, page 292.
[3a] Table XXIV in Chapter XII ante.

TABLE XLVIII

STATEMENT SHOWING ALL-INDIA ESTIMATES OF PRODUCTION OF FOODGRAINS AS ALSO THEIR WEIGHTED INDEX NUMBERS (WITH AGRICULTURAL YEAR 1949-50 AS THE BASE)

Year	Estimates of production (in thousand tons)	Weighted index numbers of production	
		Foodgrains	All agricultural commodities
1	2	3	4
1949-50	54,048	100.0	100.0
1950-51	50,022	90.5	95.6
1951-52	51 175	91.1	97.5
1952-53	58,266	101.1	102.0
1953-54	68,718	119.1	114.3
1954-55	66,960	115.0	117.0
1955-56	65,794	115.3	116.8
1956-57	68,752	120.8	124.3
1957-58	63,295	109.2	115.9
1958-59	76,103	131.0	133.8
1959-60	74,722	126.8	128.5
1960-61	79,691	135.6	139.9
1961-62	78,566	135.2	139.9

SOURCE : (for col. 2) : Brochure entitled *Area and production of Principal crops in India, Pre-war average to* 1961-62 (Summary tables) September, 1962, and (for cols. 3 and 4) Agricultural Situation in India, August, 1962, both published by the Economic and Statistical Adviser to the Government of India, Ministry of Food and Agriculture, New Delhi.

Note : (1) Figures for the production of foodgrains for the year 1949-50 to 1958-59 are the Revised Estimates and those for 1959-60 and 1960-61 are Partially Revised Estimates while those for 1961-62 are Final Estimates.

(2) Figures for the years 1959-60 to 1961-62 are subject to revision.

average for the world and the ECAFE region as a whole as also seven countries of the region individually, and higher only than Indonesia, Burma and Pakistan.

Table LI shows the outlay on different items in the three Plans.

While in theory it is conceded that the creation of an efficient agricultural system is the indispensable precondition of sustained, self-generating industrial progress, in practice, India's planners neglect the land. Land and its problems are far more difficult than the industrial sector; it is easy enough to erect any number of steel plants with foreign assistance, but to grow two blades of corn where only one grew before, is a difficult proposition. Also, agriculture yields less spectacular results and is associated in the minds of our intellectuals with backwardness and poverty. There was an abrupt change in the comparative emphasis on agriculture and industry from the First Plan to the Second. Proportion of agricultural investment was greatly reduced, and that of industrial investment correspondingly increased. And within the industrial sector, there was enormous emphasis on heavy industry which was allocated more funds than education and agriculture combined. The only change made in the Third Plan was to increase agricultural investment by a bare 3.0 per cent. As an example of lack of appreciation of the needs of agriculture, it may be pointed out that, while almost a fourth of the country's land, or some 200 million acres suffer from soil erosion, the Third Plan calls for measures to deal only with 33 million acres (11 million by contour bunding and 22 by dry farming techniques), and a mere 2 lakh are to be protected against soil salination. Such is the treatment that is being meted out to agriculture despite the fact that the value of exports of agricultural commodities (including products of fisheries, forestry and animal husbandry) works out to full one-half of the total exports and, if one takes into account also the agricultural component in textile and fibre manufactures, the proportion rises to two-thirds, and that it provides *direct employment to two-thirds* of the population and more than 70 per cent of the workers.

Food is the first necessity of man and in India it is not available today in the quantity needed. The modern conveniences in the cities, hospitals, roads, education, housing and even clothing can wait but not food. Next to people's faith in their Government, it is the most important thing for a country—even more important

TABLE XLIX

AVERAGE YIELD PER HECTARE (100 KGM.) OF IMPORTANT CROPS IN DIFFERENT COUNTRIES

Sl. No.	Countries	WHEAT				BARLEY				MAIZE				RICE (Paddy)				POTATOES			
		1934-38	Relative (India=1)	1956-60	Ratio of Col. 5 to Col. 3	1934-38	Relative (India=1)	1956-60	Ratio of Col. 9 to Col. 7	1934-38	Relative (India=1)	1956-60	Ratio of Col. 13 to Col. 11	1934-38	Relative (India=1)	1956-60	Ratio of Col. 17 to Col. 15	1934-38	Relative (India=1)	1956-60	Ratio of Col. 21 to Col. 19
1	2	3	4	5	6	7	8	9	10	11	12	13	14	15	16	17	18	19	20	21	22
1.	India	6.9	1.0	7.3	1.1	8.5	1.0	8.0	0.9	7.4§§	1.0	8.5	1.1	13.6§§	1.0	13.7	1.0	101****	1.0	69	0.7
2.	Argentina	9.8	1.4	12.7	1.3	9.4	1.1	12.1	1.3	18.1	2.4	17.8	1.0	28.5	2.1	33.4	1.2	58	0.6	80	1.4
3.	Australia	8.0	1.2	11.4	1.4	9.5	1.1	11.4	1.2	14.8	2.0	21.1	1.4	45.0	3.3	55.7	1.2	71	0.7	127	1.8
4.	Belgium	26.9†	3.9	35.9	1.3	26.3	3.1	34.4	1.3	—	—	44.4	—					201	2.0	228	1.1
5.	Brazil	9.0	1.3	6.3	0.7	12.8	1.5	9.5	0.7	13.9	1.9	12.8*	0.9	14.3	1.1	16.2*	1.1	67	0.7	54	0.8
6.	Canada	7.1	1.0	13.5	1.9	10.5	1.2	14.0	1.4	25.3	3.4	36.7	1.5					88	0.9	149	1.7
7.	Chile	10.6	1.5	13.4	1.3	14.8	1.7	16.8	1.1	13.8	1.9	19.6	1.4	38.4	2.8	26.5	0.7	85	0.8	87	1.0
8.	Denmark	30.4	4.4	39.8	1.3	29.8	3.5	35.4	1.2									170	1.7	205	1.2
9.	Finland	18.2*	2.6	17.9	1.0	15.1*	1.8	16.7	1.1									149*	1.5	160	1.1
10.	France	15.6	2.3	23.3	1.5	14.5	1.7	24.8	1.7	15.8	2.1	28.1	1.8			41.1	—	112	1.1	151	1.3
11.	Germany (Western)	22.1	3.2	31.9	1.4	21.0	2.5	29.2	1.4	30.0	4.1	29.4	1.0					166	1.6	227	1.4
12.	Greece	9.0	1.3	14.7	1.6	9.5	1.1	12.8	1.3	9.6	1.3	12.2	1.3	19.5	1.4	38.9	2.0	69‡‡‡	0.7	131	1.9
13.	Ireland	22.9	3.3	29.6	1.31	3.8	1.6	31.7	2.3	—								192	1.9	213	1.1
14.	Israel	—	—	11.4	—	2.9§	0.3	10.7	3.7	10.9‡	1.5	42.2	3.9					73§	0.7	192	2.6
15.	Italy	14.9††	2.2	17.7	1.2	11.5††	1.4	12.2	1.1	20.3††	2.7	30.0	1.5	52.1††	3.8	51.4	1.0	68††	0.7	94	1.4

16. Japan	18.8	2.7	22.6	1.2	23.0	2.7	24.7	1.1	14.6†††	2.0	21.5	1.5	36.3	2.7	45.1	1.2	107	1.0	159	1.5
17. Korea (South)	7.4**	1.1	10.0	1.4	9.9**	1.2	9.9	1.0	6.6**	0.9	5.7	0.9	22.4**	1.6	27.7	1.2	48	—	62	—
18. Mexico	7.6	1.1	14.3	1.9	5.3	0.6	7.5	1.4	5.6	0.8	8.6	1.5	21.0	1.5	20.5	1.0	—	0.5	50	1.0
19. Netherlands	30.3	4.4	39.9	1.3	27.9	3.3	39.1	1.4	15.0	2.0	31.9	2.1	—	—	—	—	175	—	261	—
20. Norway	20.1	2.9	23.2	1.2	20.1	2.4	24.6	1.2	—	—	—	—	—	—	—	—	—	1.7	212	1.2
21. Pakistan	8.5‡	1.2	7.8	0.9	7.8***	0.9	6.4	0.8	11.1§§	1.5	10.3	0.9	14.8§§	1.1	14.6	1.0	140	—	58	—
22. Sweden	24.0	3.5	23.5	1.0	21.1	2.5	23.3	1.1	—	—	—	—	—	—	—	—	158	1.4	135	1.0
23. Switzerland	23.1†	3.3	30.5	1.3	19.0	2.2	29.5	1.6	28.9	3.9	38.2	1.3	18.8	1.4	34.9	1.9	31	1.6	234	1.5
24. Turkey	10.6†	1.5	10.9	1.0	10.9	1.3	12.7	1.2	13.1	1.8	18.1	1.0	—	—	—	—	—	0.3	90	3.2
25. United Kingdom	23.1	3.3	33.2	1.4	20.9	2.5	30.4	1.5	—	—	—	—	—	—	—	—	169	1.7	196	1.2
26. U.S.A.	8.7	1.3	15.8	1.8	11.6	1.4	16.1	1.4	14.0‡‡	1.9	31.3	2.2	24.7	1.8	36.6	1.5	78	0.8	202	2.6
27. Austria	16.7	2.4	22.6	1.4	17.6	2.1	23.2	1.3	25.5	3.4	31.6	1.2	—	—	—	—	137	1.3	197	1.4

SOURCE: Food and Agriculture Organization *Year Books* 1955, 1959 and 1961.

* Unofficial figures
† Includes spelt
** Average 1930, 1934 and 1936
‡ Average 1937 and 1938
§ Palestine
*** Average 1937-39
‡‡ Includes estimates of grain equivalent of maize used for silage or fodder and maize hogged off or grazed.

§§ Average 1936-38
‡ Palestine 1935-38
††† Includes dry equivalent of maize harvested green
**** Average for 1935-39
‡‡‡ 1935-38

than arrangements for defence of its frontiers.[4] Food shortage is likely to lead to political instability, chaos and uprisings behind.

TABLE L

WORLD, ECAFE REGION AND ECAFE COUNTRIES : INDICES OF AGRICULTURAL PRODUCTION (1952/53-1956/57 = 100)

Country,* region and the world	Average 1952-53 to 1954-55	Average 1957-58 to 1959-60	Percentage increase
Japan	92	119	29.3
China : Taiwan	97	118	21.6
Federation of Malaya	96	112	16.7
Philippines	97	113	16.5
Ceylon	97	109	12.4
South Korea	99	111	12.1
Thailand	94	105	11.7
India	97	107	10.3
Indonesia	99	107	8.1
Burma	99	104	5.1
Pakistan	99	102	3.0
ECAFE region†	97	109	12.4
Total world††	97	112	15.5

SOURCE : United Nations Food and Agriculture Organization, *Production Year-book*, 1960 (Rome, 1961).

* Countries ranked in the descending order of the percentage rate of increase in index values.

† Excluding Afghanistan, mainland China and Iran.

†† Excluding mainland China.

[4] Confucius was once asked to enumerate the three things vital to a ruler. The sage replied : "Sufficiency of food, sufficiency of military power and sufficiency of popular faith in the ruler."

When asked what he would omit if only two were possible, he replied : "Omit military power." He was asked again what he would omit if only one were possible, Confucius replied : "Let the people lose their food but keep their faith."

TABLE LI

DISTRIBUTION OF OUTLAY IN THE THREE FIVE-YEAR PLANS

	Total Provision			Percentage of Total		
	First plan	Second plan	Third plan	First plan	Second plan	Third plan
I	2	3	4	5	6	7
Agriculture and Community Development	291	530	1,068	15	11	14
Major and Medium Irrigation	310*	420	650	16	9	9
Power	260	445	1,012	13	10	13
Village & Small industries	43	175	264	2	4	4
Industries and Minerals	74	900	1,520	4	20	20
Transport and Communications	523	1,300	1,486	27	28	20
Social Services and Miscellaneous	459	830	1,300	23	18	17
Inventories	..	..	200	..	..	3
Total	1,960	4,600	7,500	100	100	100

SOURCE : *Third Five-Year Plan,* issued by Planning Commission, Government of India, Delhi, 1961, pp. 33 and 58.
   * Includes flood control.

the War Front, which will demoralize even a most efficient army and make it surrender. It has been well remarked that, "had the feeding arrangements of Bourbon France given satisfaction, the Bastille would probably never have been stormed." With the population growing by nearly ten million every year and Indian agriculture not yet capable of feeding all the existing population, there is real danger of mass starvation just over time's horizon. "A hungry people," said an ancient Roman philosopher, Seneca, "listens not to reason, nor cares for justice, nor is it bent by any prayers." It will lend a sympathetic ear to the promises of Communism, and will be prepared to sacrifice freedom for bread. Mahatma Gandhi had said : "A starving man thinks first of satisfying his hunger before anything else. He will sell his liberty and all for the sake of getting a morsel of food. Such is the position of millions of the people of India. For them, Liberty, God and all such words are merely letters put together without the slightest meaning".[5] Whether Communism in India with a far lower land-man ratio than in the USSR, would necessarily solve the food problem earlier than a democracy that we are today, will be clear from the confession of Messrs. Khrushchev and Bulganin at the 20th Congress of the Communist Party in 1956 that there had been a deplorable failure of agriculture and consumer goods industries even after the successful completion of five successive five-year plans. But this truth will dawn upon our people when it would have become all too late.

Hence agriculture, at least, immediately is more important than industry—more important than giant steel or hydro-electric projects and heavy or producer goods industries. Not that anybody is opposed to industrialisation or to production of steel and electric energy which are essential to industrialisation, but because man does not live by industrial goods. Therefore, only a grudging concession to the role of agriculture that our economic planners and political leaders usually make, will not do. Agriculture is not only equally important with industrialisation : relatively it is much more important in India today than it is in more advanced countries. Also, industrialisation that we seek will come about not as an indirect but a direct consequence of agricultural prosperity and cannot come about without it at all or even slowly. Nor, as we have already seen, will industrialisation, if by it is meant only or largely heavy or mechanised industry, be able to solve our unemployment problem. And inasmuch as agriculture *directly* occupies more than 70 per cent of the workers and will always remain the most important source of employment and income—it will be a fortunate day, indeed, when the percentage comes down to 50. Without improvement in the output of agriculture there will be no *general rise in living standards even if there were rapid progress in other sectors.*

Differences in economic levels in various States of India today are largely attributable to differences in their agricultural productivity.

[5] *Young India*, dated March 18, 1926, p. 105.

A study paper of the Planning Commission has made the admission that "States which have fared well in agricultural production have generally achieved a larger measure of advance in other directions as well".

Fluctuations in national income as a whole also very largely turn on corresponding contribution of agriculture. This will be clear from a comparison of figures in Table No. XLVIII with those in Table LII. Owing to a fall in agricultural output national income in 1959-60, at constant prices, recorded an increase of 1.8 per cent only over 1958-59 whereas, owing to an exceptionally good harvest in 1960-61, national income went up by 7.1 per cent. During the year 1961-62, there was no increase in total agricultural production whereas food production registered a fall of 1.1 million tons or 0.4 per cent. With the result that national income in 1961-62 showed an increase only of 2.1 per cent as against the average annual increase of 4.8 per cent during the Second Plan period.

Table LII shows changes in the total national income, *per capita* income, total national income from agriculture and percentage distribution of income between agriculture, factory or large scale establishments, and small enterprises since 1948-49.

The importance of increased agricultural production would be indelibly impressed on our minds if we remember that the three steel plants at Durgapur, Bhilai and Rourkela, which are expected to produce 3 million tons of steel ingots yearly and of which we are so proud, and justly, would ultimately cost us Rs. 615 crores, perhaps even more, while we have, in 15 years since 1947, imported foodgrains worth Rs. 1845.4 crores.[6] And it is to be remembered that the imported foodgrains have usually to be paid for in external currencies. Had we grown our own food, we could have put up eight steel plants of equivalent size for nothing !

Agriculture, without question or equivocation, will, therefore, have to be assigned priority number I. At the same time, we must beware of whipping up the mentality of a 'crisis'. There is no cause for alarm or despair : there are many ways by which agricultural production can be increased in India.

What is most relevant, rather heartening, in this context is the fact that we are short of capital and agriculture requires comparatively little capital: it depends so greatly upon factors like land

[6] *Bulletin on Food Statistics*, Issued by Ministry of Food and Agriculture, 1961.

TABLE LII

TOTAL AND *PER CAPITA* NATIONAL INCOME AND PERCENTAGE DISTRIBUTION OF NATIONAL INCOME BY INDUSTRIAL ORIGIN

	Net national output (in Rs. 100 crores)		Per capita net output (in Rs.)		National income by industrial origin— percentage distribution		
	at current prices	at 1948-49 prices (Index no.)	at current prices	at 1948-49 prices (Index no.)	agri-culture	factory estab-lish-ments	small enter-prises
1	2	3	4	5	6	7	8
1948-49	86.5	86.5 (100.0)	249.6	249.6 (100.0)	49.1	6.3	10.1
1949-50	90.1	88.2 (102.0)	256.0	250.6 (100.4)	49.8	6.0	10.0
1950-51	95.3	88.5 (102.3)	266.5	247.5 (99.2)	51.3	5.8	9.6
1951-52	99.7	91.0 (105.2)	274.2	250.3 (100.3)	50.4	6.4	9.6
1952-53	98.2	94.6 (109.4)	265.4	255.7 (102.4)	59.0	6.5	9.9
1953-54	104.8	100.3 (116.0)	278.1	266.2 (106.7)	50.7	6.6	9.3
1954-55	96.1	102.8 (118.8)	250.3	267.8 (107.3)	45.3	7.8	10.0
1955-56	99.8	104.8 (121.2)	255.0	267.8 (107.3)	45.3	7.8	9.7
1956-57	113.1	110.0 (127.2)	283.3	275.6 (110.4)	48.8	7.9	8.7
1957-58	113.9	108.9 (125.9)	279.6	267.3 (107.1)	46.4	8.6	8.8
1958-59	126.0	116.5 (134.7)	303.0	280.1 (112.2)	49.5	7.9	8.2
1959-60	129.5	118.6 (137.1)	304.7	279.0 (111.9)	48.3	8.6	8.2
1960-61	141.6	127.5 (147.4)	326.2	293.7 (117.7)	48.7	9.3	7.9
1961-62 (Preliminary)	146.3	130.2 (150.5)	329.7	293.4 (117.5)	46.8	10.0	8.0

SOURCE : *Estimates of National Income 1948-49 to 1960-61*, January 1963, issued by Central Statistical Organisation, Department of Statistics, Cabinet Secretariat, Government of India, New Delhi.

reforms, innovations in or improvement of agricultural practices improvement of the human factor, development of scientific and technical outlook in general in the country-side, etc. etc., that is, factors other than capital investments *per se*, that the capital : output ratio in agriculture is very low, perhaps, of the order of 1:1. Non-mechanised agriculture—and that is the only type of farming that we need to consider in our country—is known to have a ratio much lower than manufacturing in general and very much lower, indeed, than heavy industry in particular. Further, what is still more significant : not only is the ratio of capital investment to added output in agriculture comparatively much less, but *the increase in output generally comes more quickly* than in most other enterprises, particularly, heavy industry.

"The heavy industry programme," says P. T. Bauer Smuts, Reader in Commonwealth Studies, Cambridge University, "is almost certain to be economically wasteful. For instance, it ignores the highly relevant consideration of the actual or prospective demand for the products of the expensive capacity. It is the agricultural sector and the consumer goods industries which must ultimately provide the domestic market for the products of heavy industry. . . In India, major branches of the consumer goods industries have for years been working far below capacity,[6a] notably because of the failure of the productivity of agriculture to rise significantly and the resulting inability to provide a growing market for industry . . . Exports may eventually supply a market for part of the output, but this is unlikely to be a major factor. Much of the capacity is capital-intensive and/or in activities which require advanced techniques and skills, so that it is improbable that India will enjoy international competitive advantages in these activities.

[6a] According to an editorial in the *Economic Weekly*, Bombay, May 20, 1961, industrial production in 1955 was less than 50 per cent of capacity in nearly half of the factory establishments. By 1960, the position had improved to the extent that production was over 50 per cent of capacity in some 60 per cent of the industries. And according to a survey, *Small Industry in a Big City : A Survey in Bombay*, by D. T. Lakdawala and J. C. Sandesara, published by the University of Bombay, 1960, as many as 85 per cent of the sample units were working below—at between one-fifth to four-fifths of their full capacity. The survey covered 1060 units, each employing less than 50 workers, the average capital employed per unit being Rs. 4,839, of which fixed capital amounted to a bare Rs. 1,781.

Moreover, other possible markets are in countries likely to be as autarkic as the Indian."[7]

To take the example of steel : while India's need for iron rods and sheets for highways, railroads, public buildings and other works, engineering industries, agricultural implements, and the like, is unquestioned, and her natural resources in this regard are ample, the decision to build three steel rolling mills under the Second Plan and to increase their number or capacity under the Third will be justified only if there is a simultaneous increase in the real incomes of the masses. For, unless there is such increase, they will not have the capacity either to pay the taxes with which public works may be executed or to purchase the products of the engineering or consumer goods industries that may be expected to absorb all the steel that is produced. So that if agricultural production does not go up—for, it is only from increased agricultural production that real incomes of the masses in India will increase—we will have to export our steel which will, perhaps, not easily find a market at economic rates. Also, it will be a fantastic situation when such a huge nation as ours comes to depend on outside food in exchange of steel !

Doubters or those who look to European or communist testimony for every policy they advocate in India may, perhaps, be silenced by what the Soviet Prime Minister had to say on this aspect of the economic problem only last year, that is, after 44 years of Communist rule—and that, let us remember again, in a country where land : man ratio is higher than in India. The *Pioneer*, Lucknow, dated January 24, 1961, carries the following report under date-line of Moscow, January 23 :

In his speech at the recent Party Central Committee meeting here, M. Nikita Khrushchev declared that the rate of progress of such industries as steel would be curbed to make more resources available for agriculture.
What was the use of a lot of steel if the rapidly growing army of consumers got only a little bread and butter, he asked the meeting.
He underlined the supreme political significance of agriculture by threatening to sack the inefficient and expel from the party and try those who try to cook their books.

Better and more food is necessary for yet another reason. If allowance is made both for quality and caloric content, the average

[7] "Problems, Paradoxes, Prospects of Indian Planning", published in the Supplement to the *Capital*, Calcutta, dated December 17, 1929.

per capita diets of North America, Oceania and West Europe are something like one and a half to two times those of India. According to the *UN Statistical Yearbook*, 1961, the average daily calorie[8] supply *per capita* in our country is only 1,890 or so, as against the 2,200 accepted by the FAO in its Second World Food Survey of 1952 as a daily minimum standard, or the 3,570, 3,490, 3,340 and 3,290 calories enjoyed in 1959 by Ireland, New Zealand, Denmark and the United Kingdom respectively, and a daily intake in excess of 2,900 calories in all countries of Europe except the Southern European countries. This inevitably means that the majority of our people are habitually or permanently undernourished, incapable of achieving full growth, health or energy. An improvement in nutritional levels, therefore, is a primary condition for economic development, for without it there can be no improvement in the quality of labour. Thus we find ourselves in a vicious circle : lack of more and better food lowers our physical efficiency, which, in turn, limits our productivity of food.

The very fact that the yields per acre in India today are much lower than in some countries with comparable climatic and soil conditions shows that they are capable of vast improvement. India contains some tracts of the richest land in the world and the small size of holdings is not an obstacle to increasing the yield per acre as the experience of China and Japan would show.

Japan has proved that it is possible to utilise science, and all that science has placed at the disposal of man, equally well on small farms as some of the Western countries have utilised it on large farms. The emphasis in Japan is on maximising the yield per unit of land by substituting land as much as possible by capital and labour. Although production and distribution are on an individual basis,

[8] The *National Herald*, Lucknow, dated May 24, 1960, carries the following report :

India is the worst fed among over forty countries which supplied statistics to the United Nations, according to the UN Statistical Year Book, 1959, just published.

The Indian consumed 1890 calories in 1954-56—the latest figures available—compared to the pre-war figure of 1950 calories in 1934-38.

According to another UN publication, however, viz., *Economic Survey of Asia and the Far East*, 1961 (Bangkok, 1962, p. 19), the figure of calorie supply in India rose from 1640 in 1948/49-1950/51 to the pre-war figure of 1950 in 1957/58-1959/60.

the Japanese farmer works so hard and well and the state has provided so many facilities by way of highly developed transport and marketing organisations, easy credit, national research and extension services, etc., that the yields per unit of land on the tiny farms of Japan are today among the highest in the world. Each farm is run as a small business and within his limited means the Japanese farmer is as anxious to make the fullest use of modern technology as large farmers in other parts of the world.

"Given three tracts of land of equal inherent productivity," says J. D. Black, "one in Japan, one in China and one in India, and each farmed at the state of the agricultural arts that is average for these countries, the Japanese tract will produce roughly a half more than the Chinese tract and the Chinese tract roughly twice as much as the Indian tract."[9]

As for reasons of our low yields : Considering the high level of cultivation and craftsmanship often achieved by an Indian peasant, it will not be just to attribute the low yield of our agriculture to his shortcomings alone. Dr. Wallick, who was Superintendent of the East India Company's Botanical Garden at Calcutta, giving his evidence[10] on the state of agricultural arts in India on 13th August, 1832, before the House of Commons' Committee, said :

The husbandry of Bengal has in a great measure been misunderstood by the Europeans out of India. The Bengal husbandry, although in many respects extremely simple and primeval in its mode and form, yet is not quite so low as people generally suppose it to be, and I have often found that very sudden innovations in them have never led to any good results. I have known, for instance, European iron ploughs introduced into Bengal with a view to superseding the extremely tedious and superficial turning of the ground by a common Bengal plough. But what has been the result ? That the soil which is extremely superficial, as I took the liberty of mentioning before, which was intended to be torn up, has generally received the admixture of the under-soil, which has deteriorated it very much.

Asked if the Indian husbandry was susceptible of any great im-

[9] *Introduction to Economics for Agriculture*, 1953, p. 344.

[10] Evidence before the Commons' Committee, 1832, Vol. II, Part I, p. 195, quoted in *The Economic History of India* (Early British Rule) by Romesh Dutt, Kegan Paul, Trench, Trubner & Co. Ltd., London, p. 277 (Sixth edition).

provement, Dr. Wallick replied : "Certainly, but not to so great an extent as is generally imagined ; for instance, the rice cultivation. I should think, if we were to live for another thousand years, we should hardly see any improvement in that branch of cultivation."

In 1889 Dr. Voelcker, Consulting Chemist to the Royal Agricultural Society of England, was deputed to India to make inquiries and suggest improvements in respect of Indian agriculture. And he wrote :

On one point there can be no question, *viz.* that the ideas generally entertained in England, and often given expression to even in India, that Indian agriculture is, as a whole, primitive and backward and that little has been done to try and remedy it, are altogether erroneous. . . At his best the Indian Ryot, or cultivator is quite as good as, and in some respects the superior of, the average British farmer ; whilst, at his worst, it can only be said that this state is brought about largely by an absence of facilities for improvement which is probably unequalled in any other country, and that the Ryot will struggle on patiently and uncomplainingly in the face of difficulties in a way that no one else would.

Nor need our British farmers be surprised at what I say, for it must be remembered that the natives of India were cultivators of wheat centuries before we in England were. It is not likely, therefore, that their practices should be capable of much improvement. What does, however, prevent them from growing larger crops is the limited facilities to which they have access, such as the supply of water and manure. But, to take the ordinary acts of husbandry, nowhere would one find better instances of keeping land scrupulously clean from weeds, of ingenuity in device of water-raising appliances, of knowledge of soils and their capabilities, as well as the exact time to sow and to reap, as one would in Indian agriculture, and this not at its best alone, but at its ordinary level. It is wonderful, too, how much is known of rotation, the system of mixed crops and fallowing. Certain it is that I, at least, have never seen a more perfect picture of careful cultivation, combined with hard labour, perseverance and fertility of resource, than I have seen in many of the halting places in my tour."[11]

Nearly 50 years later Sir John Russell, author and expert of international repute, said : "The Indian Ryot compares favourably with any of the peasant populations I have met in different parts of the world."

The opinion of Dr. Wallick, Dr. Voelcker and Sir John Russell is borne out by the report of the Krishnappa Delegation to China

[11] *Report of the Improvement of Indian Agriculture* quoted by Romesh Dutt, *ibid*, footnote, on pp. 277-78.

which, on comparing the yields in certain farms and regions in the two countries, observes :

The crops in the best areas or in best farms in India are no worse than those in the best areas and in best farms in China. For instance, in the State of Mysore, the average yield of paddy is about 2000 lbs. for the rainy season cultivation as against the all-India average of about 1,100 lbs. But in the Malahalli National Extension Block of the State the average yield of paddy in irrigated areas under improved seeds was 2,500 lbs. in 1952-53 and has gone up to 4,500 lbs. in 1953-54, and 5,500 lbs. in 1954-55 as a result of extension work. In Ramnagar Extension Block of the same State, the normal yield is 3,000 to 3,200 lbs. per acre but the Japanese method is yielding as much as 6,000 lbs. per acre. This shows that in India the proportion of indifferent and poor farmers is much greater than in China and that is the main reason why, although our best yields do not compare unfavourably with those in China, our average yield is very much lower. The main problem before our country is, therefore, that of raising the level of the average farmers to that of the best farmers (p. 90).

These quotations are not intended to suggest that there is no scope for further improvement in Indian agricultural practices. Far from it ; they only highlight two other explanations of our low agricultural output, and, thus, pose two corresponding problems, *viz.*, that of creating a desire in the overwhelming sections of the peasantry to catch up with the few best among them, *i.e.*, an urge for material progress, and of extending to them 'facilities for improvement' which, perhaps, no other farming community anywhere in the world lacks so greatly.

Fortunately for us, it is only "in any given state of agricultural skill and knowledge," as John Stuart Mill pointed out, that the Law of Diminishing Returns applies—that increase in labour does not increase the product in an equal degree. The law is to a large extent subject to the stipulation that if the soil and crops can be improved, which can be done frequently, if not continuously, a given area will yield more produce. This improvement of soil and plants can be effected by improvement in technology, that is, by introduction of innovations in farming practices through scientific knowledge and by application of more capital.

If the law of constant returns to labour applied in agriculture and production per head were to be maintained as population increases in relation to land, it is self-evident that, inasmuch as, in addition

to land, agricultural production requires both labour and capital,
there must be an increase either in capital investment, or in order
that efficiency of labour or capital or of both may be increased, an
increase in improvements in technology at the same rate as increase
in population. But, as we have already seen, it is the Law of Diminishing Returns to labour that applied. So, if the rate of increase
in capital investment or improvements in technology only equals
the rate of increase in population, a decline in output per head is
inevitable. To maintain food production per head as population
increases, either the proportion engaged in farming would have to
rise (with the result that there would be a decline in the proportion
engaged in manufacture and tertiary industries) or there must be an
increase in capital investment or improvements in technology at a
greater rate than the increase in population. But if production per
head had to rise as population increases, the rate of increase in
capital investment or improvements in technology must be greater
still by an amount more than sufficient to offset the rate at which
returns to labour decrease.

The amount of land at our disposal is practically fixed and we
have almost reached the limits of extensive cultivation ; on the
other hand, our population is increasing. So, if output of food per
head is to rise there is no alternative except to increase the yield
or productivity per acre. Need for capital investment and innovations or improvements in technology, therefore, is apparent. The
fact that from an exporter of food India has become an importer,
shows that capital investment and technological improvements in
agriculture have not kept pace with increase in population, or,
at best, in those parts of the country where the Law of Diminishing
Returns has begun to operate, have only kept pace with it. The
country would not have become an importer of food, had the rate of
capital investment in land or of technological improvements or of
both combined, been greater than the rate of population growth.
The effect of the declining land-man or rising man-land ratio can be
offset only by improving the farmer's arts and by investing more
capital. It may be pointed out that in actual practice it will frequently not be possible to distinguish between capital investments
and technological improvements, for, in most cases, the latter will
depend on the former. For example, increase in water or manure
supply is a technological improvement, but this may require capital
investment.

To re-emphasise and remind the reader : Land area being constant, agricultural production depends on two factors, *viz.*, labour
and capital. We may also add a third, *viz.*, farming arts or practices
obtaining in a particular region, which, in effect, are another name
for level of efficiency of labour and capital reached. If either of
these factors is reduced either in quantity or quality, as the case
may be, the other two or one of them has to be increased in order
that production may be maintained at the previous level. In
absence of such increase, production is bound to go down. It
follows that fewer men working a given land area, with no difference
in farming methods and capital employed per man, will result in
less product per acre and less total product. Therefore, if we seek
economic development of the country, that is, want men to be
released from agriculture for diversion to industry, commerce,
transport and other non-agricultural occupations, and further,
want production not only to be maintained at the present level
but increased, while population grows, capital in land will have to
be invested in a far greater measure and technological improvements
in agriculture effected at a far greater rate than we imagine or have
planned for. Once agricultural production is increased, say, doubled,
if not trebled—which, let us understand, is not impossible of achievement—industrialisation or development of non-agricultural resources will follow almost automatically (the necessary mental
attitudes or an urge to seek material advancement on the part of
the people, being assumed). To put it in a nut-shell : *inasmuch as
industrialisation will progress to the extent men are released from
agriculture, and men will be released to the extent agricultural production goes up, and agricultural production will go up to the extent
agricultural practices improve and more capital invested, industrialisation or economic development of the country turns on improvement in
agricultural practices we are able to effect and amount of capital
we are able to invest in land.*

We have to be clear in our mind about four basic facts if we are
intent on finding a correct solution of our low agricultural yields
and also of other related problems—firstly, that our agriculture is
already labour-intensive ; secondly, that when we talk of having
intensive agriculture in our country, it is capital-intensive agriculture that is largely meant ; thirdly, that capital in this context is
not a synonym for large machinery , and fourthly, that our agricultural arts, practices or techniques where they are inferior, will

have to be improved, that is, innovations will have to be introduced.

The use of improved farming methods or improvements in technology and greater investment of capital per man are the steps that other countries have consciously or unconsciously taken when they found their population increasing and their area of agricultural land to be limited or diminishing. The Krishnappa Delegation has found that it is exactly on these two points, viz., familiarising the peasantry with still better and improved techniques and investment of more capital that the Communist Government is—at least, in the pre-commune period—laying most stress in China. We, too, will have to do the same.

Our farmers will have to learn (and practise) the simple arts of Chinese, Japanese and Italian peasants, their methods of manuring and other cultural practices where they are superior to ours. Agricultural research has not tackled the specific problems of the small farmer, nor have even such of its results as may be beneficial to him been brought to his notice. Dissemination of education or technical knowledge will be needed in most parts of the country in order that the results of agricultural research are reached to the small or average farmer and he may be brought to the level of the best. So that research, education and extension services which will spread the knowledge of improved methods of farming, will have to proceed hand in hand.

None of our schemes, remedies or measures of agricultural improvement will make any headway unless the interest and enthusiasm of the farmers is awakened and maintained. *Once the farmers begin to desire progress* almost all difficulties will be overcome, but so long as they are apathetic and disinterested very litle can be done, our plans and schemes of financial assistance on a most liberal scale notwithstanding.[12]

While expenditure of money may be a fair measure of achievement in the spheres of heavy industry, transport and social services, it cannot be so in agriculture. The basic factors of our agriculture are intractable and cannot be easily altered. Production depends upon the active participation of nearly 5 crore (50 million) peasant families or 10 crore (100 million) workers (excluding hired labourers), nearly eighty per cent of whom are poor and illiterate. They possess small holdings, are wedded to traditional methods and

[12] See Chapter XVIII *supra*.

cannot be hustled. Conviction must precede adoption or introduction of any new techniques or practices.

As we have seen in a previous chapter, rural communities in certain parts of the country tend to expect that whatever is to be done for their improvement,is the responsibility of the Government or some outside agency. The assumption that each man is fully alive to his interests and will be willing to exert himself to the maximum extent if only the necessary guidance or assistance was offered to him, has been proved to be baseless. Experience would seem to show that many peasants have neither the desire nor the initiative to put themselves to trouble even if it were for advancing their own interests and increasing resources for maintaining their families. To change this passive attitude into one whereby people realise that they can do a good deal themselves with little or no outside help, should be the duty as the privilege of non-official leaders of the people. We agree with the Krishnappa Delegation when it says :

Technical measures can be developed by research institutes. They can be taken to the farmers' fields by the extension agency ; credit and supplies may be made available to the farmers so as to make it possible for them to adopt the measures recommended. But it is not enough to bring water to the horse. The horse must have a will to drink it. That will can be created no doubt to some extent by the official extension agency but official agencies have also their limitations. The non-official agencies of the country, especially, the political and social organisations, have to take a much greater hand in it than has been done hitherto. Although in some areas of India, farmers are diligent and keen to adopt new techniques, it must be admitted that in many areas they are apathetic and much less hardworking compared to the Chinese farmers. Our peasantry as a whole is not working hard enough nor is it always keen to work efficiently and adopt improved techniques. It is only our popular leaders and popular parties who can effectively revitalise our peasants and unless they do so we are bound to lag behind. On the other hand, if a mass enthusiasm is created by non-official workers and there are no extension agencies to follow up, or supplies and credit are inadequate, there may be also serious frustration. It is, therefore, very important that some organisation like Technique Popularisation Stations of China should be set up at the block level in our national extension areas (Report, p. 172).

The delegation has touched a very vital aspect of our public life when it reminds our popular leaders of their duty to "effectively revitalise our peasants". It cannot be seriously disputed that, had those in whose hands lies the power to make policies in India, their roots laid in the soil of their own country and their fingers on the pulse of their peasantry, we would have progressed much faster, at least, in the sphere of agriculture. But views and sentiments of the peasants are seldom shared by those at the top today. Political leadership of the country vests almost entirely in the hands of those who come from the town and, therefore, have an urban outlook.[12a] They may have an intellectual sympathy for the rural folk, but have no personal knowledge and psychological appreciation of their needs, problems and handicaps. Not only this : our leaders and the intelligentsia are nurtured on text-books written in conditions entirely different from our country, or which are mostly inspired by the ideology of Marx who had made no special study of the rural problems. That is mainly why Mahatma Gandhi's powerful advocacy in favour of a truly Indian approach to India's problems notwithstanding, we are under the spell of economic, political and social ideas and doctrines that we may have received ready-made from foreign oracles—western oracles till yesterday and eastern today.[13]

Because of their mental background and physical surroundings in which they have been brought up, our administrators—and also the political leaders—have gradually come to entertain a feeling of pity for the poor peasant because he still uses the ancient plough, the bullock, the bullock-cart and the cow-dung ! They would have him use the tractor and the artificial fertilisers and if, for reasons of low land-man ratio in the country, our farmers cannot have large areas of land each, on which 'modern' agriculture can

[12a] During the course of a conversation, an old educated *Swami* told Mr. W. S. Woytinsky, author of *India : The Awakening Giant* (Harper & Brothers, New York, 1957) : "The trouble is that ours is a country of small farmers, a rural country, but our politicians, like all intellectuals, are city people. Most of them are good, honest people. But the needs of large cities always come first with them" (p. 30).

[13] On the merest basis of Chinese claims of a 'Great Leap Forward', which was said to have doubled their country's agricultural production in 1958, certain people in India also began advocating adoption of Chinese methods in our country. But according to Dr. S. Chandrashekhar, widely-publicized methods or experiments like deep ploughing, irrigation with hot water to speed up germination, and close spacing of crops, had now been dropped quietly in China when they proved unworkable (*vide* the *National Herald*, Lucknow, dated July 4, 1959).

be practised, they would huddle them into large joint farms willy-nilly. It is from such attitudes and lack of identity with the interests of the villagers that spring unrealistic plans and schemes in agriculture which, in turn, bedevil India's entire economy. In the West the urban complexion of the political leadership or the administration is not very material inasmuch as the rural sector forms a very small part of their economy and also because in some countries, e.g., the USA, they have laid down an unwritten rule that the Minister of Agriculture shall be a person who comes from the agricultural class. The University Education Commission, 1951, presided over by Dr. Sarvapalli Radhakrishnan, had recommended that, as far as possible, "agricultural education, agricultural research and the formulation of agricultural policy shall be in the hands of persons and groups of persons, who, by intimate association, participation and experience, have *first-hand and penetrating* knowledge of agriculture" (Italics ours). Nothing came of this recommendation, however.

As regards the administration, the Patil Delegation has this to say:

Although a change in the attitude of the administration is noticeable, the old system, traditions and outlook have not yet disappeared and it becomes difficult for the administration to function on the basis of trust and cooperation as between equals. Identification with the people is made further difficult by the fact that higher services usually come from *higher classes and castes in society* (Report, pp. 139-140).

Need of a more rural-oriented leadership, therefore, both in the sphere of politics and administration—a new type of authentic Indian leadership which must rise from the villages—is clearly indicated. Says the *National Herald*, Lucknow, dated August 24, 1962: "Until the political and economic elites are freed from the fascination of the methods and solutions which have worked in more well-to-do western societies, or alternatively, until they are replaced by leaders more attuned to specific Indian problems and developments, we will merely continue to have the same mild mixture of socialism and capitalism which cannot initiate a process of dynamic growth".

To revert to the immediate subject in hand : among the 'facilities for improvement' of which Dr. Voelcker speaks, the availability of credit on reasonable terms comes foremost. Again, that is, just

as in the case of health, it is tho case of a vicious circle. Our fields
are poorly cultivated because the farmers cannot make capital investments in their land. And the farmers are poor and cannot make
investments because the fields are poorly cultivated and produce
little. Because capital investments in agriculture yield greater
return relatively to industry, it will be a mistake to think that we
need not allot large funds for agricultural development. Rather,
for some time to come, we would do well to invest the major part of
our financial resources in agriculture. One of the main reasons why
food is short in India consists in the fact that the proportion of
capital invested in land is low. Investment of capital by the farmer
himself is, in many parts of the country, extremely small, the chief
reason being the poverty of his own resources and, at least, till recently the high interest at which alone he could borrow from others.
While capital is required by the farmer in many forms and for
various purposes, the need for greater and more efficiently-managed supply of water for irrigation so that agriculture may not remain
at the mercy of the capricious monsoon, and that for adequate
manure are entitled to prior attention.

On one hand, India is blessed with one of the largest water
supplies of any country in the world and, on the other, provided
water is forthcoming, we need to grow crops all the year around.
Thus, with better management of our water resources, agricultural
production in the country can be increased manifold. But only a
small portion of the water potential has been developed : according
to the estimates of the Planning Commission, in 1960-61 we were
able to utilise only 120 million acre feet of surface water, which
was 27 per cent of the usable flow and 9 per cent of the total flow
(*vide* Third Plan, p. 188). The net sown area of the country today
stands in the neighbourhood of 325 million acres, while the area
irrigated from all sources in 1950-51 was 51.53 million acres only.
While benefit of irrigation on full development from First and Second
Plan schemes was estimated to accrue to 37.56 million acres, the
potential created by end of Second Plan was estimated at 13.243
million acres, and actual utilisation at 9.989 million acres (*vide* Third
Plan Annexure I, page 410).

The reasons for non-utilisation of our vast national water supply,
which rainfall constitutes, are mainly two : First, the rainfall is
erratic in behaviour. In some years it may fail completely, leading to drought conditions ; in others, the precipitation may be very

heavy, leading to flood conditions. In the same year, in some parts of the country it may be insufficient ; in others, much more than was needed. Second, over the greater part of India, 80 per cent of the annual rainfall is received in downpours in the four months of June, July, August and September, and not in showers spread throughout the year. With the result that while, on one hand, most of the water is lost to much-needed food production, on the other, its quick run-off causes serious damage by soil erosion. India cannot afford this waste of its life-giving resource (or the damage caused by it). Our water supply has, therefore, to be more efficiently managed and utilised.

But, inasmuch as there is lack of capital in the country, emphasis has to be placed, as far as possible, on comparatively simple and inexpensive techniques of water management—not on techniques or technologies which are costly. Greater and more immediate gains in food production can be derived by intensifying expenditure of time, effort and capital on minor irrigation works like masonry wells, tanks and contour *bundhies* than on large-scale multi-purpose river valley projects which are designed to control floods, bring more land under irrigation, generate power for industrial and agricultural use and, in certain cases, improve inland navigation. Large-scale projects take years to develop[14] and, by the time they are completed, our population would have grown so much that the wealth they will produce, distributed evenly among the people, would leave them no better-off than before. Huge capital is locked up for a long time without corresponding increase in production, which leads to inflation. The equipment needed for these large-scale projects requires much foreign exchange which is not easy to obtain. As the Third Finance Commission has observed, big irrigation or multi-purpose projects are not even an economic proposition : most of them are not able to pay their working expenses and the interest charges. Even after a major project gets into commission, as much as 10 to 15 years must elapse before water utilisation achieves anything like its maximum potential. Further, major irrigation schemes requiring the construction of enormous storage reservoirs involve the sub-

[14] Prime Minister Nehru has also now begun to doubt the utility of large projects. He said recently : "Not only do large projects take a long time to come to fruition, but they have failed to reach down to the people or to elicit their understanding and cooperation."

mergence of valuable village and forest lands in the reservoir basins and rehabilitation of the displaced villages poses difficult problems. When more than one State is affected, the problems become well-nigh insoluble. Also, we have to keep in mind the eventuality that the reservoirs, after a period of time, may be filled up with silt. This has happened to hundreds of reservoirs in the United States, Japan, Puerto Rico and Ceylon. Silting up cannot be avoided unless there is considerable development of afforestation and other sorts of erosion control in the catchment areas—all through the watersheds above the dams. Also, irrigated land is liable to become clogged with salts from the reservoir water, and to become useless. Large-scale projects should, therefore, be resorted to only where there is absolutely no alternative.

Masonry wells, tanks and *bundhies*, do not suffer from any such handicap, and yet offer a way to make tremendous increases in food production on many crores of acres of non-irrigated arable soils. They do not require foreign exchange, and bring early returns. Taken severally, they irrigate or benefit only a small acreage, but their cost also is small. The needed skills, materials and labour are all at hand. Because of the source of supply being closer to the fields, there is little loss of water in conveyance and evaporation. Problems associated with the timing of delivery or demand by the farmer do not arise, or are much easier to cope with than in the case of state tube-wells or canals. Farmers are thus saved from official control and interference. Masonry wells and even some irrigation tanks are still better exploited when fitted with Persian wheels. In addition to providing water for irrigation, tanks also have many social benefits to the immediate villages.

Discussing an article on the subject published in the *Asian Economic Review*, which brings an impressive collection of expert opinion, the *National Herald* of Lucknow, in its editorial dated September 13, 1961, said as follows :

In the alluvial plains of north India, it is clear, irrigation from well has no peer. The advantage of capital and recurring cost is, of course, in favour of wells as against canals. To allow canal water to flow unutilised means great loss to the exchequer, whereas the cost of allowing wells to lie unused is negligible. The annual upkeep of wells commanding even as much as ten thousand acres of land is relatively small compared to the upkeep cost of canal works capable of serving an equal area of land . . . The time taken in completing a large irrigation work, the foreign exchange involved in its construction, the water-logging and rise in sub-soil water as a result of continued canal irrigation over a period of years are among other factors which weigh against big irrigation projects.

A study made in the specific context of eastern districts of U.P. discloses that while irrigation has admittedly an important role to play in an agricultural economy, well irrigation is in many vital respects superior to canal irrigation. It not only suits the soil but the terrain, which is furrowed by innumerable rivulets and which does not lend itself to proper alignment of canals but permits irrigation from wells.

Tube-wells are not a profitable proposition for the state. Nor are they profitable to the very small farmer who, along with his bullocks, remains idle for a large part of the year. He could utilise his own muscles or employ his bullocks for drawing water from a well, rather than pay the state for doing it for him while he and his bullocks sit idle. Also, if not carefully sited, tube-wells may eventually exhaust the sub-soil water reserves, which will adversely affect the soil. But usually even tube-wells are more economical than large-scale projects. So are also canals supplied as they can be from perennial rivers in a manner that the necessity of constructing large dams and large reservoirs does not arise. Such canals, e.g., the Ganga system in Uttar Pradesh, are far cheaper than even tube-wells.

It is common knowledge that the available irrigation facilities are not put to optimum use in most places. Some of the simple methods which may be adopted to ensure greater utilisation of the irrigation facilities are :

(a) alignment of field channels ;
(b) dividing fields into compartments in canal-irrigated areas before irrigation ;
(c) keeping channels and *guls* clean ; and
(d) keeping the old minor irrigation works, *e.g.* wells and tanks, in good condition, through individual and community efforts.

While the net sown area in the country increased from 293.3 million acres in 1950-51 to 323.6 million acres in 1958-59, that is, by 30.3 million acres, the irrigated area during the same period increased only by (57.89—51.53 =) 6.36 million acres.[15] Reasons

[15] SOURCE : *Basic Statistics Relating to Indian Economy* (1950-51—1960-61), issued by Planning Commission, December, 1961, Table 12, p. 13.

for this slow rate of extension of the irrigated area are three: (i) delay in execution of irrigation works which are mostly of a large size, (ii) lack of utilisation of the irrigation facilities that have already been made available, and (iii) neglect or disuse of existing small irrigation works like wells and tanks that used to irrigate a very large area before our Plans were launched.

Irrigation, however, cannot be carried beyond the limits which the supply of available manure warrants. For, irrigated crops trench on the temporary fertility of the soil which must be restored either by manure or rest. Inasmuch as we cannot allow the already large area of current fallow to increase, the only course left is to increase the supply of manure in proportion to extension of irrigation.

In agriculture, it is an axiom that what is taken off the soil, must in some way be put back into it, or else the soil will suffer exhaustion. Soil is like a bank. You cannot take from it more than you deposit. Nature permits no over-drafts.

Thus, fertilisers are, perhaps, even more important than irrigation. Indeed, a careful analysis of the correlation of yield per acre of cultivated land and the quantity of fertilisers applied to land would show that increased agricultural production is, above all, the function of the quantity of manure or fertiliser. Production is more powerfully influenced by this factor than all the other factors put together. Increase in yield per acre which could be directly attributed to the application of water alone is small.

Nitrogen being the most essential plant nutrient, agricultural output is ultimately determined by the quantum of nitrogen the soil contains. Nitrogen content is determined by its humus content. It is the vast quantities of bacteria contained in the humus, which is another name for colloidal organic matter, that turn the nitrogen of the air into organic nitrate salts to feed the plants. This organic matter in the soil or humus serves—through the bacteria—as the carrier and supplier of nutrients to the crops. Humus gives life to the soil; without it the soil is, in a way, dead. It is the humus content of a soil, therefore, that represents its productive capacity and ultimately determines its fertility. To keep the soil productive it is necessary that humus be replaced as fast as it is consumed or lost.

With every crop that is harvested, the soil becomes poorer in its humus content. Further losses of humus are occasioned by leaching, that is, the removal of soluble plant nutrients by the action of percolating water. Thus, there is a constant drain on the nutrient reserves of the soil or its humus content.

Further, as a rule, tropical soils like ours contain low amounts of humus or organic matter, the reason being oxidation due to high temperatures which release nitrogen from the soil and cause a break-down of the organic matter resulting in the loss of humus. The soil in Western Europe contains, on an average, more than 5 per cent of organic matter but in our country the average is only 1.5 per cent.

This loss of organic content of the soil or lack of it in sufficient quantities can be made good by man through addition of organic matter in the form of farm-yard waste, night-soil, oil-cake, fish waste, bloodmeal, bone-meal, green manure, dry leaves and twigs or other vegetable waste, sewage, tankage, sludge, or compost made of all or some of these organic wastes—human, animal and plant.

Major crops in India today are estimated to remove annually about 4.0 million tons of nitrogen from the land, but the quantity which is reimbursed, whether by way of inorganic fertilisers or of organic manures, is less than a million tons of nitrogen in a year. The balance of 3.0 million tons of nitrogen or more is left to be made good through the natural recuperative process that takes place in the soil and outside, and through the uncollected waste products of plant and animal life. Where this recouping is not possible, the crops draw upon the original endowment of the land itself. "The extra crop in England", says Dr. Voelcker, "is . . . the produce of what is added to, and not, as in India . . . of what is taken out of it."[16] No wonder then that the fertility of our soil in many a part of our country is gradually declining. On this state of affairs Sir Albert Howard has the following remarks to make :

The using up of soil fertility is a transfer of past capital and of future possibilities to enrich a dishonest present ; it is banditry, pure and simple. Moreover, it is a mean form of banditry because it involves the robbing of future generations which are not here to defend themselves.[17]

[16] Report of Dr. Voelcker, Consulting Chemist to the Royal Agricultural Society in England, 1889, p. 41.
[17] *Farming and Gardening for Health or Disease* by Sir Albert Howard, Faber and Faber, London, pp. 69-70.

The common source of soil nitrogen available in our villages is cattle-dung or farmyard waste. Compared to Europen countries, livestock density in India is very high. According to the cattle Census of 1956, we had 307 million livestock (excluding poultry) as against 320 million acres of net area sown. Possibilities of increasing the use of organic manures of animal origin are, thus, quite large in India. It is estimated, however, that 40 per cent, more or less, of the total annual production of cattle-dung is burnt up for want of cheap fuel. About 20 per cent of the supply is lost because it is not collected, and only 40 per cent of it is left to be used for fertilising the soil. According to the Planning Commission,[18] the amount of cattle-dung annually available can be estimated at 1,200 million tons (wet weight) of which 400 million tons are used as fuel and only 215 million tons as manure, the balance being wasted. (On the basis of energy content, 400 million tons of dung is equivalent to 46 million tons of coal.) Implications of this tremendous national waste have been brought out by Shri K. C. Pant as follows :[19]

A Committee appointed by the Government of India to go into this question came out with the estimate that 200 million tons of dry cowdung having 15 per cent moisture was being burnt each year, the dry weight of this being equal to 170 million tons.[20] Assuming dry dung to contain 0.8 to 1.0 per cent nitrogen, 0.4 to 0.6 per cent phosphorous (P_2O_5), 1.0 to 1.2 per cent potash (K_2O) and 50-60 per cent organic matter, 170 million tons would contain roughly :

TABLE LIII

NUTRIENTS IN COWDUNG BURNT AS FUEL

(Figures in 'ooo tons)

	Total plant nutrients in cowdung burnt as fuel	Minimum available nutrients from cowdung burnt as fuel	Planned targets from fertiliser plants at the end of 1960-61
Nitrogen (N)	1,530	918	382
Phosphorus (P_2O_5)	850	510	120
Potash (K_2O)	1,870	1,122	30
Total	4,250	2,550	532

[18] The Third Plan, pp. 194-95. [19] *Fertilizers For More Foods*, the Hindustan Times Ltd., New Delhi, 1959.
[20] According to Dr. P.C. Bansil, cattle dung produced in the country

The value of the three 'available' plant nutrients alone lost by burning cowdung would amount to Rs. 382.5 crores each year (at an average value of Rs. 1,500 per ton of nutrient). If we give a nominal value of Re. 0.80 per ton of dry dung for its organic content, the 200 million tons of dung would have to be valued at Rs. 160 crores. The total would thus amount to 542.5 crores. On the other hand, the fuel value of the dung is equivalent to only 80 million tons of coal. In other words, the farmer who burns dung is using a fuel whose equivalent value to him as fertiliser, on a very conservative estimate, is Rs. 67.8 per ton of fuel.

For fixing 918,000 tons of nitrogen alone (see column 2 of the table) in the form of chemical fertilisers, a capital outlay of more than Rs. 250 crores will be required. For producing the other two plant nutrients, *i.e.* potash and phosphorus, besides finding the capital outlay, raw materials will have to be imported.

In the last column of the table, the targets for the production of the three plant nutrients at the end of the second Five-Year Plan have been given. It will be seen that by burning dung we are losing nearly five times the quantity of fertilisers which we plan to produce as chemical fertilisers at an investment of more than Rs. 100 crores. If dung were solely used as manure, the net annual drain on plant nutrients—estimated earlier at 6.3 million tons—would be reduced by over 40 per cent (pp. 22-23).

According to the National Council of Applied Economic Research which undertook a study of domestic fuels in India, the national loss caused by the burning of cowdung as fuel "is roughly equivalent to the burning of 12 Sindries every year." Sindri is a fertiliser factory producing 3.5 lakh tons of ammonium sulphate per annum.

The figures both of Shri K. C. Pant and the National Council of Applied Economic Research have to be upgraded by about 10.0 per cent. The number of livestock in the country has increased from 307 million in 1956 to 337 million in 1961.

Of all kinds of dung Richard B. Gregg, a believer in Mahatma Gandhi's programme for uplift of India, places the highest value on cowdung. He says :

Of all the various fertilizers, cowdung is the best. Because the cow chews its cud, the organic particles are very fine. Because the

amounts to 1,175 million tons in green weight. Dry weight is taken as 20 per cent of green weight, so that the total dry weight would be 235 million tons. Of this, 15 per cent are lost or wasted even under the best conditions of storage so that only 200 million tons are left (Vide *India's Food Resources and Population.* Vora and Co., Bombay, 1958).

cow has three stomachs, the organic matter has been not only well digested but has in it certain vitamins and other subtle elements that are missing from the dung of horses, sheep, goats or pigs, and which enrich the soil when put on it. Cow-dung contains minerals, nitrogen, phosphorus and potassium, that are the important part of chemical fertilisers. But since it also contains the rich, finely-divided organic matter which is easily assimilated by the micro-organisms of the soil, and which improves the physical structure and water-holding capacity of the soil, cow-dung is the best of all fertilisers.

If instead of being used for fuel, the cow-dung could be put on the soil, preferably after composting it with waste vegetation, then the fertility of the soil would greatly increase. Thus India could come far closer to feeding herself and be that much safer from famine.[21]

Cow—or cattle-dung, instead of being directly burnt, can provide fuel in another way, and yet serve as the much-needed manure. Cow-dung (as also night-soil and dried leaves) like any other organic matter, when it gets decomposed, produces gases, particularly, methane which is inflammable and could be used as fuel or source of energy. Germany has been the pioneer in exploiting methane gas for domestic and agricultural purposes. During the Second World War, when supplies of coal were cut off, some progressive farmers with engineering aptitude tried to explore this source of energy for heating their houses, cooking their food and operating their tractors. They developed a number of designs to serve their purpose. In our country also the idea was picked up, and research work in order to discover a gas plant to suit our conditions, started, by the Indian Agricultural Research Institute, New Delhi, the U.P. Planning Research and Action Institute, Lucknow, and other organisations. Researches at both these institutes have established that, apart from producing energy for heating, lighting and cooking, the cow-dung gas plant, which they have devised, could be harnessed to generate power for light industrial purposes like running of a mechanical chaff-cutter, a paddy-huller, a flour mill, a water-pump or a baby oil-expeller. Only an electric generator has to be connected to an internal combustion engine which can be worked with the cow-dung gas as fuel.

"Besides the use of the gas for various purposes", says Dr. Ram Das, Director, Planning Research & Action Institute, U.P., "the

[21] Richard B. Gregg's article, "One Way to Increase Food Production" published in the *National Herald*, dated March 23, 1958.

digested slurry, which comes out from a *gobar* gas plant, is a source
of excellent manure. On the basis of dry matter its contents of
nitrogen vary from 1.5 to 1.8 per cent. Since the seeds of weeds
remain in the digestion tank for a period of 15 to 30 days they lose
their germination capacity and thus the slurry obtained is superior
to farmyard manure as the latter contains live weed seeds which
affect the growth of plants."[22]

One ton of *gobar* is capable of producing 3,122 cubic feet of gas.
The gas can suffice for meeting cooking and lighting requirements
of about 30 families. The total cost of installing a unit for community use has been estimated at about Rs. 7,500. For individuals,
units costing Rs. 400 to Rs. 600 could be installed. While the
plant is easy to operate, its cost is beyond the financial means of
an ordinary farmer. It is understood, however, that work for
reducing the cost is proceeding in the U.P. Planning Research and
Action Institute, Lucknow.

Only when a cheap and easily-operated cattle-dung gas plant
has been invented or when a cheap and plentiful supply of firewood
in rural areas is available, will the farmyard manure be diverted
from the village hearth to the village field. There are several fast-
growing trees which bear the botanical names of *Casuarina equi-
setifolia, Eucalyptus citriodora, Cassia siamea, Moringa teragosperma,
Ingaldulcis, Prosopis juliflora, Prosopis spicigera, Acacia catechu*
and *Acacia arabica* and its variant, *Acacia arabica var cupressi-
formis* and which could, after waiting five years for them to grow,
supply the needed fuel. Village Panchayats could maintain a grove
of any of the trees or each peasant might have a few trees on his
holding or the boundaries of his fields. Because of their deep-rooted
system *Acacias* do not compete with farm crops for nutrition
in the upper layers of the soil and can tap the sub-soil water, and
therefore, thrive on *usar* (alkaline) lands. Their feather-like leaves
do not shade crops so as to reduce their yields. All the three *Acacias*,
the two *Prosopis'* and the *Cassia* are members of the leguminous
family of trees which grow nodules on their roots and fix nitrogen.
Therefore, they have an additional advantage of adding to soil
fertility and rendering unculturable land culturable. The *Casuarina*
and the *Eucalyptus* are non-leguminous. But they, too, have an
advantage besides providing fuel : green shoots of *Casuarina*

[22] "Utilization of *Gobar Gas*", in the *Pioneer*, dated March 11, 1962.

may be used as fodder for cattle, and *Eucalyptus* can yield oil. The *Butea frondosa* and *Aegle marmelos* are two other trees which, though not fast-growing, are suitable for planting on alkaline lands, and yield good fuel wood. The former grows wild and also serves to reclaim the alkaline *usars :* the latter yields fruits which can be used for various purposes.

Cotton-stalks could make another alternative. If we can persuade every peasant, where climate does not stand in his way, to grow, at least, one-third or one-half of an acre of cotton on his farm, as he used to when the British conquered the country, and introduce or re-introduce *charkha* in every village home, it will, in addition to fuel, give employment to his women-folk, employment to the blacksmith, the carpenter, the carder, the weaver, the dyer, etc. and save money, which the peasant would have spent on purchasing mill-made cloth from the market. Also, cotton-seeds that will be available will serve as, perhaps, the best cattle-feed, especially for the buffaloes.

Arhar and indigo stalks are yet two other good substitutes for wood. Also, tapioca stalks can serve as fuel, just as in Japan and South-East Asia.

We will also have to have new hearths or *choolhas* for our villagers—*choolhas* which will utilise all the heat, all the energy that is generated from the fuel. Today, much of this energy goes waste.[22a] Indeed, economy of fuel must be made a national slogan—a slogan of as big an importance as any other, just as it is in Japan.

Besides the cattle-dung, cattle urine is also rich in plant nutrients. Voelcker had said as long ago as in 1893 that "the value of urine is not only not fully appreciated, but is actually unknown to a large number of cultivators."[23] The position remains practically the same today. Little or no effort has so far been made to utilise this important source of manure.

In addition to cattle and buffaloes there were 110 million live-

---

[22a] According to a recent study of the energy requirements of South India, made by the National Council of Applied Economic Research, "80 per cent of the energy available to the Indian economy is dissipated in the form of waste heat ; only 20 per cent is converted to work . . . . In the case of non-commercial fuels like cow-dung and fire-wood (*sic*), 85 per cent is wasted"—The *National Herald*, Lucknow, dated January 9, 1963.

[23] *Report on the Improvement of Indian Agriculture*, p. 123.

stock in India in 1961, consisting of sheep, goats, horses, ponies, mules, donkeys, camels and pigs which are also a source of organic manure. So also is poultry.

When they die or are slaughtered, animals provide carcasses which are a source of material that could significantly contribute to increased agricultural production. Horns of animals contain 15 per cent of nitrogen. They are all exported at present. Dried blood produced from blood of fallen animals, contains 8 to 14 per cent of nitrogen. Existing slaughter-houses in the country could make available some 10,000 tons of this source of organic manure. Steamed bone meal contains 25 per cent of phosphoric acid, and is very useful for acidic soils. The fallen animals can provide 1.1 million tons of bone every year. But today hardly 20 per cent are collected, and 75 per cent of these are exported. The problem posed by the high cost of collection and transportation should now be deemed to have been solved by the introduction of the Bone Digester. The digester is not costly, and its working is said not only to be economical but profitable. It can be easily set up in the villages, if necessary, on behalf of the *Gaon Panchayats*.

Human excreta or night-soil is another source of organic manure. The Chinese who are greatly manure-minded, regard—and rightly regard—night-soil as property which has to be cherished rather than as waste material which may be thrown away. Josue De Castro comments on this trait of the Chinese thus:

The dependence of the Chinese people on human wastes is so complete that along the roads in certain remote parts of the country the traveller finds special pavilions where suggestive, poetical inscriptions invite him to rest awhile, and leave his small, personal contribution of organic matter in the receptacle provided, for the sake of the regional soil. The same traveller may be amazed as he approaches the cities to see the belts of greenery that girdle them. This wealth of vegetation is owing to the abundance of fertilizer in the cities; the sale of this material is actually one of their chief sources of income.[24]

Calculated at the rate of 11 lbs. of nitrogen which human excreta or waste expelled from the body of one person, on the average, produces in a year, 45 crores of people in the Union of India produce 2.25 million tons of nitrogen. This will serve to fertilise 112.5 million acres at 20 kgms. to an acre. We are, however, doing practically

[24] *Geography of Hunger*, 1952, p. 137.

nothing to conserve this source of nitrogen supply. No cheap, simple and easily portable latrine has yet been evolved for the villages.[25] In all cantonments, railway stations and factories, the night-soil is simply burnt and in many a big municipality we are burying it so deep in barren lands that it is lost to the plants for ever. In many a big town near about the sea and rivers we unthinkingly throw it away into the sea or river, incidentally polluting the water and making it injurious both for man and animal. A way, therefore, has to be found to utilise the night-soil, and the best way to do it is to compost it along with other waste material. If it is used in its raw form or administered to crops directly without subjecting it to hygienic processing, it breeds diseases affecting both crops and those who eat them.

Where composting of the excreta is not possible, as it is not in most villages, Mahatma Gandhi suggested that it should be buried in earth no deeper than nine to twelve inches. The way to do it was either to have fixed latrines, with earthen or iron buckets, and empty the contents in properly prepared places from day to day, or to perform the function of easing directly on to the ground dug up in squares. By this method, he went on to say, "the cost of digging is lessened and that of removal avoided altogether or certainly lessened. Add to this the fact that excreta are turned into manure in almost a week's time, for the reason that the bacteria which lie within six or nine inches of the surface of the earth, and the air and the rays of the sun, act upon the excreta and turn them into soft sweet-smelling manure. . . . By burial of the refuse we will be serving the double purpose of promoting the villagers'

[25] The Planning Research and Action Institute of Uttar Pradesh, however, claims to have recently devised a simple, cheap, clean and durable latrine which can be easily fabricated by a village mason after a short training. It consists of four parts—a pan, a water-seal trap, a bent pipe and a dome cover. They are all made of cement or mozaic and cost only Rs. 10 to 16 per set. Another Rs. 12 are needed for installing a latrine and for providing the foundation work. For a family of 5 members it takes about two years' time to fill in one pit. As soon as a pit is full, the dome cover is removed and the connecting pipe, which is a bent one, is shifted to the other side. Another pit is dug and the dome cover is placed over it. The pit which has been filled with sullage is kept covered with earth for about three months. When proper decomposition has taken place the composted faeces can then be taken out and used as manure. It is reported that the device is becoming popular with the villagers.

health[26] and their material condition through the better yield of their crops which the manure must produce" (*vide* the *Harijan*, dated March 1, 1935).

It has been estimated that the nitrogen potential available from the human and animal wastes alone would be more than sufficient to meet the needs of the country. The following table, prepared on the basis of human and livestock census of 1961, shows the total quantities of the various crop nutrients that can be available from these two sources, *but are not utilised today :*

TABLE LIV

CHEMICAL CONTENTS IN HUMAN AND ANIMAL WASTES

(In Million tons)

	Livestock* Waste (Dung and Urine)	Urban compost	Human excreta in rural areas†	Animal bones‡	Total
Nitrogen	3.48	0.044	1.1	..	4.624
Phosphoric Acid	1.14	0.004	0.73	0.149	2.023
Potash	1.50	0.064	..	..	1.564
Total	6.12	0.112	1.83	0.149	8.211

* Here 'Livestock' means only cattle, buffaloes, sheep and goats. The figures of available crop nutrients are based only on availability of 25 per cent dung out of the 60 per cent dung which is not utilised today, and of burnt ashes of another 25 per cent of dung which, unfortunately, will continue to be burnt for a long time to come. Remaining 10 per cent (out of 60 per cent) have been allowed for dung, which, in any case, will remain uncollected.

† Almost all the 360 million people living in rural India (Census, 1961) use open fields as latrines. It is assumed that about half of the crop nutrients contained in the excreta of the total rural population, which are wasted today through exposure to sun, will be available.

‡ The existing livestock population of 337 million may yield about 11 lakh tons of bones in a year, but only 5.5 lakh tons have been taken into account. Two lakh tons, however, are alone collected today.

[26] It is owing to insanitation or bad sanitation, a direct result of practice of easing themselves on the open ground, that an alarmingly large number of our villagers suffer from anaemia and other diseases. Stool surveys conducted by the State Planning Research & Action Institute

The total net area sown in the country amounts to about 325 million acres. Even if the entire area requires to be fully manured, an amount of about 31.0 lbs. per acre of nitrogen would be available from the human and animal wastes in addition to what our soils are getting today. 'Lightning discharges also,' says Dr. P. C. Bansil, 'unite nitrogen and oxygen to form oxides of nitrogen which combine with the moisture in the air and are washed down with the rain. This adds another 5 to 7 lbs. of nitrogen per acre to the soil annually from the atmosphere' (p. 114).

Dr. P. C. Bansil goes on to point out that Sir Albert Howard who had studied waste products of agriculture came to the conclusion that if all such waste could be well composted, the fields of India would be supplied with manure as required and yet leave enough material over to allow for the manufacture of the well-known *kandas* (cow-dung cakes) for fuel.[27]

Oil-cake is an important source of concentrated hygienic nitrogen, but its supply can be expanded only slightly and the cost of manuring cereal crops with this is prohibitive. The use of oil-cakes for manurial purposes would otherwise also seem to be a waste of the fats and proteins contained in them. Therefore, it would be advisable to use only non-edible cakes, like *neem mahua* and castor.

As a source of nitrogen, green manures, however, have distinct possibilities of rapid expansion. Crops like sun-hemp (*sanai*) and *Sesbania aculeata* (*dhaincha*) which grow quickly, make ideal manure nearly in all areas where rainfall is something like 30 inches or more. Where sun-hemp seed is not available, or as an alternative, other leguminous crops like *moong*, *guar* and cowpea, can be used. The crop has to be ploughed into the soil after the onset of the monsoon. It adds to the soil almost as much fertility per acre as 75 to 125 maunds of cow-dung manure. (During the monsoon season, the legumes will also serve as cover crops which will protect the soil from erosion.)

"In a major portion of the *rabi* areas, wheat fields are kept

at Chinhat in Uttar Pradesh revealed that out of 210 persons examined, 150 were found infected. Of these 159, 25 had more than one infection. Cases in which E. Histolytica responsible for dysentry was found numbered 16, and those in which hook-worms were found numbered 125.

[27] Louis E. Howard, *Sir Albert Howard in India*, London, 1953, p. 208, referred to in Dr. P. C. Bansil's *India's Food Resources and Population*, Bombay, 1958, p. 101.

fallow in the *kharif* season. Green manure in such cases," says Dr. P. C. Bansil[28], "can be raised and ploughed in time by the middle of August. Where maize precedes wheat, the green manure can be inter-cropped. For this purpose, a relatively slow-growing green manure crop like *Aeschynomene americana*[29] which is succulent and able to withstand heavy monsoon rains, seems to be better suited than the more common green manure crops."

Green manure crops are, no doubt,better suppliers of humus than other sources, but the main practical objection to growing them is that it involves expenditure in terms of time, labour and seed, and also removes moisture required for the main crop. Also, a green manure crop cannot be fitted into the time-table of double crop lands. And land in India being scarce, we have to so plan things that, as far as possible, we are able to utilise every inch of our land in both the seasons for one crop or another. Such green manures, therefore, whether from trees, shrubs or plants, have to be developed as do not compete with crops for space or soil moisture. Border planting is the obvious way out. Successful experiments to this end have been carried out at the Agricultural Research Stations of Koilpatti and Aduthurai in the State of Madras. The choice of such shrubs is dictated by their adaptability to local conditions, high drought resistance and absence of adverse root effect on the adjoining crop or crops. An additional advantage of the shrubs discovered by these stations consists in the fact that they require or can prosper in a lower rainfall, *viz.* from 20 to 30 inches a year.

In the Madras State, confidently asserts[30] Shri M. S. Sivaraman, I.C.S., Adviser, Programme Administration, Planning Commission (formerly Director of Agriculture, Madras), on every holding, irrespective of its size, it is possible to produce the complete requirements of organic manure by way of composts for use on dry lands, and green manure for use on irrigated lands by border planting of green manure plants or shrubs, perennial or annual—without in any way affecting the usual crops. Suitable shrubs and green manure plants can, in actual fact, be developed to cover or suffice for every field in every village in the country in two to three years

[28] An article entitled "Food for Soil" in the *AICC Economic Review*, dated July 1, 1959.

[29] Known as Joint Vetch in English and *Sola* or *Shola* in Bengali.

[30] "If Each Field Grows Its Manure" by M. S. Sivaraman, I.C.S., published in the *Pioneer* of May 20, 1958.

from small nucleus materials. The border planting does not require any expenditure of money and all that is required is an earnest effort to raise the shrubs on a pre-determined plan. Says Shri M. S. Sivaraman :[31]

While it takes about 3 years to set up a fertilizer factory costing Rs. 18 crores and involving a capital outlay of about Rs. 23 per acre of crop manured, plus Rs. 16 per acre every year towards the cost of fertilizer, organic manures for an acre of paddy or wheat field can be grown in 4 to 6 weeks with the help of seeds raised in one line in the preceding season along a portion of the borders of the field from a nucleus packet costing 5 *naya paise*.

As for compost: there is a nutritional cycle (खाद्य-चक्र) in Nature, without maintenance whereof Mother Earth will refuse to yield any crops at all. Nature has so ordained that whatever the earth produces is the nutrition (खाद्य) of all living things including man, but whatever part of this nutrition is left unutilised and, therefore, rejected by the body of man, beast, bird, or insect, is the nutrition of Mother Earth, which had, in the process of producing nutrition for the animal world, got exhausted and become hungry. If this night-soil and farmyard waste are composted (along with dead vegetation), that is, properly treated, and returned to the earth, the nutritional cycle becomes complete, and our fields will never disappoint us and will continue giving us an ever-enduring supply of food. One really becomes tongue-bound at the wisdom of our ancestors who gave the name of खाद (nutrition) to the farmyard and other organic waste, in fact, any kind of manure or fertiliser that is, or should be, fed to the fields regularly.

Mahatma Gandhi laid great stress on composting. The art of composting consists in collection and admixture of vegetable, animal and human wastes off the area farmed, into heaps or pits, and providing such conditions as will allow microbial action in the waste material by means of air and moisture. Compost thus prepared contains a wealth of nutrients and organisms essential for plant growth. Composting turns weeds and dead vegetation, human and animal wastes, into an asset. It improves the structure of the soil, helps soil hold more moisture, increases crop yields and improves the quality of the crops.

[31] "Why Organic Manures ?" published in the *AICC Economic Review*, dated November 15, 1958.

Writing of the secret of the successful agriculture the Chinese have practised for more than forty centuries now, Sir Albert Howard says :

The Chinese peasant has hit on a way of supplying his fields with humus by the device of making compost. Compost is the name given to the result of any system of mixing and decaying natural wastes in a heap or a pit so as to obtain a product resembling what the forest makes on its floor: this product is then put on the fields and is rich in humus. The Chinese pay great attention to the making of their compost. Every twig, every dead leaf, every unused stalk is gathered and every bit of animal excreta and the urine, together with all the wastes of the human population, are incorporated. The device of a compost heap is clever. By treating this part of the revolution of the Wheel as a special process, separated from the details of cultivation, time is gained, for the wastes mixed in a heap and kept to the right degree of moisture decay very quickly, and successive dressings can be put on the soil, which thus is kept fed with just what it needs : there is no pause while the soil itself manufactures from the raw wastes the finished humus. On the contrary, every thing being ready and the humus being regularly renewed at frequent intervals the soil is able to feed an uninterrupted succession of plants, and it is a feature of Chinese cultivation that one crop follows another without a pause ; indeed, crops usually overlap, the ripe crops being skilfully removed by hand from among the young growing plants of the succeeding planting or sowing. In short, what the Chinese farmer really does is ingeniously to extend his area. He, so to say, rolls up the floor of the forest and arranges it in a heap. The great processes of decay go on throughout that heap, spreading themselves over the whole of the internal surface of the heap, that is, over the whole of the surface implied in the juxtaposition of every piece of waste against every other. He also overcomes the smallness of the superficial area of his holding by increasing the internal surface of the pore spaces of his soil. This is what matters from the point of view of the crop—the maximum possible area on which the root hairs can collect water and food materials for the green leaf. To establish and to maintain this maximum pore space there must be abundant humus, as well as a large and active soil population.[32]

This is, however, old China ; under the Communist dispensation everything including the art and practice of agriculture has been changed.

The place of humus or organic manure in the scheme of agricul-

[32] *Farming and Gardening for Health or Diseases*, by Sir Albert Howard, Faber & Faber, London, pp. 46-47.

ture[33] and the utility of compost in improving the soil and its yield, will be easily appreciated once we understand the fundamental truth that every form of life in nature is dependent not only upon other living forms, but also upon dead-tissues of older forms. Edward H. Faulkner quotes Paul B. Sears as saying in *Deserts on the March* (Norman, University of Oklahoma Press, 1935) :[34]

The face of the earth is a grave-yard, and so it has always been. To earth each living thing restores when it dies that which has been borrowed to give form and substance to its brief day in the sun. From earth, in due course, each new living being receives back again a loan of that which sustains life. What is lent by earth has been used by countless generations of plants and animals now dead and will be required by countless others in the future.

However, after all that has been said about the utility of organic manures, as is contended by the advocates of chemical fertilisers, a careful examination will reveal that while their extensive use will, at best, help conserve soil fertility, it will not raise it—which is what should be our aim. Application of organic manures, which consist of, or are prepared from, human, animal or plant wastes and green manures or agricultural wastes, symbolises only a return to the soil of matter or nutrients already taken out of it by the plants. It amounts to compensating or making up the net loss to the soil bank, and serves merely to stabilise the soil fertility at its existing level. Even this return or compensation is not, and cannot be, complete because of the impracticability of collecting and applying to the soil all these wastes or manures at an economic cost.

Attempts must, therefore, be made to provide the soil with plant nutrients, i.e., nitrogen, phosphorus and potash from some other source or sources. Artificial fertilisers—it is contended—constitute one such source. Most agricultural scientists regard artificial fertilisers not merely as a supplementary to, but a substitute for organic manures.

We, do not, however, agree with these arguments in their entirety. Organic wastes or green manures contain much more than what they receive merely from the soil : the atmosphere also is a store-

[33] As will appear later, organic manure of any kind, particularly of the bulky kind, not only recoups the soil that may be depleted or exhausted by crops, but also helps maintain or conserve it best.

[34] *Ploughman's Folly*, Michael Joseph, 1951, p. 16.

house of equal importance from which plants draw their sustenance. Legumes draw two-thirds of nitrogen from the atmosphere and non-legumes, though they are not able to fix any atmospheric nitrogen, draw carbon, hydrogen and oxygen from the atmosphere, which also make a contribution to agricultural production. Also, organic manure is not merely a combination of nitrogen, phosphorus and potash : it is something more. Elements present in an organic manure which make foodgrains grown in a field fertilized with such manure, more tasty and health-giving than those grown in a field fertilised with artificials, cannot all be detected in a laboratory or supplied by a factory of chemicals. (Even if they are, our farmers have not the financial resources to obtain them, or the technical ability to use them.)

Further, as we have already seen in Chapter VI, the use of pure or unmixed mineral fertilisers may be risky unless they are mixed with large quantities of organic manure. Nor can or should they be used in areas which depend entirely on rainfall unless the rains are well distributed and average 30 inches and over, and such areas are few. Further—and this is the biggest limiting factor—the quantity of artificial fertiliser available in the country is not sufficient even for one-third of present irrigated area of about 62 million acres or so.

Shri M.S. Sivaraman, I.C.S., Adviser, Programme Administration, Planning Commission, who himself sees nothing wrong in the use of chemical fertilisers, would like the controversy about the comparative utility of the organic manures and inorganic fertilisers to be viewed from a practical angle. He contends that the controversy is largely academic and irrelevant in the context of our conditions. As practical men interested in increasing the agricultural production of our country without loss of time, we should, says Shri Sivaraman, address ourselves immediately to development of organic manures :

Controversy about the role of inorganic fertilisers and organic manures in agricultural production is unnecessary, if it is realized that the former are only a few stages nearer the end product of assimilation in plant nutrition. Nature produces the same products from organic manures through millions of micro-flora found in every tea-spoon of soil. Inorganic fertilisers and organic manures differ like processed from natural food : both are good and both can be bad if improperly used. The choice between the two depends not so much on their merits as plant nutrients, as on extraneous factors like scope for rapid development and for general adoption by the cultivators in their present economic set-up. The difficulties of setting apart adequate internal and external resources to step up production of fertilizers in the country or to import them from outside, have to be viewed against the background of available local alternatives in the form of cheaper organic manures. The general poverty of cultivator, his inability to go in for expensive fertilisers, the absence of adequate credit facilities, the distinct possibilities of large-scale development of organic manure for every field through a new approach that has clearly shown its merits in Southern States, are also material consideration which will have to guide our policy.[35]

Peat deposits are yet another source which is practically untapped. Says Dr. P. V. Mane :

Amongst the natural rich sources of humus, peat deposits which are common in Kerala, take the lead. Peat is a partly decomposed organic material formed under the semi-waterlogged conditions of what are known as moors or bogs. It is half-way towards the formation of coal. Natural peat, however, cannot be used as such and has its disadvantages. Its organic matter would decompose too slowly in an untreated state to be a good manure. Peat has, therefore, to be ground, dressed and treated with certain chemicals to render it neutral in reaction (against its natural reaction which is acidic) and made water-soluble to a high degree. It needs to be stabilised or replenished, if necessary, so as to contain fixed quantities of nitrogen, phosphoric acid and potash which will make it a completely balanced organic humus fertiliser.

Such a humus fertiliser will be, in its effect on the soil, at least eight to ten times better than farmyard manure or compost. It will be a soil conditioner as also a plant-feeder and will be free from weed seeds, carriers of plant diseases, germs of human or cattle diseases, and will be easier to transport and apply in the fields. It will also be economical in cost and may prove highly useful as an ingredient in fertiliser mixtures.[36]

There are also other sources of humus, *e.g.* sullage and sewage water, silt from rivers and tanks, hyacinth, and other water-weeds, in fact, all kinds of plant and herb waste—which are derived from sources other than land under actual cultivation. There is as yet little practical experience of the sullage and sewage water so that no firm statement can be made, but remarkable effects of their

[35] *Op. cit.*
[36] "Humus from Peat", *Hindustan Times,* New Delhi, dated September 7, 1961.

application on improvement of soils, especially *usar* lands, and in increasing crop yields have been observed. The silt was in common use as manure some two generations ago, but not so now. Its possibilities have to be investigated. Hyacinth and other water-weeds which infest tanks and ponds in most parts of north-western Uttar Pradesh, gradually filling them up, however, make good compost. Whether the process will pay economically has, however not yet been established.

Just as water and manure, seed is a resource of an agriculturist. If better or improved seed is sown, it will certainly give improved yields. High-yielding varieties have, therefore, to be found out and, since improved varieties have no value unless used by the cultivators, a vigorous effective seed multiplication and distribution programme has to be undertaken. Research and extension have to go hand in hand.

As already noticed in Chapter VI, crop diseases and pests are, to a large degree, the consequence of artificial fertilisers. If organic manures alone are applied, plants will grow and remain healthy. Yet when diseases do appear, they have to be controlled and eradicated : so also pests. Amongst the scientific innovations in the field of agriculture, the plant protection measures come only second to fertilisers. Among these measures, importance of control or destruction of field rats cannot be over-estimated. There is said to be a rat population of over 2,400 millions in the country causing an annual damage of over 2.6 million tons of food-grains. Cheap storage accommodation has also to be devised, which will protect agricultural produce against insect, pest and moisture.

Besides water, fertiliser, improved seed and insecticide or pesticide, capital will have to be found to provide pedigree livestock and to provide new equipment to a steadily increasing degree, for example, the simple equipment that the Italian peasant uses for dairying, rice growing, fruit growing and similar activities. Even purchase of hand-operated tools, such as the rotary weeder, pedal thresher, ground-nut decorticators and line seeding planters may require capital which the farmer is not always able to afford.

Further, as an aid to increased agricultural production, an adequate and dependable transportation system is as important as any other facility. It is as necessary to a farmer as to a trader, since without it land cannot always be put to its most advantageous use. To illustrate : it is not profitable for peasant farmers living in far away villages to grow fruits or vegetables if they cannot market their products as soon as they are produced. Also, largely for the same reason, *viz.*, want of cheap transportation facilities, mountain-sides of the Himalayas in North India are being shorn of their forests for farming purposes. The fruits and the timber grown in these parts are worth little because of high transportation costs. Moreover, food stuffs cannot be brought in for the same reason; yet food must be had at any cost and that cost is the erosion of mountain-sides wrongly used for farming, and the filling of stream channels, resulting in the flooding of productive lands in the Indo-Gangetic plains.

The resources or resource facilities that have been mentioned here are indispensable to a farmer. But his production will greatly depend on the way he uses them, that is, on his art. There is great scope for improvement of this art, at least, over most parts of India and among most agricultural communities. Improvement of the farming art or arts obviously means adoption of such improved cultural practices and such judicious use of the given or available resources as will lead or contribute to greater production than today—*greater production without further capital investment*. The improved practices include (*a*) proper tillage of land for preparation of a good seed bed, (*b*) timely sowing and proper sowing, *i.e.* sowing the seed in lines at proper distances or by dibbling, (*c*) timely irrigation, (*d*) adoption of interculture operations for eradication of weeds and conservation of moisture by maintaining proper tilth, (*e*) following a proper rotation of crops including mixed cropping, double cropping and raising green-manure crops.

Besides, adoption of soil and moisture conservation practices through contour bunding and contour sowing on slopes, *mend*-bunding in levelled fields to avoid sheet erosion and to conserve rain water, are also important.

If the farm area as also the skill of the farmer allows it, there is no practice more useful than a scientific or balanced crop rotation. Such rotation helps maintain the fertility of the soil and also ensures better yields in the long run. Evils of monoculture, *viz.*, growing of an exhausting crop year after year, are unfortunately not fully understood. Hardly any other single factor proves so ruinous to the soil fertility as monoculture, especially as being practised by the small paddy or sugarcane growers in certain parts of Uttar Pradesh where holdings are small. There is no attempt to follow any crop rotation wherein a leguminous crop would intervene. If such conditions are allowed to continue any longer, the soil would be rendered barren.

While dealing with the subject of soil exhaustion, it will be advisable to once again emphasize that large agricultural machinery serves to deplete the soil, rather than to improve or conserve it, at least, in our climatic conditions. Tropical sunshine, on the one hand, kills the micro-life in the soil, on which its fertility depends and causes more rapid oxidation of organic matter in the soil than in temperate climates. The torrential rains of the monsoons, on the other, wash away the top soil faster than the more moderate rains of European or Northern countries. If we abolish the bullock and use tractors instead, we will have to apply chemical fertilisers instead of dung or compost, which is the best form of organic matter for fertilising the soil and best means of soil conservation. Thus, with tractors taking the place of bullocks in our agricultural economy, India will soon end up with a desert. We will, therefore, do better to discourage the use of tractors and other large machinery, particularly, on lands which are already under the plough. All that we may do is, where necessary, to develop improved ploughs, harrows, seeders or seed drills, bund formers, and other implements of proved utility many of which can be made by village carpenters and blacksmiths.

In most of our cultivable area, only one crop is grown during the year. According to the figures of 1956-57, only 14.1 per cent of irrigated acreage grew more than one irrigated crop per year. Now, this is a clear waste of our land and water resources. Wherever facilities of irrigation and manuring—and these have to be increased —are available, no field should be left without double cropping. There are examples where farmers raise three to four crops in twelve months.

In areas of uncertain rain-fall or poor productivity, or where double-cropping is not possible, and on small holdings the cultivator can resort to mixed crops so that, in case there is drought or other calamity, one crop may survive or grow better than the other, and the fertility exhausted by one crop may be made up by the other, provided the latter is a leguminous crop. (Before the Britishers arrived on the scene and wanted only unmixed wheat to be exported to their country, our farmers used largely to sow wheat and gram mixed with one another). Some plants are deep-rooted and draw most of their food from far below the surface, while others have spreading roots which feed close to the surface. By mixing two such crops, both can thrive without interfering with each other. Even three crops may be grown in a field at a time, e. g. a crop like maize whose plant goes straight upwards, a second crop of small creepers as that of a pulse, and a third root crop in the space not required by the other two. Mixed cropping can, thus, serve, at least, two purposes : it acts as a sort of insurance against the vicissitudes of weather, and preserves, if not increases, the fertility of the soil. The combinations to suit the differing soils and climates have to be suggested by our research workers.

Lastly, there is a measure or an innovation which, although properly falling within the sphere of land reform, yet is mentioned here because it will help better utilize all the means of increased agricultural production suggested in this chapter. It is known as Consolidation of Holdings.

Land-holdings in India, as in many another country, lie divided into tiny plots scattered all over the arable area of the village, because of the desire of elders, in the historic past, to prevent some farmers from having all good land and others all inferior land, or land adapted only to one kind of crop. The disadvantages of the system, however, are so great that agrarian economists throughout the world have regarded consolidation—consolidation of scattered fields belonging to the same owner in a single block, or at any rate, in a smaller number of parcels than today—as the very first step towards improvement of agriculture.

As a result of consolidation, control of drainage and supply of irrigation water would become more easy, leading to better utilisation of land. It is not economical for a farmer to dig a well for every field, nor is it always possible for several farmers to co-operate in digging and using the same well. Where canal and tube-well irrigation facilities are available, the present system of scattered fields leads to disputes over timing of delivery or demand by the farmer, and also in great wastage of water which has necessarily to be carried through long channels to reach the various fields belonging to an individual.

If land belonging to one farmer were all in one piece, barriers such as fences, hedges or even ditches could be erected to obtain privacy and prevent trespassing by man and animal, thieving and gleaning. Control of pests such as rodents, insects and locusts would also be less difficult. Standing crops will thus be better tended and protected.

Disputes over boundary lines, or right to irrigation and drainage, and those arising from mistakes in land records which are facilitated by the multiplicity of small plots, will have almost been entirely eliminated, thus making litigation a thing of the past. Bullocks, which are the main capital of the farmer, would be better utilised, inasmuch as time that is wasted in taking them from one tiny plot to another, will have been saved.

Human labour, too, would be employed more efficiently and economically. It is not only the time of the bullocks that is wasted today, but that of the farmers and labourers also, if any, in going from one plot to another. To quote figures from Uttar Pradesh by end of February, 1962, 1,62,93,809 plots had been consolidated into 28,27,940 chaks,[36a] giving an average of 5.76 plots in a chak. In Domariaganj, a tahsil of Basti district where fragmentation had reached extreme limits, there were twenty-five plots on the average possessed by a farming family, with a total area of slightly over 3.0 acres of land between them. This means that the area of an average plot was 14 biswas or 600 square yards or so. After consolidation, the twenty-five plots that a family holds were reduced to two.[37] The quantum of animal and human labour that would be saved, can be imagined.

After consolidation, the farmer will, in all likelihood, shift his entire agricultural equipment to his chak (चक) or consolidated holding where he will put up a building for his own use and an enclosure for his cattle, stack the bhusa (भूसा) or chaff and cattle fodder, stock the cattle-dung, reserve a piece of land as threshing-floor, and set up a kolhu (कोल्हू) or sugar-cane pressing machine, and from where he will carry on all agricultural operations on his land that now lies compact at his feet and within his ken. He will be able to exercise far better supervision.

Thus, consolidation of holdings results in increasing the productivity of all the three factors of production in agriculture—land, capital and labour. Experience has proved that the per acre production goes up considerably.

"However, while it is easy to chronicle the beneficent results

[36a] Chak is a Hindi word for a block or compact area.

[37] 22,74,733 plots owned by some 90,000 families, covering an area of 2,84,300 acres, have been consolidated into 1,81,398 chaks.

of consolidation," says Malcolm Darling, "it is most difficult to produce them. For, everyone has to be satisfied and all conflicting interests reconciled. The ignorant have to be enlightened and the stubborn conciliated. The poor, the weak and the speechless have to be as much regarded as the rich, the strong and the vocal. Moreover, technical difficulties abound, and underlying all is the peasant's passionate love of his land with the jealousy of neighbours that passion breeds. In such circumstances, the work must be slow. The marvel is that it is done at all."[38]

The consolidation operations are already under way in several States, and good work has been done. But the entire arable area in the plains has to be covered. When this has been done, masonry wells sunk in the consolidated holdings with Persian wheels fitted to them, and the farmers taught the value of preserving the cattle dung and composting it with human and vegetable wastes, the battle for food for our increasing millions, would have been more than won.

While speaking of increased agricultural production, although the farmers' need for credit has been mentioned, we will do well to further stress and elaborate it. Owing to a difference in the nature of agriculture, on the one hand, and industry and commerce, on the other, there is a difference in the rate of turnover of capital in the two groups of undertakings. The industrialist and the trader turn their capital over several times a year; the farmer, on the other hand, requires several years to turn his capital over. Industry and commerce operate daily, but agriculture has to wait for months and, in some cases, even years before it can realise a return on expenditure. The so-called economic lag in agriculture, i.e., the period during which costs have to be met before the product is finally marketed and yields a return, is long in comparison with the lag in industry and commerce. This lag represents a period of expense and, therefore, a period of strain on the farmer's purse. Owing to the slow capital turn-over in agriculture, the farmer requires credit for comparatively long periods and the source of credit, therefore, that suits the industrialist and trader, may not, and in fact does not, suit him. The result is that the industrialist and the trader can more readily obtain financial facilities from banks, other financial institutions and investors than farmers can.

[38] *The Punjab Peasant : in Prosperity and in Debt*, p. 253.

The farmer's credit problem furthermore is accentuated by the low return which he earns on his capital. The combination of the two factors—slow turnover of, and low return on capital—demands that the farmer must be assured of cheap credit for a comparatively long period. It is for these reasons that Governments all the world over have deemed it fit to take special legislative measures for agricultural financial requirements, especially, long-term and intermediate credit, or, the farmers themselves have through cooperation tried to satisfy their credit requirements. In India, however, neither the state nor the co-operative movement has come up to the people's expectations or demands of the situation:

The percentages evidenced by the table below give an indication of the extent to which the main agencies of rural credit severally contribute to the total borrowings of the cultivators:

TABLE LV

SOURCES OF RURAL CREDIT IN INDIA

Credit Agency	Proportion of borrowings from each agency to the total borrowings of cultivators (per cent)
1. Government	3.3
2. Cooperatives	3.1
3. Commercial Banks	0.9
4. Relatives	14.2
5. Landlords	1.5
6. Agricultural Moneylenders	24.9
7. Professional Moneylenders	44.8
8. Traders and Commission Agents	5.5
9. Others	1.8

SOURCE : *Summary of the Report of All-India Rural Credit Survey* (1955), Vol. II, p. 5.

Supply of state credit in the form of *taqavi* met only 3.3 per cent of the need; the co-operatives and the banks between them, 4.0 per cent. It is true that, of the needs for which credit is required, resource facilities like water, manure and seeds are the most important, and the state has constructed canals and reservoirs and sunk tube-wells as also opened stores for supply of seeds and ferti-lisers. The resources of the state, however, are meagre and its economic operations are often costlier and necessarily hamstrung by rules and regulations. State aid in all these spheres, therefore, will have to be supplemented to a far greater extent by co-operative action on the part of the peasant farmers themselves. The contri-bution of 'cooperatives' to the credit needs of the people in 1955, *viz.* 3.1 per cent, has gone up several times since then, but as will appear later, it is not genuine co-operative credit.

It will be a mistake to believe that cooperation does not suit the genius or mental attitudes of our people. (It is only when a peasant is convinced that cooperation, which, in fact, is merely so-called, but is another name for merger and would deprive him of his indi-vidual rights in property that it becomes abhorrent to him.) A village, as our long history bears out, was always a stronger moral unit than a factory is. The sense of the community was a vital thing among the peasantry, providing a natural foundation for collaboration or co-operative action. So, in spite of agriculture being the most individualistic industry, the peasant in old India, as in some other countries, has inherited and kept up certain co-operative instincts and traditions of neighbourly collaboration. Helping each other, whether it was a matter of ploughing, bringing in the harvest, building a house or even preparing a girl's dowry 'chest', was a matter of course, a tradition, not an organised arrangement. The cost and responsibility of sugar-cane pressing, well or tank irrigation, provi-sion for drinking water, drainage, cultural centres, fairs, etc., have been shared in common from time immemorial. Cultivation of crops according to a prearranged plan and their protection from boars and other wild animals are still common features of some of our villages. Neighbourly collaboration has taken various other forms also : such as lending each other a bullock or a pair of bullocks; exchanging a day of work for other services, etc. Within a better and consciously-planned organisation, this mutual cooperation or collaboration might be still further extended and developed.

Differences or disputes amongst the villagers were settled mostly by discussion on a basis of equity guided by the village elders, the priest or the teacher, again, as a tradition and out of the self-same sense of being one community : hardly, if ever, was a matter put to vote. People versed in political economics make much of decisions by majority vote. The ancient Indian village offers a possibly higher alternative, if we believe in Government by consent, in decisions by the general sense of the community. This procedure left no sense of bitterness in the defeated party and no sense of elation in the victorious. In fact, there was no victor and no vanquished. If we want to make our village panchayats a success, the present system of decisions by majority vote will have to be greatly modified, if not abandoned altogether.

To revert to agricultural co-operatives : they can be made to serve every need and every aspect of rural life. They may, in particular, engage in one or more of the following functions :

(*i*) receiving deposits and making loans for reasonable business and personal requirements,

(*ii*) improving agricultural lands and water facilities,

(*iii*) processing, storing and transporting goods produced by its members,

(*iv*) making available rural industrial facilities,

(*v*) insuring property of its members against damage or loss and reducing other uncertainties confronting farmers,

(*vi*) making available those common services which will improve the social and living conditions, culture and health of the agricultural community,

(*vii*) conducting educational activities relating to co-operative associations and farming techniques,

(*viii*) organising collective labour, or *shramdan* to meet collective needs like building a road in one place and irrigation channel, or improving drainage elsewhere,

(*ix*) improving marketing facilities, that is, facilities for purchase of requirements (including improved seeds, improved agricultural implements or, if necessary, even machines, cattle-feeds, scientific manures, or fertilisers, if they at all need them, insecticides and domestic supplies like cloth, oil, salt, matches, soap, etc.) and sale of produce.

It is in the improvement of marketing facilities—according to Adam Smith, "the greatest of all agricultural improvements—that a co-operative society offers its members the technical advantages of a large-scale undertaking in the largest measure."

Although the small farmer labours under various disadvantages, yet experience has shown these to be commercial more than technical. He can hold his own in the field of production. It is when he enters the market that he finds it difficult to stand up to the big man. The profit that he might have gained in production is often lost in the selling. His disadvantage arises from his weak bargaining power which is fully exploited by the middleman. The fall in prices which usually occurs at harvest time represents the cultivator's inability to retain possession of the harvested crop. In the marketing of every agricultural commodity the spread between the price paid to the grower and that paid by the final consumer is very wide—to the injury of the grower—and one of the fruitful methods of enhancing the income of the grower is to rationalise the distributive trade by eliminating some, at least, of the swarm of intermediaries who render no other service except to give a push to the commodity. Co-operative marketing alone is the solution : it strengthens the economic position of an individual grower and enables him "to save time for other duties, to enjoy a wider market, to sell a properly-graded product and thereby gain the benefit of a better price, to obtain the necessary financial facilities which will enable him to spread his sales over a period of 12 months instead of disposing of his products immediately after harvest and, finally, therefore, to enjoy a wider market also in respect of time."[38a]

Cooperation is primarily the small man's instrument. It has been attended with special success among the small farmers of the densely-populated countries of Europe.

With all their advantages, however, establishment of co-operative societies is not an easy task. In India till now, we have been treating the co-operative movement as a subject or policy fit to be executed through a Government department : it has not been a people's movement at all. Government, particularly, since the Congress Resolution at Nagpur in January, 1959, has begun fixing targets for setting up societies, to be fulfilled within a given time and Government officials, in order to win position or approbation of their superiors, are busy organising societies which exist on paper only. As said earlier in Chapter X, you cannot fix targets where the will and volition of other people are concerned. A Government can build a road or a building or accomplish any other physical target within a given time, but not set up an organisation which requires willing cooperation of the would-be members for its formation and successful working. The ideological confusion from which the movement suffers, will be apparent when one finds that while, on one hand, official initiative is expected to set up the co-operatives, on the other, talk of freeing them from official control goes on. Now, this

[38a] *Economics of Agriculture* (1937), AP Van Der Post, p. 399.

is self-contradiction. If co-operatives come into being under official inspiration, they will wither away as soon as the life-giving force is withdrawn. Mahatma Gandhi commented as follows on the failure of rural development programme of Mr. Brayne, a well-meaning Deputy Commissioner of Gurgaon in the Punjab in the British days, which became apparent when he was transferred from the district :

The reason for the failure of Mr. Brayne's experiment for village re-making is not far to seek. The reform came not from within but was super-imposed from without. Mr. Brayne made use of his official position to put as much pressure as he could upon his subordinates and upon the people themselves, but he could not carry conviction by force, and conviction so essential to success was lacking. Mr. Brayne thought that results would convince the people. But that is not how reform works. The reformer's faith is strewn not with roses but with thorns, and he has to walk warily. He can but limp, dare not jump. Mr. Brayne was impatient and wanted to cover a long distance in one stride and he failed.[39]

Cooperation has to come about as a result of an urge from within the farmers themselves—as an instrument of satisfaction or fulfilment of a common need of theirs. Also, its success presupposes a consciousness and a sense of enlightened self-interest informed by a sense of public duty, that are not yet very common in our villagers. So, the co-operative societies that are now springing up under the official whip like mushrooms all over the country-side, do not pulsate with life. They will soon degenerate into instruments of the officials themselves, their props and stooges in the village.[39a] Communists in foreign countries who have no faith in democracy and free elections, have exploited co-operative slogans in order, partly, to beguile their own peasantry but, largely, to deceive the outside world. It would seem our governments also, in their anxiety for rapid economic development of the country, have fallen prey to Communist propaganda.

The relevant part of the Nagpur Resolution says :

The organisation of the village should be based on village *panchayats* and village co-operatives, both of which should have adequate powers and resources to discharge the functions allotted

---

[39] *Young India*, dated November 14, 1929.

[39a] A conference convened by the Reserve Bank recently has gone on record with the finding that members of co-operatives are mostly "passive co-operators and unscrupulous self-seekers".

to them. A number of village co-operatives may form themselves into a union. All permanent residents of the village, whether owning land or not, should be eligible for membership of the village co-operative which should promote the welfare of its members by introducing progressive farming methods and improved techniques of cultivation, developing animal husbandry and fishery and encouraging cottage industries. In addition to providing credit and discharging other servicing function, it will arrange for processing and marketing the agricultural produce of the farmers and storage and godown facilities for them. Both the panchayat and the co-operative should be spearheads of all developmental activities in the village and, more specially, should encourage intensive farming with a view to raising the per acre yield of agricultural produce.

The resolution, on the face of it, betrays a wrong approach and raises several doubts. For example, it has been said that 'co-operatives should have adequate resources.' Co-operatives, in a large part, can have only the resources its members can find from their earnings. If so, there is no meaning in using a peremptory language such as the resolution does. If the resources, or an overwhelming part of them, are to be found by Government, then the society will cease to be a co-operative enterprise. And who will do the 'allotting' of functions to a co-operative ? It should be the right of the cooperative itself, and not anybody else's. It is for would-be members and not for Government to decide for what purpose or purposes they want to come together. In the non-communist world, people possessing common interests alone have come together in order to jointly carry on functions which they could not carry on individually or could not carry on so well. The resolution, however, envisages coming together of 'all permanent residents of the village, whether owning land or not.' Such a co-operative will simply not work : economic interests of all the villagers are not common. Further, if the co-operative is to consist of all permanent residents of the village, then why have another organisation in the village, *viz.* the *Gaon Panchayat* consisting of the same membership, at all ? One organisation alone should do for both or all purposes.

Besides, peasants are aware that it is the co-operative farm which was the ultimate goal, wherein they and their lands would both lose their identity. The Nagpur Resolution queered the pitch for service co-operatives when it laid down that 'as a first step, prior to the institution of joint farming, service co-operatives should be organised throughout the country. This stage should be completed within a period of three years.' The farmer is not a fool, however ; he can see through it all. Howsoever illiterate, he cannot be wheedled into treading a path which will lead to a destination where he does not want to arrive at all. The movement for service co-operatives, therefore, labours under a psychological handicap.

The resolution says that the work of organising service co-operatives throughout the country should be completed within three years ending 1961. Now, anybody who runs, or knows anything about our peasantry will outright dismiss the idea as a chimerical one. The co-operative movement in the country was started more than 50 years ago, and we have not yet been able to make much of a success even of purely credit societies. We are afraid the same is likely to be the true of the service co-operatives into which they are being, or have been hastily converted. To state only one reason : they were and are predominantly credit societies and that, too, only in name. In fact, they are either borrowers' societies or Government credit societies. Co-operative credit societies should mean societies where farmers or artisans pool their financial resources. Some of the members make deposits of their surplus earnings with the society and others in need take loans out of these very deposits. But in the societies that are springing into existence as a command performance, the share money is insignificant and deposits not many. A large part of the money comes from the Reserve Bank at the rate of 2 per cent per annum. Members of so-called co-operative societies in the villages have to pay an interest of 8.5 per cent or so for the loans they borrow from them. The difference, viz., 6.5 per cent wasted on administration and other items is a dead loss to the nation. Also, inasmuch as a very considerable proportion of the amount of hundreds of crores of rupees that is being distributed to the farmers all over the country, will not be utilised for productive purposes, most of it will remain unrealised and ultimately will have to be written off. Need for investing capital in our agriculture is universally accepted, and has been recommended in these pages also. But the co-operatives that are being set up to order, are mere make-believes and not the genuine metal. They will do more harm than good. Compared with such co-operative credit, advance of *taqavi* (agricultural loan) directly by Government is a far better and cheaper method.

To the extent the present-day service co-operatives are supplying resource facilities to agriculturists in kind, they are dealing simply

in monopoly goods, that is, goods which are available to co-operatives alone and which private firms or individuals are forbidden to
sell or purchase. Were the latter allowed to compete, the co-operatives will soon go out of business and crumble, perhaps, and, at
least, in some parts of the country, much to the advantage of the
agriculturist.

Co-operative societies to perform the various functions envisaged
in the Nagpur Resolution, are a still far-off cry. It is easier to set
up co-operatives in the industrial and commercial spheres of the
economy, than agricultural. Even in the West, the movement
took birth in the urban centres, and it was only later on that it
slowly spread to the rural areas. Other reasons are not far to seek :
they have already been stated and lie in the deficiency of the human
factor and our social and economic conditions. Co-operatives, in
the sense of real living organisations, will, therefore, take far
longer than three years, and will come about only as an organic,
and not a hot-house growth. In fact, as already said, inasmuch
as they have been hitched to the wagon of the co-operative farms,
even the slow growth warranted by our conditions will be retarded.

Sometimes, even knowledgeable persons in the country are
heard advocating state support of agricultural prices. It is contended that the best of technical and administrative programmes
of agricultural development will not produce the desired result if
prices are allowed to fall to unremunerative levels. In as much
as, owing largely to uncertainties of weather, there is wide fluctua-
tion in yields, agricultural production cannot be adjusted to demand. This peculiarity of agriculture (coupled with the fact that
most of the farm products have a relatively low price elasticity)
is the chief cause of the farmer's poverty. Price manipulation and
guaranteeing of minimum prices to the farmer will, therefore,—
it is argued—help him much more than any other kind of assistance
by the state. The farmer will try to secure the production requisites
or resource facilities, all on his own, once he is assured of a "reasonable" return.

The argument may or may not be theoretically sound but, in
our opinion, any policy of agricultural price support, except for
limited periods and selected products, is unworkable in India. It is
an idea borrowed from the Western countries where this policy
was practised during the two World Wars with great advantage
to agricultural production. It has been practised in times of peace

also in some countries, particularly, in the USA, where the agricultural economy is faced by such over-production and surplus that a whole range of financial contrivances have been devised to maintain farm prices at a level which will provide the farmer with profits, which, in turn, can be spent in purchasing the products of the country's vast industries.

A policy of price support means that funds are transferred from the national exchequer to the pockets of the agricultural community. Now if this community is small in comparison to the general community, as it is in the UK where it constitutes only 5 per cent of the whole population and in the USA where the percentage is only 13, [39b] the policy is workable. The pockets of 95 or 87 per cent of the people can be taxed in order to subsidise the remaining 5 or 13 per cent whose survival is essential in the ultimate interest and welfare of the nation. But if those who have to be subsidised constitute 70 per cent of the people as they do in India, any policy of agricultural price support, in the final analysis, only means that the subsidy in the form of difference between the market price and price guaranteed by the state will be coming, by and large, from their own pockets. The money spent in provision of godowns and transport, payment of salaries of the huge staff that will have to be temporarily raised for this purpose and other over-head expenses, and the wastage of grain that is inevitably involved in storage, will be an unnecessary drain on the lean finances of the country. Also, it is not to be forgotten that in a poor, under-developed country like India, multiplication of government servants who cannot be adequately paid, means multiplication of corruption.

What then is the way out of the low, unremunerative agricultural prices ? There is certainly a way out—and one that should be welcome to us, *viz.*, the agricultural workers have to shift to non-agricultural occupations as they have done in all developed countries. Fall in agricultural prices *not only in a year or two but over some length of time*, means that the agricultural products are being produced in quantities surplus to the needs of the community. Also, 'fall' being a relative term, it means that agricultural prices are low in relation to prices of some other things, that is, non-agricultural goods and services. The most obvious course dictated

---

[39b] In 1962, this percentage was brought down to 10.

by common sense and economic forces, therefore, is for workers from agricultural pursuits with lower incomes to shift to non-agricultural pursuits, or industries and services, with higher incomes. But the danger is that, owing to low mobility of labour and capital employed in agriculture, this obvious course may not be followed, and the economy may find some sort of an equilibrium at a low level of productivity. It is here that or why the mental attitudes of a people are relevant. If the people are determined to raise their living standards and are not content with bare food alone, they will seek non-agricultural employments. And if the society or Government makes available the necessary facilities, *viz.*, steel, energy and the know-how, the country will achieve economic progress with ever accelerating speed. If, on the other hand, the people do not give up their fatalistic attitudes and are content with their *kismet*, nobody will be able to help them, not even the Government with their price support or any other scheme whatsoever. There will be only one alternative left, *viz.*, communism under which, our people must know, there will be little or no individual liberty to choose, refuse or hesitate. For employment in industrial and other non-agricultural enterprises, surplus labour in the villages will be recruited or conscripted in accordance with a plan. The sort of work they will do and the factory or enterprise in which they will work, will be chosen for them by the agents of the all-mighty state.

Also, in the background of our conditions, any talk of parity between agricultural and non-agricultural prices, artificially maintained, is unrealistic.

What is advocated in these pages is a co-operative society as distinct from the liberal Capitalist society as from a collectivist society of Communism—a co-operative society where small men combine amongst themselves and, on the basis of their pooled resources, find the resource facilities which the big man is able to do on the basis of his capital—where all exploiters and middle-men are eliminated, where exploitation is ended, the individuals remain free and their personalities are not merged unidentifiably in a whole.

The distinguished European thinker, count Coundenhove-Kalergi, has suggested the establishment of agricultural co-operatives as a final and lasting solution of all the ills of this war-weary world. Discussing the need for an economic revolution, he observes :

It demands a free economic system and operation. Its aim is the creation of the greatest possible number of *independent existences* bound together by the principle of cooperation. It rejects both economic anarchy and collectivism. Its model is to be found in the agricultural co-operatives, which combine all the advantages of private property with the spirit of brotherhood and reciprocal aid ; they differ as much from the collectivist factory management of the Soviet Kolhoz as they do from the anarchic misery of small isolated peasants without machinery and cooperation.[40]

That is, it is farmers' co-operatives, where the identity both of the farm and the farmer will remain unimpaired, that are needed, not co-operative farms.

[40] *Totalitarian State Against Man.*

CHAPTER TWENTY-ONE

Soil Conservation

Hordes of gullies now remind us,
    We should build our lands to stay ;
And departing leave behind us,
    Fields that have not washed away.
Then when our boys assume the mortgage
    On the land that's had our toil,
They'll not have to ask the question,
    "There's the Farm, but where's the Soil ?"[1]

                                   —Anonymous
                        (With apologies to Longfellow.)

THE LAST chapter was concerned with one of the two highly important objectives in agriculture, *viz.*, improved crop yields, which is immediate. This chapter deals with the second objective *viz.*, maintenance of soil which is long range, but closely related to our ultimate welfare.

Any nation's soil resources constitute its greatest wealth, rather the very basis of its existence. "In reality all life on the land— vegetation, trees, insects, animals and human beings—depends on the existence and healthy condition of only about eight inches of top-soil, the part that contains the soil bacteria, fungi, other microscopic forms of life, and earth worms."[1a] Failure to realise the need of soil maintenance has led many a people to ruin and convert many a prosperous country into a howling desert. Exhaustion of soil fertility is, in fact, one of the major causes of cultural decline of a country, the other three being warfare, decline of personal character, and urbanization.

As pointed out by Jacks and Whyte in Chapter VIII of their work, *The Rape of the Earth*,[1b] there are two kinds of erosion— 'vertical' and 'lateral'. The former involves the washing out of the soluble parts of the soil and the latter mainly the washing (or

[1] *Soil Erosion and its control* by Quincy Claude Ayres, C. E., First Edition, Fifth Impression, published by McGraw-Hill Book Company Inc., New York and London, 1936.
[1a] *Which Way Lies Hope ?* (1957), p. 7.
[1b] Faber and Faber, 24 Russell Square, London.

451

blowing) away of the insoluble parts. 'Vertical' erosion is always liable to occur in humid regions where the movement of water in the soil is predominantly downwards but not in arid regions where water is drawn upwards by evaporation. 'Lateral' erosion is very liable to occur on unprotected soils in arid regions because the soil pulverises and loses its water-absorbing power when it dries out. Both 'vertical' and 'lateral' erosion occur in the humid tropics owing to the effects of extreme heat and torrential rain.

Perhaps, there is nothing which a man can do to prevent completely the leaching of soluble plant nutrients, salts and minerals, from the soil through natural action of water. Yet its ill-effects can be minimised by adding to the humus of the soil through application of heavy doses of bulky organic manure like farmyard waste and by adopting a regular system of green manuring.

It is, however, lateral erosion which is the most important cause of soil loss. Man has so misused the land that the surface soil, an inch or two of which takes centuries to build, is washed away by water in one rainy season or blown away by wind in one summer. Land is uneven and hence subject to washing where rainfall is heavy and water flows rapidly. In dry areas the soil blows away. These natural phenomena combined with the misuse of land by man, which consists mainly in overcutting, over-grazing and over-ploughing, can cause rapid soil losses. In India these losses are likely to be great, for she has a tropical climate with a combination, over much of its area, of strong sunshine and alternating torrential rains and drought. The ill effects of this sort of climate are heightened after the natural covering of the soil has been removed through its misuse by man. With this covering once removed, nature in the form of wind and water rushes to take its toll.

Wind erosion is specially prominent in tracts covered by soils of single-grained structure. Next to disappearance of vegetation, it is lowering of the sub-soil water table that is responsible for wind erosion. Lowering of the water table results in intense desiccation and consequent loss in soil aggregation, *i.e.* soil texture and humus content. The prevention of this form of erosion has to be sought mostly in improving the structure of the soil through accumulation of humus. Wind erosion of cultivators' land can, therefore, be controlled, again, by adding organic material to the soil through green manuring or application of compost in liberal quantities. Adequate provision of irrigation facilities would undoubtedly be a great help. Denudation of vegetation can be made good, for example, by cultivation of crops like sugar-cane. Most of the active soil blowing or wind erosion can be controlled only by vegetation—by providing cover to the soil. And this cannot be provided unless grazing is controlled. "With controlled grazing the amount of soil cover, both for browse or cutting and for soil protection, would be enormously increased ; and it would be practical to establish wind-breaks of tall grasses, trees, or shrubs at appropriate intervals to afford protection of sandy cropland."[2]

Erosion through water takes three forms *viz.*, sheet erosion, rill and gully erosion (culminating in ravine formations) and flood erosion. Several times more plant food is carried away from farm land in the streams that drain the various water sheds than is absorbed by growing crops or grazed off by animals. Water erosion has gone on throughout the ages, but it has been greatly accelerated in recent years, particularly, in North India, owing to heavy rains. Sheet erosion is the most widespread and yet continues unnoticed. It cuts into the very vitals of the soil through removal of the surface layer and thus, in the course of years, renders the soil, in an insidious manner, totally unfit for agricultural purposes. Constant vigilance is, therefore, needed to prevent the ravages of sheet erosion. For its prevention and control, it is imperative that no piece of land in rainy season, cultivable or otherwise, is left without vegetation and without proper *mends* or embankments, if necessary, on contour lines, and that ploughing and sowing in adjoining sloping areas, if any, and where the slope is only moderate, say, 2–3 per cent, are done not parallel to the slope but across it. This will reduce the run-off and enable the water to be absorbed into the soil. Organic matter, again particularly of the bulky kind, mixed into the soil surface, will cause that surface to appropriate the rain as it falls, thus obviating not only verticular but lateral flow of water which is essential to the processes of sheet erosion. Quick-maturing legumes, for example, *moong, lobia* and ground-nut, or other cover crops which grow thick and close to the ground, sown in the rainy season, can effectively reduce sheet erosion to the minimum. Such crops will also serve as green manure. Strip cropping with legumes is also useful where the slope is not steep.

[2] Report on *India's Food Crisis and Steps to Meet It*, the Agricultural Production Team (also known as Ford Foundation Team), 1959, p. 156.

As compared with sheet erosion the ravages of gully erosion are very conspicuous. This form of erosion, to which sheet erosion, if unchecked, gradually leads, can only be prevented by starting operations right at the point of origin, or the head, by adopting widespread afforestation, controlling grazing and putting a ban on arable cultivation. The steps for checking gully erosion in the lower reaches of rivers may be of a large magnitude, totally beyond the resources of the average individual cultivator, inasmuch as they would involve erection of dams, construction of terraces, or diversions, gully-plugging by masonry chutes or adoption of other mechanical methods for reducing run-off. In these conditions it is for the state to come to the aid of the people. Co-operative efforts on the part of farmers can also yield some results.

At some places, points out the Ford Foundation Team, badly located highway culverts, broken bunds, unprotected outlets of bunds, or any other cause of water concentration produces disastrous gullying or gully erosion. It is for Government or village panchayats to remove such causes as soon as they appear, for subsequent restoration of the soil is exceedingly difficult and costly. The best way is to keep these structures in repair.

The ravined lands generally may be beyond redemption, but at the head of ravines there are sub-marginal lands which are under the full grip of active erosion. And above these lands lie the flat, productive fields. Adequate protective measures have to be taken and improved farming practices adopted to save the sub-marginal lands from becoming ravined lands, and productive fields from becoming sub-marginal. Control of grazing may be one of the most effective means of preventing further deterioration of ravined lands, and terraces, furrows, etc., of stopping the advancement of ravines, but suitable crop rotation, maintenance of fertility and good farming practices in general are equally, if not more important in checking the spread of gully erosion.

As regards floods, afforestation, particularly, in the upper reaches of the rivers is most efficacious. Devegetation and denudation of the soil is the fundamental reason for the fury of the great North Indian rivers which, feeling their marginal lands shorn of trees, begin to swallow up the loose and unprotected soil of the plains and to take revenge by over-flowing their banks. Just as the loss of the forest cover is singly the most potent cause of soil erosion and has brought increasingly destructive floods, so tree plantation is singly the most potent method that will prevent floods and conserve the soil resources as also the water resources, since no storer of water has ever been invented that is more efficient than deep, porous soil—soil which has been rendered porous and thus made a vast sponge by tree roots and vegetation. This sponge will soak up and trap the rain-drops upstream where they fell, thus minimising down-stream, flood conditions. Bunds, except of minor dimensions and at a few strategic places, are at best a palliative, which may, in course of time, prove worse than the disease they are designed to control. Nor will it be practicable to construct reservoirs of such dimensions and in such numbers on all rivers as to divert flood waters in the required volume.

The destruction of forests is responsible not only for erosion and floods : it cuts down the reserves of humidity in the soil and leads to drought conditions. According to some authorities, trees attract rain and where there are no trees, there is no rain and, therefore, no sub-soil water. There are others who do not agree with this view. But it is admitted on all hands that where there is paucity of trees, rain comes in a heavy downpour and flows away rapidly without being absorbed in the soil. Where trees are in plentiful numbers or take the form of a forest, it rains in mild showers. And when it rains in mild showers and there are trees and deep-rooted grasses on the earth below, water is led into natural underground reserves, recharging springs and wells. Decaying leaves and spreading root systems of trees make the soil an ideal store-house of sub-soil water to feed perennial springs.

Like the nutritional cycle, there is another cycle in Nature, *viz.*, the hydrologic (जल-चक्र)—the movement of water from the air to the land and eventually back to the air, usually by evaporation from the lakes, rivers and oceans—which man can help maintain by planting trees, and has to be explained to every child in the country. It was not without reason that our *Rishis* taught that tree means water and water means life, and that our unsophisticated villagers have been handing down a saying from father to son that it is a sinful act to cut down a green, living tree, while it is a virtuous act to plant one.

Says the Purana : दशकूपसमा वापी
दशवापी समोह्रदः ।
दशह्रदसमः पुत्रः
दशपुत्रसमस्तरुः ॥

The man who constructs a step-well earns the religious merit of getting ten wells dug. He who constructs a lake obtains the merit of constructing ten step-wells. A man who has a son, gets the merit of constructing ten lakes. But plant a tree and the merit you receive is the same as having ten sons.

An English poet would interrupt a destroyer of trees by addressing him thus :

> Woodman, spare that tree !
> Touch not a single bough !
> In youth it sheltered me.
> And I'll protect it now.
>
> GEORGE POPE MORRIS

Apart from providing shade and fuel and conserving soil and water resources, trees can and do greatly contribute to food production. Fruits which trees alone can supply are such a necessary complement of balanced diet. Trees also provide shelter against desiccating winds which affect crops so adversely. In fact, the maintenance of a good forest cover is essential to agriculture—to the duration and prosperity of every nation, culture or civilisation. As John Stewart Collis wrote : "Trees hold up the mountains. They cushion up the rain storms. They discipline the rivers. They maintain the springs. They foster the birds."[3] Forests also condition the weather and equalise the climate. They are the abode of wild life and add to the scenic beauty of the landscape. Finally, they supply a variety of much-needed products, such as timber for building purposes, drugs and edible, medicinal, poisonous or oil-yielding plants, gums and resins, tans and dyes, fibres, flosses and grasses, bamboos and reeds, canes (rattans), spices, cutch and *katha*, and animal products like honey and wax, lac and shellac, horns, hooves and skins. Besides material, there are non-material benefits also accruing to mankind from trees and forests. Says Henry Van Dyke :

> But the glory of trees is more than their gifts ;
> 'Tis a beautiful wonder of line that lifts,
> From a wrinkled seed in an earthbound clod,
> A column, an arch in the temple of God,
> A pillar of power, a dome of delight,

[3] *In the Triumph of the Tree*, p. 149, quoted by Richard B. Gregg in *Which Way Lies Hope* ? Navjivan Press, Ahmedabad, 1957, p. 35.

A shrine of song, and a joy of sight ;
Their roots are nurses of rivers in birth,
Their leaves are alive with the breath of the earth ;
They shelter the dwellings of man ; and they bend,
O'er his grave with the look of a loving friend.

Thus, forests are a natural asset of inestimable value to man.
In truth, where there are no trees or forests, human and animal
life also will cease to exist : the region will be reduced to a desert.
Trees, therefore, have to be planted and some of the forests allowed
to grow once again where they had been cut from, by human greed
and folly.

Van Mahotsava is one of the few movements launched since
the attainment of Independence that has gone to the root of a problem and had a psychological appeal, but it would seem to be slogging;
it is in danger of becoming a formal ritual and stands in need of
rejuvenation. If groves to be planted in future are exempted
from payment of land revenue, agricultural income tax and irrigation charges, it will give a fillip to the movement.

If we have one thing to learn from Japan, it is her care of forests.
"In order to obtain high yields", says Josue De Castro,[4] "Japan
put into practice all the agricultural techniques she could learn
from the West, and adapted them to the traditional processes
of Chinese and Japanese farming. But though these people have
always been under pressure to produce more food, they have never
robbed and abused their soil, or worked it out in a few years as has
been done in various parts of the Occident. In spite of the tremendous pressure of population, great tracts of land have been set aside
as insurance against erosion. Foreign specialists have always
wondered why Japan, with her shortage of food, particularly of proteins, never took up cattle raising. It could have been done just
as well there as in New Zealand, where the topography is very
similar to that of the Japanese Islands, by taking the same advantage of mountainous lands unsuitable for agriculture. The
reason lies in Japan's wise policy of soil conservation, a technique
that this country was the first in the world to adopt. Once the
forests had been sacrificed to pasture, waters pouring off the slopes
with nothing to stop them might well have done tremendous
damage to the soil of agricultural areas." Forests and woodlands in

[4] *Geography of Hunger*, Josue De Castro, London, 1952, p. 164.

TABLE LVI

NUMBER OF LIVESTOCK IN 1959-60

(In thousands)

Sl. No.	Country	Area of arable land and land under permanent crops, permanent meadows and pastures (in 1000 hectare)	Cattle	Cows*	Buffaloes	Bovine Animals		Goats	
						Total	(Per 100 Hectare)	Total	(Per 100 Hectare)
1.	Austria	40,52	23,08	11,32	..	23,08	57	1,75	4
2.	Australia	45,94,74	1,65,03	40,07	—	1,65,03	4	—	—
3.	Belgium	17,16	26,96	10,24	—	26,96	157	82	5
4.	Burma	86,14	52,54	3,16	10,05	62,59	73	4,29	5
5.	Canada	6,24,76	1,04,97	31,62	—	1,04,97	17	18	0
6.	Chile	59,68	29,11	5,16	—	29,11	49	13,00	2
7.	China (Mainland)	28,73,50	4,44,90†	—	2,09,40	6,54,30	23	5,15,30	18
8.	Columbia	1,81,16	1,33,90	21,99	—	1,33,90	74	2,15	1
9.	Czechoslovakia	73,27	43,03	20,72	—	43,03	59	6,62	9
10.	Denmark	31,27	33,94	14,36	—	33,94	109	4	0
11.	Fed. of Malaya	—	3,08	35	2,63	5,71	—	2,79	—
12.	Fed. Rep. Germany	1,42,54	1,24,80	56,70	—	1,24,80	87	4,14	3
13.	France	3,46,33	1,87,35	70,49	—	1,87,35	54	11,64	3
14.	Guatemala	20,55	10,62	2,43	—	10,62	52	93	5
15.	India	17,38,50	17,56,72	4,72,48	5,11,37	22,68,09	130	6,08,13	35
16.	Indonesia	1,76,81	48,05	—	29,10	77,15	44	54,36	36
17.	Iran	1,80,00	54,00	—	3,00	57,00	32	82,50	46
18.	Ireland	47,15	47,40	12,84	—	47,40	101	50	1

19.	Israel	12,10	2,24	82	—	2,24	19	1,68	14
20.	Italy	2,09,30	93,99	—	18	94,17	45	14,40	7
21.	Japan	70,20	31,63	5,19	—	31,63	45	5,61	8
22.	Netherland	23,17	35,07	16,28	—	35,07	151	1,31	6
23.	New Zealand	1,31,28	59,92	18,87	—	59,92	46	—	—
24.	Norway	10,33	11,29	5,97	—	11,29	109	1,01	10
25.	Pakistan	2,94,53	2,38,20	87,78	63,54	3,01,74	102	96,92	33
26.	Philippines	79,54	11,10	—	36,96	48,06	60	6,17	8
27.	Romania	45,47	44,50	—	1,89	46,39	102	4,46	10
28.	Sweden	42,82	25,01	12,99	—	25,01	58	8	0
29.	Switzerland	21,65	17,46	9,40	—	17,46	80	95	4
30.	Thailand	79,43	51,42	—	65,05	1,16,47	146	38	0
31.	Turkey	5,40,18	1,30,76	41,13	12,29	1,43,05	26	2,50,78	46
32.	United Arab Rep.	26,10	15,88	—	13,95	29,83	114	7,23	28
33.	United Kingdom	1,98,94	1,17,71	48,72	—	1,17,71	59	21	0
34.	U.S.S.R.	59,10,55	7,42,33	—	39	7,42,72	13	78,80	1
35.	United States	43,99,41	9,62,36	1,95,27	—	9,62,36	22	33,39	0
36.	Venezuela	2,07,24	71,62	2,80	—	71,62	35	9,21	4
37.	Yugoslavia	1,49,23	52,95	18,28	49	53,44	36	10,98	7

SOURCE: *Production Year Book of Food and Agriculture Organization*, 1961 (Vol. 15), Tables 70, 71, 74, and 75.

† Unofficial figures.

* Cows including heifers in calf kept primarily for milk.

Note: 1. Data of the countries at sl. Nos. 11 (cols. 6 & 7), 24 (col. 5), 27 (col. 7) and 30 (col. 7) relate to 1958/59.

2. Data of the countries at sl. Nos. 28 (col. 7), 32 (cols. 6 & 7) relate to 1957/58.

3. Data of the countries at sl. Nos. 4 (col. 5), 8, 11 (col. 5), 13 (col. 5), 33 (col. 7) and 36 relate to 1956/57.

4. Data of India at sl. No. 15 relate to 1960-61.

5. Data of the countries at sl. Nos. 5 (col. 7), 6 (col. 5), 10 (col. 7), 17 (col. 7), 18 (col. 7), 22 (col. 7), 27 (col.6), 34 (col. 6) and 37 (col. 7) relate to 1947/48—1951/52.

Japan cover full two-thirds of the total area of the country. The total forest area in our country covers only about 24 per cent of the land surface whereas the dictates of a balanced economy require a percentage of 33.3.

We should also, all clamour notwithstanding, take a definite decision in long-term national interest that no forests shall in future be cut down in order merely to extend cultivation or settle landless people. Our food problem will have to be solved almost entirely by intensive cultivation, rather than by bringing valuable forest land or marginal and sub-marginal land under cultivation.

India's cattle population is far in excess of the available supplies of fodder and feed. According to the live-stock census of 1961 the bovine population stands at 226.8 million, of which 175.7 million are cattle and 51.1 million buffaloes. This is 22.25 per cent of the world's total viz., 1016.6 million, and more than the bovine population of any other country as evidenced by Table LVI.

Although the density of bovine population in India is lower than in Belgium, Netherlands and Thailand, we cannot afford even the present numbers. At least, one-third, if not actually half of India's cattle population can be counted as surplus in relation to the feed supply. We could easily do with two-thirds without traction power or milk yield being affected. The Ford Foundation Team (April, 1959) estimates that if the feed and forage of, say, fifty million of the useless cattle were fed to the milch cows of India this could add a much-needed pound of milk a day to the diet of 50 million children of India. Owing to absence of any positive check on their indiscriminate breeding, on one hand, and to enactment of legislation, in various States, making the slaughter of cattle a crime, on the other, the problem of surplus and uneconomic cattle is being accentuated as time passes.

Uneconomic cattle impose a heavy cost not only in terms of deprivation of land from utilisation for human food, but also in terms of soil erosion. No single factor is as much responsible for widespread erosion of all kinds as indiscriminate and uncontrolled grazing. By their excessive grazing these cattle destroy young trees, shrubbery and grass so much as to strip the plains and hillsides clean of vegetation. That invites erosion in the rainy season, causes floods and extends the deserts. If, therefore, erosion has to be checked, grazing will have to be controlled, and grazing is difficult, if not impossible, to effectively control unless measures are instituted to greatly reduce the number of uneconomic cattle and to prevent them from multiplying. The control of grazing, points out the Ford Foundation Team (Report, p. 157), though most difficult, is one of the most important agricultural and conservation problems in India for five reasons :

(a) With controlled grazing under systems that allow grass and browse plants to recover, the total yield of forage can be increased manifold;

(b) Over-grazing leads to the replacement of good species of pasture and browse plants with poor or even unpalatable species;

(c) Severe over-grazing leaves the soil bare and exposed directly to the sun, rain, and wind. Commonly a crust forms over the surface that further reduces water infiltration. Thus, much of the water loss, soil erosion and soil blowing are direct results of over-grazing;

(d) Great opportunities for commercial timber production, for fuel trees in the village and for useful windbreaks are unrealised because of uncontrolled grazing; and,

(e) Over-grazing reduces infiltration of water and consequently the water available for wells. In Rajasthan, for example, the extreme grazing of the steep stony hills reduces infiltration so much that wells are low yielding. With controlled grazing on these hills, the increased crop production from the greater water supply for irrigation would greatly exceed the current forage production in the hills.

By developing herds and flocks of high quality, double-purpose animals, the numbers can be kept within bounds and, at the same time, their productivity greatly increased. Then grazing and consequent erosion will also be easy to control.

The cow has given us traction power in the form of bullocks and will continue to give it ; it has given us sustenance for land in the form of dung and sustenance for man in the form of milk and will continue to do so. It is the base of our agricultural economy and our health. Our civilisation, in fact, our very existence depends on agriculture. Cow, therefore, is rightly regarded as almost a member of the peasant's family and has rightly occupied a high place in our legend, in our folk-lore, in our history, in our sentiment. At the same time, its breed today has deteriorated greatly, the main reason being lack of feed and fodder . Owing to small holdings and poor agricultural yields, the farmers are able to spare only a small proportion of land for fodder crops. As regards village pastures. most of them are pastures only in name, and serve mainly as an exercise-ground for cattle and, year by year, the soil is eroded away until the land becomes a dreary waste. More and more animals are kept and there is less and less for them to eat. It is small wonder then that the village cows are poor, thriftless beasts with a phenomenally low milk yield. Table LVII shows how the milk yield of our cows compares with other countries. Even a good cow cannot compete with the buffalo, at least, in the production of *ghee* or fat which is the measure of money income that a milch-animal brings. So, as soon as its maintenance begins to cost more than what it yields, the peasant sells it to the butcher, or a middle man knowing all the while that he is sending it to the hack. This outrages the feelings of the Hindu community. So, somewhere a compromise has to be made ; a principle has to be found which will strain neither the heart of the Hindu nor the economy of the country. The best solution would seem to lie in sterilising all the scrub bulls and, if possible, uneconomic cows also so that they might not be instrumental in multiplying a useless breed, and simultaneously in upgrading the sires—the bulls. Sterilisation of the young male or a scrub bull does not require castration. A slight operation does it by tying the spermatic cord, involving but very slight and brief pain.

The day the cow ceases to be an object of utility altogether, it will disappear completely, sentiment notwithstanding. Since the horse went out of use as a result of mechanisation of the army and other transport after the first World War, it has become rare in the country, without having been butchered or eaten up by anybody. The number of horses and ponies in the Union of India came down from 15,14,000 in 1951 to 13,51,000 in 1961, that is, by 10.8 per cent, and in Uttar Pradesh from 3,71,000 in 1951 to 2,98,000 in 1961, that is, by 19.5 per cent.

On the other hand, according to the cattle censuses of Uttar Pradesh, the she-buffalo has, during the last 50 years, multiplied in numbers as compared with the cow, in spite of the fact that proportionately more buffaloes have gone to the shambles during this period than cows. This is all because, in view of the higher fat content of her milk, the housewife attaches more value to the buffalo than to the cow.

The following statement[5] shows the number of cows and buffaloes

[5] Report of the Gosamvardhan Enquiry Committee, Uttar Pradesh 1954, Part II (Appendices), p. 99.

TABLE LVII
MILK YIELD PER MILKING COW PER ANNUM
(1960)

Sl. No.	Country	Kgms.
1.	Austria	2,430
2.	Australia	2,020
3.	Belgium	3,810
4.	Burma	760
5.	Canada	2,640
6.	Chile	700
7.	China (Taiwan)	2,450
8.	Czechoslovakia	1,860
9.	Denmark	3,710
10.	Federation of Malaya	470
11.	Fed. Republic Germany	3,400
12.	Finland	3,030
13.	France	2,140
14.	Germany (Eastern)	2,680
15.	Hungary	2,260
16.	India	220
17.	Indonesia	2,140
18.	Iran	620
19.	Ireland	2,300
20.	Isreal	4,380
21.	Italy	1,560
22.	Japan	3,640
23.	Korea Rep. of	2,690
24.	Netherlands	4,280
25.	Norway	2,630
26.	Pakistan	420
27.	Peru	560
28.	Philippines	200
29.	Romania	820
30.	Sweden	3,100
31.	Switzerland	3,280
32.	Turkey	590
33.	United Arab Republic	680
34.	United Kingdom	2,990
35.	U.S.S.R.	1,820
36.	United States	3,180
37.	Yugoslavia	1,140

SOURCE : *Production Year Book* of Food and Agriculture Organisation, 1961. (Table 84)

Note : (1) Data of the countries at sl. Nos. 1, 6, 10, 13, 21 and 35 relate to 1959.

(2) Data of the countries at sl. Nos. 14, 17, 25 relate to 1958.

(3) Data of the countries at sl. Nos. 16, 22, 28, 29 and 33 relate to 1957.

slaughtered in the recognised slaughter houses of Uttar Pradesh during a period of 15 years from 1936-37 onwards :

TABLE LVIII

NUMBER OF COWS AND BUFFALOES SLAUGHTERED IN U.P.
(1936-51)

Year	Cows	Buffaloes
1936-37	1,26,828	1,12,030
1937-38	1,42,237	1,21,817
1938-39	1,18,690	1,27,914
1939-40	1,35,379	1,54,198
1940-41	1,26,331	1,80,891
1941-42	1,25,470	2,42,229
1942-43	1,17,207	2,05,148
1943-44	76,543	1,72,763
1944-45	59,233	1,60,881
1945-46	75,345	1,82,493
1946-47	81,544	1,80,737
1947-48	49,908	27,434
1948-49	19,024	1,70,774
1949-50	27,839	2,02,196
1950-51	5,086	2,32,962

In spite of a total of 25,74,000 buffaloes having been slaughtered during these 15 years as against a total of 12,87,000 cows only, the number of the former in the State (excluding hill districts), increased from 34,21,000 in 1904 to 49,88,000 in 1951, while that of the cow decreased from 69,48,000 to 61,20,000 during the same period. The live-stock census of 1961 shows that during the last decade the number of cows went up to 61,67,000 only, that is, by 0.77 per cent, while that of the she-buffaloes shot up to 54,36,000, that is, by 9.0 per cent. This, in spite of the fact that, during the period July 1951—June 1960, the number of she-buffaloes that has been slaughtered stood at 23,11,000 while, during the period July 1951—June 1955, the number of cows that had been slaughtered stood only at 15,000. In 1955 a legislation prohibiting the slaughter of cows was put on the statute book. The number of these animals, therefore, that might have been slaughtered clandestinely since then, cannot affect the conclusions to any appreciable degree.

Next, there is the goat. Of all cattle, it is the one which eats away grass and foliage far closer to the ground—rather tears them away from the very roots. It eats many shrubs, the lower branches of trees and young seedling trees entire. Just as a swarm of locusts eats up everything it comes across, so a herd of goats can, in course of time, devastate a blooming countryside and convert it into a veritable desert. The goat has, therefore, to be actively discouraged,[5a] particularly, in Rajasthan and the adjoining areas, the best means of doing it being to levy a tax which will make maintenance of goats a burden on their owners. It renders no peculiar service to the people, except as a source of milk supply to the poor man and one of the sources of meat-supply to the non-vegetarian section of our people. There are, however, other sources of milk supply, and the non-vegetarians can do, in national interest, with a little less or dearer meat.

Further, although the goat does not feed on cultivated fields, it will not be a calamity if the meat supply otherwise also diminishes, or we, as a nation, turn still more and more to a vegetarian diet. Other arguments apart, our land-man ratio would strongly tend to dictate such a course. There is not sufficient land left in India today for growing food to feed animals to be slaughtered for human consumption. Domestic animals raised for food required several times more land than was necessary to raise an equivalent amount of nutrition in the form of grains, fruits and vegetables for human consumption. Thus India already on a predominantly vegetarian diet, would seem to be living far more wisely within its own land resources than are the meat-eating peoples. Referring to the German Four-year Plan prepared by the Nazis, an eminent economist G. D. H. Cole, writes :

The virtually official institute for Konjuncturforschung has recently issued an elaborate memorandum telling the citizens what types of food they may consume, and what they are to avoid, in the interests of the nation. In this highly instructive document, the first emphasis is laid on reduced consumption of all products of animal origin, with the exception of fish and rabbits. Each hectare of soil, it is pointed out, can be made to yield a far larger food value if it is used to produce vegetable products than if animals are fed upon it. One hectare under potatoes, it is calculated, gives twenty times

[5a] Table LVI would show that India is one of the countries which have the highest density of goats in the world.

as great a value as one used for producing beef ; and one hectare under wheat is nearly ten times as productive in this sense. Accordingly, the German people is adjured to 'change over to a diet which prefers plant products, such as, potatoes, vegetables and sugar, rather than animal products'.[6]

Teachings of our ancestors in regard to vegetarianism, which, inter alia, had their roots in the basic economic facts of our soil and climate, also find confirmation in the eating habits of another ancient people, the Chinese. The author of Geography of Hunger says:

Vegetable foods are so predominant in the diet of the Chinese people that only 2 or 3 per cent of the total calories are of animal origin, compared to 39 per cent in the United States. The Chinese cannot afford to waste his limited soil in the raising of animals, and he knows it ; animals yield much less nutritional energy per acre than do plants. The Chinese knows that a vegetable eaten directly by man furnishes infinitely more energy than the same product indirectly utilized in raising livestock. Unfortunately, the task of obtaining enough energy for his basic, vital functions has always been the immediate and burning problem with him. By giving himself almost entirely to agriculture, and planting only high-energy foods such as rice, wheat and millet, the Chinese farmer still falls short of a ration of 2,250 calories daily. Where would he be if he indulged in the luxury of converting vegetable calories into animal calories ? In this conversion, the scientists have found, a very small part of the energy consumed by the animal is recovered. Fifteen per cent is recovered in producing milk, 7 per cent in eggs and only 4 per cent in beef. This is the biological determinism which keeps the Chinese from raising animals to eat. In the United States 90 per cent of the domestic animals are raised for food ; in China, only 25 per cent. Most of them serve merely to assist man in growing plants.[7]

According to Dr. M. R. Raghvendra Rao[8] of the National Chemical Laboratory, Poona, the efficiency of conversion of vegetable protein from cattle-feeds like straw, bran, grains and oil-seed cakes into animal proteins is as follows :

Milk	Eggs	Meat
40–50%	25–30%	10–15%

[6] Practical Economics, England, 1937, p. 111.
[7] Ibid., pp. 126-27.
[8] An article published in the magazine section of the Pioneer, Lucknow, dated June 1, 1958.

It is clear that a given area of land in the form of corn and other vegetable materials will support about several times as many men as will the meat obtainable from the same land. Densely-populated areas, therefore, like India, China, Japan and Indonesia can ill afford a meat diet, at least, on the Western scale. According to Mr. Richard St. Barbe Baker, a forester and ecologist, world tension, which arises mostly from uneven distribution of land, could be relieved "if we all could accept a vegetarian way of life." In fact, even if half the vast areas of land now given over to pastures in Europe, America and Oceania for raising animals for slaughter, were devoted to food production, there would be a glut of food in the world.

There are, however, two or three categories of animals which can be added to our menu without detriment to national interest, for example, birds of the air, terrestrial animals like rabbits and deers, and aquatic animal like fish, which do not compete with men for food space, and are available—particularly, of the last category —in practically inexhaustible numbers. We have a coastline of about 4,000 miles and a continental shelf more than one lakh square miles. But we are today exploiting barely 6 per cent of our fish-able marine and not more than the same percentage of our water resources.

Lastly, there are the monkey and the blue-bull to be considered. They are nothing but pests and have undoubtedly to go. Respect for life inculcated by our ancestors has its limitations. Our agricul-tural economy has reached a stage where it cannot bear unnecessary burdens—where we will have to make a definite choice whether it is the man or animal that we want to see survive. Both the monkey and the blue-bull do incalculable harm to standing crops and have nothing to recommend in their favour, except superstition.

So much for conservation of soil resources, that are already under utilisation of some sort, by promotion of proper agricultural practices, contour ploughing, terraces, strip cultivation, composting, use of night-soil, crop rotations, planting of fast-growing trees for fuel wood, restriction on grazing, etc. etc. But there are millions of acres which are utterly barren and make no contribution to the wealth or welfare of the nation. For example, there are water-logged, *usar* and weed-infested areas which can be utilised, provided there is the imagination and the will to do so.

In truth, there is no soil made by God or Nature but cannot be put to profitable use by man with the aid of science, if necessary. Says the Ford Foundation Team :

Actually all natural soils are modified by agricultural use. The cultivator makes an arable soil from either a natural soil or one already modified by use. Rarely do even the most primitive people cultivate soils without any practices to improve or maintain them. As agriculture becomes increasingly efficient through the use of science and engineering, we are less and less concerned with the productivity of soils when first ploughed. Rather, we are more and more concerned with their potential productivity in response to combined practices. Among the most productive arable soils of the world today are a high proportion that were nearly worthless in their natural state or as modified only by land clearing and tillage (page 141).

Water-logging is deleterious to the growth and the ultimate yields of crops. It also raises the spring-level, which is generally very injurious to the soil. In regions of low rainfall it is the nearness of the water-table to the surface of the soil that has mainly been responsible for the occurrence of large *usar* tracts. Nearness of water brings about accumulation of injurious salts in the surface layer, making the soil *usar* and unfit for cultivation. Drainage, therefore, should receive our earnest attention. There are places in India where millions of acres could be reclaimed and made productive by surface drainage than by developing new irrigation projects. The most obvious means by which good drainage facilities could be afforded at a cheap cost and through co-operative efforts is to desilt and deepen the *nalas* (channels), which abound in large numbers, so that these could be used both for irrigating the land and for draining away surplus water. Natural drainage of our country-side has been greatly upset by the faulty alignment of roads, canals and railways, and faulty construction of culverts, bridges and aqueducts. Also, at some places, paths made by individual farmers or village panchayats add to the problem. Where necessary, these have to be resurveyed and improved.

In the absence of adequate drainage facilities the water-table in certain irrigated areas commanded by canals, has been gradually rising in the recent years. Large areas which used to be good arable land some 20 or 30 years back have now become almost swamps or *usar*. There is a provision in the Canal Drainage Act, 1873, that for every three miles of the canal there should be two miles of drainage cuts. But in actual practice, even where this scale is rigidly followed, the drainage cuts are allowed to silt up, with the result that due to lack of drainage or to defective drainage the water-table is gradually coming nearer the surface of the soil. The absence of silt berms along the sides of the canal beds is also responsible for seepage of water in the canal-commanded areas.

The country certainly stands in need of better and greater irrigation facilities. And yet we cannot ignore the fact that there are certain regions where any sudden and marked increase in irrigation may well prove detrimental to soil formation and soil fertility. In such tracts, *e. g.*, in certain parts of Uttar Pradesh where the natural topography does not permit of satisfactory drainage and where the spring-level happens to be rather high, care must be taken to ensure that no water-logging is ultimately produced as a result of increased irrigation.

Setting up of bunds all round and intermittent impounding of water and its drainage, followed by a crop of *sanai*, or preferably, *dhaincha* for green manuring, would prove useful for amelioration of the existing *usar* conditions or formations brought about by seepage and water-logging. For this purpose it would, however, be necessary to have a fairly large supply of water at a cheap price. After the soil has been so reclaimed, care should be taken to see that a judicious crop rotation, suited to the locality, is practised and the land is never left without a crop. Prevention, however, is always better than cure : it is easier and more effective to prevent water-logging and its accompanying salt and alkali problems ahead of time, than it is to reclaim the soil after these conditions have developed.

Refractory *usar* formations can be attributed to the replacement of calcium of the clay-complex by sodium through various causes which have been in operation over very many years. Reclamation of such *usar* lands is a very expensive and tedious project, yet it does not mean that they should be left alone and no efforts made to utilise them in a profitable manner. The best use that we can make of these *usar* areas is to implement a scheme of afforestation by planting alkali-loving trees like *babool* (*cassia arabica*), *dhak* (*Butea frondosa*), etc. As has already been noticed, we need badly both firewood for use in the villages, especially with a view to releasing cattle dung for manurial purposes, and grazing-ground for our large cattle population. Both of these objectives could be achieved with a large measure of success by making use of the available areas of refractory *usar* lands for afforestation and pasture purposes.

The problem of perennial weeds has been baffling the ingenuity of agricultural experts in India and many other countries. And yet no successful programme of agricultural improvement will be complete unless and until perennial weeds of the worst kinds have been successfully eradicated. In Uttar Pradesh a large-scale campaign was in the recent past organised for eradication of *kans* in Bundelkhand by deep-ploughing with tractors. This certainly resulted in a measure of success, but proved much too expensive for the average cultivator. Also, the weeds in certain parts have come up again. Chemical weedicides have now recently been tried as an experimental measure in some parts of the country, but neither the effectiveness of those chemicals has been generally established nor is this process found to be economical. By and large, therefore, one has to fall back upon the age-old system of smothering the weeds through cultivation of such crops as have luxuriant growth, *e.g. juar*, *guar*, *dhaincha* or *sanai*. Cover crops like *lobia*, groundnut and soya bean are also helpful to a certain extent. In most cases, such a system of cropping will serve the dual purpose of putting down the troublesome weeds and adding appreciably to the fertility status of the soil.

CHAPTER TWENTY-TWO

Need for Population Control

ACCORDING to the U.N.'s *Demographic Year Book* for 1961, the world's population reached 3,120 million on July 1. There are now 22 persons for every square kilometre of land, compared with 18 only ten years ago, the report said. In 60 years the world's population has almost doubled ; at the outset of the century it was 160.8 million.

The population explosion is being aided by the fact that births now double deaths, with continuing advances in health and nutrition. In 1961, the estimated world birth rate was 36 per 1,000 population, and the estimated death rate exactly half this figure. In mid-1961, the baby boom was swelling the world population at the rate of about five million monthly. At its present growth rate, the world could touch the 4,000 million mark in under 15 years.

The latest official estimate of U.S. population was given as 185.8 million, as of April 1, 1961. The annual rate of increase in the U.S. for the 1953-60 period was figured at 1.7 per cent. The U.S. birth rate in 1961 was estimated at 23.4 per 1,000 population, the lowest in ten years. The death rate was estimated at 9.3 lowest since 1956.

The Soviet Union's population was estimated at 218 million. It had a growth rate of 1.7 per cent, same as the U.S. The Soviet Union reported the lowest regional death rate, 7.1 in 1960, and a birth rate in the year, 24.9. U.N. computors, however, declined responsibility for that figure.

India's population was estimated at 440.3 million in mid-1961.

The figures, covered in the annual *U. N. Demographic Year Book* and the latest quarterly population statistics report, also indicated that China might be near—if it had not passed—the 700 million mark.

Central America with an annual rate of growth of 2.7 per cent was listed as the fastest growing area. South-west Asia was next with 2.6 per cent. Countries of Northern and Western Europe showed an increase of only 0.7 per cent.

The most densely populated region of the world is still Central Europe, with 137 persons per square kilometre.

The Netherlands is the most tightly-packed single country, with 342 people per square kilometre, followed by England and Wales (303 per square kilometre), Belgium (302) and Japan (252).

The highest regional birth rate (48 per 1,000) and the highest death rate (27 per 1,000) were found in tropical and Southern Africa, the report stated.

The "wide open spaces" of the world are Australia, Bechuanaland, Greenland and South-West Africa, with not more than 34 persons per square kilometre.

This depicts the world picture as a whole. The intention here, however, is merely to discuss the population problem with reference to India.

Until 1947, it was the political problem that gripped the attention of our public men, but, freedom having been won, the focus of attention has now shifted from politics to economic development or eradication of poverty. The Census Report of 1961, in particular, has brought to the fore the demographic problem—the problem which our huge, increasing population poses, and the bearing that it has on our economic conditions. The population of India, according to *Census of India*, 1951, Part I-A, page 181 and *Census of India*, 1961, Paper No. I of 1962, page x has grown as follows :

TABLE LIX

STATEMENT SHOWING INDIA'S POPULATION VARIATION
AND ITS MEAN DECENNIAL GROWTH RATE

Year	Population (in million)	Variation (in million)	Mean Decennial* Growth Rate
1891	238.4	..	..
1901	238.4	0.0	..
1911	252.1	15.8	+ 5.6
1921	251.4	0.7	— 0.28
1931	279.0	27.8	+10.4
1941	318.7	39.7	+13.3
1951	361.1	42.4	+12.5
1961	439.2	78.1	+19.5

* The mean decennial growth rate is expressed as percentage of the mean population of the decade during which the growth occurred.

The year 1921 may be taken to be a water-shed, or, as, the census Commissions for 1951 aptly put it, the Great Divide in the recent demographic history of the country. If the average rates of the period, 1891-1920 are considered, India's population grew at the mean rate of 1.8 per cent per decade, while from 1921 to 1960 it grew at the mean rate of 14.0 per cent per decade. The reasons for this difference lie in the fact that of the three factors which, according to Malthus, are the main positive checks to population growth, only one had been completely eliminated at the beginning of the first period. War and banditry had been eliminated owing to the establishment of a firm and ordered political system. But the other two, disease and famine, had their full sway during the period : famine in several parts of the country occurred in 1891-92, 1895, 1896-97 and 1899 ; bubonic plague which had made its first appearance in modern times in India in 1896 could not be controlled till the end of the next decade, 1901-10 ; and the influenza epidemic of 1918 was specially severe in its ferocity. On the other hand, owing to introduction of modern public health services (however unsatisfactory and inadequate these may be, compared to other countries) resulting in the control of epidemics, and improvement of transport and communication facilities, both inside the country and outside, resulting in control of scarcity and famine conditions, which were usually local affairs and a consequence of isolation, the subsequent period 1921-60, except for the Bengal catastrophe of 1943-44, was singularly free from visitations of large-scale disease or famine.

Apart from immigration, it is the difference between the birth rate and the death rate in a particular country that governs the growth of its population. It will be seen from Table LX that the birth rate of India has been somewhat erratic ; after registering a fall in the last decade of the nineteenth century, it shot up and beat the previous record in the next decade, 1901-10. Since then it showed a downward trend till 1940, and, thereafter, would appear to have become stationary. On the other hand, the death rate since 1921 has gone on declining steeply. It is this increasing difference between the two rates since 1921 that is primarily responsible for the rapid growth of our population during the last 40 years.

We breed profusely and die profusely, or to be more correct, in view of the decline in the death rate during the last decade, have till now died profusely. The social and economic wastage these

TABLE LX

AVERAGE ANNUAL RATES PER 1,000 POPULATION*

Decade	Births	Deaths	Natural Increase	Expectation of life at birth
1881-1890	48.8	39.6	9.2	25.7
1891-1900	45.8	44.4	1.4	..
1901-1910	51.3	43.1	8.2	22.95
1911-1920	49.2	48.6	0.6	31.0
1921-1930	46.4	36.3	10.1	26.73
1931-1940	45.2	31.2	14.0	..
1941-1950	39.9	27.4	12.5	32.6
1951-1960†	40.0	18.0	22.0	45.0

* SOURCE : *Census of India*, Paper No. I of 1962, page XV, except for figures relating to the period 1891-1900 which have been taken from Kingsley Davis : *Population of India and Pakistan*, 1951, p. 85.

† Figures for this decade are estimates only.

high rates involve, or have involved hitherto, has already been referred to in a previous chapter.

So far as the growth rate of our population is concerned it has not been exceptional in any way, at least till 1940. According to Kingsley Davis, while from 1871 to 1940 the average rate of growth of India's population was approximately 0.60 per cent per year, that of the whole world from 1850 to 1940 was somewhat higher, *viz.* 0.69. India's growth rate was less than that found in Europe, in North America and in a good many particular countries. The total Indian increase during 1871-1940 was 52 per cent. The British Isles, despite heavy emigration during the same period, increased 57 per cent. Similarly, Japan during the 70 years from 1871 to 1940, experienced a growth of approximately 120 per cent and the USA a growth of 230 per cent. During the deeade 1921-30, the United States population increased 16 per cent—a rate not equalled in India till 1950. Even today, as the UN's *Demographic Year Book*, 1961, has revealed, there is not much difference between the mean decennial growth rate of India during the 1950s, viz., 19.50, and the growth rate of the world as a whole in 1961, viz., 18. The growth rate of Central America and our neighbouring countries of South West Asia is definitely higher.

The fact that there are certain countries which have a higher birth rate, or a higher rate of population growth or increase, should not, however, make us complacent. The figures given in Table LXI should awaken us to the problem with which India is faced.

Part of the area in every country consisting of mountainous, barren and other land, is unusable and will remain unusable. Also, in every country there is some area other than 'arable area and area under permanent crops', such as classified under 'permanent meadows and pastures' and 'forested area', which, directly or indirectly, maintains or nourishes human beings to-day, or, such as classified under 'unused but potentially productive area' which, as science and technology advances, will serve to do so tomorrow. Population density in the various countries in Table LXI has, therefore, been worked out with reference to three areas, *viz.*, the total area including the part which may never be used for human sustenance, the area that is being, directly or indirectly, used to-day or can be used tomorrow, and the area that is being directly used to-day. Also, all the countries in the world whose latest statistics are available and which are worth mention, have been divided into three categories : the first which have a larger total area than India, arranged in ascending order of the area; the second having almost the same or higher population density per unit of usable land area than India, arranged in ascending order of the density ; and the third having the same or a higher rate of population growth than India, arranged in ascending order of the rate.

It will be seen that, barring China, all the countries which have a larger area than India are in the fortunate position that their population density is far lower than ours. As regards the rates of population growth, those in Australia, Brazil and Canada have been inflated by immigration. The actual difference in the birth and death rates in Australia and Canada, according to U.N. Bulletin of Monthly Statistics, November, 1962, over the period 1956-61, came only to 1.39 and 1.93 per cent per annum. The corresponding figure for Brazil over the period 1940-50, based, according to U.N. *Demographic Year Book*, 1961, on the analysis of 1940 and 1950 census returns, was 2.24.

Of the remaining 24 countries, while 15 which have the same or a higher growth rate than India, have a far lower population density per unit of usable land area, 6 which have the same or a higher density, enjoy a far lower growth rate. Thus, besides China, there

TABLE LXI

COUNTRIES HAVING A LARGER AREA, HIGHER DENSITY OF POPULATION OR HIGHER RATE OF POPULATION GROWTH THAN INDIA

Sl. No.	Countries	Estimates of mid-year population in the year 1961 (in thousands)	Total land area (Sq.k.m.)	Population density per Sq.k.m. of total land area in col. 4	Usable land area (Sq.k.m.)††	Population density per Sq.k.m. of land in col. 6	Area of arable land & land under of land in permanent crops (Sq.k.m.)	Population density per Sq.k.m. of land in Col. 8	Annual rate of population growth during 1953-60 (%)
1	2	3	4	5	6	7	8	9	10
1.	India	44,16,31	32,62,930*	135	24,62,480	179	16,07,380	275	2.2¶
2.	U.S.A.	18,37,42	76,96,030	24	70,30,820	26	18,49,400	99	1.7
3.	Australia	1,05,08	77,04,160*	1	49,92,900	2	2,70,280	39	2.2
4.	Brazil	7,30,88	84,69,890	9	67,89,750	11	1,90,950	383	3.4
5.	Canada	1,82,69	91,94,230	2	57,74,750	3	4,06,000	45	2.6
6.	China (Main land)	64,65,30†	97,61,010*	66	36,39,500	178	10,93,540	591	2.3***
7.	U.S.S.R.	21,80,00	2,23,37,700	10	1,47,13,720	15	22,13,660	98	1.7¶
8.	Israel	21,83	20,260	108	12,850	170	4,120	530	3.6
9.	Italy	4,94,55	2,94,010	168	2,77,610	178	1,58,330	312	0.5
10.	Ceylon	1,01,67	64,740	157	50,840	200	15,380†	661	2.7
11.	United Kingdom	5,27,77	2,40,950	219	2,15,940	244	73,050	722	0.5
12.	Germany (F.R.)	5,40,27	2,42,780	223	2,13,530	253	85,490	632	1.2
13.	Pakistan	9,45,47	9,46,260*	100	3,30,670	286	2,94,530†	321	2.5¶
14.	Japan	9,40,50	3,69,660*	254	3,20,180	294	60,720	1,549	1.0
15.	Belgium	92,03	30,510*	302	23,070	399	9,470	972	0.6
16.	Netherlands	1,16,37	32,450*	359	25,860	450	10,390	1,120	1.3
17.	Columbia	1,44,43	11,38,360*	13	8,75,160	17	48,430	298	2.2

18.	Paraguay	18,12	4,06,750*	4	2,26,780	8	5,170	350	2.4
19.	Honduras	18,83	1,12,090*	17	78,130	24	9,970	189	2.5‡‡
20.	Rhodesia & Nyasaland (Fed.)	85,20	12,53,120*	7	10,20,030	8	3,50,640**	24	2.6
21.	Panama	10,84	74,470*	15	62,720	17	4,500	241	2.7
22.	Peru	1,03,65	12,49,050*	8	8,37,300	13	17,300	599	2.7
23.	Iraq	72,63	4,44,440*	16	2,02,020	36	54,570	133	2.9
24.	Guatemala	38,68	1,06,200	36	68,870	56	14,730	263	3.0
25.	Fed. of Malaya	71,39	1,31,080	54	1,16,630	61	21,860	327	3.0
26.	Mexico	3,60,91	19,69,270*	18	14,55,170	25	1,99,280	181	3.1
27.	British Guiana	5,82	1,96,840	3	1,96,840	3	13,880‡	42	3.1
28.	Ecuador	44,55	2,63,950	17	2,55,000	17	11,200	398	3.2
29.	Nicaragua	15,27	1,37,000	11	98,820	15	17,930‡	85	3.4
30.	Costa Rica	12,25	50,900*	24	16,790	73	2,810	436	4.1 .
31.	Venezuela	75,24	8,82,050	9	3,97,240	19	29,240	257	4.3‡‡

SOURCE : (1) For col. 3 U.N. *Monthly Bulletin of Statistics*, October, 1962 issue.

(2) For cols. 4, 6 and 8 Food & Agriculture Orga. *Production Year Book*, 1961 (Table I).

(3) For col. 10 U.N. *Demographic Year Book*, 1961 (Table 1).

† December 31, 1957 estimate.

* Land area figures were not available, hence total area figures have been taken.

†† Usable land area in col. 6 (for countries at Sls. 1, 2, 4, 5, 8, 16, 22, 25, 26, 27 and 28) includes (1) Arable land and land under permanent crops, (2) Permanent meadows & pastures, (3) Forested land, and (4) Unused but potentially productive area. For the remaining countries 'unused but potentially productive area' figures were not available and hence in their cases usable land area covers only first three types of land areas.

‡ Relate to Total Agricultural Area.

** Arable land in col. 8 includes area under permanent meadows and pastures of Northern Rhodesia; excludes fallow land owned by the native population of Southern Rhodesia.

¶ Taken from Census of India, 1961—Paper No. 1.

*** For 1953-57.   ¶¶ For 1950-60.   ‡‡ For 1953-61.

are only three countries left, *viz.*, Israel, Ceylon and Pakistan which
have both the same or a higher population density and also a
higher growth rate than India. Of these 4 countries the growth rate
of Israel, like that of Australia, Brazil and Canada, is affected
or vitiated by a heavy immigration rate of Jewish people from all
over the world. According to the U.N. *Monthly Bulletin of Statistics*,
November, 1962, the natural growth rate of this young country
over the period 1956-61, came only to 2.11 per cent per annum.

As in the case of China, the disquieting, rather alarming feature
of our situation consists in the fact that the annual growth rate
is operating on such a huge total, at present, 475 million, that the
absolute net increase, viz., 9 million, it produces yearly, is overwhelming. While India accounts only for 2.4 per cent of the world's
inhabited land area, it contains 14.1 per cent of the world's population. From 1921 to 1960, some 188 million people, just equivalent to the entire population of the USA today, were added to
India's teeming masses. The last decade alone added a huge number of 78 million ! With more than 3,65,000 square miles less of
territory as a result of the partition, India more than made up for
the population of Pakistan (75.8 million in 1951, three years and a
half after August, 1947) which she had lost on the eve of her Independence. The calculations of the Registrar General, Kingsley
Davis, Coale and Hoover as also T. Chellaswami, and the Planning
Commission Experts Committee, who had forecast for 1961 an
upper limit of 397.8, 402, 424 and 431 million respectively, have
all proved to be under-estimates.

While, on the one hand, we are faced with the rising rate of
population growth, on the other, the land area of the country
remains constant. With the result that cultivated area per head
of population, despite extension of cultivation to lands hitherto
left uncultivated, is gradually decreasing, and decreasing at a fast
rate :

1891	109
1901	103
1911	109
1921	111
1931	104
1941	94
1951	84
1961	73

While the rural industries during the British rule declined and
—it must be sorrowfully recorded—are still declining, the growth
of urban industries and services have not been able to offset the.
population increase. The relative dependence on agriculture for
employment in the country has, therefore, gone up and the number
of persons working on a given area of land (and their non-earning
dependents) has increased.

As regards the yields of food crops per acre : a study by the
Indian Council of Agricultural Research showed that, by and large,
the yield per acre, till 1950, tended to remain stationary during
the past several decades. "All the attempts at agricultural improvement . . . have served merely to postpone the diminishing returns
which inevitably follow increasing pressure on land". According to
Economic Survey of Indian Agriculture, 1960-61, published by the
Ministry of Food and Agriculture, Government of India, July 1962,
however, during the 11 years period 1950 to 1960-61, when two
Five Year Plans were executed, the productivity of all agricultural
crops has increased at the rate of 1.54 per cent per annum. Anyway,
two facts are not in dispute : the productivity of land in India is
far below most other countries ; second, till about 1920 India was
usually a surplus producer of food-grains, but for the last four
decades it has been a net importer. As we have already seen,
food-imports since independence have averaged approximately
worth Rs. 123.0 crores a year.

As regards the quality of food that our nationals are able to
get, or their levels of consumption, the following table quoted by
Horace Belshaw, in which some selected countries in pre-war years
have been rated according to 19 indicators, would make the position
clear :

TABLE LXII

LEVELS OF CONSUMPTION IN SELECTED COUNTRIES

Country	Underweighted	Weighted
United States	100	100
Canada	80.6	83.7
United Kingdom	75.6	76.6
Philippines	25.7	21.6
India	20.8	16.8
China	18.0	13.8

Horace Belshaw says :

These selected comparisons are not intended, as precise measures of differences in levels of consumption, still less of welfare, but merely to remind the reader of the rough order of size of the differences in developed and under-developed countries. There is no doubt that these are considerable. While any single indicator may be open to criticism, the general picture is one of levels of consumption which are so low that it would not seem to unduly strain the use of words, or be an undue concession to Malthus, to describe the population in many Asian countries as living pretty close to the subsistence level (*Ibid*, pp. 21-22).

The question, however, arises whether it is under-development of economic resources that India suffers from, or over-population. Those who hold the former view contend that means of life can increase as fast as population growth, and that the problem is not one of increasing population and vanishing resources, but one of under-production and mal-distribution. Malthus's apprehensions that, unless population growth is restrained by preventive checks voluntarily exercised, it will be prevented by the means of subsistence which will gradually decline, or other positive checks like disease, war and famine, have—it is pointed out—been falsified in respect of Western Europe, North America and Oceania, first, by innovations or improvements which he did not foresee ; second, by increased capital formation which became possible out of the increased income resulting from innovations. These changes enabled productive power to grow more rapidly than population. If Malthus has been proved wrong in respect of some countries, he can be proved wrong in respect of others also.

If a considerable segment of our population is under-fed, under-clothed or under-housed,—the argument proceeds—it is because of defective exploitation of our resources and not because of the niggardliness of Mother Nature—because we do not work hard and well enough. India may be faced with tremendous problems, but she is fortunate in having plenty of soil, water, sun and raw materials. The total production of food can be doubled, or even quadrupled by a marriage of modern science and technology with agriculture and food production. Research and technological advance can make it possible to cultivate land which has hitherto been considered uncultivable. Technology has produced synthetic milk without cows, and methods can be devised of converting plants directly into proteins and oils instead of through such secondary media as fish or animals.[2] What is needed is courage and skill to find food and employment for all instead of taking a defeatist attitude that there is no other solution but birth control. Twelve years ago, it is said, the whole economy of Federal Germany was shattered, her factories were in ruins, almost every worker of her 70 million was unemployed. In addition, 8 million refugees had been dumped on her from the East. But she did not sit and weep and introduce 'family planning'. Her answer was hard work. Today her difficulty is to find enough workers.[3] There is no reason why technological improvements and capital investments should not be capable of taking care of population increase in India as they have done in Germany recently or other countries of the West.

A country may be under-populated and still suffer from poverty and unemployment. "Soil productivity", says Josue De Castro, "is not an absolute. Like population density, it is variable, a function of the prevailing kind of economic organisation. The soil has neither absolute productive limits—Vogt's 'biotic potential'—nor absolute demographic limits. The relation to the soil has been handled with an inaccuracy and a blind empiricism repugnant to the scientific spirit. Earl Parker Hanson is entirely right in pointing out : 'Such neo-Malthusians as Vogt seem totally unaware that it is never a land that is over-populated in terms of inhabitants per square mile ; it is always an economy, in terms of inhabitants per square meal.' To prove it, he cites the case of Brazil" :

[2] The transformation of leaves into protein, to be eaten in many different forms, may answer the world's increasing need for food.

This suggestion was made by Mr. N. W. Pirie, Head of the Biochemistry Department at Rothamsted Experimental Station, Hertfordshire, Britain's largest agricultural research establishment.

Writing in the magazine, *Discovery*, he points out that by the end of this century world food production was likely to be more ample than today, but present and foreseeable needs were so great that every reasonable source should be tapped.

Micro-organisms rather than animals would be increasingly used for food, predicted Mr. Pirie. In 24 hours half a ton of bullock would make a pound of protein, but half a ton of yeast would make 50 tons—(*vide* the *Hindustan Times*, New Delhi, dated September 5, 1960).

[3] According to a newsletter by A. C. N. Nambiar published in the *Hindustan Times*, New Delhi, dated June 13, 1960, West Germany was, at the time, negotiating to get 1,00,000 workers from Italy.

To judge by its current low standard of living, Brazil is woefully overpopulated with 40,000,000 inhabitants. But to raise its standard of living, Brazil must diversify its economy, must industrialise, and for that it is so definitely underpopulated that the shortage of labour is one of the chief obstacles to real modernization (*Geography of Hunger*, p. 238).

Poverty of some countries is entirely due to their defective economic system. Population theories in these countries, according to Marxists, have been used almost invariably as a prop for the static view of society and against all proposals for revolutionary change—as a refuge of social reactionaries. It is pointed out : "While there are examples of low standards of living side by side with rapid population growth, this does not prove that population growth is the cause of a low standard. On the contrary, many countries have experienced a rise in national wealth and income per head of population (for example, the United States, England and Belgium) while their population increased rapidly ; and a good argument can be developed to show that population growth has been one of the main factors not only of economic betterment but also of political and cultural greatness. Examples of rapidly increasing population rising in wealth and influence abound, but there are none of a declining population doing so".[4]

The advocates of the other view hold that population change and economic development are inter-linked, that the Indian people have apparently already reached a stage where density and rapid growth of population are impeding economic development, and that economic expansion cannot for ever compensate for a constant increase in population. We may select the most desirable crops and livestock and raise them on the soils best suited to them. We may cultivate the sea as the Japanese have begun to do. But, sooner or later, food production will reach its limit. "Any attempt to compensate indefinitely on the economic side for population increase is bound to fail, because human beings live in a finite world. Atomic energy, use of sun's rays, harnessing of the tides, all may enormously increase the food supply, but they cannot for ever take care of an ever-growing population".[5]

We may educate our people, our engineers and agrarian econo-

[4] *Population Growth and Living Standards*, Albert Nevett, *International Labour Review*, pp. 445-49, November, 1954.
[5] *The Population of India and Pakistan*, 1951, p. 222.

mists may do their best, we may arrange for a re-division of the land, and we may divide up the purchasing power of the Rajas and Maharajas. But how far would these palliatives take us? Our physical resources, in the total, are limited. The basic trouble, it is contended, is excessive parenthood.

Finally, granted that we can produce food in virtually unlimited quantities—but what are we to do about space? The total land area of the globe, including desert, ice and mountain, is only fifty-six million square miles. Suppose we allot each person only one square yard for standing room. Then if world population increases by as little as one per cent per annum, W. Arthur Lewis[6] points out, there will be standing room only in as little as 1,120 years from now. Calculations for India separately will also give similar results.

In actual fact, there is partial truth in both the view-points and one need not take up an extreme position. The terms 'under-development' and 'over-population' do not connote any absolute quantities, but imply a relationship to something else, just as 'too hot', 'too high' or 'too small' do. A country is over-populated or under-populated in accordance with the ratio that the size of its population bears to the quantity of its economic resources: it is developed or under-developed in accordance with the level of exploitation of these resources. A country may have a small population-resources ratio, and yet be a poor or under-developed country if its resources have not been well or fully exploited. Another country may have comparatively a higher population-resources ratio, and yet be a rich or developed country if its resources have been better exploited. So that the level of development, or under-development of a country has little or nothing to do with the size of its population. An under-developed country is one in which there is an under-employment of the existing factors of production, and whose productivity could be increased by the simple introduction of techniques which are already known—or one in which there are, through application of existing techniques, good potential prospects of using more capital or more labour or more available natural resources, or all of these to support its present population on a higher level of living. India is obviously an under-developed country.

The economic conditions of a country are determined not by the absolute quantity of goods it produces or the absolute number of

[6] *The Theory of Economic Growth*, George Allen & Unwin Ltd., 1957, p. 309.

its inhabitants but by the ratio which the goods and the inhabitants bear to each other. If production of wealth is large as compared to the number of consumers, the country will be regarded as wealthy, howsoever numerous its population may be; if small, it will be regarded as poor, howsoever little its population may be. If production of wealth proceeds at a higher pace than does increase in population as in the USA today, levels of consumption will go on rising. If it does at a comparatively lower pace, there will be retrogression of economic standards. Horace Belshaw has put the whole matter admirably in a nutshell. He says :

> Certainly population density has a bearing on levels of consumption, but it should be defined in terms of the relationship between size of population and resources which can be utilised with existing capital at existing levels of technology, as affected by (and influencing) economic and social structure and organisation. In the same way, the problem of improving levels of consumption is not merely one of the rate of population growth, but of the rate of growth in relation to the rate of increase in capital formation and the rapidity and effectiveness of technological improvements in the utilization of natural resources, as affected by (and influencing) changes in economic and social structure.[7]

Developed countries have high consumption levels and in most cases are able to improve them still further, even though their populations are growing fast. In India which is under-developed and poor, the prospects of improvement are precarious and relatively much less; in fact, maintenance of existing levels of consumption will present not a little difficulty. Statistics prove that the gap between living levels in India and the more highly developed countries has actually widened in the last quarter of the century. This is shown *vide* Table LXIII. The two terms, '*per capita* money income' and '*per capita* product', used in the table are, in effect, identical.

The reasons for this widening gap lie, as already noted, first, in the high natural resources : man ratio in some of these countries and an industrial apparatus built on the exploitation of other people's resources in others, and, second, in greater propensity to innovate in all these countries than in India.

It is true that if economic production can advance faster than population can grow, over-population need not occur ; but from this

[7] *Population Growth and Levels of Consumption* by Horace Belshaw (1956), George Allen and Unwin Ltd., London, p. xvii, Introduction.

TABLE LXIII

GAP BETWEEN LIVING LEVELS IN INDIA AND OTHER DEVELOPED COUNTRIES

Countries	Per capita money income in rupees in 1931-32	Per capita product in US dollars in 1952-54	Per capita product in US dollars in 1960
India	65	60	69
	(1)	(1)	(1)
U.S.A.	1406	1870	2286
	(21.6)	(31.2)	(33.1)
Canada	1038	1310	1536
	(16.0)	(22.0)	(22.3)
Australia	980	950	1236
	(15.1)	(15.8)	(17.9)
France	621	740	964
	(9.5)	(12.3)	(14.0)
Germany	603	510*	927
	(9.3)	(8.5)	(13.4)
Japan	281	190	341
	(4.3)	(3.2)	(5.0)

SOURCES : Col. 2 : *Pressure of Population and Economic Efficiency in India* by D. Ghosh, Indian Council of World Affairs, Oxford University Press, 1946, p. 29.

Col. 3 : UNO Statistical Papers Series E No. 4, *Per Capita National Product of Fifty-five Countries :* 1952-54, New York, 1957.

Col. 4 : Calculated on the basis of figures given in UN *Monthly Bulletin of Statistics*, April, 1962.

* Figures relate to Western Germany alone.

Figures for Germany and Japan in 1952-54 show a decline because of the devastation and set-back caused by the Second War and occupation of the two countries by foreign forces for several years.

the conclusion, particularly in the conditions of India and other under-developed countries, that we can concentrate on economic development and ignore population, does not by any means follow. In these countries the rates of financial savings and of capital formation in relation to current population increase are so low that the prospects of growth in output being greater than growth in population are not great ; even a small diminution in the rates of population growth, therefore, may make a difference to the chances of raising levels of consumption. It is to be remembered that in spite of their economic advantage the Western societies have all taken to birth control. They have not remained content with technological innovations and increased capital formation alone.

If we adopt the same techniques, apply as much capital, possess equally skilled workers, as the advanced countries, we can produce not only enough for the existing population, but also for a larger number of people. After assessing the prospects of increased yield due to increased acreage, an increase in the area under irrigation, and methods other than irrigation, the conclusion is expressed in the Census Report for India, 1951 (p. 206), in the following terms : "Of course, there will never be a point of time at which it can be said that the last improvement has been effected. But if we draw the moral correctly from the many unmistakable signs which go to show that the law of diminishing returns is in effective operation, we should make up our minds to face the fact that our effort to keep pace with unchecked growth of population is bound to fail at some point. If the analysis of the subject . . . is even approximately valid, we should be able to go one step further and fix this point by saying that it is the time at which our total number reaches and passes 45 crores."

According to the appraisal made in the report, it might be possible to achieve an over-all increase of agricultural productivity by about one-third of its present level, which would correspond to the needs of a total population strength of 45 crores. This population figure, at the rates of 1951-60, was already reached by mid-1962, that is, 7 years earlier than 1969, as envisaged by the Census Report for 1951. The estimate of possible increase in agricultural production is also pessimistic—we will be able to produce far more and feed a far larger population. But, in the ultimate analysis, the second viewpoint is correct, that is, economic production cannot permanently be advanced in the face of an ever-increasing population. There must come a time when the total production will go up no further with further increases of man-power. Indeed, the time has arrived in many parts of the country already.

Innovations or improvement of soil and of plants can increase the product in excess of the increase of people, but there is a limit to such improvement : improvements can be effected frequently, but not continuously. The ultimate factor, the land, cannot perform miracles. There is a limit to what the land can produce—a limit to the extent to which labour and improvements brought about by scientific knowledge and capital investments can be substituted for land. Ultimately a point is reached whereafter additional expenditure and additional labour on a given area bring less and less results per unit of expenditure or per unit of labour ; so the amount of land available in a country is singly the most vital factor in terms of its population policies. If the size of our average farm continues to shrink year by year, as it is rapidly doing since 1921, we cannot be far from the point at which the most efficiently worked unit will be too small for the needs of the farmer and his family. We must, therefore, sit up and think— think furiously.

This is as regards agricultural production. As regards industrialisation, it has already been considered in a previous chapter as an employment source or an alternative to any population policy at all. The conclusion was reached that no conceivable industrialisation, at least, on the factory scale, will be able to absorb current and prospective increases in India's population. That it has not been able over the past fifty years to reduce the proportion of population dependent on agriculture is undisputed.

The principle that more men result in more product per acre and more total product, and that fewer men result in less product per acre and less total product, explains the resistance of a crowded land to manufacturing. "The evidence from India and China together with the principle which makes the evidence cohere, ought to put an abrupt stop to the recurrent proposal that the overcrowded countries undertake manufacturing as a cure for their poverty, and it ought to take the haze away from the truth that it is necessary to meet the population facts with population measures" (*Population on the Loose*, pp. 63-64).

The opinion that an increase in population will itself increase productive power per head of population derives support from the fact that population growth in the past has, in certain countries, been accompanied by improvements in levels of living. But it does not follow that the former is the cause of the latter : increase in productive power is rarely, if ever, the result of the increase in workers or population *per se*. Nations with increasing populations have risen in affluence and influence only when they have got started with industrialisation, that is, when their economic apparatus expands with still greater pace—when capital formation and technological improvements occur at a greater rate—or, at least, *pari passu* with population. England, Belgium and other countries of Western Europe built up their prosperity on the exploitation of other peoples and countries. It was only in its pioneer days when there was vacant land to cultivate and vast mineral wealth to exploit that growing population was an asset in the USA. It can be and is an asset today in certain countries of Africa and Latin America and also, perhaps, in Australia, Canada and the Soviet Union—countries where there is an abundance of virgin land and other natural resources. New factories need workers, roads must be built, towns and villages expanded, frontiers conquered. But, perhaps, there is not a single example where a nation with an increasing population has attained a position of political or cultural distinction while its economic production has not kept pace or cannot keep pace with population. Population growth by itself or at a rate higher than economic development proceeds, will only serve to lower the consumption levels, with all the misery and degradation that are associated with want.

In this connection it is worthwhile to listen to Vera Anstey's words :

First and foremost, it must be definitely recognised that general prosperity in India can never be rapidly or substantially increased so long as any increase in the income of individuals is absorbed not by a rise in the standard of life, but by an increase in the population. The population problem lies at the root of the whole question of India's economic future, and it is useless to try to bilk the fact.[8]

If every increase in our national wealth is absorbed by the increase in population, putting us back where we originally were, we will never be able to solve the problem of food supply or our economic problem in general. If levels of consumption are to rise, national real income must in the long run grow faster than population.

The existing population of the Union of India increases by ten million every year, if not more ! This increase is obviously a calamity rather than a blessing. For, these ten million people only make the economic situation harsher or more difficult for the existing population. Whatever economic improvement we are able to achieve during the year is cancelled to that extent and it is a large extent.

India's destiny in the next few years, according to a private research study, *viz.*, a recent issue of *Population Bulletin*, Washington, published by a non-Government scientific body, will be controlled by its success or failure in coping with its growth of population. It said : "A period of grace still exists for India, but the time is short. If every year no effective attack is mounted against high fertility, India moves nearer the demographic point of no return. The rising tide will swamp its economic improvement."[9]

We need not be so pessimistic about our destiny as our American friends, but at the same time we cannot afford to be complacent. While we will and should make all efforts to increase our agricultural and industrial production, we will have to so plan that our population does not increase at a pace which negates or largely negates these efforts. Work in the sphere of economic production and of population control can go on simultaneously, both being equally important. We do not have to choose between increase in population on one hand, and industrialisation or economic development of the country, on the other. On the contrary, we should industrialise our country even if we decide to control births, and we may have to restrict the growth of our population even if we can industrialise our economy. The issue is not between population control versus economic development. We can proceed from two angles at the same tine : (a) production can be increased, and (b) the rate of population expansion can be retarded. We may even, as some people contend, regard economic production as of primary and greater importance and population control as of secondary and lesser importance. But it will be a mistake to foreswear any demographic policy altogether and simply try to step up economic production, just as it would be a mistake to simply foreswear any economic policy and try to do it all on the population side. In actual practice this allocation of priorities will make no difference, for, our efforts in one direction will not stand in the way of, or counter-act our efforts in the other direction.

[9] *Hindustan Times*, New Delhi, December 16, 1958.

CHAPTER TWENTY-THREE

Means of Population Control

SLOWING DOWN of the growth rate being a logical approach to improving the Indian living standards, we should set about seriously searching for ways and means of achieving it. Demographically speaking, there are only three ways of doing this—by raising the death rate, encouraging emigration, or lowering the birth rate. Nobody can seriously recommend the first course. Human life, except under extreme group necessity, is an end in itself and not a means to an end, economic or other.

As regards emigration, with India's massive population it does not offer much of a solution. The empty lands, in relation to the size of our population, are not quite so empty as some of us wish they were. Second, as we have already seen in a previous chapter, the doors of almost all countries are already shut to India's nationals. Our people are meeting and would continue to meet with serious resistance if they seek to migrate to foreign countries on a permanent basis. But, supposing the almost impossible were to happen and there was no resistance to settlement of our people in foreign lands, large parts of the world would soon become filled with Indians which will lead to development of minority problems and serious conflicts. Third—and it is this that matters—emigration with a continuing high birth rate and declining death rate would afford no relief, as shown by the experience of Italy. Between 1880 and 1920, 4½ million people migrated from Italy to the United States and 12 million more to other countries. Yet, because the birth rate remained high, population of Italy grew, in that same period, from 29 millions to 39 millions. During the years of greatest migration the population of Italy increased faster than it did before or since. Similarly, if, say, 100 million people were to migrate out of India, the relief from population pressure would last not more than 10 years. The benefits from their departure would be very temporary, indeed, because of the balance of births over deaths of those who would remain. Improvement in medical and sanitary facilities together with measures taken to provide a certain minimum of food to the poorer sections of the community—in fact, humanitarian advances in general—by the very process of saving lives, make worse the overall tragedy of population increase, which is a clear pointer to disaster.

It needs no elaborate argument, therefore, to establish that curtailment of birth rates is the only alternative left to us. If death rates continue to fall, as they will, we will soon be in a mess unless birth rates also fall much to the same extent.

Quite apart from whether the threat of over-population will actually materialise or not, family limitation or spacing of the children is necessary and desirable in order to secure better health for the mother and better care and upbringing of children. It is obvious that excessively frequent child-bearing results in sickness and misery, drudgery and ill-health, both for the mother and for the children. Also, it is better to have fewer children who could be well fed, well educated and well brought up rather than to have many with less to eat and less good things of life to share. It should therefore, need no arguments for a husband to appreciate that he should not over-tax the strength of his wife, or for a couple to realise that they should not procreate more children than they can hope to educate and rear healthily and otherwise to suitably provide for. Contraception would enable fathers to space their children with due regard to the health of the mother and make sure that every child is a wanted child. There could not be a better form of investment, viz., giving the next generation proper care, good health and instruction. How the women think about it all will be clear from a letter which Queen Victoria wrote to her uncle, King Leopold of Belgium, who had congratulated her on giving birth to her first child in 1840 :

I think, dearest Uncle, you cannot really wish me to be the *Mamman d'une nombreuse famille*, for I think you will see with me the great inconvenience a large family would be to us all, and particularly to myself ; men never think, at least seldom think, what a hard task it is for us women to go through this very often.[1]

No doubt, millions and millions of women, in a more or less dumb sort of way, do desire release from perpetual child-bearing and all the misery that so often accompanies it.

[1] Sten S. Nilson, 'Child-Bearing and the Standard of Life,' *International Labour Review*, Vol. LXIX, No. 1, January 1954, pp. 73-76.

While it is conceded by most that birth-control may be conducive to the health of the wife and the children, it is contended that it will have an adverse effect on the health of the husband. In answer to unproven views of this type, it will suffice to quote the following conclusion of Dr. C. V. Drysdale :

Nothing can do away with the fact that as birth rates have declined (in the West) the longevity of both men and women has enormously increased—from the figures of 35 to 45 years before birth control commenced to 60 to 65 years today, and that it is still rapidly increasing. Moreover, recent figures have shown that the improvement in the death rates has taken place to a most remarkable extent, especially during the reproductive period, both in men and women.[2]

Even if it is conceded that improvement in longevity or death-rates has been brought about by means other than, or despite, birth-control, critics will admit that ill-effects of birth-control, if any, can be averted or countered by other factors within reach of man today.

The main reasons in order of importance vouchsafed by married couples to the Royal Commission on Population in UK (1949), for using birth control methods were : (a) that more children could not be afforded, (b) to space pregnancies, (c) for health reasons, and (d) that parental instincts were satisfied with the children already born.

Until recently, Communist authorities everywhere, including China, have been saying that a large population is really no problem in a socialist society. Marx had held that over-population was purely the product of a capitalist society and could not occur under socialism. In China, however, there was now a growing demand for family planning. A decision was taken in 1953 to promulgate birth-control measures throughout the country except in national minority areas. Abortion and sterilisation were approved through an official announcement in 1957. Prime Minister Chou En-lai's reason for the necessity of family planning, which he vouchsafed to the Indian Delegation to China led by Shri M. V. Krishnappa[3]in 1956, was to space the number of children suitably with a view to improv-

[2] "Judgment on Birth-Control", Eugenics Review, January, 1933, quoted in D. Ghosh's Population Pressure and Economic Efficiency in India, p.105.
[3] Para 44, Chap. II of the Report.

ing the health of the mothers and the education of the children. As soon as a good method of contraception was discovered, the Government of China intended to undertake a country-wide campaign for the adoption of family planning by the Chinese people. For what the Chinese Prime Minister may have left unsaid, the Communist government of the country might be finding reasons that have led to birth-control in other countries, valid in their circumstances also.[3a] A policy which might be right in relation to the special circumstances of Russia—and it is these policies that have usually guided Communists all over the world till now—might not be right in relation to conditions of such countries as China and India.

Through medicine, sanitation and public-health measures, man has interfered with Nature by combating diseases and prolonging his life. Since birth and death are a pair of opposites and have to keep in step with each other, he must to an equivalent degree now interfere with Nature by controlling the production of off-spring. If it is not sinful to practise medicine and sanitation, neither would it be sinful to practise birth control. From a purely physical point of view, birth control would also be easier than death control.

[3a] China's essay into the problem of population has, however, been erratic. The campaign started in early 1957 was snuffed out abruptly in November 1957 without any explanation. Chairman Mao made a brief public reference to population at the Congress in May 1958 : "Our fast expanding population is an objective fact and is our asset". Chou En-lai and Liu Shao Chi cheered "the great flesh-and-blood force of our vast population, by which we can, or soon can, do anything within the realm of human possibility". The *People's Daily*, which had said in July, 1957 that "an ideal family should have only three, or at most four children in a planned manner," claimed in August, 1958, that "China will always have room for more people because of our rich resources, good natural conditions and wide territory". Latest reports indicate that now all this has changed again. Apart from a succession of bad harvest, China has run into grave industrial difficulties and urban unemployment. Rumbles of inflation are also getting noisier. All these have prompted what might be described as "backsliding" over the issue of family planning.

The argument has now been shifted against early parenthood in the interest of young wives, the proper care and education of children, and the rest and relaxation of young husbands between their work and their self-criticism. The new party line is that no man should be a father until he is 26 and no woman a mother until 23 and that births should be spaced "according to the mother's capacity for work". Direct and explicit advice for contraception is being given. The old birth-control clinics which had fallen into relative disuse are hustling for business once more.

Gandhiji admitted the necessity of birth control but believed that there was only one sound method, *viz.*, that of abstinence. He said : "There can be no two opinions about the necessity of birth control. But the only method handed down from ages past is self-control or *Brahmacharya*. It is an infallible sovereign remedy doing good to those who practise it. And medical men will earn the gratitude of mankind, if, instead of devising artificial means of birth-control, they will find out the means of self-control. The union is meant not for pleasure but for bringing forth progeny. And union is a crime when the desire for progeny is absent."[4]

For Mahatmaji, sexual pleasure was inherently sinful. It was justified only when it served a higher purpose—reproduction. It followed that the only permissible form of birth control was abstinence or self-control. There are many Hindus (which include all religious leaders) who agree with Mahatmaji that any method which allows people to have sexual pleasure without risking the penalty of having children, is a materialistic innovation and promotes immorality. Says D. Ghose in this context :

The moral arguments which are usually advanced against birth control are two. First, it is considered unnatural and immoral ; those who use contraceptives are supposed to interfere with Nature and cheat her of her end ; they gratify their passions, and yet avoid conception which is its natural consequence. On this view of things, however, every act of human intelligence should be considered unnatural and immoral. We are constantly controlling, directing and thwarting Nature to serve our purposes rather than her own. And users of contraceptives cheat Nature far less than she cheats herself ; for, out of every 5 million sperms ejected at each orgasm, only one finds its way to the ovum to fertilize it ; the rest die after a fruitless existence. Secondly, contraceptives are supposed to promote excessive sex indulgence in and out of marriage. Some abuse there is of the freedom from the consequences of sexual union which contraceptives secure ; but the evil does not seem to be as serious as it is made out. Hosts of normal persons in the UK, for example, have not only had easy access to the means of birth control for a long time, but they have consistently applied them. But to assume that they have indulged excessively and to their undoing is in accordance neither with everyday experience nor with the Registrar-General's statistics.[5]

---

[4] *Young India,* March 12, 1925.

[5] *Pressure of Population and Economic Efficiency in India,* Indian Council of World Affairs, Oxford University Press, 1946, pp. 105-106.

For the vast mass of mankind, therefore, who cannot rise to the heights of Gandhiji, the problem becomes one of control not by abstinence, or restraint of sex instincts, but by limitation. Recent surveys have proved that public opinion in the country, both urban and rural, is in favour of fewer children. They know why the children come and yet, being fashioned of the common clay, they cannot help it. The fear of undesigned parenthood or unwanted children has not proved sufficiently powerful as a restraining force.

A Family Planning Pilot Research Project being conducted in several villages of Uttar Pradesh has revealed that 60 per cent of the mothers and 55 per cent of the fathers in these areas were eager to learn methods of family planning. About 70 per cent of the married women in these villages recorded that they do not want to have more than three or four children in all, at an average spacing of three and a half years.

Mrs. Shakuntala Paranjpye, who has been working in different parts of India for over 13 years in this sphere, said in her report to the First All-India Conference on Family Planning (Bombay, 1951) :

It has been my experience that most people, regardless of their social status, are willing and grateful to receive advice in spacing and limiting their families. In slums and rural areas I have met with the same response from people as in middle class localities. In fact, people of the working classes, whether they work in the cities or villages, have their roots in the rural parts of the land and readily realize that while they multiply, their holdings do not ; that when a tree bears too much fruit it often succumbs under the burden and in any case such fruit is of a less quality than when it bears less....[6]

A recent survey made in Baroda city (population 2,11,000) showed that from 63 per cent to 77 per cent of women, classified according to language groups, favoured birth control, and between 44 per cent and 62 per cent favoured either contraception or an operation. Those favouring control of size of family by one method or another varied from 70 per cent to 82 per cent. Those favouring control of size of family by moral restraint as well as contraception, grouped according to income instead of languages, were between 69 and 100 per cent of the total in each income group.

The Director of the United Nations Office for Population Studies in New Delhi, in 1953, published the results of a survey carried out

[6] *International Labour Review*, January 1954, pp. 73-76.

in Mysore. Here it turned out that 60 per cent of the urban and 40 per cent of the rural dwellers interviewed took a positive interest in the limitation of births ; in other areas the percentage rose as high as 70.

Addressing the fourth annual meeting of the Family Planning Board, the Union Minister of Health, Mr. Karmarkar, declared that "there is a general acceptance of the family planning programme in this country".

Another proof—if proof is at all needed—of the intense desire to limit the number of their children, can be seen in the fact that in many parts of India married women take to induced abortion[7] than which there could not be a more objectionable method of birth control. Infanticide also, which prevailed in certain communities till the last century, could in part, be traced to this desire.

The question now arises as to upon which of the married couples in particular, the obligation in India to practise birth control lies in their own as well as in the national interest. Every man—let us not forget—owes a duty not only to his wife and his children, but also to the nation. Our general aim may be defined to be : so to limit the number of births that they do not materially exceed the number of deaths and thus achieve a substantially stationary population as soon as possible.

According to the 1951 Census Report the total number of births which occurred in the course of one year in the decade, 1941-50, among about 1,000 people of India was 40. Among these 40 births, 8 births were first births ; 16 births were either first births or second births ; 23 births were either first, second or third births ; and 17 births out of 40 were either fourth births or births of higher order. Calculations made in the report show that if the number of children born to a married couple does not exceed three, the excess of births over deaths at the mortality rates of the forties will be reduced to negligible numbers and a substantially stationary population achieved. A child-birth occurring to a mother who has already given birth to three[7a] or more children (of whom at least

---

[7] As already noted, China had legalised abortion in 1957 ; so also Japan. In 1947 the birth rate in Japan was 34.3 per thousand. In 1958 it was brought down to 18 per thousand. This miracle was achieved through abortion—a method highly repugnant to many people.

[7a] Although figures are not available, yet in view of a steep reduction in death rates during 1951-60, this figure would now stand reduced.

one is alive) in our circumstances, may, therefore, well be defined as 'improvident maternity'. If the figure obtained by expressing the number of births of this nature as a percentage of all births occurring in any particular area during any particular period of time be treated as 'incidence of improvident maternity', the following table for six countries based on the latest figures shows that this incidence in India (17 births out of 40) is the highest :

TABLE LXIV

INCIDENCE OF IMPROVIDENT MATERNITY IN CERTAIN
COUNTRIES

Country	Incidence of 'improvident maternity'
1. India	42.8
2. Japan	33.9
3. France	19.7
4. U.S.A.	19.2
5 U.K.	14.3
6. Germany (Federal Republic)	12.3

A great many people in our country, then, need to practise birth control.

There are, broadly speaking, three direct methods of birth control, which may also be called preventive checks to population growth, *viz.*, delayed marriage, voluntary restraint within marriage and artificial control of conception.

Throughout India, early marriages have been until recently the rule, but a deferment of only a year or two may make a considerable difference to total fertility. According both to medical and statistical evidence, greater number of births in almost all populations occur in the comparatively early years of married life. Fertility of women in the first half (15-30 years) is greater than in the second half (30-45 years) of their child-bearing stage. The Indian Census Report, 1951, gives on page 84 the child birth indices of two classes of mothers in Travancore-Cochin (now Kerala) *viz.*, those who commence child-bearing during ages 15 to 19 and those who commence during ages 20 to 24 called Maternity Types A and B respectively, in a table as follows :

TABLE LXV

CHILD-BIRTH INDICES ACCORDING TO AGE GROUPS IN KERALA IN 1951

	Child-birth indices	
Age Group	maternity type A	maternity type B
Under 20	1.2	..
20 to 24	2.0	1.3
25 to 29	3.6	2.3
30 to 34	4.8	3.7
35 to 39	6.0	4.9
40 to 44	6.8	5.8
45 and over	7.3	6.4

The figures of this table indicate that if we can bring about a postponement of age of marriage by five years, maternity would be reduced by approximately one-eighth which will be not a negligible gain, indeed. Similar results were obtained from figures relating to Madhya Pradesh[8]

Besides observance of continence or *Bramacharya*, there is a method of birth control falling within the term 'voluntary restraint within marriage', though not in full consonance with Mahatmaji's views or strict Hindu thought, yet approvingly mentioned in the Hindu scriptures, *viz.*, the 'rhythm method', or what is known in the West, as the rule of the 'safe period'. According to this method, which is suggested in the *Brahadaranyaka Upanishad*, people are merely advised to observe abstinence during particular days, or the middle-third of every menstrual cycle. This method, however, ac-

[8] A survey made at the time of the Indian Census of 1931, however, showed that an increase in the age of marriage increased the number of children born and also the probability of their survival. While the average number of children born from wives married at the age of 15-19 was 4.1 and the survival rate 2.1, the respective figures for wives married at 20-29 years and 30 years and over stood at 4.3 and 3.1, and 5.1 and 3.6 respectively.

cording to experiments conducted under Government aegis, has been found not to be completely effective.

Artificial control of conception is of three kinds, viz., the non-appliance method, the appliance method and sterilisation. The first is more or less synonymous with *coitus interruptus*. Evidence of wide practice of this method, even in recent years, has been reported in Great Britain where an investigation into the contraceptive habits of the population was conducted in 1946-47. Among recently married couples about 43 per cent were using this method.

The second consists in the use of chemical or mechanical devices which interfere with the natural results of sexual intercourse. They are designed to immobilise or destroy the spermatozoa or to prevent them from entering the womb. The difficulty is that very little medical and biological research has been expended on improving contraceptive methods and the existing techniques—the use of douches, jellies and pessaries which represent the latest development up to this time—are not very well suited to the Indian population.

The peasants of India are too poor to purchase such devices, not able to understand them, probably would be repelled by the idea, are not careful or responsible enough to use them regularly and effectively, and do not understand the vast issues involved.[9]

So that a contraceptive adapted to the conditions of those countries like India, China and Indonesia, which need it most, does not exist at present. In fact, the position all the world over, so far as the technique of contraception is concerned, is extremely unsatisfactory. A fully satisfactory contraceptive is still to be found.

Sterilisation of either spouse is a surer method. The operation on the woman—*salpingectomy*—can be performed at any time and does not ordinarily require a long period of hospitalisation, but it is usually performed twenty-four to forty-eight hours after delivery because it is easier done at this time. Owing to the simplicity of the operation on the males, however, they are the ones who, in most cases, should be sterilised.

The severity of *vasectomy*, or the Steinach operation as also it is called, is no greater than a tooth extraction, and no more dangerous. A man who had an operation in the morning could go back to work

[9] *Which Way Lies Hope ?* First Edition, 1952, p. 62.

in the afternoon. The wide-spread notion that the operation changes
sexual activities and desires, is not well-founded. The effect is to
prevent the microscopic sperm cells from leaving the body. They
come into being as before, and the male hormone comes into being
as before ; so there is no change in sex desire or in the psychological
effects of sex relations. The sperm cells, as they disintegrate, are
taken up by the blood as impurities and thrown off like other waste
tissue. Thus, there is no disabling effect on the general health either.
It is obvious that this operation should be undergone only by those
men who want a technique of permanent conception control—say,
a father of three or four children.[10]

Until now contraceptives have been either chemical or mechanical. Research is now being directed along lines which may yield
biological contraceptives. It is hoped that birth control by an oral
pill is not more than a few years away. According to the *Statesman*,
dated May 6, 1958, the Union Government is already experimenting
with an oral contraceptive to be taken by males. Extracted from
the common field pea (*pisun sativum*) and also synthetically produced in the laboratory, the effect of the contraceptive pills on about
800 women is being observed for the last two years at the All-India
Institute of Hygiene and Public Health, Calcutta. Results so far are
stated to be very satisfactory.[11]

[10] The 'Pioneer', Lucknow, dated May 24, 1960, carried the following
report :

"LONDON, May 23—Indian birth control specialist, Dr. G. M.
Phadke's startling new method for men was described at the 23-
nation Family Planning Conference at The Hague as the 'greatest
advance in the science of birth control'.

India's representative, Dr. Sushila S. Gore, added that Dr. Phakde's
method involving a painless operation under local anaesthetic 'is
foolproof'.

The new method being tried in Government-sponsored tests on 100
men in Bombay is claimed to render the subject sterile for a year or
so. Another brief operation can restore the ability to procreate if
required.

One snag is that a cord severed during the sterilising operation tends
to rejoin itself naturally after a time, but is expected to be overcome.

The operation does not stifle the sexual instinct or prevent intercourse."

[11] According to a report in the *Pioneer*, Lucknow, of August 7, 1962,
Dr. A. K. Mukherji, Head of the Department of Physiology, Presidency
College, Calcutta, and Dr. K. C. Ghosh, formerly of Burma Medical
Service, have claimed here to have discovered a new oral contraceptive

According to an article by Robert Sheehan, entitled "A Pill to Cure Over-Population ? New Birth-Control Methods are given their First Mass Test", published in an American Magazine, *Life*, dated July 7, 1958, several US scientists, working with steroid hormones, appear to have found the answer to the problem of finding a simpler and more acceptable method of curbing fertility than the various mechanical obstruction and chemical supermicides. The compounds they have come up with are progestins. These are synthetic substitutes for the natural hormone progesterone that all women secrete when pregnant ; progesterone is known to prevent further ovulation (the release of fertilisable egg cells) during pregnancy. This is exactly what the synthetic progestin does to the non-pregnant women—it inhibits ovulation. One such progestin, in pill form, is being used in the study which is being made in Puerto Rico. To those women who followed the regimen faithfully (one pill a day for 20 days of each month), it has given 100 per cent protection against pregnancy.

At this stage the total performance of the drug is far from definitive, and no one knows what setbacks may lie ahead. That such a progestin would effectively prevent pregnancy was no great surprise to scientists. But there remain many problems to be solved, both scientific and social. Is the drug non-toxic ? Is its action selective, or might it disturb, beyond re-establishment, the delicate balance of the organism ? What about individual differences in tolerance ? How long can suppression of ovulation be continued without permanently sterilising a woman ? Scientists believe that at least five years of strictly controlled testing on at least 500 women (preferably of different ethnic groups), plus lifetime testing of an

agent, isolated from an Indian indigenous plant seed 'Genimin' generally available in Bengal and Burma.

They told pressmen that the effectiveness of this agent has been proved "extremely satisfactory" in both human subjects and experimental animals.

Dr. Mukherji said "It is safe, harmless and non-toxic both to human subjects and in animals. A single dose of 'Genimin' in soluble gelatine capsule is effective in checking conception for one year".

After application of the drug, normal menstruation cycle in all human subjects had been reported. No inhibition in sex libido was noted. After the lapse of one-year period normal conception occurred in human subjects. Dr. Mukherji added however, that they needed another two years for carrying on further research about various effects of the drug.

appropriate animal species, are needed for dependable evaluation and final approval of the habitual use of such a drug.

Second, there is the possibility of inducing temporary sterility in the male or female through hormonal control or a hypodermic injection of a hormone. It will be a perfect contraceptive which will induce loss of fecundity for a given or definite length of time and will be revocable at will.

Third, research on certain plant materials used by the ancient peoples in many parts of the world is also under way.

When as a result of any of these researches a harmless, reliable and clean contraceptive is made available, it will revolutionise the whole field of family planning and the problem of the unwanted child—a problem of such serious import to India and some other countries—would have been solved.

In the ultimate analysis, however, the issue is as much sociological as technological. A programme of family limitation cannot be a success only when the old values and sentiments of the people have been changed.

Besides the direct methods of birth control, it is said, there are, at least, two indirect factors, viz., education and increased material prosperity, which tend to reduce human fertility. In our opinion, this assumption is not correct : these factors tend to reduce the birth rates, not the fertility. Ultimately these two factors resolve into one : almost universally a people who are more prosperous are also more educated.

TABLE LXVI

VARIATION IN RATE OF DECENNIAL GROWTH OF POPULATION OF THE WORLD AND ASIA, AFRICA AND EUROPE SINCE 1751[11a]

Period	Total world population at the beginning of the period (in crores)	Rate of Decennial Growth				
		Africa	Asia	Europe	New World	World as a whole
1751-1800	72.8	Nil	4.5	5.7	12.4	4.4
1801-1850	90.5	1.8	4.4	7.0	15.5	5.1
1851-1900	117.0	4.5	4.5	8.1	16.8	6.3
1901-1950	160.8	9.3	6.8	6.0	15.1	4.0

[11a] According to U.N.'s *Demographic Year-book*, 1961, the rate of population growth during the fifties in Africa, Asia, Europe, America, and the world as a whole respectively stood at 22, 19, 8, 21, and 18.

The rate of growth for various regions and the world as a whole over the last two centuries is shown vide Table LXVI.

The table indicates that the birth rates of Europe and the New World which had been constantly increasing since 1750, have been falling fast since 1900. The theory was advanced that this fall in the birth rate among West European people and the people of the same stock in the New World was due to their rising standards of living. In fact, the law or theory was a hundred years old. It was stated by Thomas Doubleday in 1853 as follows :

There is in all societies a constant increase going on amongst that portion of it which is the worst supplied with food; in short, amongst the poorest.

Amongst those in the state of affluence and well supplied with food and luxuries, a constant decrease goes on.

This theory has, however, been disproved by the findings of the Royal Commission on Population in the United Kingdom (1949). The Commission says : "There is, thus, an overwhelming volume of evidence in this and other countries that the rates of child-bearing are at present being greatly restricted by the practice of birth control and other methods of deliberate family limitation below the level at which they would stand if no such methods were practised."[12]

Thus, an improvement of the nutritional standards or other standards of living is by no means incompatible with the maintenance of a high rate of child-bearing, if the people so desired. It is due not to education or increased material prosperity, but to the practice of contraception which, during the last 60 years, has grown and become part of the normal mode of conjugal life among the majority of the people in Western Europe and people of their stock inhabiting the New World, that their birth rates have gone down.

According to the Royal Commission the percentage of women in the United Kingdom reporting the use of any form of birth control, classified according to date of marriage, is shown in Table LXVII.

This table shows that there is a steady increase with date of marriage in the use of birth control at some time during married life. It should be noted that these percentages under-estimate the percentage of women who will eventually use birth control in the

[12] Para 87, Chapter IV of the Report.

TABLE LXVII

PERCENTAGE OF WOMEN USING BIRTH CONTROL AT SOME
TIME DURING MARRIED LIFE

Date of marriage	No. of women	Percentage who used birth control
Before 1910	161	15
1910-19	361	40
1920-24	342	58
1925-29	339	61
1930-34	440	63
1935-39	617	66
1940-47	974	55
Omitted	47	..
Total	3,281	

latter marriage cohorts,[13] since some of those not using it up to the time of the survey will subsequently adopt it. This accounts for the lower percentage in the last cohort.

Josue De Castro, the author of *Geography of Hunger* (London, Victor Gollancz Ltd., 1952), also a believer in the theory that lack of sufficient food increases the rate of population growth, refers to experiments made on rats which showed that diets inadequate in protein (or animal products) increased fecundity, and says that the way this result came about in rats was also true of human beings. And animal products or foods with high protein content being usually more expensive than starchy foods, poor people cannot get enough of them.

Table LXVIII shows, however, that there is no correlation between consumption of proteins or calories of animal origin and material prosperity on one hand, and birth rate on the other. Canada, Australia and United States consume more proteins and more calories of animal origin than most European countries, yet have a higher birth rate. India and Japan consume less protein and less calories of animal origin than all other countries shown in the table, yet have lower birth rates than many of them :

There is also one important factor which is missed in these calculation, *viz.*, the reduction in birth rates brought about in several

[13] The term, 'marriage cohort', is used to indicate groups of women married in a given set of years.

TABLE LXVIII

STATEMENT SHOWING INTAKE OF CALORIES AND PROTEIN
ESTIMATES OF NATIONAL INCOME AND CRUDE BIRTH RATES
OF 33 COUNTRIES OF THE WORLD DURING 1960-61

Sl. No.	Name of countries	CALORIES (Number Per Day)		PROTEIN (Grammes Per Day)		Per Capita National Income (in U.S. Dollars)	Crude birth rates (per 'ooo population)
		Total	Animal origin	Total	Animal origin		
1	2	3	4	5	6	7	8
1.	Ireland	3,570*†	1,464§§	96*†	57*†	530	21.4
2.	New Zealand	3,490†	1,780	110†	75†	1,285	26.5
3.	Denmark	3,340*	1,403§§	94*	59*	1,036	16.6
4.	United Kingdom	3,290*	1,283§§	87*	52*	1,071	17.5
5.	Australia	3,260*	1,369	93*	61*	1,236	22.4
6.	Canada	3,150*	1,386§§	96*	65*	1,536	26.9
7.	United States	3,120†	1,279	92†	65*	2,286	23.6
8.	Finland	3,090*	1,174§§	93*	52*	821	18.4
9.	Netherlands	3,080	893	80	47	807	20.8
10.	Austria	3,010	993	88	47	644	17.8
11.	Norway	2,980*	1,192	82*	49*	971	17.5
12.	Switzerland	2,980*	1,043§§	85*	51*	1,377	17.6
13.	Yugoslavia	2,970*†	624§§	96*†	26*†	481	23.1
14.	Argentina	2,950	1,092	91	48	378	..
15.	France	2,940*	..	98*	52*	964	18.0
16.	Germany (F.R.)	2,940	1,029§§	80	48	927	17.6
17.	Belgium	2,930*	967	87*	47*	989	16.9
18.	Sweden	2,920	1,226§§	81	53	1,377	13.7
19.	Turkey	2,830††	311	90††	14††	164 (1959)	..
20.	Israel	2,770*	499	83*	34*	911	27.1
21.	Italy	2,740	493§§	80	28	509	18.5
22.	Brazil	2,650‡	450§§	67‡	19‡	108 (1959)	..

TABLE LXVIII (contd.)

Sl. No.	Name of countries	CALORIES (Number Per Day)		PROTEIN (Grammes Per Day)		Per Capita National Income (in U.S. Dollars)	Crude birth rates (per '000 population)
		Total	Animal origin	Total	Animal origin		
2		3	4	5	6	7	8
23.	U.A.R.	2,580††	181	76††	13††	112 (1958)	..
24.	Chile	2,570‡	463§§	77‡	26‡	503	35.4
25.	Paraguay	2,500††	475§§	68††	26††	101	
26.	China Taiwan	2,310*†	277	56*†	14*†	114	39.5
27.	Venezuela	2,300	437	64	27	891	49.6
28.	Japan	2,240**	179	68**	18**	341	17.2
29.	Columbia	2,200§	418§§	48§	23§	215 (1959)	..
30.	Pakistan	2,080*	166	48*	7*	52	..
31.	Peru	2,060	288§§	52	13†	113 (1959)	32.5
32.	Phillipines	1,950†‡	176§§	49‡	15†	135	
33.	India	1,860††	112§§	50††‡	6	69	22.4

* relate to 1959-60 　　　** refers to Fiscal year, April-March
† calendar years instead of split year 　‡ relate to 1957
†† relate to 1957-58—1959-60 　　§ relate to 1956-58
　　　　　　　　　　　　　　§§ Tentative data.

SOURCE : (1) Crude Birth rates in Col. 8 has been taken from U.N. Monthly Bulletin of Statistics—September, 1962.

(2) (i) For col. 7 : United Nations Monthly Bulletin of Statistics, April 1962.

(ii) Exchange rates for conversion of National currency units into US Dollars from U.N. Monthly Bulletin of Statistics, April, 1962 and IMF International Financial Statistics March 1962.

(3) Total calories, total protein, animal origin in Cols. 3, 5 and 6 have been taken from F.A.O. Production Year Book 1961, while calories of animal origin in Col. 4 have been worked out from percentages as appear in Table 126 of U.N. Statistical Year Book—1961.

Note : Countries have been arranged in the descending order of Total calories as in Col. 3.

of the above countries by the use of contraceptives and other methods. Unless allowance is made for the births which would have occurred but for the practice of birth control, it is not possible to determine the fecundity of a people. So that it would seem to be a useless pastime to relate the birth rates with the consumption of proteins, or, for the matter of that, any other food, or with the extent of prosperity and the economic conditions obtaining in the different countries, or to draw any conclusions from the relation.

There is evidence in the Indian Census Report, 1951, also to the effect that birth rates are not governed by the social status or the economic standard of the families or classes concerned. There can be no manner of doubt that the agricultural labourers in India occupy the lowest place in the social and economic ladder. Yet, they do not have more children or grow in numbers faster than others. The following table gives the figures for Travancore-Cochin (now Kerala) for which alone these calculations were made :

TABLE LXIX

CHILD-BIRTH INDICES IN KERALA ACCORDING TO GROUPS OF POPULATION IN 1951

Maternity group	Child-birth indices	
	Age 45 and over	All ages
Agricultural land-holders and tenants' families	6.7	4.5
Agricultural Labourers' families	6.3	4.1
Non-agricultural families	6.6	4.2
Rural	6.6	4.3
Urban	6.4	4.2

We reach the same conclusion when figures relating to east and west plains of the State of Uttar Pradesh are compared. It is a well-known fact that economic conditions in the west region are somewhat better than those in the east, particularly, those in Meerut division as compared with Gorakhpur division. Residents of the former consume greater quantity of milk and milk products which contain a large percentage of protein and eat less rice which is a most starchy food, as compared with those of the latter. As regards the percentage of literacy, the figures for the two regions and divisions, taken from the Census Report of 1951, are given below :

	Percentage of literacy
West plain	10.8
East plain	9.1
Meerut Division	12.7
Gorakhpur Division	7.9

Yet, as Table LXX will show, the birth rates in the former plain and division are higher than in the latter. Figures of birth and death registration are not accurate, but there is no reason to suppose that the degree of error in one part of the State differs from that of another. In any case they may be taken as fairly indicative of the real trends.

The same results for the two plains for the year 1953 are evidenc· ed by Census of India, Paper No. I, 1955—Sample Census of Births and Deaths—1953-54, Uttar Pradesh, pages 21 and 51 :

TABLE LXXI

REGISTERED BIRTH AND DEATH RATES PER ONE THOUSAND, 1953, CORRECTED FOR OMISSIONS IN REGISTRATION

Natural division	Birth Rates		Death Rates		Growth rate
	registered	corrected	registered	corrected	
West Plain	17.6	25.8	12.0	17.2	8.6
East Plain	13.9	18.3	8.9	11.6	6.7
Uttar Pradesh	15.3	21.7	10.1	14.2	7.5

Generally, figures from Kerala and Uttar Pradesh in India should be more reliable in assessing the effect of social status, education and economic conditions on birth rates than from any other country, inasmuch as here the results of birth rates are not affected by use of contraceptives. Birth control in India today is practised only by an infinitesimal proportion of the population.

TABLE LXX

MEAN DECENNIAL RATES

Region	Population in Thousands		Percentage increase	Births per 1,000 (Registered)			Deaths per 1,000 (Registered)			Actual Growth		
	1921	1951		1921-1930	1931-1940	1941-1950	1921-1930	1931-1940	1941-1950	1921-1930	1931-1940	1941-1950
1	2	3	4	5	6	7	8	9	10	11	12	13
Meerut Division	45,09	67,19	49.2	38.7	39.3	30.3	27.8	24.6	18.3	8.5	15.0	16.0
Gorakhpur division	67,21	88,31	31.3	30.6	29.8	21.4	21.9	18.9	14.8	7.0	10.0	12.5
West Plain	167,29	227,71	36.1	38.9	39.3	29.5	28.9	25.1	18.7	6.6	13.4	11.4
East Plain	134,98	178,87	32.5	30.0	30.4	21.8	22.3	19.3	15.3	7.0	11.3	11.0
Uttar Pradesh	466,70	632,16	35.5	34.0	34.2	24.8	25.6	21.9	16.5	6.4	12.7	11.2
Corrected				39.9	38.8	34.9	32.7	26.0	23.8	6.4	12.7	11.2

SOURCE: Tables No. 40, 61, 68 and 77 of Part I-A and table No. A-II of Part II-A of Census of India, 1951, Volume II, Uttar Pradesh—Report.

The conclusion, *viz.*, that education and material prosperity do not affect fecundity of a woman, receives confirmation from English figures also :

TABLE LXXII

SPECIFIC FERTILITY OF MARRIED WOMEN IN COCHIN (1936-37) AND ENGLAND AND WALES (1931)

Age Period	Cochin	England & Wales
15-20	224	372
20-25	249	267
25-30	253	187
30-35	246	127
35-40	182	81
40-45	120	33
Total fertility	6,370	5,335

Remarks D. Ghose :[15]

If all women in the two countries marry by age 15 and if no one of them dies before completing her forty-fifth year, the average Indian woman would give birth to between 6 and 7 children and the average English woman to nearly 5½ children. The Indian woman is seen to be not so much more prolific than the English inspite of our much higher birth rate. Indeed, when we take into account the fact that while in England and Wales contraceptives are in extensive use, in India they play as yet a small part in determining the flow of births, Indian women appear to be less fecund than the English.

The English were, at the time to which the figures relate, about thirteen times more prosperous and seven times more literate than the Indian.

It would seem, therefore, that neither material prosperity nor education has anything to do with the activity of the hormones. If the birth rates in the educated and prosperous sections of the society

[15] *Pressure of Population and Economic Efficiency in India*, p. 15.

are less, it is due not to any biological change, but to change in attitudes—to the desire on their part to accumulate money and achieve social position through limitation of births. They have also the knowledge and the means to translate their desire into practice, which illiterate and poor people have not.

Horace Belshaw invites the reader's attention to the following :

The generally accepted view is that the decline in birth rates, was the result of industrialisation and urbanisation. Undoubtedly there is a relationship, but its precise nature is by no means clear. We may indicate probable causes with some degree of confidence, but they appear to be many and we are by no means sure of their relative importance . . . . New Zealand began to experience a downward trend of birth rates eighty years ago when neither greatly industrialised or urbanised nor densely populated. The trend appears to have begun earlier in the US than in the industrially more advanced and urbanised British Isles. So it is safer to regard changes in attitudes as arising out of the process of which industrialisation and urbanisation were a part, as well as out of the actual effects of these latter (pp. 25-26).

Industrialisation encourages the development of new patterns of living which lead to the control of high birth rates. Seen in this perspective, industrialisation is ultimately a means of reducing birth rates through changing the conditions of life and, thus, forcing people in their private capacity to seek the means of family limitation. Industrialisation, however, is a very slow process : even granting that it can be greatly accelerated, the time required would, nevertheless, permit huge interim growth in numbers, and thus as a population policy it has little to recommend in its favour. Industrialisation being instrumental to so many ends, its feasibility and character should be determined on grounds other than that it is found to be an indirect means of population control in its later stages.

The population problem has become the most fundamental of all human problems today, and cannot be lightly set aside. It affects every aspect of a man's social life : it affects him inasmuch as it affects the health and happiness of his family ; it affects him inasmuch as it affects the economic conditions of his country ; and, finally, it affects him in as much as it affects international security and peace, for it is the problems of population pressure that largely underlie the issues of peace and war. No matter what the apparent or immediate cause may be, many a war has its basic roots in economic differentials between nations—in uneven distribution of physical resources of the world relative to population of the various countries.

Countries that expand their population beyond the support of their food production have three courses open : either they produce industrial goods in exchange whereof they may purchase food, or reduce their population by emigrating and/or controlling their birth rates, or sink to lower levels of food consumption and, if these levels have already touched the bottom, owing to malnutrition, invite disease and starvation, with periodic visitations of epidemics and famine, so that only so many remain as can just subsist on the barest rations. Nations which are vigorous, industrialised and militarily strong, will seek either markets in which they can sell their manufactured goods and purchase their food, or *lebensraum* and, if they find an obstacle, will precipitate a war in the interest of survival. Countries like the USA and the USSR need not go to war in quest of food or *in the interest of self-preservation*. It is apparent from their land resources in comparison with their populations that they produce and should continue to produce food sufficient to feed their peoples at their present rate of reproduction, at least in the foreseeable future. If these two giants are today preparing for war, it is for reasons which are really rooted in the pugnacity or combativeness of human nature, though they might be clothed in terms of ideology. An attempt on the part of one country to win decisive hegemony leads to similar attempts by others, or preparations for self-defence out of fear. Offence, or forestalling, in certain circumstances may be the best form of defence, or baffling an attack that may be contemplated—and this leads to a vicious circle. The case of those countries which depend upon outside sources of food, like the UK and Germany, which they receive in exchange of their industrial products is, however, different. If they cannot sell the latter or purchase the former, and are unable to dump their population in open spaces or comparatively sparsely populated regions of the world, they will go to war, merits of a dispute or question notwithstanding.

The population problem, therefore, is not the concern of population experts alone, nor even that of Governments alone. It is the vital concern of every thoughtful citizen. No practical action can result unless the population policy that may be proposed has the intelligent backing of informed public opinion. The death rate can be reduced by public action taken by the few. The birth rate can be reduced or stabilised only by private action taken by the many.

In the West, family limitation propaganda was unofficial. But the situation in our country demands an all-out Government campaign using every available educational and propagandistic resource to take family planning to the very doors of our people. Owing to the furtive air that clings to the subject, there is a good deal of ignorance in the country over the whole question of conjugal relations. This furtive air has to be dissipated : solution of the population problem will be found round the corner once our people simply begin to think about it. Oswald Spengler puts it thus—"When the ordinary thought of a highly cultivated people begins to regard having children as a matter of pros and cons, the great turning point has come."

It must be recognised, however, that a direct approach to family limitation by education and propaganda is no more likely to achieve quick results than it did in the West, that alteration in population trends would take, at least, a few generations to materialise, and that there is little possibility of a change in birth rates sufficient to offset prospective decline in mortality over the next few decades. To control population is not only a matter of acquiring contraceptives and a knowledge of technique. The social and economic transformation which must accompany if not actually precede, birth control affects, and is in turn affected by a man's whole view of the meaning and purpose of life.

While, therefore, more active steps will have to be taken to tackle the problem of population control, emphasis on non-demographic measures cannot be relaxed. The difficulty in bringing about a deceleration in the rate of population growth in the next fifteen years, or so, when the battle for subsistence is going to be critical, increases the relative importance of economic development. National real income will have to be increased more rapidly than prospective population increases, not only so that consumption levels may be raised, but also so that the forces making for a retardation of population growth may be strengthened. Higher incomes, as we have seen, are likely to change demographic attitudes.

Altogether, the problem that faces India is exceedingly difficult. There is no 'open sesame' that will work the magic. While we should educate our children, marry them late and carry on propaganda in favour of family planning, all the while laying emphasis on the values of continence, benefits of observance of the 'safe period' and the advisability of an operation of either spouse (rather than on contraceptives such as obtained in the West), at least till biological contraceptives are available, we should plan simultaneously and, with a still greater vigour, for increased agricultural production and a co-ordinated and parallel development of industries, preferably agro-industries, so that each sector may generate adequate purchasing power which would help absorb the increasing production of the other sector. Action is needed on all fronts simultaneously.

Index